The Expeditions of Zebulon Montgomery Pike

Edited by ELLIOTT COUES

In Two Volumes
VOLUME II

Dover Publications, Inc.
NEW YORK

Published in Canada by General Publishing Company, Ltd., 30 Lesmill Road, Don Mills, Toronto, Ontario.

Published in the United Kingdom by Constable and Company, Ltd., 10 Orange Street, London WC2H 7EG.

This Dover edition, first published in 1987, is an unabridged version in two volumes of the work first published in three volumes in 1895 by Francis P. Harper, New York, in an edition of 1150 copies (the copy reproduced here is No. 245), with the full title: *The Expeditions of Zebulon Montgomery Pike, To Headwaters of the Mississippi River, Through Louisiana Territory, and in New Spain, During the Years 1805–6–7. A New Edition, Now First Reprinted in Full From the Original of 1810, With Copious Critical Commentary, Memoir of Pike, New Map and other Illustrations, and Complete Index, by Elliott Coues, Late Captain and Assistant Surgeon, United States Army, Late Secretary and Naturalist, United States Geological Survey, Member of the National Academy of Sciences, Editor of Lewis and Clark, etc., etc., etc.*. In addition, Volume I of the 1895 edition was titled "Memoir of the Author—Mississippi Voyage"; Volume II, "Arkansaw Journey—Mexican Tour"; Volume III, "Index—Maps." In the present edition, which combines Volumes II and III of the 1895 edition into a single Volume II, the plates have been moved to new locations, while the maps are in a special pocket in the last volume, as in the 1895 edition; corresponding alterations have been made in the listings of contents and plates.

Manufactured in the United States of America
Dover Publications, Inc., 31 East 2nd Street, Mineola, N.Y. 11501

Library of Congress Cataloging-in-Publication Data

Pike, Zebulon Montgomery, 1779–1813.
    The expeditions of Zebulon Montgomery Pike.

    Reprint. Originally published in three vols.: New ed. New York: F.P. Harper, 1895. With new pref.
    Includes index.
    1. West (U.S.)—Description and travel—To 1848. 2. United States—Exploring expeditions. 3. Mississippi River—Description and travel. 4. New Mexico—Description and travel. 5. Pike, Zebulon Montgomery, 1779–1813—Journeys—West (U.S.) I. Coues, Elliott, 1842—1899. II. Title.
F592.P636 1986   917.8'042   86-19701
ISBN 0-486-25254-X (pbk.: v. 1)
ISBN 0-486-25255-8 (pbk.: v. 2)

CONTENTS OF VOL. II.

v

PART III.

The Mexican Tour.

PIKE'S EXPEDITIONS.

Part II.

THE ARKANSAW JOURNEY.

CHAPTER I.

ITINERARY: UP THE MISSOURI AND OSAGE RIVERS, AND
THROUGH KANSAS TO THE PAWNEE VILLAGE ON THE
REPUBLICAN RIVER, JULY 15TH–SEPT. 30TH, 1806.

TUESDAY, July 15th, 1806. We sailed from the landing at Belle Fontaine [1] about 3 o'clock p. m., in two
boats. Our party consisted of two lieutenants, one surgeon,

[1] Belle Fontaine or Bellefontaine is the name of the large cemetery in the en-
virons of St. Louis, where William Clark lies buried; and probably few persons now living know its proper geographical connotation. The cemetery is
four miles from the Court House, and ten miles further is the place whose name
was given to the burying-ground on the road thither, after its original designation as the Rural Cemetery. Belle Fontaine was a place on the south bank of
the river, 14 m. north of St. Louis, in what is now St. Ferdinaud township of
St. Louis Co. (Sect. 10, T. 47 N., R. 7 E. of this county). Before there
was any such "place," or locality, Belle Fontaine was the French name of
the creek which falls in there, which had been called Ferdinand by the Spanish,
and which became known to the English as Cold Water creek, there being a
fine large spring under the bluffs, close to the Missouri. This, however, was
washed away by the encroachment of the river. We find the latter name in
Lewis and Clark, who made the first camp of their expedition on Green isl., opposite the mouth of the creek, May 14th, 1804. There was nothing then at the
place that was soon to become forever notable as the spot where was built the
first military post ever established in the newly acquired territory of Louisiana.
Much early history attaches to the locality, some of which may be here epito-
mized, mainly on the basis of Billon's Annals. In 1768, when St. Louis was but
begun, Captain Rios arrived with 25 soldiers under orders from Count Ulloa to

one sergeant, two corporals, 16 privates and one interpreter.[2]
We had also under our charge chiefs of the Osage and Pawnees, who, with a number of women and children, had been
to Washington.   These Indians had been redeemed from
captivity among the Potowatomies, and were now to be re-

establish Spanish authority in the region where things were at a standstill, if not
in distraction.   Rios was persona non grata in the infant St. Louis ; he with-
drew, and selected Belle Fontaine as a suitable location for a post.   Late in 1768
he there built a fort which he called Fort Prince Charles in honor of the son of
his king and heir apparent to the Spanish throne.   In 1769 Rios left with his men;
in 1770 Piernas came.   The Spanish presidio was soon turned into a commercial factory or trading-post.   On Sept. 10th, 1797, Governor Zenon Trudeau
granted to Hezekiah Lord a concession of 1,000 arpents of land on Belle Fontaine or Cold Water cr.; and on the site of the former Spanish fort Lord built a
house and mill.   He died in 1799 ; his estate was sold in partition in 1803,
when 600 arpents were bought by William Massey.   In 1805, General James
Wilkinson selected the place for a military establishment, and United States
troops were first cantoned in temporary quarters during the winter of 1805–6.
This was the original Cantonment Belle Fontaine.   On April 20th, 1806, General Wilkinson purchased from Massey, on behalf of the United States, five acres
of ground with the improvements, called Belle Fontaine, with the use for five
years of the ground on which had been located the cantonment, and upon these
five acres established a permanent post.   In July, 1806, he purchased the rest
of the tract of 500 arpents, which was conveyed to the United States in Mar.,
1809.   Belle Fontaine was really the parent of Jefferson Barracks ; for, after
the establishment of Forts Atkinson, Snelling, and others on the Missouri and
Mississippi frontiers, it lost its importance from a military point of view, and
was abandoned for the site of the present Jefferson Barracks.   This in 1825; on
July 4th of which year Colonel Talbot Chambers, with four companies of the 1st
United States Infantry, evacuated Belle Fontaine and proceeded to the new site
which had been selected, though the place remained for some ten years in charge
of a military storekeeper, Major John Whistler.   General Lewis Cass, Secretary
of War under Van Buren, ordered it to be sold at public auction in 1836.   It
was bought by Jamison Samuel, Dunham Spalding, H. N. Davis, and E. L.
Langham, who laid out a paper town that never came to anything.   Agriculture
finally reclaimed Belle Fontaine after the military occupancy ; it was bought for
a farm by the late Dr. David C. Tandy of St. Louis, whose son, Robert E.
Tandy, now or lately did live there.   The old road can still be traced in part
over ground where it ran more than a century ago.

    [2] The roster of the party, with some of the most notable particulars, is as
follows :

COMMISSIONED OFFICERS (2).

    1. Captain Zebulon M. Pike.   Escorted to Mexico from his post on the Rio
Conejos, with six privates, by Spanish dragoons, Feb. 26th, 1807.   His men,

turned to their friends at the Osage towns. The whole number of Indians amounted to 51.

We ascended the river about six miles, and encamped on the south side behind an island. This day my boat swung

excepting one left with Jackson, were Brown, Carter, Gorden, Menaugh, Mount-joy, Roy, and Stoute.

2. Lieutenant James B. Wilkinson. Detached to descend the Arkansaw with five men, from camp near Great Bend, Aug. 28th, 1806.

NON-COMMISSIONED OFFICERS (3).

1. Sergeant Joseph Ballenger. Went with Wilkinson.

2. Sergeant William E. Meek. Sent from Rio Conejos to relief of aban-doned men, Feb. 19th, 1807.

3. Corporal Jeremiah R. Jackson. Left in charge of post on Rio Conejos, with Carter, Feb. 26th, 1807, to await return of Meek and Miller with Vasquez, Smith, Sparks, and Dougherty.

PRIVATES (16).

1. John Boley. Went with Wilkinson, Aug. 28th, 1806.

2. Samuel Bradley. Went with Wilkinson, Aug. 28th, 1806.

3. John Brown. Left with Jackson on Rio Conejos, Feb. 26th, 1807.

4. Jacob Carter. Went with Pike, Feb. 26th, 1807.

5. Thomas Dougherty. Abandoned in Sangre de Cristo mountains with frozen feet, Jan. 22d, 1807.

6. William Gorden. Went with Pike, Feb. 26th, 1807.

7. Solomon Huddleston. Went with Wilkinson, Aug. 28th, 1806.

8. Henry Kennerman. Deserted July 19th, 1806.

9. Hugh Menaugh. Abandoned in Sangre de Cristo mountains, Jan. 27th, 1807 ; recovered on Rio Conejos, Feb. 18th, 1807 ; went with Pike, Feb. 26th, 1807.

10. Theodore Miller. Went with Meek to relief of abandoned men, Feb. 19th, 1807.

11. John Mountjoy. Went with Pike, Feb. 26th, 1807.

12. Alexander Roy. Went with Pike, Feb. 26th, 1807.

13. Patrick Smith. Left with Vasquez on the Arkansaw at site of present Cañon City, Jan. 14th, 1807.

14. John Sparks. Abandoned in Sangre de Cristo mountains with frozen feet, Jan. 22d, 1807.

15. Freegift Stoute. Went with Pike, Feb. 26th, 1807.

16. John Wilson. Went with Wilkinson, Aug. 28th, 1806.

CIVILIANS (2).

1. Dr. John H. Robinson, volunteer surgeon. Left Pike on the Rio Conejos to proceed to Santa Fé alone, Feb. 7th, 1807.

around twice ; once when we had a tow-rope on shore, which it snapped off in an instant. The Indians did not encamp with us at night. Distance six miles.[2]

July 16th. We rejoined our red brethren at breakfast, after which we again separated, and with very severe labor arrived late in the evening opposite the village of St. Charles,[4] where the Indians joined us. Distance 15 miles.

July 17th. We crossed the river to learn if any communications had arrived from St. Louis, and if there was any news of other Indian enemies of the Osages. Called at Mr. James Morrison's, and was introduced to Mr. [George] Henry, of New Jersey, about 28 years of age ; he spoke a little Spanish and French tolerably well ; he wished to go with me as a volunteer. From this place I wrote letters back to Belle Fontaine, whilst the Indians were crossing the

2. Interpreter A. F. Baronet Vasquez. Left with Smith on the Arkansaw, at site of present Cañon City, Jan. 14th, 1807.

Of these persons—

(1) Lieutenant Wilkinson, Sergeant Ballenger, and Privates Boley, Bradley, Huddleston, and Wilson descended the Arkansaw and reached New Orleans in February, 1807.

(2) Private Kennerman deserted.

(3) Dr. Robinson left Captain Pike at the post on Conejos r., and went to Mexico on his own account.

(4) Captain Pike, Sergeant Meek, Corporal Jackson, Privates Brown, Carter, Dougherty, Gorden, Menaugh, Miller, Mountjoy, Roy, Smith, Sparks, Stoute, and Interpreter Vasquez were escorted in separated parties to Mexico by Spanish dragoons. Of whom—

(5) Captain Pike, Privates Brown, Gorden, Menaugh, Roy, and Stoute were escorted back to the United States, and reached Nachitoches on or about July 1st, 1807 ; while—

(6) Sergeant Meek, Corporal Jackson, Privates Carter, Dougherty, Miller, Mountjoy, Smith, and Sparks, and Interpreter Vasquez, were still detained in Mexico at the time of Pike's return, and are not accounted for in his narrative.

(7) The 51 Indians, which raised to 74 the total of persons who left Belle Fontaine, were all dropped at their respective destinations, and no others were permanently attached to the party which reached the Rocky mts.

[3] Past present Jamestown ldg. to Carbunker's pt., off which the large Pelican isl. now separates Car of Commerce bend from Pelican bend.

[4] See L. and C., ed. 1893, p. 6, and Pike's Dissertation, etc., beyond. The village was then the seat of justice of the District of St. Charles, Louisiana Territory, as it is now of St. Charles Co., Mo. The Wabash, St. L. and Pac. R.

river.   A man by the name of Ramsay reported to the Indians that 500 Sacs, Ioways, and Reynards were at the mouth of Big Manitou [*i. e.*, the band under Pashepaho (Stabber) and Quashquame (Lance)].   This gave them considerable uneasiness, and it took me some time to do away the impression it made upon them, for I by no means believed it.   We were about sailing when my interpreter [Vasquez] was arrested by the sheriff at the suit of Manuel De Liza [or Lisa[5]], for a debt between $300 and $400, and was obliged to return to St. Louis.   This made it necessary for me to write another letter to the general.[6]   We encamped about three-fourths of a mile above the village.

July 18th.   Lieutenant Wilkinson and Dr. Robinson went with [one soldier and] the Indians across the country to the village of La Charette.[7]   Mr. George Henry engaged, under oath, to accompany me on my tour.   Wrote to the general, and inclosed him one of Henry's engagements.[8]   After we

---

R. bridged the Mo. r. here ; opposite is Bon Fils station ; also Brotherton.   St. Charles was not so called till 1784 ; the place had been known as Les Petites Côtes, where the hunter Blanchette settled about 1770 : note [41], p, 214.   In to-day's journey Pike passed the place known as Piper's (or Fifer's) ldg.: see the mark " Ferry " on his map.   The principal point was the coal hill on the south, then known as La Charbonnière, now Charbonnier pt.   A present or recent place of ferriage is Music's or Hall's ; some of the landings are Heagler's, Kemp's, and Orick's or Orrick's ; some of the present islands above the Pelicans are Charbonnier or Mullanphy, Holmes, and Vingt-une.   There was a marsh or lake on the N. side, 5 or 6 m. below St. Charles, which the French called Marais Croche, Crooked marsh ; some maps now make it Marie Croche l.

[5] M. de Lisa was one of the most noted Missourian Indian traders in those days.   This is certainly not the last, and probably not the first, time he played exactly that trick.   Pike has a good deal to say of him further on : see also L. and C., pp. lxxix, 62, 242, 256, 443, 1153, 1154, 1232, where my notes refer to further information in Brackenridge's Travels and Irving's Astoria.   Lisa was at one time associated with Captain Clark in the fur-trade.

[6] One of the two letters Pike wrote to Wilkinson formed No. 3 of the App. to Pt. 2 of the orig. ed.   See beyond, where it is given.

[7] See L. and C., ed. 1893, pp. 2, 8, 1182, 1211 ; also, p. 1257, where Charette's cr. and village are given, showing this to be a personal name.   We come to the place presently.

[8] This letter formed No. 4 of the App. to Pt. 2 of the orig. ed.   It is given beyond.

had made our little arrangements we marched by land and
joined the boats, which had sailed early [in charge of Sergeant Ballenger], at twelve o'clock.   Two of the men being
sick, I steered one boat and Mr. Henry the other, by which
means we were enabled to keep employed our full comple-
ment of oars, although we put the sick men on shore.   Encamped on the north side.   About eleven at night a tremendous thunderstorm arose, and it continued to blow and rain,
with thunder and lightning, until day.   Distance 15 miles.[9]

July 19th.   In consequence of the rain we did not put off
until past nine o'clock; my sick men marched.   I had
some reason to suspect that one of them [Kennerman[10]] intended never joining us again.   At dinner time the sick
man of my own boat came on board; I then went on board
the other, and we continued to run races all day.   Although
this boat had hitherto kept behind, yet I arrived at the encamping ground with her nearly half an hour before the
other.   The current not generally so strong as below.   Distance 14 miles.[11]

[9] This mileage would set Pike about Cottleville ldg., on the N., though I
hardly think he got quite so far.   He passed Fee Fee and Crèvecœur creeks on
the S., latter discharging from Crèvecœur l.; Little Duckett and Big Duckett
creeks, near together, on the N.; Catfish isl., behind which is Howard bend,
into which Bon Homme or Good Man's r. falls, about opposite the middle of
Green's bottom, N., 3½ m. long, separated by Green's chute from Bon Homme
isl., next above which comes Bacon's or Post's isl., and then Cottleville ldg.   If
Pike reached this place, he was 44 m. from the mouth of the Missouri, according to recent charts.

[10] Late Sergeant Henry Kennerman, reduced to the ranks for cause at Pike's
stockade on the Upper Mississippi r., Mar. 9th, 1806: see p. 181 and note [10],
p. 245.   He was posted as a deserter in various places, but we are not told he
was retaken.   He drops out of the story at this point.   With Kennerman
deserted, Vasquez arrested, and Geo. Henry engaged, the whites of the party are
now 23—2+1=22 ; Vasquez rejoins on the 21st, when the roster is again 23.

[11] Position uncertain, especially as the text of the 18th–20th cannot be squared
with the camp-marks on Pike's map.   Going by the text, which agrees with the
actual geography better than the map does, we may set Pike in the vicinity of
St. Albans.   To reach this point from his last camp he passes places on the N.
now known as Cottleville ldg., Hamburg, and Dozier's ldg.   At the last named
Femme Osage r. falls into the lower end of Dozier's bend.   The Missouri is
here 1½-2 m. broad, and mostly filled with Howell's isl., 2½ m. long, some

Sunday, July 20th. Embarked about sunrise. Wishing to ascertain the temperature of the water, I discovered my large thermometer to be missing, which probably had fallen into the river. Passed one settlement on the north side, and, after turning the point to the south, saw two more houses on the south side. We encamped [on the south] in a long reach which bore north and west. The absentees had not yet joined us. Distance 15 miles.[12]

July 21st. It commenced raining near day, and continued until four o'clock in the afternoon; the rain was immensely heavy, with thunder and lightning remarkably severe. This obliged me to lie by; for, if we proceeded with our boats, it necessarily exposed our baggage much more than when at rest, as the tarpaulin could then cover all. We set sail at a quarter past four o'clock, and arrived at the village of La

small islands, and various sand-bars. Thence on the N. or rather N. W. is a bottom 8 m. long and a mile or more deep; while on the S. E. is a nearly unbroken line of bluffs which the river washes from Port Royal (in Franklin Co., just over the border of St. Louis Co.) to St. Albans. At one place in these rocks is the cave formerly, and perhaps still, known as the Tavern: see L. and C., ed. 1893, p. 8, and Pike's map, place lettered " Cave." The small stream which makes in on the S. W. at St. Albans is still called Tavern cr.; and directly opposite is Murdoch's ldg. The Mo. R. Comm. charts of 1879 mark a place Missouriton on the N. W., 2 m. below Murdoch's ldg. Nicollet's map, pub. 1843, marks Missouriton on the N., slightly *below* mouth of Femme Osage r., about position of present Hamburg.

[12] The " point to the south " which Pike passes I take to be that opp. Cottlebaum's ldg., at the mouth of Ridenour or Fiddle cr., at the head of the difficult place called Devil's Race-ground by Lewis and Clark: see ed. of 1893, p. 8. This is a couple of miles above St. Albans, at the 55th river-mile point of recent surveys. The bluffs continue a mile or so, and then, at the mouth of Labadie's cr. or slough, begins the extensive Labadie's bottom on the S., for the Missouri crosses over to the bluffs on the N., and continues on that side to the town of Augusta, St. Charles Co. Thence the channel runs obliquely by the Augusta and Hinkley bends, between Labadie's and Hancock's bottoms, to the S. side again. Here, at Mung's or South Point isl., is the lower end of the " long reach," N. W., in which Pike says he camped. We set him on the S., at the mouth of Dubois or Wood cr., where there is now a place called South Point. This is directly opposite the line between St. Charles and Warren cos. on the N.; it is about 2 m. below Washington, Franklin Co., and at the 67th milepoint from the mouth of the Missouri. Pike maps the stream in the right place, but by the wrong name of " Ash R."

Charette at a little after the dusk of the evening. Here we found Lieutenant Wilkinson and Dr. Robinson with the Indians ; also, Baroney [Vasquez [13]], our interpreter, with letters from the general and our friends. The weather still continued cloudy, with rain. We were received in the house of Mr. Chartron, and every accommodation in his power was offered us. Distance six miles.[14]

[13] The proper name of the interpreter, whom Pike usually calls " Baroney," was A. F. Baronet Vasquez. He was b. St. Louis, 1783 ; his wife was Emily Faustine Parent. He was the son of Benito Vasquez (b. 1750) and Julia Papin (married Nov. 27th, 1774), and was the fifth child of 12 they had. He appears in army registers as Barony Vasquez, appointed to be an ensign in the 2nd Infantry Dec. 12th, 1808 ; transferred to 1st Infantry Oct. 31st, 1810 ; commissioned as second lieutenant Mar. 4th, 1811 ; promoted to a first lieutenancy July 30th, 1813 ; and resigned Oct. 1st, 1814. See also a letter about him in my Memoir of Pike, anteà.

[14] See note [7], p.361. La Charette is still the name of the stream, and of the extensive bottom on the N. side through which the river seeks the Missouri. But the settlement once so called is not to be found by this name on modern maps. Instead of this we have Marthasville (3 m. N. of which stands still the house in which Daniel Boone died), a village about a mile from the Missouri, and nearly midway between the points where La Charette cr. and Tuque cr. respectively enter the bottom. Marthasville appears on maps of 50 years ago, as for example, on Nicollet's, 1843. Gass calls the place St. Johns where he camped May 25th, 1804 ; it then had seven houses : see L. and C., ed. 1893, p. 8. St. Johns is now the name of the largest one of a cluster of islands and sand-bars in an expanded part of the Missouri, between the mouth of La Charette cr. on the N. and of St. Johns or Bourbeuse cr. on the S., 2 m. and more above the town of Washington, Franklin Co. Pike maps " St. Johns R." correctly between his " Ash R." (error for Wood or Dubois cr.) and his " Bay R." (error for Bœuf r.). Washington is the most notable place Pike passes to-day ; it is now quite a town, large enough to have started a place opposite itself, called North Washington, on Lac's pt. in Warren Co. Here is where, at the 69th river-mile point, a creek falls in on the N.; it is commonly called Tuque cr., though Sheet III. of the Mo. R. Comm. charts has " Duke " as the name. It looks like a French word, but whether it be a personal name, or derived from Toque or Turque, does not appear. It is one of two creeks which L. and C. speak of passing on the N., May 25th ; the other one of these has never been identified. But there is an old lake bed, or something of the sort, a couple of miles back of North Washington, in Hancock's bottom, under the bluffs, and I imagine this once discharged about opp. Dubois or Wood cr.—say at Rieskamp's place, on the boundary between St. Charles and Warren cos. Tuque cr. itself seems to have had more than one outlet, in the course of the several miles it meanders the low land and separates Hancock's bottom from La Charette.

July 22d. We arranged our boats, dried our lading, and wrote letters for Belle Fontaine.

July 23d. I dispatched an express to the general, with advertisements relative to Kennerman, the soldier who had deserted.[15] We embarked after breakfast, and made good progress. Lieutenant Wilkinson steered one boat and I the other, in order to detach all the men on shore, with the Indians, that we could spare. We crossed to the south side, a little below Shepherd river. Dr. Robinson killed a deer, which was the first killed by the party. Distance 13 miles.[16]

July 24th. We embarked at half past six o'clock. Very foggy. The Indians accompanied by only three of my people. Lieutenant Wilkinson being a little indisposed, I was obliged to let Baroney steer his boat. We made an

[15] Originally Docs. Nos. 5 and 6, p. 33 and p. 36 of the App. to Pt. 2. They are given beyond.

[16] To camp at New Haven, Franklin Co., a considerable town which has grown up of late years at the place formerly known as Miller's ldg., on the S., a little below Pinckney pt. Passing through Charette bend, beyond Patton's pt. and ldg., Pike comes to the mouth of the Rivière au Bœuf of the French, now Bœuf or Buffalo r., which falls in on the S. behind Bœuf, Buffalo, or Shelton's isl., about a mile below Dundee station of the Mo. Pac. R. R. This is the stream by error lettered " Bay R." on Pike's map. On rounding Emily and Miller bends, Pike comes to his camp, say at the 85th river-mile point of late surveys. Here he is 1½ m. below a place which was charted by Nicollet in 1843 as Griswold, and which may be found on maps of but few years ago, but has since disappeared. On the N., opp. Griswold, was a place called Pinckney or Pinckneyville, seat of Warren Co. about 1825, and there is still a hamlet of the same name in the vicinity. The Shepherd r. which the above text mentions falls in about a mile above Griswold and the same below the present R. R. station Etlah. This is Shepherd's cr. of L. and C., ed. 1893, p. 9, but is oftener now called Berger r. or cr. I am told by R. J. Holcombe that the word is not the common F. noun *berger*, a shepherd, but a personal name, probably of the old German pioneer Caspar Burger, a founder of the colony there ; if so, it should not have been translated into English. The word is mangled into " Boeger " on the beautiful chart of the Mo. R. Comm. It is a pity that so many cases as bad as this one mar the lettering of such fine draughtsman's work as Mr. D. W. Wellman's. Berger's or Burger's cr. comes into the bottom 2 m. above its mouth, and is there joined by Little Berger's or Burger's cr., which runs about 4½ m. in the bottom before its confluence ; the two thus make what is known as Berger's (*i. e.,* Burger's) bottom nearly an island, 6 or 7 m. long.

excellent day's journey, and encamped [on the south] five miles from [below] the Gasconade river. Killed three deer, one bear, and three turkeys. But three or four of the Indians arrived ; the others encamped a small distance below. Distance 18 miles.[17]

July 25th. We embarked at half past six o'clock, and arrived at the entrance of the Gasconade river at half past eight o'clock, at which place I determined to remain the day, as my Indians and foot people were yet in the rear, and they

[17] On rounding Pinckney pt. through the bend of that name, Pike passes the mouth of Berger's cr., opp. Yeager's ldg., crosses to the N. side of the Missouri, and sails along with Berger's bottom on his left for several miles ; he goes by Whitehouse's isl., near which L. and C. were camped May 26th, 1804, and on finishing with Berger bottom, reaches a place on the N. called Bridgeport. This is pretty old for a Missouri River town ; we find it located more than 50 years ago, and it still exists in name, but has never amounted to much. Opp. Bridgeport is Bates' isl., 2 m. long, the largest one of several at the head of Berger's bottom. In the vicinity of Bridgeport several small creeks fall in on the N. Three of these are called Lost cr., Massas (qu. Massey's?) cr., and Malhern (qu. Malheur ?) cr. Excepting Lost cr., these fall into Chenal à Loutre or Otter slough ; and this snicarty cuts off a very large piece of bottom known as Île à Loutre or Otter isl. L. and C. speak of this as nearly 10 m. long, and say that it was one of the most fertile in the whole river. The details of the river bottom along here seem to have altered a good deal since 1804, and even since Long's time ; the upper end of the slough is now a little above Hermann, near McGirk's isl. and ldg., cutting the island down to a total length of not over 7 m. The slough itself is very narrow, and hardly more than a sluggish creek, like a good many others that meander bottoms before they discharge. L. and C. speak of three creeks which fall in behind Otter isl., and one of these as having the same name. This is Rivière à la Loutre of early F. settlers, now Loutre, Louter, or Luter r., and Otter r., very curiously lettered on the Mo. R. Comm. map, as " L'Outre "—a form which only needs an accent to be decidedly *outré*. Pike maps the stream as " Otter Riv." He proceeds by Otter or Loutre Island bend to a mile or so above Hermann, and camps on the S. In finishing the bend just named he passes on the S. the county line between Franklin and Gasconade, which cuts through Bates' isl., and then on the N. the line between Warren and Montgomery cos., which cuts the upper part of Otter isl. at the lower point of Hermann isl., opp. the town of this name. This is now quite a place, and more than 50 years old. It is situated across the mouth of Rivière aux Frênes of the F., commonly called Frene cr. and Ash cr., but uncommonly appearing as " Frame " cr. on the Mo. R. Comm. map. Pike does not map Ash cr., though it is given under this name by L. and C.: for the stream he marks "Ash R." by mistake, see note [12], p. 363.

had complained to me of being without shoes, leggings, etc. Distance five miles.[18]

One of our Pawnees did not arrive until late ; the other had communicated his suspicions to me that the Oto, who was in company, had killed him : he acknowledged that he proposed to him to take out their baggage and return to St. Louis. The real occasion of his absence, however, was his having followed a large fresh trace up the Gasconade a considerable distance ; but finding it led from the Missouri, he examined it and discovered horses to have been on it ; he then left it, joined ours, and came in. This being generally the route taken by the Potowatamies, when they go to war against the Osage, it occasioned some alarm. Every morning we were awakened by the mourning of the savages, who

Loutre isl. is quite historic. A number of Americans and some French families settled there in 1805 ; first child born was Jacob Grosjean (name corrupted to Groshong) ; one b. 1806 became the local celebrity known as " old man Patton," living in 1884. Fort Clemson was built by Capt. Clemson about 1808, and maintained till after the war of 1812-15. From 1808 to 1816 there was quite a colony, whence were drawn the settlers for Boone's Lick, Howard Co. On the N. mainland the colonists, when the war broke out, were killed in part, and the rest driven to the island to be " forted up " till the peace. Fort Clemson was a Rangers' hdqrs. in the war, and from this post Capt. James Callaway, grandson of Daniel Boone, set out in March, 1815, on the expedition up Loutre r., during which he and others were killed. Daniel Boone's Spanish grant from Gov. Delassus was about 15 m. up the Loutre, and included a salt spring—the original and only genuine " Boone's Lick "; Boone's adopted son Van Bibber kept a tavern there, where Washington Irving stopped some time in the '30's ; it is now reputed a medicinal spring in the little village Mineola, near Danville, seat of Montgomery Co.

[18] Passing McGirk's ldg. and isl. N., Cole's or Coles' cr., S., Rineland and Kallmeyer's ldgs., S., to the mouth of the Gasconade, which falls in on the S., opp. Cuyler's pt., 107⅓ m. up the Missouri : see L. and C., ed. 1893, p. 9. This is much the largest tributary of the Missouri thus far reached ; Pike elsewhere allows it 200 yards' width at the mouth, and navigability at times of 100 m. He also notes that the Sac boundary started opp. its mouth : see note [14], p. 11. Gasconade City is a place on the tongue of land that makes into the Missouri on the upper side of the Gasconade ; being a mere village or hamlet, is as appropriately named as the river itself, which got its name from the way some persons bragged about their exploits when they returned to St. Louis. Beck's Gaz. speaks of pine which was cut and rafted down, but there has been none for 60 years within 150 mlies.

commenced crying about daylight, and continued for the space of an hour. I made inquiry of my interpreter with respect to this, who informed me that this was a custom not only with those who had recently lost their relatives, but also with others who recalled to mind the loss of some friend, dead long since, and joined the other mourners purely from sympathy. They appeared extremely affected; tears ran down their cheeks, and they sobbed bitterly; but in a moment they dry their cheeks and cease their cries. Their songs of grief generally run thus: " My dear father exists no longer; have pity on me, O Great Spirit! you see I cry forever; dry my tears and give me comfort." The warriors' songs are thus: "Our enemies have slain my father (or mother); he is lost to me and his family; I pray to you, O Master of Life! to preserve me until I avenge his death, and then do with me as thou pleaseth."

July 26th. We commenced at five o'clock to ferry the Indians over the Gasconade, and left the entrance of this river at half past six o'clock in the afternoon. Met five Frenchmen, who informed us that they had just left the Osage river, and that it was so low they could not ascend it with their canoe. We wrote letters and sent them back by them.[19] Dr. Robinson, Baroney, Sparks, and all the Indians encamped about one league above us. Killed one bear, two deer, one otter, three turkeys, and one raccoon. Distance 15 miles.[20]

[19] One of these letters, given beyond, formed No. 7, p. 36, of the App. to Pt. 2. of the orig. ed.

[20] Pike's map marks no camp for the 26th. The distance between Gasconade and Osage rivers is exactly 30 m. by the channel. Pike says he goes 15 m. to-day; I doubt that he went so far if he did not leave the Gasconade till 6.30 p. m. But to take the record on its face would be to set him a mile above Fisher's ldg., on the S., in the vicinity of the hamlet called Chamois, in Osage Co. On decamping and ferrying over the Gasconade, Pike first passed the mouth of Bailey's cr. (Deer cr. of L. and C.), on the S., whence the channel took him obliquely to Bluffton on the N., 5 m. above the Gasconade. The bluffs border the river for about 4 m. along here, and at one place in them is the cave which used to be known as Montbrun's Tavern: see L. and C., *l. c.* At 1 or 1½ m. above Bluffton the line between Montgomery and Callaway cos. comes

Sunday, July 27th. We embarked at half past five o'clock, and arrived at the Indians' camp at seven o'clock. They had been alarmed the day before, and in the evening sent men back in the trace, and some of the chiefs sat up all night. Breakfasted with them. About half past three o'clock encamped in sight of the Osage river. There being every appearance of rain, we halted thus early in order to give the Indians time to prepare temporary camps, and to secure our baggage. I went out to hunt, and firing at a deer, near two of the Indians who were in the woods, they knew the difference of the report of my rifle from their guns, were alarmed, and immediately retired to camp. Distance 13 miles.[21]

to the Missouri just about opp. the line between Gasconade and Osage cos. on the S.; this last strikes the river-bottom just where Bailey's cr. also does. At 5 m. above Blufton is Portland, Callaway Co., before reaching which Pike passes Little Tavern and Big Tavern creeks, which are a mile apart, on the N., and both opp. Portland isl., 2 m. long; while a mile above Portland is the mouth of Logan cr. On the S. along here is a creek whose mysteries I have never been able to fathom. This is Rush cr. of L. and C., *l. c.*, given by them as 4 m. above Montbrun's Tavern, on the S. It is called Greassy cr. by the Mo. R. Comm., and Greasy cr. by the U. S. G. S.; the latter name is probably correct. It comes into the bottom in the vicinity of Chamois, about the 121st river-mile point, meanders down for several miles, and finally discharges behind Portland isl., somewhere between the 117th and 115th m. of the Mo. R. Comm.

[21] To an interesting locality—that of the old French village, Côte sans Dessein. so called from the celebrated long narrow ledge of rocks of the same name immediately above, isolated on the N. bank of the river opposite Dodd's isl. In approaching the Osage, Pike maps two streams from the N., respectively lettered "Gr. R. au vase" and "L. R. au vase." The first of these is Grande Rivière au Vase or Grande Rivière Vaseuse of the F., which appears on the best modern maps as Au Vasse and Auxvasse r.—better talk English than such Missouri French as this, and say Big Muddy r., as L. and C. did! This considerable stream falls in a mile above Harrison's ldg., about 123½ m. by the channel from the mouth of the Missouri. The other is Little Muddy r. of L. and C., who translated Petite Rivière au Vase (or Petite Rivière Vaseuse) better than those do who now style it Au Vasse cr. or Auxvasse cr. This creek joins in the bottom-land another now called Middle r. or cr., and the two fall in together a mile above the village of St. Aubert, Callaway Co. Moreover: between the Big and the Little Muddy there is a third creek, distinct from both the others, falling in 1½ m. *below* St. Aubert. This is simply called Muddy cr. on the Mo. R. Comm. map; on that of the U. S. G. S. it is lettered Ewing's cr.

July 28th. Embarked at half past five o'clock, and at half past ten arrived at the Osage [22] river, where we stopped, discharged our guns, bathed, etc. We then proceeded on about six miles, where we waited for and crossed the Indians to the west shore; we then proceeded on to the first island, and encamped on the west side, Sans Oreille and only four or five young men coming up, the rest encamping some distance behind. Killed one deer and one turkey. Distance 19 miles.

July 29th. All the [rest of the] Indians arrived very early. Big Soldier, whom I had appointed the officer to regulate the march, was much displeased that Sans Oreille and the others had left him, and said for that reason he would not suffer any woman to go in the boat and by that means separate the party; but in truth it was from jealousy of the

A branch of this is lettered by the U. S. G. S. East Wing cr.—a name which I suspect originated in mistaking "Ewing" for "E. Wing." On the S. side of the Missouri Pike passes two small streams, both historically notable. The first of these is the one which L. and C. called Grindstone cr., when they camped at its mouth May 30th, 1804 ; but it is now known as Deer cr. It falls in behind St. Aubert's isl., a mile below St. Aubert station on the Mo. Pac. R. R., or the village now called Medora, 126⅔ m. up the Mo. r. One Carr has or had his home at the mouth of this creek. The other creek is 4¾ m. above Grindstone or Deer cr., and 1¼ m. above Shipley's ldg.; it is the one L. and C. called Bear cr., May 31st, 1804 ; Pike charted it " Bear R.," and it is now called Bear or Loose cr. I suppose " Loose " cr. to be a loose translation of F. R. à l'Ours or à l'Ourse, according to whether it was a he-bear or a she-bear which the Frenchman who first named the creek killed there. In any event this stream has given name to the village of Loose Creek and to Bear Creek isl., opposite its mouth. Four miles higher on the S., opposite the foot of Dodd's isl., is the village of Dauphine at the place where one Benêt, Bénite, Benoit, Bennet, Bonnet, Bonnot, or Bennight built his mill, 15-20 years ago. Dauphine is almost exactly opposite the site of the old French village above named, which started about 1808 and had a dozen or more families in 1811. There is a sort of settlement in this vicinity immediately at the lower end of the Côte sans Dessein, at one time known as Bennet's ldg.; people named Gray, Crews, and Maddox live or lived there. Behind the Côte are some small lakes or ponds discharging by R. aux Riveaux or Riveaux cr. (as it is called) around the upper end of the Côte, near Dearing's ldg. Hence it is only 1½ m. diagonally across the Missouri to Glenn's ldg. at the mouth of the Osage r. See L. and C., ed. 1893, p. 11.

[22] Arising in the Ozark mts. of Kansas, the Osage r. leaves that State and enters Missouri in Vernon Co., which it delimits in part from Bates Co.; tra-

men whose women went in the boats. He began by flog-
ging one of the young men and was about to strike Sans
Oreille's wife, but was stopped by him and told that he
knew he had done wrong, but that the women were innocent. We then crossed them and embarked at half past
eight o'clock. About twelve o'clock we found the Indians
rafting the river, when the first chief of the Little Osage,
called Tuttasuggy, or Wind, told me that the man whom
Big Soldier struck had not yet arrived with his wife, "but
that he would throw them away." As I knew he was
extremely mortified at the dissensions which appeared to
reign amongst them, I told him by no means [to do so];
that one of my boats should wait for the woman and her
child, but that the man might go to the devil, as a punishment for his insubordination.

I then left Baroney with one boat, and proceeded with
the other. We were called ashore by three young Indians,
who had killed some deer; and, on putting them on board,
gave them about one or two gills of whisky, which intoxicated all of them. It commenced raining about one o'clock,
and continued incessantly for three hours, which obliged us
to stop and encamp. One of our men, Miller, lost himself,
and did not arrive until after dark. Killed five deer, one
turkey, and one raccoon. Distance 14 miles.[23]

verses St. Clair and continues past the corner where this, Henry, and Benton
cos. adjoin ; traverses Benton, enters Morgan, forms a part of the boundary
between this and Camden, makes a loop through the latter and again separates
it for a short space from Morgan, then for a little distance separates Camden
from Miller, traverses the latter, enters Cole, and finally runs to the Mo. r.
between this last and Osage cos. We shall learn much more of this stream as
we follow it up in Pike's wake. There is a village called Osage City at its
mouth on the west bank ; Pike's camp is also on this side, in Cole Co., past two
small tributaries known as Caddy and Sandford's creeks, and not far above
Maries r., which comes from Pulaski through Maries (named for two French
girls) and Osage cos. to fall in on the E. or right (left hand) bank. A Spanish
fort (trading-house) was built about 1795 near the mouth of the Osage.

[23] No further indication of camp of 29th, which is also omitted by the draughtsman or engraver from Pike's map ; nor is there any notable modern locality
along here. But it must be short of where the Osage, after coursing in Cole

July 30th. After the fog dispersed I left Lieutenant Wilkinson with the party to dry the baggage, and went with Dr. Robinson and Bradley. About two o'clock we returned, set sail, and having passed the first rapid about three miles, encamped on the eastern shore. Killed three deer. Distance five miles.[24]

July 31st. We embarked early, and passed several rapids pretty well. Dined with the Indians. Two of them left us in the morning for the village, and they all had an idea of doing the same, but finally concluded otherwise. One of the Osages, who had left the party for the village, returned and reported that he had seen and heard strange Indians in the woods. This we considered as merely a pretext to come back. I this day lost my dog, and the misfortune was the greater, as we had no other dog which would bring anything out of the water. This was the dog Fisher had presented to me at Prairie des Chiens. Killed three deer and one turkey. Distance 18 miles.[25]

Aug. 1st. It having rained all night, the river appeared to have risen about six inches. We spread out our baggage to dry, but it continuing to rain at intervals all day, the things were wetter at sundown than in the morning. We rolled them up and left them on the beach. We sent out

Co., begins to separate the latter from Osage Co. Nearest present settlements, Babbtown, Osage Co., and St. Thomas, Cole Co.

[24] In Cole Co., and a mile or two above Proft's cr.; about 2 m. N. E. of St. Thomas, and 4 m. S. E. of Osage Bluff.

[25] Camp a little above Big Tavern cr., from the E., in Miller Co., on whichever side of the river it was pitched. There is no mark on Pike's map for this camp, nor those of Aug. 2d and 3d. The nearest named places to the camp of July 31st and Aug. 1st, and that of Aug. 2d (only 2 m. further), are St. Elizabeth, on Big Tavern cr., and Mary's Home, west of the Osage—both in Miller Co., but both some miles away from the river. On breaking camp this morning, Pike passed on his right the bluffs from which the hamlet of Osage Bluff takes its name ; this is about a mile north of the river. He later passed Babruly cr., from the W., whose name is obviously a corruption of Bois Brûlé ; then Sugar cr., from the E., and next Little Tavern cr., falling in from the W. a mile or two below Big Tavern cr. There was more than one cave or "tavern" in the bluff near the creek: see figure of one, where the early Osage boatmen used to put up, in the Mo. Geol. Reports.

two hunters in the morning, one of whom killed three deer; all the Indians killed three more.

Aug. 2d. The weather cleared up. The lading being spread out to dry, Dr. Robinson, myself, Bradley, Sparks, and Brown went out to hunt. We killed four deer, the Indians two. Having reloaded the boats, we embarked at five o'clock, and came about two miles. The river rose, in the last 24 hours, four inches.

Sunday, Aug. 3d. Embarked early, and wishing to save the fresh [take advantage of the rise in the river], I pushed hard all day. Sparks was lost, and did not arrive until night. We encamped about 25 paces from the river, on a sand-bar. Near day I heard the sentry observe that the boats had better be brought in; I got up and found the water within a rod of our tent, and before we could get all our things out it had reached the tent. Killed nine deer, one wildcat, one goose, and one turkey. Distance 18 miles.[26]

Aug. 4th. We embarked early and continued on for some time, not being able to find a suitable place to dry our things, but at length stopped on the east shore. Here we had to ferry the Indians over a small channel which we did not before observe; all of them, however, not arriving, we put off and continued our route. Finding our progress much impeded by our mast, I unshipped it and stripped it of its iron, and, after Lieutenant Wilkinson had carved our names on it, set it adrift, followed by the yards. This mast had been cut and made at [our wintering post on] Pine creek, Upper Mississippi. After proceeding some miles, we found the Indians on the west shore, they having rafted the river. We stopped for them to cook, after which we proceeded. The navigation had become very difficult from the rapidity of the current, occasioned by the rise of the water,

[26] Passing Cub cr., right; Humphrey's and Panther creeks, left; then the present Saline cr., on the right. This is laid down and lettered "Saline R." on Pike's map; but observe that it is *not* the Saline r. of Aug. 7th : see that date. Above Saline cr. Pike passes Dog cr., left, and then present site of Tuscumbia, seat of Miller Co., on the right; and camps at or near present site of Brockman, on the right, a mile above Bear cr., in the same county.

which rose one foot in an hour. Killed two deer. Rainy. Distance 10 miles.[27]

Aug. 5th. We lay by this day, in order to give the Indians an opportunity to dry their baggage. Dr. Robinson and myself, accompanied by Mr. Henry, went out to hunt; we lost the latter about two miles from camp. After hunting some time on the west shore, we concluded to raft the river, which we effected with difficulty and danger, and hunted for some time, but without success. We then returned to the party and found that Mr. Henry, who had been lost, had arrived one hour before us; he had met one of the soldiers, who brought him in.

To-day in our tour I passed over a remarkably large rattlesnake, as he lay curled up, and trod so near him as to touch him with my foot, he drawing himself up to make room for my heel. Dr. Robinson, who followed me, was on the point of treading on him, but by a spring avoided it. I then turned round and touched him with my ramrod, but he showed no disposition to bite, and appeared quite peaceable. The gratitude which I felt toward him for not having bitten me induced me to save his life. Killed four deer. River rises 13 inches. Rain continues.

Aug. 6th. We embarked at half past eight o'clock, it having cleared off and had the appearance of a fine day. Passed [Little] Gravel river [of Pike, now Big Gravois creek] on the west.[28] About three miles above this river the Indi-

[27] Taking Pike past a place called Bagnell, on the right, just below present Little Gravois cr., in Miller Co., and setting him somewhere about the point on the river where Miller, Morgan, and Camden cos. come together—the latter on the S., the two former on the N. side, as the river is here running E. His camp of Aug. 4th and 5th is marked on his map, on the left, just below the mouth of his Little Gravel r., which he passes on the 6th: see next note.

[28] On the right hand as Pike ascends, left bank of the Osage, and rather on the N. than W., as the general course of the river is to the E. The "Gravel" rivers of Pike require attention in identifying them with ours. The Osage is here making an ox-bow bend, which reverses points of the compass so far as a traveler's right and left are concerned. The stream now in question, Gravel r. of the above text, lettered "L. Gravel R." on the map, is that now known as Big Gravois, Gravis, or Gravel cr., running in Morgan Co., with a place called

ans left us and informed me that, by keeping a little to the south and west, they would make in 15 miles what would be at least 35 miles for us. Dr. Robinson, Mr. Henry, and Sergeant Ballenger accompanied them. Killed two deer. Distance 13 miles.

Aug. 7th. Not being detained by the Indians, we are for once enabled to embark at a quarter past five o'clock. The river having fallen since yesterday morning about four feet, we wish to improve every moment of time previous to its entire fall. We proceeded extremely well, passed the Saline [read Great Gravel [29]] river [of Pike, now Grand Auglaise creek] on the east, and encamped opposite La Belle Roche on the west shore. This day we passed many beautiful cliffs on both sides of the river ; saw a bear and wolf swimming the river. I employed myself part of the day in translating into French a talk of General Wilkinson's to Cheveux Blanche.[30] Distance 21 miles.

Gladstone near its mouth, one known as Gravois Mills higher up, and some of whose branches are called Indian, Soap, and Mill creeks. Cape Galena is 2½ m. above the mouth of this river. Present Little Gravois cr. is that one with Bagnell just below its mouth ; it is laid down by an unlettered trace on Pike's map. The correct form of the word is Gravois, being F. *gravois*, rubbish, rubble, whence "Gravel."

[29] *Not* the Saline r. of Pike's map, which was passed on the 3d. "Saline river" of the present text is a slip of the pen or memory ; Pike meant to say Great Gravel r., as correctly laid down by this name on his map on the left or south, being lettered "G. Gravel R." This is not the Great Gravel or Big Gravois cr. of present maps, but the considerable stream now known as Grand Auglaise cr.—a name also perverted from the F. word *glaise*, clay, into Glaize or Wet Glaize cr. It heads in Laclede and Pulaski cos., in close relation with sources of the Gasconade, and runs about N. N. W. through Camden Co. to fall into the Osage from the S., on the right bank of the river, on Pike's left, at or near a place called Blackman's Mills. The Osage is here turning from its E. course to N., whence it soon bends W., then loops N. and again E., where it receives present Big or Pike's Little Gravel r., and completes another ox-bow bend. Camp of the 7th, opposite the notable bluff called " La Belle Roche," is marked on Pike's map, not far above a place now called Damsel, on the other side of the Osage ; whence the Yungar is reached for breakfast on the 8th.

[30] *Sic*, usually in Pike, and I make no change. But "Cheveux Blanche " is a phrase joining a masculine plural noun to a feminine singular adjective. The English ed. alters to Cheveu Blanc ; but as doubtless the savage had more than

Aug. 8th. We embarked at 20 minutes past five o'clock.
Found the river had fallen about two feet during the night.
At the confluence of the Youngar [31] with the Osage river we
breakfasted. Encamped at night on a bar. Distance 21
miles.

Aug. 9th. We embarked at five o'clock, and at half past
six met the Indians and our gentlemen. They had met
with nothing extraordinary. They had killed in their excursion seven deer and three bear. We proceeded to an old
wintering ground, where there were eight houses, occupied
last winter by [Blank], who had not been able to proceed any
higher for want of water. Passed the Old Man's Rapids,
below which, on the west shore, are some beautiful cliffs.
Dined with the Indians, after which we passed Upper Gravel
river on the west, and Pottoe [qu. Poteau?] river on the
east. Sparks went out to hunt, and did not arrive at our
encampment, nor did the Indians. Distance 25 miles. [32]

one hair of that color, probably Cheveux Blancs would be better in form and
fact for the F. name of the person also known as White Hair.

[31] Before the Youngar is reached Pike passes on his left Linn cr.; county seat
called Linn Creek, a mile above its mouth. The name of the river has fluctuated widely. Pike has Yungar, Youngar, and also Nehemgar ; the latest G. L.
O. and U. S. G. S. maps letter Niangua. The word, whatever may be its preferable form, is the Osage name of the bear, though by some it is said to refer to
the numerous springs at the sources of the stream. It is by far the largest tributary of the Osage thus far reached ; Pike credits it with a canoe navigation of
100 m. The main stream heads in Webster Co., in relation with sources of the
Osage fork of the Gasconade, and runs through Dallas Co., also touching the W.
border of Laclede, into Camden ; its tributaries are numerous and widespread.
One called Little Niangua falls in on the W., 6 or 8 m. above the mouth of the
main river. To-day's voyage takes the Expedition past Purvis, and finishes
about 4 m. above Bolinger or Bollinger cr., from the S., on which are the Osage
Iron Works.

[32] Pike's map marks none of the places passed to-day by the names given in
his text. We have therefore a triple adjustment to make—of map with text, and
of these with modern geography. This I can do, bearing in mind that Pike
does not necessarily mention places in the order in which they are passed en
route, and that all his mileages are guessed at by the hours spent in making
them. His map marks camp of Aug. 8th a good ways above the Niangua, and
I set it 4 m. above Bolinger cr., as already said. For the 9th the map has : (1)
Big Rock cr., right ; (2) Rapids ; (3) Slave r., right ; (4) camp, right. The

Sunday, Aug. 10th.   Embarked a quarter past five o'clock, when the sun shone out very clearly; but in 15 minutes it began to rain, and continued to rain very hard until one o'clock.   Passed the Indians, who were encamped on the west shore, about half a mile, and halted for them.   They all forded the river but Sans Oreille, who brought his wife up to the boats, and informed me that Sparks had encamped with them, but left them early to return in search of us.   We proceeded after breakfast.   Sparks arrived just at the moment we were embarking.   The Indians traversing the country on the east had sent Sparks with Sans Oreille.   About two o'clock split a plank in the bottom of the batteau.   Unloaded and turned her up, repaired the breach, and continued on the route.   By four o'clock found the Indians behind a large island; we made no stop, and they followed us.   We encamped together on a bar, where we proposed halting to dry our corn, etc., on Monday. Killed four deer.   Distance 18½ miles.[33]

facts in the case are : Pearson's branch, left ; Wells' branch, right ; Proctor cr., right, on which is Proctor ; Raney, Rainey, or Rainy cr., left, with Crittenden at its mouth—none of the foregoing noted by Pike in any way ; then (1) Little Buffalo cr., right, on or near which is a place called Search ; (2) rapids along a long curved bluff, right, with three little creeks on the left ; (3) Big Buffalo cr., right, with a place called Riverview at its mouth ; (4) camp, right.   This makes about 25 m., barely over the border of Morgan into Benton Co., Big Buffalo cr. falling in just short of the same boundary ; whence it is evident that (1) Big Rock cr. of the map is (1) Little Buffalo cr., on which is Search ; (3) Slave r. of the map is (3) Big Buffalo cr., on which is Riverview ; and this last is the Upper Gravel cr. of the text.   This ends the day, for by no stretch can we get Pike past Pottoe r. of the text : see next note for this.

[33] Text gives no geography to-day, but the map shows three large streams between the camp-marks of 9th and 10th.   These are : (1) a river, left, lettered " P. R."—that is, " Pottoe " r.; (2) Francis r., right ; (3) Cardinal r., left. The facts in the case are : Knobby cr., left, small, at lower point of Williams isl., large ; (1) a large creek, left, falling in at head of Williams isl., called Beaver cr. on the G. L. O. map, Deer cr. on the U. S. G. S. map, and on which is a place named Hastain ; 2 m. above its mouth is another place called Duroc, on the S. bank of the Osage ; (2) a very large creek, right, variously called Vermilion, Coal Camp or Cole Camp cr.; (3) a very large creek, left, called Turkey cr.   These three are of the relative sizes and in the relative positions of the three that Pike charts ; so that unquestionably

Aug. 11th. We continued here to dry our corn and baggage. This morning we had a match at shooting. The prize offered to the successful person was a jacket and a twist of tobacco, which I myself was so fortunate as to win ; I made the articles, however, a present to the young fellow who waited on me. After this, taking Huddleston with me, I went out to hunt ; after traveling about 12 miles we arrived at the river, almost exhausted with thirst. I here indulged myself by drinking plentifully of the water, and was rendered so extremely unwell by it that I was scarcely capable of pursuing my route to the camp. On arriving opposite it, I swam the river, from which I experienced considerable relief. The party informed me they had found the heat very oppressive, and the mercury, at sundown, was at 25° Reaumer [Réaumur]. This day, for the first time, I saw trout west of the Allegheny mountains. Reloaded our boats and finished two new oars, which were requisite.

Aug. 12th. Previously to our embarkation, which took place at half past five o'clock, I was obliged to convince my red brethren that, if I protected them, I would not suffer them to plunder my men with impunity ; for the chief had got one of my lads' tin cups attached to his baggage, and, notwithstanding it was marked with the initials of the soldier's name, he refused to give it up. On which I requested the interpreter to tell him, " that I had no idea that he had purloined the cup, but supposed some other

" P. R." or " Pottoe " r. of Pike's map is (1) the Beaver or Deer cr.; (2) Francis r. is the Vermilion or Cole or Coal Camp cr.; and (3) Cardinal r. is the Turkey cr. It is true Pike says his Pottoe cr. was passed on the 9th ; but his map shows otherwise ; and if it had been, that is a question of the location of camp for the 9th, not affecting the identification of the streams here made. The queer name " Pottoe " I suppose to be intended for Poteau, and not a misprint for Potatoe : see the name Pomme de Terre or Potatoe for a river further on. Where Pike got his name Francis r. I have no idea. His Cardinal r. I imagine was so called by some confusion with Vermilion r.; for cardinal and vermilion are two names of a red color—in the one case worn by certain church dignitaries on their heads, in the other by cochineal insects on their bodies. Camp of the 10th (and 11th) is 3 or 4 m. above Turkey cr.

person had attached it to his baggage; but that, knowing it to be my soldier's, I requested him to deliver it up, or I should be obliged to take other measures to obtain it." This had the desired effect; for I certainly should have put my threats into execution, from this principle, formed from my experience during my intercourse with Indians, that if you have justice on your side, and do not enforce it, they universally despise you. When we stopped for dinner, one of my men took his gun and went out; not having returned when we were ready to re-embark, I left him. Passed the Indians twice when they were crossing the river. Passed some very beautiful cliffs on the W. [N. or right] shore; also Vermillion [Little Tabeau] and Grand rivers, the latter of which is a large stream, and encamped at the [first bend above it, on the E. or left-hand bank of the Osage[34]]. Distance 24 miles.

Immediately after our encampment a thunder-storm came

[34] The lacuna of the orig. text can be supplied from the map, which marks camp of the 12th as above said. On decamping this morning Pike passed what he charts as Cave cr. This is the middle one of three insignificant runs which make in on the right. "Vermillion" r. of to-day is a mistake. This is the stream Pike charts as Deep cr., on the right, immediately below Grand r., and is that now called Little Tebo, Teabo, Tabo, Tebeau, etc. These are commonly supposed to be forms of a personal name; but I am informed by R. I. Holcombe they are perversions of Terre Beau, old name of the prairie in Lafayette Co. where the "Tebo" r. that flows into the Missouri rises. The Osage tributary called Tebo, etc., falls in a mile below Grand r.; its E. fork is meandered for some miles by the Sedalia, Warsaw and Southern branch of the Mo. Pac. R. R., which then leaves the creek and strikes the Osage 2½ m. below Warsaw. This is the county seat of Benton, on the N. bank of the Osage, 2 m. below Little Tabeau cr. and three below Grand r., opposite the very large island also called Warsaw. Grand r. of the text and present maps is the largest branch of the Osage passed since the Niangua was left. It falls in on the N., a mile below Wright's isl. Some of its affluents head not far from Independence (on the Mo. r.), and others in Kansas. Its largest branch is Big cr.; others are Deep Water and Big Tabeau. Camp is in the bight of the bend that receives Grand r., between Wright's and Holloway isls.

Pike has mapped the river unmistakably along here, rendering identifications easy; but the text is not so correct, and requires the interpretation I have given. The mileages of the 10th–12th seem excessive. Here, as in various other places, he seems to have supplied the loss of orig. notes from memory.

on, which blew overboard my flag-staff and a number of
articles of my clothing, which were on top of the cabin, and
sunk them immediately. Being much fatigued and the
bank difficult of ascent, lay down in the cabin without
supper and slept all night. It continued to rain. The man
[Sparks] I left on shore arrived on the opposite bank in the
night, having killed two deer, but was obliged to leave the
largest behind. Finding he was not to be sent for, he con-
cealed his gun and deer, and swam the river.

Aug. 13th. It continued to rain. In the morning sent
a boat over for Sparks' gun and deer. Embarked at half
past nine o'clock. Stopped to dine at two o'clock. During
the time we halted, the river rose over the flat bar on which
we were; this, if we had no other proof, would convince us
we were near the head of the river, as the rain must have
reached it. We made almost a perfect circle, so that I do
not believe we were to-night three miles from where we
encamped last night. This day, for the first time, we have
prairie hills. Distance 13 miles.[35]

Aug. 14th. Embarked at half past five o'clock. Passed
the Park, which is 10 miles around, and not more than three-
quarters of a mile across, bearing from S. 5° E. to due N.
At its head we breakfasted, and just as we were about to
put off we saw and brought-to a canoe manned with three

[35] In making the circuit Pike passed two rivers which he charts by name as
"Hallico R." and "Potatoe R.," both from the S., or on his left as he ascends.
Potatoe is clearly the same name as Pomme de Terre, by which latter title is
now mapped the large stream which heads in Webster Co., cuts the N. E. corner
of Green, perhaps also the S. W. corner of Dallas, then traverses Polk and
Hickory, and in Benton falls into the bight of the bend of the Osage herein
mentioned. The natives call this river "Pumly Tar." Two miles above its
mouth it receives the Little Pomme de Terre, from the W., in the vicinity of
Fairfield. A much smaller stream, next above on the same hand, which is
received in the same bend of the Osage, is Hogle's cr. The relative situations
of these would make Pike's Hallico correspond to Pomme de Terre, and his
Potato to Hogle's. But I have no doubt he *meant* by Potato the river now
called Pomme de Terre, and we need not insist upon the reversal of names,
especially as there may be some small stream below to answer to Hallico, and
it would be nothing for Pike to pass over so small a creek as Hogle's, both in
the text and on the map.

engagees of Mr. [Chouteau], who informed us that the Little Osage had marched a war-party against the Kans, and the Grand Osage a party against our citizens on the Arkansaw river. Wrote by them to the general [36] and all friends. Gave the poor fellows some whisky and eight quarts of corn, they having had only two turkeys for four days. We left them and proceeded, passing on our east some of the largest cedars I ever saw. Came on very well in the afternoon, and encamped [37] on an island above Turkey island. Distance 28 miles.

Aug. 15th. We embarked at five o'clock, and at eight o'clock met the Indians and the gentlemen [38] who accompanied them. Found all well. They had been joined by their friends and relatives from the village, with horses to transport their baggage. Lieutenant Wilkinson informed me that their meeting was very tender and affectionate—"wives throwing themselves into the arms of their husbands, parents embracing their children, and children their parents, brothers and sisters meeting, one from captivity, the other from the towns; they at the same time returning thanks to

[36] This letter formed Doc. No. 8 of the App. to Pt. 2. The name, omission of which causes the hiatus in the text, is Chouteau. The letter was sent by one Baptiste La Tulipe, who is no doubt the man of whom we read in Frémont, Rep. 1845, p. 18 : "I had found an old companion on the northern prairie, a hardened and hardly-served veteran of the mountains, who had been as much hacked and scarred as an old moustache of Napoleon's 'old guard.' He flourished in the soubriquet of La Tulipe, and his real name I never knew."

[37] Near the N. E. corner of St. Clair Co. and the S. E. corner of Henry Co. The Park is a narrow, somewhat rectangular loop of the Osage, including some bold bluffs in its bight. The distance was much under "28" m., unless the river were then even crookeder than it is now. We have to foreshorten the mileages along here, in order to bring Pike into anything like the proper position above the mouth of Sac r. on the 16th. He passes five or six small creeks to-day, the last and largest being charted by Pike as Buckeye cr. This is Wright's, from the S., in St. Clair Co. A mile above this is a large island, which seems to be Pike's Turkey isl.; and a mile above this is another, probably that on which he camped.

[38] That is to say, Lieut. Wilkinson, Dr. Robinson, the interpreter, and one soldier, who left the boats to march across country with some of the Indians, thus avoiding the periplus of several bends in the river.

the Good God for having brought them once more together "—in short, the *tout ensemble* was such as to make
polished society blush, when compared with those savages,
in whom the passions of the mind, whether joy, grief, fear,
anger, or revenge, have their full scope. Why can we not
correct the baneful passions, without weakening the good?
Sans Oreille made them a speech, in which he remarked:
"Osage, you now see your wives, your brothers, your
daughters, your sons, redeemed from captivity. Who did
this? Was it the Spaniards? No. The French? No.
Had either of those people been governors of the country,
your relatives might have rotted in captivity, and you never
would have seen them; but the Americans stretched forth
their hands, and they are returned to you! What can you
do in return for all this goodness? Nothing; all your
lives would not suffice to repay their goodness." This man
had children in captivity, not one of whom we were able to
obtain for him.

The chief then requested that Lieutenant Wilkinson and
Dr. Robinson might be permitted to accompany them by
land, to which I consented. Wrote a letter to Cheveux
Blanche, by Lieutenant Wilkinson. When we parted, after
delivering the Indians their baggage, Sans Oreille put an
Indian on board to hunt, or obey any other commands I
might have for him. We stopped at eleven o'clock to dry our
baggage. Found our biscuit and crackers almost all ruined.
Put off at half past four o'clock, and encamped at three-
quarters past five o'clock. Distance 15½ miles.[39]

Aug. 16th. We embarked at five o'clock and came on

[39] Pike is still considerably below the present site of Osceola, at the neck of
the last remarkable bend the river makes some 6 or 7 m. (direct distance)
from that town. At present this loop is 4 or 5 m. around and about
a quarter of a mile across at the narrowest part. It receives several creeks
from the N. E., E., and S., the highest and largest now called Bear cr. In
this day's course, which does not include the circuit of the bend, Pike charts
a certain " East River," which he runs in directly from the W. This corresponds in position with the stream now called Muddy cr., but if meant for that
it is drawn much too large—half as large as Grand r. itself.

extremely well in the barge to an evacuated French hunt-
ing-camp 12 miles to breakfast, the batteaux coming up
late. We exchanged hands. About twelve o'clock passed
the Grand Fork [confluence of Sac river with the Osage,
above Osceola], which is equal in size to the one on which
we pursued our route. Waited to dine at the rocks called
the Swallow's Nest, on the W. shore, above the forks. The
batteaux having gained nearly half an hour, the crews are
convinced that it is not the boat, but men who make the
difference ; each take their own boat, after which we proceeded very well, the water being good and men in spirits.
Saw an elk on the shore ; also met an old man alone hunting, from whom we obtained no information of consequence. Encamped on the W. shore of Mine [or Mire]
river. Distance 37 miles.[40]

[40] Several points require attention in this long course, whatever its actual
length may have been. 1. Passing Osceola in the forenoon, Pike reaches his
"Grand Fork," *i. e.*, the confluence of Sac r. with the Osage, at noon. This
is clear, and the distance seems about right from the place where I set his camp
of the 15th. But the streams he charts on this course, below the forks, are not
more easily disposed of than was the "East" r. 2. Thus, on the same side
as "East" r., about halfway from this to the forks, he lays down two small
streams from the W., the lower of which he names Light cr. There are in fact
several such ; and it may be reasonable to assume that by Light cr. Pike means
the largest of them. This is the one now called Gallinipper cr., which falls in
a mile below Osceola, and which is now meandered for a few miles by both the
Kansas City, Clinton, and Springfield R. R., and the Kas. Cy. and Southern
R. R. 3. After rounding the bend above described, and passing the Bear cr.
there said, Pike passes two creeks on his left, from the S., one of which he charts
by the name of Lime r. This probably answers to the stream now called
Wablo, or Weablo, or Weaubleau cr. The other one of the two is Brushy cr.
But the identification of Lime r. with Weaubleau cr., and of Light with Gallinipper, throws both out of relative position, and introduces a difficulty which
can only be done away with by supposing an error of the map. 4. Osceola is
the seat of St. Clair Co., on the left hand going up river, 3 or 4 m. below the
mouth of Sac r. This village is notable as a point up to which steamboats
used to come, especially during our Civil War ; it was burned in Sept., 1861, by
"Jim" Lane (James Henry Lane, b. Lawrenceburg, Ind., June 22d, 1814, committed suicide at Leavenworth, Kas., July, 1866) ; pop. lately 331. 5. Two
of the little crosses which usually mark Pike's camps are superfluous for the 14th–
16th. One I cannot account for ; the other evidently marks the spot where
Bel Oiseau was killed, as there is the legend "Beloiseau Kill'd." Pike usually

We to-day passed the place where the chief called **Belle Oiseau**, and others, were killed. The Belle Oiseau was killed by the Sacs in the year 1804, in a boat of Manuel de Liza, when on his way down to St. Louis, in order to join the first deputation of his nation who were forwarded to the seat of government by Governor Lewis. A particular relation of the event, no doubt, has been given by that gentleman. This chief had a son who accompanied me to the Pawnee nation, and whose honorable deportment, attachment to our government, amiableness of disposition, and the respect and esteem in which he was held by his compeers, entitle him to the attention of our agents to his nation.

Sunday, Aug. 17th. We embarked at five o'clock and came 12 miles to breakfast. At four o'clock arrived at 10 French houses on the E. shore, where was then residing a Sac, who was married to an Osage femme and spoke French only. We afterward passed the position where Mr. [Pierre] Chouteau formerly had his fort [Fort Carondelet [41]], not a vestige of which was remaining, the spot being

calls him Belle Oiseau; but the French noun is of the same gender as the Indian himself. He was also known as Beautiful Bird. 6. The Sac is about as large as the Osage at their confluence; it runs on an average due N. course from Lawrence, through Dade and Cedar, into St. Clair Co. We are told by the old pioneer " Jack " Beard that the river was so called because a party of Sacs (probably of the Missouri River band) camped on it about 1820; in the fall of 1861 Sterling Price's rebel army were on this river for several weeks. 7. Camp is set on the left bank or right hand of the Osage, above Salt cr., right, and just below the mouth of the stream from the N. called Mine r. in the text, but lettered " Mire Cr." on the map. This is the Little Monegan, Monegau, or Monegaw cr.; the place called Monegaw Springs is in the vicinity. (The name may be preferably *Monega*, Osage word for " wolf.")

[41] Legended " Chouteau's " on the map, where the cross ✕ also does duty for to-night's camp, two miles higher up. The spot can be identified by the coal bank and shoal mentioned, though the " 41½ " m. assigned for the day's journey take us beyond the confluence of the Little Osage, and we see by to-morrow's itinerary that we are still half a day's sail short of that point. Pierre Chouteau's place was known in Spanish records as Fort Carondelet, and was built about 1790 at what is now called Halley's Bluff named for Col. Anselm Halley. It was an actual fortification with mounted swivels, which Lieut.

only marked by the superior growth of vegetation. Here the river-bank is one solid bed of stone-coal, just below which is a very shoal and rapid ripple [Kaw rapids, where was Collen or Colly ford] ; whence to the village of the Grand Osage is nine miles across a large prairie. We came about two miles above [Chouteau's], and encamped on the W. [right-hand] shore. This day the river has been generally bounded by prairies on both sides. Distance 41½ miles.

Aug. 18th. We put off at half past five o'clock. Stopped at nine o'clock to breakfast. Passed the second fork[42] of

Wilkinson speaks of in his Report (given beyond) : but it was only maintained for a few years. The post is twice noticed in the Hist. of Vernon Co., 1887, by R. I. Holcombe, who informs me that he went over the ground, including Blue Mound, Timbered Hill, and other places in the vicinity, and that some old caches in the sandstone may still be seen. 1. In the course of to-day's voyage the map shows a large stream, unnamed, falling in from the N., on the right-hand or left bank. This is evidently intended for Big Monegan or Monegaw cr.; place called Dollie at its mouth. 2. Higher up, on the other side, another nameless cr. is charted, from the S. This is Beshaw, better called Clear, cr.; quite large, coming from Barton, through Vernon, past the N. W. corner of Cedar, into St. Clair Co. 3. Above this, Pike has two traces, both from the N., unnamed. One of these doubtless represents Panther or Painter cr., in Bates Co. Here the Mo., Kan. and Tex. R. R., a branch of the Mo. Pac. R. R., crosses the Osage between Rockville on the N. and Schell City on the S. of that river. These places are 4 m. apart. A mile or two below this crossing the Osage now forms a circle circumscribing a large round island, nearly a mile in diameter, which may have been a bend in Pike's time. Several smaller streams than those just na ned fall into the Osage on either side, in the course of a few miles, as Miller, McKenzie, Shaw, Willow, and Lady's. The " 10 French houses" Pike speaks of were opp. the mouth of Lady's cr. (named for one Wm. Lady). Camp was on the N. W. side of the Osage, near Lady's cr., and thus in the vicinity of Papinsville (old Harmony Mission).

[42] A most important point in this itinerary, for here is the junction of the Little Osage with the main stream,, which latter Pike now leaves to proceed up the former to the villages, and so on into Kansas, etc. He elsewhere says : " The three branches of the [Osage] river, viz.: the large east fork [*i. e.*, Sac r., lying E. of where he now is], the middle one up which we ascended [*i. e.*, Little Osage], and the northern one [*i. e.*, main Osage]." The present confluence is at the point where Bates and Vernon cos. begin or cease to be separated by the meanders of the Osage ; for the Little Osage runs in Vernon Co., and the main Osage, above the confluence, runs in Bates. There is a conspicuous mound in the prairie, a short distance S. of this " second fork," giving name to Blue Mound township. Both forks head beyond (W. of) the

the river at twelve o'clock, the right-hand fork bearing N., about 30 yards wide ; the left, the one which we pursued, N. 60° W., and not more than 50 or 60 feet in width, very full of old trees, etc., but with plenty of water. Observed the road where the chiefs and Lieutenant Wilkinson crossed. We proceeded until one o'clock, when we were halted by a large drift quite across the river. Dispatched Baroney to the village of the Grand Osage, to procure horses to take our baggage nearer to the towns, and unloaded our boats. In about two hours Lieutenant Wilkinson, with Tuttasuggy, arrived at our camp, the former of whom presented me an express from the general[43] and letters from my friends. The chiefs remained at our camp all night. I was attacked by a violent headache. It commenced raining, and continued with great force until day. Distance 19¼ miles.

Aug. 19th. We commenced very early to arrange our

Missouri State line, in Kansas, in which State the main Osage r. bears the name of Marais des Cygnes. The " large drift " in the Little Osage which stopped the boats is marked and so legended on the map, a short distance above the forks. It seems to have been above the mouth of Muddy cr., which falls in from the N. within 2 m. of the forks, and was probably about the place where there is now some marshy ground on the W. side, opposite Horseshoe l. The latter is a mile long around the curve, and discharges by a short stream into the Little Osage, from the S., between the forks and the mouth of Muddy cr. Doubtless it was once the bed of the river. Close by this lake, an eastward bend of the Little Osage receives a creek from the S.; and beyond this was the Grand Osage village, close to which Pike established what he calls Camp Independence, on the E. side of the river, near the confluence of Marmiton or Marmaton r. This stream falls in from the S., and is rather larger than the Little Osage ; in fact, it forms with the latter the main forks. The Marmiton receives Drywood cr. a few miles above its confluence with the little Osage. The name of this river is apparently the F. word *marmiton*, scullion, from *marmite*, pot or kettle ; the settlers pronounce it " Mommytaw." For other features of the locality we may note that the river bottoms are here below the 750-foot contour line, which represents the general level of the surrounding prairie ; and that there is an isolated mound or butte of 850 feet or more on the E. side of the Marmiton and close to this river, at the first bend it makes eastward. The Marmiton is otherwise notable in the present connection, as Pike's further route goes between it and the Little Osage.

[43] A letter received from General Wilkinson by this express formed Doc. No. 9 of the App. to Part 2.

baggage, but had not finished at one o'clock, when the chief of the Grand Osage, and 40 or 50 men of his village, arrived with horses. We loaded and took our departure for the place where Manuel de Liza had his establishment, [near Fort Carondelet], at which we arrived about four o'clock, and commenced pitching our encampment near the edge of the prairie, when I was informed that three men had arrived from St. Louis sent by Manuel de Liza. I dispatched Lieutenant Wilkinson to the village with Baroney, who brought to camp the man [Jean Baptiste Duchouquette] who had charge of the others from St. Louis; he having no passport, I detained him until further consideration. Our reception by the Osage was flattering, and particularly by White Hair and our fellow-travelers. This evening there arrived in the village of the Grand Osage an express from the Arkansaw, who brought the news that a boat, ascending that river, had been fired on, had two white men killed and two wounded, and that the brother-in-law of Cheveux Blanche, who happened to be on board, was also killed. This put the whole village in mourning.

Aug. 20th. About twelve o'clock I dispatched Baroney for the chiefs of the Grand [Osage] village, in order to give the general's parole to Cheveux Blanche; also, a young man to the village of the Little Osage. Cheveux Blanche and his people arrived about three o'clock, and after waiting some time for Wind and his people, I just informed the chiefs that I had merely assembled them to deliver the parole of the general and present the marks of distinction intended for Cheveux Blanche and his son—hanging a grand medal round the neck of the latter. The packets committed to my charge for the relations of the deceased Osages were then delivered to them, the widow making the distribution. It must be remarked that I had merely requested Cheveux Blanche to come with his son, and receive the general's message; but instead of coming with a few chiefs, he was accompanied by 186 men, to all of whom we were obliged to give something to drink. When the council was over we mounted our horses, rode to the village, and halted at the quarters of the chief, where we were regaled with boiled pumpkins; then we went to two different houses, and were invited to many others, but declined, promising that I would pay them a visit previous to my departure, and spend the whole day. We then returned to camp. After inquiring of White Hair if the men of Manuel de Liza had any ostensible object in view, he informed me that they had only said to him that they expected Manuel would be up to trade in the autumn. I concluded to take the deposition of Babtiste Larme as to the manner in which he was employed by Manuel de Liza, forward the same to Dr. Brown[44] and the attorney-general of Louisiana, and permit the men to return to St. Louis, as it was impossible for me to detach a party with them as prisoners.

Aug. 21st. In the morning White Hair paid us a visit, and brought us a present of corn, meat, and grease; we invited him, his son, and son-in-law to breakfast with us, and gave his companions something to eat. I then wrote a number of letters to send by express, and inclosed the deposition of Larme. In the afternoon we rode to the village of the Little Osage, and were received by our fellow-travelers with true hospitality. Returned in the evening, when a tremendous storm of rain, thunder, and lightning commenced, and continued with extraordinary violence until half past nine o'clock. It was with great difficulty we were

---

[44] Joseph Browne, who in 1806 was first Justice of the Court of Common Pleas in and for the District of St. Louis, appointed by Governor and General Wilkinson Tuesday, Mar. 18th, 1806; in 1807 he was Territorial secretary, and sometimes acting governor. He was succeeded by Frederick Bates, appointed secretary by Jefferson, May 7th, 1807: see L. and C., p. 1236. The "Babtiste Larme" of the above paragraph is elsewhere called by Pike "Mr. Baptist Duchouquette alias Larme." Billon's Annals of St. Louis for 1764–1804, pub. 1886, p. 437, has "Jno. B. Duchouquette, usually called Batiste Lami." Among the signers of a paper relating to the erection of a Roman Catholic church in St. Louis, Oct. 30th, 1819, is found "Batiste X Duchouquete"(his mark). The alias occurs in various forms, as Lamie, Lamy, Lamme, etc. J. B. D. was son of François Lafleur Duchouquette and Céleste Barrois; b. about 1760, d. May, 1834; married Marie Brazeau, St. Louis, 1798.

enabled to keep our tents from blowing down.   The place prepared for an observatory was carried away.

Aug. 22d.   Preparing in the morning for the council, and committing to paper the heads of the subject on which I intended to speak.   The chiefs of the Little Osage arrived about one o'clock, also the interpreter of the Grand Osage, who pretended to say that the Grand Osage had expected us at their village with the Little Osage.   Cheveux Blanche arrived with his chiefs.   The ceremony of the council being arranged, I delivered them the general's parole, forwarded by express.   My reason for not delivering it until this time was in order to have the two villages together, as it was equally interesting to both.   After this I explained at large the will, wishes, and advice of their Great Father, and the mode which I conceived most applicable to carry them into effect.   Cheveux Blanche replied in a few words, and promised to give me a full reply to-morrow.   Wind replied to the same amount ; after which Cheveux Blanche addressed himself to Wind as follows : " I am shocked at your conduct, Tuttasuggy—you who have lately come from the States, and should have been wise ; but you led the redeemed captives, with an officer of the United States, to your village, instead of bringing them through my town in the first instance."   To this Wind made no reply, but left his seat shortly after, under pretense of giving some orders to his young men.   I conceived this reprimand intended barely to show us the superiority of the one and inferiority of the other ; it originated, in my opinion, from an altercation of Lieutenant Wilkinson and Cheveux Blanche, in which allusions were made by the former to the friendly conduct of the Little Chief, alias Wind, when compared to that of the latter.   I must here observe that when the chiefs and prisoners left me, accompanied by Lieutenant Wilkinson, I did not know the geographical situation of the two villages,[45]

---

[45] The village of the Little Osage Indians was about 6 m. higher up and on the other (west) side of the river of the same name.   Marmiton r. falls in between where the two villages were.   These were so well-known to the traders

but conceived that, in going to the Little Village, they would pass by the Grand Village, and of course that Lieutenant Wilkinson and the chief would arrange the affair properly.

Aug. 23d. I expected to have received from the chiefs their answers to my demands ; but received an express from both villages, informing me that they wished to put them off until to-morrow. I then adjusted my instruments. Took equal altitudes and a meridional altitude of the sun ; but, owing to flying clouds, missed the immersions of Jupiter's satellites.

Sunday, Aug. 24th. Was nearly half the day in adjusting the line of collimation in the telescopic sights of my theodolite. It began to cloud before evening, and although the sky was not entirely covered, I was so unfortunate as to miss the time of an immersion, and, although clear in the intermediate period, an emersion also. I was informed by Baroney that the Little Village had made up 11 horses for us. In the evening, however, the interpreter, accompanied by the son-in-law and son of Cheveux Blanche, came to camp, and informed me that there were no horses to be got in the village of the Big Osage.

The son-in-law spoke as follows : " I am come to give you the news of our village, which is unfortunate for us, our chief having assembled his young men and warriors and pro-

and others in Pike's time that he does not take the trouble to say exactly where they were ; nor are we favored with the precise location of Camp Independence, " near the edge of the prairie." But there is of course no question of the exact site of a village which stood for more than a century : see for example Holcombe's Hist. Vernon Co. Hundreds of Osages were buried on the mound, to which their descendents used to come from Kansas to cry over them, as late at least as 1874. Among the remains rested those of old White Hair himself, until his bones were dug up and carried off by Judge C. H. Allen of Missouri. In the vicinity of the upper village is now a place called Arthur, where the Lexington and Southern Div. of the Mo. Pac. R. R. comes south from Rich Hill, Bates Co., and continues across both Little Osage and Marmiton rivers ; a mile W. of its crossing of the former, on the S. of that river, is the present hamlet called Little Osage. All Pike's positions of Aug. 18th–Sept. 1st are in the present Osage township.

posed to them to furnish horses, etc. They have generally refused him; but I, who am the principal man after Cheveux Blanche, will accompany you." The son: "Our young men and warriors will not take pity on my father, nor on me, nor on you, and have refused to comply with your request; but I will accompany you with two horses to carry provision for your voyage." The interpreter: "The Cheveux Blanche was ashamed to bring you this answer, but will again assemble his village and to-morrow come and give you the answer." I replied: "That I had made the demand without explanation, merely to let the Osage act agreeably to their inclination, in order that we might see what disposition they would exhibit toward us; but why do I ask of their chiefs to follow me to the Pawnees? Is it for our good, or their own? Is it not to make peace with the Kans? To put their wives and children out of danger? As to their horses which they may furnish us with, I will pay them for their hire; but it is uncertain whether I can pay them here, or give them an order on the Superintendent of Indian Affairs at St. Louis; but this I do not now wish them to be made acquainted with."

Aug. 25th. In the morning we were visited by Cheveux Blanche and three or four of his chiefs, who were pleased to accord to my demands. He found much difficulty in informing me that in all his village he could only raise four horses, but that we should be accompanied by his son and son-in-law. I then expressed to him the difference of our expectations from the reality. He remained until after twelve o'clock, when I went to the Little Osage village, and was received with great friendship by the chief. Remained all night at the house of Tuttasuggy. Took the census.[46]

Aug. 26th. Rose early and found my friends in council, which was merely relative to our horses. The chief then

[46] This census of the Grand Osage village was contained in a letter which in the orig. ed. formed Doc. No. 12 of the App. to Pt. 2, being a folded table opp. p. 52, with a tabular "recapitulation" on p. 53. The matter is given beyond.

declared their determination to me, and that he himself gave me one horse, and lent me eight more to carry our baggage to the Pawnees. Sold the old batteau for $100 in merchandise, which I conceived infinitely preferable to leaving her to the uncertain safeguard of the Indians. About this time we received the news that the party of Potowatomies were discovered to be near the towns. I gave them the best advice I was capable of giving, and then returned to our camp.

Aug. 27th. Spent in arranging our baggage for the horses. Received four horses from the Little Village and two from the Big Village. In the evening Lieutenant Wilkinson rode to the Grand Village. I observed two immersions of Jupiter's satellites.

Aug. 28th. Writing to the secretary at war and the general, and making arrangements for our departure. Visited by Wind and Sans Oreille.

Aug. 29th. Forenoon writing letters. In the afternoon Dr. Robinson and myself went to the Grand Village, at which we saw the great medicine dance. Remained at the village all night.

Aug. 30th. Returned to the camp after settling all my affairs at the town. Sealed up our dispatches and sent off the general's express.[47] In the afternoon we were visited by the principal men of the Little Village and the chief, to whom I presented a flag, and made the donations which I conceived requisite to the different Indians, on account of horses, etc.

Sunday, Aug. 31st. Arranging our packs and loading our horses, in order to fit our loads, as we expected to march on the morrow. Up late writing letters.

Sept. 1st. Struck our tents early in the morning, and commenced loading our horses. We now discovered that an Indian had stolen a large black horse which Cheveux

---

[47] Three letters from Pike to Wilkinson which went by this express formed Docs. Nos. 10, 11, 12 of App. to Pt. 2. One of them is dated from "Camp Independence," by which we learn the name Pike gave his station : see beyond.

Blanche had presented to Lieutenant Wilkinson. I mounted a horse to pursue him; but the interpreter sent to town, and the chief's wife sent another in its place. We left the place about twelve o'clock with 15 loaded horses,[48] our party consisting of two lieutenants, one doctor, two sergeants, one corporal, 15 privates, two interpreters, three Pawnees, and four chiefs of the Grand Osage, amounting in all to 30 warriors and one woman. We crossed the Grand Osage fork and a prairie N. 80° W. five miles to the fork of the Little Osage.[49] Joined by Sans Oreille and seven Little Osage, all of whom I equipped for the march. Distance eight miles.

Sept. 2d. Marched at six o'clock. Halted at ten o'clock and two o'clock on the side of the creek [Little Osage river], our route having been all the time on its borders. Whilst there I was informed by a young Indian that Mr. C. Chouteau had arrived at the towns. I conceived it proper for me to return, which I did, accompanied by Baroney, first to the Little Village; whence we were accompanied by Wind to the Big Village, where we remained all night at the lodge of Cheveux Blanche. Mr. Chouteau gave us all the news, after which I scrawled a letter to the general and my friends.

Sept. 3d. Rose early, and went to the Little Village to breakfast. After giving my letters to Mr. Henry, and arranging my affairs, we proceeded, and overtook our party

[48] So far as the white men are concerned, the party is identical with that which left Belle Fontaine (see the roster, pp. 358–360), excepting Kennerman, deserted, which reduced the privates from 16 to 15, and further excepting the additional interpreter, one Noel alias Maugraine. (Mr. George Henry, who is left here, was engaged after the start, and therefore does not affect this count.)

[49] By "Grand Osage fork" Pike means the stream on which was the Grand Osage village, *i. e.*, Little Osage r. By "fork of the Little Osage" his actual implication is Marmiton r., near which was the Little Osage village—though the phrase happens to be verbally applicable, as the Marmiton is the fork of the Little Osage r. Pike's course "N. 80° W." at the start would seem to conflict with the dot-line on his map; but this is simply due to faulty projection of the streams: see next note. Observe also that the course of Sept. 1st is simply a swing-around to the mouth of the Marmiton, whence Pike revisits the Grand Osage village. There is no camp-mark for this day; the first + set is camp of the expedition of Sept. 2d, before Pike had rejoined his party.

at two o'clock.   They had left their first camp about four miles.   Our horses being much fatigued, we concluded to remain all night.   Sent out our red and white hunters, all of whom only killed two turkeys.   Distance four miles.[50]

Sept. 4th.   When about to march in the morning one of our horses was missing ; we left Sans Oreille, with the two Pawnees, to search for him, and proceeded till about nine o'clock ; stopped until twelve o'clock, and then marched. In about half an hour I was overtaken and informed that Sans Oreille had not been able to find our horse ; on which we encamped, and sent two horses back for the load.   One of the Indians, being jealous of his wife, sent her back to the village.   After making the necessary notes, Dr. Robinson and myself took our horses and followed the course of a little stream until we arrived at the Grand [51] river,

[50] Which the party had made on the 3d before Pike joined them.   Their camp of the 2d is the first one marked on the map, and this of the 3d is the second one so marked.   This we know from the position marked for the 6th, just over the divide, and three camps ahead of this of the 3d.   Pike is now first fairly en route.   The faulty projection of his map makes him seem to go E. of S. till the 6th, and then turn W. abruptly.   The course of the Little Osage is practically from W. to E., and Pike ascends it the whole way, having it at a considerable distance to his right.   His trail is over the prairie between the Little Osage and Marmiton rivers.   This is to be particularly noted, as some have vaguely supposed Pike "followed up the Osage river," *i. e.*, the main Osage (Pike's " North fork "), and then wondered how he came where we presently find him.   In fact, he goes almost due W. from Missouri over into Kansas.   Camp of the 3d was in the vicinity of the present town of Little Osage.   Gregg's map, on which Pike's trail is traced for the most part with all the accuracy that the small scale allows, starts him into Kansas too far S.—a good way S. of Fort Scott, which is correctly located on the Marmiton.

[51] Misleading, at first sight ; but " Grand river " here means that stream on which was the Grand Osage village.   Pike and Robinson simply took an excursion of 6 m. to the Little Osage and back to camp, supposed to be 13 m. from that of the 3d.   It was considerably past Rinehart, and probably in the vicinity of Hoover, a place 2 m. E. of the inter-State line ; or perhaps just over this boundary, which here runs on a meridian of longitude (about 94° 37').   This vicinity is notable as the scene of the raid of old John Brown in Dec., 1859, when this extraordinary compound of saint and sinner, whose prophetic visions of the coming struggle had startling distinctness, killed a man and stole some negroes and horses.   Pike has entered or will immediately enter the N. E. portion of Bourbon Co., Kas., in the vicinity of places called Hammond, Fulton,

which was distant about six miles.   We here found a most delightful basin of water, of 25 paces' diameter and about 100 in circumference, in which we bathed; found it deep and delightfully pleasant.   Nature scarcely ever formed a more beautiful place for a farm.   We returned to camp about dusk, when I was informed that some of the Indians had been dreaming and wished to return.   Killed one deer, one turkey, one raccoon.   Distance [made by the main party]13 miles.

and Barnesville.   The two former of these are on the Kansas City, Fort Scott, and Gulf R. R.   I suppose Pike to be about 10 m. N. N. E. of Fort Scott, the county seat of Bourbon.   This is a well-known city, on Marmiton r., at the point where Mill cr. falls in.   Its military name is a legacy from former days, the fort having been built in 1842 ; pop. now about 12,000.

From the present station we have to trail Pike clear across Kansas to a point on the Republican Fork of the Kansas r., just over the middle of the northern boundary of the State.   This is not easy.   It would be impossible to do so with precision, had we only the slender thread of text to guide us.   His Indians took him a roundabout way by the Smoky Hill r.   The whole country is flat, with a complicated river-system ; Pike cuts through it, incessantly *crossing* creeks and rivers, not one of which does he follow for any considerable distance after he leaves the Osage basin.   The names of the many small towns and stations, as well as of the small streams, will be recognized by few non-residents. Fortunately we have the trace dotted on his map, and though this is far out of drawing for absolute geography, its relative positions are recognizable for the most part.   I am satisfied that the course I lay down for Pike is true to his route in all its main features.   The whole of this Kansan route would be in the Missourian watershed, were it not for the northward extension of the Arkansan basin in the drainage of the Neosho and Vermilion rivers.   This Pike enters as soon as he leaves the Osage basin, crosses, and quits before reaching the Smoky Hill : see the two places legended " Dividing Ridge," etc., on his map.   If we suppose, what I see no reason to question, that his camp-marks are all right, his marches of Sept. 5th to 17th may be summarized as follows : Sept. 5th, further up Little Osage r.; 6th, over divide to Arkansan waters of the Neosho r.; 7th, approaching the Neosho ; 8th, across this river ; 9th, further along S. of it ; 10th, across subdivide of Vermilion river basin ; 11th, heading this river, and across subdivide into Neosho basin again ; 12th, across Cottonwood fork of the Neosho ; 14th, further along this fork ; 15th, across divide from these Arkansan to Missourian waters again ; 16th, nearing Smoky Hill r.; 17th, across this river. (Total distance from the Osage villages about 210 m., by Pike's mileages of Sept. 1st-17th about 250 m.)   The counties crossed are Bourbon, Allen, Woodson, Coffey, Lyon, Chase, Marion, Dickinson, and Saline.   Further details in following notes.

Sept. 5th. In the morning our Little Osage all came to a determination to return, and, much to my surprise, Sans Oreille among the rest. I had given an order on the chiefs for the lost horse to be delivered to Sans Oreille's wife, previously to my knowing that he was going back; but took from him his gun, and the guns from all the others also.

In about five miles we struck a beautiful hill, which bears south on the prairie; its elevation I suppose to be 100 feet. From its summit the view is sublime to the east and south-east. We waited on this hill to breakfast, and had to send two miles for water. Killed a deer on the rise, which was soon roasting before the fire. Here another Indian wished to return and take his horse with him; which, as we had so few, I could not allow, for he had already received a gun for the use of his horse. I told him he might return, but his horse would go to the Pawnees.

We marched, leaving the Osage trace, which we had hitherto followed, and crossed the hills to a creek that was almost dry. Descended it to the main [Little Osage] river, where we dined [vicinity of Harding]. The discontented Indian came up, and put on an air of satisfaction and content.

We again marched about six miles further, and encamped at the head of a small creek, about half a mile from the water. Distance 19 miles [approaching Xenia, Bourbon Co., Kas.[52]].

Sept. 6th. We marched at half past six o'clock, and arrived at a large fork of the Little Osage river, where we

---

[52] The whole of this way is W. up along the S. side of the Little Osage, for the most part at a considerable distance from the river, which here has a northward convexity. But for some miles after leaving Camp Independence, Pike must have kept pretty close to the south side of the Little Osage, to avoid the unnumbered mounds into which the country further to his left is broken. The hill to which Pike came in the forenoon represents a rise from the general 750-foot level hitherto traveled to about 1,100 feet. From its southern slopes, Mill and Wolverine creeks gather to flow into the Marmiton at and near Fort Scott; while from the other side some small runs seek the Little Osage. Camp is in Bourbon Co., somewhere in the vicinity of Xenia, Zenia, or Hay, a small place near a branch of the Little Osage.

breakfasted [vicinity of Xenia].   In the holes of the creek we discovered many fish, which, from the stripes on their bellies and their spots, I supposed to be trout and bass; they were 12 inches long.   This brought to mind the necessity of a net, which would have frequently afforded subsistence to the whole party.   We halted at one o'clock and remained until four o'clock.   Being told that we could not arrive at any water, we here filled our vessels.   At five o'clock arrived at the dividing ridge, between the waters of the Osage and the Arkansaw, alias White river,[53] the dry branches of which interlock within 20 yards of each other. The prospect from the dividing ridge to the east and southeast is sublime.   The prairie rising and falling in regular swells, as far as the sight can extend, produces a very beautiful appearance.   We left our course, and struck down to the southwest on a small [tributary of Elm] creek, or rather a puddle of water.   Killed one deer.   Distance 20 miles.

Sunday, Sept. 7th.   We left this at half past six o'clock,

[53] Pike does not mean that the Arkansaw r. itself is otherwise called White r., but the waters of the Arkansaw River basin he has reached are those of a river called the White, which is perfectly true.   He elsewhere calls this Grand r.   He also discusses whether this White r. be a tributary of the Arkansaw or of the Mississippi, and comes to the latter erroneous conclusion.   This White or Grand r. of Pike is the Neosho ; a large stream which waters much of southeastern Kansas, leaves the State in Cherokee Co., enters Indian Territory, and falls into the Arkansaw on the boundary between the Cherokees' and the Creeks' country.   Its general course is S. E., then S.   Pike lays it down pretty well on his map, by the name of Grand r., and I find it so charted on various modern maps.   Pike runs it into the Arkansaw all right, and makes its Cottonwood fork the main stream, out of all proportion to the little creek he traces for the other fork ; but there is not much difference in the two streams, which unite in Lyon Co. some 8 m. below Emporia.   From the vicinity of Xenia, in Bourbon Co., Pike has to-day continued about W., by or near the station Bayard of the Mo., Kas., and Tex. R. R., in Allen Co.   Having thus headed all Osage (Missourian) waters, he strikes and crosses the divide, and camps on the head of a small tributary of Elm cr., a branch of the Neosho (Arkansan waters).   I suppose his camp to be at a point about equidistant from Bayard and two other places called respectively La Harpe and Wise—perhaps rather Bayard, La Harpe, and Morantown.

before which we had a difficulty with the son of the chief, which was accommodated. At nine o'clock we came on a large fork [of Elm creek] and stopped for breakfast. Proceeded on and encamped on a fine stream [Deer creek?], where we swam our horses and bathed ourselves. Killed four deer. Distance 15 miles.[54]

Sept. 8th. Marched early, and arrived at a grand fork of the White river.[55] The Indians were all discontented; we had taken the wrong ford; but, as they were dispersed through the woods, we could not be governed by their movements. Previously to our leaving the camp, the son of Cheveux Blanche proposed returning, and offered no other reason than that he felt too lazy to perform the route. The reason I offered to prevent his going was ineffectual, and he departed with his hunter, who deprived us of one horse. His return left us without any chief or man of consideration, except the son of Belle Oiseau, who was but a lad. The former appeared to be a discontented young fel-

[54] The two streams concerned in Pike's approach to the Neosho are Elm and Deer creeks. Elm is the large forked one which falls in close below Iola, county seat of Allen. Deer cr. is the next above, falling in about 4 m. above Elm cr. Pike's map indicates that, after passing some insignificant heads of Elm cr., he got into its forks, then crossed its north branch near Iola, and camped on Deer cr., very near the junction of this with the Neosho. I do not know whether horses can swim in Deer cr.; if not, the only alternative stream would be the Neosho itself. But the map sets Pike on the east branch of Deer cr., and there I leave him.

[55] The Neosho, Neozho, or Neocho r. "A grand fork of the White river" is ambiguous; but becomes intelligible if we remember that he has just spoken of the "Arkansaw, alias White river." Pike's ideas of what he calls "White" and "Grand" r. were not clear. There is no stream in his present vicinity large enough to be dignified as the "grand fork" of the Neosho itself; we must understand him to mean the Neosho, as being itself a grand fork of whatever he meant by "White" r. The Neosho was long and often called Grand r.; "Neosho or Grand R." is lettered on Gregg's map. Pike never says where he crossed the Neosho, nor in fact does he inform us that he ever crossed it—unless it was when he swam his horses. But that was on the 7th. However these uncertainties be regarded, two facts are certain: Pike was across the Neosho on the 8th, and he crossed it between Iola and the town of Neosho Falls, Woodson Co. I think the crossing was a little above the mouth of Deer cr.

low, filled with self-pride ; he certainly should have considered it as an honor to be sent on so respectable an embassy as he was. Another Indian, who owned one of our horses, wished to return with him, which was positively refused him ; but fearing he might steal him, I contented him with a present. We marched, and made the second branch [North Big creek], crossing one prairie 12 miles, in which we suffered much with drought. Distance 22 miles.[56]

Sept. 9th. Marched at seven o'clock, and struck a large [Eagle] creek at 11 miles' distance. On holding a council, it was determined to ascend this creek to the highest point of water, and strike across to a large river of the Arkansaw [watershed]. We ascended 4½ miles, and encamped. Killed one cabrie [antelope, *Antilocapra americana*], two deer, and two turkeys. Distance 12 miles.[57]

[56] West for a few miles, then about northwest, up along the Neosho, but at several miles' distance from that river, on the dry prairie, and passing from Woodson into Coffey Co. As to the "second branch" on which is camp : Pike charts three streams passed to-day, running to his right into the Neosho, and marks his camp on the third one of these. I take these to be Turkey, South Big, and North Big creeks ; and suppose that Pike camped on the last of these. It is true that these all three unite in one before falling into the Neosho ; but Pike passed them too high up to observe their connections. Turkey cr. is practically a separate one, as it falls into Big cr. only about one-quarter of a mile above the mouth of it ; and the connection of North and South creeks, much higher up, may be implied in his speaking of the "second branch" on which was camp (Turkey cr. then answering to a first branch). The single mouth of the three streams here in mention falls into the Neosho about 2 m. west of Leroy. If it seems rather a stretch to get Pike some distance up North Big cr. to-day, it may be remembered that the place he crossed the Neosho was not determined with precision ; and that we have to find him to-morrow, at 11 miles' distance, on a large creek up which he can go over the divide to the heads of Verdigris r. There seems to be no alternative.

[57] The total of 12 m. does not agree with the text, which calls for 11+4½=15½. Eagle cr. seems to have been struck about on the boundary between Coffey and Lyon cos., where Four Mile cr. falls into it. It is a considerable stream, which heads in the divide about Olpe (a place on the A. T. and S. Fé R. R.), is increased by Harper, Hoosier, and other tributaries, and runs E. into the Neosho a mile and a half above Strawn (a place on the Mo. Pac. R. R.). To reach Eagle cr. from North Big cr. Pike passed opposite Burlington, seat of Coffey Co., several miles to his right, and headed the small Otter cr., on or near which is a place called Patmos.

Sept. 10th. Marched early. Struck and passed the divide between the Grand [Neosho] river and the Verdegris [or Vermilion] river. Stopped to breakfast on a small stream of the latter; after which we marched and encamped on the fourth small stream [tributary of Vermilion river]. Killed one elk, one deer. Distance 21 miles.[58]

Sept. 11th. Passed four branches and over high hilly prairies. Encamped at night on a large branch of Grand river. Killed one cabrie, one deer. Distance 17 miles.[59]

Sept. 12th. Commenced our march at seven o'clock. Passed very ruff [rough] flint hills. My feet blistered and

[58] It may not be possible to decide which of the several branches of Eagle cr. Pike went up to the divide. To send him up the main branch, past Olpe, agrees best with his 21 m. to-day ; but in that case he must have breakfasted late. There is a sharp elbow in his dotted trail, which would seem to indicate that he made a turn from his former course over the divide. Aside from any questions of detail, which perhaps could not be decided even by a resident of the region traversed, we have Pike safe on the headwaters of Vermilion or Verdigris r. (it has these alternative names on recent maps). It heads in the divide which Pike has crossed, by numerous small tributaries, several of which Pike charts. Among them are Haldemand and Tate, heading opposite branches of Eagle cr., and further on Moon, Rock, Fawn, and Camp creeks. The Verdigris is of a size smaller than the Neosho, W. of which it runs in an approximately parallel course ; it leaves Kansas through Montgomery Co., enters Indian Territory, and in the country of the Creek Indians falls into the Arkansaw 8 m. above the mouth of the Neosho. Pike lays it down well, especially the fan-shaped leash of branches in which it heads, but runs it into the Arkansaw in common with the Neosho. The Verdigris has of course its proper basin or drainage within the more general watershed of the Neosho and other Arkansan as distinguished from Missourian waters. The rim of this basin is the divide Pike crosses over to-day. He camps on one of the small headwaters, probably Fawn or Camp cr., in the close vicinity of the places called Elco and Verdigris.

[59] Pike has headed Verdigris r., and recrossed the brim of its basin into the Neosho basin again. In cutting off this small segment of the Verdigris basin he passed from Lyon into Chase Co., " over high hilly prairies," *i. e.*, the divide, and continued westward till he struck "a large branch of Grand r." We discover later that Pike takes Cottonwood r. to be the main Grand, *i. e.*, Neosho r., which I do not see that it is not, though the other one retains the name of Neosho above their confluence. The stream he strikes is the S. fork of Cottonwood r. This heads in the same hilly country, by tributaries known as Little Cedar, Thurman, and Mercer creeks, in relation or opposition to the uttermost sources of Verdigris r., and flows N. to fall into the main Cottonwood 4 m. below Cottonwood Falls, county seat of Chase. Pike probably

very sore. I stood on a hill, and in one view below me
saw buffalo, elk, deer, cabrie, and panthers. Encamped on
the main [Cottonwood] branch of Grand [Neosho] river,
which had very steep banks and was deep. Dr. Robinson,
Bradley, and Baroney arrived after dusk, having killed three
buffalo, which, with one I killed, and two by the Indians,
made six; the Indians alleging it was the Kans' hunting
ground, therefore they would destroy all the game they
possibly could. Distance 18 miles.[60]

Sept. 13th. Late in marching, it having every appearance of rain. Halted to dine on a branch of Grand river.

came on this stream somewhere in the vicinity of Baker or Crocker cr., between
places called Matfield Green and Bazar.

Cottonwood " creek " was originally so named at the point where it was
struck on the old Santa Fé caravan road, and because it showed the first trees
of that kind to be found in traveling westward on that route. The crossing was
at or near present town of Durham, Marion Co. It was some time before the
true connection of the Cottonwood with the Neosho was made out. At
Council Grove the traders knew they were on a head of the Neosho or Grand r.,
though they called it Council Grove cr. They kept on W. to " Diamond
springs " (on a head of Six Mile or present Diamond cr.), and thence to " Lost
spring" on their " Willow" cr. (a head of present Clear cr., which falls into
the Cottonwood at Marion) ; the next stream they struck being this Cottonwood cr., at or near Durham : see a note beyond, where I undertake, perhaps
rashly, to recover the old caravan road in terms of modern geography.

[60] If Pike bore as much N. of W. as his dotted trail seems to indicate, the
mileage would fetch him on Cottonwood r. about the situation of Cedar Grove
and Cedar Point, which are within a mile or two of each other and of the
boundary between Chase and Marion cos., and about 6 m. down river from
Florence, Marion Co. He is evidently in the loop which the Cottonwood
makes S. E. from Marion to Florence, and then gradually N. E. to the vicinity
of Cottonwood Falls. If the old Kansas Indian trail the map lays down could
be recovered or identified, it would serve to locate him still more precisely.
He crosses the Cottonwood and camps on its left bank. If we attentively
regard the camp-marks of the 12th and 13th, we find them close together, N.
of the Cottonwood, S. of a creek flowing E., and W. of a pair of creeks flowing S. These requirements are fulfilled, if we take the one running E. to
be Middle creek, which falls in by Elmdale, 10 m. below Cedar Grove ; and
the other two, those that fall in together at Marion, 12 m. (direct) above Cedar
Grove. It is true there are several creeks nearer, on the same side, as Silver,
Bruno, and Martin, but these are all smaller than such as Pike usually charts,
and, moreover, he could not go his 9 m. to-morrow in any direction without
getting beyond them.

Marched again at half past two o'clock, and halted at five, intending to dispatch Dr. Robinson and one of our Pawnees to the village to-morrow. Killed six buffalo, one elk, and three deer. Distance nine miles.[61]

Sunday, Sept. 14th. The doctor and Frank, a young Pawnee, marched for the village at daylight; we at half past six o'clock. Halted at one o'clock. On the march we were continually passing through large herds of buffalo, elk, and cabrie ; and I have no doubt that one hunter could support 200 men. I prevented the men shooting at the game, not merely because of the scarcity of ammunition, but, as I conceived, the laws of morality forbid it also. Encamped at sunset on the main branch [Cottonwood] of White river, hitherto called Grand river. Killed one buffalo and one cabrie. Distance 21 miles.[62]

Sept. 15th. Marched at seven o'clock ; passed a very large Kans encampment, evacuated, which had been occupied last summer. Proceeded on to the dividing ridge between the waters of White river and the Kans [more exactly, from basin of the Cottonwood to that of the Smoky Hill]. This ridge was covered with a layer of stone, which was strongly impregnated with iron ore, and on the W. side of said ridge we found spa springs. Halted at one o'clock, very much against the inclination of the Osage, who, from the running of the buffalo, conceived a party of Kans to be near. Killed two buffalo. Distance 18 miles.[63]

[61] Camp in the close vicinity of Marion, seat of the county of that name. The Indian trail seems to have run past or through Marion. We can confidently locate Pike within 3 m. of the town on the night of the 13th ; and Marion thus furnishes an excellent fixed point whence to trace him on to Smoky Hill r. The two streams which unite at Marion, and run through the place as one, are called Brook Luta and Clear cr.

[62] Continuing past Marion, up the Cottonwood, which he has to his left, Pike camps near Durham, Marion Co. This town is on the river, and through it runs the Chic., Kas. and Neb. R. R. The route seems to have sheered off from the river a little to the right, more in line with Brook Luta than with the Cottonwood itself : see next note.

[63] Passing north between Cottonwood r. on his left and Brook Luta on his right, Pike makes the divide in the vicinity of Tampa, Marion Co. This is a village

Sept. 16th. Marched late, and in about 4½ miles' distance came to a very handsome branch of water [Hobbs branch of Gypsum creek], at which we stopped and remained until after two o'clock, when we marched and crossed two branches [main Gypsum and Stag creeks]. Encamped on a third. At the second [Gypsum] creek, a horse was discovered on the prairie, when Baroney went in pursuit of him on a horse of Lieutenant Wilkinson, but arrived at our camp without success. Distance 13 miles.[64]

on the head of Brook Luta ; the railroad last named goes through it, and Pike crosses the line of this railroad between Durham and Tampa. He is flanking the higher hills (1,500 feet or more) in which the main Cottonwood heads, by leaving them to the left or W. This is a somewhat roundabout way from the vicinity of Durham to that of Bridgeport on the Smoky Hill, where Pike strikes this river early on the 17th ; but it is evident that he did not go straight between these points, for they are only about 25 m. (direct) apart, and we have to account for 18+13+6=37 m. on the 15th, 16th, and morning of the 17th. These mileages adjust themselves to a nicety by the way I make out. I suppose he crossed the divide between Tampa and Kuhnbrook, Marion Co., thus passing from Arkansan to Missourian waters, as he says. Kuhnbrook is a little place on one of the heads of the large Turkey cr., which runs N. into the Smoky Hill r. opp. Abilene. Rhoades is the next place on this branch of Turkey cr., and in passing to its vicinity Pike crosses from Marion into Dickinson Co. He continues on, bearing to the vicinity of Elmo and Banner. These are places near another head of Turkey cr., and both on the Mo. Pac. R. R.; they are within a mile of each other. Pike keeps on a piece, westerly, and sets camp in the vicinity of Carlton, Dickinson Co. Carlton is between the two forks of Holland cr., next W. of Turkey cr., with which Holland runs parallel to fall into the Smoky Hill r. opp. Abilene. Carleton is 7 m. due E. of Gypsum City, which latter is on a creek of that name Pike next strikes.

[64] Pike camps on a branch of Gypsum creek. This is a large stream which heads in close relation with the uttermost sources of Cottonwood r., in the vicinity of Canton, McPherson Co., and flows due N. into the Smoky Hill, between the mouths of Solomon and Saline rivers. It is larger than either Turkey or Holland cr., and much branched. It runs about halfway between Holland cr. and the Smoky Hill, parallel with both ; for the latter, having made a bold sweep from the W., curves N. past Lindsburg and Bridgeport to Salina, and thence E. to receive first the Saline, next Gypsum, and then Solomon r. On Gypsum cr. are Chico and Gypsum City, 10 and 12 m. above its mouth ; and Pike strikes it a few miles further up or S. of these towns. Pike charts its headwaters elaborately, and sets his camps of the 15th and 16th among the five branches he lays down. Probably one of these should be taken for Holland cr.; the other four are less easily identified. From his position in the

Sept. 17th. Marched early and struck the main S. E. [Smoky Hill] branch of the Kans river at nine o'clock ; it appeared to be 25 or 30 yards wide, and is navigable in the flood seasons. We passed it six miles to a small branch to breakfast. Game getting scarce, our provision began to run low. Marched about two o'clock, and encamped at sundown on a large branch [Mulberry creek]. Killed one buffalo. Distance 21 miles.[65]

vicinity of Carlton Pike passes W. from Dickinson into Saline Co., comes first to Hobbs cr., next upon Gypsum itself and Stag cr., in quick succession ; crossing these three he continues W. to another branch of Gypsum cr., namely, that one now meandered by the Mo. Pac. R. R. between Gypsum City and Bridgeport. He camps on the latter, 6 m. E. of the Smoky Hill.

[65] " We passed it six miles to a small branch to breakfast " is a dubious phrase which I understand to mean that Pike went 6 m. to a small branch to breakfast, and then crossed the Smoky Hill r. at once—at nine o'clock. This crossing was in the immediate vicinity of Bridgeport, and perhaps at the very place the Council Grove, Smoky Valley and Western branch of the Mo. Pac. R. R. crosses to run into Bridgeport. Two insignificant runs fall into the river from the east within 3 m. below Bridgeport ; the first of them is named Pawnee cr. Crossing the river, Pike proceeds up it, but a little W. of N., and bearing somewhat away from it ; he passes Dry cr., which lower down runs through the county seat Salina, and camps on Mulberry cr., 2 or 3 m. due W. of that city, and about the same distance below the point where Spring cr. falls into Mulberry. This stream skirts north of the city, receives Dry cr., and falls into Saline r. a mile or two further. Salina is a large place, one of the best known in the State, where four great railroad lines meet—the U. P., Mo. P., A., T. and S. F., and C., R. I. and P. Six or 8 m. due W. of the place where Pike crossed the river are the Smoky hills, or Smoky Hill Buttes, celebrated in story if not in song. The great river named from these conspicuous landmarks is the main southern fork of Kansas r., as the Republican is the northern. Its uttermost sources are in Colorado. Receiving uncounted tributaries in its long course, it runs E. in Kansas through Wallace, Logan, Gove, Trego, Ellis, Russell, and Ellsworth, loops S. into McPherson and out again N. into Saline Co., makes an elbow at Salina and continues E. through Dickinson into Geary Co., where it joins its mate between Junction City and Fort Riley, thus composing the Kansas. Two of its largest branches are the Saline and Solomon.

This finishes the first section of Pike's Kansas route from the Little Osage to Salina. The rest of the way to the Pawnee Republic is northward, crossing in succession Saline r., Salt cr., Solomon r., Buffalo cr., and White Rock cr., striking the Republican r. in Webster Co., Neb., near the S. border of that State. The distance is less than the 97 m. Pike makes of it. His map is extremely faulty ; he seems to have gone about N. W., though his actual route was very

Sept. 18th. Marched at our usual hour, and at twelve o'clock halted at a large branch [Saline river] of the Kans [Smoky Hill], which was strongly impregnated with salt. This day we expected the people of the [Pawnee] village to meet us. We marched again at four o'clock. Our route being over a continued series of hills and hollows, we were until eight at night before we arrived at a small dry branch [of Covert creek]. It was nearly ten o'clock before we found any water. Commenced raining a little before day. Distance 25 miles.[66]

little W. of N. It also runs Saline and Solomon rivers far apart into the Republican, instead of the Smoky Hill, magnifies Salt cr. out of all proportion, and minimizes both Buffalo and White Rock cr.

As a bit of authentic history which may interest those in Salina who have reason to be proud of the growth of their city during one generation, I will transcribe a passage from my own field notebook, made when I was staging from Leavenworth to Santa Fé, in 1864 : "Sunday, May 29th. Left Junction City and came to a place called Salina—three houses and a pig stye."

Fort Riley, as above mentioned, was begun by Major Edmund Augustus Ogden, who had selected the site and was occupied with the work when he died there Aug. 3d, 1855, in the epidemic of cholera then raging. He was born at Catskill, N. Y., Feb. 20th, 1810 ; removed to Unadilla, N. Y., and from there entered West Point July 1st, 1827 ; he became second lieutenant of the 1st Inf., July 1st, 1831 ; first lieutenant, Dec. 17th, 1836 ; was transferred to the 8th Inf., July 7th, 1838 ; promoted to be captain, Dec. 1st, 1839 ; and was breveted major for meritorious conduct. His first duty was at Prairie du Chien ; his marriage with Captain Gustavus Loomis' daughter Eliza, at Fort Snelling, is said to have been the first ceremony of the kind between white persons in Minnesota ; he served faithfully and with distinction in the Black Hawk, Florida, and Mexican wars, and for many years discharged arduous and responsible duties in the quartermaster department. For several years immediately preceding his death he was stationed at Fort Leavenworth.

[66] Saline r., distinctively called Great or Grand Saline, has been already noted. Pike crosses this, and proceeds to "a small dry branch" of the next river, to camp for three days. This river is the one he calls Little Saline, and is now known as Covert or Salt cr., a branch of Solomon r. which falls into the Solomon 4 m. below Minneapolis, Ottawa Co. Pike's map connects it correctly, but magnifies its size ; for the stream which he passed on returning from the Pawnee village, and which he lays down as a head of his Little Saline, is a branch of the Great Saline. Pike probably crossed Saline r. in the vicinity of Culver, where the railroad now does, then soon passing from Saline into Ottawa. The small branch of Salt cr. on which he camped was one of several such in the vicinity of Ada.

Sept. 19th. It having commenced raining early, we secured our baggage and pitched our tents. The rain continued without any intermission the whole day, during which we employed ourselves in reading the Bible and Pope's Essays, and in pricking on our arms with India ink some characters, which will frequently bring to mind our forlorn and dreary situation, as well as the happiest days of our life. In the rear of our encampment was a hill, on which there was a large rock, where the Indians kept a continual sentinel, as I imagine to apprise them of the approach of any party, friends or foes, as well as to see if they could discover any game on the prairies.

Sept. 20th. It appearing as if we possibly might have a clear day, I ordered our baggage spread abroad to dry; but it shortly after clouded up and commenced raining. The Osage sentinel discovered a buffalo on the prairies; upon which we dispatched a hunter on horseback in pursuit of him, also some hunters on foot; before night they killed three buffalo, some of the best of which we brought in and jerked or dried by the fire. It continued showery until afternoon, when we put our baggage again in a position to dry, and remained encamped. The detention of the doctor and our Pawnee ambassador began to be a serious matter of consideration.

Sunday, Sept. 21st. We marched at eight o'clock, although there was every appearance of rain, and at eleven o'clock passed a large [Little Saline river of Pike, now Covert] creek, remarkably salt. Stopped at one o'clock on a fresh branch of the salt creek. Our interpreter having killed an elk, we sent out for some meat, which detained us so late that I concluded it best to encamp where we were, in preference to running the risk of finding no water. Distance 10 miles.

Lieutenant Wilkinson was attacked with a severe headache and slight fever. One of my men had been attacked with a touch of the pleurisy on the 18th, and was still ill. We were informed by an Osage woman that two of the Indians were conspiring to desert us in the night and steal some of our horses, one of whom was her husband. We engaged her as our spy. Thus were we obliged to keep ourselves on our guard against our own companions and fellow-travelers—men of a nation highly favored by the United States, but whom I believe to be a faithless set of poltrons, incapable of a great and generous action. Among them, indeed, there may be some exceptions.

In the evening, finding that the two Indians above mentioned had made all preparations to depart, I sent for one of them, who owned a horse and had received a gun and other property for his hire, and told him " I knew his plans, and that if he was disposed to desert, I should take care to retain his horse; that as for himself, he might leave me if he pleased, as I only wanted men with us." He replied " that he was a man, that he always performed his promises, that he had never said he would return; but that he would follow me to the Pawnee village, which he intended to do." He then brought his baggage and put it under charge of the sentinel, and slept by my fire; but notwithstanding I had' him well watched.

Sept. 22d. We did not march until eight o'clock, owing to the indisposition of Lieutenant Wilkinson. At eleven waited to dine. Light mists of rain, with flying clouds. We marched again at three o'clock, and continued our route 12 miles to the first branch of the Republican Fork. [?] Met a Pawnee hunter, who informed us that the chief had left the village the day after the doctor arrived, with 50 or 60 horses and many people, and had taken his course to the north of our route; consequently we had missed each other. He likewise informed us that the Tetaus [misprint for Tetans, and that a mistake for Ietans, *i. e.,* Comanches] had recently killed six Pawnees, the Kans had stolen some horses, and a party of 300 Spaniards had lately been as far as the Sabine; but for what purpose was unknown. Distance 11 miles.[67]

[67] An error is here evident, and I suspect some confusion of the diary of the 21st and 22d. 1. "Distance 11 miles," for the whole 22d, is necessarily wrong, if

Sept. 23d. Marched early and passed a large fork of the Kans [*i. e.*, Smoky Hill] river, which I [correctly] suppose to be the one generally called Solomon's. One of our horses fell into the water and wet his load. Halted at ten o'clock on a branch of this fork. We marched at half past one o'clock, and encamped at sundown on a stream [Buffalo creek] where we had a great difficulty to find water. We were overtaken by a Pawnee, who encamped with us. He offered his horse for our use. Distance 21 miles.[68]

Sept. 24th. We could not find our horses until late, when we marched. Before noon met Frank, who had accompanied Dr. Robinson to the village, and three other Pawnees, who informed us that the chief and his party had only arrived at the village yesterday, and had dispatched them out in search of us. Before three o'clock we were joined by several Pawnees; one of them wore a scarlet coat, with a small medal of General Washington, and a Spanish medal also. We encamped at sunset on a middle-sized branch [White Rock creek], and were joined by several Pawnees in the evening, who brought us some buffalo meat. Here we

12 m. were made in the afternoon, and this, too, after marching from eight to eleven in the forenoon. 2. Aside from the fact that there is no branch of the Republican fork in this vicinity, the map shows that Pike did not reach Solomon r. till the 23d, and the text of that day confirms this. Camps of the 21st and 22d were both in the space traversed between Salt cr. and Solomon r., less than 20 m. at the furthest. 3. The difficulty disappears if for " 12 miles," etc., of the above questionable clause, we read " 2 miles to the first branch of Solomon river on our route." This would set Pike on one of the small creeks that fall into the right bank of Solomon r. in the vicinity of Glasco, Simpson, and Asherville. A former name of Solomon r. was Nepeholla, used, *e. g.*, by Gunnison, P. R. R. Rep. II. 1855, p. 17. Capt. J. W. Gunnison came to the mouth of Solomon's fork July 6th, 1853, from Westport, Mo., by the Wakarusa River route, striking the Kansas r. at Fort Riley, crossing there, and continuing through Abilene ; he was en route to the great bend of the Arkansaw by the usual Smoky Hill route.

[68] Taking Pike northward across Buffalo cr. I suppose this was crossed somewhere in the vicinity of Jamestown, Republic Co. In this position the Republican r. itself is only 5 or 6 m. to his right, and the rest of the journey is simply following up this river obliquely on about a N. W. course, at a somewhat increasing distance from it, until he nears it to approach the village.

saw some mules, horses, bridles, and blankets, which they obtained of the Spaniards. Few only had breech cloths, most being wrapped in buffalo robes, otherwise quite naked. Distance 18 miles.[69]

Sept. 25th. We marched at a good hour, and in about eight miles struck a very large road on which the Spanish troops had returned, and on which we could yet discover the grass beaten down in the direction which they went.

When we arrived within about three miles of the village, we were requested to remain, as the ceremony of receiving the Osage into the towns was to be performed here. There was a small circular spot, clear of grass, before which the Osage sat down. We were a small distance in advance of the Indians. The Pawnees then advanced within a mile of us, halted, divided into two troops, and came on each flank at full charge, making all the gestures and performing the maneuvers of a real war charge. They then encircled us around, and the chief advanced in the center and gave us his hand ; his name was Caracterish. He was accompanied by his two sons and a chief by the name of Iskatappe. The Osage were still seated ; but Belle Oiseau then rose, came forward with a pipe, and presented it to the chief, who took a whiff or two from it. We then proceeded ; the chief, Lieutenant Wilkinson, and myself in front ; my sergeant, on a white horse, next with the colors ; then our horses and baggage, escorted by our men, with the Pawnees on each side, running races, etc. When we arrived on the hill over the town we were again halted, and the Osage seated in a row ; when each Pawnee who intended so to do presented them with a horse and gave a pipe to smoke to the Osage to whom he had made the present. In this manner were

[69] To White Rock cr., west of White Rock, a town on the creek and on the boundary between Republic and Jewell cos. This stream runs east through these, and falls into the Republican r. opposite Republic City. In getting here, Pike seems by his map to have crossed several small streams *running to his left*, and into a stream he runs into Solomon r. I suppose these to be some branches of Marsh cr., a sluggish tributary of Buffalo cr. from the N. W.

eight horses given. Lieutenant Wilkinson then proceeded
with the party to the [Republican] river above the town,
and encamped. I went up to our camp in the evening,
having a young Pawnee with me loaded with corn for my
men. Distance 12 miles.[70] As the chief had invited us to
his lodge to eat, we thought it proper for one to go. At
the lodge he gave me many particulars which were interesting to us, relative to the late visit of the Spaniards.

I will attempt to give some memoranda of this expedition,
which was the most important ever carried on from the
province of New Mexico, and in fact the only one directed

---

[70] Finishing the journey to the Pawnee Republic village, whence the great
river on which it was situated took its name. Its ultimate sources are in Colorado, like those of the Smoky Hill r. Its main course then cuts off the extreme
N. W. corner of Kansas, by running through Cheyenne Co.; whereupon the
stream enters Nebraska, and skirts the southern border of this until it dips into
Kansas across the N. border of Jewell Co., whence it continues E. into Republic Co., turns S. in this to Cloud Co., E. through this to Clay Co., and S. E.
through this to Geary Co., where it is joined by the Smoky Hill, as already noted.
The whole journey thus made from the Osages to the Pawnees foots up, by
Pike's distances, about 350 m. In a letter to the Secretary of War he calls it
" 375 "; but this is simply offhand. He also claims that his Osages led him
roundabout 100 m. through their fear of the " Kans." Pike's land mileages
seem to me more correct than those excessive ones he assigns to his navigation.
I suppose this journey to have been between 300 and 325 m.

I must emphasize here the fact that I have failed in every attempt to locate
the precise site of the Pawnee village. One would suppose it well known ; I find
that it is not, and have yet to discover the ethnographer or geographer who can
point it out. Correspondence addressed to persons now living in the vicinity
was as fruitless as my exploration of the sources of official knowledge in Washington, where several friends interested themselves in my behalf to no purpose.
I know of no closer indication than that afforded by Gregg's map of 1844. This
letters " Old Pawnee Village " on the S. bank of the Republican, halfway between long. 98° and 99° W., and thus, as I judge, about opposite the present
town of Red Cloud, Webster Co., Neb. Gregg runs the Republican entirely S.
of lat. 40° N., *i. e.*, in Kansas ; but the place where Pike struck it was certainly
in that portion of its course which runs in Nebraska, just over the Kansas line.
Gregg in fact gives his river a recognizable northward convexity along here, and if
it does not overreach 40°, that is a fault of absolute, not relative, position. We
are here much less concerned with latitude than with longitude. The river is running approximately from W. to E., in Webster Co., and the main point is how
far W. the village was, as that would affect details of the route from the last

N. E. (except that mentioned by the Abbe Raynal [71] in his History of the Indies) to the Pawnees—of which see a more particular account hereafter. In the year 1806 our affairs with Spain began to wear a very serious aspect, and the troops of the two governments almost came to actual hostilities on the frontiers of Texas and the Orleans territory. At this time, when matters bore every appearance of coming to a crisis, I was fitting out for my expedition from St. Louis, where some of the Spanish emissaries in that country transmitted the information to Majar. Merior [*sic*] and the Spanish council at that place, who immediately forwarded the information to the then commandant of Nacogdoches, Captain Sebastian Rodreriques [*sic*], who forwarded it to Colonel [Don Antonio] Cordero, by whom it was transmitted to [General Don Nimesio Salcedo, at Chihuahua,] the seat of government. This information was personally communicated to me, as an instance of the rapid means they possessed of transmitting information relative to the occurrences transacting on our frontiers. The expedition was then determined on, and had three objects in view:

point at which I have been able to locate Pike. It will be necessary to discover the exact situation of the Pawnee village before the cloud over the end of this journey can be dispelled, and the beginning of the journey from the village to Great Bend on the Arkansaw can be set in a clear light. For the present I can only tentatively assume longitude 98° 30' W. (See Scandia, in the Index.)

[71] Guillaume Thomas François Raynal, commonly called Abbé Raynal, b. Aveyron, France, Apr. 12th, 1713, d. Paris, Mar. 6th, 1796—a philosophical freethinker and historian, who wrote too much sense and truth to suit his official superiors, and was consequently unfrocked. It is a curious fact in the history of the most Tammany-like machine for the propagation of painful superstitions ever known in the Western world—excepting perhaps Brigham Young's similarly organized scheme—that whenever one of its members begins to think for himself they make him take off his gown and wear trousers openly. The irony in the case seems to escape the professional nurserymen in that hot-house. The abbé wrote various works ; his most celebrated one, to which Pike refers, is : Histoire Philosophique et Politique des Établissements et du Commerce des Européens dans les Deux Indes, 1770, repub. 1780-85—a book whose strength and other merits may be inferred from the fact that it had the honor of being burned by Parliamentary order ; though its author was simply exiled, the times being already a little out of joint for roasting heretics along with their heresies.

1st. To descend the Red river, in order, if he met our expedition, to intercept and turn us back; or, should Major Sparks [72] and Mr. [Thomas] Freeman have missed the party from Nacogdoches, under the command of Captain Viana, to oblige them to return and not penetrate further into the country, or make them prisoners of war.

2d. To explore and examine all the internal parts of the country from the frontiers of the province of New Mexico to the Missouri between the La Platte [sentence unfinished].

3d. To visit the Tetaus, Pawnees republic, Grand Pawnees, Pawnee Mahaws, and Kans. [73] To the head chief of each of those nations the commanding officer bore flags, a commission, grand medal, and four mules; and with all of them he had to renew the chains of ancient amity which was said to have existed between their father, his most Catholic majesty, and his children the red people.

The commanding officers also bore positive orders to oblige all parties or persons, in the above-specified countries,

[72] Richard Sparks of Pennsylvania had been a captain in the levies of 1791, when he was appointed a captain of infantry, March 7th, 1792; he was arranged to the 3d Sub-legion, Sept. 4th, 1792, to the 3d Infantry, Nov. 1st, 1796, and transferred to the 2d Infantry Apr. 1st, 1802; he became major July 29th, 1806, lieutenant-colonel Dec. 9th, 1807, and colonel July 6th, 1812; he was honorably discharged June 15th, 1815, and died July 1st, 1815.

[73] 1. As already indicated, "Tetaus" and "Tetans" are Pike's names for Comanches, also variously known as Ietans, Jetans, Hietans, Aiatans, etc., and also by the Sioux name Padoucas, adopted by the French; they called themselves Num, meaning simply "people." Some of their other names are Kaumains, Choumans and Comandes; we now write Comanches or Camanches indifferently, thus adopting a form of the Spanish name, whose meaning is unknown. These Indians are of the Shoshonean family; they number about 150, on the Kiowa, Comanche, and Wichita Reservation in Oklahoma; there were some 2,500 when they were placed in a reservation in 1868; they had been noted, time out of mind, as wide-ranging, lawless, and warlike freebooters. 2. Pike above mentions three of the four principal tribes of the Pawnee confederation, i. e., of the middle group of Caddoan stock, who are: (1) Pawnee proper, Grand Pawnee, or Tcawi; (2) Pawnee Republicans or Republican Pawnees (giving name to the great branch of the Kansas r.); (3) Pawnee Loups, Pawnee Mahas, Pawnee Wolves, or Skidis; (4) Tapage or Pitahauerat: see further, L. and C., ed. 1893, pp. 55-57. (3) Pike's Kans are entirely different Indians, of Siouan stock, Dhegiha group: for these see l. c., pp. 33, 34.

either to retire from them into the acknowledged territories of the United States, or to make prisoners of them and conduct them into the province of N. Mexico. Lieutenant Don Facundo Malgares, the officer selected from the five internal provinces to command this expedition, was a European (his uncle was one of the royal judges in the kingdom of New Spain), and had distinguished himself in several long expeditions against the Apaches and other Indian nations with whom the Spaniards were at war; added to these circumstances, he was a man of immense fortune, and generous in its disposal, almost to profusion; possessed a liberal education, high sense of honor, and a disposition formed for military enterprise. This officer marched from the province of Biscay with 100 dragoons of the regular service, and at Santa Fe, the place where the expedition was fitted out, he was joined by 500 of the mounted militia of that province, armed after the manner described by my notes on that subject, and completely equipped with ammunition, etc., for six months; each man leading with them (by order) two horses and one mule, the whole number of their beasts was 2,075. They descended the Red river 233 leagues; met the grand bands of the Tetaus, and held councils with them; then struck off N. E., and crossed the country to the Arkansaw, where Lieutenant Malgares left 240 of his men with the lame and tired horses, while he proceeded on with the rest to the Pawnee republic. Here he was met by the chiefs and warriors of the Grand Pawnees; held councils with the two nations and presented them the flags, medals, etc., which were destined for them. He did not proceed to the execution of his mission with the Pawnee Mahaws and Kans, as he represented to me, from the poverty of their horses and the discontent of his own men; but, as I conceive, from the suspicion and discontent which began to arise between the Spaniards and the Indians; the former wished to revenge the death of Villineuve and party, while the latter possessed all the suspicions of conscious villainy deserving punishment. Malgares took with him all the traders he found there from our country, some of whom, having been sent to Natchitoches, were in abject poverty at that place on my arrival, and applied to me for means to return to St. Louis. Lieutenant Malgares returned to Santa Fe the   of October, when his militia was disbanded; but he remained in the vicinity of that place until we were brought in, when he, with dragoons, became our escort to the seat of government [in Chihuahua].

Sept. 26th. Finding our encampment not eligible as to situation, we moved down on to the prairie hill, about three-fourths of a mile nearer the village. We sent our interpreter to town to trade for provisions. About three o'clock in the afternoon 12 Kans arrived at the village, and informed Baroney that they had come to meet us, hearing that we were to be at the Pawnees' village. We pitched our camp upon a beautiful eminence, whence we had a view of the town and all that was transacting. In the evening Baroney, with the chief, came to camp to give us the news, and returned together.

Sept. 27th. Baroney arrived from the village about one o'clock, with Characterish, whose commission from the Governor of New Mexico was dated Santa Fe, June 15th, 1806, and three other chiefs, to all of whom we gave a dinner. I then made an appropriate present to each, after which Lieutenant Wilkinson and myself accompanied them to town, where we remained a few hours, and returned. Appointed to-morrow for the interview with the Kans and Osage.

Sunday, Sept. 28th. Held a council of the Kans and Osage, and made them smoke of the pipe of peace. Two of the Kans agreed to accompany us. We received a visit from the chief of the village. Made an observation on an emersion of one of Jupiter's satellites.

Sept. 29th. Held our grand council with the Pawnees, at which were present not less than 400 warriors, the circumstances of which were extremely interesting. The notes I took on my grand council held with the Pawnee nation were seized by the Spanish government, together with all my speeches to the different nations. But it may be interesting to observe here, in case they should never be returned, that the Spaniards had left several of their flags in this village, one of which was unfurled at the chief's door the day of the grand council; and that among various demands and charges I gave them was, that the said flag should be delivered to me, and one of the United States' flags be received and hoisted in its place. This probably was carrying the pride of nations a little too far, as there had so lately been a large force of Spanish cavalry at the village, which had made a great impression on the minds of the young men, as to their power, consequence, etc., which my appearance with 20 infantry was by no means calculated to remove.

After the chiefs had replied to various parts of my discourse, but were silent as to the flag, I again reiterated the demand for the flag, adding " that it was impossible for the nation to have two fathers; that they must either be the children of the Spaniards, or acknowledge their American father." After a silence of some time an old man rose, went to the door, took down the Spanish flag, brought it and laid it at my feet; he then received the American flag, and elevated it on the staff which had lately borne the standard of his Catholic Majesty. This gave great satisfaction to the Osage and Kans, both of whom decidedly avow themselves to be under American protection. Perceiving that every face in the council was clouded with sorrow, as if some great national calamity were about to befall them, I took up the contested colors, and told them " that as they had shown themselves dutiful children in acknowledging their great American father, I did not wish to embarrass them with the Spaniards, for it was the wish of the Americans that their red brethren should remain peaceably around their own fires, and not embroil themselves in any disputes between the white people ; and that for fear the Spaniards might return there in force again, I returned them their flag, but with an injunction that it should never be hoisted again during our stay." At this there was a general shout of applause, and the charge was particularly attended to.

Sept. 30th. Remained all day at the camp, but sent Baroney to town, who informed me on his return that the chief appeared to wish to throw great obstacles in our way. A great disturbance had taken place in the village, owing to one of the young Pawnees, Frank, who lately came from the United States, having taken the wife of an Osage and run away with her. The chief, in whose lodge the Osage put up, was extremely enraged, considering it a breach of hospitality to a person under his roof, and threatened to kill Frank if he caught him.

CHAPTER II.

ITINERARY, CONTINUED: FROM THE PAWNEE VILLAGE
THROUGH KANSAS AND COLORADO TO PIKE'S PEAK,
OCT. IST–NOV. 30TH, 1806.

WEDNESDAY, Oct. 1st. Paid a visit to town and had a very long conversation with the chief, who urged everything in his power to induce us to turn back. Finally, he very candidly told us that the Spaniards wished to have gone further into our country, but he induced them to give up the idea; that they had listened to him and he wished us to do the same; that he had promised the Spaniards to act as he now did, and that we must proceed no further, or he must stop us by force of arms. My reply was, " that I had been sent out by our great father to explore the western country, to visit all his red children, to make peace between them, and turn them from shedding blood; that he might see how I had caused the Osage and Kans to meet to smoke the pipe of peace together, and take each other by the hand like brothers; that as yet my road had been smooth, with a blue sky over our heads. I had not seen any blood in our path; but he must know that the young warriors of his great American father were not women, to be turned back by words; that I should therefore proceed, and if he thought proper to stop me, he could attempt it; but we were men, well armed, and would sell our lives at a dear rate to his nation; that we knew our great father would send his young warriors there to gather our bones and revenge our deaths on his people, when our spirits would rejoice in hearing our exploits sung in the war-songs of our chiefs." I then left his lodge and returned to camp, in considerable perturbation of mind.

Oct. 2d. We received advice from our Kans that the chief had given publicity to his idea of stopping us by force of arms, which gave serious reflections to me, and was productive of many singular expressions from my brave lads, which called for my esteem at the same time that they excited my laughter. Attempted to trade for horses, but could not succeed. In the night we were alarmed by some savages coming near our camp at full speed; but they retreated equally rapidly, on being hailed with fierceness by our sentinels. This created some degree of indignation in my little band, as we had noticed that all the day had passed without any traders presenting themselves, which appeared as if all intercourse was interdicted. I wrote to the secretary at war, the general, etc.

Oct. 3d. The intercourse again commenced. Traded for some horses, and wrote for my express.

Oct. 4th. Two French traders arrived at the village in order to procure horses to transport their goods from the Missouri to the village. They gave us information that Captains Lewis and Clark,[1] with all their people, had descended the river to St. Louis; this diffused general joy through our party. Our trade for horses advanced none this day.

Sunday, Oct. 5th. Buying horses. Preparing to march, and finishing my letters.

Oct. 6th. Marched my express.[2] Purchasing horses and preparing to march on the morrow.

Oct. 7th. In the morning we found two of our newly purchased horses missing. Sent in search of them; the Indians brought in one pretty early. Struck our tents and commenced loading our horses. Finding there was no

---

[1] On the other hand, Lewis and Clark first heard of Pike's expedition on Sept. 10th, 1806, when they were nearing the Big Nemaha on their way down the Missouri, and met a boat with a trader bound for the Pawnee Loups : see L. and C., p. 1206.

[2] Letters to Generals Dearborn and Wilkinson, sent by this express, formed Docs. Nos. 13 and 14 in the App. to Pt. 2. of the orig. ed. They are given beyond.

probability of our obtaining the other lost one, we marched at 2 p. m.; and as the chief had threatened to stop us by force of arms, we made every arrangement to make him pay as dearly for the attempt as possible. The party was kept compact, and marched by a road round the village, in order that, if attacked, the savages would not have their houses to fly to for cover. I had given orders not to fire until within five or six paces, and then to charge with the bayonet and saber, when I believe it would have cost them at least 100 men to have exterminated us, which would have been necessary. The village appeared all to be in motion. I galloped up to the lodge of the chief, attended by my interpreter and one soldier, but soon saw there was no serious attempt to be made, although many young men were walking about with their bows, arrows, guns, and lances. After speaking to the chief with apparent indifference, I told him that I calculated on his justice in obtaining the horse, and that I should leave a man until the next day at twelve o'clock to bring him out. We then joined the party and pursued our route.

When I was once on the summit of the hill which overlooks the village, I felt my mind relieved from a heavy burden; yet all the evil I wished the Pawnees was that I might be the instrument, in the hands of our government, to open their ears and eyes with a strong hand, to convince them of our power.

Our party now consisted of two officers, one doctor, 18 soldiers, one interpreter, three Osage men, and one woman, making 25 warriors. We marched out and encamped on a small branch [of Rock creek], distant seven miles, on the same route we came in.[3] Rain in the night.

[3] Camp is on one of the tributaries of Rock cr., close to that of Sept. 24th, if not on the same spot.

The route now taken by the expedition is very little W. of S., to strike the Arkansaw r. at the most convenient point. Thus it diverges westerly from the route by which the Pawnee Republic was approached, which was W. of N. The two make a ∧ whose legs rest on the Smoky Hill fork at the two points where this was crossed in going and returning, with the apex at the village.

Oct. 8th. I conceived it best to send Baroney back to the village with a present, to be offered for our horse, the chief having suggested the propriety of this measure ; he met his son and the horse with Sparks. Marched at ten o'clock, and at four o'clock came to the place where the Spanish troops encamped the first night they left the Pawnee village. Their encampment was circular, having only small fires round the circle to cook by. We counted 59 fires ; now if we allow six men to each fire, they must have been 354 in number.[4] We encamped on a large branch of the second [Solomon's] fork of the Kans river. Distance 18 miles.[5]

Oct. 9th. Marched at eight o'clock, being detained until that time by our horses being at a great distance. At eleven o'clock we found the forks of the Spanish and Pawnee roads,

The main streams crossed between the Republican and Smoky Hill forks are Solomon and Great Saline rivers. Pike is also on the trail of the Spaniards who have just raided United States territory to the Pawnees ; he marks their camps, as far as he can find them out, with a O, to distinguish them from his own, marked X.

The party which leaves the Pawnees, so far as the white men are concerned, only differs from that which left Belle Fontaine by the absence of the deserter, Kennerman : see note [2], p. 358. The express which Pike dispatched therefore consisted of some of his Indians.

[4] This close calculation was doubtless based in part on information Pike already possessed. We have been told that Malgares started on his raid with 100 dragoons and 500 militia, of which 600 men 240 had been detached, leaving 360. The "large branch" on which was camp was probably one of the heads of Livingston cr.

[5] "Distance 18 miles" would never bring Pike to any branch of the Solomon. His error here is a puzzling one until it is detected by reference to the map. That sets his camp-mark high up on the same creek, several branches of which he had on his left when he went up E. of it, Sept. 24th. It is *Buffalo cr.*, which Pike erroneously runs into Solomon r., and so seems never to have passed before. See back, note [68]. I suppose he struck Buffalo cr. below Mankato, somewhere in the vicinity of Jewell and very likely between these places. He seems to be holding about S. S. W., and to-morrow strikes Solomon r. But, as already explained, note [70], p. 410, precision in this matter is impossible, without knowing exactly where the Pawnee village stood, so as to have a fixed initial point of the journey. I understand that there was a certain "Pawnee trail" once well known from this village to Great Bend on the Arkansaw. If this be now determinable, it will represent Pike's route with a closer approximation to accuracy than I have been able to follow it out.

and when we halted at twelve o'clock, we were overtaken by the second chief, Iskatappe, and the American chief with one-third of the village. They presented us with a piece of bear-meat.

When we were about to march, we discovered that the dirk of the doctor had been stolen from behind the saddle. After marching the men, the doctor and myself, with the interpreter, went to the chief and demanded that he should cause a search to be made; it was done, but when the dirk was found, the possessor asserted that he had found it on the road. I told him that he did not speak the truth, and informed the chief that we never suffered a thing of ever so little value to be taken without liberty. At this time the prairie was covered with his men, who began to encircle us around, and Lieutenant Wilkinson with the troops had gained half a mile on the road. The Indian demanded a knife before he would give it up; but as we refused to give any, the chief took one from his belt and gave him, took the dirk and presented it to the doctor, who immediately returned it to the chief as a present, desired Baroney to inform him he now saw it was not the value of the article but the act we despised, and then galloped off.

In about a mile we discovered a herd of elk, which we pursued; they took back in sight of the Pawnees, who immediately mounted 50 or 60 young men and joined in the pursuit. Then, for the first time in my life, I saw animals slaughtered by the true savages with their original weapons, bows and arrows; they buried the arrow up to the plume in the animal. We took a piece of meat and pursued our party; we overtook them and encamped within the Grand or Solomon Fork, which we had crossed lower down on the 23d of September, on our route to the Pawnees. This was the Spanish encamping ground. Distance 18 miles.[6]

In the evening two Pawnees came to our camp, who had

[6] To the Solomon r., in the vicinity of Beloit, Mitchell Co. The stream which Pike lays down across his trail of to-day is perhaps Plum cr., which falls in below Beloit.

not eaten for three days, two of which they had carried a sick companion whom they had left this day ; we gave them for supper some meat and corn, and they immediately departed in order to carry their sick companion this seasonable supply.   When they were coming into camp, the sentinel challenged, it being dark ; they immediately, on seeing him bring his piece to the charge, supposing he was about to fire on them, advanced to give him their hands; he, however, not well discerning their motions, was on the point of firing ; but being a cool, collected little fellow, called out that there were two Indians advancing on him, and asked if he should fire.   This brought out the guard, when the poor affrighted savages were brought into camp, very much alarmed, for they had not heard of a white man's being in their country, and thought they were entering one of the camps of their own people.

Oct. 10th.   Marched at seven o'clock and halted at twelve o'clock to dine.   Were overtaken by the Pawnee chief whose party we left the day before, who informed us the hunting-party had taken another road, and that he had come to bid us good-by.   We left a large ridge on our left, and at sundown crossed it. . . . [? [7]]   From this place we had an extensive view of the southwest ; we observed a creek at a distance, to which I meant to proceed.   The doctor, interpreter, and myself arrived at eight o'clock at night ; found water and wood, but had nothing to eat.   Kindled a fire in order to guide the party ; but they, not being able to find the route and not knowing the distance, encamped on the prairie without wood or water.

Oct. 11th.   Ordered Baroney to return to find the party and conduct them to our camp.   The doctor and myself went out to hunt, and on our return found all our people had arrived, except the rear-guard, which was in sight.

---

[7] Hiatus in the text, probably from missing or illegible MS.; no course or distance for to-day.   But the map shows a march, and sets camp among the heads of a small stream.   This is perhaps Salt cr., high up, somewhere in the icinity of Saltville, Paris, or Victor.

Whilst we halted five Pawnees came to our camp and brought some bones of a horse which the Spanish troops had been obliged to eat at their encampment on this creek. We took up our line of march at twelve o'clock, and at sundown the party halted on the Saline. I was in pursuit of buffalo, and did not make the camp until near ten o'clock at night. Killed one buffalo. Distance 12 miles.[8]

Sunday, Oct. 12th. Here Belle Oiseau and one Osage left us, and there remained only one man and woman of that nation. Their reason for leaving us was that our course bore too much west, and they desired to bear more for the hunting-ground of the Osage. In the morning we sent out to obtain the buffalo meat, and laid by until after breakfast. Proceeded at eleven o'clock ; and crossing the [Grand Saline] river two or three times, we passed two camps where the Spanish troops had halted. Here they appeared to have remained some days, their roads being so much blended with the traces of the buffalo that we lost them entirely. This was a mortifying stroke, as we had reason to calculate that they had good guides, and were on the best route for wood and water. We took a southwest direction, and before night were fortunate enough to strike their roads on the left ; and at dusk, much to our surprise, struck the east [Smoky Hill] fork of the Kans, or La Touche de la Cote Bucanieus. Killed one buffalo. Distance 18 miles.[9]

Oct. 13th. The day being rainy, we did not march until

[8] Perhaps to vicinity of Lincoln, seat of the county so called. The map has an extra camp-mark, on the head of what Pike calls "Little Saline river."

[9] In saying that he crossed the (Grand Saline) river "two or three times," Pike does not mean that he meandered that stream on his march, but that he or some of his party were hunting about for the Spanish trail which he was so eager to follow, and which here became blind. His map marks O O, the two Spanish camps he found. His was on the north bank of Smoky Hill r., whose other name in the text, "La Touche de la Cote Bucanieus," possibly stands for La Fourche de la Côte du Kansas, *i. e.*, that fork of the Kansas which runs along the dividing ridge or coteau—which is perfectly true of the Smoky Hill fork. Pike struck the Smoky Hill in Russell or Ellsworth Co. Camp of the 13th is about on the border of Russell and Barton cos., in the vicinity of Forest Hill and Dubuque.

two o'clock; when, it having an appearance of clearing off, we raised our camp [and crossed the Smoky Hill river]; after which we marched seven miles and encamped on the head of a branch of the river we had left. Had to go two miles for water. Killed one cabrie.

Oct. 14th. It having drizzled rain all night, and the atmosphere being entirely obscured, we did not march until a quarter past nine o'clock, and commenced crossing the dividing ridge between the Kans and Arkansaw rivers.[10] Arrived on a branch of the latter at one o'clock; continued down it in search of water until after dusk, when we found a pond on the prairie, which induced us to halt. Sparks did not come up, being scarcely able to walk with rheumatic pains. Wounded several buffalo, but could not get one of them. Distance 24 miles.

Oct. 15th. In the morning rode out in search of the south trace, and crossed the low prairie [Cheyenne Bottoms], which was nearly all covered with ponds, but could not dis-

[10] The approximation of Missourian and Arkansan waters is here very close. The Arkansaw makes its great bend northward into Barton Co., whose county seat is named Great Bend accordingly. The courses of the Smoky Hill and Arkansaw are for many miles approximately parallel, and only some 30 m. apart in air-line distance; the numerous tributaries of each arise all along the ridge which forms the divide between these waters. Pike has crossed the divide, and is now on one of the headwaters of Cow cr., a large affluent of the Arkansaw, which traverses Barton and Rice cos. in a southeasterly course, and falls in at Hutchinson, Reno Co. His camp appears to have been somewhere in the vicinity of Claflin, Barton Co., on the Kas. and Col. R. R. The stream is laid down on his map. It is by far the largest tributary of the Arkansaw between the Little Arkansaw and Walnut creeks. It was the last stream to be crossed on the old Santa Fé caravan road before the Arkansaw was reached. This road also crossed the several tributaries of Cow cr. in the vicinity of Lyons, Rice Co. One of these, between Lyons and Chase, was called Little Cow cr. We find another, E. of Lyons, marked on modern maps as "Jarvis" cr., and given as Charez or Owl cr. in Beckwith's Report of 1853, P. R. R. Rep. II. 1855, p. 22. Two of these names refer to Don Antonio José Chavez, who left Santa Fé in February, 1843, en route for Independence, Mo., but was brutally murdered and robbed in this vicinity, on or about April 12th, by a party of 15 men who represented themselves to be Texan troops under the command of one John McDaniel. Particulars of this outrage are given by Gregg, Comm. Pra. II. 1844, pp. 166–169.

cover it.   Finding Sparks did not arrive, sent two men in search of him, who arrived with him about eleven o'clock. At twelve o'clock we commenced our line of march, and at five o'clock Dr. Robinson and myself left the party at a large [Walnut [11]] creek, having pointed out a distant wood to Lieu-

[11] Walnut (Big or Wet Walnut) cr. is that large northern affluent of the Arkansaw which runs E. from Lane through Ness and Rush into Barton Co., and falls into the river 4 m. below Great Bend, county seat of Barton. A branch of this, called Little or Dry Walnut cr., runs E. from Rush into Barton, and falls into Walnut cr. about 4 m. from the mouth of the latter. Great Bend is on the N. bank of the Arkansaw, and thus between that river and Little Walnut cr. The way in which, and the precise point at which, the Expedition struck the Arkansaw could hardly be discovered from the text of the 15th–18th ; we are not even told till the 18th that we are on the Arkansaw, as the 15th mostly, and the 16th and 17th entirely, are taken up with the wanderings of the lieutenant and doctor, who got lost. The key to the situation is not found till the 23d, when it is luckily recited that a trip was made from the camp on the Arkansaw " about 20 miles to a large branch [or fork] on the right." This is the well-known Pawnee fork of the Arkansaw, where was old Fort Larned, a noted place, and where is now Larned, seat of Pawnee Co. So the Expedition struck the Arkansaw 20 m. below Larned, in the very suburbs of the present city of Great Bend. This locality about the mouth of Walnut cr. became early noted, not only as the place of northernmost deflection of the Arkansaw, but also as the first objective point on that river, where the old Santa Fé caravan road struck that river. It also became the site of Fort Zara, or Zarah—to be found on some maps as Fort Sarah—which was built in 1853 on the high ground between Walnut and Cow creeks, about 5 m. N. of the road. On July 12th of that year, Capt. Gunnison reached the great bend by the Smoky Hill route from Fort Riley, having been preceded in arriving there three days by his companion, who came over the regular Santa Fé route ; Lieut.-Col. E. V. Sumner, 1st Dragoons, and other officers, arrived from Mexico the same night ; and on the spot was camped Captain and Bvt.-Major Edward Johnson, 6th Infantry, about to build the fort, as that 100 m. further up the Arkansaw (Fort Atkinson) was to be abandoned. Col. John Garland of the 8th Infantry passed by in July of that year. Pike's approach was : Being in camp of the 14th on some head of Cow cr., the Expedition started on the 15th at noon, and marched five hours, about 15 m., on a W. S. W. course, thus crossing the Cheyenne Bottoms above said, and coming to Walnut cr. just above the mouth of the Little Walnut above described. Pike pointed out a wood and told Wilkinson to go there to camp, while he and the doctor would go up Walnut cr. a piece to hunt for the Spanish trail. Either mistaking the wood intended, or finding himself so near the Arkansaw, Wilkinson went on to that river and camped the party on its north bank, a mile or two above where Great Bend now stands. Pike and the doctor went shooting buffalo, and it got pretty late ; they returned to where Pike had told Wilkinson

tenant Wilkinson for our encampment, in order to search
some distance up it for the Spanish trace.   Killed two buffalo and left part of our clothing with them to scare away
the wolves.   Went in pursuit of the party.   On our arrival

to camp, and found nobody there ; so they bivouacked on the spot.   In the
morning they went up Little Walnut cr. to search, but did not go far from those
two buffalo they had killed ; in fact they got rattled at finding no camp, turned
about and went *down* Little Walnut cr. to its mouth (which is what text of the
16th means by " their junction "—confluence of the two creeks).   On the morning of the 17th, being thoroughly alarmed, and imagining that the party must
be higher up the Little Walnut, they started up again, but probably went a
very little way in the rain ; for they were overtaken early on the 18th by two
men whom Wilkinson had sent in search of them, and then they were only
" about three " miles from the camp on the Arkansaw.   It is not likely they
were at any moment 10 m. from the spot where they had left the party.

Pike's map shows nothing but the trail of the party, no camp being marked
after that of the 12th, on the other side of the Smoky Hill r.   The trail
makes a sharp elbow at the point where, having come down Cow cr. on the
14th, they turned from that stream on the 15th.   Besides Cow cr., three
others appear in succession to the W.   The first is Walnut cr.; the second
is Little Walnut, a branch of the first, run separately into the Arkansaw ; while
the third is Ash cr., which falls in above camp.   Cow cr. is brought in too near
the next one.   On the south side of the Arkansaw is marked the station of the
19th–27th, with the legend : " Here we struck the Arkansaw from whence
L^t. Wilkinson descended the river in skin canoes and Capt. Pike went up by
land with his party."   This ends map I. of the Arkansaw, etc., and map II. of
the same connects at this point, the first stream laid down being Pawnee fork,
and the first camp that of the 29th.   Camp of the 28th falls between the two
maps, and is not shown.   The Spanish trail, which Pike lost on Smoky Hill
r., was all the while a little to the W. or right of the party, and is recovered on
the S. side of the Arkansaw, on the 30th.

Pike elsewhere says of his journey from the Pawnees to the Arkansaw that it
was on a general course S. 10° W. 150 m., but might have been made in 120.
His deviation from the most direct route was in bearing a little too far W. to cross
the Saline and Smoky Hill, and then some needless meandering across the divide
to the Arkansaw.   But he struck the latter exactly at the right point ; for Great
Bend is where the old Smoky Hill and Cimarron route from Leavenworth to
Santa Fé reached the Arkansaw.   There was of course nothing on the spot in
Pike's time—nor was there even in 1864, when I first passed the place, excepting a miserable shack the stage company had built.   The nearest settlement at
that time was Fort Larned.   My journal of May 31st, 1864, refreshes my memory : "At 2 p. m. we brought up at Fort Larned—mean place, built of adobe
and logs, with a drunken officer in command ; everybody half drunk already ;
and all were whole drunk by bed-time."

at'the [Little Walnut] creek appointed for the encampment, did not find them.   Proceeded down it for some miles, and not finding them, encamped, struck fire, and then supped on one of our buffalo tongues.

Oct. 16th.   Early on horseback; proceeded up the [Little Walnut] creek some distance in search of our party, but at twelve o'clock crossed to our two buffaloes; found a great many wolves at them, notwithstanding the precautions taken to keep them off.   Cooked some marrow-bones and again mounted our horses, and proceeded down the creek to their junction.   Finding nothing of the party, I began to be seriously alarmed for their safety.   Killed two more buffalo, made our encampment, and feasted sumptuously on the marrow-bones.   Rain in the night.

Oct. 17th.   Rose early, determining to search the [Little Walnut] creek to its source.   Very hard rain, accompanied by a cold northwester all day.   Encamped near night without being able to discover any signs of the party.   Our sensations now became excruciating, not only for their personal safety, but for fear of the failure of the national objects intended to be accomplished by the expedition.   Our own situation was not the most agreeable, not having more than four rounds of ammunition each, and being 400 miles in the nearest direction from the first civilized inhabitants.   We, however, concluded to search for the party on the morrow, and if we did not succeed in finding them, to strike the Arkansaw, where we were in hopes to discover some traces, if not cut off by the savages.

Oct. 18th.   Commenced our route at a good time, and about ten o'clock discovered two men on horseback in search of us—one my waiter.   They informed us the party was encamped on the Arkansaw, about three miles south of where we then were; this surprised us very much, as we had no conception of that river being so near.   On our arrival we were met by Lieutenant Wilkinson, who, with all the party, was greatly concerned for our safety.   The Arkansaw, on the party's arrival, had not water in it six inches deep, and the stream was not more than 20 feet wide ; but the rain of the two days covered all the bottom of the river, which in this place is 450 yards from bank to bank. These are not more than four feet in height, bordered by a few cottonwood trees ; on the north side is a low swampy prairie ; on the south, a sandy sterile desert at a small distance. In the afternoon the doctor and myself took our horses and crossed the Arkansaw, in order to search for some trees which might answer the purpose to make canoes ; found but one, and returned at dusk. It commenced raining at twelve o'clock.

Sunday, Oct. 19th. Finding the river rising rapidly, I thought it best to secure our passage over [from the N. to the S. bank]; we consequently made it good by ten o'clock. Rain all day. Preparing our tools and arms for labor and the chase on the morrow.

Oct. 20th. Commenced our labor at two trees for canoes, but one proved too much doated.[12] Killed two buffalo and one cabrie. Discharged our guns at a mark, the best shot a prize of one tent and a pair of shoes. Our only dog was standing at the root of the tree, in the grass ; one of the balls struck him on the head and killed him. Ceased raining about twelve o'clock.

Oct. 21st. Dr. Robinson and myself mounted our horses, in order to go down the river to the entrance of the three last creeks we had crossed on our route ; but meeting with buffalo, we killed four ; also, one cabrie. Returned to the camp and sent for the meat.

Oct. 22d. Having sat up very late last evening, expecting the sergeant and party, who did not arrive, we were very anxious for them ; but about ten o'clock Bradley arrived and informed us that they could not find the buffalo which we had killed on the prairie. They all arrived before noon. In the afternoon we scaffolded some meat, and nearly completed the frame of a skin canoe, which we concluded to build. Overhauled my instruments and made some rectifications preparatory to taking an observation, etc.

[12] Doted or unsound : see L. and C., ed. 1893, p. 951.

Oct. 23d. Dr. Robinson and myself, accompanied by one man, ascended the river with an intention of searching for the Spanish trace ; at the same time we dispatched Baroney and our two hunters to kill some buffalo, to obtain the skins for canoes. We ascended the river about 20 miles to a large branch [Pawnee fork [13]] on the right. Just at dusk gave chase to a buffalo and were obliged to shoot 19 ball sinto him before we killed him. Encamped on the fork [at Larned, Pawnee Co.].

Oct. 24th. We ascended the right branch [Pawnee fork] about five miles [old Fort Larned], but could not see any sign of the Spanish trace ; this is not surprising, as the river bears southwest, and they no doubt kept more to the west from the head of one branch to another. We returned and on our way killed some prairie-squirrels [*Cynomys ludovicianus*], or wishtonwishes, and nine large rattlesnakes [*Crotalus confluentus*], which frequent their villages. On our arrival, found the hunters had come in a boat, one hour before, with two buffalo and one elk skin.

[13] Pawnee fork is larger than Walnut cr. It runs through several counties on a general E. course, and falls in at Larned, seat of Pawnee Co. When I was in the country, 30 years ago, the three principal branches were called Heth's, Buckner's, and Shaff's. A branch now rejoices in the name of Guzzler's Gulch. Saw-mill cr. is a long but slight tributary which falls in close to the mouth of the main stream. Pike crosses the mouth of Pawnee fork on the 29th ; the Spaniards had crossed it higher up. He lays it down as a short, forked stream. Larned is now a city of some importance, and a rival of Great Bend ; it is the natural development of which old Fort Larned was the germ ; it is built mainly on the N. or left bank of Pawnee fork, but has lately crossed that stream, and also extended in the adjoining Arkansaw bottom. The locality became noted with the establishment of the Santa Fé trade in the '20's, and later on was a point of strategic importance in our relations with hostile or unruly Indians. The main road passed here en route for Santa Fé, in continuation both of the earliest caravan road and of the later Smoky Hill stage route ; it offered a good camping place, which traders, troops, and other travelers generally occupied. Another reason for stopping was that the river was not easy to cross when full. Thus, when Emory and Abert were here, July 13th, 1846, one of Kearny's expressmen, A. E. Hughes, was drowned in it (J. T. Hughes, Doniphan's Exp., 1887, p. 21). But it varied much ; July 13th, 1853, Gunnison and Beckwith found it 20 feet wide, with a fair current, and a depth of only a foot or two.

The wishtonwish of the Indians, prairie-dogs of some travelers, or squirrels, as I should be inclined to denominate
them, reside on the prairies of Louisiana in towns or villages, having an evident police established in their communi-
ties. The sites of their towns are generally on the brow of
a hill, near some creek or pond, in order to be convenient to
water, and that the high ground which they inhabit may not
be subject to inundation. Their residence, being under
ground, is burrowed out, and the earth, which answers the
double purpose of keeping out the water and affording an
elevated place in wet seasons to repose on, and to give them
a further and more distinct view of the country. Their holes
descend in a spiral form ; therefore I could never ascertain
their depth; but I once had 140 kettles of water poured
into one of them in order to drive out the occupant, without
effect. In the circuit of the villages they clear off all the
grass, and leave the earth bare of vegetation ; but whether
it is from an instinct they possess inducing them to keep the
ground thus cleared, or whether they make use of the herbage as food, I cannot pretend to determine. The latter
opinion I think entitled to a preference, as their teeth designate them to be of the graminivorous species, and I know of
no other substance which is produced in the vicinity of their
positions on which they could subsist ; and they never extend their excursions more than half a mile from the burrows. They are of a dark brown color, except their bellies,
which are white. Their tails are not so long as those of our
gray squirrels, but are shaped precisely like theirs ; their
teeth, head, nails, and body are the perfect squirrel, except
that they are generally fatter than that animal. Their villages sometimes extend over two and three miles square, in
which there must be innumerable hosts of them, as there is
generally a burrow every ten steps in which there are two or
more, and you see new ones partly excavated on all the borders of the town. We killed great numbers of them with
our rifles and found them excellent meat, after they were exposed a night or two to the frost, by which means the rank-

ness acquired by their subterraneous dwelling is corrected. As you approach their towns, you are saluted on all sides by the cry of "wishtonwish," from which they derive their name with the Indians, uttered in a shrill and piercing manner. You then observe them all retreating to the entrance of their burrows, where they post themselves, and regard every, even the slightest, movement that you make. It requires a very nice shot with a rifle to kill them, as they must be killed dead, for as long as life exists they continue to work into their cells. It is extremely dangerous to pass through their towns, as they abound with rattlesnakes, both of the yellow and black species; and strange as it may appear, I have seen the wishtonwish, the rattlesnake, the horn frog [*Phrynosoma douglasi*], with which the prairie abounds (termed by the Spaniards the cammellion [camaleon, *i. e.*, chameleon], from their taking no visible sustenance), and a land-tortoise, all take refuge in the same hole. I do not pretend to assert that it was their common place of resort; but I have witnessed the above facts more than in one instance.[14]

Oct. 25th. Took an observation; passed the day in writing, and preparing for the departure of Lieutenant Wilkinson.

Sunday, Oct. 26th. Delivered out a ration of corn by way of distinction of the Sabbath. Preparing for our departure.

Oct. 27th. Delivered to Lieutenant Wilkinson letters for the general[15] and our friends, with other papers, consisting of his instructions, traverse tables of our voyage, and a draught

[14] This is an early but not the first account of the animals, and has been much cited, particularly as authority for the name wishtonwish (which J. Fenimore Cooper misapplied to the whippoorwill in one of his novels). The date of Pike's observation is subsequent to that of Lewis and Clark, but its publication was prior by four years; both these notices are antedated by Gass, 1807: see L. and C., ed. 1893, p. 111.

[15] A letter which Lieutenant Williamson bore to his father from Pike formed Doc. No. 15 of the App. to Pt. 2. of the orig. ed., and is given beyond in its proper place.

of our route to that place complete, in order that if we were lost, and he arrived in safety, we might not have made the tour without some benefit to our country.   He took with him, in corn and meat, 21 days' provisions, and all the necessary tools to build canoes or cabins.   Launched his canoes.   We concluded we would separate in the morning, he to descend [the river], and we to ascend to the mountains.

Oct. 28th.   As soon as possible all was in motion, my party crossing the river to the north side, and Lieutenant Wilkinson launching his canoes of skins and wood.   We breakfasted together, and then filed off ; but I suffered my party to march, while I remained to see Lieutenant Wilkinson sail.   This he did at ten o'clock, having one skin canoe, made of four buffalo skins and two elk skins, which held three men besides himself and one Osage.   In his wooden canoe were one soldier, one Osage, and their baggage ; one other soldier marched on shore.[16]   We parted with " God bless you " from both parties ; they appeared to sail very well.   In the pursuit of our party, Dr. Robinson, Baroney, one soldier, and myself, killed a brelau [blaireau, badger, *Taxidea americana*] and a buffalo ; of the latter we took only his marrow-bones and liver.   Arrived where our men had encamped, about dusk.   Distance 14 miles.[17]

[16] The five soldiers who descended the Arkansaw with Lieutenant Wilkinson were : Sergeant Ballenger ; Privates Boley, Bradley, Huddleston, Wilson. Lieutenant Wilkinson's separate report of his journey hence to the Arkansaw Post formed one of the Documents of the App. to Pt. 2 of the orig. ed., and will be found beyond, where it is annotated in due course.

Those who proceeded to the horrors of the mountains in midwinter and subsequent capture by the Spaniards were : Captain Pike ; Dr. Robinson ; Interpreter Vasquez ; Sergeant Meek ; Corporal Jackson ; Privates Brown, Carter, Dougherty, Gorden, Menaugh, Miller, Mountjoy, Roy, Smith, Sparks, Stoute —16 all told : compare date of Oct. 7th, p. 419 and note [2], p. 360.

Pike now starts up the Arkansaw, to which he holds till he reaches the site of Pueblo, Col.

[17] Taking the party past Pawnee rock and the mouth of Ash cr., to a point about midway between the latter and the mouth of Pawnee fork.   They traveled on the left or N. side of the river, approximately along the track of the A., T. and S. F. R. R., passing Dundee station and the small town of

Oct. 29th. Marched after breakfast and in the first hour's march passed two fires, where 21 Indians had recently encamped, in which party, by their paintings on the rocks, there were seven guns. Killed a buffalo, halted, made fire, and feasted on the choice pieces of meat. About noon discovered two horses feeding with a herd of buffalo; we attempted to surround them, but they soon cleared our fleetest coursers. One appeared to be an elegant horse. These were the first wild horses we had seen. Two or three hours before night struck the Spanish road; and, as it was snowing, halted and encamped the party at the first woods on the bank of the river. The doctor and myself then forded it, the ice running very thick, in order to discover the course the Spaniards took; but owing to the many buffalo roads, could not ascertain it. It evidently appeared that they had halted here some time, as the ground was covered with horse-dung for miles around. Returned to camp. The snow fell about two inches deep, and then it cleared up. Distance 12 miles.[18]

Pawnee Rock; Hubbard cr., on the other side of the river, is also passed, and camp is set a little beyond it, over the border of Barton Co., in Pawnee Co. The town of Pawnee Rock takes its name from the remarkable natural object of the same designation, also sometimes called Painted rock, which was a great landmark in old times. This is the most prominent point of a sandstone ridge of notably reddish color and in part scoriaceous; it is about 20 feet high, and stands off to the right of the road as you go up—about 2 m. from the Arkansaw r., before you come to the crossing of Ash cr. It was a convenient place for the Indians to exercise their pictographic art, and when the road came to be traveled by the whites the rock was soon covered with inscriptions of names, dates, and the like. It is about 9 m. by the road from the town of Pawnee Rock to the crossing of Pawnee fork.

[18] Passing Pawnee fork and Larned, Pawnee Co., to camp on the left or N. W. bank of the Arkansaw, about 5 m. beyond. Here is the place where the old Santa Fé road forked, in the days of the caravans and stages. The main road followed up the Arkansaw; but the right-hand road sheered off from the river to take up what was known as the "dry route"—a sort of cut-off which looked promising and became a regular stage-road, but was no great advantage when you had to go slowly and camp out, as the lesser distance was offset by lack of wood at all times, and of water at most seasons. Having been over this road, I can certify to the remarks of Gunnison and Beckwith, P. R. R. Rep. II., 1855, p. 24: "Five miles from camp [on Pawnee Fork] the road

Oct. 30th. In the morning sent out to kill a buffalo, to have his marrow-bones for breakfast, which was accomplished. After breakfast the party marched up on the north side; the doctor and myself crossed with considerable difficulty, on account of the ice, to the Spanish camp, where we took a large circuit in order to discover the Spanish trace, and came in at a point of woods south of the river, where we found our party encamped. We discovered also that the Spanish troops had marked the river up [*i. e.*, left an up-river trail], and that a party of savages had been there not more than three days before. Killed two buffalo. Distance 4 miles. [Opposite Garfield, Pawnee Co., where Big Coon creek falls in.[19]]

Oct. 31st. Fine day; marched at three quarters past nine o'clock, on the Spanish road. Encamped, sun an hour high, after having made 16 miles [opposite Kinsley, Edwards Co.[20]].

forks . . . . and one branch follows near by the windings of the Arkansas, to secure grass and water, while the other appears to push off for a ' short cut ' and ' dry route ' to Fort Atkinson, near which they again unite on the Arkansas river ; but this appearance is deceptive ; for after going a few miles it turns abruptly southward, and follows but a few miles from, and parallel with, the other road, keeping it generally in sight, as it does also the trees and sand-hills upon the banks of the Arkansas river, and is, except in the rainy season, without good grass and badly watered." The air-line distance of the " dry route," from the point where Pike is now to Dodge City, is about 54 m.; the actual travel is nearer 60. The ground passed over is that sometimes watered by the Coon creeks, and the road coincides to some extent with that now traversed by the A., T. and S. F. R. R. Of late the face of the country has been modified by the Eureka Irrigating Canal, which starts from the Arkansaw at Ingalls, hugs the river more or less closely to the bluffs below Dodge City, and then starts off across country in the direction of Spearville and Kinsley.

[19] Pike camps to-night about opposite Garfield, a railroad station and small village on the left or N. W. bank of the river. He started up on that side (having the river to his left), but crossed over on the 30th, and will continue the whole way to Pueblo up the right bank, having the river on his right. The general course of the river being from W. to E., its right bank is on the S., and thus N. of Pike.

[20] Kinsley, county seat of Edwards, is something of a town in these parts, situated a mile or two W. of the river on that one of the Coon creeks which runs oftener than the other one does, and which, when it has any water to dis-

We observed this day a species of crystallization on the road, when the sun was high, in low places where there had been water settled ; on tasting it found it to be salt ; this gave in my mind some authenticity to the report of the prairie being covered for leagues. Discovered the trace of about 20 savages who had followed our road ; and of horses going down the river. Killed one buffalo, one elk, one deer.

Nov. 1st. Marched early ; just after commencing our line, heard a gun on our left. The doctor, Baroney, and myself being in advance, and lying on the ground waiting for the party, a band of cabrie came up among our horses, to satisfy their curiosity ; we could not resist the temptation of killing two, although we had plenty of meat. At the report of the gun they appeared astonished, and stood still until we hallowed [hallooed] at them to drive them away. Encamped in the evening on an island.[21]

Upon using my glass to observe the adjacent country, I observed on the prairie a herd of horses. Dr. Robinson and Baroney accompanied me to go and view them ; when within a quarter of a mile they discovered us, and came

charge, falls into the Arkansaw at Garfield, after skirting the river for many miles. The nomenclature of Big and Little Coon creeks is reversed on some maps. I find that I was camped on one of them, 24 m. from Fort Larned, June 1st, 1864, under which date my old journal calls it " a puddlesome slough on the prairie." Thirty years ago it was good buffalo country, and consequently bad Indian country. A note I penciled June 3d, 1864, runs thus : " Our route since leaving Larned has been mostly along the north bank of the Arkansaw. Queer river that—a great ditch, chock full of grassy islets, stretching through the treeless prairie like a spotted snake, some seasons so dry you can't wet your foot in it for miles, and have to dig for a drink, sometimes a raging flood 200 yards wide. Traveling without military escort is risky. The Cheyennes are on the rampage ; Comanches and Kiowas too." On the 6th, nearing Fort Lyon, we passed an Indian camp ; " it was a band of Arapahoes, at war with the Cheyennes."

[21] No mileage for to-day. By Pike's map, camp is at an elbow of the river, which denotes that curve the Arkansaw makes in passing from Ford into Kiowa Co. There is no place to name in this vicinity, and the best maps, on a scale of 2 m. to the inch, do not give any island hereabouts. We will allow Pike 16 m., and set camp in Ford Co., just over the border of Kiowa.

immediately up near us, making the earth tremble under them ; this brought to my recollection a charge of cavalry. They stopped and gave us an opportunity to view them; among them there were some very beautiful bays, blacks, and grays, and indeed of all colors. We fired at a black horse, with an idea of creasing[22] him, but did not succeed; they flourished round and returned again to see us, when we returned to camp.

Sunday, Nov. 2d. In the morning, for the purpose of trying the experiment, we equipped six of our fleetest coursers with riders and ropes, to noose the wild horses, if in our power to come among the band. They stood until we came within forty yards of them, neighing and whin-neying, when the chase began, which we continued about two miles, without success. Two of our horses ran up with them ; but we could not take them. Returned to camp. I have since laughed at our folly ; for taking wild horses in that manner is scarcely ever attempted, even with the fleetest horses and most expert ropers. See my account of wild horses and the manner of taking them, in my disserta-tion on the province of Texas. Marched late. Killed one buffalo. River turned to north by west. Hills changed to the north side. Distance 13½ miles.[23]

Nov. 3d. Marched at ten o'clock. Passed numerous

---

[22] To " crease " a horse is to hit him with a bullet somewhere along the nape of the neck, close enough to the cervical vertebræ to stun him by the shock to the spinal cord, or to the ligamentum nuchæ, yet not to inflict permanent injury. When this is nicely done the horse falls as if killed, and is roped before he recovers. But it takes a very good shot, like " driving the nail," " snuffing the candle," " barking the squirrel," and other feats of skill which our backwoodsmen used to practice.

[23] Since he left Great Bend, Pike has had hilly country continuously on his left, with only a very narrow river-bottom on that side, in comparison with the breadth of the low-lying land on the W. or N. In fact, it is this series of countless thousands of hills and hillocks which causes the deflection of the river northward, thus making the " great bend." The place where the change occurs, and where Pike camps, is at Ford, a town in the county of that name, on the S. bank of the Arkansaw, or rather on the E. and S. bank of Mulberry cr. a stream from the S. W., which winds around the town on the W. and N., and

herds of buffalo, elk, some horses, etc., all traveling south.
The river bottoms full of salt ponds ; grass similar to our
salt meadows.   Killed one buffalo.   Distance 25½ miles.[24]

falls into the Arkansaw a mile or so lower down.   A branch of the Chic., Kas.,
and Neb. R. R. runs through Ford from Bucklin to Dodge City, Ensign, and
Montezuma.

[24] Taking Pike past the site of old Fort Dodge and of present Dodge City,
nearly to the boundary between Ford and Gray cos.—say halfway from Dodge
to Cimarron, and thus about opp. Howell station of the A., T., and S. F. R. R.
Dodge started on the N. bank, but has overgrown the river, and is now built
up on both sides, with two bridges across.   Dodge is 17 m. by rail above Ford,
and almost exactly on the 100th meridian—probably some of the houses are built
on each side of this line of longitude.   At or near Dodge were the long-noted
"Caches," of which most of the early travelers speak, but which seem to have
been latterly lost sight of.   I cannot locate the exact spot, but it ought to be
easily recoverable by those who have the data I happen to lack.   The place
used to be spoken of as near the meridian just said—though that does not help
us at all, as the maps of those days were mostly 30′ out of the way in longitudes.
Thus, even Gunnison and Beckwith's route-map of 1853 runs the line E. of the
mouth of Mulberry cr. where Ford now stands, and thus about 99° 40′.   Gregg's
is much closer than this, though it is on a much smaller scale ; his 100th line runs
midway betwixt the mouth of Mulberry cr. and the "Caches."   Wislizenus'
route-map, accompanying his report to Congress (Senate Misc. Doc. No. 26,
30th Congr., 1st Sess., pub. 1848) is closer still ; for the "Caches" are marked
scarcely W. of 100°.   Wislizenus gives us another clew, as he marks "Fort
Mann" at the "Caches."   The "Caches" were also about the place where the
dry cut-off, described in note [18] above, reached the Arkansaw—in short, everything points to the immediate vicinity of Fort Dodge as the place where these
caches were located.   "The history of the origin of these 'Caches' may be of
sufficient interest to merit a brief recital," as Gregg says, Comm. Pra. I. 1844,
p. 67, where, and on p. 19, we have the account.   In 1812 was fitted out the
first expedition which attempted to reach Santa Fé by following the account of
Pike's journey now before us.   This consisted of about a dozen men, among
them two named Beard and Chambers, who had succeeded in reaching Santa Fé
with the others, and had returned to the United States in 1822 (Chambers had
done so by way of the Canadian r.).   These two interested some St. Louis
capitalists to join an enterprise in the Santa Fé trade, and then undertook to
return to Santa Fé in the fall of 1822 with a small party and an assortment of
merchandise.   "Reaching the Arkansas late in the season, they were overtaken
by a heavy snowstorm, and driven to take shelter on a large island.   A rigorous
winter ensued, which forced them to remain pent up in that place for three long
months.   During this time the greater part of their animals perished ; so that,
when the spring began to open, they were unable to continue their journey with
their goods.   In this emergency they made a *cache* some distance above, on the

Nov. 4th. This day brought to our recollection the fate of our countrymen at Recovery,[25] when defeated by the Indians, in the year 1791. In the afternoon discovered the north side of the river to be covered with animals ; which, when we came to them, proved to be buffalo cows and calves. I do not think it an exaggeration to say there were 3,000 in one view. It is worthy of remark that in all the extent of country yet crossed, we never saw one cow, and that now the face of the earth appeared to be covered with them. Killed one buffalo. Distance 24½ miles.[26]

north side of the river, where they stowed away most of their merchandize. From thence they proceeded to Taos, where they procured mules, and returned to get their hidden property. Few travelers pass this way without visiting these mossy pits, many of which remain partly unfilled to the present day."

[25] Alluding to the terrible defeat of General Arthur St. Clair's army by Indians on a branch of the Wabash r., in present Darke Co., Ohio, Nov. 4th, 1791. This was the most disastrous battle ever lost by the whites to the Indians, surpassing Braddock's defeat on the Monongahela in 1755. On Dec. 25th, 1793, General Anthony Wayne, who had become commander-in-chief in 1792, and taken command of the Army of the West, sent a detachment of soldiers to take possession of the field where General St. Clair had been defeated, built a fort there, and named the place Recovery, because it was then first recovered from the Indians, who had retained possession after the disaster above named. June 29th, 1794, General Wayne sent troops with supplies to Fort Recovery from Greenville, where he was then stationed. The detachment reached the fort and deposited its supplies in safety, but was immediately attacked, and the fort itself was invested by Indians, assisted by whites from Canada. The battle raged June 30th and July 1st, when the assailants were repulsed, not without great loss on our side. Among those who fell was the gallant McMahon, who had commanded the expedition to Fort Recovery. For further information see : Howe's Hist. Coll. Ohio, under head of Darke Co.; Burnet's Notes of the N. W. Terr., chap. vii ; Albach's Annals of the West, p. 642. Present Fort Recovery is a village in Mercer Co. O., on a branch of the Wabash r., close to the Indiana State line.

[26] Camp past Cimarron and Ingalls, but not far W. of the latter—5 m., perhaps. These are two towns on the N. bank, respectively 18 and 26 m. above Dodge City. Ingalls is the seat of Gray Co. The Amer. Sp. word *cimarron* means something wild, runaway, or unreclaimed, like *maroon*, and is applicable to an animal, a person, a place, etc. It designated the wild sheep of the Rocky Mountains (*Ovis montana*), gave name to one of the largest branches of the Arkansaw, and was early associated with a certain route from the Arkansaw to Santa Fé. The name of J. J. Ingalls was long prominent in Kansas politics and in national statesmanship, and at one time associated with the too-true

Nov. 5th. Marched at our usual hour; at the end of two miles shot a buffalo and two deer, and halted, which detained us so long that we foolishly concluded to halt this day and kill some cows and calves, which lay on the opposite side of the river. I took post on a hill, and sent some horsemen over, when a scene took place which gave a lively representation of an engagement. The herd of buffalo being divided into separate bands covered the prairie with dust, and first charged on the one side, then to the other, as the pursuit of the horsemen impelled them;

statement that "purity in politics is an iridescent dream." Notwithstanding the injunction against truth-telling which the consequences of the scholarly senator's remark imply, I wish to speak as accurately as possible regarding the points at which the Cimarron route left the Arkansaw. There were two of these places, both of which Pike passes to-day, where the river was forded, and the road thus crossed from the N. to the S. bank. These became known as the Lower and Upper Crossings of the Arkansaw ; they were 8 m. apart ; the lower one was 18 m. and the upper one 26 m. above Fort Atkinson ; they thus correspond to the positions of Cimarron and Ingalls, respectively. The river is now bridged at each town. The Lower Crossing was the earlier one, most used by the traders from 1834 till the closing of the Mexican ports in 1843 ; after the war the Upper Crossing seems to have been generally chosen. Thus, we find Gunnison and Beckwith saying in 1853, P. R. R. Rep. II. 1855, p. 26 : "Seventeen miles from the fort [Atkinson] there is a ford, sometimes used by the trains and parties going to and from New Mexico by the Cimmaron [*sic*] route ; but the principal ford for that route is 8 m. above this." Writing of 1846, Dr. Wislizenus speaks of moving "about 20 miles" up the Arkansaw from the Caches, and arriving "at the usual fording place," *i. e.*, the lower one. "This track," says Gregg, Comm. Pra. I. 1844, p. 311, "which has since remained permanent, was made in the year 1834. Owing to continuous rains during the passage of the caravan of that year a plain trail was then cut in the softened turf, on the most direct route across this arid desert, leaving the Arkansas about 20 miles above the 'Caches.' This has ever since been the regular route of the caravans ; and thus a recurrence of those distressing sufferings from thirst, so frequently experienced by early travellers in that unhospitable region, has been prevented." The first camp S. of the Arkansaw was usually made in the vicinity of the Sand Hills, at a place called the Battle-ground after 1843, in which year the defeat of the Mexicans by the Texans under Colonel Snively occurred on that spot ; it was some 12–15 m. from the river. The roads from the two fords came together at no great distance from the Arkansaw (perhaps in the vicinity of Ulysses, seat of Grant Co.) ; having thus headed the Crooked Creek branch of Cimarron, the road crossed Sandy cr. not far above its confluence with the Cimarron, and so reached that river.

the report and smoke from the guns added to the pleasure of the scene, which in part compensated for our detention.

Nov. 6th. Marched early, but was detained two or three hours by the cows which we killed. The cow buffalo was equal to any meat I ever saw, and we feasted sumptuously on the choice morsels. I will not attempt to describe the droves of animals we now saw on our route; suffice it to say that the face of the prairie was covered with them, on each side of the river; their numbers exceeded imagination. Distance 16 miles.[27]

Nov. 7th. Marched early. The herbage being very poor, concluded to lay by on the morrow, in order to recruit our horses. Killed three cow buffalo, one calf, two wolves, one brelaw. Distance 18 miles.[28]

Nov. 8th. Our horses being very much jaded and our situation very eligible, we halted all day; jerked meat, mended mockinsons, etc.

Sunday, Nov. 9th. Marched early. At twelve o'clock struck the Spanish road, which had been on the outside of us, and which appeared to be considerably augmented. On our arrival at the camp, found it to consist of 96 fires, from which a reasonable conclusion might be drawn that there were from 600 to 700 men. We this day found the face of the country considerably changed, being hilly, with springs; passed numerous herds of buffalo and some horses. Distance 27 miles.[29]

[27] Past Pierceville, a village and station on the A., T., and S. F. R. R., just over the line between Gray and Finney cos.; camp 3 or 4 m. short of Garden City, seat of the latter county.

[28] Past Garden City and Sherlock; camp on or near the boundary between Finney and Kearney cos., in the vicinity of Deerfield, a place on the railroad. Most of the older maps mark hereabout the large island in the Arkansaw called Chouteau's, somewhat W. of the 101st meridian, and apparently near Deerfield.

[29] Vicinity of Harland, seat of Kearney Co. In saying that the Spanish road had been "on the outside" of the party, Pike gives us to understand that it had run along to his left, a little further from the river, though since the 30th of Oct. he had been also traveling on the S. side of the Arkansaw, having that river on his right. Nevertheless, the map marks the two trails as identical,

Nov. 10th. The hills increased; the banks of the river covered with groves of young cottonwood; the river itself much narrower and crooked. Our horses growing weak; two gave out; bring them along empty; cut down trees at night for them to browse on. Killed one buffalo. Distance 20 miles.[03]

Nov. 11th. Marched at the usual hour. Passed two old camps, and one of last summer, which had belonged to the savages, and we supposed Tetaus. Passed a Spanish camp where it appeared they remained some days, as we conjectured, to lay up meat, previously to entering the Tetau country, as the buffalo evidently began to grow much less numerous. Finding the impossibility of performing the voyage in the time proposed, I determined to spare no pains to accomplish every object, even should it oblige me to spend another winter in the desert. Killed one buffalo, one brelaw. Distance 24 miles.[31]

Nov. 12th. Was obliged to leave the two horses, which entirely gave out. Missed the Spanish road. Killed one buffalo. Distance 20 miles.[32]

the Spanish camps alternating with the American all along. There has been little to note along this stretch of the river, where no stream of any consequence falls in on either side. Pike here remarks a change, in the beginning of hilly country ; extensive sand-hills are skirting the river on the S., in Kearney Co., and thence into Hamilton.

[30] Vicinity of Syracuse, seat of Hamilton Co.

[31] Last day's journey in Kansas, passing from Hamilton Co., over the inter-State line, into Prowers Co., Colorado. Pike's mileages along the whole course from Great Bend are remarkably close. I designedly ran them off day by day, without any checking by known positions, to see when he would strike the inter-State line, about 5 m. beyond which is the first identifiable named stream ; expecting then to hark back, much as usual, and make the requisite adjustments of camps by proportionate lengths of each. But I find no occasion for this ; his own mileages fix his camp of the 11th as nearly as possible on the line, and we have three identifiable streams in the course of his march on the 12th. To-day's camp is between Coolidge, Hamilton Co., Kas., and Hollys, Prowers Co., Col., 2 m. W. of the former, 4 m. E. of the latter, in lat. 38° 02′ N., long. 102° 02′ W.

[32] In Colorado Pike first comes opp. Hollys, a village on the N. bank and station of the A., T., and S. F. R. R. Below this are some small runs on the

Nov. 13th. We marched at the usual hour. The river-banks began to be entirely covered with woods on both sides, but no other species than cotton-wood. Discovered very fresh signs of Indians, and one of our hunters informed me he saw a man on horseback, ascending a ravine on our left. Discovered signs of war-parties ascending the river. Wounded several buffalo. Killed one turkey, the first we have seen since we left the Pawnees. [Supposed distance 12 miles.[33]]

Nov. 14th. In the morning, Dr. Robinson, one man and

N., among them one called Cheyenne cr.; and Wild Horse cr. falls in on that side a mile above Hollys.   He then crosses Two Butte cr., a much larger stream, from the S., arising in Las Animas Co. about the elevations from which it takes name, running through the N. W. corner of Baca and traversing Prowers to fall in a mile above the mouth of Wild Horse cr., opposite the large island there.   Continuing, Pike crosses Granada cr., from the S., which falls in where the railroad crosses the Arkansaw and runs into the station named Adana. If he held straight on the best road, keeping to the left of the extensive bottoms along here, he went through the present sites of Granada, a village 4 m. W. of Adana, on Wolf cr., and of Manville, a station 2 m. further along.   Camp was set about halfway between Manville and Carlton, a place 4 m. beyond.   Several runs or washes make in along here on each side, but seldom carry as much water as the ditches which have been brought from the Arkansaw through and by Granada.   Pike charts Two Butte cr., and one that answers either to Granada or Wolf cr.: notice the pair he lays down, S., with the legend " Cotton Wood becomes frequent " lettered across Two Butte cr.

The Wild Horse cr. above mentioned appears on Gregg's map by the name of " Lit. Sand Cr."

[33] No mileage to-day ; and the omission is not easily supplied.   On the 15th Pike camps at the mouth of Purgatory r., and it took him 34 m. by his reckoning to get there from his camp of the 13th.   Therefore, camp of the 13th was about 12 m. from that of the 12th, and thus within a mile or two of Lamar.   I shall so suppose it to have been.   This sets Pike past the " point of red rocks and one large [Big Sandy] creek," which he speaks of as having passed on the 14th, but it agrees with the map, which sets a camp-mark for the 13th past Big Sandy cr.   There is evidently a confusion of the record of the 13th and 14th, perhaps in the flurry of the Indian sign ; all things considered, I shall set camp of the 13th, hypothetically, 2 m. short of Lamar : and that of the 14th at the station Prowers, 10 m. further ; whence it is about 24 m. for the 15th to Purgatory r.   The points passed on the 13th and 14th are most conveniently discussed together : see next note.   The site of Fort Aubrey (named for or by F. X. Aubrey ?), on the N. bank, was probably passed on the 13th.

myself, went up the ravine in which the man was supposed
to have been seen, but could make no important discovery.
Marched at two o'clock; passed a point of red rocks and
one large creek.[34] Distance 10 miles.

Nov. 15th. Marched early. Passed two deep creeks[35]

[34] From his camp of the 12th Pike passes the village and station Carlton, opposite which the small Cottonwood cr. falls in from the N., and proceeds to his
own " large creek " and " point of rocks." This stream is Big Sandy cr., from
the N.; Pike lays it down very well. It is quite a river or river-bed, which
when it runs drains from the high country known as the Arkansaw Divide, *sc.*
between Arkansan and Missourian waters, in El Paso, Elbert, and Lincoln cos.
The stream further traverses Cheyenne and Kiowa cos., and seeks the Arkansaw in Prowers Co., 2 or 3 m. below the point of rocks Pike notices. This is
a place where a bold headland abuts against the river on the south, rising rapidly from 3,575 to more than 3,800—that is, some 300 feet above the general level
of the river bottom. A run known as Clay cr. comes around the bluff on the W.
The next above is Willow cr., S., on which Lamar stands between irrigating
ditches derived from the Arkansaw, and the next above is Dry cr., S., halfway
between Lamar and Prowers station. Here is camp of the 14th, just over the
border of Prowers, in Bent Co. Pike's map legends " Broken with small
Ravines & Creeks " on the country passed over.

[35] This statement conflicts with Pike's map, which lays down only one stream
between the two camp-marks that stand for the 14th and 15th. But the text
is right, and *both* these camp-marks are misplaced. One belongs just below
.Mud cr., and the other at Purgatory r., where there is no sign of one, though
this is the most exactly locatable station since we left Great Bend. Pike's
" two deep creeks " are Mud and Caddoa ; his " many points of rocks " appear
on any good topographical map. There is a series of such between Prowers
and Mud cr., on the S., opposite which Graveyard cr. falls in, N. Two very
notable points of rocks, a mile apart, are separated by Caddoa cr.; and
Limestone cr. falls in from the N., 2 or 3 m. below these. These bluffs extend to the village of Caddoa, 2 m. up, in a bottom left by their recession from
the river, before they again close in on the river in two bold headlands, 1 or 2
m. above Caddoa. The country on the N., across the river, is also bluffy for
several miles along here. The elevations close to the river are 3,800 to 3,900
feet, and higher further back on both sides. Above the Caddoan bluffs a
creek which Pike charts falls on the S. This is lettered Blue cr. on late G. L.
O. maps, and Rule cr. on those of Hayden and Powell. Caddoa cr. heads
about the N. W. corner of Baca Co., and takes a northerly course to the Arkansaw ; Blue or Rule cr. is the larger one of the two ; some of its affluents
are near those of Caddoa and upper reaches of Two Butte cr., about Shell Rock
cañon in Baca Co., but its real source is further south in Las Animas Co.,
where Johnny cr. and others head. Its course is northerly, but with an eastward trend, about parallel with Purgatory r. About an hour before **Pike**

and many high points of rocks; also, large herds of buffalo.

At two o'clock in the afternoon I thought I could distinguish a mountain to our right, which appeared like a small blue cloud ; viewed it with the spy glass, and was still more confirmed in my conjecture, yet only communicated it to Dr. Robinson, who was in front with me ; but in half an hour they appeared in full view before us. When our small party arrived on the hill they with one accord gave three cheers to the Mexican mountains.[36] Their appearance can easily be imagined by those who have crossed the Alleghenies ; but their sides were whiter, as if covered with snow, or a white stone. Those were a spur of the grand western chain of mountains which divide the waters of the Pacific from those of the Atlantic ocean; and it [the spur] divides the waters which empty into the Bay of the Holy Spirit from those of the Mississippi, as the Alleghenies do those which discharge themselves into the latter river and the Atlantic. They appear to present a natural boundary between the province of Louisiana and New Mexico, and would be a defined and natural boundary.

reached this large river he passed opposite the place where Fort Lyon was later built, on the bluff around which the Arkansaw there sweeps closely. In 1864 Lyon was the first inhabited place on the Arkansaw west of Larned, though there had been trading-posts or certain other temporary dwellings at various points, especially at the upper end of the Big Timbers, say 12 m. E. of Fort Lyon. These were a large body of cottonwoods extending thence several miles down the river on its N. side, and formed a noted resort of various Indian tribes. Hence the woods became well known to travelers along the Arkansaw, whose itineraries almost always speak of the "Big Timbers" as they approach the Purgatory on their way to Bent's fort. Pike's text of the 13th is no doubt the earliest indication of these woods.

Gregg's map lays down three large creeks from the S. between his Big Sand cr. and Purgatory r. The first of these is called Mulberry ; the other two are nameless. The three appear to correspond to the Mud, Caddoa, and Blue creeks just described.

[36] The main chain of the Rocky mts., with Pike's Peak towering to the right : see L. and C., ed. 1893, p. 328. Pike has before him the Front range of the Rockies, northward, or to the right ; and southward, or to the left, the Sangre de Cristo range. The sources of Arkansan waters are between these ;

Before evening we discovered a fork [Purgatory river] on the south side bearing S. 25° W.; and as the Spanish troops appeared to have borne up it, we encamped on its banks, about one mile from its confluence, that we might make further discoveries on the morrow, Killed three buffalo. Distance 24 miles.[37]

Sunday, Nov. 16th. After ascertaining that the Spanish troops had ascended the right branch or main river, we marched at two o'clock. The Arkansaw appeared at this place to be much more navigable than below, where we first struck it; and for any impediment I have yet discovered in the river, I would not hesitate to embark in February at its mouth and ascend to the Mexican mountains, with crafts properly constructed. Distance 11½ miles.[38]

while on the other side of the last named range are those of the Rio Grande. The " cheers to the Mexican mountains " were given at an alt. of 3,900 feet.

[37] Purgatory r., also called in English Picket-wire, in French Rivière Purgatoire, and in Spanish Rio Purgatorio and Rio de Las Animas, is charted by Pike as the " 1st Fork," with the legend " Here the Mountains are first seen." This very large branch or fork of the Arkansaw heads in that southward continuation of the Sangre de Cristo range which is known as the Culebra range, about Trinchera, Culebra, and other peaks, where it connects with sources of the Rio Culebra, a tributary of the upper Rio Grande. Its own tributaries are very numerous and extensive. The main river runs N. E. from Las Animas Co., through the S. E. corner of Otero Co., and joins the Arkansaw in Bent Co., between the site of Fort Lyon and that of Las Animas, present county seat of Bent. Pike camped where the railroad now crosses ; and his journey since the 12th has been practically along the present railroad line.

[38] It is certain that Pike was on Purgatory r. on the 15th, and certain that he did not reach his " Grand Forks " (present site of Pueblo, at junction of Fountain r.) till evening of the 23d. The distance between these points, along the river, is between 90 and 100 m. Pike's ostensible mileages are : for the 16th, 11½ ; 17th, 23½ ; 18th and 19th, none ; 20th, 18 ; 21st, 21 ; 22d, 17 ; and 23d, 19 ; total, 110 m. We have, therefore, to reduce these mileages by about one day's journey. Observe, also, that only *four* camps are marked for the 16th–22d ; there should be *five*, and with that for the 23d, *six*. Thus the text and map do not agree, and some error is evident, though what it is we have no means of deciding with confidence. I am inclined to think that the difficulty lies at the start from the " 1st Fork " (Purgatory r.), when so much of the day was occupied in searching for the Spanish trail, and the " 11½ " m. assigned may have been little if any actual advance. If we proceed upon this supposition, there will be no trouble in adjusting mileages to bring in the

Nov. 17th. Marched at our usual hour; pushed on with
an idea of arriving at the mountains, but found at night no
visible difference in their appearance from what we did yesterday. One of our horses gave out and was left in a ravine,
not being able to ascend the hill; but I sent back for him
and had him brought to the camp. Distance 23½ miles.[39]

missing camp by the 20th; after which all possible error is removed by the
identifiable points. I shall, therefore, set camp of the 16th scarcely above the
mouths of Adobe and Horse (formerly Dry) creeks, which fall in close together
on the north, 7 and 8 m. above Purgatory r. Neither of these is noticed by Pike,
though each is larger than some of the streams he charts. But they were across
the river, and Pike had a bad case of Spanish trail on the brain, aggravated by
anxiety about Indian sign.

[39] The mileage hardly requires any adjustment, from the position I have
assigned for the 16th, to set camp of the 17th in the close vicinity of Rocky
Ford, a village and station on the railroad, where Pike remains on the 18th and
19th. Rocky Ford is 5 m. above Timpas cr. (which he charts as the first
stream from the left above his " 1st Fork "). Timpas or Timpa is a large
creek which heads in Las Animas Co. and runs N. N. E. into the Arkansaw at
the upper point of that very large island above La Junta.

The most notable point passed to-day is the historic site of Bent's old fort, on
the N. bank of the Arkansaw, 7 or 8 m. E. of the Timpas. It was a position
of great consequence in the days of staging from Fort Leavenworth and other
points on the Missouri to Taos, Santa Fé, and other New Mexican places.
Most of the early itineraries, both commercial and military, speak of Bent's fort,
and the advantages of this location for a post were more than once urged upon the
attention of the War Department. It was on an emigrant road, in the heart of
an Indian country overrun with various tribes; was a sort of focus for several
widely divergent termini; was in the vicinity of good building material, and had
plenty of fuel, grass, and water. Mr. Bent himself destroyed it in 1849, when
he abandoned it for sufficient reasons; but some of the chimneys and adobe
walls long stood to mark the spot. Thus it was Bent's " old " fort when I
passed by, about 30 years ago. Gregg's, Wislizenus', and in fact most maps of
the period mark the fort, some of them giving also a certain Fort William
alongside it. The structure is described as " quite complete " by Lieut. J. W.
Abert, who was here in August, 1846, at which time he met such noted plains-
men as Capt. Walker of California renown, Marcellus St. Vrain, and " Bill "
Garey. Col. Price's regiment was here about the same time. The several
columns of Gen. S. W. Kearny's Army of the West, which invaded and subju-
gated New Mexico and California, coming from Fort Leavenworth by the
Arkansaw route, concentrated in camp a few miles below the fort, Aug. 1st,
1846. Kit Carson knew the place well, and Frémont found him not far
away from here in July, 1843. A view of Bent's fort as it appeared in 1846 is
given by John T. Hughes, in his admirable Doniphan's Expedition, 8vo, Cin-

Nov. 18th. As we discovered fresh signs of the savages, we concluded it best to stop and kill some meat, for fear we should get into a country where we could not kill game. Sent out the hunters; walked myself to an eminence whence I took the courses to the different mountains, and a small sketch of their appearance. In the evening, found the hunters had killed without mercy, having slain 17 buffalo and wounded at least 20 more.

Nov. 19th. Having several buffalo brought in, gave out sufficient to last this month. I found it expedient to remain and dry the meat, as our horses were getting very weak, and the one died which was brought up on the 17th. Had a general feast of marrow-bones, 136 of them furnishing the repast.

Nov. 20th. Marched at our usual hour ; but as our horses' loads were considerably augmented by the death of one horse and the addition of 900 lbs. of meat, we moved slowly and made only 18 miles.[40] Killed two buffalo and took some choice pieces.

cinnati, 1847, p. 35.   The old route into Santa Fé left the Arkansaw close by Bent's fort, went S. W. between Purgatory r. and Timpas cr., struck the latter at a place then as now called Iron Springs, and so on through the Raton mts., not very different from the way the A., T., and S. F. R. R. now takes. A glimpse at the kind of a road this used to be is had from the following extract from my diary : " *Tuesday, June 7th*, 1864.   Bent's old fort.   Cold ride in the rain from 3 a. m. to 5 p. m., when we brought up at the fort.   Here was our crossing of the Arkansaw.   Recent hard rains made the river unfordable ; so we had to ferry ourselves over the surging tide in a frail skiff—ticklish business.   However, we got safe across, with all our worldly goods—the latter nothing to speak of, and stood shivering while the ramshackled hack that met us on the other side was loaded and hitched up.   This storm and the ferriage began a series of mishaps that reached to Fort Stanton in New Mexico, and made the driver swear that ' the grace of God had petered out on the other side of the Arkansaw.'   Kept on to Iron Springs ; road miry, pace snaily."

The name of Bent's Fort is preserved as that of a place nearly opposite (a little above) the present station Robinson, which latter is exactly on the boundary between Bent and Otero cos.   Above this is La Junta, on the S., seat of the county.   Several creeks fall in on the S. along here, the largest one of them named Crooked cr.

[40] Taking the Expedition just beyond the mouth of the Apishapa, Apishipa, or Apishpa r., to the present station Rockdale.   This stream is charted by

Nov. 21st. Marched at our usual hour; passed two Spanish camps, within three miles of each other. We again discovered the tracks of two men, who had ascended the river yesterday. This caused us to move with caution; but at the same time increased our anxiety to discover them. The river was certainly as navigable here, and I think much more so, than some hundred miles below; which I suppose arises from its flowing through a long course of sandy soil, which must absorb much of the water, and render it shoaler below than above, near the mountains. Distance 21 miles.⁴¹

Pike ; *a camp-mark is set just above it,* assuring us that the difficulty we had is already adjusted. It is a large river, or rather a long-bedded water-course (like many others which start well, but run out in the thirsty soil), heading about the Spanish Peaks, and reaching the Arkansaw at the foot of Apishapa bluffs (4,675 feet), between Rockdale and Catlin. Three miles off, across the Arkansaw, is the station Olney of the Mo. Pac. R. R., which here comes to the river. In old days a point opposite the mouth of the Apishapa was a good camp on the Cherokee trail to the gold-diggings on Cherry cr., with the Huerfano mountains and Spanish Peaks in sight.

[41] To a point on the river, in Pueblo Co., between Nepesta and the Huerfano, short of which river Pike's camp-mark is set. Pike charts the Huerfano as his " 2nd Fork." We also notice that he marks *two* Spanish camps, O O, for the day's march, as called for by the text, though they are by no means set down " within three miles of each other." Nepesta is only a hamlet and station, but serves to mark a well-known crossing of the Arkansaw. The A., T., and S. F. R. R. now crosses here, meeting the Mo. Pac. R. R., and the two tracks run together into Pueblo. The Huerfano is a great river, which heads in the Sangre de Cristo range, among the mountains of the Sierra Blanca range, and by various other affluents, as Muddy cr. and others, heading in the very passes of the Sangre range which we shall have to discuss when Pike's forlorn and frostbitten party reaches them. Some other tributaries drain from the W. side of the Wet mts. The union of these in Huerfano Park starts the river out of the mountains by Huerfano pass ; in the plains it receives Cucharas r., a tributary of nearly equal size, from further S., and their united stream seeks the Arkansaw on a N. E. course. A place called Jackson is on the river near its mouth ; opposite, across the Arkansaw, is Booneville.

The place above mentioned by the name Nepesta reminds me to say that Rio Napeste was a Spanish name of the Arkansaw r. itself, at least in its upper or Colorado reaches. One of Pike's own maps letters " Rio de Napesi," a phrase reappearing as " Rio de Nanesi " on Lewis and Clark's map of 1814 ; and yet other forms of the name occur. The phrase is obviously Spanish, but the word itself I do not recognize as such—very likely it is derived from the Ute Indian language. Humboldt's map letters " Rio de Napestle."

Nov. 22d. Marched at our usual hour, and with rather more caution than usual. After having marched about five miles on the prairie, we descended into the bottom—the front only [42] ; when Baroney cried out *"Voila un Savage !"* We observed a number running from the woods toward us ; we advanced to them, and on turning my head to the left I observed several running on the hill, as it were to surround us; one with a stand of colors. This caused a momentary halt ; but perceiving those in front reaching out their hands, and without arms, we again advanced ; they met us with open arms, crowding round to touch and embrace us. They appeared so anxious that I dismounted from my horse; in a moment a fellow had mounted him and was off. I then observed that the doctor and Baroney were in the same predicament. The Indians were embracing the soldiers. After some time tranquillity was so far restored, they having returned our horses all safe, as to enable us to learn they were a war-party from the Grand Pawnees, who had been in search of the Tetaus ; but not finding them, were now on their return. An unsuccessful war-party, on their return home, are always ready to embrace an opportunity of gratifying their disappointed vengeance on the first persons whom they meet.

Made for the woods and unloaded our horses, when the two partisans endeavored to arrange the party ; it was with great difficulty that they got them tranquil, and not until there had been a bow or two bent on the occasion. When in some order, we found them to be 60 warriors, half with fire-arms, and half with bows, arrows, and lances. Our party was 16 total. In a short time they were arranged in a ring, and I took my seat between the two partisans ; our colors were placed opposite each other ; the utensils for

---

[42] The " front only," a phrase italicized in the original, means that only the vanguard of the army met the insolent Pawnees. This probably consisted of Pike, Robinson, and Vasquez ; the rest of the invading forces, being 13 rank and file, main column and rearguard combined, having not yet come up to engage the enemy.

smoking were paraded on a small seat before us; thus far all was well. I then ordered half a carrot of tobacco, one dozen knives, 60 fire steels, and 60 flints to be presented them. They demanded ammunition, corn, blankets, kettles, etc., all of which they were refused, notwithstanding the pressing instances of my interpreter to accord to some points. The pipes yet lay unmoved, as if they were undetermined whether to treat us as friends or enemies; but after some time we were presented with a kettle of water, drank, smoked, and ate together. During this time Dr. Robinson was standing up to observe their actions, in order that we might be ready to commence hostilities as soon as they. They now took their presents and commenced distributing them, but some malcontents threw them away, by way of contempt.

We began to load our horses, when they encircled us and commenced stealing everything they could. Finding it was difficult to preserve my pistols, I mounted my horse, when I found myself frequently surrounded; during which some were endeavoring to steal the pistols. The doctor was equally engaged in another quarter, and all the soldiers in their positions, in taking things from them. One having stolen my tomahawk, I informed the chief; but he paid no respect, except to reply that " they were pitiful." Finding this, I determined to protect ourselves, as far as was in my power, and the affair began to take a serious aspect. I ordered my men to take their arms and separate themselves from the savages; at the same time declaring to them that I would kill the first man who touched our baggage. On which they commenced filing off immediately; we marched about the same time, and found they had made out to steal one sword, tomahawk, broad-ax, five canteens, and sundry other small articles. After leaving them, when I reflected on the subject, I felt myself sincerely mortified, that the smallness of my number obliged me thus to submit to the insults of lawless banditti, it being the first time a savage ever took anything from me with the least appearance of force.

After encamping at night the doctor and myself went about one mile back, and waylaid the road, determined in case we discovered any of the rascals pursuing us to steal our horses, to kill two at least; but after waiting behind some logs until some time in the night, and discovering no person, we returned to camp.   Killed two buffalo and one deer.   Distance 17 miles.⁴³

Sunday, Nov. 23d.   Marched at ten o'clock; at one o'clock came to the third fork [St. Charles river], on the south side, and encamped at night in the point of the grand forks [confluence of Fountain river].   As the river appeared to be dividing itself into many small branches, and of course must be near its extreme source, I concluded to put the party in a defensible situation, and ascend the north fork [Fountain river] to the high point [Pike's Peak] of the blue mountain [Front range], which we conceived would be one day's march, in order to be enabled, from its pinical [pinnacle], to lay down the various branches and positions of the country.   Killed five buffalo.   Distance 19 miles.⁴⁴

⁴³ The Huerfano (Orphan) r., marked " 2nd Fork " on Pike's map, is passed to-day without remark—no doubt Pike was thinking more of Pawnees than of geography.   In consequence of the fracas, little progress was made ; probably less than 17 m., as we see by the mileage assigned to the 23d.   Camp can be set little if any beyond the site of old Fort Reynolds, which stood on the S. bank of the river, about opposite the mouth of Black Squirrel or Chico cr. This falls in from the N., on a course parallel with that of Fountain r.; it arises by several heads in the Arkansaw divide, N. E. of Colorado Springs, opposite heads of Kiowa and Bijou creeks (branches of the South Platte) ; at its mouth is Chico sta. (Nyburg), on the N. side of the Arkansaw, 12 m. E. of Pueblo. Nearly opposite the mouth of the Huerfano is Booneville ; this locality used to be a regular camping-ground on the old Cherokee trail, and here was a ford across the Arkansaw, opposite Charles Audebee's (or Autobee's) house.

⁴⁴ Pike's Third Fork, charted " 3d Fork," is the San Carlos or St. Charles r. His Grand Forks is the confluence of Fountain r. with the Arkansaw, at present city of Pueblo—perhaps the best known place where we have found him since the Expedition started.   The Charles arises in the Wet mts., where also heads its main branch, called Greenhorn r., as in fact the Charles itself often used to be.   Their streams unite in the prairie 8 m. S. of Pueblo, and fall into the Arkansaw 7 m. E. of that city, or about halfway to Fort Reynolds. It was in this vicinity that the old Cherokee trail forked, the right-hand road taking up toward the gold diggings, while the other kept on to Pueblo.   The

Nov. 24th.   Early in the morning we cut down 14 logs,

Greenhorn mt., about which the San Carlos heads, has an ascertained altitude
of 12,230 feet.   Fountain r. is still called Fontaine r. by those who prefer
French to English, and used to be more elaborately styled La Rivière de la
Fontaine qui Bouille, River of the Boiling Spring—not that the water is hot,
but that it bubbles as it wells out of the rocks, as if it were boiling.   " This
spring," says Marcy, Pra. Trav. 1859, p. 300, " or, rather, springs, as there are
two, both of which boil up out of solid rock, are among the greatest natural
curiosities that I have ever seen.   The water is strongly impregnated with salts,
but is delightful to the taste, and somewhat similar to the Congress water."
But before General Marcy's time the springs had become noted.   On the 17th
of July, 1843, they were visited by Frémont, who describes them at length in
his Rep., orig. ed. 1845, p. 117 ; Mr. Charles Preuss, of his party, thought the
water resembled that of the Seltzer Springs in the Grand Duchy of Nassau.
About nine-tenths of the solid matters in solution is chalk.   When I was at
Manitou Springs, a few years ago, it was a common sight to see people in the
electric cars with bottles of the water, which had already become an extensively
advertised commercial article.   Fountain r. has also its Spanish name of Rio
Almagre or Almagra, meaning red ocher or other reddish earth.   It is formed
of two main courses which head about Pike's Peak and other elevations of the
same outlying (Front) range of the Rockies, called respectively Fountain and
Monument cr.; these unite at Colorado Springs.   Monument cr., coming
southward in the foothills, is composed of various others, called Beaver, Dead
Man's, West Monument, Crystal, etc.   Fountain cr., which comes eastward
from Pike's Peak itself and that vicinity, seeks the plains by the villages of
Manitou Springs and Colorado City, and the city of Colorado Springs (seat of
El Paso Co.)—for such are the respective designations of these places, now
well known to tourists and especially valetudinarians.   At Manitou Springs it
receives Ruxton cr., through Ingleman cañon, now traversed by the cogwheel
Manitou and Pike's Peak R. R.; item, it receives Glen " Erie " (Eyrie) cr.,
which runs through the little mountain park called Garden of the Gods—a spot
not favorable to agriculture and one whose alleged proprietors maintain their
wonted alibi.   Visitors who now inspect the natural curiosities hereabouts,
including a cave of very respectable dimensions and disagreeable atmosphere,
go up a carriage road which follows for some distance what was an old Indian
trail between South Park and the plains.   Fountain r., thus composed, runs S.
along the E. base of the R. mts., receiving small affluents all along on either
hand, as Bear, N. Cheyenne, S. Cheyenne, Sand, Jimmy's Camp, and Little
Fountain creeks, and falls into the Arkansaw at Pueblo, as already said.   It is
Pike's " North Fork " of the Arkansaw, and this is the stream nearly parallel
with which he proceeds via Turkey cr. toward the " high point of the blue
mountain," *i. e.*, Pike's Peak.   His breastwork was built on the S. side of the
Arkansaw, slightly above the confluence of Fountain r., and thus within present
city limits of Pueblo—though the built-up portions of South Pueblo are mostly
a mile or so from the confluence.   A suburb of South Pueblo is called Besse-

and put up a breast work,[45] five feet high on three sides and

mer, where stand the great smelters and other evidences of that commercial energy which has caused Pueblo to be sometimes styled "the Pittsburg of the West," though the pure air is not to be compared with the smutty gas one breathes at the old site of Fort Duquesne. A mile from Bessemer is Lake Minnequa, a resort of the Pueblonians for boating, beer, and music. Pueblo has retained for more than half a century a name that was originally not a proper but a common noun. Thus we read in Frémont, Rep. 1845, p. 116 : "Continuing down the [Fountain] river, we encamped at noon on the 14th [of July, 1843] at its mouth, on the Arkansas river. A short distance above our encampment, on the left bank of the Arkansas, is a *pueblo*, (as the Mexicans call their civilized Indian villages,) where a number of mountaineers, who had married Spanish women in the vicinity of Taos, had collected together, and occupied themselves in farming, carrying on at the same time a desultory Indian trade. They were principally Americans, and treated us with all the rude hospitality their situation admitted." Frémont calls the river "Fontaine-qui-bouit" (not *Bouille*). I understand that Pueblo was known at one time, during the '40's, as Hardscrabble—a name now given to another place, for which see a note beyond. I am told by Mr. Maguire that "Jimmy's Camp"—now the name of a creek above said—was a traditionally well-known place where one "Jimmy" had a small trading outfit, mainly for the Utes ; he was killed by the Plains Indians. Present Jimmy Camp is a hamlet about Corral Bluffs, 9 m. due E. of Colorado Springs.

[45] This was a slight structure, occupied only for a few days, and soon disappeared. But it is notable as the first wooden building of an American in present Colorado, and very probably our flag first flew in that State over these logs. There was no trace of it to be found in 1819, according to Long. It was built on the S. side of the Arkansaw, a little above the then confluence of Fountain r., within the present city of Pueblo (South Pueblo). The precise spot has never been recovered, and probably never will be. Changes in the river may have soon washed it away, or left it at some unrecognizable point on the prairie. The Arkansaw here has suffered great changes in details of its course, and is liable to inundation : witness the disastrous flood this year (1894), which almost drowned the city itself. In this connection I may cite part of an interesting letter with which I am favored by Mr. C. H. Small of the Board of Trade of Pueblo, whose knowledge of real estate in that city is probably unsurpassed. It refers to the discovery by excavation of an old fort which cannot by any possibility be Pike's, yet in the course of human nature is liable to become so considered by some, and in due time to enter history as such. Mr. Small says : " A fort was once built on the south side of the Arkansas just north of the Farris Hotel—between this hotel and the Santa Fé R. R. tracks at Union Avenue. The channel of the river changed in the seventies to a more southerly and straighter course. The occupants of the fort were all massacred by Indians on one occasion. In laying a pipe on Union Avenue two years ago [1892], one or more skeletons were exhumed, doubtless the remains of those massacred. This was at the depth of ten feet below the present level of the street, and

the other thrown on the river. After giving the necessary orders for their government during my absence, in case of our not returning, we marched at one o'clock, with an idea of arriving at the foot of the mountain; but found our- selves obliged to take up our night's lodging under a single cedar which we found in the prairie, without water and extremely cold. Our party besides myself consisted of Dr. Robinson, and Privates Miller and Brown. Distance 12 miles.[46]

directly in front of the Farris Hotel ; the logs of the old fort were come upon at the same time.   The grade of the street had been raised five feet, about 1885." Mr. Small's letter is dated Feb. 23d, 1894.   In further correspondence on this subject I am given to understand that this fort was an adobe structure built by the American Fur Co., on what is now Union Avenue.   On Christmas Day, 1854, a drunken spree ended in a free fight, in which all the whites were killed by the Indians but one, who fled to a smaller post on the Arkansaw at the mouth of the St. Charles, 7 or 8 m. off, whence a burying-party came next day.   For a long time there was also an adobe tower or lookout on top of the hill, about present intersection of Second and Summit streets ; but it has entirely disappeared.

[46] Pike starts up the W. bank of Fountain r., but soon bears N. W., directly through the present city, in the direction of Turkey cr.   This is a stream which runs (when it runs anywhere) parallel with Fountain r., 10 to 15 m. further W.; it heads about Cheyenne Peak, the foremost though not the highest of the Front range in the vicinity of Pike's Peak.   The air-line distance of Pike's Peak from Pueblo is about 50 m.; the distance over any ground by which the summit could be reached would be as far again.   In making this side-trip our hero proceeds with the determination expressed in the modern slang phrase, "Pike's Peak or bust !"   We must remember that he knew nothing of mountains, so to speak, from personal experience, and had never in his life been higher than some pass in the Alleghanies, perhaps about the elevation of the ground on which he built his breastwork (say 4,700 feet).   In the prairie close by Colorado Springs there stands a little knob, up which a man could run in a few minutes, and which has been dubbed in derision, "Mt. Washington," because it is exactly as high as that celebrated peak in the White mts. of New Hamp- shire—6,288 feet.   Though Pike never surmounted his eternal monument, he overcame all those dangers, difficulties, and hardships which did "bust" many a later, less hardy, and less resolute adventurer who "bucked against the Rockies."   Tourists and invalids have now the option of ascending to the summit of his peak from Colorado Springs by stage, or from Manitou Springs by the cogwheel railroad, which has been in operation since July, 1891.   By the latter mode of conveyance I have ascended the Rigi in Switzerland, as well as Mt. Washington in my native State ; but neither of these afforded the sensa-

Nov. 25th. Marched early, with an expectation of ascending the mountain, but was only able to encamp at its base, after passing over many small hills covered with cedars and pitch-pines. Our encampment was on a [Turkey] creek, where we found no water for several miles from the mountain; but near its base, found springs sufficient. Took a meridional observation, and the altitude of the mountain. Killed two buffalo. Distance 22 miles.[47]

Nov. 26th. Expecting to return to our camp the same evening, we left all our blankets and provisions at the foot of the [Cheyenne] mountain. Killed a deer of a new species [*Cariacus macrotis*], and hung his skin on a tree with some

tion I experienced upon the summit of Pike's Peak, looking far down upon the greatest elevation he attained on the present excursion. His 12 m. N. W. to-day sets him on the prairie between Fountain r. and Turkey cr., nearer the latter. The present road from Pueblo to Turkey cr. strikes the usually dry bed of the latter at about 17 miles' distance, follows up the E. bank to the foot of the mountain, crosses there, keeps on past East Turkey cr. through Dead Man's cañon, crosses the heads of Little Fountain cr., and continues to skirt the E. base of the range, past Cheyenne Peak to Colorado Springs. Up to the cañon, at least, this is exactly the route Pike took to reach Mt. Cheyenne.

[47] In the hilly country along the E. side of Turkey cr., and then on that creek, heading straight for Cheyenne Peak ; camp on the creek when he came to water, probably about where West Turkey cr. falls in ; altitude perhaps 6,000 feet. The situation is now in the ravine of the creek, with elevations of 6,500 feet on the right, and others 7,000 to 8,000 feet on the left and ahead. The creek receives small tributaries from the left all along, each gulch having its little stream, or bed of one. One of the largest of these is West Turkey cr., running S. E. from altitudes of about 9,500 feet. Further along comes down the parallel stream of East Turkey cr., heading S. from Mt. Rosa from altitudes of about 10,500 feet, and falling in by Dead Man's cañon. The summit of the Cheyenne mt. is due N. of Pike's present position, at an air-line distance of 10 or 12 m.; Mt. Rosa bears N. by W., somewhat further off. The situation is such that, if Pike should keep straight ahead, through Dead Man's cañon, he would run across Little Fountain cr., and proceed to climb Cheyenne mt. from the S.; but if he should bear to the left, up some one of the Turkey Creek affluents I have mentioned or alluded to, he would much sooner reach what he would be likely to call "the summit of the chain" (see text of the 27th)—that is, an altitude of about 9,000 feet, with Mt. Rosa bearing N. and the summit of Cheyenne mt. N. N. E., each at an air-line distance of 6 or 8 m. I think this was most probably his route ; but do not see that we have the data to establish the fact.

meat. We commenced ascending; found it very difficult,
being obliged to climb up rocks, sometimes almost perpendicular; and after marching all day we encamped in
a cave, without blankets, victuals, or water.[48] We had

[48] Pike's expectation of climbing his peak and getting back to his camp on
Turkey cr. in one day may serve to console some who have thought they would
like to take a stroll before breakfast to the same peak from the Antlers Hotel in
Colorado Springs. Though Pike's actual footsteps in these mountains be not recoverable with exactitude, there is no uncertainty as to *about* where he was on the
26th and 27th, when he climbed S. of Mts. Cheyenne and Rosa to an altitude
of about 9,000 feet, and then returned. Mt. Cheyenne is the foremost of the
group of peaks in this part of the Front range ; it stands out in such bold relief
that uninformed visitors to Colorado Springs often mistake it for Pike's Peak.
But its altitude is only 9,407 or 9,948 feet, as estimated by different authorities,
and thus considerably less than that of various other peaks in the vicinity.
Some of these are : Cameron Cone, 10,685 or 11,560 feet ; Mt. Rosa, 11,427
or 11,572 feet ; Mt. Pisgah, given as 10,487 feet ; Pilate Peak, given as 12,420
feet. The two last named are further W. and S.; Cheyenne, Cameron, and
Rosa form angles of a triangle, E. of Pike's Peak, that " grim sentinel of the
Rockies," as it is styled by some, or the " Grand Peak," as Pike calls it, which
towers over all the rest to the generally accepted altitude of 14,147 feet. These
figures can easily be recalled to mind if one remembers that twice seven is 14.
This peak is due W. of Colorado Springs, at an air-line distance of 12 m.
Visitors are driven to the summit by way of the Cascade carriage road, running
up Cascade cañon from a point in the Ute Pass 11 m. from Colorado Springs.
This stage route is a trifle over 17 m. from Cascade, or a total of about 28 m.
from the Antlers Hotel, Colorado Springs. During the season when the crop
of pink-toed tender-foots is harvested, wagons make the round trip in one day,
9 a. m.–6 p. m., spending an hour at the Halfway House and another at the
Peak. This is said to be the highest stage-line in the United States. There is
also a road up Bear Creek cañon to the Seven Lakes, but not to the Peak, and
no line of stages is regularly run on it. The Cheyenne Mountain road also
goes to these lakes, and has been run through to the mining camp on Cripple
cr., which lately made such a noise in Colorado. This is S. W. of the peak,
about 18 air-line miles from Colorado Springs. The Pike's Peak Cog Railway
takes a much shorter, steeper, and straighter course than the stage road, by way
of Ingleman cañon and Ruxton cr. The cog line starts from Manitou, 6¼ m.
from Colorado Springs, and is 8¾ m. long. The round trip is made in about
five hours, two hours each way, with one hour between, on the summit. This
is ample time ; for tourists find Pike's Peak a convenient place to leave as soon
as they have paid twenty-five cents for a cup of the worst coffee in the world,
and tried in vain to stand up against a wind of 50 or 60 m. an hour. Those
who may be more interested in Pike's Peak at a distance are referred to a dainty
booklet entitled Legends of the Pike's Peak Region, 8vo, Denver, 1892 ; it is

a fine clear sky, while it was snowing at the bottom. On
the side of the mountain we found only yellow and pitch-
pine. Some distance up we found buffalo; higher still the

full of quaint local lore, especially of the traditions of the only mountain Pike
climbed part way up. Among all the myths that cling to the Peak, obscuring
the facts in the case like the clouds that mantle the mountain, the very basic
one—that one on which the mountain rests, so to speak—is the universal
tradition that the brave young officer discovered and ascended the Peak which
upholds his name. One wishes that such laurels as he earned and well deserved
had been plucked from an eminence unknown and unattained before. But
Pike's Peak had been long and well known to the Spaniards ; it was the Ultima
Thule of their possessions ; and for that matter, was not Pike at the very time
in pursuit of the Spanish troops under Malgares, who had gone along just
before him? It is true that Pike, Robinson, Brown, and Miller—the four
whose names are thus linked should be upheld together—are the first white men
known to have come within " the distance of 15 or 16 miles " of the peak, as it
seemed to them, when the " Grand Peak " appeared " as high again as what we
ascended and would have taken a whole day's march to arrive at its base."
This is the testimony of the hero of the occasion ; his evidence is alike incisive
and decisive. So far as we are informed by authentic history, Pike's Peak was
first surmounted by Dr. Edwin James, Mr. Wilson, and two other men, July
13th and 14th, 1820, during Major S. H. Long's expedition to the Rocky mts.,
when it was named James' Peak. When, where, and by whom the mountain
was first called Pike's Peak is unknown, to me at least ; but its earliest appearance in print should be discoverable. The date is probably somewhere in
the '40's, or still earlier. The name was certainly in verbal use in the '30's.
Mr. Oliver P. Wiggins, now of Denver, who was on the plains in 1838, heard
only " Pike's Peak," as a phrase already in common speech. Gregg's map of
1844 legends " Pikes Peak (or James')." Beckwith's Report of 1853, pub. 1855,
p. 30, has only " James'." The alternative names ran parallel for some years.
G. K. Warren states, Pac. R. R. Rep. XI., 1855, p. 24 : " Captain Frémont, in his
report and map of explorations in 1843 and 1844, calls it Pike's Peak, probably
because it was so called by the white people in the country at the time ":
see also George Frederick Ruxton's Adventures, etc., London, Murray, 1861,
but written much earlier. Governor Alva Adams, in the address already cited,
p. 13, discusses the point as " one of the historical mysteries," and adds : " The
name of Pike's Peak begins to appear in the literature of the prairies and mountains about the middle of the century, but it was not irrevocably christened
until the Pike's Peak gold excitement, when the name was fixed to remain as
long as men love to listen to stories of valor." Whether it originated spontaneously or was formally introduced, it will probably never die ; the alliteration of
the words would be enough to keep the phrase in the mouths of the people, let
alone its justice and propriety. As for any Spanish claim which may hereafter
be established respecting prior discovery or ascent of the peak, the following

new species of deer, and pheasants [dusky grouse, *Dendra-gapus obscurus*].

Nov. 27th. Arose hungry, dry, and extremely sore, from the inequality of the rocks on which we had lain all night, but were amply compensated for toil by the sublimity of the prospect below. The unbounded prairie was overhung with clouds, which appeared like the ocean in a storm, wave piled on wave and foaming, while the sky was perfectly clear where we were. Commenced our march up the mountain, and in about one hour arrived at the summit of this chain. Here we found the snow middle-deep; no sign of beast or bird inhabiting this region. The thermometer, which stood at 9° above zero at the foot of the mountain, here fell to 4° below zero. The summit of the Grand Peak, which was entirely bare of vegetation and covered with snow, now appeared at the distance of 15 or 16 miles from us. It was as high again as what we had ascended, and it would have taken a whole day's march to arrive at its base, when I believe no human being could have ascended to its pinical. This, with the condition of my soldiers, who had only light overalls on, no stockings, and were in every way ill provided to endure the inclemency of the region; the bad prospect of killing anything to subsist on, with the further detention of two or three days which it must occasion, determined us to return. The clouds from below had now ascended the mountain and entirely enveloped the summit, on which rest eternal snows. We descended by a long, deep ravine, with much less difficulty than contemplated. Found all our baggage safe, but the provisions all destroyed. It began to snow, and we sought shelter under the side of a projecting rock, where we all four made

extract from the Legends already cited is pertinent : "From Pike's Peak to Popocatepetl the land is a palimpsest, dotted with ruins of remotest antiquity, the relics of a people whose records are replete with poetry and strange romance. Their manuscripts enrich the archives of Mexico and Madrid, and yet we learn but little of them. They moulder in the missions of the suspicious Spanish priests, or among the mystic treasures of the Pueblos, and are decaying unread."

a meal on one partridge and a piece of deer's ribs the ravens had left us, being the first we had eaten in that 48 hours.

Nov. 28th. Marched at nine o'clock. Kept straight on down the [Turkey] creek to avoid the hills.⁴⁹ At half past one o'clock shot two buffalo, when we made the first full meal we had made in three days. Encamped in a valley under a shelving rock. The land here very rich, and covered with old Tetau [Comanche] camps.

Nov. 29th. Marched after a short repast, and arrived at our camp before night; found all well.

Sunday, Nov. 30th. Marched at eleven o'clock; it snowed very fast, but my impatience to be moving would not permit my lying still at that camp. The doctor, Baroney, and myself went to view a Tetau encampment, which appeared to be about two years old; and from their having cut down so large a quantity of trees to support their horses, we concluded there must have been at least 1,000 souls. Passed several more in the course of the day; also one Spanish camp. This day came to the first cedar and pine. Killed two deer. Distance 15 miles.⁵⁰

⁴⁹ The trail of this excursus, as dotted on Pike's map, would be enough to show how far he was from reaching the summit of the " Highest Peak " there delineated, in the absence of any other data. Such an affair as this would never have been understated or underdrawn intentionally. Yet the dot-line leaves him further from the peak than I am inclined to think he actually was ; but it is obviously incorrect in detail, and thus no offset to the explicit text. The wide looping of the trail merely indicates a " round trip" from Pueblo and return. The only considerable difference in Pike's going and coming was, that in the latter case he " kept straight down the creek to avoid the hills," over which he had before trudged. The map exaggerates the size of Turkey cr., as well as of Fountain r. It is possible that someone thoroughly familiar with the topography of the mountains at the heads of Turkey and Little Fountain creeks may yet work out Pike's trail in exact detail.

⁵⁰ Up S. bank of the Arkansaw, past places called Goodnight, Rock Cañon, Vegas, and Meadows ; also past Rock and Peck's or Willow Springs creeks, both S., to a point near but short of the mouth of Turkey cr., N.

CHAPTER III.

ITINERARY, CONCLUDED: IN THE MOUNTAINS OF COLO-
RADO ON HEADWATERS OF THE ARKANSAW AND RIO
GRANDE, DECEMBER 1ST, 1806–FEBRUARY 26TH, 1807.

MONDAY, Dec. 1st. The storm still continuing with violence, we remained encamped; the snow by night was one foot deep. Our horses were obliged to scrape it away to obtain their miserable pittance, and to increase their misfortunes the poor animals were attacked by the magpies, which, attracted by the scent of their sore backs, alighted on them, and in defiance of their wincing and kicking, picked many places quite raw. The difficulty of procuring food rendered those birds so bold as to alight on our men's arms and eat meat out of their hands. One of our hunters went out, but killed nothing.

Dec. 2d. It cleared off in the night, and in the morning the thermometer stood at 17° below zero (Reaumer [Réaumur]), being three times as cold as any morning we had yet experienced. We killed an old buffalo on the opposite [north] side of the river, which here was so deep as to swim horses. Marched and found it necessary to cross to the north side, about two miles up, as the ridge joined the river.[1] The ford was a good one, but the ice ran very bad, and two of the men got their feet frozen before we could get accommodated with fire, etc. Secured some of

---

[1] Crossing the river from S. to N. above the mouth of Turkey cr., somewhere about the place now called Swallows, below the mouth of Rush cr., and where the bluffs come down to the Arkansaw. The D. and R. G. R. R. now makes a crossing a little higher up. Passing up the N. bank, opp. Red cr., S., the party continued to Carlisle Springs and camped in that vicinity, just over the border of Frémont Co. Red cr. is lettered "Bed" on the G. L. O. map of 1892.

our old buffalo and continued our march. The country being very rugged and hilly, one of our horses took a freak in his head and turned back, which occasioned three of our rear-guard to lie out all night ; I was very apprehensive they might perish on the prairie. Distance 13 miles.

Dec. 3d. The weather moderating to 3° below zero, our absentees joined, one with his feet frozen, but were not able to bring up the horse. I sent two men back on horseback. The hardships of last voyage [*i. e.*, that up the Mississippi, winter of 1805-6] had now begun ; and had the climate only been as severe as the climate then was, some of the men must have perished, for they had no winter clothing. I wore myself cotton overalls, for I had not calculated on being out in that inclement season of the year.

Dr. Robinson and myself, with assistants, went out and took the altitude of the north mountain [Pike's Peak], on the base of a mile. The perpendicular height of this mountain, from the level of the prairie, was 10,581 feet, and admitting that the prairie was 8,000 feet from the level of the sea, it would make the elevation of this peak 18,581 feet ; equal to some and surpassing the calculated height of others for the peak of Teneriffe, and falling short of that of Chimborazo only 1,701 feet. Indeed, it was so remarkable as to be known to all the savage nations for hundreds of miles around, to be spoken of with admiration by the Spaniards of New Mexico, and to be the bounds of their travels N. W. In our wandering in the mountains it was never out of sight, except when in a valley, from the 14th of November to the 27th of January.[2]

After this, together with Sparks, we endeavored to kill a cow, but without effect. Killed two bulls, that the men

[2] The excessive estimate of the height of Pike's Peak, 18,581 instead of 14,-147, was in part due to a misapprehension of the elevation of the prairie whence the observation was taken. This was assumed to be 8,000, but is really little, if any, over 5,000. The altitude of Pico de Teyde, the volcanic Peak of Teneriffe, in the Canary isls., is given on good authority as 12,200 ; and that of Mt. Chimborazo, one of the highest peaks in the Ecuadorean Andes, is placed at 20,498 feet by Whymper, who ascended it in 1880.

might use pieces of their hides for mockinsons. Left Sparks out. On our return to camp found the men had got back with the strayed horse, but too late to march.

Dec. 4th. Marched about five o'clock; took up Sparks, who had succeeded in killing a cow. Killed two buffaloes and six turkeys. Distance 20 miles.[3]

Dec. 5th. Marched at our usual hour. Passed one very bad place of falling rocks; had to carry our loads. Encamped on the main branch of the river [as distinguished from Grape creek], near the entrance of the South [Wet] mountain. In the evening walked up to the mountain. Heard 14 guns at camp during my absence, which alarmed me considerably; returned as quickly as possible, and found that the cause of my alarm was their shooting turkeys. Killed two buffaloes and nine turkeys. Distance 18 miles.[4]

    [3] Passing Beaver cr., N., with places called Beaver Depot and Beaver at and near its mouth ; passing opp. Hardscrabble cr., S., with a place called Adobe at its mouth, where one of the two railroads now makes a crossing ; continuing up N. bank, past Ute or Brush Hollow cr., N., and Eight Mile cr., N., to camp below Six Mile cr., N., about opposite the mouth of Coal cr., S., where is now the town of Florence.

    [4] Passing opposite mouth of Oak cr., S., Six Mile cr., N., and Chandler cr., S., then coming to the "bad place of falling rocks," which is where a bluff point comes down to the river—all these places within 2 or 3 m. of camp ; and continuing past Oil cr., N., to camp within the present limits of Cañon City, Fremont Co.   This is already a considerable village, and is growing.   It nestles directly at the foot of the mountains, under the shadow of Noonan's and Frémont's Peaks, and derives its name from the remarkable formation which the text presently describes.   This is the Grand Cañon of the Arkansaw, a part of which is well known to tourists as the " Royal Gorge," because it has been exploited so much on the folders of the D. and R. G. R. R.   But it is worthy of exploitation, and does not disappoint the expectations raised by the advertisements of the " scenic line of the world."   Cañon City is almost in the very jaws of this vast chasm, through which the Arkansaw has forced its way to issuance on the plains.   It was practically impassable, even afoot, until a way was hewn and blasted for the railroad which now traverses its whole length.   Both trails which lead west from Cañon City get around the terrible place ; one on the north starts up Sand cr., past Noonan's and Frémont's Peaks, and swings around to Parkdale at the head of the cañon ; and the other, on the south, crosses Grape cr., traverses Webster Park, and comes down Copper cr. to Parkdale.   Next after Pueblo, the basis of the Pike's Peak trip, as we have seen, Cañon City is the most notable place on Pike's Arkansaw route.   The

Dec. 6th. Sent out three different parties to hunt the Spanish trace, but without success. The doctor and myself followed the river into the mountain, where it was bounded on each side by the rocks of the mountain, 200 feet high, leaving a small valley of 50 or 60 feet [in the "Royal Gorge"]. Killed two buffaloes, two deer, one turkey.

Sunday, Dec. 7th. We again dispatched parties in search of the trace. One party discovered it, on the other side of the river, and followed it into the valley of the river at the entrance of the mountain, where they met two parties who were returning from exploring the two branches [5] of the river, in the mountains; of which they reported that they had ascended until the river was merely a brook, bounded on both sides with perpendicular rocks, impracticable for horses ever to pass them; they had then recrossed the river to the north side, and discovered, as they supposed, that the Spanish troops had ascended a dry valley to the right. On their return they found some rock-salt, samples of which were brought me. We determined to march the morrow to the entrance of the valley, there to examine the salt and the road. Killed one wildcat.

Dec. 8th. On examining the trace found yesterday, conceived it to have been only a reconnoitering party, dispatched

party stops here awhile to scout about, before starting for South Park ; and to this place they return afterward, build a blockhouse, leave two men, and start on their perilous adventures by way of Grape cr. to the Sangre de Cristo range and so to the Rio Grande.

[5] One of these is, of course, the main Arkansaw, in the Royal Gorge ; the other, on the left, or S., is Grape cr., which runs through the Wet mts. to its confluence with the Arkansaw a mile or so above Cañon City, under Noonan's Peak. Grape cr. used to be called Pike's fork of the Arkansaw, as by Gregg, 1844 ; but this name lapsed. Bringing it in for a moment, we find the "forks" of the Arkansaw to be : 1st fork of Pike, Purgatory r.; 2d fork of Pike, Huerfano r.; 3d fork of Pike, St. Charles r.; Grand forks of Pike, confluence of Fountain r. with the Arkansaw ; Pike's fork of some books, Grape cr. From his present position at Cañon City, Pike explores the Royal Gorge and Grape cr. to some little extent, and abandons them both ; he scouts about for the Spanish trail, and having found it, as he supposes, starts N., up Oil cr., very likely by the present road from the town to that stream.

from the main body ; and on analyzing the rock-salt, found it to be strongly impregnated with sulphur.   There were some very strong sulphurated springs at its foot.   Returned to camp ; took with me Dr. Robinson and Miller, and descended the river, in order to discover certainly if the whole [Spanish] party had come by this route.   Descended about seven miles on the south side [of the Arkansaw].   Saw great quantities of turkeys and deer.   Killed one deer.

Dec. 9th. Before we marched, killed a fine buck at our camp as he was passing. Found the Spanish camp about four miles below ; and, from every observation we could make, conceived they had all ascended the river.   Returned to camp, where we arrived about two o'clock. Found all well ; would have moved immediately, but four men were out reconnoitering.   Killed three deer.

Dec. 10th. Marched and found the road over the mountain to be excellent. Encamped in a dry ravine.⁶ Obliged to melt snow for ourselves and horses ; and as there was nothing else for the latter to eat, gave them one pint of corn each.   Killed one buffalo.

Dec. 11th. Marched at ten o'clock, and in one mile struck a branch [Oil creek] of the Arkansaw on which the supposed Spaniards had encamped, where there was both water and grass. Kept up this branch, but was frequently embar-

⁶ A mountain trail with no course or distance given is not encouraging to follow.   In earlier studies of Pike, I had supposed he reached South Park by way of Currant cr., as he might have done.   But no doubt remains in my mind that he took the Oil Creek route. If we regard his map attentively, we see that he went up along a large creek which he fetches into the Arkansaw *below* the blockhouse he built on his return to Cañon City, and which is certainly Oil cr.   Camp of Dec. 10th is therefore in a " dry ravine" within " one mile " of Oil cr.— perhaps at the first ravine above where Wilson cr. falls in from the left, or on Wilson cr. itself. Oil cr. is a very well known stream, on the banks of which oil works have been established, and at whose mouth is a place called Reno, about 4 m. below Cañon City.   It heads by two main branches and many small tributaries in the mountains S. of Ute Pass, W. of Pike's Peak, and about Saddle and Thirty-nine Mile mt., and runs S. about 50 m. into the Arkansaw. Pike goes up Oil cr. and takes the western one of its two main branches, crosses a divide, and strikes the South Platte r. in South Park.

rassed as to the trace; at three o'clock, having no sign of it, halted and encamped, and went out to search it; found it about one mile to the right. Distance 15 miles.

Dec. 12th. Marched at nine o'clock. Continued up the same branch [Oil creek] as yesterday. The ridges on our right and left appeared to grow lower, but mountains appeared on our flanks, through the intervals, covered with snow. Owing to the weakness of our horses, we made only 12 miles.[7]

Dec. 13th. Marched at the usual hour; passed large springs, and the supposed Spanish camp; crossed at twelve o'clock a dividing ridge,[8] and immediately fell on a small

---

[7] Pike has gone N. from Cañon City some 30 or 35 m., having Oil cr. on his right, and having crossed certain of its tributaries from the west known as Wilson, South Oil, and High creeks. He is now camped on West Oil cr. (the western one of the two main branches), at or near a place called Truro. This is a sufficiently well known locality, in a nest of mountains whence Oil cr. gathers several affluents from various directions. On another branch of the creek is the place called Alnwick, near where Riggs used to have his ranch, or in the same place. West Oil cr. is also called Ten Mile cr.; another small stream is Martin's or Slate cr. Some of the surrounding points are : Mt. Pisgah, 10,322 or 10,487 feet high; Rhyolite Peak, 10,860 ; Dome Rock or the Needle, 9,463 feet—these on Pike's right as he faces N., and S. W. to W. of his peak ; while on his left are in succession : Iron Knoll or Trachyte Knob (lettered " Trackite " on G. L. O. map, 1892) ; Saddle mt.; Thirty-nine Mile mt., 11,000 feet ; Chalcedony Buttes, 10,400 and 10,200 feet. Now the usual way out of this place is N. by Alnwick or Rigg's ranch, between Dome Rock and Saddle mt., over a divide about 9,200 feet high, known as Two Creek or Twin Creek Pass, which fetches out on S. Platte waters at Florissant, on the W. border of El Paso Co.; but Pike takes a route to the left, up West Oil or Ten Mile cr.

[8] Between Arkansan and Missourian waters, in a broad sense ; between the Oil Creek branch of the Arkansaw and the South Platte r., in a stricter sense; more exactly still, between West Oil or Ten Mile cr. and one of several small spring runs that make into the S. Platte. Pike makes the pass between Ten Mile mt. (right) and Thirty-nine Mile mt. (left), at an elevation of something over 9,000 feet. The difference between this Oil Creek way into South Park and the way by Currant cr. is that, had he come up the latter, he would have made Currant Creek Pass, 9,550 feet, between Thirty-Nine Mile mt. (right) and Chalcedony Buttes (left) ; it is simply a matter of " cotoying " (flanking) Thirty-nine Mile mt. E. or W. By the way he came, he strikes the South Platte r., in South Park, Park Co., at the very nearest approach it makes to the point he left on the Arkansaw—that is to say, at the elbow it makes where, after flowing S. E. through South Park, it turns sharp N. E. and enters what

branch running N. 20° W. There being no appearance of
wood, we left it and the Spanish trace to our right, and
made for the hills to encamp. After the halt I took my
gun and went out to see what discovery I could make. After
marching about two miles north, fell on a river 40 yards
wide, frozen over; which, after some investigation, I found
ran northeast. This was the occasion of much surprise, as
we had been taught to expect to meet with the branches
of Red river, which should run southeast. Query: Must it
not be the headwaters of the river Platte? [Answer: You
are on the South Platte, at the head of Eleven Mile cañon.]
If so, the Missouri must run much more west than is generally represented; for the Platte is a small river, by no means
presenting an expectation of so extensive a course. One
horse gave out and was left. Distance 18 miles.

Sunday, Dec. 14th. Marched; struck the river, ascended
it four miles, and encamped on the north side.⁹ The prairie,

is called the Upper or Eleven Mile cañon. These particulars are assured: for
Pike finds that the river " ran northeast." Camp of Dec. 13th is set in the
hills 2 m. south of the river, near the head of the cañon just said.

Pike's route from Cañon City and back to that place has been a subject of
much doubt and discussion, in which some very wild notions have been indulged by those who had any opinion whatever as to where he went on this
round trip. It has even been mooted whether he was ever on the South
Platte, or even in South Park at all. A cautious and tentative statement is ventured in the 1889 Denver reprint of the London ed. of the Travels, where my
friend Mr. Maguire says in his new Preface: " The exact line of march of the
party from the time it reached the foot of the Grand Cañon [" Royal Gorge "]
of the Arkansas is not easy to trace. It is likely that it reached the Platte in
the South Park, and quite possible that it penetrated to the headwaters of the
Gunnison." I do not profess to be able to trail a mosquito over a granite
bowlder, but I think we shall be able to discover precisely where Pike went
on this trip, where he entered South Park, his course through it, the place
where he left it, and how, after ascending the Arkansaw for two days, he
descended this river to Cañon City. Every one of Pike's camps can be fixed
within 2 or 3 m., and some of them with absolute precision. He was never
on the Gunnison, or any other Pacific waters. One who wishes to satisfy himself on all these points needs only to study Pike's text with Sheet vii. of Hayden's Atlas of Colorado.

⁹ At or near the place now called Howbert, on the N. bank of the S. Platte.
This great river has its uttermost source in that section of the Continental

being about two miles wide, was covered for at least six miles along the banks of the river with horse-dung and the marks of Indian camps, which had been made since cold weather, as was evident by the fires which were in the center of the lodges. The sign made by their horses was astonishing, and would have taken a thousand horses some months. As it was impossible to say which course the Spaniards had pursued, amongst this multiplicity of signs, we halted early, and discovered that they or the savages had ascended the river. We determined to pursue them, as the geography of the country had turned out to be so different from our expectations. We were somewhat at a loss which course to pursue, unless we attempted to cross the snow-capped mountains to the southeast of us, which was almost impossible. Burst one of our rifles, which was a great loss, as it made three guns which had burst ; five had been broken on the march, and one of my men was now armed with my sword and pistols. Killed two buffaloes.

Dec. 15th. After repairing our guns we marched, but were obliged to leave another horse. Ascended the river, both sides of which were covered with old Indian camps, at which we found corn-cobs. This induced us to believe that those savages, although erratic, must remain long enough in

Divide which bounds South Park on the N. W., above the sources of the Arkansaw, and in the southward continuation of the same mountains. The latter, bounding South Park on the W., and known as the Park range, are not the Continental Divide, because the Arkansaw r. here intervenes, and the Divide separates the Arkansan water-shed from that of Gunnison r. Having gathered its numerous tributaries from these mountains, the South Platte sweeps southeastward across South Park, and then turns abruptly northeastward to leave the Park by the Eleven Mile Cañon already mentioned, finds its way through the Front range south of Denver, and runs in the prairie till it joins the North Platte in Lincoln Co., Nebraska. The Col. Mid. R. R. now runs from Colorado Springs, past Florissant, through Eleven Mile cañon, and skirts the South Platte across South Park, on its way to the already notable mining camp Leadville, which no doubt has a future as well as a past ; the Denv., S. P., and Pac. R. R. traverses South Park from N. to S.; and each of these roads leaves the park on the S. through Trout Creek Pass, where Pike did also when he struck over for the Arkansaw. These points will appear more clearly as we proceed to trail the Expedition through South Park.

one position to cultivate this grain, or obtain it of the Spaniards. From their sign they must have been extremely numerous, and possessed vast numbers of horses. My poor fellows suffered extremely with cold, being almost naked. Distance 10 miles.[10]

Dec. 16th. Marched up the river about two miles and killed a buffalo; when, finding no road up the stream, we halted and dispatched parties in different courses, the doctor and myself ascending high enough to enable me to lay down the course of the river into the mountains. From a high ridge we reconnoitered the adjacent country, and concluded, putting the Spanish trace out of the question, to bear our course southwest, for the head of Red river.[11] One of our party found a large camp, which had been occupied by at least 3,000 Indians, with a large cross in the middle. Query: Are those people Catholics? [Answer: No—party of Comanches and Kiowas, among whom was James Pursley.]

Dec. 17th. Marched; and on striking a left-hand fork of the river we had left, found it to be the main branch [of the South Platte]; ascended it to some distance, but finding it to bear too much to the north, we encamped about two miles from it, for the purpose of benefiting by its water. Distance 15 miles.[12]

Dec. 18th. Marched, and crossed the mountain [one of

[10] Further up the N. bank of the S. Platte, to vicinity of the C. M. R. R. station, Sulphur Springs.

[11] Which could never be struck on any such course as this. To go hence S. W. would take the Expedition over the Park range to the Arkansaw, thence over the Continental Divide to the headwaters of the Gunnison, and so on.

[12] Hartsell's or Hartzell's ranch was located in the crotch of the forks Pike passed, and the town or railroad station by this name is now 2 m. above, on the N. bank of the S. fork, or Little Platte r. The two forks are of approximately equal size; but the N. or right-hand fork is the main one. The other, left-hand one, which Pike goes up a very short distance, and finds it does not suit him, is formed by the confluence of various creeks, among which may be named High, Herring's (Agate cr. of Hayden), Buffalo, and Long Gulch. Camp is set about 2 m. west of Hartsell's, near where High cr. falls into this branch of the S. Platte.

the Trout Creek Pass hills] which lay southwest of us ; in a distance of seven miles arrived at a small spring.   Some of our lads observed that they supposed it to be Red river, to which I then gave very little credit.   On entering a gap in the next mountain [of the Park range], came past an excellent spring, which formed a fine [Trout] creek.   This we followed through narrows in the mountains for about six miles. Found many evacuated camps of Indians, the latest yet seen. After pointing out the ground for the encampment, the doctor and myself went on to make discoveries, as was our usual custom, and in about four miles' march we struck what we supposed to be Red river [but was the Arkansaw], which here was about 25 yards wide, ran with great rapidity, and was full of rocks.   We returned to the party with the news, which gave general pleasure.   Determined to remain a day or two in order to examine the source.   Snowing. Distance 18 miles.[13]

Dec. 19th.   Marched down the creek near the opening of the prairie, and encamped ;[14] sent out parties hunting, etc.,

[13] Pike has actually got on the old San Juan road, which he follows more or less nearly out of South Park, as does also a branch of the Col. Midl. R. R. He enters those outliers of the Park range called the Trout Creek Pass hills, gets over the range itself by this pass, supposed to be 9,800 feet high, and goes down Trout cr.   Some named places near or on his route are Salt Works, Mill Top, Higgins', and McGee's.   Camp on Trout cr., in the vicinity of the last named place.

[14] Merely shifting camp a little distance down Trout cr. from the gorge to the open country, about the mouth of the creek, through which the Arkansaw here flows.   It is a very well known place.   The D. and R. G., the Col. Midl., and the D., S. P., and P. R. R. come together here ; in the immediate vicinity are places called Charcoal (about where, I suppose, camp was set), Midway, and Schwanders ; a little below is Nathrop, where the D., S. P. and P. R. R. starts over the Continental Divide for Gunnison; and a little above is Buena Vista, seat of Chaffee Co., which Pike entered when he made the Trout Creek Pass.   The Arkansaw is here flowing about S. S. E.   The Continental Divide is directly W., 15 to 20 m.; the mountains that make it are the Sawatch range, some of whose peaks along here are : Mt. Princeton, 14,190 feet, nearest Pike's camp ; Mt. Antero, 14,245 ; Mt. Shavano, 14,230 ; Mt. Keyes, 13,700.   Arnold's cr. falls in a little below Trout cr., on the same side ; while from the Sawatch mts. come Chalk and Cottonwood creeks, respectively below and above camp.   Pike is going to descend the Arkansaw from this station to Cañon City ; but he first

but had no success.   Still snowing and stormy; making preparations to take an observation.

Dec. 20th.   Having found a fine place for pasture on the river, sent our horses down to it with a guard; also, three parties out hunting, all of whom returned without success. Took an observation.   As there was no prospect of killing any game, it was necessary that the party should leave that place.   I therefore determined that the doctor and Baroney should descend the river in the morning; that myself and two men would ascend; and that the rest of the party should descend after the doctor, until they obtained provisions and could wait for me.

Sunday, Dec. 21st.   The doctor and Baroney marched; the party remained for me to take a meridional observation; after which we separated.   Myself and the two men who accompanied me, Mountjoy and Miller, ascended 12 miles [16] and encamped on the north side.   The river continued close to the north mountain [Park range], running through a narrow rocky channel in some places not more than 20 feet wide and at least 10 feet deep.   Its banks were bordered by yellow pine, cedar, etc.

Dec. 22d.   Marched up [the Arkansaw] 13 miles,[18] to a

starts his people in that direction, while with two men he makes a little recon-
naissance up river, in the narrow valley between the Sawatch and Park ranges.

[15] Pike stepped off the ties of the Col. Midl. R. R., if he went up the N. side
of the river, and those of the Denver and Rio Grande, if he passed on the other
side.   His camp was between the station Fisher of the former railroad, and
Riverside of the latter, below the mouth of Pine cr., which comes down from
Mt. Harvard.   To reach this point, he passed Buena Vista and the stations
Dornick and Americus ; also, the place where one Leonard had his ranch, and
there used to be a toll-gate—for an old mail route passed by here.   Two streams
he passed were Cottonwood cr., on the left, coming down from between Mts.
Princeton and Yale, latter 14,187 feet ; and next Seven Mile or Sweetwater cr.,
on the right, down a branch of which came the old California road.   He is
under the shadow of Mt. Harvard, of the Sawatch range, 14,375 feet high,
and Marmot Peak in the Park range.

[16] The highest point on the Arkansaw ever reached by the Expedition, and
that only by three of its members.   This is the nearest Pike ever came to
Pacific waters ; and it is close enough to have easily started the erroneous tradition.   This has been given currency in General A. W. Greely's sketch, and very

large point of the mountain, whence we had a view at least 35 miles, to where the river entered the mountains; it being at that place not more than 10 or 15 feet wide, and properly speaking, only a brook. From this place, after taking the course and estimating the distance, we returned to our camp of last evening. Killed one turkey and a hare.

Dec. 23d. Marched early, and at two o'clock discovered the trace of our party on the opposite side of the river; forded it, although extremely cold, and marched until some time in the night, when we arrived at the second night's en-

lately also supported by Governor Alva Adams, in his address, July 12th, 1894, p. 13, where we read: " He wandered west over routes we cannot identify until he must have found the Tomichi, a tributary of the Gunnison, and the only time Pike touched Pacific waters." But let us see about this. Assuming the substantial accuracy of Pike's mileages for the 21st and 22d, or at any rate, that they were not *understated*, and taking the Trout Creek camp to have been 6 m. below Buena Vista, his uttermost point may be fixed within a mile or two of Twin Lakes station on the D. and R. G. R. R. This place takes name from the two beautiful lakes which lie from 2 to 5 m. westward. This deter- mination would be more particularly acceptable, as the point indicated falls almost exactly on the boundary between Chaffee and Lake cos. I think, very probably, that the " large point of the mountain," on turning which Pike viewed the further course of the Arkansaw, was that sharp spur which projects to the river on the left, 3 m. above Granite station and Cache cr., and at the foot of which falls in the discharge stream from the lakes. Pike could have seen up river a good way from any elevation in this vicinity, though by no means " at least 35 miles." I doubt that the course of any river in these parts is continu- ously visible for this distance ; besides, there is no 35 m. of the Arkansaw above Twin Lakes. The Arkansaw is composed from three branches which unite west of Leadville—the middle, Tennessee fork, heading in the Continental Divide, in and near Tennessee Pass, in relation with heads of Eagle r., a tribu- tary of the Grand ; the east fork, heading about Frémont Pass with Ten Mile cr., a tributary of Blue r. and so of the Grand ; which two, having joined, are joined by the west or Lake fork. There is little to choose between the middle and east forks, as to which is the ultimate " source " of the Arkansaw. Both are now meandered by the D. and R. G. R. R., the east one also by the Denver, Leadville and Gunnison division of the U. P.; while the Col. Midl. goes along the west fork. Below the junction of this fork the Arkansaw receives various small tributaries, chiefly from the Park range on the east, as those from the gulches known as Iowa, Thompson, Empire, Union, Weston, and Granite ; the corresponding streams on the other side, from the Sawatch range, mostly fall into the west fork, as Half Moon cr. and others ; but one which gathers from Mt. Elbert falls into the main river 2 m. above the discharge of Twin Lakes.

campment [17] of our party. Our clothing was frozen stiff,
and we ourselves were considerably benumbed.

Dec. 24th. The party's provisions extended only to the
23d, and their orders were not to halt until they killed some
game, and then wait for us; consequently they might have
been considerably advanced. About eleven o'clock met
Dr. Robinson on a prairie, who informed me that he and
Baroney had been absent from the party two days without killing anything, also without eating; but that over-
night they had killed four buffaloes, and that he was in search
of the men. I suffered the two lads [Miller, Mountjoy]
with me to go to the camp where the meat was, as we had
also been nearly two days without eating. The doctor and
myself pursued the trace and found them encamped on
the river-bottom. Sent out horses for the meat. Shortly
afterward Sparks arrived and informed us he had killed
four cows. Thus, from being in a starving condition, we
had eight beeves in our camp.[18]

The lesser of these two is fed by Lake and other small streams, and discharges
into the greater one, which in turn discharges into the Arkansaw. The lakes
are about 1½ and 2½ m. in their respective diameters. Between the two is a
place called Interlaken, reminding one of the fact that Colorado is often styled
the Switzerland of America.

[17] We must guess as well as we can where this was. Pike, Miller, and Mountjoy started early from their camp below Pine cr., about Riverside station, and
made a forced march well into the night. We may credit them with 25 m., and
suppose them to be below Nathrop (which is on Chalk cr.), and somewhere in
the vicinity of Brown's cr., which falls in from the left.

[18] It is specially desirable to fix this Christmas camp, if not for the sentiment
of the thing, then because it is our initial point for the whole journey hence
down the Arkansaw to Cañon City. From anything that has preceded we do
not know where it was, within 10 m. But on the 26th Pike notes a " large
stream " from the south, at 7½ m. This is the South Arkansaw, which falls
in very near the well-known town of Salida. Salida is 7 m. by rail below a
station called Brown Cañon, which latter is a little above Squaw cr. Between
Salida and Brown Cañon the country is open and park-like among the mountains—just the sort of a place where buffalo would herd in the winter. The
seasonable supply of eight beeves was got in consequence, and I have no doubt
that Christmas was spent in the immediate vicinity of Brown Cañon. The
mountain fastnesses about the headwaters of the Arkansaw long continued to
be wintering-grounds for the buffalo. Thus we find one of the most experi-

We now again found ourselves all assembled together on Christmas Eve, and appeared generally to be content, although all the refreshment we had to celebrate that day with was buffalo meat, without salt, or any other thing whatever. My little excursion up the river had been in order to establish the geography of the sources of the supposed Red river. As I well knew that the indefatigable researches of Dr. Hunter, [William] Dunbar, and [Thomas] Freeman had left nothing unnoticed in the extent of their voyage up said river, I determined that its upper branches should be equally well explored. In this voyage I had already ascertained the sources of the [Little] Osage and White [Neosho] rivers, been round the head of the Kans river [*i. e.*, above the confluence of its Smoky Hill and Republican forks], and on the head-waters of the [South] Platte.

Dec. 25th. It being stormy weather and having meat to dry, I concluded to lie by this day. Here I must take the liberty of observing that, in this situation, the hardships and privations we underwent were on this day brought more fully to our mind, having been accustomed to some degree of relaxation, and extra enjoyments. But here, 800 miles from the frontiers of our country, in the most inclement season of the year—not one person clothed for the winter—many without blankets, having been obliged to cut them up for socks, etc., and now lying down at night on the snow or wet ground, one side burning whilst the other was pierced with the cold wind—such was in part the situation of the party, whilst some were endeavoring to make a miserable substitute of raw buffalo hide for shoes, etc. I will not speak of diet, as I conceive that to be beneath the serious consid-

enced officers of our army making the following remark : " Although generally regarded as migratory in their habits, yet the buffalo often winter in the snows of a high northern latitude. Early in the spring of 1858 I found them in the Rocky mountains, *at the head of the Arkansas and South Platte rivers*, and there was every indication that this was a permanent abiding place for them," says Marcy, Pra. Trav. 1859, p. 234, half a century after Pike's fortunate find. The herd now preserved in Yellowstone Park has no trouble with the deepest snows and coldest weather of that region.

eration of a man on a voyage of such a nature. We spent the day as agreeably as could be expected from men in our situation.

Caught a bird of a new species [*Conurus carolinensis*], having made a trap for him. This bird was of a green color, almost the size of a quail, had a small tuft on its head like a pheasant, and was of the carnivorous species; it differed from any bird we ever saw in the United States. We kept him with us in a small wicker cage, feeding him on meat, until I left the interpreter on the Arkansaw, with whom I left it. We at one time took a companion of the same species and put them in the same cage, when the first resident never ceased attacking the stranger until he killed him.

Dec. 26th. Marched at two o'clock and made 7½ miles to the entrance of the mountains.[19] On this piece of prairie the river spreads considerably, and forms several small islands; a large stream [South Arkansaw] enters from the south. As my boy and some others were sick, I omitted pitching our tent in order that they might have it; in consequence of which we were completely covered with snow on top, as well as that part on which we lay.

Dec. 27th. Marched over an extremely rough road; our horses received frequent falls, and cut themselves considerably on the rocks. From there being no roads of buffalo, or signs of horses, I am convinced that neither those animals, nor the aborigines of the country, ever take this route, to go from the source of the river out of the mountains; but that

[19] Down the Arkansaw, past Squaw cr., right, and some runs in the park he traversed, also past the stations Bellevue and Salida, to the mouth of the South Arkansaw r., where the so-called Arkansaw hills on the north close in against the Sangre de Ćristo range on the south, thus straitening the valley. The S. Arkansaw heads about Mts. Shavano and Keyes; its principal branch is Poncho or Puncho cr. There was a good road up both these streams, which are now meandered by railroads. Had Pike known it, he could have struck up the S. Arkansaw to Poncho cr., and up this by Poncho Pass into Homan's Park. This is *west* of the great Sangre de Cristo range, and is in fact the upper part of the San Luis valley or basin of the Upper Rio Grande, which Pike only reaches by a roundabout way, after subjecting himself and his men to almost incredible sufferings. But it is easy to be wise after the event.

they must cross one of the chains to the right or left, and find a smoother tract to the lower country. Were obliged to unload our horses and carry the baggage at several places. Distance 12½ miles.[20]

Sunday, Dec. 28th. Marched over an open space [Pleasant Valley]; and, from the appearance before us, concluded we were going out of the mountains; but at night encamped at the entrance of the most perpendicular precipices on both sides, through which the river ran and our course lay. Distance 16 miles.[21]

Dec. 29th. Marched; but owing to the extreme ruggedness of the road, made but five miles.[22] Saw one of a new species of animal on the mountains; ascended to kill him, but did not succeed. Finding the impossibility of getting along with the horses, made one sled, which with the men of three horses, carries their load [*i. e.*, on which the men dragged the loads of three horses].

Dec. 30th. Marched; but at half past one o'clock were obliged to halt and send back for the sled loads, as the men had broken it and could not proceed, owing to the waters running over the ice. Crossed our horses twice on the ice. Distance eight miles.[23]

Dec. 31st. Marched; had frequently to cross the river on the ice; horses falling down, we were obliged to pull them

[20] To a point on the Arkansaw about the mouth of Badger cr., from the N.; vicinity of station Wellsville or Badger.

[21] Camp in vicinity of that elbow which the river makes, nearly from S. E. to E. N. E., and near where there is a way up a creek from the S. over the S. de C. range by Hayden's Pass. The position is short of Bernard and even of Oak Grove cr.

[22] Only to the vicinity of Bernard cr. (past Cotopaxi). Pike's mileages appear excessive for the actual advance made, in comparison with modern schedules; but he has to step over much ground for comparatively little progress. All his distances to Jan. 5th require adjustment, or we should fetch him out a long way below Cañon City.

[23] Camp about the mouth of Texas cr., a considerable stream from the S., which falls in three or four miles below the mouth of Corral or Carroll cr., another large one from the N.; Texas Creek station and a place called Ford in the vicinity.

over on the ice.   The river turned so much to the north as
almost induced us to believe it was the Arkansaw.   Distance 10¾ miles.²⁴

Jan. 1st, 1807.   The doctor and one man marched early,
in order to precede the party until they should kill a supply
of provision.   We had great difficulty in getting our horses
along, some of the poor animals having nearly killed themselves in falling on the ice.   Found on the way one of the
mountain rams [bighorn, *Ovis montana*], which the doctor
and Brown had killed and left in the road.   Skinned it with
horns, etc.   At night ascended a mountain, and discovered
a prairie ahead about eight miles, the news of which gave
great joy to the party.

Jan. 2d.   Labored all day, but made only one mile ; many
of our horses were much wounded in falling on the rocks.
Provision growing short, left Stoute and Miller with two
loads, to come on with a sled on the ice, which was on the
water in some of the coves.   Finding it almost impossible to
proceed any further with the horses by the bed of the river,
ascended the mountain and immediately after were again
obliged to descend an almost perpendicular side of the mountain ; in effecting which, one horse fell down the precipice,
and bruised himself so miserably that I conceived it mercy
to cause the poor animal to be shot.   Many others were
nearly killed with falls received.   Left two more men with
loads, and tools to make sleds.   The two men we had left
in the morning had passed us.

Jan. 3d.   Left two more men to make sleds and come
on.   We pursued the river, and with great difficulty made

²⁴ Camp in the vicinity of the station Spikebuck.   The river here bears
noticeably to the N. E.   A little further along there is a sharp turn to the
S. E., at Parkdale.   This place is at the head of the Grand Cañon proper, or
Royal Gorge, by rail 10 m. above Cañon City, 22 below Cotopaxi, and 46
below Salida; total, 56 m. from what is practically the same as Pike's camp
of Dec. 26th to that of Jan. 5th, when he reaches Cañon City.   These figures
may be here compared with his mileages, which are : 12½+16+5+8+10¾+
1+6+8+7=74¼.   Details aside, the routes are identical ; and a discrepancy
of 17 or 18 m. is not more than would be expected under the circumstances.

six miles by frequently cutting roads on the ice, and covering it with earth, in order to go round precipices, etc. The
men left in the morning encamped with us at night; but
those of the day before we saw nothing of. This day two
of the horses became senseless from the bruises received on
the rocks, and were obliged to be left.[25]

Sunday, Jan. 4th. We made the prairie about three
o'clock, when I detached Baroney and two soldiers with
the horses, in order to find some practicable way for them to
get out of the mountains light. I then divided the others
into two parties of two men each, to make sleds and bring
on the baggage. I determined to continue down the river
alone, until I could kill some sustenance, and find the two
men who left us on the 2d inst., or the doctor and his companion; for we had no provision, and everyone had then
to depend on his own exertion for safety and subsistence.
Thus we were divided into eight different parties, viz.:
1st. The doctor and his companion; 2d. The two men
with the first sled; 3d. The interpreter and the two men
with the horses; 4th. Myself; 5th, 6th, 7th, 8th, two men
each, with sleds at different distances; all of whom, except
the last, had orders, if they killed any game, to secure some
part in a conspicuous place, for their companions in the
rear. I marched about five miles on the river, which was
one continued fall through a narrow channel, with immense
cliffs on both sides.[26] Near night I came to a place where

[25] For the past three days the party has been struggling with cumulative
difficulties that threaten to become insurmountable, and are already strung
along miles apart in the mountains. Yet Pike is only at the head of the Royal
Gorge—that Grand Cañon of the Arkansaw which he had before noted from its
lower end and regarded as impassable for horses. Parkdale is the place where
Currant cr. falls in on the N. or left. This is the large creek which heads in
the mountains about South Park, and which we have heard of before, when the
Oil Creek route to that park was in question: see back, note [6], p. 464. Now
we see more clearly than before that Pike never went up Currant cr. This has
two principal branches, both from the W., one called Cottonwood and the other
Tallahassee (Hayden), Tallahassa (Wheeler), or Talahsee (G. L. O., 1892,
brought into the Arkansaw as a separate tributary).

[26] It should be noted here that not one of the eight straggling parties managed

the rocks were perpendicular on both sides, and there was no ice, except a narrow border on the water. I began to look about, in order to discover which way the doctor and his companion had managed, and to find what had become of the two lads with the first sled, when I discovered one of the latter climbing up the side of the rocks. I called to him; he and his companion immediately joined me. They said they had not known whether we were before or in the rear; that they had eaten nothing for the last two days, and that this night they had intended to have boiled a deer-skin to subsist on. We at length discovered a narrow ravine, where was the trace of the doctor and his companion; as the water had run down it and frozen hard, it was one continuous sheet of ice. We ascended it with the utmost difficulty and danger, loaded with the baggage. On the summit of the first ridge we found an encampment of the doctor, and where they had killed a deer; but they had now no meat. He afterward informed me that they had left the greatest part of it hanging on a tree, but supposed the birds had destroyed it. I left the boys to bring up the remainder of the baggage, and went out in order to kill some subsistence; wounded a deer, but the darkness of the night approaching, could not find him. I returned hungry, weary, and dry, and had only snow to supply the calls of nature. Distance 8 miles.

Jan. 5th. I went out in the morning to hunt, while the two lads were bringing up some of their loads still left at the foot of the mountain. Wounded several deer, but was surprised to find I killed none. On examining my gun discovered her bent, owing, as I suppose, to some fall on the

to get through the cañon itself. Some came over the mountains on the N., and the rest over those on the S. Pike alone essayed the gorge, but only got halfway through. Next morning he escaped by scrambling up a small side cañon which occurs on the N. side, and came down on the N. of Noonan's Peak. This is the mountain that overhangs Cañon City, standing guard at the throat of the gorge. Dr. Robinson and his man came that way too. Vasquez and his men brought the horses the other way, across Webster Park, and had an easier time of it. It was three days before all the party got in.

ice or rocks; shortly afterward received a fall on the side of a hill, which broke her off by the breach. This put me into *désespoir*, as I calculated on it as my grandest resource for the great part of my party; returned to my companions sorely fatigued and hungry. I then took a double-barreled gun and left them, with assurances that the first animal I killed, I would return with part for their relief. About ten o'clock rose [that is, I surmounted] the highest summit of the [Noonan] mountain, when the unbounded spaces of the prairie again presented themselves to my view; and from some distant peaks I immediately recognized it to be the outlet of the Arkansaw, which we had left nearly one month since. This was a great mortification; but at the same time I consoled myself with the knowledge I had acquired of the sources of La Platte and Arkansaw rivers, with the river to the northwest, supposed to be the Pierre Jaun [Roche Jaune, Yellowstone [27]], which scarcely any person but a madman would ever purposely attempt to trace further than the entrance of those mountains which had hitherto secured their sources from the scrutinizing eye of civilized man.

I arrived at the foot of the mountain and bank of the river, in the afternoon, and at the same time discovered, on the other shore, Baroney with the horses; they had found quite an eligible pass [through Webster Park], and had killed one buffalo and some deer. We proceeded to our old camp [Cañon City], which we had left the 10th of December, and reoccupied it. Saw the traces of the doctor and

[27] Pike's map shows "Yellow Stone River Branch of the Missouri," with his trail looped up to it. This of course is an egregious error, as the Yellowstone is much further off, beyond anything that Pike sighted when he was highest on the Arkansaw, Dec. 22d. Next N. of him there, and on the W. of the Continental Divide, was Grand r., which unites with the Green to form the Colorado of the West. This arises in Middle Park. North of this again, in North Park, are the headwaters of the North Platte; and the southernmost heads of the Yellowstone are still beyond these. The mountains which Pike legends "White Snow" are the Sawatch range, continued southward by the Sangre de Cristo range. All this part of Pike's map is too defective to be of any use in tracing

his companion, but could not discover their retreat. This was my birth-day, and most fervently did I hope never to pass another so miserably. Fired a gun off as a signal for the doctor. Distance seven miles.

Jan. 6th. Dispatched the two soldiers back with some provision to meet the first lads and assist them on, and sent the interpreter hunting. About eight o'clock the doctor came in, having seen some of the men. He had been confined to the camp for one or two days, by a vertigo which proceeded from some berries he had eaten on the mountains. His companion brought down six deer, which they had at their camp ; thus we again began to be out of danger of starving. In the afternoon some of the men arrived, and part were immediately returned with provisions, etc. Killed three deer.

Jan. 7th. Sent more men back to assist in the rear, and to carry the poor fellows provisions ; at the same time kept Baroney and one man hunting. Killed three deer.

Jan. 8th. Some of the different parties arrived. Put one man to stocking my rifle ; others were sent back to assist up the rear. Killed two deer.

Jan. 9th. The whole party were once more joined together, when we felt comparatively happy, notwithstanding the great mortification I experienced at having been so egregiously deceived as to the Red river. I now felt at considerable loss how to proceed, as any idea of services at that time from my horses was entirely preposterous. After various plans formed and rejected, and the most mature delibera-

the trip just ended, and I have not had occasion to adduce it in support of the text since we started up Oil cr. The dotted trail loops up the Arkansaw far beyond the point Pike reached, and a number of the camps he made are omitted. The best delineation of Pike's route in South Park and about the headwaters of the Arkansaw is that traced on Josiah Gregg's map of the Indian Territory, etc., in his Commerce of the Prairie, 1844. This loops Pike around the Park, thence almost to the source of the Arkansaw, and back down this river—which is quite right. This case must be more accentuated, because tradition *will* have it that Pike got over on Pacific waters—not a drop of which he ever saw.

tion, I determined to build a small place for defense and deposit; [28] leave part of the baggage, horses, my interpreter, and one man [Smith]; and with the balance, our packs of Indian presents, ammunition, tools, etc., on our backs, cross the mountains on foot, find the Red river, and then send back a party to conduct the horses and baggage by the most eligible route we could discover; by which time the horses would be so recovered as to be able to endure the fatigues of the march. In consequence of this determination, some were put to constructing the blockhouse, some to hunting, some to taking care of horses, etc. I myself made preparations to pursue a course of observations which would enable me to ascertain the latitude and longitude of this situation, which I conceived to be an important one. Killed three deer.

Jan. 10th. Killed five deer. Took equal altitudes and angular distances of two stars, etc., but do not now recollect which. Killed three deer.

[28] Marked " □ Block house" on Pike's map. Lewis and Clark's map of 1814 letters " □ Block House U. S. Factory in 1806" on the same spot on the " Rio de Nanesi," *i. e.*, the Arkansaw. The building stood on the N. bank of the Arkansaw, doubtless within present limits of Cañon City. All trace of the structure seems to be gone, and I doubt that the precise spot will ever be recovered. My correspondence with several persons in Cañon City and vicinity has availed nothing. But the location at Cañon City is unquestionable.

The terrible trip Pike now ventures to make should not have been attempted in the dead of winter, with his miserable outfit. Pike was brave to excess, as we know; that and the mysterious *crux* of the orders he had from Wilkinson about the Spanish business must excuse this particular piece of foolhardihood. A more experienced mountaineer, with any concern for his own life, to say nothing of the lives of his men, would not have bucked up against those mountains under such circumstances. If he had had to hunt for the unknown sources of a river which came eastward from there, he would have backed out of the mountains, gone down the Arkansaw a piece, struck south at his convenience till he found his river, and then considered the chances of being able to follow it up to its source. That Red r. of which Pike is supposed to have gone in search was never found, for the simple reason that there is no such river in that part of the world—as probably Pike himself knew. He had a chip on each shoulder for some Spaniard to please knock off; his coat-tails were dragging all over the R. mts. for some Spaniard to please step on; and he would rather have broken some Spanish heads than have discovered the head of any river.

Sunday, Jan. 11th. Ascertained the latitude and took the angular distances of some stars. Killed four deer.

Jan. 12th. Prepared the baggage for a march by separating it, etc. Observations continued.

Jan. 13th. Weighed out each man's pack. This day I obtained the angle between sun and moon, which I conceived the most correct way I possessed of ascertaining the longitude, as an immersion and emersion of Jupiter's satellites could not be obtained. Killed four deer.

Jan. 14th. We marched our party, consisting of 18 [read 12][29] soldiers, the doctor, and myself, each of us carrying 45 pounds and as much provision as he thought proper, which, with arms, etc., made on an average 70 pounds. Left Baroney and one man, Patrick Smith [in the blockhouse at Cañon City].

We crossed the first ridge, leaving the main branch of the river to the north of us, and struck on the south fork [Grape creek], on which we encamped, intending to pursue it through the mountains, as its course was more southerly. Distance 13 miles.[30]

[29] This " 18 " is a misprint for 12. There were but 16 persons all told, of whom 2 are left when Pike, Robinson, and 12 soldiers proceed to tempt fate. The 12 were : Sergeant Meek, Corporal Jackson, Privates Brown, Carter, Dougherty, Gorden, Menaugh, Miller, Mountjoy, Roy, Sparks, Stoute.

[30] The " South fork " of the Arkansaw, afterward sometimes called Pike's fork, as for example on Gregg's map, 1844, and which he now proceeds to ascend, is Grape cr. This considerable stream arises on the eastern slopes of the Sangre de Cristo range, waters the Wet Mountain valley, receives various tributaries from the western slope of the Wet mts., and traverses a gorge in the latter to fall into the Arkansaw from the S. W., about a mile above Cañon City. The general course is about N. from its uttermost head in the S. de C. range, in the vicinity of Music Pass. Here its watershed is separated, on the E. side of the range, by a divide, on the other side of which are certain sources of the Huerfano r. ; while on the west of the S. de C. range the connection is with " Meadow " (qu. Medano?) cr., a tributary of San Luis cr., in the valley of the latter name, and consequently in the basin of the Rio Grande— that " Red river " which Pike seeks in vain. To-day he strikes Grape cr. at or near present site of Williamsburg, a station on the railroad which once meandered Grape cr. to Silver Cliff, but was washed out and abandoned. This is a good way below the entrance of Pine cr., a branch which falls into Grape cr.

Jan. 15th. Followed up this branch and passed the main ridge of what I term the Blue [now Wet] mountains. Halted early. The doctor, myself, and one hunter went out with our guns; each killed a deer, and brought them into camp. Distance 19 miles.[31]

Jan. 16th. Marched up the [Grape] creek all day. Encamped early, as it was snowing. I went out to hunt, but killed nothing. Deer on the hill; the [Wet] mountains lessening. Distance 18 miles.[32]

Jan. 17th. Marched about four miles, when the great White mountain [33] presented itself before us, in sight of

from the W. This may seem short for the "13" m. of the text ; but if anyone should think so, he has only to start from Cañon City to change his mind by the time he finds himself on Grape cr. by the present best trail. Besides, we shall soon see that we have to shorten up all of Pike's mileages in this rough country.

[31] Past Pine cr., to some point on Grape cr. short of the boundary between Frémont and Custer cos., probably in the vicinity of Soda Springs or the station Grape. Pike is flanking a mountain as well as meandering a crooked creek ; and, aside from any question of typographical error, we have to adjust his whole set of ostensible mileages by the topography of the country. If we should apply the figures he gives to the flat face of the map, we should run him clear over into New Mexico before he reaches his camp on the Conejos in Colorado.

[32] Over the line from Frémont into Custer Co., past Grape and Blackburn, to camp about the mouth of Silver cr. This heads about Mt. Tyndall and Mt. Herring, and by another branch N. of these ; it runs N. W. and then N. to fall into Grape cr., between Blackburn and Gove. Camp is 6 or 8 m. (air-line) due N. of Round mt. and town of Silver Cliff ; but much further by the meanders of the creek or either of the roads through the mountains.

[33] "White" and "Snow" are Pike's names for what he regarded as a continuous chain from as far N. as he knew anything about it, to the Sierra Blanca of New Mexico. That is to say, the names cover the whole Sawatch range, along the Continental Divide, and the Sangre de Cristo range ; which latter separates the Arkansaw from the Rio Grande basin, and ends on the S. with the bold elevations of the Sierra Blanca, or White mts. of modern geography. In saying that the "great White mountain presented itself," Pike means that he has reached a point in the Wet Mountain valley where he has the Sangre de Cristo range immediately before him, on the W. In this direction are the heads of the Texas cr., already mentioned (p. 475), and of Swift or Dutch cr., draining eastern slopes of the mountains, two of the nearest points of which are Electric Peak and Monte Rito Alto, the latter 12,863 or 12,989 feet high, according to whether Lieut. Wheeler or Dr. Hayden made the most accurate determination.

which we had been for more than one month, and through
which we supposed lay the long-sought Red river. We
now left the [Grape] creek on the north of us, and bore
away more east, to a low place in the [Wet] mountains.
About sunset we came to the edge of a prairie which
bounded the foot of the [Wet] mountains. As there was
no wood or water where we were, and the woods from the
skirts of the [Sangre de Cristo] mountains appeared to be
at no great distance, I thought proper to march for it; in
the middle of said prairie crossed the creek [recrossed
Grape creek from N. E. to S. W.], which now bore east.
Here we all got our feet wet. The night commenced extremely cold, when we halted at the woods at eight o'clock,
for encampment. After getting fires made, we discovered
that the feet of nine of our men were frozen; and, to add to
this misfortune, both of those whom we called hunters
were among the number. This night we had no provision.
Reaumer's [Réaumur's] thermometer stood at 18½° below
zero. Distance 28 miles.[34]

[34] This is the most difficult itinerary of the whole trip, and much depends upon
its correct recovery. It is out of the question to take " 28 miles " at its face value ;
the difficulty must be adjusted. Pike's trail shows with substantial accuracy
his three camps of the 14th, 15th, and 16th, along Grape cr. ; then a long loop
S. E. and back S. W. to a point on Grape cr. again, above two creeks coming
down from the Sangre range. I think these creeks can be identified ; this
would fix to-day's camp with sufficient precision. I base my conclusions on
Pike's whole set of mileages for this trip, as applied to the topography of the
route. Thus we have, going up Grape cr., 13+19+18=50 m. ; with 4 more
miles on the 17th, making 54 to the point where this creek is left. Further on
come (28—4=)24+0+0+0+0+8+8+9+0+0+14=63 m., which puts Pike
over the Sand Hill Pass on the 27th. Finally, we have 15+17+24+18=74
m., in the San Luis valley to the stockade on the Rio Conejos ; total, 191 m.
The three sections of this route—the Grape Creek course, the Wet Mountain
Valley course, the San Luis Valley course—are practically, therefore, in the ratio
of 5 : 6 : 7 ; and such figures must be made to fit the known geography of the
route. I make the journey of the 17th as follows : Pike proceeds up Grape
cr. a short distance, leaves it, flanks Round mt., and passes by or near the
present site of Silver Cliff, seat of Custer Co.; continues S. E. across the valley
or prairie to the base of the Wet mts., in the vicinity, not immediate, of Mt.
Robinson, Mt. Brinley, and Rosita, where the mines of the latter name were or
are ; where, not liking the place, as there was no fuel, he turns about S. W. and

Sunday, Jan. 18th. We started two of the men least injured; the doctor and myself, who fortunately were un-
touched by the frost, also went out to hunt something to
preserve existence. Near evening we wounded a buffalo
with three balls, but had the mortification to see him run off
notwithstanding. We concluded it was useless to go home
to add to the general gloom, and went amongst some rocks,
where we encamped and sat up all night; from the intense
cold it was impossible to sleep. Hungry and without cover.

Jan. 19th. We again took the field, and after crawling
about one mile in the snow, got to shoot eight times among
a gang of buffalo; we could plainly perceive two or three to
be badly wounded, but by accident they took the wind of us,
and to our great mortification all were able to run off. By
this time I had become extremely weak and faint, it being
the fourth day since we had received sustenance, all of which
we were marching hard, and the last night had scarcely
closed our eyes to sleep. We were inclining our course to a
point of woods, determined to remain absent and die by ourselves rather than return to our camp and behold the misery
of our poor lads, when we discovered a gang of buffalo coming along at some distance. With great exertions I made
out to run and place myself behind some cedars. By the
greatest of good luck, the first shot stopped one, which we
killed in three more shots; and by the dusk had cut each of

repasses the valley at a right angle to his other course through it, recrosses Grape
cr. a little below the confluence of Rosita cr., and camps under the Sangre de
Cristo range, somewhere about Spring cr. or Horse cr. This day was disastrous,
as a culmination of misery already endured by the handful of half-naked and
more than half-starved adventurers, for whom still more acute suffering was in
store. The wonder is not at any error in distances, but that any intelligible
itinerary of such a journey has reached us from the splendidly brave young
fellow, who so rashly led his companions into a death-trap. But for the buffalo
which were wintering in the Wet Mountain valley, not a man would have
escaped with his life. Whatever the exact spot, this is the place where poor
Sparks and Dougherty were abandoned with frozen feet. What they endured
may be imagined from the mute messages Pike afterward received from them—
a present of some of the bones which came away from their gangrenous feet
after sphacelus had set in.

us a heavy load, with which we determined immediately to proceed to the camp, in order to relieve the anxiety of our men and carry the poor fellows some food.

We arrived there about twelve o'clock, and when I threw my load down, it was with difficulty I prevented myself from falling; I was attacked with a giddiness of the head, which lasted for some minutes. On the countenances of the men was not a frown, nor a desponding eye; all seemed happy to hail their officer and companions, yet not a mouthful had they eaten for four days. On demanding what were their thoughts, the sergeant replied that on the morrow the most robust had determined to set out in search of us and not return unless they found us, or killed something to preserve the lives of their starving companions.

Jan. 20th. The doctor and all the men able to march; returned to the buffalo to bring in the balance of the meat. On examining the feet of those who were frozen we found it impossible for two of them [Sparks and Dougherty] to proceed, and two others only without loads, by the help of a stick. One of the former was my waiter, a promising young lad of twenty, whose feet were so badly frozen as to present every probability of losing them. The doctor and party returned toward evening, loaded with the buffalo meat.

Jan. 21st. This day we separated the four loads which we intended to leave, and took them some distance from camp, where we secured them. I went up to the foot of the mountain to see what prospect there was of being able to cross it, but had not more than fairly arrived at its base when I found the snow four or five feet deep; this obliged me to determine to proceed and *côtoyer* the mountain [keep alongside the base of the Sangre de Cristo range] to the south, where it appeared lower, until we found a place where we could cross.

Jan. 22d. I furnished the two poor lads who were to remain with ammunition, made use of every argument in my power to encourage them to have fortitude to resist their fate, and gave them assurance of my sending relief as soon as possible. We parted, but not without tears.

We pursued our march, taking merely sufficient provisions for one meal, in order to leave as much as possible for the two poor fellows who remained. They were John Sparks and Thomas Dougherty. We went on eight miles and encamped on a little creek,[35] which came down from the mountains. At three o'clock went out to hunt, but killed nothing. Little snow.

Jan. 23d. After showing the sergeant a point to steer for, the doctor and myself proceeded on ahead in hopes to kill something, as we were again without victuals. About one o'clock it commenced snowing very hard; we retreated to a small copse of pine, where we constructed a camp to shelter us; and, as it was time the party should arrive, we sallied forth to search for them. We separated, and had not marched more than one or two miles, when I found it impossible to keep any course without the compass continually in my hand, and then was not able to see more than 10 yards. I began to perceive the difficulty even of finding the way back to our camp; and I can scarcely conceive a more dreadful idea than remaining on the wild, where inevitable death must have ensued. It was with great pleasure I again reached the camp, where I found the doctor had arrived before me. We lay down and strove to dissipate the ideas of hunger and misery by thoughts of our far distant homes and relatives. Distance eight miles.[36]

Jan. 24th. We sallied out in the morning, and shortly after perceived our little band marching through the snow about two and a half feet deep, silent and with downcast

[35] By Pike's map, this should be the next to the last creek before Grape cr. is headed—the first one above Horse cr. If so, the party are in the vicinity of the place now called Blumenau.

[36] About to the ultimate forks of Grape cr. The S. end of the Wet Mountain valley is a sort of pocket where the Wet mts. connect with the Sangre range by intermediate elevations (as Promontory Bluffs, etc.). Creeks come into the valley from the E., S., and W., converging to compose Grape cr., the ultimate tributary of which is now known as Cottonwood cr. The border of this

countenances. We joined them and learned that, finding the snow to fall so thickly that it was impossible to proceed, they had encamped about one o'clock the preceding day. As I found all the buffalo had quit the plains, I determined to attempt the traverse of the mountain, in which we persevered until the snow became so deep that it was impossible to proceed ; when I again turned my face to the plain, and for the first time in the voyage found myself discouraged.

This was also the first time I heard a man express himself in a seditious manner ; he [John Brown] exclaimed that "it was more than human nature could bear, to march three days without sustenance, through snows three feet deep, and carry burdens only fit for horses," etc. As I knew very well the fidelity and attachment of the majority of the men, and even of this poor fellow (only he could not endure fasting), and that it was in my power to chastise him when I thought proper, I passed it unnoticed for the moment, determined to notice it at a more auspicious time.

We dragged our weary and emaciated limbs along until about ten o'clock. The doctor and myself, who were in advance, discovered some buffalo on the plain, when we left our loads on the snow, and gave orders to proceed to the nearest woods to encamp. We went in pursuit of the buffalo, which were on the move. The doctor, who was then less reduced than myself, ran and got behind a hill and shot one down, which stopped the remainder. We crawled up to the dead one and shot from him as many as 12 or 14 times among the gang, when they removed out of sight. We then proceeded to butcher the one we had shot; and after procuring each of us a load of the meat, we marched for the camp, the smoke of which was in view. We arrived

pocket, on the S., is the boundary between Custer and Huerfano cos.—an irregular line continuing on the W. along the main ridge of the Sangre range, and on the E. along that ridge of the Wet mts. which divides sources of Hardscrabble cr. and St. Charles and Greenhorn rivers from those of the Huerfano.

at the camp, to the great joy of our brave lads, who immediately feasted sumptuously.

After our repast I sent for the lad who had presumed to speak discontentedly in the course of the day, and addressed him to the following effect: "Brown, you this day presumed to make use of language which was seditious and mutinous. I then passed it over, pitying your situation, and attributing it to your distress rather than your inclination to sow discontent among the party. Had I reserved provisions for ourselves, while you were starving; had we been marching along light and at our ease, while you were weighed down with your burden ; then you would have had some pretext for your observations. But when we were equally hungry, weary, emaciated, and charged with burdens which I believe my natural strength is less able to bear than any man's in the party; when we were always foremost in breaking the road, in reconnoitering, and in the fatigues of the chase, it was the height of ingratitude in you to let an expression escape which was indicative of discontent. Your ready compliance and firm perseverance I had reason to expect, as the leader of men and my companions in miseries and dangers. But your duty as a soldier called on your obedience to your officer, and a prohibition of such language, which for this time I will pardon ; but assure you, should it ever be repeated, by instant death will I avenge your ingratitude and punish your disobedience. I take this opportunity likewise to assure you, soldiers generally, of my thanks for the obedience, perseverance, and ready contempt of every danger which you have generally evinced. I assure you nothing shall be wanting, on my part, to procure you the rewards of our government and the gratitude of your countrymen." They all appeared very much affected, and retired with assurances of perseverance in duty, etc. Distance nine miles.

[37] Taking the party over the low divide mentioned in the last note, from Custer into Huerfano Co., and from the Grape Creek watershed to that of the Huerfano. The exact spot is perhaps not determinable, but it was not far from

Sunday, Jan. 25th. I determined never again to march with so little provision on hand; as, had the storm continued one day longer, the animals would have continued in the mountains; we should have become so weak as not to be able to hunt, and of course have perished. The doctor went out with the boys, and they secured three of the buffalo; we commenced bringing in the meat, at which we continued all day.

Jan. 26th. Got in all the meat and dried it on a scaffold, intending to take as much as possible along and leave one of my frozen lads with the balance, as a deposit for the parties who might return for their baggage, etc., on their way back to Baroney's camp.

Jan. 27th. We marched, determined to cross the [Sangre de Cristo] mountains, leaving Menaugh [38] encamped with our deposit. After a bad day's march through snows, in some places three feet deep, we struck on a brook which led west. This I followed down, and shortly came to a small stream [Sand creek], running west, which we hailed with fervency as the waters of Red river. Saw some sign of elk. Distance 14 miles. [39]

Jan. 28th. Followed down the ravine and discovered

Bradford, a place on Muddy cr., one of the first two forks of the Huerfano. The map shows that Pike has headed Grape cr. and got into another basin, from which he starts a river running out on the prairie to the Arkansaw. This is by mistake made out to be his "3d Fork," *i. e.*, the St. Charles and Greenhorn; it is really his "2d Fork," *i. e.*, the Huerfano.

[38] If we call the roll to-day we find: Vasquez and Smith left at Cañon City on the 14th; Sparks and Dougherty left at camp of the 22d; Menaugh left at camp of the 26th; present on the 27th, Pike, Robinson, Meek, Jackson, Brown, Carter, Gorden, Miller, Mountjoy, Roy, Stoute = 11.

[39] The Expedition crosses the Sangre de Cristo range to the basin of the Rio Grande, and is about to enter the San Luis valley. The matter of the pass by which they came has been much mooted and left in doubt. Thus we find Maguire saying in the preface to the Denver ed. of Pike, p. xi: "Whether this pass was the Mosca or the Medano (known also as 'Sandhill') or whether it was one still farther to the north as thought by some, cannot be definitely established." Governor Adams in his Address, p. 17, says "Medano or Music Pass." I think it is certain that the Expedition made the Sand Hill Pass, and I hope to be able to settle the question. The three passes to which

after some time that there had been a road cut out; on many trees were various hieroglyphics painted. After marching some miles, we discovered through the lengthy

Maguire refers, and the only ones to be considered for a moment, are the following, in order from N. to S.

1. A pass from Antelope cr., one of the heads of Grape cr., in Custer Co., over to a tributary of San Luis r. in Saguache Co., not traversing any portion of Huerfano Co., or barely touching the extreme N. W. corner of this county—in fact, Custer, Huerfano, and Saguache cos. meet in this pass, and Muddy as well as Antelope cr. heads there. This is the " one still farther to the north " to which Maguire alludes. It is the one marked " Music Pass " on the G. L. O. and U. S. G. S. maps of 1892 (but not the Music Pass of Hayden's map). This seems to me so far N. as to be out of the question, if any reliance is to be placed on either Pike's mileages or his map. Even after the utmost reduction of his distances that can be made with any regard to the topography of the region, we fetch him out of the Grape Creek basin, into that of the Huerfano, and thus well along in Huerfano Co. His map bears this out completely. Observe that on the 24th he has *crossed* the head of Grape cr., left it a good way behind him, and marked his camp near the head of the other stream—the Huerfano. Notice also that from this camp of the 24th–26th the trail makes a sharp elbow *west*, and goes through the Sangre range in a gap next *below* that one in which he makes Grape cr. head. Again, if he had made this northernmost pass he would have come out N. of the Sand Dunes, and had these on his left as he went S. in the San Luis valley; whereas, we find them on his right as he comes down from the mountains to the S. of them. Finally, the mileages of the San Luis Valley route do not fit so well from this pass as from the next one. These facts seem to me to prove that Pike made no pass N. of the sand-hills.

2. The Sand Hill Pass, also rightly Medano and wrongly Modenos Pass, called Music Pass by Hayden, and Williams' Pass by Gunnison and Beckwith, is that which connects Navajo or Greaser cr. (br. of Muddy cr.) with a certain tributary (Medano or Sand cr.) of the San Luis r. This is on the boundary between Huerfano and Saguache cos., about 5 m. (air-line) S. of Music Pass. The Huerfano gathers its waters in the valley called Huerfano Park. The three principal tributaries, from the N. to N. W., are Turkey, Wilson's, and Muddy creeks. The place Bradford, already named as that to the vicinity of which we traced the Expedition, without reference to any question of a pass, is on Muddy cr., and a road goes direct from this place through this pass. That branch of Muddy cr. by some called Navajo cr. drains from this pass, and Greaser cr. also heads in its immediate vicinity. Across the divide, which sinks to an altitude of about 9,800 feet at the pass, Medano or Sand cr. drains S. W. and then S. between the Sand Dunes and the mountains, in the San Luis basin (Saguache Co.). That Pike took this route I have no question. There seems also to have been no doubt in the minds of Captain Gunnison and Lieutenant Beckwith, who quote Pike on their approach to this pass, Aug. 25th, 1853, and add : " The course of Williams' Pass as we entered it [from the sand-hills] is

vista, at a distance, another [the San Juan] chain of mountains; and nearer by, at the foot of the White mountains which we were then descending, sandy hills [the

N. 58° E., but it soon bends to the left to N. 27° E. We passed up it only about three-fourths of a mile. Its width is about 250 yards, rising gradually as far as we could see. Its walls of rock rise on either side to a height of some hundreds of feet, and are nearly vertical. Our guides represent it as continuing for 14 miles, both in character and direction as here described ; beyond that it is more abrupt, terminating at its summit less favorably for a road than Roubideau's Pass. It is followed by a large Indian trail." (P. R. R. Rep. II., 1855, p. 43.)

3. Mosca or Musca Pass, also called Fly Pass by some, translating the Spanish, and by others Robideau's Pass, 6 or 8 m. in an air-line S. of the Sand Hill Pass, is a lower and better one. It connects the Bear Creek branch of May cr. (the latter a tributary to the Huerfano) with the branch of Mosca cr. on the other side of the divide. There is a place called Sharpsdale on Bear or May cr., whence a road goes W. up to the pass, and others N. to Bradford, E. through Poison cañon to Gardner on the Huerfano at the mouth of Muddy cr., and also E. down May cr. and along the Huerfano to Point of Rocks and Malachite, and so on to Gardner. On the subject of Mosca Pass Maguire's remarks seem to me judicious, and I transcribe them to express my concurrence in his decision : " In the early days of the settlement of the country the Mosca was well travelled by the Southern Utes on their journeys to the Plains, and their ' hieroglyphics,' of which Pike speaks, were to be seen cut in the bark of the aspen trees ; but from the fact that on reaching San Luis valley on January 28th, 1807, the party marched some considerable distance on a course lying between the sand dunes and the mountains, the evidence would seem to warrant the belief that the pass used was north of the Mosca."

There are other passes of this range, as the one called Sangre de Cristo, and the Veta Pass (which latter is now utilized by the D. and R. G. R. R.). But these are altogether too far S., and have never been brought in question. There seems to be no named or used pass from the head of the Huerfano itself. The ultimate heads of this river drain N. from Cerro Blanco and Baldy Peak, with collateral sources thence along the line between Huerfano and Costello cos. to Grayback and Iron mts., etc., besides those from the W. on the line between Huerfano and Saguache cos. in the direction of Mosca Pass.

In view of the above considerations, we will proceed with Pike through Medano or Sand Hill Pass into San Luis valley (or Park). This is a plain between the Sangre de Cristo range on the E. and N. E., and on the W. and N. W. the San Juan and Sawatch ranges. It has a total length of about 110 m. from Poncho Pass on the N. to Taos valley on the S., with a maximum breadth of about 45 m., and an area of upward of 3,000 square miles. The general elevation is between 7,500 and 8,000 feet. The Rio Grande enters this valley at about the middle of its W. side, running E. and then sweeping in a long curve S.

Dunes]. We marched on the outlet of the mountains, left the sandy desert to our right, and kept down between it and the mountain. When we encamped, I ascended one of the largest hills of sand, and with my glass could discover a large river [the Rio Grande], flowing nearly N. by W. and S. by E., through the plain [San Luis valley]. This river came out of the third chain of mountains, about N. 75° W.; the prairie between the two mountains bore nearly N. and S. I returned to camp with the news of my discovery. The sand-hills extended up and down the foot of the White mountains about 15 miles, and appeared to be about five miles in width. Their appearance was exactly that of the sea in a storm, except as to color, not the least sign of vegetation existing thereon. Distance 15 miles.[40]

Jan. 29th. Finding the distance too great to attempt crossing immediately to the river, in a direct line, we marched obliquely to a copse of woods, which made down a considerable distance from the mountains. Saw sign of horses. Distance 17 miles.[41]

Jan. 30th. We marched hard, and arrived in the evening

[40] The billows of sand which Pike has on his right as he comes down Sand cr. from Sand Hill (Music, Medano) Pass are very remarkable formations, which alone would fix his position in the lack of any other data. West of these Dunes are several streams of the San Luis system, flowing southward to form sinks called the San Luis lakes, though Pike's map runs them into the Rio Grande. His camp is on or near Sand cr., at about the point where this and Mosca cr. join, or perhaps a little further along. Mosca cr. is the one that comes down from Mosca Pass, and if Pike had made this pass he would have fetched out in the valley at about the same spot—at or near Montville.

[41] About S., along the W. base of the Sierra Blanca, which is simply the continuation of the Sangre de Cristo range. Some of the summits Pike has on his left are : Grayback Peak, 12,387 feet ; Bald, Baldy, or Old Baldy mt., 14,125 feet ; and Cerro Blanco itself, 14,431 feet, giving name to the group. Pike goes from the vicinity of Montville past Zapato cr., probably on the present road through the town of the latter name on the creek, and camps in the valley at the place where timber reaches furthest from the mountains. A present road curves S. E. from this point, around to the S. of the range, where was built Fort Garland, probably 12 or 15 m. S. E. of to-night's camp. This was a sort of focal point to which roads converged from various points, and especially was it on the most direct route from any place in the lower part of the

on the banks of the Rio del Norte, then supposed to be Red river. Distance 24 miles.[42]

Jan. 31st. As there was no timber here we determined on descending until we found timber, in order to make transports to descend the river with, where we might establish a position that four or five might defend against the insolence, cupidity, and barbarity of the savages, while the others returned to assist the poor fellows who had been left behind at different points. We descended 18 [13] miles, when we met a large west branch [Rio Conejos], emptying into the main stream, about five miles up which branch we took our station. Killed one deer. Distance 18 miles.[43]

San Luis valley through Sangre de Cristo Pass to the Huerfano, and so on. Garland was on Ute cr., a branch of Trinchera cr., which latter falls into the Rio Grande about 3 m. above the Rio Conejos.

[42] Pike reaches the Rio Grande on a S. W. course, about the present position of the town of Alamosa, whence railroads now radiate in or converge from four directions. These branches of the Denver and Rio Grande system come from the E. through the Veta Pass, from the N. directly down the San Luis valley, from the N. W. down the Rio Grande, and from the S. up the same river. A few miles S. of Alamosa, Alamosa and La Jara creeks fall in close together, from the W. These are both indicated by a single unlettered trace on Pike's map. Next below Trinchera cr. falls in on the E. This is the one called Rio de la Culebra on Pike's map, which correctly brings it in above the one from the W. (Rio Conejos) on which he established himself. The Rio Culebra is the next one, from the E., below Trinchera and Conejos, and above Rio Costilla. Pike lays down the Costilla by its proper name, omits the Culebra, and calls the Trinchera by the name of the latter. In English, Rio Conejos would be Rabbit r.; Culebra, Snake r.; Costilla, Rib r.; and Trinchera, Cut-bank r. Alamosa should imply that the river so called were shaded with elms, though cottonwood (*Populus angustifolia*) is the actual growth. La Jara is properly the rock-rose (*Cistus creticus*), but as a name of this creek it refers to willow-brush.

[43] Of which about 13 (misprinted " 18 ") was down the Rio Grande, the rest up the Rio Conejos; Trinchera cr. (the one from the E., which Pike's map letters " Rio de la Culebra ") was passed a short distance above the Conejos. The latter is a large stream from the W. which arises in the San Juan range, in the vicinity of Conejos Peak (13,183 feet), leaves the mountains by the foot of Prospect Peak (6,837 feet), is joined in the San Luis hills by San Antonio cr. (its principal branch), and then seeks the Rio Grande by winding about the northern ends of the hills just named. The data already given, with those

Sunday, Feb. 1st.   Laid out the place for our works, and went out hunting.

Feb. 2d.   The doctor and myself went out to hunt, and with great difficulty, by night, at the distance of seven or eight miles from camp, killed one deer, which we carried in.

Feb. 3d.   Spent in reading, etc.

Feb. 4th.   Went out hunting, but could not kill anything. One of my men killed a deer.

Feb. 5th.   The doctor and myself went out to hunt.

details which the text presently offers, serve to fix the present station with pre-cision—about 5 m. up the Conejos, on its N. bank, at a point where it was not fordable, and directly S. of which was a high hill.   A sufficiently large map, such as Sheet X of the Hayden survey, shows exactly these topographical details, and also marks two ranches in the immediate vicinity : see also Pike's own map.   Under these circumstances it seems to me wasted ingenuity to find Pike's blockhouse in some other place ; yet its locality has been disputed. Maguire puts the case well : " The exact locality of the site (a notable spot in Western history) is in dispute, owing to the discovery many years ago of the remains of an ancient log structure further W. on the Conejos, which some suppose to have been Pike's fortress ; but everything in the narrative, as well as in the Spanish records, indicates the prairie opposite the mineral springs and high hill on the S. bank of the Conejos as the spot where the flag of the United States is first recorded as floating above the soil of Colorado."   Gregg's map locates the place approximately, with the legend " □ Pike's Stockade Whence taken to Santa Fé.   Feb. 1807 "

Concerning the exact location of Pike's post on the Conejos, I am favored with the following letter (cited in substance) from Mr. Maguire, an old resident of the San Luis valley :

" DENVER, COLO., *April 18th, 1894.*
" MY DEAR SIR :
" . . . As to the disputed stockade on the Conejos : I am entirely familiar with that country, and had fixed it as having been situated in the prairie on the N. bank of the stream due across from what is known as the Ojo Caliente. Before writing the preface to the Denver reprint of Pike, I had made up my mind to that, although it was contended in the neighborhood that the stockade had been situated some 14 or 15 m. from the mouth of the stream.   This supposi-tion was due to the fact that Lafayette Head, the oldest American settler on the Conejos, who came there early in the fifties, was lieutenant-governor of this state, and a man of high standing and much authority, had asserted that the fort had been built much further up the stream than the site I had accepted.   In 1890 I saw Mr. Head upon the subject, and he told me that when he first came to the country there still existed on the Conejos the remains of a structure of cottonwood logs laid horizontally, which he had seen, and which was so old that

After chasing some deer for several hours, without success, we ascended a high hill which lay south of our camp, whence we had a view of all the prairies and rivers to the north of us. It was at the same time one of the most sublime and beautiful inland prospects ever presented to the eyes of man. The prairie, lying nearly north and south, was probably 60 miles by 45. The main river, bursting out of the western mountain, and meeting from the northeast a large branch [San Luis creek] which divides the chain of

the logs would scarcely bear the weight of one's foot. Upon this evidence, with or without suggestion from some source, he concluded it was Pike's fort, and so gave out ; whence the prevalent impression. That Mr. Head saw this structure there is no question. I have no idea what it was, or when or by whom built ; but it would be useless to pursue this matter, because Mr. Head is positive that the location was on the *south* side, and therefore the structure cannot have been Pike's. The Ojo Caliente above mentioned is on the property of Mr. A. W. McIntire, as is also the prairie opposite, on the north bank of the river. Mr. McIntire is a Pike enthusiast, very much interested in the case. When in Denver recently he startled me by stating that we had been in error as to the exact location, as he had become convinced it was about half a mile below the Ojo Caliente. This half-mile bears a remarkable relation to the statement in your letter to me : ' I have it probably within half a mile.' Mr. McIntire says that the depression caused by digging the moat is still visible. The place is on the north bank of the Conejos, opposite some warm or mineral springs flowing out of the hill on the south side ; and Mr. McIntire informs me that the spot is a little north of the center of Sect. 7, T. 35, R. 11.

" Very truly yours,
"W. M. MAGUIRE."

Later correspondence on this subject with Mr. Maguire includes a letter and sketches from Gov. McIntire, who is satisfied that he has the exact site. He marks it on a township map which he transmits, as on the middle of the W. line of the N. W. ¼ of the N. E. ¼ of Sect. 7, T. 35, R. 11, just across the Conejos, under a hill from out of which flows a mineral or thermal spring which never freezes, at a point so chosen that the current in the river would not cut the ditch around the work. Gov. McIntire's sketch represents the ditch as 2½-3 feet deep, 68 steps long (including an unbroken place of 13 steps), and of semicircular figure ; the two ends of this figure against the river, in a small deep bend, so that the river and the ditch inclose an oval space 37 steps in the longest diameter. This seems large for such a temporary work as Pike started, but he tells us that it was never finished, and Gov. McIntire is persuaded that the ditch is not a natural formation. I am therefore led to believe that he has found the right spot.

mountains, proceeds down the prairie, making many large
and beautiful islands, one of which I judge contains 100,000
acres of land, all meadow ground, covered with innumerable
herds of deer.   About six miles from the mountains [San
Luis hills] which cross the prairie at the south end, a branch
[Alamosa or La Jara creek] of 12 steps wide pays its tribute
to the main stream from the west course.   Due W. 12°.
N. 75°. W. 6° [*sic*].   Four miles below is a stream [Trin-
chera creek] of the same size, which enters on the east and
up which was a large road ; its general course is N. 65° E.
From the entrance of this was about three miles, down to
the junction of the west fork [Rio Conejos], which waters
the foot of the hill on the north, while the main river wound
along its meanders on the east.   In short, this view combined the sublime and the beautiful.   The great and lofty
mountains, covered with eternal snows, seemed to surround
the luxuriant vale, crowned with perennial flowers, like a
terrestrial paradise shut out from the view of man.

Feb. 6th.   The doctor, having some pecuniary demands
in the province of New Mexico, conceived this to be the
most eligible point for him to go in, and return previous to
all my party having joined me from the Arkansaw, and that
I was prepared to descend to Nachitoches.   He therefore
this day made his preparations for marching to-morrow.
I went out hunting, and killed at three miles' distance a deer
which, with great difficulty, I brought in whole.   We continued to go on with the works of our stockade or breastwork, which was situated on the north bank of the west
branch, about five miles from its junction with the main
river, and was on a strong plan.

The stockade was situated in a small prairie on the west
fork [Conejos river] of the Rio [Grande] del Norte.   The
south flank joined the edge of the river, which at that place
was not fordable ; the east and west curtains were flanked
by bastions in the northeast and northwest angles, which
likewise flanked the curtain of the north side of the work.
The stockade from the center of the angle of the bastions

was 36 feet square. Heavy cottonwood logs, about two feet in diameter, were laid up all round about six feet, after which lighter ones, until we made it 12 feet in height; these logs were joined together by a lap of about two feet at each end. We then dug a small ditch on the inside all round, making it perpendicular on the internal side and sloping next the work. In this ditch we planted small stakes, about six inches in diameter, sharpened at the upper end to a nice point, and slanted them over the top of the work, giving them about 2½ feet projection. We then secured them above and below in that position, which formed a small pointed frise, which must have been removed before the works could have been scaled. Lastly, we had dug a ditch round the whole, four feet wide, and let the water in all round. The earth taken out, being thrown against the work, formed an excellent rampart against small-arms, three or four feet high. Our mode of getting in was to crawl over the ditch on a plank, and into a small hole sunk below the level of the work near the river for that purpose. Our port-holes were pierced about eight feet from the ground, and a platform was prepared to shoot from. Thus fortified, I should not have had the least hesitation of putting the 100 Spanish horse at defiance until the first or second night, and then to have made our escape under cover of the darkness; or made a sally and dispersed them, when resting under a full confidence of our being panic-struck by their numbers and force.

Feb. 7th. The doctor marched alone for Santa Fe; and as it was uncertain whether this gentleman would ever join me again, I at that time committed to paper the following testimonial of respect for his good qualities, which I do not, at this time, feel any disposition to efface. He has had the benefit of a liberal education, without having spent his time, as too many of our gentlemen do in colleges, in skimming on the surfaces of sciences, without ever endeavoring to make themselves masters of the solid foundations. Robinson studied and reasoned; with these qualifications he possessed a liberality of mind too great ever to reject an hypothesis because it was not agreeable to the dogmas of the schools; or adopt it because it had all the eclat of novelty. His soul could conceive great actions, and his hand was ready to achieve them; in short, it may truly be said that nothing was above his genius, nor anything so minute that he conceived it entirely unworthy of consideration. As a gentleman and companion in dangers, difficulties, and hardships, I in particular, and the expedition generally, owe much to his exertions.

The demands which Dr. Robinson had on persons in New Mexico, although legitimate, were in some degree spurious *in his hands*.[44] The circumstances were as follows: In the

[44] That our friend Robinson was, in plain English, a spy, is incontestible. If he had any other object in joining the Expedition, it is certain that he had no other in leaving it than to find out what he could about New Spain for the benefit of his own country. Had it been in actual war times he could have been hanged or shot by the Spaniards without violation of the customs of nations. As it was, Pike felt so apprehensive for Robinson's personal safety that when the two met in New Mexico Pike at first affected not to know Robinson, for fear of putting him in jeopardy, and he denied point-blank to the Spanish authorities that Robinson was one of the party. They had parted on the Conejos with a perfect understanding on such points ; indeed, General Whiting calls it " in pursuance of a previous scheme " that Robinson set out alone for Santa Fé ; meanwhile, Pike sat down on the Conejos to wait for the Spaniards to come and catch him. The ostensible object of Robinson's visit to Mexico was fictitious ; Pike says himself that the commercial claim Robinson pretended to have was worthless " in his hands." Whiting observes that " it was transferred to Dr. Robinson, who was to make it a pretext for a visit to the place, and a cover for observing its trade and resources, for the benefit of his countrymen. He regarded the excursion as a romantic adventure, and in that mood detached himself from the protection of his friend and commanding officer." (Life of Pike, p. 272.)

The *ultima ratio* of Pike's presence on the Rio Grande in Spanish territory will probably always remain in question, unless some documentary evidence, not yet forthcoming, should turn up to show whether he came there by accident or design. Perhaps the safest ground to take would be to suppose it the particular accident of a general design. His open and official instructions required him to " approximate " to the Spanish possessions ; he was to spy out all the land and see how it lay, politically as well as geographically; hunt up the Comanches; and make a counter-demonstration to Malgares' spirited raid, involving a reconnoissance in force as a military operation. This may all be true of the

year 1804, William Morrison, Esq., an enterprising merchant of Kaskaskias, sent a man by the name of Babtiste La Lande, a Creole of the country, up the Missouri and La Platte, directing him if possible to push into Santa Fe.   He

general design of his expedition, but it may as easily be true that he lost his way in searching for the Red river, and only found his way to the Rio Grande by accident.   This seems to be the view of his biographer, General Whiting, who was a very competent critic of Pike's military career, and who wrote in comparatively short historical perspective, though he does not seem to have possessed, or at any rate to have utilized, any private sources of information. Whiting fully acquits Pike of intentional errancy, and gives no hint that he is keeping anything back that would support any other view of the case than that which he presents, without apparent reserve or arrière-pensée.   Some of his expressions may be here cited.   Speaking of Pike's seeing a Mexican newspaper with an account of Burr's conspiracy, he remarks, p. 277 : "This afforded a clew to the suspicions with which his movements on the Mexican frontier had most naturally been regarded.   It was not surprising that he should have been looked upon as forming one of the ramifications of the revolutionary scheme which that distinguished individual had projected. . . It was true, that he had been found, with a belligerent aspect, in the Mexican country ; but his apology was ready, and, no doubt, acceptable ; while he knew that the Mexican authorities had lately violated, in a similar way, the soil of the United States, for which no apology could be rendered . . . His misapprehensions of the geography of the country, which led him to establish himself in such a suspicious manner, on a foreign river, were excusable, bewildered as he was among mountains and streams that were likely to confuse all calculations.   Still, it was natural for the Mexican authorities to regard his conduct, at first, as the result of a design, rather than a mistake, particularly when taken in connection with Colonel Burr's contemporaneous movements ; and their treatment of him must be considered under the circumstances, as having been marked by much consideration."   General Wilkinson also alludes to the assertion that had been made, that the expedition which resulted in the orders he had given Pike "was a premeditated coöperation with Burr."   The Mexicans, it seems, were not alone in their suspicions and expressions to that effect.

However the bottom facts of Pike's coming on the Rio Grande may turn out to be, it is certain that after he had been captured and taken to Mexico under the diplomatic disguise of a polite invitation to visit the governor, who had heard of his having lost his way, hastened to send to his rescue, etc., Pike turned spy and informer with great agility and signal success.   He kept his temper well in hand, except on one or two occasions ; and in several instances showed that art which diplomacy has been defined to be.   He bore himself with courage, dignity, and much fertility of resources ; while that duplicity and prevarication which he confesses his conscience condoned, if it did not justify, were never indulged from personal considerations, but from his intense patriotism.

sent in Indians, and the Spaniards came out with horses and carried him and his goods into the province. Finding that he sold the goods high, had land offered him, and the women kind, he concluded to expatriate himself and con-

His love of his country was the crucible in which he assayed his own motives ; that was fervid enough to relax the rigidity of morals he professed and practiced on all ordinary occasions, and induce a certain ethical elasticity, so to speak, if not actually to melt all scruples. Patriotism must sometimes shake hands with Jesuitism in this wicked world ; and the majesty of the flag, like the glory of God, must be maintained by human means. Abstract questions of the adaptation of means to ends are best left with casuistry. Pike's methods, while he was the distinguished guest of a half-hostile foreign power, may be questioned by some, but his motives by none ; and as for his ends, we know that nothing succeeds like success. The results are well summed by his biographer, p. 282, in words which I will cite :

" At the time Captain Pike explored those regions of our wide-spread interior, almost nothing authentic was known of them. More satisfactory information of the headwaters of the Mississippi than was in the possession of the public was highly desirable, and his narratives relating to them were read with interest. But his accounts of the Mexican territories were looked for with much more interest, and when they came out were received with avidity. The jealous policy of Spain had surrounded her provinces with guards and restraints, that rendered them almost inaccessible. Their condition and prospects were veiled from all foreign observation ; and at the time Captain Pike obtained, through an unintentional aberration from his prescribed route, access to them, unusual attention was turned upon the Mexican country by the events of Burr's conspiracy. This extraordinary transaction had awakened an intense curiosity respecting a region which was known to abound with gold, and which precious metal was supposed to have been its ultimate object. The trial of Colonel Burr was beginning, or in progress, when Captain Pike returned, and was known to have visited the El Dorado, on which this individual was said to have fixed an eye of cupidity and ambition. Scarcely anything had been heard of Mexico since the conquest of Cortes, excepting vague reports of the unbounded wealth that flowed from its mines into the public and private coffers of Spain. It is not strange, then, that Captain Pike's tour through some of its provinces should have been regarded as a rare and most opportune work. His statements were of course founded on hasty and imperfect observations, it being obvious from his journal, that, from the time he left Santa Fe, until he reached the United States, he was under a surveillance, and could only take notes by stealth. He could neither survey attentively what passed beneath his eye, nor inquire about that which he did not see, without exciting suspicion and provoking a rebuke. Still, with an acute eye, and a retentive memory, he appears to have gathered up many new and interesting facts, that were well received at the time."

vert the property of Morrison to his own benefit. When I was about to sail, Morrison, conceiving that it was possible that I might meet some Spanish factors on the Red river, intrusted me with the claim, in order, if they were acquainted with La Lande, I might negotiate the thing with some of them. When on the frontiers, the idea suggested itself to us of making this claim a pretext for Robinson to visit Santa Fe. We therefore gave it the proper appearance, and he marched for that place. Our views were to gain a knowledge of the country, the prospect of trade, force, etc.; while, at the same time, our treaties with Spain guaranteed to him, as a citizen of the United States, the right of seeking the recovery of all just debts or demands before the legal and authorized tribunals of the country, as a franchised inhabitant of the same, as specified in the 22d article of said treaty.

In the evening I dispatched Corporal Jackson with four men, to recross the mountains, in order to bring in the baggage left with the frozen lads, and to see if they were yet able to come on. This detachment left me with four men only, two of whom had their feet frozen; they were employed in finishing the stockade, and myself to support them by the chase.

Sunday, Feb. 8th. Refreshing my memory as to the French grammar, and overseeing the works.

Feb. 9th. Hunting, etc.

Feb. 10th. Read and labored at our works.

Feb. 11th. Hunting. Killed three deer.

Feb. 12th. Studying.

Feb. 13th. Hunting. Killed two deer.

Feb. 14th. Crossed the [Conejos] river and examined the numerous springs which issued from the foot of the hill, opposite our camp. These were so strongly impregnated with mineral qualities, as not only to keep clear of ice previous to their joining the main branch, but to keep open the west fork until its junction with the main river and for a few miles afterward, while all the other branches in the neighborhood were bound in the adamantine chains of winter.

Sunday, Feb. 15th. Reading, etc. Works going on.

Feb. 16th. I took one man and went out hunting; about six miles from the post, shot and wounded a deer.

Immediately afterward I discovered two horsemen rising the summit of a hill, about half a mile to our right. As my orders were to avoid giving alarm or offense to the Spanish government of New Mexico, I endeavored to avoid them at first; but when we attempted to retreat, they pursued us at full charge, flourishing their lances; and when we advanced, they would retire as fast as their horses could carry them. Seeing this, we got in a small ravine, in hopes to decoy them near enough to oblige them to come to a parley; which happened agreeably to our desires, as they came on, hunting us with great caution. We suffered them to get within 40 yards—where we had allured them; but they were about running off again, when I ordered the soldier to lay down his arms and walk toward them, at the same time standing ready with my rifle to kill either who should lift an arm in an hostile manner. I then hollowed to them that we were "Americans," and "friends," which were almost the only two words I knew in the Spanish language; when, with great signs of fear, they came up, and proved to be a Spanish dragoon and a civilized Indian, armed after their manner, of which we see a description in the Essai Militaire.[45] We were jealous of our arms on both sides, and acted with great precaution.

They informed me that this was the fourth day since they had left Santa Fe; that Robinson had arrived there, and been received with great kindness by the governor. As

---

[45] It is uncertain to what work we are here referred. There may be some old military treatise, well known in Pike's time, to which he thus alludes; but I think it most likely that he means his own Observations on New Spain, which formed a part of the App. to Pt. 3 of the orig. ed. of this work, and which included a considerable account of the military establishment of that country. If so, the " Essai Militaire " in question will be found beyond.

I knew them to be spies, I thought proper to inform them merely that I was about to descend the river to Nachitoches. We sat on the ground a long time, till, finding they were determined not to leave us, we rose and bade them adieu. But they demanded where our camp was; and, finding they were not about to leave us, I thought it most proper to take them with me, thinking we were on Red river, and of course in the territory claimed by the United States.[46]

We took the road to my fort, and as they were on horseback, they traveled rather faster than myself; they were halted by the sentinel, and immediately retreated much surprised. When I came up, I took them in, and then explained to them, as well as possible, my intention of descending the river to Nachitoches; but at the same time told them that if Governor Allencaster would send out an officer with an interpreter who spoke French or English, I would do myself the pleasure to give his Excellency every reasonable satisfaction as to my intentions in coming on his frontiers. They informed me that on the second day

[46] My editorial function becomes extremely distasteful, with Pike's reiterated insistence upon affecting to believe himself upon the Red r., and expecting us to believe him. See note [44], and imagine Dr. Robinson starting off alone to walk from the Red r. into Santa Fé! I have blinked the business thus far, but I cannot keep my eyes shut to the end of this chapter, as there is worse to come in the miserable straits to which Captain Pike reduces himself through his awkwardness and inexperience in telling lies. He bluffs the thing through, to be sure; but at the present juncture he catches himself in the meshes of his own falsification. For, supposing he had really been on the Red r., as he declared he believed; he had *crossed that river*, and gone 5 m. up a stream on the other side of it; so he was absolutely in Spanish territory, and this he must have known perfectly well. On the 22d he says, p. 507, that he "began to think it was time we received a visit from the Spaniards or their emissaries," which shows that he was expecting to be caught. When they come, he makes a show of resistance by blustering a little, then hauls down his flag and goes with them peaceably enough—probably not only a willing captive, but one who had all along intended and desired to be taken into the enemy's country for purposes of his own. And back of this sorry scene there looms the sinister shadow of General James Wilkinson, the traitor and conspirator with Aaron Burr—let the curtain fall.

they would be in Santa Fe, but were careful never to suggest an idea of my being on the Rio del Norte. As they
concluded, I did not think as I spoke. They were very
anxious to ascertain our numbers, etc.; seeing only five
men here, they could not believe we came without horses.
To this I did not think proper to give them any satisfaction, giving them to understand we were in many
parties, etc.

Feb. 17th. In the morning, our two Spanish visitors
departed, after I had made them some trifling presents,
with which they seemed highly delighted. After their
departure, we commenced working at our little stockade, as
I thought it probable the governor might dispute my right
to descend the Red river, and send out Indians, or some
light party, to attack us; I therefore determined to be as
much prepared to receive them as possible.

This evening the corporal and three of the [four] men
arrived, who had been sent back to the camp of the frozen
lads. They informed me that two men would arrive the next
day, one of whom was Menaugh, who had been left alone on
the 27th of January [and the other of whom was the fourth
one of the soldiers who had gone as a relief-party under
Corporal Jackson]; but that the other two, Dougherty and
Sparks, were unable to come in. They said that they
[Dougherty and Sparks] had hailed them [the relief-party]
with tears of joy, and were in despair when they again left
them, with the chance of never seeing them more. They
sent on to me some of the bones taken out of their feet,
and conjured me, by all that was sacred, not to leave them
to perish far from the civilized world. Ah! little did they
know my heart, if they could suspect me of conduct so
ungenerous. No! before they should be left, I would for
months have carried the end of a litter, in order to secure
them the happiness of once more seeing their native homes,
and being received in the bosom of a grateful country.
Thus those poor lads are to be invalids for life, made infirm
at the commencement of manhood and in the prime of their

course, doomed to pass the remainder of their days in misery and want. For what is the pension? Not sufficient to buy a man his victuals. What man would even lose the smallest of his joints for such a trifling pittance?

Feb. 18th. The other two boys [Menaugh and the fourth member of the relief-party] arrived. In the evening I ordered the sergeant [Meek] and one man [Miller] to prepare to march to-morrow for the [stockade on the] Arkansaw, where we had left our interpreter [Vasquez, with Patrick Smith], horses, etc., to conduct them on, and on his return to bring the two lads [Dougherty and Sparks] who were still in the mountains.

Feb. 19th. Sergeant William E. Meek marched with one man, whose name was Theodore Miller, and I took three other men to accompany him some distance, in order to point out to him a pass [47] in the mountain which I conceived more eligible for horses than the one by which we came. I must here remark the effect of habit, discipline, and example, in two soldiers soliciting a command of more than 180 miles, over two great ridges of mountains covered with snow, inhabited by bands of unknown savages, in the interest of a nation with which we were not on the best understanding. To perform this journey, each had about ten pounds of venison. Only let me ask, What would our soldiers generally think, on being ordered on such a tour, thus equipped? Yet those men volunteered it with others, and were chosen; for which they thought themselves highly honored. We accompanied them about six miles, and pointed out the pass alluded to, in a particular manner. But the corporal afterward reported that the new one which I obliged him to take was impassable, he having been three days in snows nearly middle deep.

We then separated and, having killed a deer, sent one of

---

[47] Doubtless the more eligible Mosca Pass instead of the Sand Hill Pass : see note [39], p. 492. A clause in Pike's next sentence is so singularly constructed as to leave the sense obscure ; he simply means to call attention to the fact that Meek and Miller had asked him to order them on that trip.

the men back to the fort with it. With the other two, I kept on my exploring trip down the river on the east side, at some leagues from its banks, intending to return up it. At nine o'clock at night we encamped on a small creek[48] which emptied into the river from a nearly due east course.

Feb. 20th. We marched down the river for a few hours; but, seeing no fresh sign of persons, or any other object to attract our attention, took up our route for the fort. Discovered the sign of horses and men on the shore. We arrived after night and found all well.

Feb. 21st. As I was suspicious that possibly some party of Indians might be harboring round, I gave particular orders to my men, if they discovered any people, to endeavor to retreat undiscovered; but if not, never to run, and not to suffer themselves to be disarmed or taken prisoners, but conduct whatever party discovered them, if they could not escape, to the fort.

Sunday, Feb. 22d. As I began to think it was time we received a visit from the Spaniards or their emissaries, I established a lookout guard on the top of a hill all day, and at night a sentinel in a bastion on the land side. Studying, reading, and working at our ditch to bring the river round the works.

Feb. 23d. Reading, writing, etc.; the men at their usual work.

Feb. 24th. Took one man with me and went out on the Spanish road hunting; killed one deer and wounded several others. As we were a great distance from the fort, we encamped near the road all night. Saw several signs of horses.

Feb. 25th. Killed two more deer, when we marched for our post. Took all three of the deer with us, and arrived about nine o'clock at night, as much fatigued as ever I was in my life. Our arrival dissipated the anxiety of the men, who began to be apprehensive we were taken or killed by some of the savages.

---

[48] Rio Culebra of present maps—next below Trinchera cr.

Feb. 26th. In the morning was apprized of the approach
of strangers by the report of a gun from my lookout guard.
Immediately afterward two Frenchmen arrived. My sentinel halted them, and ordered them to be admitted, after
some questions. They informed me that his Excellency,
Governor [Joachin R.] Allencaster, had heard it was the
intention of the Utah Indians to attack me; had detached
an officer with 50 dragoons to come out and protect me;
and that they would be here in two days. To this I made
no reply: but shortly after the party came in sight, to the
number, as I afterward learned, of 50 dragoons and 50
mounted militia of the province, armed in the same manner
with lances, escopates,[49] and pistols. My sentinel halted
them at the distance of about 50 yards. I had the works
manned. I thought it most proper to send out the two
Frenchmen to inform the commanding officer that it was
my request he should leave his party in the small copse of
woods where he was halted, and that I would meet him
myself in the prairie in which our work was situated. This
I did, with my sword on me only. I was then introduced
to Don Ignatio Saltelo and Don Bartholemew Fernandez,
two lieutenants, the former the commandant of the party.
I gave them an invitation to enter the works, but requested
the troops might remain where they were. This was complied with. When they came round and discovered that to
enter they were obliged to crawl on their bellies over a
small draw-bridge, they appeared astonished, but entered
without further hesitation.

We first breakfasted on deer, meal, goose, and some biscuit which the civilized Indian who came out as a spy had
brought me. After breakfast the commanding officer
addressed me as follows:

" Sir, the governor of New Mexico, being informed you
had missed your route, ordered me to offer you, in his
name, mules, horses, money, or whatever you might stand in

---

[49] Escopets or escopettes: the carbine or short rifle used by Spanish-
Americans.

need of to conduct you to the head of Red river; as from
Santa Fe to where it is sometimes navigable is eight days'
journey, and we have guides and the routes of the traders
to conduct us."

"What," said I, interrupting him, "is not this the Red
river?"

"No, Sir! The Rio del Norte."

I immediately ordered my flag to be taken down and
rolled up, feeling how sensibly I had committed myself in
entering their territory, and conscious that they must have
positive orders to take me in.

He now added that he "had provided 100 mules and
horses to take in my party and baggage, and how anxious
his Excellency was to see me at Santa Fe." I stated to
him the absence of my sergeant [Meek, with Miller], the
situation of the balance of the party [Vasquez and Smith
in the stockade on the Arkansaw; Dougherty and Sparks
in the mountains with frozen feet], and that my orders
would not justify my entering into the Spanish territory.
He urged still further, until I began to feel myself a little
heated in the argument; and told him, in a peremptory
style, that I would not go until the arrival of my sergeant
with the balance of the party. He replied, "that there was
not the least restraint to be used; that it was only necessary his Excellency should receive an explanation of my
business on his frontier; that I could go now, or on the
arrival of my party; that, if none went in at present, he
should be obliged to send in for provisions; but that, if I
would now march, he would leave an Indian interpreter and
an escort of dragoons to conduct the sergeant [Meek, and
the five other absentees—Miller of the relief-party, Vasquez,
Smith, Sparks, Dougherty] into Santa Fe." His mildness
induced me to tell him that I would march, but must leave
two men [Jackson and Carter] to meet the sergeant and
party, to instruct him as to coming in, as he never would
come without a fight, if not ordered.

I was induced to consent to this measure by the conviction that the officer had positive orders to bring me in ; and as I had no orders to commit hostilities, and indeed had committed myself, although innocently, by violating their territory, I conceived it would appear better to show a will to come to an explanation than to be in any way constrained ; yet my situation was so eligible, and I could so easily have put them at defiance, that it was with great reluctance I suffered all our labor to be lost without once trying the efficacy of it.   My compliance seemed to spread general joy through their party, as soon as it was communicated ; but it appeared to be different with my men, who wished to have "a little dust," as they expressed themselves, and were likewise fearful of treachery.

My determination being once taken, I gave permission for the Spanish lieutenant's men to come to the outside of the works, and some of mine to go out and see them.   The hospitality and goodness of the Creoles and Metifs began to manifest itself by their producing their provision and giving it to my men, covering them with their blankets, etc.

After writing orders to my sergeant [Meek], and leaving them with my corporal [Jackson] and one private [not named (Carter)], who were to remain, we [50] sallied forth, mounted our horses, and went up the river about 12 miles, to a place where the Spanish officers had made a camp deposit, whence we sent down mules for our baggage, etc.

WASHINGTON CITY, January, 1808.

[50] The roll-call now is :

1. Interpreter Vasquez and Private Smith on the Arkansaw.   (2.)

2. Privates Dougherty and Sparks in the mountains, with frozen feet.   (2.)

3. Sergeant Meek and Private Miller gone to the relief of the foregoing.   (2.)

4. Corporal Jackson and one man (Private Carter) left on the Rio Conejos to await the coming of the foregoing six.   (2.)

5. Dr. Robinson gone ahead to Santa Fé.   (1.)

6. Pike therefore sallies forth under escort of the Spanish dragoons with the following : Privates Brown, Gorden, Menaugh, Mountjoy, Roy, Stoute.   (7.)

Total 16, present or accounted for.

CHAPTER IV.

PIKE'S DISSERTATION ON LOUISIANA.[1]

FROM the entrance of the Missouri, on the south bank the land is low until you arrive at Belle Fontaine, four miles from its entrance. In this distance are several strata of soil, one rising above the other. As the river is cutting off the north point, and making land on the south, this is well timbered with oak, walnut, ash, etc.

From Belle Fontaine to St. Charles the north side of the Missouri is low, bounded on its banks by timbered land extending from half a mile to one mile from the river. Six miles below St. Charles, on the south side, in front of a village called Florissant, is a coal hill, or, as it is termed by the French, La Charbonniere. This is one solid stone hill, which probably affords sufficient fuel for all the population of Louisiana. St. Charles is situated on the west side of the Missouri, where the hill first joins the river, and is laid out parallel to the stream.

The main street is on the first bank, the second on the top of the hill. On this street is situated a round wooden

[1] Chapter IV consists of an article which came first in the App. to Pt. 2 of the orig. ed., pp. 1–18. This had no number among the various pieces of which that Appendix was made up ; but as it came first, and the next piece was No. 2, the lack of numeration was a mere inadvertence, and it is to be taken *pro formâ* as No. 1. It was lengthily entitled : "A Dissertation On the Soil, Rivers, Productions, Animal and Vegetable, with General Notes on the Internal Parts of Louisiana, compiled from observations made by Capt. Z. M. Pike, in a late tour from the mouth of the Missouri, to the Head Waters of the Arkansaw and Rio del Norte, in the years 1806 and 1807 ; including Observations on the Aborigines of the Country." Such notes as I should otherwise have to offer on the substance of this Dissertation are for the most part already made in the foregoing three chapters of the Itinerary. The present chapter may therefore be passed without remark, excepting in so far as concerns some new points that come up for notice.

tower, formerly occupied by the Spaniards as a fort or guard-house, now converted into a prison. From this tower you have an extensive view of the river below. St. Charles consists of about 80 houses, principally occupied by Indian traders or their engagees. It is the seat of justice for the district of St. Charles.

From St. Charles to the village of La Charrette, the west side is generally low, but with hills running parallel at a great distance back from the river; the south side is more hilly, with springs. Scattering settlements are on both sides.

La Charrette is the last settlement we saw on the Missouri, although there is one above, at a saline on the west side. From La Charrette to the Gasconade river, you find on the north low land heavily timbered; on the south, hills, rivulets, and a small number of small creeks, with very high cane. The Gasconade is 200 yards wide at its entrance; it is navigable at certain seasons 100 miles. At the time we were at it, it was backed by the Mississippi,[2] but was clear and transparent above their confluence. On the side opposite their confluence commences the line between the Sac Indians and the United States. [See p. 339, and note [14], p. 11.]

From the Gasconade to the entrance of the Osage river, the south side of the river is hilly but well timbered. On the north are low bottoms and heavy timber. In this space of the Missouri, from its [the Gasconade's] entrance to the Osage river, we find it well timbered, rich in soil, and very proper for the cultivation of all the productions of our Middle and Western States. It is timbered generally with cottonwood, ash, oak, pecan, hickory, and some elm; but the cottonwood predominates on all the made bottoms. From the entrance of the Osage river to the Gravel river, a distance of 118 miles, the banks of the Osage are covered

---

[2] Read Missouri—"Mississippi" being the slip of a pen which had so often written the latter word. The clause means that muddy backwater from the Missouri ran some way into the Gasconade.

with timber and possess a very rich soil. Small hills, with rocks, alternately border the eastern and western shores; the bottoms being very excellent soil, and the country abounding in game. From thence to the Yungar, the river continues the same in appearance; the shoals and islands being designated on the chart. The Yungar, or Ne-hem-gar, as termed by the Indians, derives its name from the vast number of springs at its source; it is supposed to be nearly as extensive as the Osage river, navigable for canoes 100 miles, and is celebrated for the abundance of bear which are found on its branches. On it hunt the Chasseurs du Bois of Louisiana, Osage, and Creeks or Muskogees, a wandering party of whom have established themselves in Louisiana; and between whom and the French hunters frequent skirmishes have passed on the head of the Yungar.

A few miles above this river the Osage river becomes narrower, and evidently shows the loss experienced by the deficiency of [gain not as yet acquired from] the waters of the Yungar. On the east shore is a pond of water, about 20 paces from the bank of the river, and half a mile in circumference; it was elevated at least 20 feet above the surface of the river. This appeared the more singular, as the soil appeared to be sandy, whence it would be concluded that the waters of the pond would speedily discharge through the soil into the river; but there appeared to be no reason for any such deduction.

Thence to a few miles below the Park (see chart [and diary of Aug. 14th]), the banks of the river continue as usual. We now, for the first time, were entertained with the sight of prairie land; but it still was interspersed with clumps of woodland, which diversified the prospect.

In this district the cliffs, which generally bordered one of the sides of the river, were covered with the largest and most beautiful cedars I ever saw. Thence to the Grand Forks [confluence of Little with main Osage], the banks of the river continue the same; but thence up to the Osage town, there is a larger proportion of prairie. At the place where Mr. Chouteau formerly had his trading-establishment, the east bank of the river is an entire bed of stone-coal; whence by land by the villages is but nine miles, but by water at least 50. The country round the Osage villages is one of the most beautiful the eye ever beheld. The three branches of the river, viz.: the large east fork [Sac river], the middle one [Little Osage], up which we ascended, and the northern one [main Osage], all winding round and past the villages, giving the advantages of wood and water, and at the same time the extensive prairies crowned with rich and luxuriant grass and flowers, gently diversified by the rising swells and sloping lawns, present to the warm imagination the future seats of husbandry, the numerous herds of domestic animals, which are no doubt destined to crown with joy those happy plains. The best comment I can make on the navigation of the Osage river is a reference to my chart and journal on that subject. From the last village on the Missouri to the prairies on the Osage river we found plenty of deer, bear, and some turkeys. Thence to the towns there are some elk and deer, but near the villages they become scarce.

From the Osage towns to the source of the [Little] Osage river there is no difference in the appearance of the country, except that on the south and east the view on the prairies becomes unbounded, and is only limited by the imbecility of our sight. The waters of the White [Neosho] river and the [Little] Osage are divided merely by a small ridge in the prairie, and the dry branches appear to interlock at their head. From thence to the main branch of the said [Neosho] river the country appeared high, with gravelly ridges of prairie land. On the main White river is large timber and fine ground for cultivation. Hence a doubt arises as to the disemboguing of this stream. Lieutenant Wilkinson, from some authority, has drawn the conclusion that it discharges itself into the Arkansaw a short distance below the Vermilion river; but from the voyages of Captain Maney [Many] on White river, the information of hunters, Indians, etc., I am rather induced to believe it to be the White river of the Mississippi, as at their mouths there is not so great a difference between their magnitude; and all persons agree in ascertaining [asserting] that the White river heads between the Osage, Arkansaw, and Kansas rivers, which would still leave the Arkansaw near 800 miles more lengthy than the White river. From the proofs, I am perfectly confident in asserting that this was the White river of the Mississippi which we crossed.[3] At the place where we traversed it, the stream was amply navigable for canoes, even at this dry season (August) of the year.

Up this river to the dividing ridges between it and the Verdigrise river, the bottom is of some magnitude and importance; but the latter river is bounded here in a narrow bed of prairie hills, affording not more than sufficient timber for firewood for a limited number of inhabitants for a few years. From the Verdigrise our course again lay over gravelly hills and a prairie country, but well watered by the branches of the Verdigrise and White (alias Grand) rivers. From this point to the source of White river there is very little timber, the grass short, prairies high and dry. From the head of White river over the dividing ridge between that and the eastern [Smoky Hill] branch of the Kans river, the ridge is high, dry, and has many appearances of iron ore, and on the west side are some spaw springs [spas]. Here the country is very deficient of water. From the east branch of the Kans river (by our route) to the Pawnee

[3] The river which the Expedition crossed was of course the Neosho, which Wilkinson was correct in stating to fall into the Arkansaw a short distance below the Vermilion or Verdigris—"a quarter of a mile," his Report says. Pike's wrong conclusion is not here animadverted upon, as it has been set right before; but I wish to note that the "White river of the Mississippi" has given rise to much confusion, from the very simple circumstance that it is a branch both of the Mississippi and of the Arkansaw. It runs into the very crotch between these two, and has a sort of a delta of its own, as well as a double debouchment. Various maps consulted on this point, as I have never been on the spot, differ in that some run White r. into the Arkansaw, some into the Mississippi, and some into both these rivers. The latter seems to be the present arrangement; but this may have repeatedly altered in former times.

Republic on the Republican fork (see chart), the prairies are low, with high grass; the country abounds with salines, and the earth appears to be impregnated with nitrous and common salts. The immediate border of the Republican fork near the village is high ridges, but this is an exception to the general face of the country. All the country between the forks of the Kans river, a distance of 160 miles, may be called prairie, notwithstanding the borders of woodland which ornament the banks of those streams, but are no more than a line traced on a sheet of paper, when compared to the immense tract of meadow country.

For some distance from the Osage villages you only find deer, then elk, then cabrie, and finally buffalo. But it is worthy of remark that although the male buffaloes were in great abundance, yet in all our route from the Osage to the Pawnees we never saw one female. I acknowledge myself at a loss to determine whether this is to be attributed to the decided preference the savages give to the meat of the females, so that consequently they are almost exterminated in the hunting-grounds of the nations, or to some physical causes; for I afterward discovered the females with young in such immense herds as gave me no reason to believe they yielded to the males in numbers.

From the Pawnee town on the Kansas river to the Arkansaw, the country may almost be termed mountainous; but want of timber gives the hills less claim to the appellation of mountains. They are watered and created, as it were, by the various branches of the Kans river. One of those branches, a stream of considerable magnitude (say 20 yards), which I have designated on the chart by the name of Saline, was so salt, where we crossed it on our route to the Arkansaw, that it salted sufficiently the soup of the meat which my men boiled in it. We were here very eligibly situated; had a fresh spring, issuing from a bank near us; plenty of the necessaries of life all around, viz.: buffalo; a beautiful little sugar-loaf hill, for a lookout post; fine grass for our horses; and a saline in front of us.

As you approach the Arkansaw on this route within 15 or
20 miles, the country appears to be low and swampy ; or
the land is covered with ponds extending out from the river
some distance.   The river at the place where I struck it is
nearly 500 yards wide, from bank to bank, those banks not
more than four feet high, thinly covered with cottonwood.
The north side is a swampy low prairie [Cheyenne Bottoms],
and the south a sandy sterile desert.   Thence, about half-
way to the mountains, the country continued with low
prairie hills, and scarcely any streams putting into the river ;
and on the bottom are many bare spots on which, when the
sun is in the meridian, is congealed a species of salt sufficiently thick to be accumulated, but so strongly impregnated
with nitric qualities as to render it unfit for use until puri-
fied.   The grass in this district, on the river bottoms, has
a great appearance of the grass on our salt marshes.   From
the first south fork ([Purgatory river] see chart) the borders
of the river have more wood, and the hills are higher,
until you arrive at its entrance into the mountains.   The
whole of the timber is cottonwood, from the entrance of the
Arkansaw into the mountains to its source, a distance of
about 170 miles by the meanders ; it is alternately bounded
by perpendicular precipices and small, narrow prairies, on
which the buffalo and elk have found the means to arrive,
and are almost secure from danger from their destroyer—
man.   In many places the river precipitates itself over
rocks, so as at one moment to be visible only in the foaming and boiling of its waters—at the next moment it
disappears in the chasms of the overhanging precipices.
The Arkansaw[4] river, taking its meanders agreeably to

[4] The route from the Missouri, at or near the mouth of the Kansas—that
is, from old Westport (now Kansas City), Mo., and Independence, Mo.—to the
great bend of the Arkansaw, near the mouth of Walnut cr., was established as
an overland highway during the '20's, when it began to be regularly taken by
the traders' caravans en route to Santa Fé.   The trade attained such proportions
that some years merchandise of the value of $250,000 and $450,000 was hauled
over this road : see Gregg's statistics for 1822–43, Comm. Pra., II. 1844, p. 160.
Pack-animals or wagons were used, 1822–25, but after that wagons only ; and

Lieutenant Wilkinson's survey of the lower part, is 1,981 miles from its entrance into the Mississippi to the mountains, and from thence to its source 192 miles, making its total length 2,173 miles: all of which may be navigated with proper boats, constructed for the purpose, except the

these soon wore a road as plain as a turnpike.   It will be interesting to go over this road, and identify the camping-grounds of those hardy pioneers by the modern names of the places on and near their route ; especially as no railroad now follows this primitive trace exactly.   It held a pretty straight westward course, bearing all the while southward ; the distance from the usual starting place (Independence, Mo.) was called 300 m. roundly, but is somewhat less than this.   The most noted point on the route was Council Grove, so called since 1825, when the U. S. Commissioners Reeves, Sibley, and Mathers, who there treated with the Osages, gave the place its present name.   In the most general terms, the road followed the divide between Kansan waters on the N., or right hand going W., and on the other, first those of the Osage (a branch of the Missouri), then those of the Neosho (a branch of the Arkansaw), and finally those of the Arkansaw itself.   But the route was nearly everywhere in the latter water-shed ; after the first few miles, every stream crossed ran to the left.   In some places, the divide between the two sets of streams had little breadth ; one place was called The Narrows, the approximation was so close. The wagon-train that started from Independence usually left " the States " the first day out, and entered " the Indian territory "—that is, it went from the present State of Missouri into the present State of Kansas ; and all the rest of the way to Great Bend was through the latter.   Let us look up some maps and itineraries of half a century ago—say Gregg's, pub. 1844 ; Wislizenus', of 1846 ; and Beckwith's, 1853—to see what sign-posts they set up.   These point to such places as the following, in regular order from E. to W.: Independence and Westport, Mo.—Big Blue camp—Round Grove, Lone Elm, The Glen— Bull cr., Black Jack cr. and pt., Willow springs, and The Narrows—two Rock creeks in succession—One Hundred and Ten Mile cr.—Bridge cr.—Dwissler's or Switzler's cr.—five creeks to which the names First Dragoon, Second Dragoon, Soldier, Prairie Chicken, Elm, and One Hundred and Forty-two Mile attach in some itineraries and are to be collated with Fish and Pool, or Fish and Pleasant Valley, of others—Bluff cr.—Big Rock cr.—Big John spring and cr.—*Council Grove,* on its own cr.—another Elm cr.—Diamond spring and cr.—Lost spring and Lost or Willow cr.—Cottonwood cr.—two or three Turkey creeks in succession—Little Arkansaw r.—several Little Cow creeks, among them one called Chavez or Charez and Owl—Big Cow cr.—approach to the Arkansaw r. at Camp Osage—up the Arkansaw to Walnut cr. and thus to Great Bend.   From such *indicia* as these it may not be difficult to reopen the road in terms of modern geography.   1. Independence maintains its independence as the seat of Jackson Co., Mo., 2 or 3 m. S. of the Missouri r., and about the same E. of Big Blue cr.; but Westport is practically absorbed in the suburbs of Kansas City,

192 miles in the mountains.   It has emptying into it several
small rivers navigable for 100 miles and upward.   Boats
bound up the whole length of the navigation should embark
at its entrance on the 1st of February, when they would
have the fresh [high water] quite to the mountains, and

Mo.   Starting from Independence, the first halt on the prairie, after crossing
Big Blue r., was likely to be " Big Blue camp." This was about the heads of
Brush cr., a small tributary of the Big Blue from the W., and in the vicinity of
present Glenn.   Being nearly on the present inter-State boundary, it was the
" jumping-off place " from " the States," where the traveler entered " the Indian
territory." The military road between Forts Towson (on Red r.) and Leavenworth passed by.   A little to the N. W. was the Shawnee agency and mission,
on a branch of Turkey cr., the first tributary of the Kansas from the S.;
Shawnee is there now, and other places on Turkey cr. are called Merriam,
South Park, and Rosedale ; the Kansas City, Fort Scott, and Gulf R. R.
meanders Turkey cr. into Kansas City.   The position is about lat. 38° 59′ N.
and long. 94° 35′ W.   2. About 5 m. further S. W. the road passed by Lenexa,
Johnson Co., and a camp could be made on a head of Indian cr., which is
a small stream joined by Tomahawk cr. before it reaches the Big Blue.   The
road continued S. W., approximately by the present S. Kan. R. R., and thus
past Olathe, now seat of Johnson Co., where six tracks diverge in various
directions.   This is in the center of the county, near the head of Indian cr., on
the head of Mill cr., a tributary of the Kansas, and near the head of a branch
of Cedar cr., another Kansan affluent.   3. " Round Grove," " Lone Elm," or
" The Glen " was a camping-place on one of the heads of Cedar cr., between
Olathe and the village of Gardner ; it was reckoned 15 m. from Big Blue camp,
and 22 m. from Westport.   Thus far the Santa Fé route coincided with the even
more celebrated " Oregon trail."   But at a point beyond Gardner, in the
direction of Edgerton, and 6 or 8 m. from Round Grove, the road forked—
that is, the Oregon trail struck off to the right in the N. W. direction of the
Kansas, while the Santa Fé trail kept on the left-hand fork westward.   4. Bull
cr. is still so called, or specified as Big Bull cr. to distinguish it from Little
Bull cr. which, with other tributaries, such as Rock, Ten Mile, and Wea, it
receives before it falls into Marais des Cygnes (main Osage) r.   This is the
creek on which is Paola, seat of Miami Co., near the junction of Wea cr., and it
was the first of the Osage waters which the road crossed.   The crossing was high
up on its main course, between Gardner and Edgerton, whence the road continued W. from Johnson into Douglas Co.   5. From the crossing of Bull cr. it
is 9 m. to Black Jack cr. and pt., so called from the kind of oak (*Quercus
nigra*) which grows there.   Black Jack is still the name of a place between the
heads of Captain cr. (tributary of the Kansas) and Rock cr. (a branch of Bull
cr.) ; it is 3 m. due E. of Baldwin City.   6. " Willow springs " was a noted
camping place W. of Baldwin City, on one of the heads of Ottawa cr., which
flows southward into the Marais des Cygnes r., a little below Ottawa, county

meet with no detention. But if they should start later, they would find the river 1,500 miles up nearly dry. It has one singularity which struck me very forcibly at first view, but which, on reflection, I am induced to believe is the same case with all the rivers which run through a low, dry, sandy

seat of Franklin. The distance of Willow springs from the crossing of Black Jack cr. is 10½ m. Willow springs seems to be the same place that was called Wakarusa pt., or was at any rate very near it. Here the approximation of Kansan and Osage waters is very close, and this is the place which consequently became known as "The Narrows." The interlocking is between several heads of the Ottawa cr. just said and some tributaries of Cole cr., a branch of the Wakarusa. Camp could also be made at a place called Hickory pt., short of Willow springs by 3 or 4 m. 7. Two "Rock" creeks were passed at distances given as 9 and 12 m. from Willow springs by some writers, and quite differently by others; some also mention but one "Rock" cr. Eight Mile cr. was headed if not crossed by the road; and beyond this the road crossed one or both heads of Appanoose cr. These creeks are tributaries of the Marais des Cygnes, falling in a mile apart at Ottawa and just beyond. Part of the uncertainty about these "Rock" creeks arose from the fact that they often ran dry, were woodless, and thus ineligible for camping-grounds; hence they would often be passed without remark. The names seem to me to apply rather to the two forks of the Appanoose than to the main fork of the latter and to Eight Mile cr. 8. One Hundred and Ten Mile cr., which still floats its long name, was so called because it was taken to be 110 m. from Fort Osage, our earliest establishment of the kind on the Missouri. This was built in Sept., 1808, at Fort Point (present Sibley: see L. and C., ed. 1893, p. 30), and was sometimes called Fort Clark. The creek in mention was crossed at a point taken to be 24 m. from Willow springs, and thus in the vicinity of present Scranton, Osage Co. It is a branch of the Dragoon cr. we have next to consider. 9. Continuing nearly due W., the road crossed several heads of present Dragoon cr., in the vicinity of Burlingame, Osage Co. This is a comparatively large creek, which runs southeastward to fall into the Marais des Cygnes near Quenemo. That one of the several heads of Dragoon cr. on which Burlingame is situated is now called Switzler's cr.; the next beyond is the main source of Dragoon cr., into which a branch called Soldier's cr. falls, about 2 m. W. of Burlingame, But none of the older itineraries I have consulted speak of either "Dragoon" or "Soldier's" cr.; instead of which, they give a certain Bridge cr., as crossed 8 m. W. of One Hundred and Ten Mile cr. This is precisely the distance given by Beckwith for his "Dwissler's" cr. No doubt "Switzler" and "Dwissler" are the same person's names; but whether this has always been applied to the same creek may well be doubted. The "First Dragoon" cr. is now Dragoon cr.; the "Second Dragoon" cr. is now Soldier's cr.; these were passed near their confluence. 10. In the next few miles the road crossed in rapid succession several heads of the Marais des Cygnes itself, thus finishing with the Osage water-shed.

soil in warm climates, as I observed it to be the case with the Rio del Norte, viz.: for the extent of 400 or 500 miles before you arrive near the mountains, the bed of the river is extensive and a perfect sand-bar, which at certain seasons is dry, or at least the water is standing in ponds not afford-

Three of these are now known as Onion, Chicken or Prairie Chicken, and Elm ; the latter is the main head, and seems to be the one which appears as " Fish " cr. in the early narratives—the name by which it is mapped both by Gregg and by Wislizenus. A fourth head of the Marais des Cygnes which the road crossed is that now known as One Hundred and Forty-two Mile cr., which joins the main stream much lower down than the other three. This is mapped by Gregg as Pool cr. and by Wislizenus as Pleasant Valley cr. All four of these streams are crossed in Lyon Co., the boundary between this and Osage Co. having been passed at long. 95° 50′ 57″ W. nearly. 11. The road continued across Big Rock cr., having first passed its branch, Bluff cr. This is a tributary of the Neosho. It is probable that the Bluff cr. of early writers refers to the main Big Rock rather than to the branch now called Bluff, as it is the last one they give before coming to—12. Big John cr., another tributary of the Neosho, which was crossed immediately before Council Grove was reached ; on which account, as well as for its beautiful spring and eligible camping-ground, it early became noted under the name it still bears. 13. Council Grove, now the seat of Morris Co. This was always the most marked place on the route—a sort of halfway station between the Missouri settlements and the great bend of the Arkansaw. Its area was indefinitely extensive along the wooded bottom-land of the Neosho, or, as it was called here, Council Grove cr.; but as the situation became peopled, settlement was made chiefly on the W. or right bank of the stream, at the mouth of Elm cr., a tributary from the W. This is not far from the center of a tract about 45 m. square known as the Kansas Trust Lands, of which the Kansas Diminished Reserve is a southwestern portion. Council Grove is only some 8 m. from the boundary between Lyon and Morris Co., which runs on a meridian close by the course of Big Rock cr. 14. The road continued W. up the left or N. bank of Elm cr. for about 8 m., crossed it at or near present station Milton of the Topeka, Salina, and Western R. R., and went on S. W. to Diamond spring, about 8 m. further. This was a camping place high up on the waters of Diamond or, as it is also called, Six Mile cr., a branch of the Cottonwood. 15. Hence W. about 16 m. to Lost spring, on Lost or Clear cr.—that branch of the Cottonwood which falls in at Marion. This place is a little over the border of Marion Co., and a town or station Lost Spring perpetuates the name, at the point where the Chicago, Kansas, and Nebraska R. R. crosses a branch of the A., T., and S. F. R. R. 16. From Lost spring the route turned S. W. 17 m. to the Cottonwood, approximately by the present railroad line, and struck that river at or near Durham, Marion Co. 17. Continuing S. W. and then bearing more nearly W., the road passed by or near Canton and thence to McPherson, both in the county of the latter name.

ing sufficient to procure a running course; but when you come nearer the mountains you find the river contracted, a gravelly bottóm, and a deep, navigable stream. From these circumstances it is evident that the sandy soil imbibes all the [not evaporated] waters which the sources project from the mountains, and renders the river in dry seasons less navigable 500 than 200 miles from its source.

The borders of the Arkansaw river may be termed the terrestrial paradise of our territories for the wandering savages. Of all countries ever visited by the footsteps of civilized man, there never was one probably that produced game in greater abundance. We know that the manners and morals of the erratic nations are such (the reasons I leave to be given by the ontologists) as never to give them a numerous population; and I believe that there are buffalo, elk, and deer sufficient on the banks of the Arkansaw alone, if used without waste, to feed all the savages in the United States territory one century. By the route of the Arkansaw and the Rio Colorado of California, I am confident in asserting, if my information from Spanish gentlemen of information is correct, there can be established the best communication, on this side of the Isthmus of Darien, between the Atlantic and Pacific oceans; as, admitting the utmost, the land car-

Both are situated among the heads of Turkey cr., a branch of the Little Arkansaw; two or three of these were crossed. When two were noted, it used to be by the names of Little and Big Turkey creeks; map names are now Running Turkey, Turkey, and West Turkey; McPherson is on the last of these, some 25 m. from the crossing of the Cottonwood. The Turkey creeks vary very much in character with season and the weather. 18. The road continued about 20 m. to the crossing of the Little Arkansaw, in the vicinity of the place now called Little River. 19. In 10 m. the road reached one of the tributaries of Cow cr., and it was 10 more before all of these were passed; there are five or six of them, and some hardly ever run water. One of them is now called "Jarvis" cr.: see note [10], p. 424. Another is known as Long Branch; between this and Little Cow cr. is Lyons, seat of Rice Co., and beyond this Big Cow cr. is crossed. 20. The road now makes for the Arkansaw on a due W. course, and comes on to that river at a place which was known as Camp Osage, in the vicinity of present Ellinwood, Barton Co. This town is only 3 m. from the mouth of Walnut cr., and the city of Great Bend is a mile or two beyond that.

riage would not be more than 200 miles, and the route may be made quite as eligible as our public highways over the Alleghany mountains. The Rio Colorado is to the great Gulph of California what the Mississippi is to the Gulph of Mexico, and is navigable for ships of considerable burden, to opposite the upper parts of the province of Senora.

From the Arkansaw to the Rio del Norte, by the route I passed, the country was covered with mountains and small prairies, as per chart ; but the game became much more scarce, owing to the vicinity of the Spanish Indians and the Spaniards themselves.

In this western traverse of Louisiana, the following general observations may be made, viz.: that from the Missouri to the head of the [Little] Osage river, a distance in a straight line of probably 300 miles, the country will admit of a numerous, extensive, and compact population ; thence, on the rivers Kanses, La Platte, Arkansaw, and their various branches, it appears to me to be only possible to introduce a limited population on their banks. The inhabitants would find it most to their advantage to pay attention to the multiplication of cattle, horses, sheep, and goats, all of which they can raise in abundance, the earth producing spontaneously sufficient for their support, both winter and summer, by which means their herds might become immensely numerous ; but the wood now in the country would not be sufficient for a moderate share of population more than 15 years, and it would be out of the question to think of using any of it in manufactures ; consequently, the houses would be built entirely of mud-brick [adobe], like those in New Spain, or of the brick manufactured with fire. But possibly time may make the discovery of coal-mines, which would render the country habitable.

The source of La Platte is situated in the same chain of mountains with the Arkansaw (see chart), and comes from that grand reservoir of snows and fountains which gives birth on its northeastern side to the Red river of the Missouri (the yellow stone river of Lewis [and Clark], its great southwestern branch), and La Platte ; on its southwestern side it produces the Rio Colorado of California ; on its east the Arkansaw; and on its south the Rio del Norte of North Mexico. I have no hesitation in asserting that I can take a position in the mountains, whence I can visit the source of any of those rivers in one day.[5]

Numerous have been the hypotheses formed by various naturalists to account for the vast tract of untimbered country which lies between the waters of the Missouri, Mississippi, and the Western Ocean, from the mouth of the latter river to 48° north latitude. Although not flattering myself to be able to elucidate that which numbers of highly scientific characters have acknowledged to be beyond their depth of research, still I would not think I had done my country justice did I not give birth to what few lights my examination of those internal deserts has enabled me to acquire. In that vast country of which I speak, we find the soil generally dry and sandy, with gravel, and discover that the moment we approach a stream the land becomes more humid, with small timber. I therefore conclude that this country never was timbered ; as, from the earliest age the aridity of the soil, having so few water-courses running through it, and they being principally dry in summer, has never afforded moisture sufficient to support the growth of timber. In all timbered land the annual discharge of the leaves, with the continual decay of old trees and branches, creates a manure and moisture, which is preserved from the

[5] This wild notion was a pet of Pike's, which he indulged to the extent of embodying it in the title of his book, and making his map fit it. No man can go, afoot or on horseback, in anything like one day, from any possible position, to the sources of all those rivers. It can be taken as an indication of the really close approximation of certain pairs of rivers, which drain from opposite sides of the same range, or made elastic enough to suit the situation about Mt. Lincoln, where some heads of the Grand, the Arkansaw, and the South Platte approximate ; but the other rivers are entirely out of the question. Owing to Pike's ignorance of the existence of the *North* Platte, all that he says in various places of his hypothetical Yellowstone comes nearer the facts in the case of the Platte. " La Platte " he only knew from the sources of the *South* Platte.

heat of the sun not being permitted to direct his rays perpendicularly, but only to shed them obliquely through the foliage. But here a barren soil, parched and dried up for eight months in the year, presents neither moisture nor nutrition sufficient to nourish the timber. These vast plains of the western hemisphere may become in time as celebrated as the sandy deserts of Africa; for I saw in my route, in various places, tracts of many leagues where the wind had thrown up the sand in all the fanciful form of the ocean's rolling wave, and on which not a speck of vegetable matter existed.

But from these immense prairies may arise one great advantage to the United States, viz.: The restriction of our population to some certain limits, and thereby a continuation of the Union. Our citizens being so prone to rambling and extending themselves on the frontiers will, through necessity, be constrained to limit their extent on the west to the borders of the Missouri and Mississippi, while they leave the prairies incapable of cultivation to the wandering and uncivilized aborigines of the country.

The Osage appear to have emigrated from the north and west; from their speaking the same language with the Kans, Otos, Missouries, and Mahaws, together with their great similarity of manners, morals, and customs, there is left no room to doubt that they were originally the same nation, but separated by that great law of nature, self-preservation, the love of freedom, and the ambition of various characters, so inherent in the breast of man. As nations purely erratic must depend solely on the chase for subsistence, unless pastoral, which is not the case with our savages, it requires large tracts of country to afford subsistence for a very limited number of souls; consequently, self-preservation obliges them to expand themselves over a large and extensive district. The power of certain chiefs becoming unlimited, and their rule severe, added to the passionate love of liberty and the ambition of young, bold, and daring characters who step forward to head the malcontents, and

like the tribes of Israel, to lead them through the wilderness
to a new land—the land of promise which flowed with milk
and honey, alias abounded with deer and buffalo—these
characters soon succeed in leading forth a new colony, and
in process of time establishing a new nation. The Mahaws,
Missouries, and Otos remained on the banks of the Missouri
river, such a distance up as to be in the reach of that
powerful enemy, the Sioux, who, with the aid of the smallpox, which the former nations unfortunately contracted by
their connection with the whites, have reduced the Mahaws,
formerly a brave and powerful nation, to a mere cipher,
and obliged the Otos and Missouries to join their forces, so
that these now form but one nation. The Kanses and
Osage came further to the east, and thereby avoided the
Sioux, but fell into the hands of the Iowas, Sacs, Kicka-
pous, Potowatomies, Delawares, Shawanese, Cherokees,
Chickasaws, Chactaws, Arkansaws, Caddoes, and Tetaus ;
and what astonished me extremely is that they have not
been entirely destroyed by those nations. But it must only
be attributed to their ignorance of the enemies' force, their
want of concert, wars between themselves, and the great
renown the invaders always acquire, by the boldness of their
enterprise, in the minds of the invaded.

Their government is oligarchical, but still partakes of the
nature of a republic ; for, although the power nominally is
vested in a small number of chiefs, yet they never undertake any matter of importance without first assembling the
warriors and proposing the subject in council, there to be
discussed and decided on by a majority. Their chiefs are
hereditary, in most instances, yet there are many men who
have risen to more influence than those of illustrious ancestry, by their activity and boldness in war. Although there
is no regular code of laws, yet there is a tacit acknowledgment of the right which some have to command on certain
occasions, whilst others are bound to obey, and even to
submit to corporeal punishment ; as is instanced in the
affair related in my diary of July 29th, when Has-ha-ke-da-

tungar or Big Soldier, whom I had made a partisan to regulate the movements of the Indians, flogged a young Indian with arms in his hands. On the whole, their government may be termed an oligarchical republic, where the chiefs propose and the people decide on all public acts.

The manners of the Osage are different from those of any nation I ever saw except those before mentioned of the same origin, having their people divided into classes. All the bulk of the nation being warriors and hunters—with them these terms being almost synonymous—the remainder is divided into two classes, cooks and doctors; the latter of whom likewise exercise the functions of priests or magicians, and have great influence in the councils of the nation by their pretended divinations, interpretations of dreams, and magical performances. An illustration of this will be better given by the following anecdote of what took place during my stay at the nation, in August, 1806: Having had all the doctors or magicians assembled in the lodge of Ca-ha-ga-tonga, alias Cheveux Blancs, and about 500 spectators, they had two rows of fires prepared, around which the sacred band was stationed. They commenced the tragicomedy by putting a large butcher-knife down their throats, the blood appearing to run during the operation very naturally; the scene was continued by putting sticks through the nose, swallowing bones and taking them out of the nostrils, etc. At length one fellow demanded of me what I would give if he would run a stick through his tongue, and let another person cut off the piece. I replied, "a shirt." He then apparently performed his promise, with great pain, forcing a stick through his tongue, and then giving a knife to a bystander, who appeared to cut off the piece, which he held to the light for the satisfaction of the audience, and then joined it to his tongue, and by a magical charm healed the wound immediately. On demanding of me what I thought of the performance, I replied I would give him 20 shirts if he would let me cut off the piece from his tongue; this disconcerted him a great deal, and I was sorry I had made the observation.

The cooks are either for the general use, or attached particularly to the family of some great man; and what is the more singular, men who have been great warriors and brave men, having lost all their families by disease, in the war, and themselves becoming old and infirm, frequently take up the profession of cook, in which they do not carry arms, and are supported by the public or their particular patron.

They likewise exercise the functions of town criers, calling the chiefs to council and to feasts; or if any particular person is wanted, you employ a crier, who goes through the village crying his name and informing him he is wanted at such a lodge. When received into the Osage village you immediately present yourself at the lodge of the chief, who receives you as his guest, where you generally eat first, after the old patriarchal style. You are then invited to a feast by all the great men of the village, and it would be a great insult if you did not comply, at least as far as to taste of their victuals. In one instance, I was obliged to taste of 15 different entertainments the same afternoon. You will hear the cooks crying, " come and eat "—such an one " gives a feast, come and eat of his bounty." Their dishes were generally sweet corn boiled in buffalo grease, or boiled meat and pumpkins; but San Oriel [Sans Oreille], alias Tetobasi, treated me to a dish of tea in a wooden dish, with new horn spoons, boiled meat, and crullers; he had been in the United States. Their towns hold more people in the same space of ground than any places I ever saw. Their lodges are posted with scarcely any regularity, each one building in the manner, directions, and dimensions which suit him best, by which means they frequently leave only room for a single man to squeeze between them; added to this, they have pens for their horses, all within the village, into which they always drive them at night, in case they think there is any reason to believe there is an enemy lurking in the vicinity.

The Osage lodges are generally constructed with upright posts, put firmly in the ground, of about 20 feet in height, with a crotch at the top; they are about 12 feet distant from each other ; in the crotch of those posts are put the ridge-poles, over which are bent small poles, the ends of which are brought down and fastened to a row of stakes about five feet in height ; these stakes are fastened together with three horizontal bars, and form the flank walls of the lodge. The gable ends are generally broad slabs, rounded off to the ridge-pole. The whole of the building and sides are cov-ered with matting made of rushes, two or three feet in length and four feet in width, which are joined together, and entirely exclude the rain. The doors are on the sides of the building, and generally are one on each side. The fires are made in holes in the center of the lodge, the smoke ascend-ing through apertures left in the roof for the purpose. At one end of the dwelling is a raised platform, about three feet from the ground, which is covered with bear-skins, generally holds all the little choice furniture of the master, and on which repose his honorable guests. In fact, with neatness and a pleasing companion, these dwellings would compose a very comfortable and pleasant summer habitation, but are left in the winter for the woods. They vary in length from 36 to 100 feet.

The Osage nation is divided into three villages, and in a few years you may say nations, viz.: the Grand Osage, the Little Osage, and those of the Arkansaw.

The Little Osage separated from the Big Osage about 100 years since, when their chiefs, on obtaining permission to lead forth a colony from the great council of the nation, moved on to the Missouri ; but after some years, finding themselves too hard pressed by their enemies, they again obtained permission to return, put themselves under the protection of the Grand village, and settled down about six miles off. (See chart.)

The Arkansaw schism was effected by Mr. Pierre Choteau, 10 or 12 years ago, as a revenge on Mr. Manuel De Sezei [Liza or Lisa], who had obtained from the Spanish govern-ment the exclusive trade of the Osage nation, by the way of the Osage river, after it had been in the hands of Mr.

Choteau for nearly 20 years. The latter, having the trade of the Arkansaw, thereby nearly rendered abortive the exclusive privilege of his rival. He has been vainly promising to the government that he would bring them back to join the Grand village. But his reception at the Arkansaw village, in the autumn of 1806, must have nearly cured him of that idea. And in fact, every reason induces a belief that the other villages are much more likely to join the Arkansaw band, which is daily becoming more powerful, than the latter is to return to its ancient residence. For the Grand and Little Osage are both obliged to proceed to the Arkansaw every winter, to kill the summer's provision; also, all the nations with whom they are now at war are situated to the westward of that river, whence they get all their horses. These inducements are such that the young, the bold, and the enterprising are daily emigrating from the Osage village to the Arkansaw village. In fact, it would become the interest of our government to encourage that emigration, if we intend to encourage the extension of the settlement of Upper Louisiana ; but if the contrary (our true policy), every method should be taken to prevent their elongation from the Missouri.

They are considered by the nations to the south and west of them as a brave and warlike nation ; but are by no means a match for the northern nations, who make use of the rifle, and can combat them two for one ; whilst they again may fight those armed with bows, arrows, and lances, at the same disproportion.

The humane policy which the United States have held forth to the Indian nations, of accommodating their differences and acting as mediators between them, has succeeded to a miracle with the Osage of the Grand village and the Little Osage. In short, they have become a nation of Quakers, as respects the nations to the north and east of them, at the same time that they continue to make war on the naked and defenseless savages of the west. An instance of their forbearance was exhibited in an attack made on a hunting-party of the Little Osage, in the autumn of 1808, on the grand river of the Osage, by a party of the Potowato-mies, who crossed the Missouri river by the Saline, and found the women and children alone and defenseless. The men, 50 or 60, having found plenty of deer the day before, had encamped out all night. The enemy struck the camp about ten o'clock in the morning, killed all the women and boys who made resistance, also some infants, the whole number amounting to 34 ; and led into captivity near 60, 46 of whom were afterward recovered by the United States and sent under my protection to the village. When the men returned to camp, they found their families all destroyed or taken prisoners. My narrator had his wife and four children killed on the spot; yet, in obedience to the injunctions of their great father, they forebore to revenge the blow.

As an instance of the great influence the French formerly had over this nation, the following anecdote may be inter-esting : Chtoka, alias Wet Stone, a Little Osage, said he " was at Braddock's defeat, with all the warriors who could be spared from both villages ; that they were engaged by Mr. M'Cartie, who commanded at Fort Chartres,[6] and who sup-plied them with powder and ball ; that the place of rendez-vous was near a lake and large fall (supposed to be Niagara) ; the Kans did not arrive until after the battle ; but the Otos were present. They were absent from their villages seven months, and were obliged to eat their horses on their return."

[6] This " Mr. M'Cartie " was Le Chevalier Macarty, Makarty, etc., who in 1751 succeeded Le Sieur de St. Clair as major-commandant of the Illinois. He was by birth an Irishman, became a major of engineers, and served about nine years in the position indicated. The far-famed Fort Chartres is called by Wal-lace " the only great architectural work of the French in the entire basin of the Mississippi, over which, in succession, had proudly floated the flags of two pow-erful nations." Old Fort Chartres, or De Chartres, supposed to have been so named for the Duc de Chartres, son of the then Regent of France, was built in 1719 and 1720, under the direction of Pierre Duqué de Boisbriant, the king's lieutenant for France, at the expense of the Company of the West ; it at once became military headquarters and the center of authority, and was long promi-nent in the French history of Illinois. It was rebuilt in 1753-56 during Major Macarty's incumbency, upon the plans of the French engineer Saucier, at

The Osage raise large quantities of corn, beans, and pump-kins, which they manage with the greatest economy, in order to make them last from year to year. All the agricul-tural labor is done by women.

If the government think it expedient to establish factories for the Grand and Little villages, equidistant from both, which would answer for the Grand and Little villages, the other establishment should be on the Arkansaw, near the entrance of the Verdigrise river, for the Arkansaw Osage, as stated by Lieutenant Wilkinson.

The Pawnees are a numerous nation of Indians, who reside on the rivers Platte and Kans. They are divided into three distinct nations, two of them being now at war ; but their manners, language, customs, and improvements are in the same degree of advancement. On La Platte reside the Grand Pawnees, and on one of its branches the Pawnee Loups, with whom the Pawnee Republicans are at war. [See note [73], p. 412.]

Their language is guttural, and approaches nearer to the language of the Sioux than the Osage ; and their figure, tall, slim, with high cheek-bones, clearly indicates their Asiatic origin. But their emigration south, and the ease with which they live on the buffalo plains, have probably been the cause of a degeneracy of manners, for they are neither so brave nor so honest as their more northern neighbors. Their govern-ment is the same as the Osages', an hereditary aristocracy, the father handing his dignity of chieftain down to his son ;

an estimated cost of 5,000,000 livres ; and this " new Chartres " is described as a " huge structure of masonry, an object of wonder and curiosity to all who ever beheld it "—some of these being antiquarians of the present day. The his-toric fortress suffered encroachments of the Mississippi for several years ; it was finally dilapidated during a freshet in 1772, then evacuated by the British gar-rison, which removed to Fort Gage, and never reoccupied. We have many memorials of the progress of its decay, as well as of the period of its greatness : see Wallace's Illinois and Louisiana under French rule, 1893, pp. 270, 271, 313–318, which include various important references, notably to Pittman, whose description of the fort as it was in 1766 is transcribed, and to Beck's Gazetteer, giving a plan of the fort from observations made in 1820. The name stands for a steamboat landing near Prairie du Rocher, Randolph Co., Ill.

but their power is extremely limited, notwithstanding the long life they have to establish their authority and influence. They merely recommend and give council in the great assemblage of the nation.

They are not so cleanly, neither do they carry their internal policy so far as, the Osage ; but out of the bounds of the village it appeared to me that they exceeded them ; as I have frequently seen two young soldiers come out to my camp and instantly disperse a hundred persons, by the strokes of long whips, who were assembled there to trade with my men.   In point of cultivation [agriculture], they are about equal to the Osage, raising a sufficiency of corn and pumpkins to afford a little thickening to their soup during the year.   The pumpkin they cut into thin slices and dry in the sun, which reduces it to a small size, and not more than a tenth of its original weight.

With respect to raising horses, the Pawnees are far superior to the Osage, having vast quantities of excellent horses which they are daily increasing, by their attention to their breeding mares, which they never make use of; and in addition they frequently purchase from the Spaniards.

Their houses are a perfect circle, except where the door enters, whence there is a projection of about 15 feet ; the whole being constructed after the following manner: First, there is an excavation of a circular form made in the ground, about 4 feet deep and 60 in diameter, where there is a row of posts about 5 feet high, with crotches at the top, set firmly in all round, and horizontal poles from one to the other.   There is then a row of posts, forming a circle about 10 feet wide in the diameter of the others, and 10 feet in height ; the crotches of these are so directed that horizontal poles are also laid from one to the other ; long poles are then laid slanting upward from the lower poles over the higher ones, and meeting nearly at the top, leaving only a small aperture for the smoke of the fire to pass out, which is made on the ground in the middle of the lodge.   There is then a number of small poles put up around the circle, so as

to form the wall, and wicker-work is run through the whole.
The roof is then thatched with grass, and earth is thrown up
against the wall until a bank is made to the eaves of the
thatch ; that is also filled with earth one or two feet thick,
and rendered so tight as entirely to exclude any storm,
and make the houses extremely warm.   The entrance is
about six feet wide, with walls on each side, and roofed like
our houses in shape, but of the same materials as the main
building.   Inside there are numerous little apartments constructed of wicker-work against the wall, with small doors ;
they have a great appearance of neatness, and in them the
members of the family sleep and have their little deposits.
Their towns are by no means so much crowded as the Osage,
giving much more space ; but they have the same mode of
introducing their horses into the village at night, which
makes it extremely crowded.   They keep guards with the
horses during the day.

They are extremely addicted to gaming, and have for that
purpose a smooth piece of ground cleared out on each side
of the village for about 150 yards in length, on which they
play the three following games :   One is played by two
players at a time, and in the following manner :   They have
a large hoop about four feet in diameter, in the center of
which is a small leather ring ; this is attached to leather
thongs which are extended to the hoop, and by that means
kept in its central position ; they also have a pole about six
feet in length, which the player holds in one hand ; he then
rolls the hoop from him, and immediately slides the pole
after it ; and the nearer the head of the pole lies to the
small ring within the hoop, when they both fall, the greater
is the cast.   But I could not ascertain their mode of count-
ing sufficiently to decide when the game was won.   Another
game is played with a small stick, with several hooks, and a
hoop about four inches in diameter, which is rolled along
the ground, and the forked stick darted after it, the value
of the cast being estimated by the hook on which the ring
is caught.   This game is gained at 100.   The third game

alluded to is that of la platte, described by various travelers [as the platter or dish game]; this is played by the women, children, and old men, who, like grasshoppers, crawl out to the circus to bask in the sun, probably covered only with an old buffalo robe.

The Pawnees, like the Osage, quit their villages in the winter, making concealments under ground of their corn, in which [caches] it keeps perfectly sound until spring. The only nations with whom the Pawnees are now at war are the Tetaus, Utahs, and Kyaways. The two latter of these reside in the mountains of North Mexico, and shall be treated when I speak of the Spanish Indians. The former generally inhabit the borders of the Upper Red river, Arkansaw, and Rio del Norte. The war has been carried on by those nations for years, without any decisive action being fought, although they frequently march with 200 or 300 men.

The Pawnees have much the advantage of their enemies in point of arms, at least one-half having firearms, whilst their opponents have only bows, arrows, lances, shields, and slings. The Pawnees always march to war on foot; their enemies are all cavalry. This nation may be considered as the one equidistant between the Spanish population and that of our settlements in Louisiana, but are at present decidedly under Spanish influence, and, should a war commence to-morrow, would all be in their interest. This circumstance does not arise from their local situation, because they are all situated on navigable waters of the Missouri ; nor from their interest, because from the Spaniards they obtain nothing except horses and a few coarse blankets of W. Mexico ; whilst from us they receive all their supplies of arms, ammunition, and clothing—but all those articles in very small quantities, not more than half having blankets, and many being without breech-cloths to cover their nakedness. But the grand principle by which the Spaniards keep them in their influence is fear, frequently chastising their small parties on the frontiers. Their sending out the detachment of 600 horsemen, in 1806, has made such an impression that the

Spaniards may safely calculate on the Pawnees in case of war. This detachment took with them some of the Pawnees to Chihuahua, at the same time that I entered the Spanish provinces. But, by our withholding their supplies of arms, ammunition, and clothing for one or two years, bringing on their backs the Osage and Kans, the Pawnees would be in great distress, and feel the necessity of a good understanding with the United States.

If there should ever be factories established for their accommodation, these should be at the entrances of La Platte and Kans rivers, as those waters are of so uncertain navigation (only in freshets) that it would be folly to attempt any permanent establishments high up them ; and to make those establishments useful to the Pawnees, we must presuppose our influence sufficient to guarantee them peace and a safe passage through the nations of the Kans, Otos, and Missouries—the former on the Kans river, the two latter on the river Platte. My journal will give various other striking traits of the national character of the Pawnees, and my dissertation on the subject of the Spanish claims will further elucidate the political and relative situation of that nation.

The Kans are a small nation, situated on a river of that name (see the chart), and are in language, manners, customs, and agricultural pursuits, precisely similar to the Osage ; with whom I believe them, as before observed, to have had one common origin. It may be said, however, that their language differs in some degree, but not more than the dialect of our Eastern States differs from that of the Southern. But in war they are yet more brave than their Osage brethren ; being, although not more than one-third of their number, their most dreaded enemies, and frequently making the Pawnees tremble.

The Tetaus, or Camanches as the Spaniards term them, [called] Padoucas by the Pawnees, are a powerful nation who are entirely erratic, without the least species of cultivation, and subsist solely by the chase. But their wanderings are confined to the frontiers of New Mexico on the

W., to the nations on the Lower Red river on the S., to the Pawnees and Osage on the E., and to the Utahs, Kyaways, and various unknown nations on the N. This nation, although entirely in our territories, is claimed exclusively by the Spaniards, and may be said to be decidedly in their interest, notwithstanding the few who lately paid a visit to Natchitoches.

They are the only nation bordering on the Spanish settlements whom that nation treats as an independent people. They are by the Spaniards reputed brave—indeed, they have given some very strong evidences of this; for when I first entered the province of New Mexico, I was shown various deserted villages and towns beaten down, which had been destroyed by the Tetaus in an invasion of that province, when they were at war with the Spaniards about ten years since.

From the village of Agua Caliente (see chart) they carried off at one time 2,000 head of horses; but they now have an excellent understanding with the Spaniards, which Don Facundo Malagare's [Malgares'] late expedition has served very much to increase. He personally related his rencounter with the Tetaus in the following manner: Having been personally apprised of each other's approximation, and appointed a time for the Indians to receive him on an extensive prairie, he sallied forth from his camp with 500 men, all on white horses, excepting himself and his two principal officers, who rode jet black ones, and was received on the plain by 1,500 of the savages, dressed in their gay robes, and displaying their various feats of chivalry. I leave this subject to the judicious, whether the circumstance would not be handed down to the latest posterity as an instance of the good will and respect which the Spaniards paid their nation, as no doubt Malgares had policy sufficient to induce them to believe that the expedition was principally fitted out with a view to pay them a visit. As I was not in their country, and did not meet with any of the wandering parties, I shall not attempt to describe their manners and customs; but in my statistical tables I shall include them, agreeably to the best information obtained of their nation.

I shall here conclude my account of the nations with whom I became acquainted in our boundaries; as I conceive the Spanish Indians require a different discussion and attention from a different point of view, as their missionaries have succeeded with them beyond what we can form an idea of. My diary will present numerous additional circumstances, to form an idea of those savages, their manners, customs, principles, and biases, political and local.

WASHINGTON CITY, January, 1808.

CHAPTER V.

WILKINSON'S REPORT ON THE ARKANSAW.[1]

NEW ORLEANS, April 6th, 1807.

SIR: Agreeably to your order dated in June, 1806, I took my departure from Belle Fontaine, under the command of Lieutenant Pike, early in July [15th]. The Missouri being well up, we found the navigation as favorable as could have been expected. On the 28th of the same month we reached the mouth of the Osage river, which we found a pellucid, tranquil stream, with the exception of a few trifling ripples, and a fall of about six feet in two-thirds of a mile, called the Old Man's Rapid. The river abounds with various kinds of good fish, especially the soft-shelled turtle [*Trionyx* or *Aspidonectes ferox*], which we took in great numbers. The banks of the river are generally formed by craggy cliffs, and not unfrequently you perceive stupen-

---

[1] The following Report was written by Lieutenant Wilkinson at a time when it was expected I had been cut off by the savages. It consequently alluded to transactions relative to the Expedition previous to our separation, which I have since corrected. But the adventures of his party, after our separation, are given in his own words.—Z. M. P.

The above explanatory note by Pike stood alone on p. 19 of the App. to Pt. 2 of the orig. ed. Wilkinson's Report, of which Chapter V. now consists, formed Doc. No. 2 of that Appendix, running pp. 20-32. It rehearses the movements of Pike's party to Oct. 28th, 1806, when the two officers separated at Great Bend, and Wilkinson started down the Arkansaw. It thus serves to some extent to check Pike's narrative, but is chiefly notable in this respect for some discrepancies which I have been unable to adjust. Lieutenant Wilkinson's health was not good during his descent of the Arkansaw, and he endured much hardship; to which causes is doubtless due in part the lack of anything very notable in his Report. James Biddle Wilkinson was the son of General James Wilkinson of Maryland. He entered the army as a second lieutenant of the 4th Infantry, Feb. 16th, 1801; was transferred to the 2d Infantry, Apr. 1st, 1802; became first lieutenant Sept. 30th, 1803, and captain Oct. 8th, 1808, and died Sept. 7th, 1813.

dous rocks projecting over the water, out of which issue excellent springs. The most remarkable natural curiosity which I observed is a pond of water, about 300 toises [2] in circumference, six miles above the Yanga [Yungar, Ne-hemgar, or Niangua river], on a rising piece of ground, con-siderably above the level of the river, which keeps one con-tinued height, is perfectly pure and transparent, and has no outlet by which to discharge.

On the 12th of August the Osages appeared dissatisfied with the tedious movement of our barges, and expressed a wish to cross the prairie to their villages, in case an escort were allowed them. I immediately volunteered my services, and we parted with the boats at the mouth of Grand river [the branch of the Osage], the spot where our ransomed prisoners were taken the preceding winter by the Potowato-mies. We reached the village of the Little Osages after a fatiguing and laborious march of six days across an arid prairie.

When within a mile of the town, the chief Tuttasuggy, or Wind, desired that a regular procession might be ob-served; he accordingly placed me between himself and his first warrior, and the ransomed captives followed by files. Half a mile from the village we were met by 180 horsemen, painted and decorated in ·a very fanciful manner; they were considered as a guard of honor, and on our approach opened to the right and left, leaving a sufficient space for us to pass through. A few yards in advance, on the right, I perceived 60 or more horsemen painted with blue chalk; when the chief observed them, he commanded a halt, and sent forward his younger brother Nezuma, or Rain that Walks, with a flag and silk handkerchief as a prize for the swiftest horseman. At a given signal they started off at full speed, the two foremost taking the flag and handker-chief, and the rest contenting themselves with having shown their agility and skill. As I entered the village I was

[2] The toise is an old French measure of length equal to six French feet or 1.949 meter, and therefore to about 6.4 English feet.

saluted by a discharge from four swivels which the Indians
had taken from an old fort [Fort Carondelet: see note ⁴¹,
p. 384] erected by the Spaniards on the river, and passed
through a crowd of nearly a thousand persons, part of
whom I learned were of the Grand village. I was immediately, but with ceremony, ushered into the lodge of
Soldier of the Oak, who, after having paid me some very
handsome compliments, courteously invited me to eat of
green corn, buffalo-meat, and water-melons about the size
of a 24-pound shot, which, though small, were highly
flavored.

After Lieutenant Pike's arrival with the boats, we formed
our camp on the bank of the river, equidistant from the
villages of the Grand and Little Osages, and he selected
a situation for making his observations, which he did not
complete until the 28th of the month. The 29th and 30th
were devoted to packing as conveniently and carefully as
possible the mathematical instruments and a small quantity
of provisions. On the 1st of September we commenced our
march for the Pawnee Republic, and entered on that vast
and extensive prairie which lies between the Missouri and
the Rio del Norte.

We coursed the [Little] Osage river to its source, and
almost immediately crossed some of the small branches of
Grand [Neosho] river, which enters the Arkansaw about
700 miles from the Mississippi. After passing Grand river,
which we found to be 60 or 80 yards wide, we marched
a whole day [week ³] before we reached the waters of the
Kansas, and were agreeably surprised to find ourselves on
the bank of a bold running stream [Smoky Hill fork].
Between this and the village of the Pawnees we crossed
two strongly impregnated salines. We then passed over
a sandy country almost destitute of herbage; and after
a painful march under an oppressive sun, over an irregular

³ The party reached and crossed the Neosho Sept. 9th, and struck the Smoky
Hill fork of the Kansas r. on the morning of the 16th: see those dates in
Pike's itinerary, and notes there.

and broken surface, we arrived at the town of the Republi-can Pawnees on the 25th of September.

We the day before were met by a number of warriors whom curiosity had led thus far to see us, among whom was the third consequential character of the Republican party ; for you must know that the village is composed of the followers of a dissatisfied warrior who first made this establishment, and the adherents of a regular chief of the Grand Pawnees who migrated thither some few years since with his family, and usurped the power of the Republican warrior.   To such a pitch does this party spirit prevail that you easily perceive the hostility which exists between the adherents of the two chiefs.

Early on the morning of the 25th we were joined by a few more savages of distinction, headed by the brother of Characterish, or White Wolf, chief of the nation, who was to act as master of the ceremonies to our formal entry. Preparatory to our march, we had our men equipped as neatly as circumstances would admit.   About mid-day we reached the summit of a lofty chain of ridges, where we were requested to halt and await the arrival of the chief, who was half a mile from us, with 300 horsemen, who were generally naked, except buffalo robes and breech cloths, and painted with white, yellow, blue, and black paint.   At tne word of the chief the warriors divided, and, pushing on at full speed, flanked us on the right and left, yelling in a most diabolical manner.   The chief advanced in front, accompanied by Iskatappe, or Rich Man, the second great personage of the village and his two sons, who were clothed in scarlet cloth.   They approached slowly, and when within 100 yards the three latter halted ; Characterish advanced in great state, and when within a few paces of us stretched out his hand and cried, " *Bon jour.*"   Thus ended the first cere-mony.   We moved on about a mile further, and having gained the summit of a considerable hill, we discovered the village directly at its base.   We here were again halted, and the few Osages who accompanied us were ordered in front and seated in rank entire. The chief squatted on his hams in front of them and filled a calumet, which several different Indians took from him and handed the Osages to smoke. This was called the horse-smoke, as each person who took the pipe from the chief intended to present the Osages a horse. Mr. Pike and Dr. Robinson afterward accompanied the chief to his lodge, and I moved on with the detachment and formed our camp on the opposite bank of the Republican fork of the Kansas river, on a commanding hill which had been selected as the most favorable situation for making observations, though very inconvenient on account of wood and water, which we had to transport nearly a quarter of a mile.

At a council held some few days after our arrival, Lieutenant Pike explained to them the difference of their present situation and that of a few years past ; that now they must look up to the president of the United States as their great father ; that he [Pike] had been sent by him [Jefferson] to assure them of his good wishes, etc.; that he perceived a Spanish flag flying at the council-lodge door, and was anxious to exchange one of their great father's for it ; and that it was our intention to proceed further to the westward, to examine this, our newly acquired country. To this a singular and extraordinary response was given—in fact, an objection started in direct opposition to our proceeding further west ; however, they gave up the Spanish flag, and we had the pleasure to see the American standard hoisted in its stead.

At the same council Characterish observed that a large body of Spaniards had lately been at his village, and that they promised to return and build a town adjoining his. The Spanish chief, he said, mentioned that he was not empowered to council with him ; that he came merely to break the road for his master, who would visit him in the spring with a large army ; that he further told him the Americans were a little people, but were enterprising, and one of those days would stretch themselves even to his town ; that they took the lands of Indians, and would drive off their game ; " and how very truly," said Characterish, " has the Spanish chieftain spoken ! " We demanded to purchase a few horses, which was prohibited, and the friendly communication which had existed between the town and our camp was stopped. The conduct of our neighbors assumed a mysterious change ; our guards were several times alarmed, and finally appearances became so menacing as to make it necessary for us to be on our guard day and night.

It was obvious that the body of Spaniards, who preceded us but a few weeks in their mission to this village, were the regular cavalry and infantry of the province of Santa Fee, as they had formed their camps in regular order; also we were informed they kept regular guards, and that the beats of their drum were uniform morning and evening. The Spanish leader, further, delivered to Characterish a grand medal, two mules, and a commission bearing the signature of the governor, civil and military, of Santa Fee. He also had similar marks of distinction for the Grand Pawnees, the Pawnee Mahaws, Mahaws Proper, Otos, and Kanses.

On the 6th of October we made some few purchases of miserable horses at the most exorbitant prices, and on the 7th, unmoved by the threats of the chief relative to our proceeding further to the west, we marched in a close and compact body until we passed their village, and took the large beaten Spanish trace for the Arkansaw river. We passed the following day [8th] an encampment of the Spaniards, where we counted 69 fires. On the 9th, as usual, made an easy march ; and about noon, when we halted to refresh ourselves, were overtaken by 300 Pawnees, on their way to the salines of the Kanses to hunt buffalo. Their every act showed a strong disposition to quarrel, and in fact they seemed to court hostility ; but, finding us without fear and prepared, to a man, they offered no outrage. Having grazed our horses an hour, we parted from this turbulent band, slung our packs, proceeded to Solomon's Fork of the Kanses, and pitched our tents on an old encampment of the

Spaniards whose trace we were following, as we found the next morning [10th] many tent-pins made of wood different from any in that country.   At mid-day Lieutenant Pike, Dr. Robinson, and the interpreter Baroney pushed on to search for water, and I remained with the troops.   I pushed on as briskly as our poor half-famished horses would permit, but at nightfall could discover nothing of Mr. Pike, and had not a tree in view.   This induced me to quicken my pace ; and, as darkness had rendered my compass useless, I coursed by the polar star ; but the horizon becoming overcast, I halted on a naked stony prairie, without water or grass for our horses.   On the following morning [11th] I directed my course more to the southward, and about ten o'clock came to the [which ?] creek and encampment of Lieut. Pike.   Late in the evening of the same day [11th], after passing over a mountainous tract of country, we reached the Grand Saline, which we found so strongly impregnated as to render unpalatable corn boiled in it.   On the 12th, after a distressing day's march, we reached the Second or Small Saline, and on the following day [13th] encamped on the most western [Smoky Hill] branch of the Kanses river.[4]

We were detained, on the morning of the 13th [14th], by a small rain ; but as time was pressing, we marched about

[4] There are material discrepancies between Wilkinson's and Pike's accounts of the 11th, 12th, 13th, and 14th, not easy to reconcile, even supposing the two officers were separated a part of the time.   Pike comes first to what he calls "Little Saline" r., and then to Great Saline on the 11th ; Smoky Hill r., 12th ; 7 m. beyond it to head of a branch of it, 13th ; over the divide, 14th, to Cow cr.; and is lost on Walnut cr., 15th.   His map puts a camp-mark on Little Saline, date uncertain ; one on Great Saline, 11th ; one on Smoky Hill r., 12th ; and none for 13th, 14th, or 15th.   Wilkinson comes first to Grand Saline, 11th ; "Second or Small Saline," 12th ; Smoky Hill, 13th ; over divide and on to a branch of the Arkansaw, also on the 13th ; reaches Arkansaw 14th, about midnight.   We have here a day miscounted ; reverse sequence of the two Saline rivers ; and several camp-marks misplaced or missing.   All this adds to the trouble we found in trying to follow Pike's itinerary, and I do not see how the difficulty can be adjusted.   What seems certain is : 1. Great Saline r. reached or crossed on the 11th ; Smoky Hill r. reached or crossed on the 12th ; divide crossed and camp on Cow cr., 13th, 14th ; Wilkinson on the Arkansaw at midnight of the 15th, when Pike and Robinson were lost on Walnut cr.

noon, crossed the dividing ridge of the Kanses and Arkansaw rivers, and halted on a small branch of the latter.   For several days past we had been so bewildered by buffalo paths that we lost the Spanish trace ; and this being an object of moment, we resolved to make search for it.   Accordingly, on the following day [15th] at noon, Mr. Pike and Dr. Robinson struck off from the party on a due west course, and I marched the detachment for a copse of wood which we could barely discern in the southwest, and reached it about midnight.   At day-break I was awakened by my old and faithful Osage, who informed me that we were on the banks of the Arkansaw river.   I immediately arose, and discovered my tent to have been pitched on the margin of a watercourse nearly 400 yards wide, with banks not three feet high, and a stream of water running through it about 20 feet in width and not more than six or eight inches deep.

I remained here four days in great anxiety and suspense, as neither Mr. Pike nor Dr. Robinson made their appearance, nor could be found, although I had all my hunters out in search of them.   But I was agreeably surprised on the fifth [5] day, early in the morning, by their arrival.   It appeared that our apprehensions were mutual, as they expected I had been cut off, and I believed they had been murdered.

On the 17th it commenced raining and continued for several days, during which time the river rose so much as to fill its bed from bank to bank.   Lieutenant Pike having determined that I should descend the Arkansaw, we cut down a small green cottonwood, and with much labor split out a

---

[5] Again a discrepancy from Pike.   According to his diary he left the party at 5 p. m., 15th, with Dr. Robinson ; was lost, 16th and 17th ; found and brought to Wilkinson's camp on the Arkansaw, 18th ; so Wilkinson could have remained but two days in suspense, which was relieved on the third day.   As Pike himself informs us that he " corrected " Wilkinson's Report for the time they were together, yet evidently failed to make it fit his own, we may be excused if we do not succeed in the attempt.   On some points I suspect Wilkinson came nearest the facts.   He did not lose his notes and supplement from memory, as Pike was forced to do ; he was not hunting for the Spanish trail, nor for buffalo ; and he did not get bewildered on Walnut cr.

canoe, which being insufficient, we formed a second of buffalo and elk skins.

After the rain had ceased the weather became extremely cold, and on the 27th, in the evening, a severe snow-storm commenced and continued nearly all night. In the morning [of the 28th [6]] the river was almost choked with drifting ice; but the sun bursting out at noon, the ice disappeared, and I took leave of Mr. Pike, who marched up the river at the moment I embarked on board my newly constructed canoe. Unfortunately, we had not proceeded more than 100 yards when my boats grounded, and the men were obliged to drag them through sand and ice five miles, to a copse of woods on the southwestern bank. I here hauled up my canoe, formed a kind of cabin of it, and wrapped myself up in my buffalo-robe, disheartened and dissatisfied with the commencement of my voyage. The night was severely cold, and in the morning [29th] the river was so full of ice as to prevent all possibility of proceeding. The day continued stormy, with snow from the northwest.

On the 30th the river was frozen up, and toward evening the water had run off and left the bed of the river covered with ice. This circumstance determined me to leave my canoes and course the river by land. Accordingly, on the 31st of October, after having thrown away all my clothing and provision, except half a dozen tin cups of hard corn for each man, I slung my rifle on my shoulder, and with my buffalo-robe at my back and circumferentor in my hand, I recommenced my march with a light and cheerful heart. My only apprehension was that I might meet with detached bands of the Pawnees, who, I am confident, would have brought me and my five men [Ballenger, Boley, Bradley,

[6] Both accounts fortunately agree on this notable date—the day on which Pike started up the Arkansaw and Wilkinson down the same river. The distance made by the latter on the 28th sets him about the mouth of Antelope cr., a small run that makes in on the right or south a mile above the mouth of Walnut cr. Here he remained on the 29th and 30th. There is obviously no possibility of following him closely through his benumbed voyage; we can only check his course at the most notable points.

Huddleston, Wilson] to action; and what the consequence of this would have been is very obvious.

On the 1st, 2d, and 3d of November I marched over high and barren hills of sand; at the close of each day passed strongly impregnated salines, and perceived the shores of the river to be completely frosted with nitre. The face of the country, as I descended, looked more desolate than above, the eye being scarcely able to discern a tree; and if one was discovered, it proved to be a solitary cottonwood, stinted in growth by the sterility of the soil. The evening of the 3d instant I encamped on the bank of the river, without a tree or even a shrub in view. On the 4th we experienced a heavy rain; but hunger and cold pressed me forward. After marching 10 miles I reached a small tree, where I remained in a continued rain for two days [5th, 6th], at the expiration of which time, having exhausted my fuel, I had again [7th] to push off in a severe storm, and formed my camp at the mouth of a bold running stream [probably Cow creek [7]], whose northern bank was skirted by a chain of lofty ridges.

On the 8th, in the morning, it having cleared up, I began my march early, and it appeared as if we had just gotten into the region of game; for the herds of buffalo, elk, goat [antelope], and deer surpassed credibility. I do solemnly assert that, if I saw one, I saw more than 9,000 buffaloes during the day's march.

On the 10th, in the évening, after a severe day's march, I encamped on the bank of a large creek [probably Little Arkansaw [8]], and discovered for the first time on the river a species of wood differing from the cotton tree. I assure you

[7] and [8] Wilkinson's "bold running stream" and his "large creek" are probably identifiable by the above data; but in my ignorance of these details I can only presume, without knowing, that he means Cow cr. and the Little Arkansaw, these being the two principal tributaries of the Arkansaw in Kansas below Great Bend. Cow cr. is the same stream whose headwaters Pike and Wilkinson came upon before they reached Great Bend: see note [10], p. 424; but it falls in much lower, at Hutchinson, Reno Co., Kas. The Little Arkansaw is that river at whose mouth is Wichita, seat of Sedgwick Co., Kas. Both these

the sight was more agreeable than a person would imagine ; it was like meeting with an old acquaintance from whom I had been separated a length of time. I even began to think myself approximating civilized settlements, although I was just entering on the hunting-ground of the Osages.

The buffaloes and goats disappeared on the 12th, or rather we had passed their range and entered that of the deer only. Our marches were through rich narrow bottoms from 150 to 200 yards wide.

On the 15th, discovering timber sufficiently large to form canoes, I felled a couple of trees, and commenced splitting out. I would have proceeded further by land, but as my men were almost worn out with fatigue, and as the game grew scarce, I conceived it most advisable to rest for a short time, and kill my winter's store of meat. This I effected by the 24th, and on the same day completed the canoes. On the 25th I again attempted the navigation of the river, but was as unfortunate as at first ; for my boat grounded, after floating a few hundred yards, and the men were consequently compelled to ply with their shoulders instead of their paddles.

The following day I passed the Negracka [read Ninnescah [9]], at whose mouth commence the craggy cliffs which line a great part of the shores of the Arkansaw.

streams course very obliquely to the Arkansaw, from the N. W., and fall in on the left bank.

[9] "Negracka " is here an error ; Wilkinson means the Ninnescah, Nenescah, or Nenesquaw r., which falls in from the W. on the right hand ; town of Whitman, Sumner Co., Kas., at its mouth. This is the only instance I have ever known of the misapplication of the name Negracka, which belongs absolutely to, and was long the current name of, the Salt fork of the Arkansaw : see next note. Thus, we read in Morse's Gazetteer, 1821, p. 499 : " Negracka River . . . falls into the Arkansaw from the N. W. It is 100 yards wide." The Nenescah is a smaller stream than this. It is lettered " Ne-ne-sesh, or Good Riv." on a map of the Indian Terr., etc., Engineer Bureau, War Dept., Oct., 1866. Between his Negracka or the Nenescah r., and his Neskalonska or the Salt fork of the Arkansaw, Wilkinson passes the following streams : 1. Slate cr., from the N. W., traversing Sumner Co. obliquely ; 2. Walnut cr. (formerly Whitewater r.), from the N., with an average course nearly due S., through Butler and Cowley cos., Kas., to fall in at Arkansaw City ; 3. Grouse cr., from

On the 28th the provision canoe overset, and I lost nearly all my stock of meat; this accident was rendered the more distressing by an almost total loss of my ammunition, which unfortunately was in the same canoe.

On the 30th, I fell in with a band of Grand Osages, who were in pursuit of buffalo cows; the chief of the party insisted on my remaining with him a day, and sent out his young men to hunt for me. In the afternoon two Indians of the Osage nation joined us, with a horse and mule, and brought me a message from Tuttasuggy, or Wind, who it appeared was lying very ill, about 20 miles across the prairie, and wished to see me. As he was a particular favorite of mine, I left my canoes in charge of the men, and passed with a guide to the chief's temporary village. I found him extremely unwell, with what I conceived to be a dropsy, for his abdomen was very much swollen. He seemed gratified at the sight of me, and observed that he was poor and pitiful, for the reason that he was a friend to the Americans. He said that Chouteau, upon arrival at their villages last fall, had treated him like a child; had taken on to Washington his younger brother Nezuma, or Rain that Walks, and intended making him [Nezuma] chief of the nation; that Chouteau told him he [Tuttasuggy] was a "bad man," and an "American" [*i. e.*, a friend of the Americans]; that the Spaniards were going to war with America, and in a short time would claim all this country again; and that he [Chouteau] prevented the traders from allowing credit, whereby his [Tuttasuggy's] family were much distressed—as I clearly perceived, for they were even destitute of a whole blanket.

This Nezuma, whom Chouteau took on to Washington

the N. E., in Cowley Co., its mouth nearly on the boundary between Kansas and Oklahoma; 4. Chilockey or Chilocco cr., over the Oklahoma line, school reservation there; 5. Deer cr., from the W., very small; 6. Beaver cr., from the N. E., whose mouth is at the Kaw or Kansas Agency; 7. South Coon cr., from the N., but falling in on the right, very small; 8. Turkey cr., from the N., but mouth on the right, between Cross and Ponca stations of the Arkansaw branch of the A., T., and S. F. R. R.

last fall with his wife, I am better acquainted with than perhaps Mr. Chouteau himself. In the first place, I marched
with him from St. Louis to his town, and he started with us
to visit the Pawnees ; but the mean and pitiful wretch got
alarmed and sneaked off without even advising us of his
departure. He has no more command in the village than
a child, is no warrior, and has not even the power to control
the will of a single man of his nation. Whether this youth
is entitled to a grand medal, you may judge from the
foregoing statement. Indeed, Sir, our grand medals have
become so common that they do not carry with them the
respect which they should. I recollect that one of the
deputation who was at the seat of government, the year
before last, came out with a large medal and an intermediate-
sized one. On our arrival at the villages, I calculated on
his acting a conspicuous part ; but, to my utter astonishment, he was not permitted to sit among the chiefs, or even
the warriors, at the council.

You well know, Sir, how particular the Spaniards, and
the British especially, have been in their distribution of
medals ; and if I mistake not, an Iowa chief, who had been
to the seat of government and there received a small medal,
returned it in preference to giving up a large British medal
which he valued more, because it was a certain distinguishing mark of a chief.

You gave to Mr. Pike an intermediate-sized medal for one
of the Pawnee chiefs ; this he presented to Iskatappe, who,
having remarked the medals pendent from the necks of the
two Pawnee young men who had been to Washington,
demanded of what utility it would be to him. The only
Spanish medals in the Pawnee nation are those worn by
Characterish, or White Wolf, and his son.

The following sarcastic remark was made by the son of
Bel Oiseau, a chief of the first standing among the Grand
Osages while living, who unfortunately was killed by the
Sacs on his way to Washington with the first deputa-
tion. The son of White Hairs, with Shenga Wassa, or

Beautiful Bird [Bel Oiseau], was to accompany us to the Pawnee village ; but the former proved recreant, and at the crossing of Grand [Neosho] river said he would return home. " Shame on you !" said the latter ; " what a pity it is so great and honorable a medal should be disgraced by so mean a heart !"

You will pardon this digression, but I would wish to convince you, from what I have seen of Indians, how very requisite it is to use the utmost caution in the distribution of our presents and marks of distinction.

Before I set out to visit Tuttasuggy, the ice had commenced drifting in large sheets, and on my return I found it running from shore to shore. However, I pushed off and drifted with it.

The night of the 2d of December was intensely cold, but hunger obliged me to proceed, and we fortunately reached the mouth of the Neskalonska [Salt fork of the Arkansaw [10]]

[10] " Neskalonska " is a name I have failed to find elsewhere, but fortunately there is no question of the river to which Wilkinson applies it. This is Salt fork, the third largest branch of the Arkansaw from the W.—the Cimarron being second, and the Canadian first in size. Wilkinson's " Neskalonska " and his " Grand Saline or Newsewtonga " are respectively Salt fork and Cimarron r. of present nomenclature. Notwithstanding their great size and importance, and the fact that they fall into the Arkansaw about a degree of latitude and of longitude apart, they have been completely confused by geographers, on whose maps almost every name of each has been misapplied to the other. Salt fork is the upper and smaller one of the two, which falls in through the Ponca Reservation, at or near Ponca P. O. and Ponca Agency, in Oklahoma. Cimarron r. is the lower and larger one ʻof the two, which falls in through the Indian Territory at a point on the boundary of Oklahoma. Salt fork has been called : Salt fork ; Salt r.; Salt cr.; Saline fork ; Saline r.; Saline cr.; Red fork ; Red r.; Little Arkansaw r. (duplicating a name : see note [8], p. 548) ; Nescutango r.; Negracka r. (its usual name for many years) ; Semerone, Cimarone, Cimmaron, Cimarron r.—the last four variants of the same word, and like Nescutango, properly belonging only to the next, viz.: Cimarron r. This has been called : Red fork ; Saline r.; Grand Saline r.; Jefferson r.; Nesuketong, Nesuketonga, Nesuhetonga, Nescutanga, Newsewketonga r.; Cimmaron, Cimarron r. On analyzing the comparative applicability of these names, I find that " Salt " or " Saline " belongs most properly to the upper and smaller stream, for which we now use it, and when applied to the lower is usually qualified as Grand Saline ; that " Red " is misapplied to both indifferently ; that " Little Arkansas " is

river without accident or injury, excepting that one of my men got frosted. This day we passed two salines which enter on the southwestern side.

The severity of the weather increased, and the river froze over on the morning of the 3d. This circumstance placed me in a situation truly distressing, as my men were almost

only applied to the upper, and "Jefferson" only to the lower stream; that "Negracka" is absolutely the name of the upper one alone; that "Nesuketonga" and its variants are almost entirely confined to the lower one; and finally that "Cimarron" in its variations is equally common to both, though in present usage it is absolutely restricted to the lower one.

These data rest upon the examination of a large lot of old maps with special reference to the points involved, with the assistance of Mr. Robert F. Thompson of the Indian Bureau at Washington. These maps show a curious reversal in the *size* of the two rivers, the earlier and poorer ones making the upper stream the larger of the two, and conversely. Furthermore, the tendency has always been to call the *larger* one "Cimarron" and "Red," no matter which its position. Aside from this, the most sharply contrasted pairs of names are "Salt" and "Negracka" for the upper stream, and "Red" and "Nesuketonga" for the lower one. Thus, to be more specific: 1. John Melish's map of the U. S., engr. by J. Vallance and H. S. Tanner, pub. Philada., 1820, has Negracka, upper, larger; Jefferson, lower, smaller. 2. H. S. Tanner's map of N. Amer., in the New American Atlas, pub. Philada., 1823, map dated 1822, has Negracka or Red r., upper, larger; and Nesuhetonga or Gr. Saline, lower, smaller. 3. The American Atlas, pub. Philada., H. C. Carey and I. Lea, 1823, has a map of the U. S., with Negracka or Red Fork, upper, larger, and Grand Saline, lower, smaller; also, a map of the Arkansaw, etc., drawn by Major S. H. Long, with Negracka or Red Fork, upper, larger; and Nesuketonga or Grand Saline, lower, smaller; also, a map of Mexico, etc., based on Humboldt, etc., by J. Finlayson, with these very same names. 4. A. Finlay's map of North America, pub. Philada., 1826, has upper larger stream Negracka or Semerone R.; lower one, very small, Grand Saline. 5. A map of Mexico in Anthony Finlay's Atlas, pub. Philada., 1830, has Negracka, upper and larger; the lower smaller one unnamed. 6. A map of North America in Tanner's Atlas, pub. Philada., Carey and Hart, 1843, has Negracka, upper and larger; Gr. Saline, lower and smaller; the map of Mexico and Guatemala, in this atlas, represents the two as Red Br. and Saline. 7. On Josiah Gregg's map of the Indian Territory, etc., in Morse's N. A. Atlas, pub. N. Y., Harper and Brothers, 1844, also accompanying Gregg's Commerce of the Prairies, the two rivers are represented of about the same size, the upper one being lettered Cimarron R. and Salt Fork; the lower, Red Fork of the Arkansas R. This is a notably good map for its date, and in the matter now under examination may be taken as the turning-point to a better understanding of the facts in the case. 8. On a map of Texas, etc., pub. Philada., S. Augustus Mitchell, 1846, the upper and

naked; the tatters which covered them were comfortless,
and my ammunition was nearly exhausted. The men
solicited me to hut, but I was resolved by perseverance and
exertion to overcome, if in my power, the obstacles opposed
to my progress.

The Neskalonska is about 120 yards wide, shoal and narrow at its mouth, but deepens and spreads after you turn

still larger river appears as Cimarone or Salt Fork; the lower, as Red Fork.
9. On a map of Mexico issued by H. S. Tanner, 3d ed., 1846, the upper,
larger stream is given as Semerone, Negracka, or Red River; the lower, as
Saline. 10. On a map of the U. S. in Harper's Statistical Gazetteer of the World,
by J. Calvin Smith, pub. N. Y., Harper and Brothers, 1855, the upper stream
is called Cimarron or Salt Fork; the lower, Red Fork of Arkansas. 11.
Emory's beautiful map of the Western U. S., pub. 1857–58, has Salt Fork
for the upper and much smaller stream, and Red Fork of the Arkansas for
the other. 12. A map of Kansas, etc., in Mitchell's Atlas of 1861, represents the
upper stream as Cimarron River, the lower as Red Fork of the Arkansas.
13. The map of N. A. in Johnston's Family Atlas, pub. N. Y., Johnston and
Ward, 1864, shows the two in a peculiar manner, and calls the upper one
Semerone, the lower one Nesuketong. 14. The Office of Indian Affairs has
on file a very fine map of the Indian Territory, drawn by Ado Hunnius from
the reconnoissance of Lieutenant J. C. Woodruff in 1852, and from a War
Dept. map of 1866, on which the upper and now *smaller* river appears as Salt
Creek or Nescutanga, or Salt Fork of the Arkansas, and the much larger lower
one as Cimarron River or Red Fork of the Arkansas. 15. The War Dept.
map of the Indian Territory, Engineer Bureau, Oct., 1866, letters for the
smaller upper stream Nescutango R. and Little Arkansas R.; for the other,
Cimarron River and Red Fork of Arkansas River. 16. A manuscript map by
John C. McCoy, on file in the Office of Indian Affairs, has Red Fork for the
upper, and Ne se ke tonga for the lower one. 17. On a cabinet map of the
U. S., pub. Chicago, Rufus Blanchard, 1868, the upper one is called Little
Arkansas River, the lower one being styled Red Fork of Arkansas River.
18. A map of the U. S. in Mitchell's Atlas of 1874 shows the upper and larger
stream as Cimmaron or Salt Fork, and the smaller lower one as Red Fork;
the map of Texas in the same atlas shows only the latter, given as Red Fork
of Arkansas. 19. The General Land Office map of the Indian Territory, 1879,
letters for the upper river Salt Fork of Arkansas R., and for the other Red Fork
of the Arkansas or Cimarron River; the same Office's map of Oklahoma, 1894,
has Salt Fork of Arkansas River for the one, and Cimarron River for the other.

The consensus of the above, aside from the eccentricities and errors involved,
is reducible to Salt fork or Negracka r. for the upper one, and Red fork,
Nesuketonga, or Cimarron r. for the other one, of these two important streams.
One of the curiosities in the matter is the constancy of the form of the word
Negracka, as well as its restriction to a single river.

the first point. On this stream the Grand and Little Osages form their temporary fall hunting-camps, and take their peltries. When the severity of winter sets in, the Grand Osages retire to Grosse Isle, on the Verdigrise or Waseti-hoge;[11] and the Little Osages to one of its small branches called Possitonga, where they remain during the hard weather, and thence return to their towns on the Neska or [Little] Osage river.

On the 6th the ice began to drift, and I immediately pushed off with it; but as my evil stars would have it, my boats again grounded. Being in the middle of the river, my only alternative was to get out and drag them along for several miles, when we halted to warm our benumbed feet and hands. The next day several large cakes of ice had blocked up the river, and we had to cut our way through them with axes; the boats as usual grounded, and the men, bare-legged and bare-footed, were obliged to leap into the water. This happened so frequently that two more of them got badly frosted.

On the 8th one of my canoes was driven on a bank of ice during a snow-storm, and did not overtake me until the evening of the 9th, in so shattered a condition that she could hardly be kept above water, and the poor fellows who were in her were almost frozen.

On the 10th, about noon, I passed the Grand Saline or Newsewketonga [Cimarron river[12]], which is of a reddish

[11] The Verdigris, Vermilion, or Wasetihoge r. has been already noticed, when Pike's party reached its headwaters in Kansas: see note [58], p. 400. The present nomenclature of its principal branches is: 1. Hominy cr., in the Osage and Cherokee countries of the Indian Territory, with a main fork, Bird cr., site of the Osage Agency; 2. Caney r., or the Little Verdigris, falling in by the Blue Mounds in the Cherokee country, and formed of two main forks known as Big and Little Caney creeks, both of which head in Kansas; 3. Elk r., heading in the Kansan county of that name, and falling in above Independence, in Mont-gomery Co., Kas.; 4. Fall r., one of the terminal forks of the Verdigris, and on which is Fredonia, Wilson Co.

[12] See note [10] for synonymy. The Cimarron is a very large river, which drains from the eastern slopes of the great mountains in New Mexico and runs thence through southwestern portions of Kansas, loops into Oklahoma Territory

color, though its water is very clear. About two days'
march up this river, you find the prairie grass on the S. W.
side incrusted with salt, and on the N. E. bank, fresh-water
springs, and lakes abounding with fish. This salt the
Arkansaw Osages obtain by scraping it off the prairie with
a turkey's wing into a wooden trencher. The river does
not derive its name from its saline properties, but from the
quantities that may always be found on its banks, and is at
all seasons of the year potable.

On the 20th, in the afternoon, we passed another Saline
[river [13]] with water equally as red as that of the Newsewketonga, and more strongly impregnated with salt.

After encountering every hardship to which a voyage is
subject in small canoes at so inclement a season of the year,
I arrived on the 23d inst., in a storm of hail and snow, at
the wintering-camp of Cashesegra or Big Track, [or Big
Foot] chief of the Osages who reside on Verdigrise river.

On the following day I gave him your talk and received
his reply, which it is unnecessary to recount fully, as it was
merely a description of his poverty and miserable situation.
He however said that he had been informed the United
States intended to erect factories on the Osage river, and
that he was anxious to have one near to his own village;
and for that purpose he was willing to give the United
States the tract of country lying between the Verdigrise
and Grand [Neosho] rivers. A factory, with a garrison of

from Meade Co., Kas., loops back into Kansas in Clarke Co., and thence
through the S. W. corner of Comanche Co. into Oklahoma again, traverses this
Territory, and joins the Arkansaw between the Osage and Creek countries, at
a certain point on the line between Oklahoma and the Indian Territory.

In passing from Salt fork to the Cimarron, we have first, Red or Red Rock
cr., a sizable stream from the W. or right ; places called Redrock and Otoe on
it ; second, Buck cr., left, from the N., once known as Suicide cr.; third, Gray
Horse cr., small, left, from the N. E.; fourth, Black Bear cr., large, from the
W., on the right. The Pawnee Agency is on this stream, which some maps
wrongly run into the Cimarron instead of the Arkansaw.

[13] This is not easily determined, as there are several small streams of similar
character between the Cimarron and the Verdigris, among them those called
Polecat, Snake, Cane, and Caney (or Pocan) creeks.

troops stationed there, would answer the double purpose of keeping in order those Indians, who are the most desperate and profligate part of the whole nation, more fully impressing them with an idea of our consequence, and gaining more firmly their friendship. It also would tend to preserve harmony among the Chactaws, Creeks, Cherokees, and Osages of the three different villages, who are in a constant state of warfare; further, it would prevent the Osages making excursions into the country of the poor and peaceably disposed Caddoes, and might have some effect in confining the Spaniards to their own territorial limits.

On the 27th I passed the mouths of the Verdigrise and Grand [Neosho [14]] rivers, the former being about 100 and the latter 130 yards wide; those streams enter within a quarter of a mile of each other. Below the mouth of Grand river commence the rapids, which continue for several hundred miles down the Arkansaw.

About 58 or 60 miles up the Verdigrise is situate the Osage village.[15] This band, some four or five years since, were led by the chief Cashesegra [Big Foot] to the waters of the Arkansaw, at the request of Pierre Chouteau, for the purpose of securing their trade, the exclusive trade of the Osage river having at that time been purchased from the Spanish governor by Manuel Lisa of St. Louis. But though Cashesegra be the nominal leader, Clermont, or the Builder of Towns, is the greatest warrior and most influential man, now more firmly attached to the interests of the Americans than any other chief of the nation. He is the lawful

[14] For these two rivers, see back, notes [53], [55], pp. 397, 398, and following to p. 402; also, note [11], p. 555.

[15] This was the so-called "Arkansaw band" of Osages, the circumstances of whose secession from the Osage village on the Little Osage r. are mentioned by Pike elsewhc.e, as well as by Wilkinson in the present instance. The faction seems to have been fomented by Chouteau through jealousy of Lisa's exclusive right to trade on the Osage r. The affair must have been notorious at the time, as various authors speak of the settlement of this Osage band on the Verdigris or, as it was also called, Vermilion r. Among them are Lewis and Clark: see ed. 1893, p. 12.

sovereign of the Grand Osages ; but his hereditary right was usurped by Pahuska or White Hair [Cheveux Blancs], while Clermont was yet an infant. White Hair, in fact, is a chief of Chouteau's creating, as well as Cashesegra ; and neither has the power or disposition to restrain their young men from the perpetration of an improper act, fearing lest they should render themselves unpopular.

On the 29th I passed a fall [Webber's] of near seven feet perpendicular. At evening I was visited by a scout from an Osage war party, and received from them a man by the name of M'Farlane, who had been trapping up the Pottoe [Poteau]. We passed about noon this day the mouths of the river des Illinois,[16] which enters on the N. E. side, and of the Canadian [17] river, which puts in from the S. W. The latter river is the main branch of the Arkansaw, and is equally large.

[16] This Illinois r., still so called, heads in Washington and Benton cos., Ark., crosses the W. border of the State N. of 36°, and runs through the Cherokee country in the Indian Territory, to fall into the Arkansaw a short distance above the mouth of the Canadian. Between the Illinois and Canadian rivers, on the E. side of the Arkansaw, opposite the mouth of Elk cr., is a place called Webber's Falls, with reference to the falls of which Wilkinson speaks.

[17] The main fork of the Arkansaw, and scarcely a lesser stream. This is one of the six or seven large rivers which have shared the name " Red " or its equivalent, though less frequently than some of the others. This is because the Mexicans called it Rio Colorado at its headwaters, which they knew very well ; and because, down to 1820, these were supposed to be those of the true " Red river of Natchitoches," a branch of the Mississippi. The discovery that this Rio Colorado or Red r. was the source of the Canadian was made by Major Long, who followed it down, thinking he was on the Red r. of Natchitoches, and was not undeceived till he found its confluence with the Arkansaw. This is noted in 1844 by Gregg, and in 1855 by Warren ; it was the third attempt made by the United States Government to discover the sources of the true Red r., Captain Sparks having been first, in 1806, and Pike second. " Canadian," as applied to the main fork of the Arkansaw, has no more to do with the Dominion of Canada in history or politics than it has in geography, and many have wondered how this river came to be called the Canadian. The word is from the Spanish Rio Cañada, or Rio Cañadiano, through such a form as Rio Cañadian, whence directly "Canadian" r., meaning " Cañon " r., and referring to the way in which the stream is boxed up or shut in by precipitous walls near its headwaters. These drain from E. slopes of the Raton and other great mountains in New Mexico E. of Taos and Santa Fé, by such streams as the Vermijo (Bermejo), Little Cimarron, Pouñel or Poñi, Rayado, and Ocaté, which join

On the 31st I passed the mouth of the Pottoe,[18] a deep though narrow stream which puts in on the S. W., and also the river au Millieu [Milieu[19]], that enters from the N. E.

On the evening of the 6th of January I reached the plantation of a Mr. Labomme, and was more inhospitably treated than by the savages themselves.

On the 8th I passed the two upper Arkansaw or Quapaw[20]

above the cañada, and the Moro, which falls in further down. Leaving New Mexico the great river courses eastward through Texas, enters Oklahoma at long. 100° W. (near lat. 36° N., vicinity of Antelope hills), traverses this territory to about long. 98° W., separates it from the Indian Territory to beyond long. 97° W., and runs in the latter to join the Arkansaw near long. 95° W., in the vicinity of Webber's falls, at a point on the boundary between the Cherokee and Chocktaw countries, about 40 m. E. of the Arkansaw State line. Its principal branch is the North fork, which as far as it goes is a parallel stream, skirting the Canadian for hundreds of miles at no great distance northward of the main stream.

[18] Poteau or Potteau r. marks a notable point in this barren itinerary, as it falls in on the boundary between the Indian Territory and Arkansas, immediately above the important and well-known Fort Smith. This is situated on the right bank of the Arkansaw, in Sebastian Co., which the river divides from Crawford Co. Poteau is F. for post, and the name may refer to some early landmark of that sort : see note [33], p. 378. Small tributaries of the Arkansaw between the Canadian and Poteau rivers are Vine cr., left ; Sans Bois and Cache creeks, right ; Sallison and Skin creeks, left—in the order here named.

[19] Wilkinson's "river au Millieu" is apparently that now called Lee or Lee's cr., which makes in between Fort Smith and Van Buren, seat of Crawford Co. It courses mostly in Arkansaw, but loops into and out of the Indian Territory. Four of its branches are called Cove, Brushy, Webber, and Garrison. The F. phrase Rivière au Milieu, equivalent to " Middle " or " Half-way " r., does not seem to have been much used anywhere in the U. S., though it is a still current voyageurs' designation of several different streams in British America.

[20] For the Quapaw or Kwapa Indians, see L. and C., ed. 1893, pp. 12 and 98, notes. Together with the Kansas, Osages, Omahas, and Poncas, they constitute a division of the Siouan stock called Dhegiha—a word equivalent to "autochthon." Dr. Sibley gives the names of the three Kwapa villages as Tawanima, Oufotu, and Ocapa : London ed. 1807, p. 53. Quapaw, Kwapa, Ocapa, Oguoppa, Quappa, Kappa, Ukaqpa, etc., are all forms of their name of themselves, meaning "those who went down river." Our knowledge of the village is traced back to Joliet and Marquette, July, 1673 ; the name Akansa, adopted in some form by the French, is what the Kwapas were called by the Illinois Indians, and the origin of our Arkansas or Arkansaw. The form Acanza is found on Vaugondy's map, 1783. About 230 Kwapas still live in Oklahoma and the Indian Territory.

villages, and on the 9th, after passing the lower Quapaw town, and a settlement of Chactaws, arrived at the post of Arkansaw.[21]

The surface of the country between the Osage towns and the Pawnee village is generally broken and naked ; the soil sterile, and abounding with flint and lime stones. As you approach the waters of the Kanses, it becomes hilly and sandy. The same may be said of the country between the Pawnee village and the Arkansaw ; but after passing the ridge which separates the waters of the Kanses and Arkansaw, the surface becomes more regular and less stony.

Below the Verdigrise the shores of the Arkansaw are gen-

[21] Arkansas Post perpetuates the name of the oldest establishment of whites in the lower Mississippi valley. The present village is on the N. bank of the Arkansaw r., in the county and State of Arkansas, 73 m. S. E. of Little Rock, the capital. Though never a locality of much importance, its place in history is secure and permanent. Early in the year 1685, Henri de Tonti, the famous trusty lieutenant of La Salle, was reinstated in command of Fort St. Louis of the Illinois, with titles of captain and governor, by order of the French king Louis XIV. Tonti learned that La Salle was in trouble somewhere in New Spain (Texas), and organized an expedition for his relief. On Feb. 16th, 1686, he left Fort St. Louis, with 30 Frenchmen and 5 Indians, descended the Illinois and Miss. rivers to the Gulf, and scoured the coast for miles, but saw no sign of his great chief. He wrote a letter for La Salle, which he committed to the care of a chief of the Quinipissas for delivery, should opportunity offer, and retraced his way up the Miss. r. to the mouth of the Arkansaw, which latter river he ascended to the village of the Arkensa Indians. There, on lands which La Salle had already granted him, he stationed six of his men, who volunteered to remain in hopes of hearing from the distant commander. This was the origin of the Poste aux Arkansas. La Salle was murdered by the traitor Duhaut, one of several ruffians among his own men who conspired to his foul assassination, some say on one of the tributaries of the Brazos, at a spot which has been supposed to be perhaps 40–50 m. N. of present town of Washington, Tex.; the date is Mar. 19th or 20th, 1687. Seven of the survivors of La Salle's ill-starred colony at Fort St. Louis of Texas, reached Arkansas Post after a journey computed at the time to have been 250 leagues, in the summer of 1687, and found Couture and De Launay, two of the six whom Tonti had stationed there the year before. (See Wallace, Hist. Ill. and La., etc., 1893.) This Tonti (or Tonty), b. about 1650, died at Mobile, 1704, was the son of Lorenzo Tonti, who devised the Tontine scheme or policy of life insurance. Arkansas Post was the scene of Laclede's death, June 20th, 1778. The place was taken by the Unionists from the Confederates, Jan. 11th, 1863.

erally lined with cane [*Arundinaria macrosperma*], and consequently rich bottoms. I was informed by the Indians that the country to the northwest of the Osage village abounds with valuable lead mines, but I could make no discovery of any body of mineral.

The survey from the Arkansaw post to the Mississippi I fear is not correct, as I was so ill when I descended that part of the river as to be confined to my blanket.

The chart which accompanies this report, of the course of the Arkansaw, I hope will prove satisfactory, not only to yourself, but the president.

I have the honor to subscribe myself,

Your faithful and obliged,

Humble and obedient servant,

[Signed] JAMES B. WILKINSON,

1st Lieut. 2d U. S. Regt. of Infantry.

His Excellency

GENERAL JAMES WILKINSON,

Commander-in-Chief of the U. S. Army.

CHAPTER VI.

CORRESPONDENCE.

Art. 1. Letter, Wilkinson's Instructions to Pike.[1]

ST. LOUIS, June 24th, 1806.

SIR: You are to proceed without delay to the cantonment on the Missouri [at Belle Fontaine], where you are to embark the late Osage captives and the deputation recently returned from Washington, with their presents and baggage, and are to transport the whole up the Missouri and Osage rivers to the town of the Grand Osage.

The safe delivery of this charge at the point of destination constitutes the primary object of your expedition; therefore you are to move with such caution as may prevent surprise from any hostile band, and are to repel with your utmost force any outrage which may be attempted.

Having safely deposited your passengers and their property, you are to turn your attention to the accomplishment of a permanent peace between the Kanses and Osage nations; for which purpose you must effect a meeting between the head chiefs of those nations, and are to employ such arguments, deduced from their own obvious interests, as well as the inclinations, desires, and commands of the presi-

---

[1] General Wilkinson's instructions to Lieutenant Pike were conveyed in the form of two letters, of June 24th and July 12th, respectively, made in the orig. ed. pp. 107–110 of main text of Pt. 2, though they were set in smaller type as a sort of preface or introduction. But as no such preliminary is observed in the other two parts of the book, and as these orders are in the form of letters from the general to his lieutenant, I think they are preferably brought in here. By this single transposition the whole of the correspondence relating to the Arkansaw expedition is brought together in chronological order to form the present Chapter VI.

dent of the United States, as may facilitate your purpose and accomplish the end.

A third object of considerable magnitude will then claim your consideration. It is to effect an interview and establish a good understanding with the Yanctons, Tetaus, or Camanches.

For this purpose you must interest White Hair, of the Grand Osage, with whom and a suitable deputation you will visit the Panis republic, where you may find interpreters, and inform yourself of the most feasible plan by which to bring the Camanches to a conference. Should you succeed in this attempt—and no pains must be spared to effect it— you will endeavor to make peace between that distant powerful nation and the nations which inhabit the country between us and them, particularly the Osage ; finally, you will endeavor to induce eight or ten of their distinguished chiefs to make a visit to the seat of government next September, and you may attach to this deputation four or five Panis and the same number of Kanses chiefs.

As your interview with the Camanches will probably lead you to the head branches of the Arkansaw and Red rivers, you may find yourself approximated to the settlements of New Mexico. There it will be necessary you should move with great circumspection, to keep clear of any hunting or reconnoitering parties from that province, and to prevent alarm or offense ; because the affairs of Spain and the United States appear to be on the point of amicable adjustment, and moreover it is the desire of the president to cultivate the friendship and harmonious intercourse of all the nations of the earth, particularly our near neighbors the Spaniards.[2]

[2] On the subject of our then strained relations with New Spain I have examined much unpublished manuscript in the Archives of the Government at Washington, but most of it has become a matter of well-known history, needless to bring up here. It is well understood that Pike had secret instructions from the traitor, General Wilkinson, over and beyond those which were ostensible ; and no doubt the main purpose of his Expedition was to open the way to Santa Fé, with reference to such military operations as then seemed probable. It is certain that General Wilkinson contemplated the possibility if not the prob-

In the course of your tour, you are to remark particularly upon the geographical structure, the natural history, and population of the country through which you may pass, taking particular care to collect and preserve specimens of everything curious in the mineral or botanical worlds, which can be preserved and are portable.   Let your courses be regulated by your compass, and your distances by your watch, to be noted in a field-book; and I would advise you, when circumstances permit, to protract and lay down in a separate book the march of the day at every evening's halt.

The instruments which I have furnished you will enable you to ascertain the variation of the magnetic needle and the latitude with exactitude; and at every remarkable point I wish you to employ your telescope in observing the eclipses of Jupiter's satellites, having previously regulated and adjusted your watch by your quadrant, taking care to note with great nicety the periods of immersions and emersions of the eclipsed satellites.   These observations may enable us, after your return, by application to the appropriate tables, which I cannot now furnish you, to ascertain the longitude.

It is an object of much interest with the executive to ascertain the direction, extent, and navigation of the Arkansaw and Red rivers; as far, therefore, as may be compatible

ability of invading New Mexico.   Take as evidence the following extract of a letter he wrote to the Secretary of War, dated St. Louis, Nov. 26th, 1805 :

" . . . Our situation at New Orleans is a defenceless one, & Colonel Freeman's removal of two Companies from Fort Adams to that city leaves us without the means of offence above Batton Rouge, which I do [not] like, but Freeman felt himself too feeble to stand alone without those Companies—I most ardently implore we may not be forced to War, because I seek repose & we are not indeed prepared for it, that is against European troops—yet if we must draw the sword, the whole of the troops destined to operate West of the Mississippi should be mounted, whether Gun-men or sword-men, because every Man of the Enemy will be found on Horse Back, and the composition should be such as I have described in a former Letter—If any thing should be done from this Quarter direct, and I might be indulged to recommend my officers, to plan & Lead the expedition, If I do not reduce New Mexico, at least, in one Campaign, I will forfeit my Head."

with these instructions and practicable to the means you may command, I wish you to carry your views to those subjects; and should circumstances conspire to favor the enterprise, that you may detach a party with a few Osage to descend the Arkansaw under the orders of Lieutenant Wilkinson, or Sergeant Ballinger, properly instructed and equipped to take the courses and distances, to remark on the soil, timber, etc., and to note the tributary streams. This party will, after reaching our post on the Arkansaw, descend to Fort Adams and there await further orders; and you yourself may descend the Red river, accompanied by a party of the most respectable Camanches, to the post of Nachitoches, and there receive further orders.

To disburse your necessary expenses and to aid your negotiations, you are herewith furnished six hundred dollars' worth of goods, for the appropriation of which you are to render a strict account, vouched by documents to be attested by one of your party.

Wishing you a safe and successful expedition,
          I am, Sir,
               With much respect and esteem,
                    Your obedient servant,
                         [Signed] JAMES WILKINSON.
     LIEUTENANT Z. M. PIKE.

---

*Art. 2.   Letter, Wilkinson's Additional Instructions
to Pike.*

CANTONMENT [BELLE FONTAINE], MISSOURI,
                              July 12th, 1806.
SIR :
     The health of the Osages being now generally restored, and all hopes of the speedy recovery of their prisoners from the hands of the Potowatomies being at an end, they have become desirous to commence their journey for their villages; you are therefore to proceed to-morrow.
     In addition to the instructions given you on the 24th

ultimo, I must request you to have the talks under cover delivered to White Hair and Grand Peste, the chief of the Osage band which is settled on the waters of the Arkansaw, together with the belts which accompany them. You will also receive herewith a small belt for the Panis and a large one for the Tetaus or Camanches.

Should you find it necessary, you are to give orders to Maugraine, the resident interpreter at the Grand Osage, to attend you.

I beg you to take measures for the security and safe return of your boats from the Grand Osage to this place.

Dr. Robinson will accompany you as a volunteer. He will be furnished medicines, and for the accommodations which you give him he is bound to attend your sick.

Should you discover any unlicensed traders in your route, or any person from this territory, or from the United States, without a proper license or passport, you are to arrest such person or persons and dispose of their property as the law directs.

My confidence in your caution and discretion has prevented my urging you to be vigilant in guarding against the strategy and treachery of the Indians; holding yourself above alarm or surprise, the composition of your party, though it be small, will secure to you the respect of a host of untutored savages.

You are to communicate, from the Grand Osage and from every other practicable point, directly to the secretary of war, transmitting your letters to this place under cover, to the commanding officer, or by any more convenient route.

I wish you health and a successful and honorable enterprise, and am,

Yours with friendship,

[Signed]   JAMES WILKINSON.

LIEUTENANT Z. M. PIKE.

Art. 3.[3] *Letter, Pike to Wilkinson.* (*Orig. No. 3, pp. 32, 33.*)

ST. CHARLES, July 17th, 1806.

DEAR SIR :

We arrived here last evening all well, except some of the soldiers from fatigue, as in the present state of the water we are obliged to row altogether.

We were disappointed in obtaining any information from St. Louis, or baggage for our Panis. I do not know how it will be digested by them. We likewise were disappointed in receiving a line from you, as we had here expected, and in the hopes of which I shall yet detain until twelve o'clock and then take my departure. Our Osage conduct themselves pretty well, and are very obedient to orders ; at first they had an idea a little too free relative to other people's property, but at present stand corrected.

I understood from you that they were equipped by Mr. Tillier with everything necessary for their voyage to their towns ; consequently, although they have been applying to me for a variety of articles, none of which have they been gratified with, but powder and ball, which is necessary for their own defense.

The general will pardon this scrawl ; and should he send an express after us, please to let Mrs. Pike know of the opportunity.

I am, dear Sir,

With high respect,

Your obedient servant,

[Signed] Z. M. PIKE, Lt.

GENERAL WILKINSON.

---

[3] Art. 3 bears the same number that this piece had in the orig. ed., and the same is the case with all the following articles of the present chapter, with one exception, where transposition of Orig. Nos. 8 and 9 to make Arts. 9 and 8 is required to preserve the chronological order. All these letters are from Pike to Wilkinson, excepting my Art. 8, Orig. No. 9, which is from Wilkinson to Pike, and one to General Dearborn. Pike's letters are in the nature of reports of progress to his commanding general and the Secretary of War. They ceased, of course, upon his separation from Lieutenant Wilkinson, and nothing further was heard of or from him till his return from Mexico, in July, 1807.

Art. 4. Letter, Pike to Wilkinson. (Orig. No. 4, p. 33.)

ST. CHARLES, July 19th [*i. e.*, 18th], 1806.
In the morning.

DEAR GENERAL :

Inclosed you have one of the articles subscribed by Mr.
[George] Henry, mentioned in my note of yesterday.[4] I
hope the general may approve of the contents.

Lieutenant Wilkinson and Dr. Robinson marched with
one soldier this morning, and the boats have proceeded
under the conduct of [Sergeant] Ballenger; I shall overtake
them in an hour or two.

Numerous reports have been made to the Indians [we
have with us], calculated to impress them with an idea that
there is a small army of their enemies waiting to receive us
at the entrance of the Grand Osage. But I have partly
succeeded in scouting the idea from their minds.

No news of Chouteau, nor Panis' trunks.

I am, dear General,
Your obedient servant,
[Signed] Z. M. PIKE, Lt.

GENERAL WILKINSON.

———

Art. 5. Letter, Pike to Wilkinson. (Orig. No. 5, pp. 33–35.)

VILLAGE DE CHARETTE, July 22d, 1806.

DEAR GENERAL :

I have the honor to acknowledge the receipt of your two
obliging favors of the 18th and 19th inst. The particular
contents of each shall be punctually attended to.

I assure you, Sir, that I am extremely pleased with the
idea that Messrs. [Blank] and [Blank] will meet with their
merited reward, and I on my part am determined to show
them that it is not their sinister movements that can de-

---

[4] There is no allusion to this matter in the letter as originally printed, where
a long row of asterisks indicates the elision of what it was not thought prudent
to publish at that time.

range the objects of our voyage; the greatest embarrassment they have yet occasioned me has been by the detention of the Panis' baggage, who have been much mortified on the occasion. But I question much if, under similar impressions and circumstances, many white men would have borne their loss with more philosophy than our young savages.

I conceive that I cannot dispose of one of my guns better than to give it to Frank, whose fusee was left at Chouteau's; also, each of them a soldier's coat; this is all the remuneration I will pretend to make them, and I hope it may bring them to a good humor.

You will probably be surprised at the slow progress we have made, but are already informed of the cause of our detention at St. Charles. Since then we have been detained two days on account of the rain; and although we were able to prevent the water from entering immediately on the top of the boat where covered, yet the quantity which she made at both ends occasioned so much dampness under the loading as to injure both my own corn and that of the Indians, with other small articles which they had at various times taken from under the loading and not returned to their proper places; but they appear satisfied that we have paid all possible attention to prevent injury to their baggage—as much as, and indeed more than, to our own.

In consequence of the above, and with a design to write you, I halted here to-day, which I hope we shall usefully employ in drying our baggage, cleaning our arms, and putting ourselves in a posture of defense. Lieutenant Wilkinson has experienced no inconvenience from his march by land with the Indians; and the event has proved the necessity of some officer accompanying them, as he informs me. He found it necessary to purchase some beeves for their consumption on the route, for which he drew on the superintendent of Indian affairs, and will write to you more particularly on the subject. They were absent from the boat four days; and had he not been with them, they

would have supplied themselves by marauding, to the great
offense of our good citizens.

I am informed that a party of 40 Sacs were at Boon's
Lick, above the Osage river, a few days since; but I by no
means conceive they were on the route to intercept us, as
the people pretend at this place.

Three days since one of my men [Kennerman] complained of indisposition, and went on shore to march; he
has never joined the party, and from various reasons I conceive has deserted. I have therefore inclosed an adver-
tisement which, if the general will please to cause to be
posted at St. Louis, Kaskaskias, and Lusk's Ferry on the
Ohio, I conceive he will be caught. I have written to
Captain Daniel Bissell [5] on the occasion; but hope the
general will enforce my request to that gentleman, as to his
[Kennerman's] being brought to trial. I was much mortified at the event, not only on account of the loss of the
man, but that my peculiar situation prevented me from
pursuing him and making him an example.

With respect to the Tetaus, the general may rest assured,
I shall use every precaution previous to trusting them; but
as to the mode of conduct to be pursued towards the Span-

---

[5] There were two Bissells, both of Connecticut, and of the same or similar
rank in the army, often confused in records of the time, unless their first names
are given, as in this instance; 1. Daniel Bissell became an ensign in the 1st
Infantry, Apr. 11th, 1792; was arranged to the 1st sub-Legion Sept. 4th, 1792;
promoted to a lieutenancy Jan. 3d, 1794; assigned to the 1st Infantry Nov. 1st,
1796; made a captain Jan. 1st, 1799; lieutenant-colonel, 1st Infantry, Aug.
18th, 1808; colonel, 5th Infantry, Aug. 15th, 1812; brigadier-general, Mar.
9th, 1814; honorably discharged June 1st, 1821, and died Dec. 14th, 1833.
2. Russell Bissell became a lieutenant of the 2d Infantry Mar. 4th, 1791; was
arranged to the 2d sub-Legion Sept. 4th, 1792; made captain Feb. 19th, 1793;
assigned to the 2d Infantry Nov. 1st, 1796; transferred to the 1st Infantry
Apr. 1st, 1802; promoted to be major of the 2d Infantry Dec. 9th, 1807, and
died Dec. 18th, 1807. Two other Connecticut Bissells who became army
officers a little later were Lieutenant Hezekiah W., who entered in 1801 and
died in 1802; and Captain Lewis, who entered as an ensign in 1808 and
resigned in 1817. One Daniel Bissell of Vermont served as a first lieutenant
for about a year, 1799–1800, and in still later years there have been several
other army officers of the same surname.

iards, I feel more at a loss, as my instructions lead me into
the country of the Tetaus, part of which is no doubt claimed
by Spain, although the boundaries between Louisiana and
New Mexico, have never yet been defined, in consequence
of which, should I encounter a party from the villages near
Santa Fe, I have thought it would be good policy to give
them to understand, that we were about to join our troops
near Natchitoches, but had been uncertain about the head
waters of the rivers over which we passed; but, that now, if
the commandant approved of it, we would pay him a visit of
politeness, either by deputation, or the whole party, but if
he refused, signify our intention of pursuing our direct route
to the post below; but if not I flatter myself secure us an
unmolested retreat to Natchitoches.   But if the Spanish
jealousy, and the instigation of domestic traitors should
induce them to make us prisoners of war, (in time of peace)
I trust to the magnanimity of our country for our libera-
tion and a due reward to their opposers, for the insult and
indignity offered their national honor.   However, unless they
give us ample assurances of just and honorable treatment,
according to the custom of nations in like cases, I would
resist, even if the inequality was as great as at the affair of
Bender [town in Russia], or the streights of Thermopylæ.[6]

[6] The above is such an important paragraph that I reproduce it verbatim
from the original, though it is so badly constructed as to be very obscure.   The
obscurity, however, is simply bad grammar, not intentional veiling of anything;
and as the sentences cannot be conveniently reconstructed in the text, I would
read as follows:

" With respect to the Ietans, the general may rest assured that I shall be
very cautious about trusting them.   I feel more at a loss how to conduct myself
with the Spaniards, for my instructions send me to the Comanche country, part
of which is no doubt claimed by Spain, though the boundaries between Louisiana and New Spain have never been settled.   Consequently, should I meet a
Spanish party from the villages near Santa Fé, I think it would be good policy
to give them to understand (1) that my party was going to join our troops near
Natchitoches, but had mistaken the Rio Grande for Red river; (2) that if it
would be agreeable to the Spanish commandant, some or all of us would pay
him a polite visit; and (3) that if he did not wish us to do this, we would go
direct to Natchitoches.   In any event, I flatter myself that I shall get out of the
scrape somehow.   But if Spanish jealousy of Americans, and the Aaron Burr

Will you pardon the foregoing as the enthusiasm of a youthful mind, yet not altogether unimpressed by the dictates of prudence?

I hope the general will be persuaded that with his son I shall act as I would to a brother, endeavoring in all cases to promote his honor and prosperity.

In consequence of indisposition, etc., Lieut. Wilkinson will steer one boat and I the other.

I am, dear General,
        Your sincere friend,
            And obedient humble servant,
                    [Signed] Z. M. PIKE.
GENERAL J. WILKINSON.

Art. 6. Letter, Pike to Wilkinson. (Orig. No. 6, p. 36.)

VILLAGE DE CHARETTE, Evening of July 22d, 1806.
DEAR SIR :

Finding no prospect of meeting with a private conveyance of our letters in time sufficient to find you previous to our setting sail, which would be entirely too late to secure my deserter and give you the other information they contain, I have hired the bearer to ride express to Belle Fontaine, for which I have promised him $8 ; which, taking into view his ferriages, etc., cannot be deemed high, and I hope the

conspiracy, cause us to be made prisoners of war (in time of peace), I trust that you will see that we are released, and they are punished for the insult. Moreover, if I do not feel assured they will treat us well in Mexico, I will fight them, no matter how many there are, before I will let them take us there."

This sort of talk is not that, mixture of youthful enthusiasm with prudence for which Pike begs Wilkinson's pardon in the next paragraph ; but the determination of a resolute young fellow to obey orders to the best of his ability, and accomplish if possible the purpose of the secret instructions given him by General Wilkinson. It is also what boys call a " dead give away "; for here, at the outset of his Expedition, Pike is talking about going to New Mexico, intending to deceive the Spaniards he expected to meet there, and weighing the chances of their good or bad treatment of himself and party. I forbear to characterize the ethics of the situation ; the discerning reader will be able to look through this hole in a grindstone, and form his own conclusions : see also note [46]. p. 504.

general will please to order the military agent to discharge the same.

The weather has at length become settled, and we set sail to-morrow with our boats newly and much better arranged.

I am, General, with sincere esteem,
And high respect,
Your obedient servant,
[Signed]   Z. M. PIKE.
GENERAL WILKINSON.

Art. 7.   Letter, Pike to Wilkinson.   (Orig. No. 7, p. 36.)

FIVE LEAGUES BELOW THE RIVER OSAGE, July 26th, 1806.
DEAR GENERAL :

I halt a moment, in order to say we have arrived thus far all safe, although our savages complain much of fatigue, etc.

The bearer had been sent by Mr. Sangonet [Charles Sanguinet, Sr.] to examine the Osage river, and reports that they could not get their canoes up the river more than 60 miles.   If so, we have a bad prospect before us ; but go we will, if God permits.

We have been detained several days by the Indians.
I am, dear General,
Your obedient servant,
[Signed]   Z. M. PIKE.
GEN. JAMES WILKINSON.

Art. 8. Letter, Wilkinson to Pike.   (Orig. No. 9, pp. 38–40.)

CANTONMENT MISSOURI [at Belle Fontaine],
Aug. 6th, 1806.
SIR :

In consequence of the receipt of the inclosed letters, I have thought proper to send you an express, to enable you to announce to the Osage the designs of their enemies, that they may take seasonable measures to circumvent them. You will not fail, in addition to the within talk, to enhance our paternal regard for this nation by every proper expression; but are to keep clear of any conflict in which they may be involved, though you are to avoid the appearance of abandoning them. If it should be the Potowatomies' intention to carry their threat into execution, it is probable they will not attempt to make the blow before the falling of the leaves; and in the mean time the Osages should establish a chain of light scouts along the coast of the Missouri, to ascertain with certainty the approach of their enemy.

It is reduced to a certainty that [Manuel de Lisa] and a society of which he is the ostensible leader have determined on a project to open some commercial intercourse with Santa Fe; and as this may lead to a connection injurious to the United States, and will, I understand, be attempted without the sanction of law or the permission of the executive, you must do what you can consistently to defeat the plan. No good can be derived to the United States from such a project, because the prosecution of it will depend entirely on the Spaniards, and they will not permit it, unless to serve their political as well as their personal interests. I am informed that the ensuing autumn and winter will be employed in reconnoitering and opening a connection with the Tetaus, Panis, etc.; that this fall or the next winter, a grand magazine is to be established at the Osage towns, where these operations will commence; that [Lisa] is to be the active agent, having formed a connection with the Tetaus. This will carry forward their merchandise within three or four days' travel of the Spanish settlements, where they will deposit it under a guard of 300 Tetaus. [Lisa] will then go forward with four or five attendants, taking with him some jewelry and fine goods. With those he will visit the governor, to whom he will make presents, and implore his pity by a fine tale of sufferings which have been endured by the change of government; that they are left here, with goods to be sure, but not a dollar's worth of bullion, and therefore they have adventured to see him, for the purpose of praying his leave for the introduction of their property into the province. If he assents, then the whole of the goods will be carried forward; if he refuses, then [Lisa] will invite some of his countrymen to accompany him to his deposit, and having there exposed to them his merchandise, he will endeavor to open a forced or clandestine trade; for he observes, the Spaniards will not dare to attack his camp. Here you have the plan, and you must take all prudent and lawful means to blow it up.

In regard to your approximation to the Spanish settlements, should your route lead you near them, or should you fall in with any of their parties, your conduct must be marked by such circumspection and discretion as may prevent alarm or conflict, as you will be held responsible for consequences. On this subject I refer you to my orders. We have nothing new respecting the pending negotiations in Europe; but from Colonel [T. H.] Cushing I understand the Spaniards below are behaving now with great courtesy.

By the return of the bearer you may open your correspondence with the secretary of war [General Dearborn]; but I would caution you against anticipating a step before you, for fear of deception and disappointment. To me you may, and must, write fully and freely, not only giving a minute detail of everything past worthy of note, but also of your prospects and the conduct of the Indians. If you discover that any tricks have been played from St. Louis, you will give them to me with names, and must not fail to give particulars to the secretary of war, with names, to warn him against improper confidence and deception. Inclose your dispatch for me to Colonel [T.] Hunt, and it will follow me by a party which I leave for the purpose. It is interesting to you to reach Nachitoches in season to be at the seat of government pending the session of Congress; yet you must not sacrifice any essential object to this point. Should fortune favor you on your present excursion, your importance to our country will, I think, make your future life comfortable.

To show you how to correct your watch by the quadrant, after it has been carefully adjusted, preparatory to your observing the eclipses of the satellites of Jupiter, I send you a very simple plan, which you will readily understand : a basin of water, in some place protected from the motion of the air, will give you a fairer artificial horizon than mercury. I think a tent, with a suitable aperture in the side of it, would do very well. I have generally unroofed a cabin.

Miranda has botched his business. He has lost his two schooners captured, and himself in the Leander returned to Jamaica. The French have a squadron of four frigates at Porto Rico, and five sail of the line with Jerome Bonaparte at Martinique. I consider them lost.

Your children have been indisposed ; but Mrs. Pike writes you. She appears well. My regards to your associates, and may God protect you.

[Signed] J. WILKINSON.

LIEUTENANT PIKE.

Art. 9. Letter, Pike to Wilkinson. (Orig. No. 8, p. 37.)

PARK ON THE OSAGE RIVER, Aug. 14th, 1806.

DEAR SIR :

I send this letter by Baptiste la Tulip [note [36], p. 381], who informs me he bears letters to Chouteau, informing him that a party of Little Osages have marched to war against the Kanses, and a party of Grand Osages left the village expressly to make war on the white people on the Arkansaw. This latter step White Hair did everything in his power to prevent, but could not. If true, what are we to think of our *bons amis*, the Osage?

But to [Manuel de Lisa] must we ascribe the stroke against the Kanses. He I am informed sent a message to the Osage nation to raze the Kanses village entirely. On this subject I intended to have been more particular, and substantiate it by proofs; but present circumstances seem to give credit to it.   On my arrival at the village, more particular inquiry shall be made on the subject.

Yesterday morning Lieutenant Wilkinson, the doctor, interpreter, and one soldier, marched with the Indians, as they were very apprehensive of an attack.   The people in the canoe heard them crying and saw them on their march.

Nothing extraordinary has yet taken place on our route, except our being favored with a vast quantity of rain, which I hope will enable us to ascend to the village.

What face will the Indians receive us with?   And to whom are we to ascribe their hostile disposition, unless to the traitors of St. Louis?

Lieutenant Wilkinson is in very good health, and will lament his having missed this opportunity of assuring his parents of his love and affection.

I am, dear General,
Your obedient servant,
[Signed] Z. M. PIKE.

GEN. JAMES WILKINSON.

Art. 10.   Letter, Pike to Wilkinson.   (Orig. No. 10, pp. 40–42.)

CAMP INDEPENDENCE, NEAR THE OSAGE TOWNS,
Aug. 28th, 1806.

DEAR GENERAL :

You will no doubt be much surprised to perceive by the date of this letter that we are still here ; but we have been unavoidably detained by a variety of circumstances.

I had the happiness to receive your express the day of my arrival, the bearer having arrived the night before, and have attended particularly to its contents.

On the 19th inst. I delivered your parole to Cheveux Blanche, and on the 21st held a grand council of both towns, and made the necessary communications and demands for horses, on the subjects of making peace with the Kans, accompanying me to the Panis,[and Wilkinson] down the Arkansaw, and [to ascertain] if there were any brave enough to accompany me the whole voyage.

They requested one day to hold council in the villages, previous to giving an answer. It was three before I received any; their determination was as follows: From the Grand Osage village, or [that of] Cheveux Blanche, we are accompanied by his son, and Jean La Fon [Le Fou], the second chief of the village, with some young men not known, and he furnishes us four horses.

The Little Osage sends the brother of the chief, whom I really find to be the third chief of the village, and some young men unknown, and furnishes six horses. This is their present promise, but four of the ten are yet deficient. With these I am merely capable of transporting our merchandise and ammunition. I shall purchase two more, for which I find we shall be obliged to pay extravagant prices.

I sincerely believe that the two chiefs, White Hair and Wind, have exerted all their influence; but it must be little, when they could only procure 10 horses out of 700 or 800.

I have taken an exact survey of the river to this place, noting particular streams, etc., a protracted copy of which Lieutenant Wilkinson forwards by this opportunity. Since our arrival here I have ascertained the variation of the compass to be 6° 30′ E.; the latitude, by means of several observations, 37° 26′ 17″ N.; and by an observation on three different nights I obtained two immersions of Jupiter's satellites, which will enable us to ascertain every geographical object in view.

On the same night I arrived near the village, Mr. Baptist Duchouquette, alias Larme, with two men, in a small canoe, arrived and went immediately to the lodge of White Hair, whose conduct, with that of our resident interpreter, appears in my estimation to have changed since I sent Lieutenant Wilkinson to demand to see Baptist's passport, if he had one, and if not, to bring him to camp; which was done. I detained him two days, until I had made an inquiry of White Hair, who said he had merely mentioned to him that Labardie was coming with a quantity of goods. Finding I could substantiate nothing more criminal against him than his having entered the Indian boundaries without a passport, and not being able to send him back a prisoner, I detained him a sufficient time to alarm him, then took his deposition (a copy of which is inclosed to the attorney-general), and wrote Dr. Brown on the occasion, requesting him to enter a prosecution against these men [see note ⁴⁴, p. 388, Aug. 20th, 1806].

Barroney informs me that he has not the least doubt that [Lisa] was at the bottom of this embassy, although in the name of [Labardie]; as after the arrival of Baptist, the Indians frequently spoke of [Lisa] and declared that if he had come he could have obtained horses in plenty.

Our interpreter, Maugraine, also, I do believe to be a perfect creature of [Lisa]; he has almost positively refused to accompany me, although I read your order on the subject, alleging he was only engaged to interpret at this place, notwithstanding he went last year to the Arkansaw for Mr. Chouteau without difficulty. I have not yet determined on the line of conduct to be pursued with him ; but believe, on his giving a positive refusal, I shall use military law. What the result will be is uncertain; but to be thus braved by a scoundrel will be lessening the dignity of our government. He is married into a powerful family, and appears, next to White Hair, to have the most influence in the Grand [Osage] village. The general will please to observe that much of the foregoing rests on conjecture, and therefore will give it its due weight. But to him I not only write as my general, but as a paternal friend, who would not make use of my open communications, when not capable of being substantiated by proofs.

We have heard nothing of the Potowatomies; but should they come in a few days, they will meet with a warm reception, as all are ready to receive them.

Since my arrival here many Spanish medals have been shown me, and some commissions. All I have done on the subject is merely to advise their delivery below, when they would be acknowledged by our government. Many have applied for permission to go to Saint Louis ; none of which I have granted except to the son of Sans Orielle, who goes down to make inquiry for his sister.

I have advanced our express some things on account, and forward his receipts ; also, some trifles to Barroney, whom I have found to be one of the finest young men I ever knew in his situation. He appears to have entirely renounced all his Saint Louis connections, and is as firm an American as if born one ; he of course is entirely discarded by the people of Saint Louis; but I hope he will not suffer for his fidelity.

On the chart forwarded by Lieutenant Wilkinson is noted the census which I caused to be taken of the village of the Little Osage ; that of the big one I shall likewise obtain— they are from actual enumeration. Lieutenant Wilkinson, if nothing extraordinary prevents, will descend the Arkansaw, accompanied by Ballenger and two men, as the former is now perfectly acquainted with the mode of taking courses and protracting his route, and the latter appears as if he had not the proper capacity for it, although a good dispositioned and brave man.

I am, dear Sir,
Your obedient servant,
[Signed]   Z. M. PIKE, Lt.

GEN. WILKINSON.

Art. 11.   Letter, Pike to Wilkinson.   (Orig. No. 11, p. 43.)

[OSAGE TOWNS], Aug. 29th, 1806.

DEAR SIR :

I will continue my communications by relating that Wind has come in and informed me that the other two horses which he promised have been withdrawn by their owners. He appeared really distressed, and I conceive I do him justice in believing that he is extremely mortified at the deceptions which have been passed on him.

It is with extreme pain that I keep myself cool amongst the difficulties which those people appear to have a disposition to throw in my way; but I have declared to them that I should go on, even if I collected our tents and other baggage which we will be obliged to leave together, and burnt them on the spot.

I have sold the batteau which I brought up, and which was extremely rotten, for $100 in merchandise, the price at this place; which I conceive was preferable to leaving her to destruction, as I am afraid I do the barge (for which I demanded $150), although I leave her under the charge of Wind, and shall report her to Colonel [Thomas] Hunt.

I shall dispatch the express to-morrow, as he complains much of the detention, etc., and as I hope nothing worthy of note will occur at this place previous to our departure. I hope the general will believe me to be and, should this be my last report, to have been, his sincerely attached friend and obedient servant,

[Signed]   Z. M. PIKE, Lt.

GEN. WILKINSON.

Art. 12.   Letter, Pike to Wilkinson.   (Orig. No. 12, pp. 43, 44.)

OSAGE TOWNS, Aug. 30th, 1806.

DEAR SIR :

I have brought Mr. Noal, alias Maugraine, to reason, and he either goes himself or hires, at his expense, a young man who is here who speaks the Panis language, and in many other respects is preferable to himself; but he will be the bearer of the express to Saint Louis.

Cheveux Blanche requested me to inform you that there is an Osage murderer in his village, who killed a Frenchman on the Arkansaw; but owing to the great dissensions and schism of the Arkansaw faction, he is fearful to deliver him up without some of his friends having agreed to it, and his authority being strengthened by a formal demand from you; when he assures me he shall be brought down a prisoner. Indeed Cheveux Blanche appears to be very delicately situated, as the village on the Arkansaw serves as a place of refuge for all the young, daring, and discontented; added to which, they are much more regularly supplied with ammunition, and, should not our government take some steps to prevent it, they will ruin the Grand village, as they are at liberty to make war without restraint, especially on the nations who are to the west, and have plenty of horses. The chief says he was promised, at Washington, that these people should be brought back to join him; but, on the contrary, many of his village are emigrating there.

Owing to the difficulty of obtaining horses, Mr. Henry returns from this place. In descending the Mississippi I will request him to pay his respects to you.

I last evening took the census of the Grand village, and found it to be: men, 502; boys, 341; women and girls, 852; total, 1695; lodges, 214.

The express waits, which I hope the general will accept as an excuse for this scrawl, having written him fully on the 28th and 29th inst.

I am, dear General,
Your ever sincere friend
and obedient servant,
GEN. J. WILKINSON. [Signed] Z. M. PIKE, Lt.

---

*Art. 13. Letter, Pike to Dearborn. (Orig. No. 13,
pp. 45, 46.)*

PAWNEE REPUBLIC, Oct. 1st, 1806.
SIR :
We arrived here on the 25th ult., after a tedious march of 375 miles, the distance, as I conceive, being very much aug-

mented by the Osages who accompanied us leading us too
far to the south, owing to their great fear of the Kans. We
suffered considerably with thirst, but our guns furnished us
amply with buffalo meat.

We delivered in safety to the chief the two young Pawnees who had lately visited Washington, and caused to be
explained to the nation the parole which they bore from the
president of the United States.

On our arrival, we found the Spanish and American flags
both expanded in the village, and were much surprised to
learn that it was not more than three or four weeks since
a party of Spanish troops, whose numbers were estimated
by the Indians of this town at 300, had returned to
Santa Fe. We further learned that a large body of troops
had left N. Mexico, and on their march had met with the
villagers of the Pawnee Mahaws, who were on one of their
semi-annual excursions ; that they encamped together, and
entered into a treaty ; but after this the Pawnees raised their
camp in the night, and stole a large portion of the Spaniards' horses. This circumstance induced them to halt on
the Arkansaw with the main body of the troops, and to send
forward the party who appeared at this village. They proposed to this chief to join a party of his warriors to their
troops, march to and entirely destroy the village of the Pawnee Mahaws; this proposition he had prudence enough to
reject, although at war with that nation. The Spanish
officer informed him that his superior, who remained on the
Arkansaw, had marched from Santa Fe with an intention of
entering into a treaty with the following nations of Indians,
viz.: The Kanses, Pawnee Republic, Grand Pawnees, Pawnee Loups, Otos, and Mahaws; and had with him a grand
medal, commissions, and four mules for each ; but by the
stroke of the Pawnee Mahaws the plan was disconcerted,
except only as to this nation. The commissions are dated
Santa Fe, 15th of June, 1806, signed governor-general, etc.,
etc., of New Mexico, and run in the usual style of Spanish

commissions to savages, as far as I was capable of judging of their contents.

The chief further informed me that the officer who commanded said party was too young to hold councils, etc.; that he had only come to open the road; that in the spring his superior would be here, and teach the Indians what was good for them; and that they would build a town near them. In short, it appears to me to have been an expedition expressly for the purpose of striking a dread into those different nations of the Spanish power, and to bring about a general combination in its favor. Under these impressions, I have taken the earliest opportunity of reporting the infringement of our territory, in order that our government may not remain in the dark as to the views of her neighbor.

I effected a meeting at this place between a few Kans and Osages, who smoked the pipe of peace and buried the hatchet, agreeably to the wishes of their great father; in consequence of which a Kans has marched for the Osage nation, and some of the latter propose to accompany the former to their village; whether this good understanding will be permanent, I will not take on me to determine; but at least a temporary good effect has succeeded.

From the Osage towns, I have taken the courses and distances by the route we came, marking each river or rivulet we crossed, pointing out the dividing ridges, etc. The waters which we crossed were the heads of the [Little] Osage, White [Neosho], and Verdigrise rivers, [the two last] branches of the Arkansaw, and the waters of the [Smoky Hill fork of the] Kans river. The latitude of this place, I presume, will be in about 39° 30′ N., and I hope to obtain every other astronomical observation which will be requisite to fix its geographical situation beyond dispute. I expect to march from here in a few days; but the future prospects of the voyage are entirely uncertain, as the savages strive to throw every impediment in our way, agreeably to the orders received from the Spaniards. Being seated on the ground, and writing on the back of a book, I hope will plead my excuse for this scrawl.

I am, Sir,
With high respect,
Your obedient servant,
[Signed]   Z. M. PIKE, Lt.

THE HON. HENRY DEARBORN,
Secretary War Department.

Art. 14.   Letter, Pike to Wilkinson.   (Orig. No. 14, pp. 47–50.)

PAWNEE REPUBLIC, Oct. 2d, 1806.

DEAR GENERAL :

Inclosed you have a copy of my letter from this place to the secretary of war, in order that, should you think any communication on the contents necessary, you may have a perfect command of the information given the war department, and will be the more capable of illustrating the subject.

You will perceive by said communication, that we were led considerably out of our course by our guides, in my opinion not less than 100 miles ; this was entirely owing to the pusillanimity of the Osage, who were more afraid of the Kans than I could possibly have imagined.

You will likewise perceive the council which took place between those nations under our auspices, and its effects, but which I candidly confess I have very little hopes will be productive of a permanent peace, as none of the principal men of either nation were present ; but as both are anxious for a cessation of hostilities, perhaps it may have the desired effect.

Two of the Kans chiefs have said they will pursue the voyage with me agreeably to my orders.   I do not yet know whether they will descend the Arkansaw with Lieut. Wilkinson, or continue on to Red river with me ; but they have their own selection.

The general will no doubt be struck with some surprise to perceive that so large a party of Spanish troops have been so lately in our territory. No doubt at first you would conclude that it must have been militia; but when informed that their infantry were armed with muskets and bayonets and had drums, that the men wore long mustaches and whiskers which almost covered the whole of their faces; that their cavalry were armed with swords and pistols, and that regular guards and patrols were kept by horse and foot, you may probably change your opinion.

The route by which they came and returned was by no means the direct one from Santa Fe, and why they should have struck so low down as the Grand Saline, unless they had an idea of striking at the village of the Grand Pest, or conceived the Saline to be in their territory, I cannot imagine.

On our arrival here, we were received with great pomp and ceremony by about 300 men on horseback, and with great apparent friendship by the chief. The Osage (one chief and four warriors) were presented with eight horses; the Kans who arrived two days after were also presented with horses. The day after, we assembled the four principal chiefs to dine, after which I presented the principal with a double-barreled gun, gorget,[7] and other articles (this man wore the grand Spanish medal); gave to the second the small medal you furnished me, with other articles; and to each of the others a gorget in their turn. Those presents I conceived would have a good effect, both as to attaching them to our government and in our immediate intercourse.

At the council which was held a day or two afterward I presented them with merchandise which at this place should be valued at $250; and after explaining their relative situation as to the Spanish and American governments, I asked on my part, if they would assist us with a few

---

[7] A sort of ornamental neck-band, such as used to be worn by some officers with insignia of rank, and somewhat like those still affected by Free Masons and other ecclesiastical or civic orders on occasions of ceremony.

horses, a Tetau prisoner who spoke Pawnee to serve as an interpreter, an exchange of colors, and finally, for some of their chiefs to accompany us, to be sent on to Washington. The exchange of colors was the only request granted at the time ; and for particular reasons, which Lieut. Wilkinson related, I thought proper to return them to the chief. After spending two or three anxious days, we were given to understand that our requests could not be complied with in the other points, and were again strongly urged by the head chief to return the way we came, and not prosecute our voyage any further. This brought on an explanation as to our views toward the Spanish government, in which the chief declared that it had been the intention of the Spanish troops to proceed further toward the Mississippi, but that he objected to it, and they listened to him and returned ; he therefore hoped we would be equally reasonable. Finding me still determined on proceeding, he told me in plain terms (if the interpreter erred not) that it was the will of the Spaniards we should not proceed ; which I not answering, he painted innumerable difficulties which he said lay in the way ; but finding all his arguments had no effect, he said " it was a pity," and was silent.

This day I have sent out several of my party to purchase horses, but know not yet how we shall succeed, as the Kans have intimated an idea that the chief will prohibit his people from trading with us.

The Pawnees and the Tetaus are at war ; the latter killed six of the former in August last ; consequently effecting any communication with the Tetaus by means of this nation is impossible.

If God permits, we shall march from here in a few days, and on the Arkansaw I shall remain until I build two small canoes for Lieut. W[ilkinson], whose party will consist of Ballenger and two or three men, with three Osage. Those canoes will be easily managed, and in case of accident to one, the other will still be sufficient to transport their baggage.

I am informed that in a few days he will meet French hunters, and probably arrive at the village of the Grand Pest in a fortnight; as all the Osage nation are apprised of his descent, I conceive he will meet with no insurmountable difficulties.* The Tetaus are at open war with the Spaniards, so that could we once obtain an introduction, I conceive we should meet with a favorable reception. Yet how it is to be brought about I am much at a loss to determine; but knowing that, at this crisis of affairs, an intimate connection with that nation might be extremely serviceable to my country, I shall proceed to find them, in hopes to find some means, through the French, Osage, and Pawnee languages, of making ourselves understood.

Any number of men who may reasonably be calculated on would find no difficulty in marching by the route we came, with baggage wagons, field artillery, and all the usual appendages of a small army; and if all the route to Santa Fe should be of the same description, in case of war I would pledge my life and what is infinitely dearer, my honor, for the successful march of a reasonable body of troops into the province of New Mexico.

I find the savages of this country less brave, but possessing much more duplicity and by far a greater propensity to lying and stealing, than those I had to pass through on my last [Mississippi] voyage.

I am extremely doubtful if any chief of those nations can be induced to prosecute the voyage with us, as their dread of the Tetaus and the objections of the Pawnees seem to outweigh every argument and inducement to the contrary.

OCT. 3D.

The Pawnee chief has induced the Kans to return to their villages, by giving them a gun and promising horses, with many frightful pictures drawn [of what would happen] if they proceeded.

The Osages lent me five horses, which their people who

* This was erroneous, but it was my impression at the time. (Orig. note.)

accompanied us were to have led back; but receiving fresh ones from the Pawnees, they would not be troubled with them. In fact, it was a fortunate circumstance, as four of the horses I obtained of the Osage have such bad backs they cannot proceed, and we will be obliged to leave them ; and not purchasing here with facility, I would have been obliged to sacrifice some of our baggage. I therefore sent them a certificate for each horse, on the Indian agent below, which I hope the general will order him to discharge.

I know the general's goodness will excuse this scrawl, as he is well acquainted with the situation it must be written in, and at the same time, believe me to be his sincere friend and

Most obedient humble servant,
[Signed] Z. M. PIKE, Lt.

GENERAL J. WILKINSON.

Art. 15.[8]   *Letter, Pike to Wilkinson.*   (*Orig. No. 15,*
pp. 50–53.)

ON THE ARKANSAW, latitude 37° 44′ 9″ N., Oct. 24th, 1806.
DEAR GENERAL :

Our party arrived here on the 15th inst., myself and Dr. Robinson on the 19th [18th by Itinerary, p. 427]. We, having been out to seek the trace of the Spanish troops, missed the party, and were not able to join them until the 4th [3d] day.

The river being very regular, Lieut. Wilkinson had calculated to proceed on the day following on the most direct route for the Red [*sic*] river ; but shortly after my joining, considerable rain fell and raised the river, and we have been ever since preparing wooden and skin canoes for that

---

[8] To this Art. 15 belongs the following table headed Statistical Abstract of the Indians, etc., which in the orig. ed. was directed to be bound facing p. 53. This page was followed by blank p. 54, the leaf of the book thus represented being simply an overrunning of the matter of the original folder. All that Recapitulation which was on p. 53 is embodied in the table which now forms pp. 590, 591.

English.	Indian.	French.	Warriors.	Women.	Children.	Villages.	Probable Souls.	Lodges of Roving Bands.	Fire Arms.	Primitive Language.	Traders or Bands with whom they traffic.	Value of Merchandise for Annual Consumption	Annual Peltry, Packs.	Species of Peltry.
I. Osage 1. Grand village *	Wasbasha	Osage Grand Osage	502	852	341 M.	1	1695	214	500	Osage	St. Louis	$10000	1000	Deer, bea otter, beaver, few buffalo
[2. Little village *]	Wasbasha	Petit Osage	250	241	174 F. 159 M. 333	1	824	102	250	Osage	St. Louis	8000	300	do.
[3. Arkansaw village †]	Wasbasha	Osages Total	500 1252	700 1793	300 M. 974	1 3	1500 4019	200 516	450 1209	Osage	Arkansaw r.			
II. Kans ‡	Kansa	Kan [Total]	465	500	600	1	1565	204	450	Osage	St. Louis	8000	250 deer 15 beaver 100 otter	Deer, beaver, o ter, bea buffalo
III. Pawnee 1. Republican village *	Pawnane	Panis	508	550	560	1	1618	44	200	Pawnee	St. Louis and Kans	8000		Deer, bu falo, a fe beaver an otter
2. Grand Village ‡	Pawnane	Panis	1000	1120	1000	1	3120	90	300	Pawnee	St. Louis ; possibly once in 3 years Spaniards	15000		do.
3. Loup village ‡	Pawnane	Panis Pawnees total	485 1993	500 2170	500 2060	1 3	1485 6223	40 174	200 700	Pawnee	do.	8000		do.
IV. Tetan ‡	Camanches	[Total] [Grand total]	2700 6410	3000 7463	2500 6134	7	8200 20007	1020 1914	270 2620	Camanche	Spaniards of N. Mexico	30000		Buffalo robes an horses

* Census taken by myself ; men counted, women and children estimated.　　† Estimat

Captain Z. M. Pike in His Tour of Discovery in the years 1806 and 1807.

...est Positions ...r Trading ...sts.	With whom at war.	With whom at peace, or in alliance.	Names of the Chiefs or Principal Men.			Remarks.
			Indian.	French.	English.	
ddle branch Osage r., bet. ...nd and Little ...ages	Tetaus, Potowatomies, Arkansaws, Cherokees, Chickasaws, Chactaws, Creeks, Padoucas, Caddoes	Little Osage, All the Pawnees, Sacs, Reynards, Delawares, Shawanese, Kickapous, Otos, Missouries, Mahaws, etc.; Kans uncertain	Cahagatonga	Cheveux Blanche	White Hair	Grand and little medals, colors, etc.; first chief
			Watchawaha	Jean La Fon		Second Chief, son-in-law to White Hair
			Tawangaha	Fils de Canard	He who drives villages	Literally from the Indian
			Ichesohungar		Wise Family	Son of Cheveux Blanche
			Hapause		Pointed Horn	First Soldier
			Chaporanga	Bonnet du Bœuf		
			Gihagatche		The Chief himself	
			Shenga Wassa	Belle Oiseau	Beautiful Bird	Accompanied me to the Pawnees
			Wasaba Tunga	Sans Nerve	Without Nerve	
			Ogahawasa		Son-in-Law	
			Tourmansara		Heart of the Town	
ddle branch Osage r., bet. ...nd and Little ...ages, and ...ve Gr. Osage ...the Arkan-, and on the ...e of the Mis-...ri	do.	do.	Tuttasuggy	Le Vent	The Wind	First chief of Little Osage
			Watchkesingar	Soldat de Chien	Soldier's Dog	Second chief of Little Osage
			Nezuma		Rain which Walks	Brother of first chief
			Tetobasi	Sans Oreille	Without Ears	First Soldier
			Tarehem		Yellow Skin Deer	49 Little Osages killed since under our government
			Maugraine		Big Rogue	
	do.	do.				
...trance of ...ns r., or at ...e village	None, if at peace with Osage	All their neighbors				
do.	Tetaus and Indians of N. Mexico; Panis Loups	Kans, Osages, and all Indians of the East	Characterish	Loup Blanche	White Wolf	
			Iskatappe	Homme Riche	Rich Man	
			—	—	Republican Chief	
					Two Sons of Characterish	
...trance of La ...tte	Tetaus and Indians of N. Mexico	do.				
do.	Tetaus and Indians of N. Mexico, and Pawnee Republic	do.				
...gh up Red r. ...d near the ...s. on the ...kansaw	Pawnees, Utahs, Osage, Kans	With all Spanish Indians				

...rnished by Grand Osage chiefs.   ‡ On information.   (Z. M. P.)

gentleman and party to descend in. The river is between 300 and 400 yards in width, with generally flat low banks, not more than two or three feet high, and the bed a sand-bank from one side to the other. The want of water will present the greatest obstacle to the progress of the party who descend the Arkansaw, as they have no cause to fear a scarcity of provision, having some bushels of corn on hand, and can at their option take as much dried meat as they think proper, hundreds of pounds of which are lying on scaffolds at our camp; and they are likewise accompanied by the choice of our hunters.

Under these circumstances, and those stated in my letter from the Pawnees, I can assert with confidence there are no obstacles I should hesitate to encounter, although those inseparable from a voyage of several hundred leagues through a wilderness inhabited only by savages may appear of the greatest magnitude to minds unaccustomed to such enterprises. Lieut. Wilkinson and party appear in good spirits, and show a disposition which must vanquish every difficulty.

We were eight days traveling from the Pawnee village to the Arkansaw, our general course S. 10° W. Several days we lay by nearly half, owing to various circumstances; my course made it 150 miles, but I could now march it in 120. Lieut. Wilkinson has copied and carries with him a very elegant protracted sketch of the route, noting the streams, hills, etc., that we crossed; their courses, bearings, etc.; and should I live to arrive, I will pledge myself to show their connections and general direction with considerable accuracy, as I have myself spared no pains in reconnoitering or obtaining information from the savages in our route.

From this point we shall ascend the river until we strike the mountains, or find the Tetaus; thence bear more to the S. until we find the head of the Red river, where we shall be detained some time; after which nothing shall cause a halt until my arrival at Natchitoches.

I speak in all those cases in the positive mood, as, so far

as lies in the compass of human exertions, we command the power; but I pretend not to surmount impossibilities, and I well know the general will pardon my anticipating a little to him.

The general will probably be surprised to find that the expenses [9] of the expedition will more than double the contemplated sum of our first calculations; but I conceived the Spaniards were making such great exertions to debauch the minds of our savages, economy might be very improperly applied, and I likewise have found the purchase of horses to be attended with much greater expense than was expected at St. Louis. For those reasons, when I advert to the expenses of my two voyages, which I humbly conceive might be compared with the one performed by Captains Lewis and Clark, and the appropriations made for theirs, I feel a consciousness that it is impossible for the most rigid to censure my accounts.

I cannot yet say if I shall sacrifice my horses at Red river, but every exertion shall be made to save them for the public; some, if in good condition, would be fine ones, and average between $50 and $60. Should the fortune of war at length have honored me with a company, [10] I hope the general will recollect his promise to me, and have my command attached to it; and on my arrival I shall take the liberty of soliciting his influence, that they may obtain the

[9] An itemized account of the Congressional appropriation for, and estimated expenses of, Lewis and Clark's Expedition, is given on p. xxi of the 1893 ed. of L. and C. So far as I have been able to inform myself, we lack the data which would enable us to make the comparison which Pike modestly conceives might be favorable to his own expeditions. To whatever sum may have been expended on the part of the United States for the Mississippian voyage and the Arkansaw journey, as performed under the orders of General Wilkinson, is to be added the cost of the enforced Mexican tour, in so far as this was paid by the United States on the strength of claims for reimbursement presented by the Spanish authorities. On this latter score I have found some curious unpublished documents in the archives of the War Department at Washington. Certain of these items will be found beyond in proper connection with the official correspondence on the subject.

[10] Pike's expected promotion to a captaincy occurred Aug. 12th, 1806.

same or similar rewards, as those who accompanied Capt. Lewis; as I will make bold to say that they have in the two voyages incurred as great dangers, and gone through as many hardships.

Dr. Robinson presents his respectful compliments, and is sanguine of the success of our expedition.

I am, dear General,

Your ever attached friend

and obedient servant,

[Signed] Z. M. PIKE.

GENERAL J. WILKINSON.

PIKE'S EXPEDITIONS.

Part III.

THE MEXICAN TOUR.

CHAPTER I.

ITINERARY: THROUGH NEW MEXICO ON THE RIO GRANDE
TO EL PASO, FEB. 27TH–MAR. 21ST, 1807.

FRIDAY, Feb. 27th, 1807. In the morning I discovered
that the Spanish lieutenant [Don Ignatio Saltelo] was
writing letters addressed to the governor and others; on
which I demanded if he was not going on with me to Santa
Fe. He appeared confused and said, No; that his orders
were so positive as to the safe conduct and protection of my
men, that he dare not go and leave any behind; that his
companion [Don Bartolomé Fernandez] would accompany me to Santa Fe with 50 men, while he with the others
would wait for the sergeant [Meek] and his party. I replied
that he had deceived me, and had not acted with candor;
but that it was now too late for me to remedy the evil.

We marched about eleven o'clock, ascending the Rio del
Norte [read Rio Conejos] five miles more, S. 60° W., when
we went round through a chain of hills and bore off to the
south. We proceeded nine miles further, when we crossed
the main branch of that stream, which was now bearing
nearly west toward [or east from] the main chain of the
third chain of mountains [San Juan range]. We encamped
on the opposite side. Intensely cold; obliged to stop

frequently and make fires. Snow deep. Distance 15 [5+9=14] miles.[1]

Feb. 28th. We marched late. One of the Frenchmen informed me that the expedition which had been at the Pawnees had descended the Red river 233 leagues, and from thence crossed to the Pawnees expressly in search of my party. This was afterward confirmed by the gentleman who commanded the troops. He then expressed great regret at my misfortunes, as he termed them, in being taken, and offered his services in secreting papers, etc. I took him at his word, and for my amusement thought I would try him ; so I gave him a leaf or two of my journal, copied,

---

[1] The Mexican Tour trips at the start with misstatements which must have puzzled many a reader, as they did the present editor. Reference to p. 510 will show that yesterday, Feb. 26th, Pike "went up the river about 12 miles." He does not say *what* river ; but as he was on the Conejos, we naturally take that to be the one he ascended that day—and we are right. But to-day he speaks of " ascending the Rio del Norte five miles *more*," implying that yesterday's march was up this river, as to-day's is said to be. Then we are confronted by the statement that to-day's course is " S. 60° W."—a direction in which it is impossible to ascend the Rio del Norte to any distance. The difficulty vanishes at once, if for " Rio del Norte" we read *Rio Conejos*. This emendation is confirmed by Pike's map, which contradicts the above text, showing no détour up the Rio Grande ; the dotted trail goes from the stockade directly up Rio Conejos, to a point on its N. or left bank marked " 1st. Camp "—*i. e.*, the " place of deposit " to which the Spaniards took him on the 26th. This place, where the Spaniards had established themselves when they sent for Pike, was on the direct road by which they had come from Santa Fé, and not far from the present town of Conejos, though probably somewhat further down the river of that name. The road which now crosses the river at the town holds the course of a trail which ran N. to the Saguache mts. and through Cochetope Pass to the Gunnison and Grand rivers, and so on. This was formerly much used by the Utes en route to Santa Fé, and was no doubt in existence in 1807. Conejos, seat of the county so named, is a very well-known place on the river, in the plain between the San Luis hills on the E. and the foothills of the San Juan range on the W.; it is directly under Prospect Peak (9,900 feet ; air-line 8 m.). Roads concenter here from various directions ; that hence to Fort Garland, 35¼ m. N. E., crosses the place where Pike had his stockade; that S. W. to old Fort Lowell is 49½ m. Some small places in the vicinity of Conejos are called Guadalupe, Servilleta, San Rafael, San José, and Brazos. The route pursued hence is the old main road S. down the Rio Grande, but at a considerable distance W. of that river for the present (along long. 106° W. nearly).

which mentioned the time of my sailing from Belle Fontaine, and our force. This I charged him to guard very
carefully and give to me after the investigation of my
papers at Santa Fe. This day we saw a herd of wild
horses. The Spaniards pursued them and caught two
colts, one of which the Indians killed and ate ; the other
was let go. We pursued our journey over some hills, where
the snow was very deep, and encamped at last on the top
of a pretty high hill, among some pines. We left the river,
which in general ran about six, eight, and 10 miles to the
left or east of us. Saw great sign of elk. Distance 36
miles.[2]

Sunday, Mar. 1st. We marched early. Although we
rode very hard we only got to the village of L'eau Chaud,
or Warm Spring [Ojo Caliente], some time in the afternoon.
The distance was about 45 miles. The difference of climate
was astonishing ; after we left the hills and deep snows, we
found ourselves on plains where there was no snow, and
where vegetation was sprouting.

The village of Warm Springs, or Aqua [Agua] Caliente
in their language, is situated on the eastern branch [bank] of
a creek of that name,[3] and at a distance presents to the eye

[2] Soon after leaving Conejos the party crossed Rio San Antonio, or San
Antonio cr. (the main branch of Rio Conejos), below the confluence of Los
Pinos cr., past places of both these names, and at lat. 37° N. went from the
present State of Colorado into the present Territory of New Mexico. This river
heads E. of the Tierra Amarilla, in the mountain range of which Brazos Peak,
over 11,000 feet, is a conspicuous elevation. The most notable feature of the
day is Cerro San Antonio, nearly 11,000 feet high, standing out from the range.
They skirted its E. base, among the hills of which Pike speaks, between it and
the Buffalo buttes, as the D. and R. G. R. R. now does, and where is the station
Volcano. S. W. of the peak are the Ortiz hills. Camp was set at or near the
present station Tres Piedras (Three Rocks).

[3] Or Rio Caliente, as the name of the stream is now usually rendered. This
is formed by various tributaries from the N. and N. W. (Rita Servilleta, Valle-
cita, etc.), and joins the Rio Chama from the W., about 5 m. above their
common entrance into the Rio Grande opp. San Juan. There are various other
hot or warm springs than the one at which Pike stopped, and this one is 10 m.
or so W. of the railroad station called Ojo Caliente. At various points near the
Rio Grande, at a considerable distance to Pike's left, are numerous isolated ele-

a square inclosure of mud walls, the houses forming the
walls.   They are flat on top, or with extremely little ascent
on one side, where there are spouts to carry off the water of
the melting snow and rain when it falls ; which, we were

vations, some of which are Cerros Olla, Chifle, Montoso, Cristobal, Taoses, and
Orejas.   Since Pike entered New Mexico, on crossing lat. 37° on the 28th, his
route has been practically along the W. border of Taos Co., so named from the
well-known Tañoan pueblo or town of Taos, frequently mentioned by him as
Tons, Tous, Toas, etc., as his printer happened to fancy, while his engraver
made it " Yaos" on the map of New Spain.   This is on a branch of Taos cr.;
when Pike passes its latitude to-day, he is about 20 m. W. of it.   Some places
passed along Caliente cr., to his right, are Petaca, Servilleta, and Cueva
Springs.   The name Taos has several different implications : for a river, Rio de
Taos ; for the country through which this river flows ; for a town at the junction of its principal forks, otherwise San Fernandez ; for a place 3 m. S. E. of
this, Rancho de Taos ; and for another place about the same distance N. E.,
Pueblo de Taos.   San Fernandez de Taos was a Mexican adobe town, which
had some 600–800 pop. in 1846, and was the capital of the Department of
Taos.   The old Indian pueblo of Taos, to which the insurgents had retreated
Jan. 7th, 1847, after the skirmishes of Cañada and Embuda, became noted during the war as the scene of a bloody siege and capture : see Ex. Doc. No. 41,
30th Cong., 1st Sess., pub. 1848, p. 457.

   In approaching the subject of the New Mexican Pueblo Indians it is necessary
at the outset to free the mind from the traditional error that because these live
in towns known as "pueblos," therefore they are one kind of Indians.   I shall
recur to the subject in a later connection.   Here I wish to cite an early instance
of the recognition of an all-important ethnological fact on the part of Lieutenant
James H. Simpson, U. S. T. E., whose interesting Journal of a Military Re-
connaissance from Santa Fé, New Mexico, to the Navajo country, etc., in 1849,
was published in 1850 as one of the collection of papers forming Ex. Doc.
No. 64, 31st Congr., 1st Sess., 8vo, Washington, pp. 56–168, many pll. and
maps.   He speaks on p. 57 of " the singular and, as I believe, the hitherto
unknown fact . . . that among the 10,000 (estimated) Pueblo Indians who
inhabit New Mexico, as many as *six* distinct dialects obtain, no one showing
anything more than the faintest, if any, indications of a cognate origin with the
other."   He sharply but justly brings to book the English author Ruxton, for
the grossly erroneous statement (Mex. and the R. Mts., p. 194) that " the
Indians of northern Mexico, including the Pueblos, belong to the same family—
the Apache. . . All these speak dialects of the same language, more or less
approximating to the Apache, and of all of which the idiomatic structure is the
the same."   A statement more at variance from the facts in the case could
hardly be penned.   Those Pueblo Indians whom Pike now or presently meets
represent two distinct linguistic families, the Keresan and the Tañoan ; and we
shall have several others to note in due course.   The influence of the church

informed, had been but once in two years previous to our
entering the country.   Inside of the inclosure were the different streets of houses of the same fashion, all of one story ;

upon the pueblo system has of course not escaped well-informed ethnographers,
but I suspect they have not always given it full credit for the hand it had in first
founding, then maintaining in misery, and finally fetching to grief, some of these
sorry settlements of inoffensive Indians, who had escaped the Apaches on one
side and the Navajos on the other, to be herded about some mud joss-house and
fleeced as fast as they acquired any substance worth stealing.   The business
began early, and the way of it is something of a historical curiosity.   A man
named Alessandro Farnese—the one who was pope 1534-49, and who undertook
to regulate the morals of various persons, besides Henry VIII., with indifferent
success—once made a discovery so astonishing that he must have been inspired.
Papa Paulo III. promptly published his find in a bull which was only saved
from being Irish by the fact that it was Latin : for this ethnological pronunci-
amento a todos los fieles cristianos, que las presentes letras vieren declared in
due and solemn form que los indios son hombres y capaces de sacramentos—*i. e.*,
told all the faithful to whom this exquisite tomfoolery came that Indians were
human and could be humbugged.   That was June 9th, 1537, and that settled it—
the hint was enough to set upon the savages the horde of corrupt, profligate,
and extortionate ecclesiastics who have cursed the country from that day to this.
The first business of these people was always to build a church in which to
brandish the crucifix at those who had escaped the tomahawk, and pray for the
souls of those whose superstitions were thus played upon while their property
was preyed upon—for churches cannot be built and priests supported unless
somebody sweats for it.   I hardly think that Indians thus huddled around a
church, in abject terror alike of their natural and their supernatural enemies,
outside and inside the pueblo, were any better off for self-defense than they
would have been had they been left to their natural resources—though many
have so fancied ; for the numerical strength of such an aggregation would have
been just as effective without that edifice, and tame Indians are no match for
wild ones.   The process of converting an Indian to Christianity simply mixes
his metaphors and muddles his mind, by substituting for the superstitions he
thinks he understands other mysteries which the priests themselves declare to be
incomprehensible.   The advantage of this to the Indian is not easily discerned,
and some of its disadvantages are obvious.   For example, the priests are
responsible for a considerable amount of fornication and fœticide—I do not
mean so much by their personal habits as by their keeping so many of their
parishioners too poor to pay for marriages and baptisms.   By the year 1680, the
papal plan and the church method had worked so well that the converted Indians
undertook to prove themselves men, capable of the very real sacrament of manhood ; for they revolted against the intolerable yoke, killed a great many of
their oppressors, and drove these ill-omened birds of prey from their repast for
a while.

the doors were narrow, the windows small, and in one or two houses there were talc lights [window-panes of that material].   This village had a mill near it, situated on the little creek, which made very good flour.   The population consisted of civilized Indians, but much mixed blood.

Here we had a dance which is called the fandango ; but there was one which was copied from the Mexicans, is now danced in the first societies of New Spain, and has even been introduced at the court of Madrid.

This village may contain 500 souls.   The greatest natural curiosity is the warm springs, which are two in number, about 10 yards apart, each affording sufficient water for a mill-seat.   They appeared to be impregnated with copper, and were more than 33° above blood heat.   From this village the Tetaus drove off 2,000 horses at one time, when at war with the Spaniards.

Mar. 2d.   We marched late, and passed several little mud-walled villages and settlements, all of which had round mud towers of the ancient shape and construction, to defend the inhabitants from the intrusions of the savages.   I was this day shown the ruins of several old villages which had been taken and destroyed by the Tetaus.   We were frequently stopped by the women, who invited us into their houses to eat; and in every place where we halted a moment there was a contest who should be our hosts.   My poor lads who had been frozen were conducted home by old men, who would cause their daughters to dress their feet, provide their victuals and drink, and at night give them the best bed in the house.   In short, all their conduct brought to my recollection the hospitality of the ancient patriarchs, and caused me to sigh with regret at the corruption of that noble principle by the polish of modern ages.

We descended the creek of Aqua Caliente about 12 miles, where it joined the river of Conejos [Rio Chama[4]] from the

---

[4] Pike joins Rio Caliente with the Chama (Conejos in the text, by error) too near Ojo Caliente and too far from San Juan, but the sum of his figures is about right.   Rio Caliente does not seem to be as well populated now as it was in his

west. This river was about 30 yards wide, and was settled
for 12 miles above its junction with the Aqua Caliente, as
the latter was in its whole course from the village of that
name.   From where they form a junction it was about 15
miles to the Rio del Norte, on the eastern branch [read
bank] of which was situated the village of St. John's [San
Juan], which was the residence of the president priest of
the province, who had resided in it 40 years.

The house-tops of the village of St. John's were crowded,
as well as the streets, when we entered, and at the door of
the public quarters we were met by the president priest.
When my companion, who commanded the escort, received
him in a street and embraced him, all the poor creatures
who stood round strove to kiss the ring or hand of the holy
father; for myself, I saluted him in the usual style. My
men were conducted into the quarters, and I went to the
house of the priest, where we were treated with politeness.
He offered us coffee, chocolate, or whatever we thought
proper, and desired me to consider myself at home in his
house.

As I was going, some time after, to the quarters of my
men, I was addressed at the door by a man in broken English: "My friend, I am very sorry to see you here; we are
all prisoners in this country and can never return; I have
been a prisoner for nearly three years, and cannot get out."
I replied: "that as for his being a prisoner, it must be for
some crime; that with respect to myself I felt no apprehension; and requested him to speak French, as I could hardly
understand his English."   He began to demand of me so
many different questions on the mode of my getting into

day; Los Gallegos is a present place on this stream. The confluence of the
two is at the point of a butte, with the Black mesa immediately to the left or
E.; some of the present places thence to the Rio Grande are Cuchilla, Chili,
and San José, all on the W. side of Rio Chama, off his route, and not noted by
him; the site of Chama itself was on the other side, near the mouth. The
St. John's of the text, charted "Sⁿ Juan 1000," is the Tañoan pueblo San Juan,
pop. now 400. He crosses to this place on the E. side of the Rio Grande,
where there was a ford or ferry; the railroad crosses there now, at Española.

the country, my intention, etc., that by the time I arrived in the room of my men, I was perfectly satisfied of his having been ordered by some person to endeavor to obtain some confession or acknowledgment of sinister designs in my having appeared on the frontiers, and some confidential communications which might implicate me. As he had been rather insolent in his inquiries, I ordered my men to shut and fasten the door. I then told him that I believed him to be an emissary sent on purpose by the governor, or some person, to endeavor to betray me; that all men of that description were scoundrels, and never should escape punishment, whilst I possessed the power to chastise them— immediately ordering my men to seize him, and cautioning him, at the same time, that, if he cried out, or made the least resistance, I would be obliged to make use of the saber which I had in my hand. On this he was so much alarmed, that he begged me for God's sake not to injure him; he also said that he had been ordered by the government to meet me, and endeavor to trace out what and who I was, and what were my designs, by endeavoring to produce a confidence in him, by his exclaiming against the Spaniards and complaining of the tyranny which they had exercised toward him. After this confession, I ordered my men to release him, and told him that I looked upon him as too contemptible for further notice; but that he might tell the governor, the next time he employed emissaries, to choose those of more abilities and sense; and that I questioned if his Excellency would find the sifting of us an easy task.

This man's name was Baptiste Lalande; [5] he had come

---

[5] I have not succeeded in identifying Baptiste Lalande. One Alexis Lalande (his X mark) appears among signers of a document executed at St. Louis, Oct. 30th, 1819; and on Sept. 16th, 1809, the same was one of a jury that convicted John Long of murdering one George Gordon the previous June 26th; and Alexis subsequently swore he neither spoke nor knew English. The William Morrison of the same paragraph is easily discovered. He was the oldest one of several brothers who came from Doylestown, Bucks Co., Pa.; had been associated with his uncle, Guy Bryan, in business in Philada.; came to Kaskaskia about 1785, and became prominent as a merchant there, in Cahokia, and

from the Illinois to the Pawnees, to trade with goods furnished him by William Morrison, a gentleman of the Illinois, and thence to New Mexico with the goods which he
had procured, and established himself ; he was the same man
on whom Robinson had a claim. He returned into the
priest's house with me, and, instead of making any com-
plaint, he in reply to their inquiries of who I was, etc., informed them that when he left Louisiana I was governor of
the Illinois. This I presume he took for granted from my
having commanded for some time the post of Kaskaskias,
the first military post the United States had established in
that country since the peace ; however, the report served
to add to the respect with which my companion and host
treated me.

I had at this place the first good meal, wine, etc., which, with
the heat of the house, and perhaps rather an immoderate use
of the refreshments allowed me, produced an attack of something like cholera morbus, which alarmed me considerably,
and made me determine to be more abstemious in future.

This father was a great naturalist, or rather florist ; he had
large collections of flowers, plants, etc., and several works
on his favorite studies, the margins and bottoms of which
were filled with his notes in the Castilian language. As I
neither had a natural turn for botany sufficient to induce
me to puzzle my head much with the Latin, nor understood
Castilian, I enjoyed but little of the lectures which he continued to give me for nearly two hours on those subjects ;
but, by the exercise of a small degree of patience, I entirely
acquired the esteem of this worthy father, he calling me
his son, and lamenting extremely that my faith had not
made me one of the holy Catholic church.

The father, being informed that I had some astronomical
instruments with me, expressed a desire to see them. All
that I had here was my sextant and a large glass which

in St. Louis ; married (1) a lady of Illinois ; (2) in 1813, a daughter of General
Daniel Bissell, U. S. A.; died 1837, at Kaskaskia ; was grandfather of Hon.
William R. Morrison. (Billon's Annals, 1804–1821, pub. 1888, p. 219.)

magnified considerably, calculated for the day or night;
the remainder of my instruments being with my sergeant
and party. On his examining the sextant, and my showing him the effect of it in the reflection of the sun, he,
as well as hundreds who surrounded us, appeared more surprised at the effect of the instrument than any nation of
savages I was ever among. Here an idea struck me as
extraordinary—how a man who appeared to be a perfect
master of the ancient languages, a botanist, mineralogist,
and chemist, should be so ignorant of the powers of reflection and the first principles of mathematics. But my friend
explained that enigma, by informing me of the care the
Spanish government took to prevent any branch of science
from being made a pursuit, which would have a tendency
to extend the views of the subjects of the provinces to the
geography of their country, or any other subject which
would bring to view a comparison of their local advantages
and situations with other countries.[6]

St. John's was inclosed with a mud wall, and probably
contained 1,000 souls; its population consisted principally
of civilized Indians, as indeed does that of all the villages
of New Mexico, the whites not forming one-twentieth part
of the inhabitants.

Mar. 3d.[7] We marched after breakfast, B. Lalande ac-

[6] In the orig. ed. this paragraph appears as Doc. No. 7, p. 69, of the App. to
Pt. 3, to which Pike refers the reader by a footnote. But as it is out of place
there, and also so short, I simply run it into the present and proper context.

[7] The defective itinerary of Mar. 3d requires attention. We see that Pike
crossed the river to San Juan, whence he goes down the E. side to Santa Fé.
But first for the places he marks on the W. side within the distance to Santa
Fé, and which are: 1. Abicu, pop. 500; 2. Cia, pop. 450; and 3. Gomez, pop.
500. 1. Abicu is marked as if it stood near the mouth of Rio Chama, in the
vicinity of present San Antonio and San José; but its exact location is not difficult to discover. For this is the town now called Abiquiu, 20 m. by the road
up the Rio Chama from the Rio Grande, on the S. side of the Chama, at the
mouth of Frijoles (Beans) cr. It is on the long and well-known trail which led
up the valley of the Chama and so on over the mountains en route to Los
Angeles, Cal. 2. Cia or Sia is a Keresan pueblo, with a present pop. of about
100. 3. Gomez is the Tañoan pueblo Jemez, misplaced too near the Rio Grande:

companying us, and in about six miles came to a village
[Santa Cruz], where I suppose there were more than 2,000
souls. Here we halted at the house of a priest, who, understanding that I would not kiss his hand, would not present
it to me. The conduct and behavior of a young priest
who came in was such as in our country would have been
amply sufficient forever to have banished him from the
clerical association—strutting about with a dirk in his boot,

see note beyond for this and for Cia. The Jemez trail from San Ildefonso
passes the ruins of an old pueblo (called by the Spanish equivalent Pueblo
Viejo), on the edge of the mesa, say 1½ m. W. of the Rio Grande and 5 m.
S. W. of San Ildefonso. There is also within this distance the Tañoan pueblo
of Santa Clara, with a present pop. of over 200, on the W. side of the Rio
Grande, a mile below the mouth of Santa Clara cr. From San Juan to Santa
Fé there are or were two roads ; a lower, which hugs the Rio Grande for some
distance before it turns away from the river, and an upper, more direct course,
probably that which Pike took. In either case, he crossed the two small
streams or arroyos now known as Cañada and Nambe. Along his route he
passed three villages, which are marked on the map and mentioned without
name in the text. 1. The first of these, Santa Cruz, 5 or 6 m. from San Juan,
is marked on the map " Village 1200 "; in 1846 it had only 300 or 400. It is
situated on the Cañada near its mouth ; higher up on the same are the Chimayo
settlements and Potrero. 2. The next, 7¼ m. further, mapped as " Village
600," is Pojoaque or Pojuaque, a Tañoan pueblo situated about 6 m. up Nambe
cr. At the mouth of this stream stood and stands another Tañoan pueblo, San
Ildefonso ; while Nambe, yet another village of the same family, was located
on the same creek about 3 m. above Pojoaque. These have all declined during
the century, the Indian pop. of Pojoaque being lately given as 20, that of San
Ildefonso 148, that of Nambe 79. 3. The next village, " 17 m." further, marked
on the map " Village 600," is Tesuque (Tesugue, Zesuqua, etc.), likewise a
Tañoan pueblo, now of less than 100 Indians. There appear to have been two
establishments of this name, 3 or 4 m. apart, both on a branch of Nambe cr.;
the furthest on, falling in best with Pike's 17 m. from Pojoaque, is only some
6 m. from Santa Fé. Between Pojoaque and Tesuque Pike passed by
Cuyamanque or Cuyamunge : and he entered Santa Fé from the N., by the
site of old Fort Marcy.

It should be particularly observed in this place that Pike has *two* maps of this
part of the Rio Grande, which are discrepant in several material respects. One
is his Louisiana map, which he runs down to take in the Rio Grande to Santa
Fé. On this his trail is dotted as if it were the lower one, hugging the Rio
Grande from Santa Cruz past Santa Clara (and Polvaredo) to San Ildefonso,
before it turned off to Santa Fé, and with the above three villages all on his
left as he passed ; the above village of Abicu is lettered Abricu, and a certain

a cane in his hand, whispering to one girl, chucking another under the chin, going out with a third, etc.

From this village [Santa Cruz] to another small village [Pojoaque], of 500 inhabitants, is seven miles. At each of those villages is a small stream, sufficient for the purpose of watering their fields. At the father's house we took coffee. From this village [Pojoaque] it was 17 miles to another [Tesuque], of 400 civilized Indians. Here we changed horses and prepared for entering the capital [Santa Fé[8]],

village of " Pino " is set at the mouth of Rio Santa Fé. I have here gone by his New Spain map, which may be presumed to be his best delineation of Rio Grande country, and which certainly fits in best with the text which we here follow.

To finish reckoning the towns Pike maps north of Santa Fé, we must note the following : 1. " Enbudo 500 " on both maps. 2. " Tranpa 450 " on one map, and " Tramha 450 " on the other. 3. " Pecucio 500 " on one map, and " Pecucis 500 " on the other. These places all lie off to the N. E., in the direction of Taos. 1. Embudo or Embuda is a town on a creek of the same name, which makes into the Rio Grande from the E., about 25 m. by the road from San Juan. The location is a couple of miles above the mouth of the creek, which falls into the Rio Grande at a place called Rinconada on account of its cornered or shut-in site among the surrounding mesas. It is near the scene of an engagement in Jan., 1847, when Captain John H. K. Burgwin of the 1st U. S. Dragoons defeated the insurgents ; he died Feb. 7th of wounds received Feb. 4th in the assault on Taos. 2. Trampas is a town on the creek of that name, a main tributary of the Embudo, 8 or 10 m. above the town of Embudo. You pass Trampas about halfway on the main upper road from Santa Fé to Taos, about 7 m. N. of Truchas. 3. Picuris is an old Tañoan pueblo, on another branch of this same Embudo cr., with a present pop. of 100.

All the foregoing places are under the shadow of the lofty mountains to the E., whence the several streams named also make down into the Rio Grande valley. Some of their peaks are : Lake, 12,400 feet ; Baldy, 12,600 feet ; the Cone, 12,700 feet ; Truches, 13,100 feet ; and the more isolated " U. S." mountain, 10,700 feet. On the other side of this range are the headwaters of Rio Cañada—that great fork of the Arkansaw better known as the " Canadian " r., without the *tilde :* see note [17], p. 558.

[8] Santa Fé is not " on the Rio Grande," as often loosely said, but at least 20 m. (direct) E. of that river, and considerably further than this up from the mouth of the small stream on which it is situated, in a rather out-of-the-way place. This creek, Rio de Santa Fé, or Rio Chacito, comes down from the lofty Santa Fé mts. under which the town nestles, and runs with a general S. W. course into the Rio Grande between the town of Peña Blanca and the old pueblo of Cochiti—places 3 m. apart. Cochiti is a Keresan pueblo on the W.

which we came in sight of in the evening. It is situated along the banks of a small [Santa Fé] creek, which comes down from the mountains, and runs west to the Rio del Norte. The length of the capital on the creek may be estimated at one mile; it is but three streets in width.

Its appearance from a distance struck my mind with the same effect as a fleet of the flat-bottomed boats which are seen in the spring and fall seasons, descending the Ohio river. There are two churches, the magnificence of whose steeples form a striking contrast to the miserable appearance of the houses.[9] On the north side of the town is the square of soldiers' houses, equal to 120 or 140 on each flank. The public square is in the center of the town; on the north side of it is situated the palace, as they term it, or government house, with the quarters for guards, etc. The

bank of the Rio Grande; present pop. perhaps 250. Peña Blanca, often called Piña Blanca, on the E. bank, is a place where the Rio Grande can be forded, to take the old road from Santa Fé to Fort Wingate.

Santa Fé was first entered and occupied by the Army of the West under General Stephen Watts Kearny, Aug. 18th, 1846—his cowardly Excellency Don Manuel Armijo having blustered and promptly evacuated the place on the approach of our forces. The site of Fort Marcy was selected by Lieutenants W. H. Emory and J. F. Gilmer, in a commanding position 600 yards from the plaza of the town, and the work began on the 23d. On Sept. 22d General Kearny issued his manifesto for the government of New Mexico, under the authority of the President of the United States; appointing as governor Charles Bent (soon afterward cruelly massacred at Taos), and as secretary Donaciano Vigil; other territorial officers appointed were Richard Dallum, Francis P. Blair, Charles Blummer, Eugene Lertensdorfer, Joab Houghton, Antonio José Otero, and Carl Bavbien—the last three as judges of the supreme court. A copy of the original document, in Spanish, is given in Lieutenant J. W. Abert's report Ex. Doc. No. 41, 30th Cong., 1st Sess., pub. 1848, p. 453. The population of Santa Fé at that time was somewhere about 3,000; it is now only a little over 6,000. It was probably the site of a pueblo before 1500; but the present town has no authentic history back of 1608, when it was founded by Juan de Oñate as a capital or seat of government. The town may boast an unbroken record as such from that day to this, in spite of changing hands several times.

[9] Lieutenant J. W. Abert supposes that these were those long known as the parroquia or parish church, and the capilla de los soldados or military chapel: Ex. Doc. No. 41, 30th Cong., 1st Sess., pub. 1848, p. 454, where an account of them and services held in them, as these were in 1846, may be read. A plate shows the parish church, with "Fort Marez" (Marcy) in the distance.

other side of the square is occupied by the clergy and public officers. In general the houses have a shed before the front, some of which have a flooring of brick; the consequence is that the streets are very narrow, say in general 25 feet. The supposed population is 4,500 souls. On our entering the town the crowd was great, and followed us to the government house. When we dismounted we were ushered in through various rooms, the floors of which were covered with skins of buffalo, bear, or some other animal. We waited in a chamber for some time, until his Excellency appeared, when we rose, and the following conversation took place in French :

Governor. Do you speak French ?

Pike. Yes, sir.

Governor. You come to reconnoiter our country, do you?

Pike. I marched to reconnoiter our own.

Governor. In what character are you ?

Pike. In my proper character, an officer of the United States army.

Governor. And this Robinson—is he attached to your party?

Pike. No.

Governor. Do you know him?

Pike. Yes; he is from St. Louis. (I understood the doctor had been sent 45 leagues from Santa Fe, under a strong guard. The haughty and unfriendly reception of the governor induced me to believe war must have been declared, and that if it were known Dr. Robinson had accompanied me, he would be treated with great severity. I was correct in saying he was not attached to my party, for he was only a volunteer, who could not properly be said to be one of my command.)

Governor. How many men have you ?

Pike. Fifteen.

Governor. And this Robinson makes sixteen ?

Pike. I have already told your Excellency that he does not belong to my party, and shall answer no more interrogatories on that subject.

Governor. When did you leave St. Louis?

Pike. July 15th.

Governor. I think you marched in June.

Pike. No, sir!

Governor. Well! Return with Mr. Bartholomew to his house; come here again at seven o'clock, and bring your papers.

On which we returned to the house of my friend Bartholomew, who seemed much hurt at the interview.

At the door of the government house, I met the old Frenchman to whom I had given the scrap of paper on the 27th of February. He had left us in the morning, and, as I suppose, hurried in to make his report, and I presume had presented this paper to his Excellency. I demanded, with a look of contempt, if he had made his report? To which he made reply in a humble tone, and began to excuse himself; but I did not wait to hear his excuses. At the hour appointed we returned, when the governor demanded my papers. I told him that I understood my trunk had been taken possession of by his guard. He expressed surprise, immediately ordered it in, and also sent for one Solomon Colly, formerly a sergeant in our army, and one of the unfortunate company of [Captain Philip] Nolan. We were seated, when he ordered Colly to demand my name, to which I replied. He then demanded in what province I was born. I answered in English, and then addressed his Excellency in French, and told him that I did not think it necessary to enter into such a catechising; that if he would be at the pains of reading my commission from the United States, and my orders from my general, it would be all that I presumed would be necessary to convince his Excellency that I came with no hostile intentions toward the Spanish government; that, on the contrary, I had express instructions to guard against giving them offense or alarm; and that his Excellency would be convinced that myself and party were rather to be considered objects on which the so much celebrated generosity of the Spanish nation might be exercised, than proper subjects to occasion the opposite sentiments.

He then requested to see my commission and orders, which I read to him in French ; on which he got up and gave me his hand, for the first time, and said he was happy to be acquainted with me as a man of honor and a gentleman ; that I could retire this evening and take my trunk with me ; and that on the morrow he would make further arrangements.

Mar. 4th. I was desired by the governor to bring up my trunk, in order that he might make some observations on my route, etc. When he ordered me to take my trunk over night, I had conceived that the examination of papers was over. As many of my documents were intrusted to the care of my men, and I found that the inhabitants were treating the men with liquor, I was fearful they would become intoxicated, and through inadvertency betray or discover the papers. I had therefore obtained several of them and put them in the trunk, when an officer arrived for myself and it, and I had no opportunity of taking them out again before I was taken up to the palace. I discovered instantly that I had been deceived, but it was too late to remedy the evil.

After examining the contents of my trunk, he informed me that I must, with my troops, go to Chihuahua, province of Biscay, to appear before the commandant-general. He added : " You have the key of your trunk in your own possession ; the trunk will be put under charge of the officer who commands your escort." The following conversation then took place :

Pike. If we go to Chihuahua we must be considered as prisoners of war ?

Governor. By no means.

Pike. You have already disarmed my men without my knowledge ; are their arms to be returned or not ?

Governor. They can receive them any moment.

Pike. But, sir, I cannot consent to be led three or four

hundred leagues out of my route, without its being by force of arms.

Governor. I know you do not go voluntarily; but I will give you a certificate from under my hand of my having obliged you to march.

Pike. I will address you a letter on the subject.[10]

Governor. You will dine with me to-day, and march afterward to a village about six miles distant, escorted by Captain Anthony D'Almansa, with a detachment of dragoons, who will accompany you to where the remainder of your escort is now waiting for you, under the command of the officer [Don Facundo Malgares] who commanded the expedition to the Pawnees.

Pike. I would not wish to be impertinent in my observations to your Excellency; but pray, sir! do you not think it was a greater infringement of our territory to send 600 miles in the Pawnees', than for me with our small party to come on the frontiers of yours with an intent to descend Red river?

Governor. I do not understand you.

Pike. No, sir! any further explanation is unnecessary.

I then returned to the house of my friend Bartholomew and wrote my letter to his Excellency, which I had not finished before we were hurried to dinner.

In the morning I received from the governor, by the hands of his private secretary, $21, notifying to me that it was the amount of the king's allowance for my party to Chihuahua, and that it would be charged to me on account of my subsistence. From this I clearly understood that it was calculated that the expenses of the party to Chihuahua would be defrayed by the United States. I also received by the same hands, from his Excellency, a shirt and neck-cloth, with his compliments, wishing me to accept of them, " as they had been made in Spain by his sister and never

[10] The governor's certificate and Pike's remonstrance, here in mention, were given in the App. to Pt. 3, of which they formed Docs. Nos. 9 and 8, and will be found in due course, beyond.

worn by any person." For this I returned him my sincere acknowledgments; and it may not be deemed irrelevant if I explain at this period the miserable appearance we made, and the situation we were in, with the causes of it.

When we left our interpreter and one man [Vasquez and Smith] on the Arkansaw, we were obliged to carry all our baggage on our backs; consequently, that which was the most useful was preferred to the few ornamental parts of dress we possessed. The ammunition claimed our first care; tools were secondary; leather, leggings, boots, and mockinsons were the next in consideration. Consequently, I left all my uniform, clothing, trunks, etc., as did the men, except what they had on their backs; conceiving that which would secure the feet and legs from the cold to be preferable to any less indispensable portion of our dress. Thus, when we presented ourselves at Santa Fe, I was dressed in a pair of blue trousers, mockinsons, blanket coat, and a cap made of scarlet cloth lined with fox-skin; my poor fellows were in leggings, breech cloths and leather coats, and there was not a hat in the whole party. This appearance was extremely mortifying to us all, especially as soldiers; although some of the officers used frequently to observe to me, that "worth made the man," etc., with a variety of adages to the same amount. Yet the first impression made on the ignorant is hard to eradicate; and a greater proof cannot be given of the ignorance of the common people, than their asking if we lived in houses, or in camps like the Indians, and if we wore hats in our country. Those observations are sufficient to show the impression our uncouth appearance made amongst them.

The dinner at the governor's was rather splendid, having a variety of dishes and wines of the southern provinces; and when his Excellency was a little warmed with the influence of cheering liquor, he became very sociable. He informed me that there existed a serious difficulty between the commandant-general of the internal provinces and the Marquis Caso Calvo, who had given permission to Mr. [William] Dunbar to explore the Ouchata [Washita], contrary to the general principles of their government; in consequence of which the former had made representations against the latter to the court of Madrid. After dinner his Excellency ordered his coach; Captain D'Almansa, Bartholomew, and myself entered with him, and he drove out three miles. He was drawn by six mules and attended by a guard of cavalry. When we parted his adieu was, " remember Allencaster, in peace or war."

I left a note for my sergeant, with instructions to keep up good discipline and not be alarmed or discouraged. As I was about leaving the public square, poor Colly, the American prisoner, came up with tears in his eyes, and hoped I would not forget him when I arrived in the United States.

After we left the governor we rode on about three miles to a defile, where we halted for the troops. I soon found that the old soldier who accompanied us and commanded our escort was fond of a drop of the cheering liquor, as his boy carried a bottle in his cochmelies [read cojinillos], a small leather case attached to the saddle for the purpose of carrying small articles.[11] We were accompanied by my friend Bartholomew. We ascended a hill and galloped on until about ten o'clock; it was snowing hard all the time. Then we came to a precipice, which we descended with great difficulty, from the obscurity of the night, to the small village,[12] where we put up in the quarters of the priest, he being absent.

[11] Pike has the thing all right, but under a curious name I never saw elsewhere, and might not have recognized, had I not happened to hear *cojinillo* myself in New Mexico. This word is probably provincial or dialectal, as it is not found in ordinary Sp. dictionaries ; in form it is a diminutive of *cojin*, name of a certain saddle-pad or cushion, precisely equivalent to E. " pillion." It turns up now and then in books about Mexico, as for example : " The *corazas* [covers] of travelling saddles are also provided with several pockets called *coginillos*—a most excellent contrivance for carrying a lunch or a bottle, or anything to which convenient access may be desired," Gregg, Comm. Pra., I. 1844, p. 214.

[12] Marked " Vitior 200 " on Pike's map. I do not recognize this name, but it is easy to pick out Pike's road to San Domingo, which he reaches to-morrow, and locate his Vitior at or within a mile of a place on the Rio Santa Fé now

After supper, Captain D'Almansa related to me that he had served his Catholic majesty 40 years to arrive at the rank he then held, which was that of a first lieutenant in the line and a captain by brevet, whilst he had seen various young Europeans promoted over his head. After the old man had taken his *quantum sufficit* and gone to sleep, my friend and myself sat up for some hours, he explaining to me their situation, the great desire they felt for a change of affairs and an open trade with the United States. I pointed out to him with chalk on the floor the geographical connection and route from North Mexico and Louisiana, and finally gave him a certificate addressed to the citizens of the United States, stating his friendly disposition and his being a man of influence. This paper he seemed to estimate as a very valuable acquisition, as he was decidedly of opinion we would invade that country the ensuing spring ; and not all my assurances to the contrary could eradicate that idea.

Mar. 5th. As it snowed very hard in the morning, we did not march until eleven o'clock. In the meantime, Bartholomew and myself paid a visit to an old invalid Spaniard, who received us in the most hospitable manner, giving us chocolate, etc. He made many inquiries as to our government and religion, and of [Bartholomew], who did not fail to give them the brightest coloring ; he being enthusiastic in their favor from his many conversations with me, and drawing comparisons with his own country. What appeared to the old veteran most extraordinary was that we ever changed

called La Bajada, which is 7¾ m. from San Domingo. In starting from Santa Fé for the Rio Grande at this point, you do not follow down the creek (Rio de Santa Fé or Rio Chacito), but bear away from it on higher ground between it and Arroyo Hondo, pass a little place called Agua Fria, and then have a choice of two roads. One of these bears off more to the left, and strikes the creek at the hamlet of Cieneguilla, whence you follow the creek in the cañon to La Bajada ; but the straighter road keeps on S. W., crosses the creek higher up, cuts across the mesa south of Tetilla Peak, and suddenly pitches down into the creek at the mouth of the cañon, where La Bajada is situated. This is what I suppose Pike means by saying he ascended a hill and then descended a precipice. If he went that way, he rode 15 m. from Santa Fé to " Vitior " or La Bajada. (See Vitior in Index.)

our president. I was obliged to draw his powers on a nearer affinity with those of a monarch than they really are, in order that they might comprehend his station and that there was a perfect freedom of conscience permitted in our country. He, however, expressed his warm approbation of the measure. In the priest's house at which we put up were two orphan girls, who were adopted by him in their infancy and at this time constituted his whole family.

I bid adieu to my friend Bartholomew, and could not avoid shedding tears ; he embraced me and all my men.

We arrived at the village of St. Domingo [18] at two o'clock. It is, as I supposed, nine miles [to this place, which is situated] on the east side of the Rio del Norte, and is a large village, the population being about 1,000 natives, generally governed by its own chief. The chiefs of the villages were distinguished by a cane with a silver head and black tassel. On our arrival at the public house Captain D'Almansa was waited on by the governor, cap in hand, to receive his orders

[18] Present Santo Domingo, or San Domingo, is at the mouth of Galisteo cr., with the pueblo immediately below it, on the E. bank of the Rio Grande, 4 or 5 m. below Peña Blanca. Pike charts it by name, and lays down this creek. The plate opp. p. 462 of Lieutenant Abert's report shows the pueblo as it was in 1846. Part of the road from Santa Fé to San Domingo was bad, on account of the rocks in the cañon of the little stream, and the sandy dunes near the pueblo. On getting out of the cañon onto the plain, Pike had on his left the Sandia range, while ahead, but somewhat to the right, rose the Jemez mts. The Galisteo was probably quite dry. There were no trees to be seen till the cottonwood fringe of the Rio Grande came into view. The pueblo did not vary much for a century. It had about 800 pop. when I passed through in 1864 ; a very recent census yielded 690. As Pike says, these Indians are " of the nation of Keres," i. e., of the Keresan family. Had he taken the ford across the Rio Grande, which was used here at times when the water was not more than three or four feet deep, though 300 yards wide, and gone westward about 26 m. to the Rio Jemez, he would have come upon the Tañoan town of Jemez, a dead-alive little place, which has held its population of 400 or 500 for many generations, and long sustained its old adobe church. Twelve miles above Jemez, at a place on the river called Ojos Calientes from its hot springs, were and may still be seen the ruins of another church, a view of which, as they appeared in 1849, is given on pl. 15 of Simpson's report already cited. Jemez is the place Pike means by the " Gomez 300 " which he charts ; only it is located too near the Rio Grande on his map. (See Santo Domingo in Index.)

as to furnishing our quarters and ourselves with wood, water, provisions, etc. The house itself contained nothing but bare walls and small grated windows, which brought to my recollection the representations of the Spanish inhabitants given by Dr. [John] Moore [the Scottish writer, 1730–1802], in his travels through Spain, Italy, etc. This village, as well as those of St. Philip's and St. Bartholomew, [San Felipe and San Bartolomé] is of the nation of Keres [or Queres] many of whom do not yet speak good Spanish.

After we had refreshed ourselves a little, the captain sent for the keys of the church; and when we entered it, I was much astonished to find, inclosed in mud-brick walls, many rich paintings, and the saint (Domingo) as large as life, elegantly ornamented with gold and silver. The captain made a slight inclination of the head, and intimated to me that this was the patron of the village. We then ascended into the gallery, where the choir are generally placed. In an outside hall was placed another image of the saint, less richly ornamented, where the populace repaired daily and knelt to return thanks for benefactions received, or to ask new favors. Many young girls, indeed, chose the time of our visit to be on their knees before the holy patron. From the flat roof of the church we had a delightful view of the village; the Rio del Norte [and Jemez mountains] on the west; the mountains of St. Dies [San Diaz, *i. e.*, Sandia] to the south; the valley round the town, on which were numerous herds of goats, sheep, and asses—upon the whole, this was one of the handsomest views in New Mexico.

Mar. 6th. Marched down the Rio del Norte on the east side. Snow one foot deep. Passed large flocks of goats. At [opposite] the village of St. Philip's [San Felipe [14]] we

[14] Marked "Sⁿ. Philip de queres 1000" on the map, on the W. side of the Rio Grande. This is the pueblo of San Felipe, situated 7 m. S. of San Domingo, opp. the mouth of Tuerto cr., which falls in from the E., a little below the gulch or ravine called Arroyo del Espinazo. The town of Covero, or Cubero, is 5 m. above, on the same (W.) side of the Rio Grande. The large stream which Pike lays down on that side, just below his St. Philip's, is the Rio Jemez, which falls in between Algodones and Bernalillo. The word "queres" of the map is

crossed [the Rio Grande to the town over] a bridge of eight
arches, constructed as follows: the pillars made of neat
woodwork, something similar to a crate, and in the form of
a keel-boat, the sharp end or bow to the current; this crate
or butment was filled with stone, in which the river lodged
sand, clay, etc., until it had become of a tolerably firm con-
sistency. On the top of the pillars were laid pine logs,
lengthways, squared on two sides; being joined pretty
close, these made a tolerable bridge for horses, but would
not have been very safe for carriages, as there were no
hand-rails.

On our arrival at the house of the father, we were received
in a very polite and friendly manner; and before my departure we seemed to have been friends for years past. During our dinner, at which we had a variety of wines, we were
entertained with music, composed of bass drums, French
horns, violins, and cymbals. We likewise entered into a
long and candid conversation as to the Creoles, wherein he
spared neither the government nor its administrators. As
to government and religion, Father Rubi displayed a liberality of opinion and a fund of knowledge which astonished
me. He showed me a statistical table on which he had, in
a regular manner, taken the whole province of New Mexico

the same as Keres of the above text; *i. e.*, San Felipe is a town of the Keresan
nation. The place is on the W. side of the Rio Grande, which here straitens
to 100 yards or so, about 6 m. above Algodones. Pike's town was no doubt
the *present* San Felipe—the one at the foot of the mesa, and not that commonly
called old San Felipe, about a mile off, upon the edge of the mesa; for this
was in ruins half a century if not a century ago, and the pueblos are all slow to
change, either for better or worse. It has taken nearly 100 years to reduce San
Felipe from the population which Pike estimated at 1000 to the 550 of a very
recent census. It has been more Mexicanized than some of the other Indian
towns. Lieutenant Abert, speaking of the bridge which Pike mentions, says
that when he was there, Oct. 10th, 1846, it had been entirely swept away, and
the people had to ford the Rio Grande. The plate opp. p. 461 of his report
shows some of them in the act. Another view of San Felipe is given in the
same volume. opp. p. 39, in the report of Lieutenant W. H. Emory, who says
that "the hardships, trials, and perseverance of the gallant Pike" came forcibly
to his mind when he first caught sight of the Rio Grande, Sept. 2d, 1846, at
San Domingo, whose population he judged to be about 600.

by villages, beginning at Tous [Taos], on the northwest, and ending with Valencia on the south, giving their latitude, longitude, and population, whether natives or Spaniards, civilized or barbarous, Christians or pagans, numbers, names of the nations, when converted, how governed, military force, clergy, salary, etc.—in short, a complete geographical, statistical, and historical sketch of the province. Of this I wished to obtain a copy, but perceived that the captain was somewhat surprised at its having been shown to me. When we parted, we promised to write to each other, which I performed from Chihuahua.

Here was an old Indian who was extremely inquisitive to know if we were Spaniards; to which an old gentleman called Don Francisco, who appeared to be an inmate of Father Rubi's, replied in the affirmative. "But," said the Indian, "they do not speak Castillian." "True," replied the other; "but you are an Indian of the nation of Keres, are you not?" "Yes." "Well, the Utahs are Indians also?" "Yes." "But still you do not understand them, they speaking a different language." "True," replied the Indian. "Well," said the old gentleman, "those strangers are likewise Spaniards, but do not speak the same language with us." This reasoning seemed to satisfy the poor savage; and I could not but smile at the ingenuity displayed to make him believe there was no other nation of whites but the Spaniards.

Whilst at dinner, Father Rubi was informed that one of his parishioners was at the point of death, and wished his attendance to receive his confession.

We took our departure, but were shortly after overtaken by our friend, who, after giving me another hearty shake of the hand, left us. Crossed the river and passed two small hamlets and houses on the road to the village of St. Dies,[15]

---

[15] Marked "S Dies 500" on the map, on the E. side of the Rio Grande, to which Pike recrossed from San Felipe. The Spanish form would be San Diaz, but the pueblo is best known as Sandia or Zandia, a name also applied to the great mountain which rises on the E. As a Spanish word, *sandia* means

opposite the mountain of the same name, where we were received in a house of Father Rubi, this making part of his domains.

Mar. 7th. Marched at nine o'clock through a country better cultivated and inhabited than any I had yet seen. Arrived at Albuquerque,[16] a village on the east side of the Rio del Norte. We were received by Father Ambrosio Guerra in a very flattering manner, and led into his hall. From thence, after taking some refreshments, we went into

"watermelon," and appeared in print as the name of this village in 1626. The aboriginal name of the pueblo is Nafiap, and its mission name was Nuestra Señora de los Dolores de Sandia. This is a Tañoan town, with a present population of about 150. The situation is 12 m. above Albuquerque. Pike speaks of two small hamlets he passed to reach St. Dies. In 1864, when I passed over the road, there was a mean place called Algodones, of 30 or 40 houses and some 200 or 300 people, and 6 m. below this was a rather better one named Bernalillo. This is doubtless what Pike charts as "S Bernilla 500." Bernalillo is present name of a station of the A., T., and S. F. R. R. Simpson relates that when he passed Sandia in 1849 he noticed in the space of a mile northward from the pueblo some 60 or 70 piles of stones which were said to mark the places where as many Navajos had fallen in battle with the Pueblonians some years before.

[16] Old Albuquerque, to be distinguished from the present contiguous or adjacent city of the same name, one of the best-known places on the Rio Grande between Santa Fé and El Paso. In coming to this town Pike passed sites of several places now named, though none of any note—as Corrales (on the opposite or W. side of the river, whence there is a road 18⅔ m. to pueblo of Cebolleta) ; Alameda (where the river could be crossed to strike the Corrales-Cebolleta road) ; Ranchos d'Albuquerque ; Los Griegos ; and finally Candelaria. The word Albuquerque, or more properly Alboquerque, is the same as the name of the very celebrated Portuguese son of Mars and soldier of fortune, Affonso d'Alboquerque, who flourished in the latter part of the fifteenth century and early in the sixteenth (b. 1453, d. Dec. 16th, 1515). It is commonly pronounced on the spot Albykirky, and sometimes Albykirk. The old town was in existence about 1700, and now has some 1,750 pop.; the new one is a thing of yesterday, so to speak, but already a notable railroad center, capital of Bernalillo Co., with nearly 4,000 pop., and scheduled as 58 m. from Santa Fé. Near Albuquerque there was a ford to a place called Atrisco, whence the road led westward to Fort Wingate ; while eastward from Albuquerque a road went to the Tijeras cañon, which marks off the Sandia range proper from the elevation S. of this cañon called Monte Largo. Tijeras cr., when it runs, falls into the Rio Grande about 8 m. below Albuquerque. Sandival, a place that appears on various maps, was Sandival's hacienda, a couple of miles S. of Albuquerque, on an upper and dryer road than the one usually taken southward.

an inner apartment, where he ordered his adopted children of the female sex to appear.　They came in by turns— Indians of various nations, Spanish, French, and finally two young girls, whom from their complexion I conceived to be English.　On perceiving I noticed them, he ordered the rest to retire, many of whom were beautiful, and directed those to sit down on the sofa beside me.　Thus situated, he told me that they had been taken to the east by the Tetaus and passed from one nation to another, until he purchased them, at that time infants; they could recollect neither their names nor language, but, concluding they were my country-women, he ordered them to embrace me as a mark of their friendship, to which they appeared nothing loath.　We then sat down to dinner, which consisted of various dishes, excel-lent wines, and, to crown all, we were waited on by half a dozen of those beautiful girls who, like Hebe at the feast of the gods, converted our wine to nectar, and with their ambrosial breath shed incense on our cups.　After the cloth was removed some time, the priest beckoned me to follow him, and led me into his sanctum sanctorum, where he had the rich and majestic images of various saints, and in the midst the crucified Jesus, crowned with thorns, with rich rays of golden glory surrounding his head—in short, the room being hung with black silk curtains, served but to aug-ment the gloom and majesty of the scene.　When he con-ceived my imagination sufficiently wrought up, he put on a black gown and miter, kneeled before the cross, took hold of my hand, and endeavored gently to pull me down beside him.　On my refusal, he prayed fervently for a few minutes and then rose, laid his hands on my shoulders, and, as I con-ceived, blessed me.　He then said to me, " You will not be a Christian.　Oh! what a pity! oh! what a pity!"　He then threw off his robes, took me by the hand and led me out of the company smiling; but the scene I had gone through had made too serious an impression on my mind to be eradicated until we took our departure, which was in an hour after, having received great marks of friendship from the father.

Both above and below Albuquerque, the citizens were beginning to open canals, to let in the water of the river to fertilize the plains and fields which border its banks on both sides; where we saw men, women, and children, of all ages and sexes, at the joyful labor which was to crown with rich abundance their future harvest and insure them plenty for the ensuing year. Those scenes brought to my recollection the bright descriptions given by Savary of the opening of the canals of Egypt. The cultivation of the fields was commencing and everything appeared to give life and gayety to the surrounding scenery.

We crossed the Rio del Norte [at Atrisco [17]], a little below the village of Albuquerque, where it was 400 yards wide, but not more than three feet deep and excellent fording. At Father Ambrosio's was the only chart we saw in the

[17] No crossing of the Rio Grande is indicated on Pike's map anywhere along here, his trail being dotted continuously on the E. side of the river. But it is quite certain that he crossed a little below old Albuquerque to Atrisco. There was here a ford, regularly used when the water was not too high. The railroad now crosses some miles lower down, between Isleta station and Isleta. Atrisco was a very well-known name, in consequence of the ford, before the days of the railroads, but is hardly to be found on ordinary maps of to-day. When I first crossed the Rio Grande, June 23d, 1864, our outfit was ferried over some 20 m. below Albuquerque, between places called Los Pinos on the E. and Las Lunas on the W. "Los Pinos" is short for Bosque or Alamo de los Pinos, as they called the large fine grove of cottonwoods there, but I do not think there were any pines. A couple of miles below was the hacienda of Mariano Chavez, brother of the unfortunate A. J. Chavez who was murdered near the Little Arkansaw : see note [10], p. 424 ; M. Chavez was dead himself before 1847. The place where Pike so joyfully met the blooming Robinson is left open to question in the present text. If by the "next village" he means the next one he came to after leaving Albuquerque, this was certainly at or near the site of Atrisco. This is really the implication ; otherwise we should have to go a good ways down the W. bank of the Rio Grande, to site of present Pajarito, or perhaps Isleta, at which latter place is now the junction of the Atl. and Pac. with the A., T., and S. F. R. R. The doubt is cleared away by the text of the 8th, where it appears that Pike visited Tousac (see next note) 3 m. from the village where Robinson was, and on the same (W.) side of the river, where the troops had been sent over night ; and was then carted back over to the E. side of the river. He simply visited across the Rio Grande, as he had done at San Felipe, and then returned to continue his regular journey down the E. side. But neither of these two cases is put very clearly at first blush in the narrative.

province that gave the near connection of the sources of the Rio del Norte and the Rio Colorado of California, with their ramifications.

On our arriving at the next village, a dependency of Father Ambrosio's, we were invited into the house of the commandant. When I entered, I saw a man sitting by the fire reading a book; with blooming cheeks, fine complexion, and a genius-speaking eye, he arose from his seat. It was Robinson! Not that Robinson who left my camp on the headwaters of the Rio del Norte, pale, emaciated, with uncombed locks and beard of eight months' growth, but with fire, unsubdued enterprise, and fortitude. The change was indeed surprising. I started back and exclaimed, " Robinson!" " Yes." " But I do not know you," I replied. " But I know you," he exclaimed; " I would not be unknown to you here, in this land of tyranny and oppression, to avoid all the pains they dare to inflict. Yet, my friend, I grieve to see you here and thus, for I presume you are a prisoner." I replied " No! I wear my sword, you see; all my men have their arms, and the moment they dare to ill-treat us we will surprise their guards in the night, carry off some horses, make our way to Appaches, and then set them at defiance."

At this moment Captain D'Almansa entered, and I introduced Robinson to him as my *companion de voyage* and friend, he having before seen him at Santa Fe. He did not appear much surprised, and received him with a significant smile, as much as to say, " I knew this." We then marched out to the place where the soldiers were encamped, not one of whom would recognize him, agreeably to orders, until I gave them the sign. Then it was a joyful meeting, as the whole party was enthusiastically fond of him. He gave me the following relation of his adventures after he left me:

" I marched the first day up the branch [Rio Conejos] on which we were situated, as you know we had concluded it would be most proper to follow it to its source and then cross the mountains [San Juan range] west, where we had conceived we should find the Spanish settlements, and at night encamped on its banks. The second day I left it a little, bore more south, and was getting up the side of the mountain, when I discovered two Indians, for whom I made. They were armed with bows and arrows, and were extremely shy of my approach ; but after some time, confidence being somewhat restored, I signified a wish to go to Santa Fe, when they pointed due south, down the river I left you on. As I could not believe them, I reiterated the inquiry and received the same reply.   I then concluded that we had been deceived, and that you were on the Rio del Norte, instead of the Red river.   I was embarrassed whether I should not immediately return to apprise you of it; but concluded it to be too late, as I was discovered by the Indians, whom if I had not met, or some others, I should have continued on, crossed the mountains to the waters of the Colorado, and descended these, until from their course I should have discovered my mistake.   I therefore offered them some presents to conduct me in ; they agreed, conducted me to the camp where their women were, and in about five minutes we were on our march.   That night we encamped in the woods ; I slept very little, owing to my distrust of my companions. The next day, at three o'clock, we arrived at the village of Aqua Caliente, where I was immediately taken into the house of the commandant, and expresses were dispatched to Santa Fe.   That night I was put to sleep on a mattress on the floor. The next day we departed early, leaving my arms and baggage at the commandant's, he promising to have them forwarded to me at the city.   On our arrival at Santa Fe, the governor received me with great austerity at first, entered into an examination of my business, and took possession of all my papers. After all this was explained, he ordered me to a room where the officers were confined when under an arrest, and a non-commissioned officer to attend me when I walked out into the city, which I had free permission to do.   I was supplied with provisions from the governor's table, who had promised he would write to Baptiste Lalande to come down and

answer to the claim I had against him ; whose circumstance
I had apprised myself of.   The second day the governor
sent for me, and informed me that he had made inquiry as
to the abilities of Lalande to discharge the debt, and found
that he possessed no property ; but that at some future
period he would secure the money for me.   To this I made
a spirited remonstrance, as an infringement of our treaties
and a protection of a refugee citizen of the United States
against his creditors.   But it had no other effect than to
obtain me an invitation to dinner, and rather more respectful treatment than I had hitherto received from his Excellency ; who, being slightly afflicted with dropsy, requested
my advice as to his case.   For this I prescribed a regimen and
mode of treatment which happened to differ from the one
adopted by a monk and practicing physician of the place,
and thus brought on me his enmity and ill offices.   The
ensuing day I was ordered by the governor to hold myself
in readiness to proceed to the internal parts of the country,
to which I agreed ; determining not to leave the country in
a clandestine manner, unless they attempted to treat me
with indignity or hardship ; and conceiving it in my power
to join you on your retreat, or find Red river and descend it,
should you not be brought in ; but, in that case, to share
your destiny.   Added to this I felt a desire to see more of
the country, for which purpose I was willing to run the risk
of future consequences.   We marched the ensuing day,
I having been equipped by my friend with some small
articles of which I stood in need, such as I would receive
out of the numerous offers of his country.   The fourth day
I arrived at the village of St. Fernandez, where I was
received and taken charge of by Lieutenant Don Faciendo
Malgares, who commanded the expedition to the Pawnees,
and whom you will find a gentleman, a soldier, and one of
the most gallant men you ever knew.   With him I could no
longer keep up the disguise, and when he informed me, two
days since, that you were on the way in, I confessed to him
that I belonged to your party.   We have ever since been

anticipating the pleasure we three will enjoy in our journey to Chihuahua; for he is to command the escort, his dragoons being now encamped in the field, awaiting your arrival. Since I have been with him I have practiced physic in the country in order to have an opportunity of examining the manners, customs, etc., of the people, to endeavor to ascertain their political and religious feelings, and to gain every other species of information which would be necessary to our country or ourselves. I am now here, on a visit to this man's wife, attended by a corporal of dragoons as a guard, who answers very well as a waiter, guide, etc., in my excursions through the country; but I will immediately return with you to Malgares."

Thus ended Robinson's relation, and I in return related what had occurred to the party and myself. We agreed upon our future line of conduct, and then joined my old captain in the house. He had been persuaded to tarry all night, provided it was agreeable to me, as our host wished Robinson to remain until the next day. With this proposition I complied, in order that Robinson and myself might have a further discussion before we joined Malgares, who I suspected would watch us closely. The troops proceeded to the village of Tousac that evening.

Sunday, Mar. 8th. Marched after taking breakfast and halted at a little village, three miles distant, called Tousac,[18] situated on the west side of the Rio del Norte. The men informed me that, on their arrival over night, they had all been furnished with an excellent supper; and after supper, wine and a violin, with a collection of the young people to a dance. When we left this village the priest sent a cart down to carry us over, as the river was nearly four feet deep. When we approached the village of St. Fernandez [19] we were

[18] " Tousac 500 " is marked nearly opposite Albuquerque, at or near present site of Atrisco. What this can be, unless it is Atrisco itself, or some old place close by, I do not know. The name reminds us of Tesuque (see note [7], p. 605), but the place here meant is obviously not that one. (See Tousac in Index.)

[19] " S. Fernandez 500 " is marked on the map as the first village below Albu-

met by Lieutenant Malgares, accompanied by two or three other officers ; he received with the most manly frankness and the politeness of a man of the world.   Yet my feelings were such as almost overpowered me, and obliged me to ride by myself for a short period in order to recover myself. Those sensations arose from my knowledge that he had been absent from Chihuahua ten months, and it had cost the king of Spain more than $10,000 to effect that [capture of myself and party] which a mere accident and the deception of the governor had accomplished.

Malgares, finding I did not feel myself at ease, took every means in his power to banish my reserve, which made it impossible on my part not to endeavor to appear cheerful. We conversed as well as we could, and in two hours were as well acquainted as some people would be in the same number of months. Malgares possessed none of the haughty Castillian pride, but much of the urbanity of a Frenchman ; and I will add my feeble testimony to his loyalty, by declaring that he was one of the few officers or citizens whom I found who were loyal to their king, who felt indignant at the degraded state of the Spanish monarchy, and who deprecated a revolution or separation of Spanish America from the mother country, unless France should usurp the government of

querque on the E. side. I do not recognize the name, nor can I find it on any one of several maps examined. No distance being given for the 8th, I am left entirely at a loss. But in no event can Pike have passed Peralta, a well-known place, and he is probably not far short of it. We may therefore note some places between Albuquerque and Peralta.   Pajarito Arriba and Pajarito Bajo (Upper and Lower Pajarito) are two towns 3 m. apart, 3 and 6 m. below Atrisco, on the W. side of the river ; and Tijeras or Tijera cr. or arroyo comes to the river from the E. about a mile below Pajarito Bajo. Three m. beyond this last town is Padillas, a Mexican town near the foot of the mesa, and three beyond this is Isleta—both on the W. side. None of these places was of importance ; but Isleta is now a station on the A., T., and S. F. R. R., which makes a crossing of the Rio Grande to it from Isleta station on the E. side ; and in the immediate vicinity of Isleta is the junction of the A. and P. R. R.   Below Isleta station, on the E., are the Ranchitos d'Isleta ; next is Los Pinos, already mentioned, then Chavez, and a mile from this stands Peralta.   The latter was known at one time as Ontero's hacienda.

Spain. These are the men who possess the heads to plan, the hearts to feel, and the hands to carry this great and important work into execution. In the afternoon our friend wrote the following notification to the alcaldes of several small villages around us:

"Send this evening six or eight of your handsomest young girls to the village of St. Fernandez, where I propose giving a fandango, for the entertainment of the American officers arrived this day.

"[Signed]   DON FACIENDO."

This order was punctually obeyed, and portrays more clearly than a chapter of observations the degraded state of the common people. In the evening, when the company arrived, the ball began after their usual manner, and there was really a handsome display of beauty.

It will be proper to mention here, that when my small paper trunk was brought in, Lt. Malgares struck his foot against it, and said: "The governor informs me this is a prisoner of war, or that I have charge of it; but, sir, only assure me that you will hold the papers therein contained sacred, and I will have nothing to do with it." I bowed assent; and I will only add that the condition was scrupulously adhered to, as I was bound by every tie of military and national honor, and, let me add, gratitude, not to abuse his high confidence in the honor of a soldier. He further added that "Robinson being now acknowledged as one of your party, I shall withdraw his guard and consider him as under your parole of honor." Those various marks of politeness and friendship caused me to endeavor to evince to my brother soldier that we were capable of appreciating his honorable conduct toward us.

Mar. 9th. The troops marched about ten o'clock. Lt. Malgares and myself accompanied Captain D'Almansa about three miles back on his route to Santa Fe, to the house of a citizen, where we dined; after which we separated. I wrote by the captain to the governor in French, and to Father Rubi in English. D'Almansa presented me with his cap and whip, and gave me a letter of recommendation to an officer at Chihuahua. We returned to our quarters and, being joined by our waiters, commenced our route.

Passed a village called St. Thomas [San Tomas, or Tomé [20]], one mile distant from camp. The camp was formed in an ellipsis, the two long sides presenting a breastwork formed of the saddles and heads of the mules, each end of the ellipsis having a small opening to pass and repass at; in the center was the commandant's tent. Thus, in case of an attack on the camp, there were ready-formed works to fight from. Malgares' mode of living was superior to anything we have an idea of in our army; having eight mules loaded with his common camp equipage, wines, confectionery, etc. But this only served to evince the corruption of Spanish discipline; for, if a subaltern indulged himself with such a quantity of baggage, what would be the cavalcade attending an army? Dr. Robinson had been called over the river to a small village to see a sick woman, and did not return that night. Distance 12 miles.

Mar. 10th. Marched at eight o'clock, and arrived at the village Sibilleta; passed on the way the village of Sabinez on the west side, and Xaxales, on the same [W.] side, Sibilleta [21] is situated on the east side, and is a regular

[20] " S. Thomas 500 " on Pike's map, a mile beyond which was camp of the 9th. As 12 m. advance was made to-day, St. Thomas and St. Fernandez were places 11 m. apart. Los Pinos, Peralta, and Valencia are all places within 3 m. of one another, and more or less nearly opposite Las Lunas, on the west, long a notable point of crossing of the Rio Grande, and present seat of Valencia Co. It is situated in the San Clemente tract, and near it are Las Lunas hills. Five miles below Valencia, on the E. side of the Rio Grande, is Tomé hill, a conspicuous butte on the edge of the mesa, in lat. 34° 45'. Tome and the Tomé ranches are 2 or 3 m. further south. These stretched along the river for more than a mile, presenting at times well cultivated and well irrigated grainfields.

[21] " Sibilleta 1000," which Pike marks on his trail on the E. bank of the Rio Grande, is otherwise Cibolleta, La Joya de Cibolleta, or old La Joya, within the area of the Cevilleta or Joya Grant, and in Socorro Co. (next county S.

square, appearing like a large mud wall on the outside, the doors, windows, etc., facing the square ; it is the neatest and most regular village I have yet seen, and is governed by a sergeant, at whose quarters I put up.

of Valencia). Present La Joya is across the river, on the W. side ; the railroad goes through it. Beyond old La Joya is Joya cañon, on the E. All these places are a few miles S. of the confluence of the Rio Puerco with the Rio Grande, on the W. The Puerco is a sizable stream, or dry bed of one, on a general S. course, crossed at 23 m. distance in going W. from Las Lunas along the old road to Zuñi, Fort Wingate, etc. Where I crossed, it was a sluggish thread of dirty yellow water which one could bestride ; but it is some 75 m. long, and important in furnishing bounds to several of the land grants in Valencia and Bernalillo cos. There is no trace of the Puerco on Pike's map, though he lays down both Rio Chama and Rio Jemez. Before coming to the confluence of the Puerco he passed a number of places now named, which may be taken up thus : On the E. side are Constancia, Casa Colorada, Vellita, and Las Nutrias, with several others of less note. Casa Colorada ("Red House") gives name to the grant next south of Tomé Grant ; it is on the Rio Grande, 4 m. above the mouth of that considerable stream, high up on which are the ruins of Abo. On the W. side, where the railroad now runs, a principal place is Belen, in the vicinity of which were others which were called Ranchos de Belen, and Pueblitos de Belen ; nearly opposite the last, but directly on the W. bank of the river, is Jarales. Next above the Belen pueblito, on the railroad, is Trejos, and next below it is San José. Below the last named is a point of woods, called in Spanish Punto del Bosque, and here is a place named Bosque. Rancho Sabinal, Sabinal station, and a certain Pueblito succeed one another, bringing us about opposite the above said Las Nutrias.

Along this whole stretch of the Rio Grande, from Peralta nearly to La Joya, a range of mountains extends in the E. offing, say 15–20 m. air-line to their summits. This is the Manzano range, running N. and S.; some of its peaks, up to 10,000 feet, are called Mosca, Capilla, Osha, and Manzano. The range continues S. under the name of Cerro Montoso. Roads start from many places on the Rio Grande to go through the cañons or passes in these mountains.

We have also to attend to Sabinez and Xaxales of the above text, and with these may note several other pueblos Pike charts in this region.

1. Sabinez, or Sabinal, or Savinal, was a place near the W. bank of the Rio Grande, in the vicinity of present Sabinal station on the railroad, about 10 m. above new La Joya, and somewhat less above the mouth of Rio Puerco.

2. "Xaxales 300" is marked a few miles S. of Sabinez, at or near the place on the railroad now called Pueblito, 6 or 8 m. above new La Joya. "Xaxales" is the same word as Jarales (otherwise Gerrales), but does not seem to have denoted the place now called by the latter name.

3. Next W. of Sabinez and Xaxales, but well off the Rio Grande, Pike marks "Seguna 250." This is the large, old, and still flourishing Keresan

Mar. 11th. Marched at eleven o'clock; came 12 miles [22] and encamped, the troops having preceded us. Lieutenant Malgares, not being well, took medicine. The village we stayed at last night being the last, we entered the wilder-

pueblo of Laguna, with a present pop. of over 1,100. It is so called from the little lake or laguna hard by, on a branch of the Rito San José (a branch of the Rio Puerco). This pueblo is on the main road from the Rio Grande to Zuñi and so on. An old Navajo trail takes or took off N. from Laguna, up another branch of the same rito, in the course of which latter is a cluster of small pueblos, as Povete, Pojuate, or Paguate; Moquino; Cebolleta; and Cebolletita; there were also various ruined pueblos here and there in the region watered by the Rito San José and its several trickling affluents. Covero is a pueblo not far W. N. W. of Laguna.

4. Pike marks "Cequimas 500" some distance S. W. of Laguna. This is the old and well-known Keresan pueblo of Acoma, on another affluent of the San José system, with a present pop. of about the same as it had in his time. Plates of Acoma and various other towns illustrate Lieut. J. W. Abert's report, Ex. Doc. 41, 30th Congr., 1st Sess., pub. 1848. (See Cequimas in Index.)

5. "Zumi 300" is charted near both of the foregoing, and E. of the continental divide. This is an error of location, for the pueblo meant is that of Zuñi or Suinyi, one of the largest and on the whole the best known of all the Indian towns in New Mexico. It is situated on the Rio Zuñi, tributary to the Colorado river system, and, therefore, on the Pacific slope. The place is famous as the very heart of the region where the "Seven Cities of Cibola" stood at the dawn of the historic period in Spanish invasion of this country; one of the seven having furnished at least a part of the present site of Zuñi. The Zuñian people, to the number of some 1,600, alone represent a distinct nation of pueblonians, called the Zuñian family: see a note beyond.

6. West of his line of continental-divide mountains Pike locates two pueblos, or rather Indian villages, by the names of "Cumpa" and "Chacat." These are not far apart, and both approximate to the four Moki villages he charts: see a note beyond for the Mokis. The identification of Cumpa may be in question; but Chacat evidently stands for what Pike learned of the old establishments in the Cañon de Chaco, or de Chasco. This is in N. W. New Mexico, and in such extent of the cañon as has running water is the Rio Chaco, tributary of Rio San Juan, a branch of the Colorado Grande which enters above the mouth of the Colorado Chiquito, in Utah. This cañon once harbored a large population in several different establishments, all long since gone to ruins; and the Chaco people have been the subjects of much disputed history. An excellent account of the ruins is contained in Simpson's Report, pp. 73-86; views of some of them are given on several plates. On his map the names of 10 of the 12 he locates stand as Pintado, Wejegi, Una Vida, Hungo Pavi, Chetho Kette, Bonito, Del Arroyo, Nos. 8 and 9 blank, Peñasca Blanca.

[22] Past Joya cañon to the vicinity of La Joyita, near the S. border of the

ness and the road became rough, small hills running into the river, making valleys; but the bottoms appear richer than those more to the north.

Mar. 12th. Marched at seven o'clock; passed, on the west side of the river, the mountains of Magdalen, and the Black mountains on the east.[23] Passed the encampment of a cara-

Joya Grant. This is a small town near which some black basaltic bluffs reach down close to the river. It is not to be confounded with the village of similar name, La Joya, a few miles further on.

[23] The Black mts. of Pike's text, Sierra Obscura of his map, are in the series of ranges along the E. side of the Rio Grande, at varying but always considerable distances. These are in general but not exact continuation of the San Diaz or Sandia mts., and take, in different parts of their extent, other names, as Cerro Manzano, Cerro Montoso, etc.; the name Sierra Oscura or Black range being now restricted to a short chain between the Chupadera mesa on the N. and the San Andreas chain on the S. Though there is of course no such linear continuity of these ranges as Pike's Sierra Obscura seems to represent, yet I think Pike hit off the mountains wonderfully well, considering the stealthy circumstances under which he observed them. All through " the captivity " in New Spain he had to make his notes furtively, and then conceal them—in other words, he stole and hid away his information. His Sierra Obscura is all the better delineated by his marking certain southern portions of the chain with the names " Sierra de el Sacramento " and " Sierra de Guadelupe "—these being ranges which he was never near, if in fact he ever laid eyes on them. They are those called to-day the Sacramento and Guadalupe ranges, trending S. E. toward the Rio Pecos, down to lat. 32° or thereabouts ; they are special southward extensions of the huge nest of mountains which bound for a great distance the water-shed of the Pecos, and are broken into many lesser ranges and peaks, as the White range (Sierra Blanca), the Nogal, Capitan, Carrizo, Jicarilla, etc. In perhaps no point is Pike's (qu : Humboldt's ?) map clearer than where he runs his " Montagnes de Salines " N. between his Sierra Obscura on the E. and the Rio Grande on the W.; for this is the San Andreas range, which extends continuously southward from the Sierra Oscura of present geography, and whose southern portions now bear the names of the Organ and Franklin mts., ending only near El Paso. The Organ mts. were better and have been long known by the Spanish name of Sierra de los Organos, exactly as lettered by Pike. This curious name originated in the fancied resemblance of the columnar trap formations to the pipes of an organ. Wislizenus and Hughes both call them the " Organic " mts. Their fastnesses were favorite and habitual lurking-places of the Mescalero Apaches—those murderous freebooters and desperadoes who used to descend upon the peaceful pueblos and the Spanish settlements. " The Assyrian came down like the wolf on the fold," and so did the Apache, not only from the Organ mts. and other parts of the San Andreas or Salinas range, but also from all the mountains above mentioned as lying further east. Ob-

van going out with about 15,000 sheep from the other provinces, from which they bring back merchandise.   This expedition consisted of about 300 men, chiefly citizens, escorted
by an officer and 35 or 40 troops; they are collected at
Sibilleta and separate there on their return.   They go out
in February and return in March ; a similar expedition goes
out in the autumn, but during the other parts of the year no
citizen travels the road, the couriers excepted.   At the pass
[El Paso] of the Rio del Norte they meet and exchange
packets, when both return to their own provinces.   Met a

serve that Pike thrice locates Apaches among these mountains, lettering "Apaches
Faraone," " Apaches Mescaleros," and "Apaches Mescalorez."   He also locates
what he calls " Indiens Ietans " ; these are the Comanches, usually given in his
text as " Tetaus," who played the part of Vandals to the Goths of the Apaches—
twin scourges during the whole historic period and down to our own day, under
the leadership of chiefs whose characters recall the popular impressions of
Attila the Hun.   The only serious criticism to be passed on this part of Pike's
map is the way he runs a great river in the country of his Ietans and Mescaleros, between his Sierra Obscura and his Montagnes de Salines, *i. e.*, in the
deserts E. of his San Andreas range and W. of the other mountains.   But this
is simply his misapprehension of such information as he had of the course of
the Pecos ; for his " Rio Puerto " is a mistake for Rio Puerco, and this was a
long current though mistaken name of the Pecos, to be found on various maps
and in different itineraries of comparatively recent dates.   It is hardly necessary to add that the Pecos lies eastward of all the mountains now under consideration ; there is no such river where Pike lays down his " Rio Puerto."   That
region is a horrid desert, where such waters as may start from the mountains on
either hand soon run out by evaporation and absorption, or lose themselves
in those salty sinks and alkaline wastes whence originated, in fact, the former
name of " Saline " or " Salinas " mts. for the San Andreas range.
    As to the " Mountains of Magdalen " of Pike's text: We observe that he
maps two isolated elevations on his right, W. of the Rio Grande, respectively
lettered " Sierra Magillez " and " Sierra Christopher."   These clearly correspond to two of the most conspicuous elevations, Mt. Magdalen and Old Baldy,
of the range which continues to be known as that of the Magdalen mts. or Sierra
Magdalena.   These are a short but high range directly W. of the county town
Socorro, whence a branch of the railroad now runs into them to the place
called Magdalena.   This range rises 20 m. and more from the river ; in this
interval a series of lesser elevations stretches northward, taking at successive
points the names of Socorro, Limitar, Polvadero, and Ladron—the two last of
these being separated by the arroyo of the Rio Salado, coming to the Rio
Grande from the W. in the vicinity of the Joya cañon from the E.
    The position of Pike's camp of the 12th is not easily determined, as he gives

caravan of 50 men and probably 200 horses, loaded with goods for New Mexico. Halted at twelve o'clock and marched at three. Lt. Malgares showed me the place where he had been in two affairs with the Appaches; one he commanded himself, and the other was commanded by Captain D'Almansa; in the former there were one Spaniard killed, eight wounded, and 10 Appaches made prisoners; in the latter 52 Appaches were wounded and 17 killed, they being surprised in the night. Malgares killed two himself, and had two horses killed under him.

Mar. 13th. Marched at seven o'clock; saw many deer. Halted at eleven o'clock and marched at four o'clock.[24]

no mileage and names no place. But it was not far below Socorro, and perhaps in the close vicinity of Bosquecito. His *Sierra* Christopher (W. of the river) is to be carefully distinguished from what he further on calls the "mountain of the Friar Christopher," *i. e.*, Fra Cristobal, on the E. of the river: see note[25], pp. 635, 636, and note[30], p. 639.

When Pike passed a couple of miles below Parida, on the E. side of the Rio Grande, he had to climb a steep hill close to the river. From the top of this there is a fine view to be had of various places. Nearly opposite is Socorro, on the W. bank; Limitar is visible, 6 or 8 m. higher up on that side; while about 4 m. below is the site of the ruins of Las Huertas (the Orchards). Socorro was long one of the largest and most important places on the Rio Grande. It had a population of 2,000 about the middle of this century.

[24] No mileage for to-day, nor even number of hours on the march; no named point. In fact Pike's itinerary from Santa Fé thus far hardly gives a natural feature—not even the mouth of the Rio Puerco; we have to check it as best we can by a few names of towns now nearly a century old, and not always indicating a present location, together with what we may suppose to have been ordinary days' journeys. Camp of the 13th may be set somewhere within the limits of the present Bosque del Apache Grant, a good ways below Bosquecitos and San Pedro on the E., or San José and San Antonio on the W. A view of the Bosque faces p. 499 of Abert's report. The grant named is a small triangular area whose N. base is the S. border of the Socorro Grant, whose W. side adjoins the E. border of the Armendaris Grant, and whose apex is at or near Mt. Pascal (Cerro San Pascual). Old Fort Conrad was built on the W. side of the river, nearly opposite but a little above Valverde. Valverde was inhabited during the first quarter of this century, but the inhabitants were killed or driven off by the Apaches and Navajos, and it showed nothing but its ruins in 1846, as delineated on the plate of Abert's report, facing p. 506. Writing of 1839, Gregg says, Comm. Pra. II. 1844, p. 71: "We passed the southernmost settlements of New Mexico, and 20 or 30 miles further down the river we

This day one of our horses threw a young woman and ran off, as is the habit of all Spanish horses, if by chance they throw their rider; many of the dragoons and Malgares pursued him. Being mounted on an elegant horse of Malgares', I joined in the chase, and notwithstanding their superior horsemanship overtook the horse, caught his bridle, and stopped him, when both of the horses were nearly at full speed. This act procured me the applause of the Spanish dragoons, and it is astonishing how much it operated on their good will.

Mar. 14th. Marched at ten o'clock, and halted at a mountain ["of the Friar Christopher," p. 639, *i. e.*, Fra Cristobal]; distance 10 miles.[25] This is the point from which

came to the ruins of Valverde. This village was founded about 20 years ago, in one of the most fertile valleys of the Rio del Norte. It increased rapidly in population, until it was invaded by the Navajoes, when the inhabitants were obliged to abandon the place after considerable loss, and it has never since been repeopled." This locality, in a narrow, sandy valley, some 15 m. by the road above Fra Cristobal mt., used to be a point of departure in various directions from the Rio Grande, and the name occurs continually in the history of scouts on reconnoissances in this region before our Civil War; it was the general rendezvous of Doniphan's forces, preparatory to his invasion of Mexico and capture of Chihuahua; and it was the scene of a battle, for gallant and meritorious services in which action a particular friend of mine, Allen Latham Anderson, was brevetted major, Feb. 21st, 1862.

[25] To-day's itinerary brings up a number of interesting and important points, not evident at first sight. Below Valverde and San Pascual mt. Pike comes to a section of the river which has made much history. Along here, above and below Valverde, within a very few miles of one another, are the sites of Fort Conrad and old Fort Craig, both on the W. bank of the river; the position of the present places known as Arny, San Marcia, and Plaza Grande on the W., with La Mesa and Contadero on the E.; the present crossing of the railroad to the Mesa Prieta, from points higher up on the W.; and below this the Rio Grande crossing known as Paraje ferry, near the place of that name on the E. But we are mainly concerned to discover Pike's "point from which the road leaves the river"; and why at this point his escort should have abandoned the main road due S., two days' journey, to take him across the river and then S. W., by a rough and roundabout way for several days till, bearing S. E., the route should strike the S. end of the direct road which had been left at its N. end. If we should imagine some dark Spanish mystery here, we should be mistaken; for Malgares simply took Pike that way to avoid the terrible Jornada del Muerto—

the road leaves the river for two days' journey bearing due south, the river here taking a turn southwest; by the river it is five days to where the roads meet. We marched at four o'clock, and eight miles below crossed the river to the west side; two mules fell in the water. Unfortunately, they carried the stores of Lieutenant Malgares, by which

that Macabresque march which too often proved to be literally a " journey of the dead." It is now, as it was then, the great highway directly N. and S.; but what is now bowled over at ease in a few hours by rail, was then the toilsome, perilous, and sometimes fatal journey through an awful desert. When I was in New Mexico, 30 years ago, officers and others who had made this jornada were never weary of descanting upon the terrors of that "ninety miles without a drop of water," as it was commonly said to be. The trip is not quite so far as this, between the points where the river is usually left and regained; but it is not much less, and lives often hung upon the uncertainty whether any water could be found at a midway point known as Laguna del Muerto, or Lake of the Dead. The route of the Jornada is like the string of a bow whose arc is the Rio Grande, stretched straight up and down the desert between the river on the W. and the San Andreas range on the E., or rather between this range and those mountains on the W. of itself which close in on the E. bank of the river, cause its deflection, and render travel along its left (E.) bank difficult or impossible. Hence the crossing of the river at a point above them, to go along the right or W. bank, as Malgares did, was the alternative to the Jornada del Muerto. The mountains in mention are a barren range which begins to hug the river in the vicinity of Paraje, below Contadero, and is known as the Fra Cristobal range; this, or rather the northern end of it, is the " mountain of the Friar Christopher," of which Pike speaks. The chain continues southward (with only partial interruption, in the vicinity of Fort McRae), as the Sierra de los Caballos, or Horse range. Pike lays down ranges at three separate points, lettered " Las Pennuclas" (for Los Penáculos, the Pinnacles), " Horse Mⁿ." and " Death Mⁿ."; the first of these being an elevation of the Cristobal range, probably that now called Cristobal Peak, and the second and third being parts of the Caballos range. Whatever the exact point at which the main road left the river when Pike passed, it was near if not at the same point whence the Jornada has begun for half a century at least, and which took the name Fra Cristobal from the mountain. Thus, we read in Gregg, Comm. Pra. II. 1844, pp. 71–72: " Our next camping place deserving of mention was *Fray Cristóbal*, which, like many others on the route, is neither town nor village, but a simple isolated point on the river-bank—a mere *parage*, or camping-ground . . . thus being the threshold of the famous *Jornada del Muerto*." The words of Dr. Wislizenus on this subject are to precisely the same effect, Mem., 1848, p. 38: " This camping place is known as *Fray Cristobal;* but as there is neither house nor settlement here, and

means we lost all our bread, an elegant assortment of bis-
cuits, etc.   Distance 18 miles.

Sunday, Mar. 15th.   Marched at half past ten o'clock.

one may fix his camp close on or some distance from the river, the limits of
Fray Cristobal are not so distinctly defined as those of a city, and generally the
last camping place on or near the Rio del Norte before entering the *Jornada
del Muerto* is understood by it." Doniphan's troops were more than three
days in making the jornada : Hughes, Don. Exp., 1847, p. 95. Here the road
left the river valley by a contadero, and passed on to the desert. The first
lap of the jornada was 26 m. to the Laguna del Muerto, usually dry, sometimes
holding water after a rain. (Pike lays this down rather too far N., as the
" Lago del munto " by mistake of the engraver.) Thus when Gregg passed in
1839, " there was not even a vestige of water," *l. c.*, p. 73. " The marshes,"
he continues, " said by some historians to be in the vicinity, are nowhere to be
found ; nothing but the firmest and dryest table land is to be seen in every
direction. To procure water for our thirsty animals, it is often necessary to
make a halt here, and drive them to the Ojo del Muerto (Dead Man's Spring),
five or six miles to the westward, in the very heart of the mountain ridge that
lay between us and the river. This region is one of the favorite resorts of the
Apaches, where many a poor arriero has met with an untimely end. The
route which leads to the spring winds for two or three miles down a narrow
cañon or gorge, overhung on either side by abrupt precipices, while the various
clefts and crags, which project their gloomy brows over the abyss below, seem
to move the murderous savage to deeds of horror and blood." The second lap
of the jornada was 28 m. to a place called Perillo (qu : same as Barilla ?), to be
found on present maps as Point of Rocks, where water may be found in holes.
The third stage was 23 m., finishing the jornada in the vicinity of Fort Selden.
This total of 77 m.—easily becoming the " 90 " of tradition—could be made
in two days, as Pike says ; the usual method being to cover the distance in three
marches of a night, next day, and the following night. The road itself is not
bad ; only the possibility or probability of 77 m. without water made it a terror.
As may be seen even from the map on the railroad folder, the jornada was
nearly coincident with the present line from Contadero due S.; but the
track leaves the river a little higher up, and strikes it again also higher up, at
Rincon. The first portion of the track runs through mal pais, as they call
ground strewn with rough and gritty fragments of lava, which makes traveling
bad ; there is a station called Lava from this circumstance, and also a certain
Lava Butte, near the station Pope. The rails continue by Crocker and Round
mt. to the station Eagle, whence a road goes off W. to the Fort McRae reservation ; stations further along are Cutler, Upham, and Granada, the last being near
the Point of Rocks, formerly called Perillo, near where the stage station used to
bě ; whence the run is into Rincon, at a point on the river opposite Angostura,
where Pike comes along on the 17th. A camping-ground on the river, at this
end of the jornada, was known as Robledo (Oaks).

Made 28 miles, the route rough and stony; course S. 20° W.[26]

Mar. 16th. Marched at seven o'clock, and halted at twelve. Passed on the east side the Horse mountain, and the Mountain of the Dead.[27] Came on a trail of the appear-

[26] The whole of this way is bad, being cut across by a series of arroyos or gulches making down from the San Mateo and Mimbres ranges. These mountains are a part of the general chain which Pike maps in linear continuity as one which forms the "Dividing Ridge between the Waters of Rio del Norte and those of the Gulf of California"—that is, the Continental Divide. At one point in these ranges Pike legends very conspicuously "Grand Copper Mines, worked." It is also shown on the map of Lieut.-Col. Philip St. George Cooke, of his route from the Rio Grande to the Gila, etc., in 1846–47, Ex. Doc. No. 41, 30th Cong., 1st Sess., pub. 1848; and a "view of the copper mine" forms the subject of the plate opp. p. 59 of the same volume, in Lieut. W. H. Emory's report: see also *ibid.*, A. R. Johnston's report, pp. 577, 578 fig. The headwaters of the Rio Gila are across the divide of the Mimbres range. As the party goes down the valley of the Rio Grande, say from the Nogal arroyo or the site of the village now called San José, opposite Fra Cristobal, 6,600 feet, they have the range of the latter name on the left, or E., immediately across the river, while the San Mateo peak, 10,200 feet, towers on the N. W.

[27] Before coming to his Horse mt., Pike passed several points of note. He crossed Rio Alamoso or Cañada Alamosa near camp (unless he was already beyond it), and next Rio Cuchillo Negro. Between these two, but off on the E. side of the river, was built Fort McRae, in the southern foothills of the Fra Cristobal range (vicinity of Elephant Butte and Ojo del Muerto). There is or was a crossing of the Rio Grande from the fort, called Fest's ferry. Horse mt. of Pike is now called Caballo Cone; it rises at the N. extremity of the range of the Horse mts., usually known by the Spanish name of Sierra de los Caballos. The Mt. of the Dead is another elevation of this range, but which one is less easily determined. It was at or near the S. end of this range; see the positions of "Horse Mⁿ." and "Dead Mⁿ." on the map. Pike also marks a mountain close to his trail, on the W., by the name of "Rabledillo." This I take to be Cerro Cuchillo Negro, opposite Caballo Cone, between Rio Cuchillo Negro and Rio Palomo (Pigeon cr.). The latter is crossed at its mouth (Los Palomos); Rio Animas is crossed (Brent's); and several arroyos or dry washes are passed, till the party is well down on the W. side of the Horse range, within some 25 m. of where the Rio Grande will be crossed to-morrow. Camp is apparently between the mouths of Rio Perchas and Cienega Apache, which fall in near together on the W. Hillsborough, seat of Sierra Co. (which Pike entered when he left Socorro Co. on the 15th), is situated about 20 m. up Rio Perchas. Near this camp, and nearly opposite his Dead mt., Pike marks an elevation by the name of "La Ranchero," which appears to be that which approaches the Rio Grande most closely between Cienega Apache and White Water cr. In any event, this is

ance of 200 horses, supposed to be the trail of an expedition from the province of Biscay, against the Indians.

Mar. 17th. Marched at ten o'clock, and at four in the
afternoon crossed the river to the east side; saw several
fresh Indian tracks; also, the trail of a large party of
horses, supposed to be Spanish troops in pursuit of the
Indians. Marched down the river 26 miles;[28] fresh sign of

one of the foothills of the Mimbres range, as are several others Pike maps in
this vicinity. See next note.

[28] Not 26 m. after crossing the river, but from last camp, from which it is
about 26 m. to make the crossing. In this trip Pike turns the W. and S. flank
of the Sierra de los Caballos or Horse mts., having these first E. and then N. of
his route (on his left all the way). In so doing he passes from Sierra into Dona
Ana Co., and goes by a number of notable points, some of which he maps. On
the W. side of the river, in Dona Ana Co., at or near present Santa Barbara,
was the site of old Fort Thorn and the old Indian Agency; Beck's ferry was
also hereabouts. Pike sets four mountains on his right, at different distances to
the W. and S. These are lettered (1) " Esterolargo," (2) " S. Jacomb," (3) " La
Salmera," (4) " Piadro." These are some of the most elevated points in the
rugged and irregularly broken country to the south of the Horse and Mimbres
ranges; and their relative positions as mapped by Pike agree so well with those
of certain well-known elevations that identifications may be attempted : (1)
Esterolargo seems to correspond to the Cerro Magdalen, between Fort Selden
on the E. and old Fort Cummings on the W. (2) is in the position of the Good
Sight mts., about half-way between the Magdalens and Fort Cummings. A
branch of the A., T., and S. F. R. R., from Rincon on the Rio Grande to
Deming, runs past the Magdalens (station Sellers) and thence through the Good
Sight mts. by Burr's Pass (station Nutt), between Good Sight Peak and Sunday
Cone. Fort Cummings was built in that southern extension of the Mimbres
range known as Cooke's range : leave railroad for the fort at Cummings station,
or keep on past Coleman to Deming, etc. (3) is Cerro Robledo, on W. bank of
the Rio Grande, immediately S. of Fort Selden. (4) may be intended for the
Florida mts., on the boundary between Dona Ana and Grant cos., directly S. of
Fort Cummings 20 and 30 m., not so far S. E. of Deming. Pike crosses the
Rio Grande from W. to E., at or near where the railroad now crosses in passing
between stations Hatch (Colorado) and Rincon ; camp at this place or in its
immediate vicinity, about opposite town of Angostura.

The practically identical language of Mar. 17th and 18th shows that Pike has
duplicated an entry, and consequently that one day's march has been lost.
This loss is irretrievable, so far as I can discover. Furthermore, we have no
mileages for the 19th and 20th. Under these circumstances the best we can do
is to march him into El Paso in three laps, set three camps *ex hypothesi*, and
note in due order the places on the road over which we know he passed.

Indians, also of a party of horses.   Country mountainous on both sides of the river.

Mar. 18th.   Marched down the river 26 miles;[29] fresh sign of Indians, also of a party of horses.   Country mountainous on both sides of the river.

Mar. 19th.   Struck out east about three miles and fell in with the main road [continuing from the Jornada del Muerto], on a large flat prairie, which we left at the mountain of the Friar Christopher.[30]

[29] To camp at some point between Fort Selden and Dona Ana, probably not far beyond the site of the former post.   The Military Reservation upon which this long noted fort was established includes a tract a few miles square on both sides of the river, between the Cerro Robledo on the S. and San Diego mt. on the N. and N. W.; eastward are some elevations known as the Dona Ana hills; the Cerro Magdalen is due W., but at a much greater distance.   A few miles below Rincon and Angostura the river enters the Selden cañon, where it is straitened between Mt. San Diego on the E. and highlands on the W.; the railroad traverses this cañon, with the stations Tonuco near its head and Randall below ; the position of the fort is between the latter and Leasburg, on the E. bank of the river.   Pike's map shows a marked bend or loop of the dotted trail of the 18th, and I suppose this indicates where he went around Mt. San Diego. There used to be a place called San Diego here, about opposite the point where the old Cooke trail left the river.   Dona Ana was founded on the E. bank of the river, say 60 m. by road from El Paso.   This town was started in or about 1839, by settlers from El Paso, and 10 years later had a population of 300, mostly Mexicans, who required the protection of the military from the Apaches.   The railroad passes by but not through the present town, which has given name to the county, though the county seat is at Las Cruces.   Both of these places are included in the Dona Ana Bend Colony tract.

The Cooke trail above mentioned is that made by Lieut.-Col. Philip St. George Cooke, commanding the Mormon battalion of the Army of the West on the march from Santa Fé, N. M., to San Diego, Cal., under the guidance of Antoine Leroux, in the autumn of 1846.   It will be found very clearly traced, from the point of departure from the Rio Grande to the Pima villages on the Gila, on the sketch-map accompanying that officer's report to General Kearny, Ex. Doc. No. 41, 30th Congr., 1st Sess., pub 1848, pp. 549–563.   It is a roundabout way which loops far S. and strikes the San Pedro several days' march above the confluence of that stream with the Gila, follows the San Pedro down a piece northward, then strikes westward to Tucson, and so on N. W. to the Gila at the Pima villages.   The distance is represented to have been 544 m.

[30] Fra Cristobal, that is, but to be distinguished from Pike's *Sierra* Christopher : see note [23], p. 633, and note [25], p. 635.   The road which Pike thus struck was in direct continuation of the Jornada del Muerto, on the way to El

Mar. 20th.   Halted at ten o'clock, at a salt lake.   Marched until two o'clock; halted for the day.[31]   Vegetation began

Paso, and led by Las Cruces, present seat of Dona Ana Co.   This has been for many years one of the best-known places on the Rio Grande between Santa Fé and El Paso ; it is located a little off the river, on the E. side.   In the vicinity of Las Cruces, on the E. bank of the river, is Messilla, another well-known town.   The party proceeded past Tortugas and Bosquecito, to a point somewhere beyond the site of old Fort Fillmore, and probably within the present limits of the Brazito tract.   This camp might be fixed more exactly by one who could say how far short it was of a certain salt lake likely to be reached at 10 a. m. next day.   The route along here, as indeed from Fort Selden, is practically coincident with that of the railroad.   Brazito became the famous name of a battle-ground, after Christmas Day of 1846, when Colonel Doniphan's regiment defeated and routed a superior force of Mexicans who attacked him.   A spirited account of this engagement is given by John T. Hughes, Don. Exp. 1847, pp. 96–99, including a plan of the battle-ground.   The engagement lasted half an hour, about 3 p. m.   The spot is given as "25 m." from El Paso, opposite a large island in the Rio Grande, and also opposite a pass between the lower end of the Organ mts. and others called the "White" mts.   The Mexicans numbered about 1,300 men, of whom 71 were killed, 5 taken prisoners, and not less than 150 wounded, including their general, Ponce de Leon ; the American casualty was 8 wounded—none killed.

On Pike's left as he passes stand the Organ or Organon mts., as now so called in strictness, being that southward continuation of the San Andreas range which is marked off by a gap from the rest of the chain.   This gap is the San Augustin Pass ; place there called Organ, 15 m. E. by N. from Dona Ana.   Pike charts these mountains : see note [23], p. 631.   They run about S., and as the river is here bearing S. S. E., the two approach within 10 to 5 m. in the vicinity of the place where Fort Fillmore stood.   Pike's "Sierra de la Cola," as laid down close to the river, but due E. of El Paso, appears to correspond with what is now known as the Franklin range, around which the river finally turns E. to escape from all confinement.   Along the Rio Grande itself his map marks nothing whatever from the vicinity of Fort Selden to El Paso.   But we are now approaching some of the most important points of the whole route.

[31] In the vicinity of Montoyo, Tex., in the extreme W. corner of the State. Passing successively Mesquite, Herron, and Lyndon, on the railroad, with San Miguel (Baca Grant), La Mesa, and Chamberino in succession on the other side of the river, Pike comes to the station Anthony and the parallel of 32° N.; on crossing which he goes from Dona Ana Co., N. M., into El Paso Co., Tex., as he proceeds down the left or E. bank of the river ; had he been on the other side he would have remained in New Mexico until he entered present Chihuahua at lat. 31° 47′ N.   For the course of the Rio Grande itself makes the irregular boundary of Texas for 15 or 20 m., from the point where the parallel of 32° N. strikes the river from the E., to that where the parallel of 31° 47′ N. leaves the river on the W.   This break or fault (as a miner would say of a lead that acted

to be discoverable on the 17th, and this day the weeds and grass were quite high.

Mar. 21st. Marched in the morning and arrived at the passo [El Paso[32]] del Norte at eleven o'clock, the road lead-

so) of the straight border between Texas and New Mexico, where the boundary slips 13′ S. down the Rio Grande, is one of the politico-geographical curiosities of the situation, which would only be fully understood upon mastering the complicated history of the U. S. and Mexican Boundary Survey in all the bitterness of its personal episodes. Some of these points are considered in the following note. From lat. 31° 47′ N. on the Rio Grande, in the immediate vicinity of El Paso, Tex., and of El Paso del Norte (Ciudad Juarez), in Chihuahua, the river forms the boundary between the United States and the Republic of Mexico— that is, between Texas and the Mexican States of Chihuahua, Coahuila, Nuevo Leon, and Tamaulipas—on a circuitous but in general S. E. course to the Gulf of Mexico.

[32] The celebrated place to which our friend has thus been conducted by his friends, the enemy, must not be confounded with our little town of El Paso, Tex. This grew up yesterday, so to speak ; that dates from about 1680, as a Spanish settlement begun after the great Pueblo revolt, when Governor Otermin's people were driven out of Santa Fé. Before Pike was welcomed by the civil and ecclesiastical dignitaries of El Paso del Norte, he crossed the great river, and thus passed from the State of Texas into that of Chihuahua, as these are now bounded. He would have said that he simply went across the river which flows in the province of North or New Mexico of the kingdom of New Spain, and had not yet reached the province of New Biscay. But aside from any of the political affairs which spoil the complexion of the maps, El Paso is one of the most remarkable positions in North America, unique in some respects. With regard to the tide of emigration which set westward by southern lines of travel to the California of the forty-niners, it is comparable with that place by which, from time immemorial, the nations have passed from Asia into Europe, along what has been fitly styled the "highway of the world." But El Paso is not only a half-way house from the Gulf of Mexico to that of California ; it is the continental cross-roads. For the ebb and flow of human tides set with conflicting currents, north and south, long before the first page of American history was traced, and will continue forever in motion by El Paso. There is the turning-point of that great river which was Rio del Norte above this pass, and Rio Grande or Rio Bravo below. "El Paso" is certainly, as it always has been, the place of fording or crossing the river—Gregg says it was called by Americans "The Pass," and speaks of "Pass wine" and "Pass whiskey," as they named the liquors made there—but that is not the implication of the name. "El Paso" is the mountain-pass—el paso del Rio del Norte—the place where the river passes from the mountains to the plains. We have traced it from Pike's stockade on the Conejos, in the San Luis valley, almost due S., in an immense

ing through a hilly and mountainous country. We put up

trough of several hundred miles' length, during the whole of which distance it has been seen to be closely confined to its mountain bed, hemmed in on the W. by the continental divide or its several outliers, on the E. by successive ranges of not less dignity and importance. In all this course it receives no more than mere creeks from the eastern side ; while from the W. its tributaries are comparatively few and small rivers. But at El Paso the river turns out of bed, so to say, with hardly a figure of speech, to go all abroad in the open country, drawing to itself large tributaries on its way to the sea. Yet it has another strait-jacketing to suffer in forcing its way through the last mountains that rise to obstruct its course. The struggle begins near the entrance of the Rio Conchas and in the vicinity of Presidio del Norte, one of the oldest establishments in northern Mexico ; it continues for many miles through a series of cañons in the Bofecillos, San Carlos, and other mountains. During this passage the river makes a sharp elbow from S. E. northward, and then with a bold sweep recovers its former course ; it receives its tribute from the Pecos, its largest branch ; then, freed from its last fetters and augmented in force, the Rio Grande winds its way to the Gulf, having well won the title " Bravo." Such action is the more to be applauded if we remember that above the cañon-formations the river sometimes sinks exhausted into the ground, and its bed may become for many miles a wagon-road. The great flexures of the river lie within about a degree of latitude (29° to 30° N.), and the series of cañons is between the 102d and 105th meridians. Major Emory speaks of that great bend of the river as " one of the most remarkable features on the face of the globe—that of a river traversing at an oblique angle a chain of lofty mountains, and making through these, on a gigantic scale, what is called in Spanish America a cañon—that is, a river hemmed in by vertical walls," U. S. and Mex. B. Surv. I. 1857, p. 42. With due deference, and no desire to derogate from the dignity, either of the Rio Grande or of its cañonation, I do not see that we have not several parallel cases in this country, some of which are on a scale of not inferior magnitude. The essential features of the case are those of a great river which has once left its bed in mountains about its origin, traversed open country, and then forced its way through cañon-formation in another range or spur. The Arkansaw, heading in the continental divide, breaks out upon the plain at Cañon City, through a chasm in another range. The South Platte traverses South Park, and the North Platte, North Park, to seek the plains through other mountains than those in which they respectively head. The Yellowstone has its upper cañon and then comes out at Livingston through a lower one. The Missouri itself leaves its sources far remote from the range through which it finally makes its exit from Lewis and Clark's Gates of the Rocky Mountains. And just think of the Columbia !

Pike has nothing to say of any place on the Rio Grande opposite the Mexican town of El Paso, at or near where El Paso stands in Texas. But the valley has been settled and cultivated from remote antiquity, and the clustering of the population at various points gave rise to towns or pueblos, all of

at the house of Don Francisco Garcia, who was a merchant

which, of course, had names, though several of these have lapsed forever. Maps now nearly half a century old mark on the Texan side several places by the names of Frontera, La Frontera, or Las Fronteras ; Isleta, a Tañoan pueblo (in what is now Texas—distinguish from the other Tañoan pueblo, Isleta, in New Mexico); Socorro ; San Elceario, or Elizario ; also, Franklin and Fort Bliss—all these before there was any El Paso in Texas. Present maps show, below Montoyo, Santa Teresa, Frontera, El Paso, Isleta, San Elizario, and so on down the river along the railroad. As to the germ of the American town of El Paso, we find that Captain S. G. French, in 1849, came up the Rio Grande " to the intersection of the Santa Fé road at the rancho opposite El Paso"; and again : " El Paso is wholly situated in Mexico—there being, excepting the three villages on the island [San Elizario, Socorro, Isleta], but three houses on the American side." French's mileages by odometer in coming up the river on the Texan side, are : San Elizario to Socorro, 5.45 m.; Socorro to Isleta, 3.10 ; Isleta to Upper Ford, 7.05 ; Upper Ford to Coon's Hacienda, 7.09 ; total, 22.69, or 22⅔ m. from San Elizario to where the Santa Fé road came to the river to cross to El Paso, Mex. (Reports of Reconn., etc., 8vo, Washington, 1850, p. 53—not a book very easy to find.) A table of distances in the reverse direction and bringing in two more of the above names, is furnished by Major Emory, U. S. and M. B. S., I. 1857, p. 135 : Franklin (opposite El Paso) to Fort Bliss, 2 m.; Fort Bliss to Isleta, 12.14 ; Isleta to Socorro, 3.10 ; Socorro to San Elceario, 5.45 ; total, 22.69, or 22⅔ m., as before. If these were independent measurements, the odometers must have been good, as well as the road ; but I cite them both to show that Coon's Hacienda, Franklin, and El Paso, Tex., were the same place, opposite El Paso, Mex., and that Fort Bliss was built 2 m. lower down. Writing of the early fifties, Emory also states, *op. cit.*, p. 91 : " From San Elceario up to El Paso, a distance by the sinuosities of the river of 30 miles, but by air-line of only 20 miles, is almost one continuous settlement of Mexicans and Pueblo Indians, with here and there an American farmer and trader." His estimates of the population all along, from El Paso, Mex., to San Elceario, are : El Paso (including the very ancient Tañoan pueblo of Sinecu, supposed to have been built before the Spaniards came), 4,000 ; Franklin (present El Paso, Tex.), 200 ; Socorro, 300 ; San Elceario, 1,200 ; with 1,300 at places still further down, making a total of 7,000. Isleta does not figure in this census. This population was mostly mixed, with little pure Spanish, or Indian either. The commercial importance of El Paso as a port of entry may be inferred from Emory's statement that, before the ports on the lower Rio Bravo were opened, for some years as much as $2,000,000 worth of goods passed into Mexico this way ; figures supposed to have been reduced more than one-half at the time of which he wrote. He describes the town of El Paso, Mex., as " one extended vineyard in the hands of many proprietors." The little town of Frontera, above mentioned, acquired some consequence in 1852 from the erection there in 1851 of one of the astronomical stations at which Major Emory, U. S. Commissioner, and

and a planter; he possessed in the vicinity of the town

Don José Salazar y Larregui, Comisionado Mexicano, determined the initial point of the boundary W. of the Rio Grande along the par. of 31° 47′ N. The position of Frontera, as decided and agreed upon by the Joint Commission, was lat. 31° 48′ 44.31″ N., long. 106° 33′ 04.5″ W. That of El Paso, Mex., or more exactly, of the cathedral in that place, was lat. 31° 44′ 15.7″ N., long. 166° 29′ 05.4″ W. Frontera was thus about 4 minutes N. and W. of El Paso, and the boundary started W. between these two places at a point 3.41 m. about N. W. of El Paso, and 2.70 m. about S. E. of Frontera; the total distance between these two places being 6.11 m. As the Rio Grande itself was the natural boundary agreed upon from the Gulf of Mexico to the point where the river should intersect the parallel of 31° 47′, the various questions that were to be determined concerned only the boundary thence W. across country to the Gulf of California and so on to the Pacific. Two different boundaries were in diplomatic agreement for some years before either of them was ascertained on the ground. These were those provided for by the treaty of Guadalupe Hidalgo, Feb. 2d, 1848, ratified Aug., 1848, and by the Gadsden treaty of Dec. 30th, 1853, ratified June 30th, 1854. Under the former of these, two abortive attempts were made to establish two different lines W. of the Rio Grande; and it was fortunate for us that neither of them succeeded. The old treaty was made in the dark, on our part at least, being based upon the ignorance of geography which Disturnell's map displayed in 1847. The old treaty line started on paper from the Rio Grande at a point some miles above Frontera, went W. on a certain parallel of latitude, hypothetical on the ground, for about 180 m., through the Chiricahua mts., and then turned due N. along a never-determined meridian till it struck Rio Gila, which was thence the boundary W. to the Rio Colorado. The line agreed upon by U. S. Commissioner John B. Weller and General Conde, the Comisionado Mexicano, started W. from the Rio Grande at a point in the vicinity of Dona Ana, ran along a parallel for the same distance as the other, and then turned N. on a meridian to the Gila, striking the latter at a point further down that river—further N. W., that is, owing to the difference of longitude of the initial point on the Rio Grande. Both of these were paper-lines, assumed when the two governments were feeling for S. and W. borders of New Mexico as laid down on Disturnell's map; for Article V. of the G. H. '48 treaty provided that from the intersection of the Rio Grande with the S. border of New Mexico (wherever that might be) the line should run W. along the whole S. border of New Mexico, and then turn N. along the W. border of the same to the Gila. This was decidedly a case of *obscurum per obscurius*, so far as laying down an actual line was concerned, for nobody knew where the S. and W. borders of New Mexico were, within several minutes of latitude and longitude. The Weller–Conde line above noted started from the Rio Grande at lat. 32° 22′, near Dona Ana, and went due W. upon an assumed S. boundary of N. M. In 1851 such an initial point had been agreed upon; a monument erected; and actual survey begun by Col. J. D. Graham. The other assumed S. boundary of N. M., along

20,000 sheep and 1,000 cows.   We were received in a most

which a line was projected W. of the Rio Grande from an initial point in the
vicinity of Frontera, was very near 31° 47′.   Both luckily failed to go into
effect.   Such a comedy of errors, beginning on a false basis, was conducted
through a tissue of blunders to an inevitable and fortunate fiasco.   The work
of the old boundary survey was prosecuted under a series of commissioners—
John B. Weller ; John C. Frémont, who accepted the appointment, but never
got on the ground, and did nothing but resign ; John R. Bartlett ; and Robert
B. Campbell.   It wound up in 1853 as an ignominious and acrimonious failure,
for which net result Congress had appropriated $787,112.   This was expensive,
but profitable in the end ; for the event proved that a different boundary would
come cheap at that or almost any other price.   Almost down to 1848, the topography of the country between the Rio Grande and the Colorado of the West
was practically unknown to Americans.   But adventurers, traders, and emigrants
had begun to set their faces toward the west along our borders ; and the question of the most practicable southern route became one of great and growing
importance.   The War Department put exploring parties in the field ; and
through the labors of such officers as Emory, Abert, Parke, Marcy, Sitgreaves,
Simpson, Whipple, Michler, J. E. Johnston, S. G. French, W. F. Smith, F. T.
Bryan, and others, new light was thrown upon a vast region, to much of
which El Paso was the key.   Among other things, Emory developed the fact
that there could be no thoroughfare through U. S. territory in the vicinity of
32° N., the country being practically impassable by any means of transportation
then available along the parallel of 32°, N. of the projected boundary.   The
G. H. treaty ’48, to use Emory's words, " fixed a line north of that parallel which
cut off entirely the communication by wagons between the rivers [Rios Grande
and Gila] ; and leaving out of view the considerations involved in securing
railway routes to the Pacific, it was a line which sooner or later must have been
abandoned.   No traveller could pass, nor could a dispatch be sent, from a
military post on the Rio Bravo to one on the Gila, without passing through
Mexican territory."   Our Mexican neighbors evidently knew their country, as
well as what they were about, much better than we did, until we learned to
our cost what the matter was.   The already notorious errors of the Disturnell
map made any adjustment of the difficulty on that basis impossible, and some
different understanding between the two countries became an obvious necessity.
This was effected by the Gadsden treaty of 1853, which provided for the
reconstruction of the international line on paper, and its determination on the
ground.   By the provisions of this agreement, the line was to run up the Rio
Grande, as already defined by the G. H. treaty ’48, to the point where the middle
of the river should intersect the parallel of 31° 47′ N. ; thence due W. 100 m. ;
thence due S. to the parallel of 31° 20′ N. ; thence due W. to the meridian of
111° W. ; thence in a straight line to a point on the Colorado r. 20 English
miles below the confluence of the Gila ; thence up the Colorado r. to the intersection of the already existing U. S. and Mexican line across California to the
Pacific.   The concessions represented by these terms were all-important to us ;

hospitable manner by Don Pedro Roderique Rey, the lieutenant-governor, and Father Joseph Prado, the vicar of the
place.   This was by far the most flourishing place we had

they not only secured the required practicable highway from the Rio Grande to
the Gila, but added 26,185 sq. m. to U. S. territory, as was discovered when
the line was run.   This tract lies between the parallels of 31° 20′ and 33° 30′
N., and between the meridians of 106° 30′ and 114° W.; it may be called, in a
phrase, so much of the U. S. as lies S. of the Gila, in New Mexico and mainly
in Arizona.   William Hensley Emory was commissioned by President Pierce,
Aug. 4th, '54, to carry out the provisions of the treaty on the part of the U. S.,
and Don José Salazar y Larregui was appointed to the same official functions
on the part of Mexico.   Major Emory was required to meet the Mexican
commissioner at El Paso by Oct. 1st, 1854, and the commission took the field
without delay.   Congress appropriated $168,130, Aug. 14th, '54, and $71,450,
Mar. 3d, '55 ; total, $239,580, for running and marking the line.   When the
work had been done, Jan. 1st, 1856, Major Emory reported an unexpended balance of $98,454.59.   He had also to turn in, as unexpended balance of certain ap-
propriations for the old commission (altogether $58,100), the sum of $37,345.53 ;
total to his credit, $135,800.12, remaining of the sum of $239,580+$58,100=
$297,680, of which he had the disbursement and was responsible.   It thus appears
that his whole work cost the government only $161,879.87 ; it was finished within
the time estimated by the government for its completion, and largely within the
amounts appropriated for the purpose.   The boundary run by Emory and
Salazar, respectively, agreed upon by them jointly, and accepted by both governments, is at present in effect.   It starts from the Rio Grande between El Paso
and Frontera, at 31° 47′, and runs W. on that parallel 100 m., to a certain spot
commonly referred to by the name of Carrizalillo, as that of the nearest named
locality ; thence it drops meridionally to the parallel of 31° 20′, at a nameless
place in the mountains ; thence it runs due W. to the intersection of the 111th
meridian at a well-known place, Los Nogales ; whence it runs obliquely to the
Colorado r., at a point which is (roundly) 20 m. S. of Fort Yuma by the
channel of the river—Yuma being on the W. bank, and practically opposite the
mouth of the Gila.   Aside from any question of the 25,185 sq. m. and
the desirable right of way thus secured, under the provisions of the Gadsden
treaty, the abrogation of the 11th article of the G. H. treaty was all-important
to the U. S.   " This article," to use Major Emory's words, " made it incumbent
on the United States to keep the Indians living within our own territory from
committing depredations on the Mexicans, and by implication imposed on the
United States the obligation of indemnity for all losses resulting from failure
to carry out the provisions of the treaty.   No amount of force could have kept
the Indians from crossing the line to commit depredations, and I think that
one hundred millions would not pay the damages they have inflicted.   Whole
sections of country have been depopulated and the stock driven off and killed ;
and in entire States the ranches have been deserted and the people driven into
the towns.   It is true, all this has not been done since the war [with Mexico],

been in. For a more particular account of its situation, population, etc., see Appendix to Part III. [now Chap. IV.].

and would form no just claim against the United States ; but those conversant with the history of Mexican claims will at once admit that the United States would have been fortunate if she could have escaped with paying real claims for depredations, whether committed before or after the war. I should not be true to history if I did not state what is within my own personal knowledge— that companies were formed, and others forming, composed of persons of wealth, influence, and adroitness, who projected extensive schemes for the purchase of these claims, with the view of extorting them from the Congress of the United States." Not the least admirable feature of the present treaty, and one which was of equal moment to all respectable citizens of both countries, was the fullness of the powers it vested in the two commissioners. For Art. I. has : " That line shall be alone established upon which the commissioners may fix, their consent in this particular being considered decisive and an integral part of this treaty, without necessity of ulterior ratification or approval, and without room for interpretation of any kind by either of the parties contracting." This kept the dirty hands of professional politicians out of the affair, and left it to be settled by two honorable and able men, free to act at their best judgment and discretion, besides being competent to the requisite scientific work in astronomy and geodesy. The joint commission, in session on the spot, agreed upon the initial point of 31° 47′ N. on the W. bank of the Rio Grande, Jan. 10th, 1855 ; they marked it and agreed to erect the monument there. The corner-stone was laid Jan. 31st, in the presence of each other and of various civil and military dignitaries. The commissioners reconvened at Fort Bliss, Aug. 14th–16th, 1855, to consider the operations which had meanwhile been carried on by themselves and their respective assistants ; whereupon they agreed to declare and did declare the line surveyed, marked, and established as far W. as the 111th meridian, and from the 111th meridian to the Colorado r.; they further agreed, etc., that the whole of the line should be declared fully established, etc., and the field-work concluded, whenever each should notify the other that certain topographical work then in progress had been completed by Lieutenant Michler and Señor Jimenez ; whereupon, having no further business, the commission adjourned to meet in Washington, D. C., Apr. 1st, 1856. The required notifications were exchanged Oct. 15th and Dec. 18th, 1855. The work had been done, and subsequent proceedings were only in the nature of formalities between the two governments. My authority for the facts embodied in this note is of course the U. S. and M. B. S. Report unless otherwise stated. I have been led into this sketch of affairs of 40 years ago, partly by their intrinsic interest, but mainly because they show the state of things at a period of time equidistant between Pike's and the present day.

CHAPTER II.

𝕾UNDAY, Mar. 22d.   Remained at the Passo.

Mar. 23d.   Mass performed; left the Passo at three o'clock, to Fort Elisiaira [Elizario], accompanied by the lieutenant-governor, the vicar, and Allencaster, a brother of the governor.   Malgares, myself and the doctor took up our quarters at the house of Capt. [Blank], who was then at Chihuahua; but his lady and sister entertained us in a very elegant and hospitable manner.   They began playing cards and continued until late the third day.   Malgares, who won considerably, would send frequently $15 or $20 from the table to the lady of the house, her sister, and others, and beg their acceptance, in order that the goddess of fortune might still continue propitious; in this manner he distributed $500.

Around this fort were a great number of Appaches, who were on a treaty with the Spaniards.   These people appeared to be perfectly independent in their manners, and were the only savages I saw in the Spanish dominions whose spirit was not humbled—whose necks were not bowed to the yoke of their invaders.   With those people Malgares was extremely popular.   I believe he sought popularity with them and all the common people, for there was no man so poor or so humble, under whose roof he would not enter; when he walked out, I have seen him put a handful of dollars in his pocket, and give them all to the old men, women, and children before he returned to his quarters; but to equals he was haughty and overbearing.   This conduct he pursued through the whole provinces of New Mexico and

Biscay, when at a distance from the seat of government; but I could plainly perceive that he was cautious of his conduct as he approached the capital [city of Chihuahua]. I here left a letter for my sergeant.

Mar. 24th. Very bad weather.

Mar. 25th. The troops marched, but Lt. Malgares and my men remained.

Mar. 26th. Divine service was performed in the morning, in the garrison, at which all the troops attended under arms. At one part of their mass, they present arms; at another, sink on one knee and rest the muzzle of the gun on the ground, in signification of their submission to their divine master. At one o'clock, we bid adieu to our friendly hostess, who was one of the finest women I had seen in New Spain. At dusk arrived at a small pond made by a spring which arose in the center, called the Ogo mall a Ukap, and seemed formed by providence to enable the human race to pass that route, as it was the only water within 60 miles on the route. Here we overtook Sergeant Belardie with the party of dragoons from Senora and Biscay, who had left us at Fort Elisiaira, where we had received a new escort. Distance 20 miles.[1]

[1] The difficulty of trailing Pike in Mexico is twofold. His notes, hasty and stealthy under the circumstances, are necessarily meager, and rather excite than satisfy our curiosity to know more. Worse than this, all the maps of Mexico are poor. I have probably before me the best maps that exist ; they do not compare with those we have used for most parts of Pike's route. The most helpful one I have found is that in Senate Misc. Doc. No. 26, 30th Cong., 1st Sess., accompanying a Memoir of a Tour to Northern Mexico, connected with Col. Doniphan's Expedition, in 1846 and 1847, by A. Wislizenus, M. D., Washington, Tippin and Streeper, 1848, 8vo, pp. 141. The author was a German scientist, interested in geography, geology, and botany. He went over much of the identical route which Pike traveled,—as far as Parras, near Saltillo,—and has left a luminous itinerary, for the publication of which we are indebted to the good sense of Thomas H. Benton. This I shall draw heavily upon, and wish to make my grateful compliments to its author in the beginning of this route.

The *Fort* " Elisiaira " which Pike has just left must not be confounded with the place on the river called Elizario, Eleazario, Elceario, etc., and described in my last note. He is starting S., on the main road, and the place where the

Mar. 27th. Arrived at Carracal [Carrizal], at twelve o'clock,[2] Distance 28 miles; the road well watered and the situation pleasant. The father-in-law of our friend gambling dovetailed so well with religion was the Presidio San Elizario, on the boundary between the then Provinces of North Mexico and New Biscay. Two roads led from El Paso to Carrizal, the principal place en route to Chihuahua. One of these went down the Rio Grande for several miles before it turned S. from that river, taking this roundabout way to avoid Los Medanos (the Sand Hills, of which more presently). The other, which Pike took, went directly S., approximately by the way the railroad goes now. To the right is a range of mountains; the valley of the Rio Grande recedes to the left; the way is over a sandy, shrubby plain, in some places so strewn with a kind of white lime-stone as to have given the name Tierra Blanca. Camp is at the place which Pike calls by the extraordinary term of " Ogo mall a Ukap " and charts as " Ojo Malalka." Both these terms are otherwise rendered Ojo de Malayuque and Samalayuca; and all these, with others I could cite, are forms of the name of the same spring or pool which was a usual first camp out from El Paso. It was in most seasons a necessary halt, on account of water in this long arid stretch, as well as a desirable one to make before encountering the Sand Hills. Pike charts two other bodies of water, off the road to the right or W., by the names of " Lago de la Condelaria " and " Lac de Susma "; there are several such, in fact, known as Palomas, Guzman, Durazno, Santa Maria, etc. Guzman is the same word as Pike's " Susma," and a personal name very well known indeed in Mexican history; but whether the same lake is another question. Candelaria is the present name of a station on the railroad below Los Medanos.

   [2] Pike gives us nothing from Samalayuca to Carrizal, and we must fill the lacuna from other sources of information. The way grows gradually hillier and sandier, till it becomes all hills and sands. These are Los Medanos, dreaded for the difficulty of hauling loaded wagons through them, though not so bad on horseback or with pack-mules. Gregg describes the entourage, Comm. Pra., II. 1844, p. 79, as " a stupendous ledge of sand-hills, across which the road passes for about six miles. As teams are never able to haul the loaded wagons over this region of loose sand, we engaged an *atajo* of mules at El Paso, upon which to convey our goods across. These Médanos consist of huge hillocks and ridges of pure sand, in many places without a vestige of vegetation. Through the lowest gaps between the hills the road winds its way." This description calls to mind the Medano or Sand Hill Pass: see note [39], p. 491. Wislizenus is even more vivid, Mem. p. 44 : " Having arrived at the foot of the sand hills, we commenced travelling very slow. There was nothing around us but the deepest and purest sand, and the animals could only get along in the slowest walk, and by resting at short intervals. At last my animals were exhausted; they would move no more, and we had not yet reached half of our way. In this dilemma I put my own riding-horse to the wagon. Mr. Jacquez lent me some additional mules, and forward we moved again. In the meanwhile dark night had come on, illuminated only by lightning, that showed us for a while the most appalling

commanded six or seven years here.   When we arrived at
fort, the commandant, Don Pedro Rues Saramende, received
Robinson and myself with a cold bow, and informed Malgares that we could repair to the public quarters.   To this

night-scene—our wagons moving along as slow and solemn as a funeral procession ; ghastly riders on horseback, wrapped in blankets or cloaks ; some tired
travellers stretched out on the sand, others walking ahead, and tracing the road
with the fire of their cigarritos ; and the deepest silence, interrupted only by the
yelling exclamations of the drivers, and the rolling of distant thunder.   The
scene was impressive enough to be remembered by me ; but I made a vow the
same night, that whenever I should undertake this trip again, I would rather go
three days around, than travel once more over the sand hills with a wagon.
About midnight, at last we reached the southern end of the sand hills, and
encamped without water."

This bad place was about 6 m.   Beyond it, some 15 (?) m., is a fine spring of
water a few yards to the left, called Ojo Lucero or Venus' spring.   A place on
the railroad in this vicinity is named Rancheria.   Further on is seen, at some
distance to the right of the road, a square mound 20 feet high, with a warm
spring on its level top.   Beyond this, on the left, is Laguna de Patos, or
Duck l., a considerable body of water, which is the sink of the Rio Carmen.
The other road from El Paso to Carrizal joins the main road in this vicinity.
San José is a place on the railroad, opposite this lake.   Off to the right, in the
mountain chain above mentioned, rises a conspicuous picacho.   Carrizal is
a small town, like most places in Mexico (pop. 300 or 400 in 1839), but for some
time supported a presidio or garrison as a protection from Indians, and was also
walled in ; but neither of these defenses seems to have troubled the Apaches
much.   Turning to Pike's map, we find he marks " Presidio de Carracal " on
a branch of a large " Rio de Carracal," which he runs N. E. into the Rio
Grande.   But this is the Carmen r. just said, which runs into Duck l. not far
from where Pike makes it head, and probably never reaches the Rio Grande.
Yet it is liable to freshets and may greatly overflow its usual limits.   Gregg
struck one when he passed this way in 1839 and describes it, *l. c.*: " Just as we
passed Lake Patos, we were struck with astonishment at finding the road ahead
of us literally overflowed by an immense body of water, with a brisk current, as
if some great river had suddenly been conjured into existence by the aid of
supernatural arts.   A considerable time elapsed before we could unravel the
mystery.   At last we discovered that a freshet had lately occurred in the streams
that fed Lake Patos and caused it to overflow its banks, which accounted for
this unwelcome visitation.   We had to flounder through the mud and water for
several hours before we succeeded in getting across."   The spring which Pike
marks " Ojo de Lotario " (Lothario) is that above named as Lucifer or Venus ;
and the hill delineated close by it is probably intended for the mound above
said.   He marks the road which leads from Carrizal to Sonora " Camino a
Senora."

Malgares indignantly replied that he should accompany us, and turned to go, when the commandant took him by the arm, made many apologies to him and us, and we at length reluctantly entered his quarters.   Here for the first time I saw the gazettes of Mexico, which gave rumors of Colonel [Aaron] Burr's conspiracies, the movements of our troops, etc.; but which were stated in so vague and undefined a manner as only to create our anxiety without throwing any light on the subject.

Mar. 28th.   Marched at half past three o'clock, and arrived at the Warm Springs [Ojos Calientes] at sundown ; crossed one little fosse on the route.[3]

Sunday, Mar. 29th.   Marched at ten o'clock, and continued our route, with but a short halt, until sundown, when we encamped without water.   Distance 30 miles.

Mar. 30th.   Marched before seven o'clock ; the front arrived at water at eleven o'clock ; the mules, at twelve. The spring[5] on the side of the mountain, to the east of the

[3] Pike's " little fosse " is no doubt the acequia below Carrizal.   Ojo Caliente is present name of a station on the railroad between Carmen station and Las Minas ; and the warm springs where Pike camps are those at or near Alamo de Peña, 10–12 m. below Carrizal, a mile short of the crossing of Rio Carmen. Gregg and Wislizenus both describe the springs in similar terms, as forming a large basin of clear, pure, lukewarm water in porphyritic rocks, with a sandy bottom, fed from various sources, and overrunning in a rivulet into the Carmen. " It forms," says Gregg, Com. Pra., II. p. 80, " a basin some 30 feet long by about half that width, and just deep and warm enough for a most delightful bath at all seasons of the year.   Were this spring . . . anywhere within the United States it would doubtless soon be converted into a place of fashionable resort."   Wislizenus determined a temperature of 82° F., the air being 84½° F.   Hughes in Doniphan's Exp., p. 108, also describes the spring and states that it was formerly the seat of a princely hacienda, " belonging to Porus, a Spanish nabob," who at one time had on his estate 36,000 head of stock.

[4] A long, hard march over a plain waterless except in rainy weather, and a dry camp ; for though Pike is past the place he marks " Les Coquillas," he stops short of the Ojo de Callejon.

[5] This spring is found on various maps by the names of " Gallejo," " Gallego," etc., also applied to a station on the railroad.   Hughes gives the word as " Guyagas."   I suppose the proper name to be Ojo de Callejon, which might be translated Pass spring—for the mountains on each side of the road here close in somewhat, leaving a pass or *puerta* between them.   Otherwise, the word is

road, is a beautiful situation.   I here saw the first ash timber
I observed in the country.   This water is 52 miles from the
Warm Springs.   Yesterday and to-day saw cabrie [antelope,
Antilocapra americana].   Marched 15 miles further and
encamped without wood or water ; passed two other small
springs to the east of the road.

Mar. 31st.   Marched early and arrived at an excellent
spring at ten o'clock.   The roads from Senora, Tanos
[qu: Yanos?], Buenaventura, etc., join about 400 yards
before you arrive at this spring.[6]

Arrived at the village of [hiatus][7] at night, a large and

callejo or *calleyo,* meaning pitfall.   This spring is off to the left, and sometimes
discharges water enough to make a rivulet, which crosses the road.   One of the
other two springs which Pike speaks of passing is no doubt that known as
Callejito.

[6] The   text does not agree with the map, for on the latter a " Camino a
Senora " (road to Sonora) is brought into an unnamed " Ojo " which Pike has
already passed.   There may have been more than one such road.   In any
event, the spring which Pike passes on the 31st is that marked on his map
" Aqas nueva," *i. e.,* Aguas Nuevas or Agua Nueva.   A station on the railroad
has the latter name.

[7] The hiatus in the text is to be filled by El Peñol or Hacienda del Petrero ;
Pike marks " Delpetrero " on his map, the last place he notes before reaching
Chihuahua.   Neither of those names appears on the late maps before me, but
both were formerly employed for the well-known locality.   Wislizenus maps
El Peñol, where he camped Aug. 22d, 1846, and speaks of the place as a large
hacienda, 28 m. from his last camp (probably the same as Pike's of the 30th)
and about 40 m. from Chihuahua.   " The creek of the same name passing by
the hacienda is the principal affluent of the lake of Encinillas ; by the rains it
was swelled to a torrent, and its roaring waves, rushing over all obstacles,
sounded in the stillness of night like a cataract."   Pike has not a word of this lake,
though it is usually a conspicuous feature of the great plain he has just traversed,
to the W. of the road.   He maps it, quite small, by the name of " Lago de
Sⁿ. Martin."   Laguna de las Encinillas, in English Lake of Live Oaks, is a
body of water whose extent varies greatly according to season and the weather,
being sometimes 15 or 20 m. long, though usually less than this ; Wislizenus
estimated its length when he saw it to be 15 m., with a width of 3 m. on an
average.   Gregg says, *tom. cit.,* p. 81 : " This lake is ten or twelve miles long
by two or three in width, and seems to have no outlet during the greatest
freshets, though fed by several small constant-flowing streams from the surrounding mountains.   The water of this lake during the dry season is so strongly
impregnated with nauseous and bitter salts as to render it wholly unpalatable
to man and beast.   The most predominant of these noxious substances is a

elegant house, for the country; here were various labors
carried on by criminals in irons. We here met with a
Catalonian, who was but a short time from Spain, whose
dialect was such that he could scarcely be understood by
Malgares, and whose manners were much more like those
of a citizen of our Western frontiers than of a subject of
a despotic prince.

Apr. 1st.[8]   In the morning Malgares dispatched a courier

species of alkali, known there by the title of *tequesquite*. It is often seen
oozing out from the surface of marshy grounds, about the table plains of all
Northern Mexico, forming a grayish crust, and is extensively used in the manufacture of soap, and sometimes by the bakers even for raising bread."

[8] As Pike has not a word of the route from El Peñol to Chihuahua, we may
supply the omission from other sources. The approach to the capital presented
then, as it does now, a number of both artificial and natural features. There
were several settlements, as, for instance, Encinillas at the S. end of the lake,
and Sauz beyond this. Both of these are places to be found marked by the
same names now; the railroad runs through them. Further on, the road
crossed the Arroyo Seco, usually a dry gulch, as its name says, but sometimes
a creek not easily crossed, owing to depth of water. It flows eastward to fall
into the Sacramento a few miles below. About 3 m. beyond this arroyo is the
valley of the Sacramento, memorable since the battle which was won by the
Americans under Colonel Doniphan on Sunday the 28th of February, 1847. Says
Wislizenus, Mem. p. 47 : " The mountains above the Sacramento approach
each other from the east and west, and narrow the intermediate plain to the
width of about six miles ; and on the Sacramento itself, where new spurs of
mountains project, to about 3 miles. The road from the Arroyo Seco to the
Sacramento leads at first over a high plain ; but as soon as the Sacramento
comes in sight, it descends abruptly to its valley and to the left bank of the
creek. Near where the road begins to descend, a ravine, with an opposite
long hill, runs to the left or east of it, and a level plain spreads out to the right
or west of it. On the hill towards the east was a continuous line of batteries
and intrenchments, and the principal force of the Mexican army was there collected. On the opposite plain from the west, the American troops, who had
above the Arroyo Seco already turned to the right to gain a more favorable
position, advanced in open field against their entrenched and far more numerous
enemies. How the American artillery with the first opening of their fire struck
terror into the Mexican ranks ; how the brave Missourians then, on horseback
and on foot, acted by one impulse, rushed through the ravine up to the cannon's
mouth, and, overthrowing and killing everything before them, took one battery
after the other, till the whole line of entrenchments was in their possession and
the enemy put to complete flight ; how they crossed from here to the Sacramento
and stormed on its right bank the last fortified position, on a steep hill, till not

with a letter to the Commandant-general Salcedo, to inform him of our approach, and also one to his father-in-law.

Apr. 2d. When we arrived at Chihuahua, we pursued our course through the town to the house of the general. I was much astonished to see with what anxiety Malgares anticipated the meeting with his military chief. Having been on the most arduous and enterprising expedition ever undertaken by any of his Majesty's officers from these provinces, and having executed it with equal spirit and judgment, yet was he fearful of his [Salcedo's] meeting him with an eye of displeasure. He appeared to be much more agitated than ourselves, although we may be supposed to have also had our sensations, as on the will of this man depended our future destiny, at least until our country could interfere in our behalf. On our arrival at the general's, we were halted in the hall of the guard until word was sent to the general of our arrival, when Malgares was first intro-duced. He remained some time, during which a French-man came up and endeavored to enter into conversation with us, but was soon frowned into silence, as we conceived he was only some authorized spy. Malgares at last came

a Mexican was left to oppose them, and all their cannon, ammunition, and trains were abandoned to the victors—these are facts well known in the history of that campaign, and will immortalize the brave volunteers of Missouri." A full account of the battle is given by the historian of Doniphan's Expedition, p. 110 *seq.*, with a plan of the ground. The U. S. forces were 924 all told, with 6 pieces of artillery ; their loss was 1 killed and 11 wounded, 3 mortally. The Americans had 140 additional men, teamsters and others, raising the total to 1,164. Of the 924, 117 were of the artillery, 93 were of an escort, and the remainder of the 1st Regt. Missouri mounted volunteers. The Mexicans had 4,224 men, and 16 pieces of artillery ; their loss was 320 killed, 560 wounded, 72 prisoners. Hughes' article cited includes Colonel Doniphan's official report.

The Sacramento is the stream upon two small tributaries of which Chihuahua is situated, at their junction, about 20 m. from the scene described. The river is usually fordable. The road leads over a level plain, which widens somewhat southward, down the valley of the river, with steep, rough mountains on either hand. The capital first comes in sight about 10 m. off, in a sort of pocket where the mountains come together from each side, as if to close up the valley below ; but there is an outlet to the E. through which the Sacramento r. runs to join the Rio Conchos.

out and asked me to walk in. I found the general sitting at his desk; he was a middle-sized man, apparently about 55 years of age, with a stern countenance ; but he received me graciously and beckoned to a seat.

He then observed, " You have given us and yourself a great deal of trouble."

Captain Pike. On my part entirely unsought, and on that of the Spanish government voluntary.

General Salcedo. Where are your papers ?

Captain Pike. Under charge of Lieutenant Malgares.

Malgares was then ordered to have my small trunk brought in, which being done, a Lieutenant Walker came in, who is a native of New Orleans, his father an Englishman, his mother a French woman, and who spoke both those languages equally well, also the Spanish. He was a lieutenant of dragoons in the Spanish service, and master of the military school at Chihuahua. This same young gentleman was employed by Mr. Andrew Ellicott,[9] as a deputy surveyor on the

---

[9] B. Bucks Co., Pa., Jan. 24th, 1754, of Quaker parentage (his father was one of those who had land on the Patapsco, and founded Ellicott's Mills, now Ellicott City, near Baltimore, Md., 1774) ; became a distinguished astronomer, surveyor, and civil engineer, and died professor of mathematics at West Point, N. Y., Aug. 29th, 1820. He did an immense amount of surveying and boundary-running, mostly of important and official public character, in New York, Pennsylvania, Maryland, Virginia, and elsewhere ; in 1790, was directed by Washington to lay out the city of that name ; in 1792 became surveyor-general of the U. S.; and in 1796 was appointed by Washington U. S. Commissioner under the treaty of San Lorenzo el Real, to run the southern boundary between the U. S. and New Spain. This is the work to which Pike alludes, though he is a little out in his dates, as witness the following title : The Journal of Andrew Ellicott, late Commissioner on behalf of the United States during part of the year 1796, the years 1797, 1798, 1799, and part of the year 1800 : for determining the boundary between the United States and the possessions of his Catholic Majesty in America, containing, . . . etc., Philada., Budd and Bartram, 1803, 1 vol. 4to, pp. i–viii, 1–299, with 6 maps, and Appendix, pp. 1–151, 1 leaf errata, and 8 more maps. Ellicott wrote this book, excepting the Appendix, at Lancaster, Pa., June to Nov., 1802 ; and while he was there in 1803 he coached Captain Meriwether Lewis in the use of astronomical instruments : see L. and C., ed. 1893, p. xxii and p. xxiv. Going down the Ohio to the scene of his official functions, Dec. 17th, 1796, Ellicott says, p. 21 : " I passed the mouth of the Tennessee, and in two hours afterwards arrived at Fort Massac, and was politely

Florida line between the United States and Spain, in the years 1797 and '98. General Salcedo then desired him to assist me in taking out my papers, and requested me to explain the nature of each ; such as he conceived were relevant to the expedition he caused to be laid on one side, and those

received by the commandant Captain Pike," etc. This was Zebulon Pike, father of Zebulon M.: see the Memoir, *anteà*. The fort stood on the N. (right) bank, about lat. 37° 14' ; early F. history obscure and not all of it authentic ; site supposed to have been first occupied *ca.* 1711 : see Beck's Gaz., 1823, p. 114, and John Reynolds' Own Times, 2d. ed. p. 16, with description of the place as it was in 1855. In descending the Ohio in 1758 the F. officer Aubry halted on the N. bank, at the old site, called 36 m. above the mouth of the river, to build a new post, which was garrisoned with 100 men and called Fort *Marsiac* after the first commandant. Thus the name is not Massac, as usually said, and still less is it derived from the apocryphal *massacre* which various historians have exploited. This fort was the last establishment of the F. on the Ohio, being kept up till they evacuated the country under the Treaty of Paris, 1763 ; it was a U. S. post till after the war of 1812–14, and during our occupancy became known as the old Cherokee fort. Pike alludes in the present work to a certain *Nolan*, who is easy to identify, but not to find out much about. Ellicott met him at the mouth of the Ohio, in Jan., 1797 : " Mr. Philip Nolan, so well known for his athletic exertions, and dexterity in taking wild horses, stopped at our camp on his way from New Madrid to fort Massac," says this author, p. 29, with a footnote stating that Nolan " was killed by the Spaniards in the spring of 1801," after taking a very active part in various disturbances in that quarter. Ellicott passed down the Miss. r., past the Chickasaw bluffs (L. and C., ed. 1893, p. xl. and p. lii), and at Natchez encountered a bigger bluff in the shape of an individual who described himself in his pronunciamentos as his Excellency Francis Lewis Hector, Baron de Carondelet, Knight of the Order of Malta, Major General of his Armies, Commandant General of Louisiana and West Florida, Inspector of the Troops, Militia, etc., etc., etc. (though what his triplicate etceteras were is not given to ordinary mortals to know). This climacteric functionary was supported by a lesser luminary who filled the rôle of Don Manuel Gayoso de Lemas, Brigadier of the Royal Armies, Governor of Natchez and its dependencies, with three-ply etceteras as before (though he was dead before Aug., 1799). These two formidable obstructions to navigation, as an engineer might say, were not overcome by our surveyor-general for nearly a year, during which period they kept him busy with Spanish diplomacy. As I read the correspondence it seems to have largely consisted in saying they hoped God would bless and keep him forever, when they really hoped the devil would fly away with him before breakfast ; and he had to silence both the caterwauling choristers before he could proceed with his scientific work. This he was free to do on the Spanish evacuation of the forts at Natchez and Nogales (Walnut Hills) in Jan., 1798.

which were not of a public nature on the other; the whole either passing through the hands of the general or of Walker, except a few letters from my lady. On my taking these up, and saying they were letters from a lady, the general gave a proof that, if the ancient Spanish bravery had degenerated in the nation generally, their gallantry still existed, by bowing; and I put them in my pocket. He then informed me that he would examine the papers, but that in the meanwhile he wished me to make out and present to him a short sketch of my voyage,[10] which might probably be satisfactory. This I would have positively refused, had I had an idea that it was his determination to keep the papers, which I could not at that time conceive, from the urbanity and satisfaction which he appeared to exhibit on the event of our interview. He then told me that I would take up my quarters with Walker, in order, as he said, to be better accommodated by having a person with me who spoke the English language; but the object, as I suspected, was for him to be a spy on our actions and on those who visited us.

Robinson all this time had been standing in the guard-room, boiling with indignation at being so long detained there, subject to the observations of the soldiery and gaping curiosity of the vulgar. He was now introduced, by some mistake of one of the aides-de-camp. He appeared and made a slight bow to the general, who demanded of Malgares who he [Robinson] was. He replied, "A doctor who accompanied the expedition." "Let him retire," said the governor; and he went out.

The general then invited me to return and dine with him, and we went to the quarters of Walker, where we received several different invitations to take quarters at houses where we might be better accommodated; but, understanding that the general had designated our quarters, we were silent.

We returned to dine at the palace, where we met Malgares, who, besides ourselves, was the only guest. He had

---

[10] This paper was given in full in the App. to Pt. 3, of which it originally formed Doc. No. 13, pp. 73–77, and will be found beyond.

at the table the treasurer, Truxillio [qu.: Trujillo?], and a priest called Father Rocus.

Apr. 3d. Employed in giving a sketch of our voyage for the general and commandant of those provinces. Introduced to Don Bernardo Villamil; Don Alberto Mayner, lieutenant-colonel, and father-in-law to Malgares; and Don Manuel Zuloaga, a member of the secretary's office, to whom I am under obligations of gratitude, and shall remember with esteem. Visited his house in the evening.

Apr. 4th. Visited the hospital, where were two officers, who were fine-looking men, and I was informed had been the gayest young men of the province. They were moldering away by disease, and there was not a physician in his Majesty's hospitals who was able to cure them; but after repeated attempts, all had given them up to perish. This shows the deplorable state of medical science in the provinces. I endeavored to get Robinson to undertake the cure of these poor fellows, but the jealousy and envy of the Spanish doctors made it impracticable.

Sunday, Apr. 5th. Visited by Lieutenant Malgares, with a very polite message from his Excellency, delivered in the most impressive terms, with offers of assistance, money, etc., for which I returned my respectful thanks to the general. Accompanied Malgares to the public walk, where we found the secretary, Captain Villamil, Zuloaga, and other officers of distinction. We here likewise met the wife of my friend Malgares, to whom he introduced us. She was, like all the other ladies of New Spain, a little *en bon point*, but possessed the national beauty of eye in a superior degree. There was a large collection of ladies, amongst whom were two of the most celebrated in the capital—Señora Maria Con. Caberairi, and Señora Margeurite Vallois, the only two ladies who had spirit sufficient, and their husbands generosity enough, to allow them to think themselves rational beings, to be treated on an equality, to receive the visits of their friends, and give way to the hospitality of their dispositions without restraint. They were consequently the envy of other ladies, and the subject of scandal to prudes; their houses were the rendezvous of all the fashionable male society ; and every man who was conspicuous for science, arts, or arms, was sure to meet a welcome. We, as unfortunate strangers, were consequently not forgotten. I returned with Malgares to the house of his father-in-law, Lieutenant-Colonel Mayner, who was originally from Cadiz, a man of good information.

Apr. 6th. Dined with the general. Writing, etc. In the evening visited Malgares and the secretary. After dinner wine was set on the table, and we were entertained with songs in the French, Italian, Spanish, and English languages. Accustomed as I was to sitting some time after dinner I forgot their *siesta*, or repose after dinner, until Walker suggested the thing to me, when we retired.

Apr. 7th. Dined at Don Antonio Caberairi's, [qu.: Cabrera's?] in company with Villamil, Zuloaga, Walker, etc. Sent in the sketch of my voyage to the general. Spent the evening at Colonel Mayner's with Malgares.

Apr. 8th. Visited the treasurer, who showed me the double-barreled gun given by Governor [Wm. C. C.] Claiborne, and another formerly the property of [Captain Philip] Nolan [see note [9], p. 657, and legend on Pike's map].

Apr. 9th. In the evening I was informed that David Ferro [11] was in town and wished to speak to me. This man had formerly been my father's ensign, and was taken with Nolan's party at the time the latter was killed. He possessed a brave soul, and had withstood every oppression, since being made prisoner, with astonishing fortitude. Although his leaving the place of his confinement, the village of St. Jeronimie [San Jeronimo], without the knowledge of the general, was in some measure clandestine, yet a countryman, an acquaintance, and formerly a brother soldier, in

[11] David Fero, Jr., of New York, was an ensign of the 3d sub-Legion from May 12th, 1794, to Nov. 1st, 1796, when he was assigned to the 3d Infantry, in which he became a lieutenant Oct. 3d, 1798, and from which he resigned July 22d, 1799.

a strange land, in distress, had ventured much to see me—
could I deny him the interview from any motives of delicacy? No; forbid it, humanity! forbid it, every sentiment
of my soul!

Our meeting was affecting, tears standing in his eyes. He
informed me of the particulars of their being taken, and
many other circumstances since they had been in the
country. I promised to do all I could for him consistently
with my character and honor, and their having entered the
country without the authority of the United States. As he
was obliged to leave town before day, he called on me at my
quarters, when I bid him adieu, and gave him what my
purse afforded, not what my heart dictated.

Apr. 10th. In the evening at Colonel Maynor's. Captain Rodiriques [Rodriguez] arrived from the province of
Texas, where he had been under arrest one year, for going
to Natchitoches with the Marquis Cassa Calvo [Marques de
Casa Calva].

Apr. 11th. Rode out in the coach with Malgares; was
hospitably entertained at the house of one of the Vallois,
where we drank London porter. Visited Secretary Villamil.

Sunday, Apr. 12th. Dined with the doctor, at Don Antonio Caberarie's, with our usual guests. In the evening at
the public walks.

Apr. 13th. Nothing extraordinary.

Apr. 14th. Spent the forenoon in writing; the afternoon
at Don Antonio Caberarie's.

Apr. 15th. Spent the evening at Colonel Maynor's [qu.:
Mayron's?] with our friend Malgares. Wrote a letter to
Governor Salcedo on the subject of my papers.[12]

Apr. 16th. Spent the evening at the secretary's, Don
Villamil's.

Apr. 17th. Sent my letter to his Excellency. Spent the
evening with my friend Malgares.

---

[12] This appeal and remonstrance was given in the App. to Pt. 3, where it
originally formed Doc. No. 14, pp. 78, 79, dated Apr. 14th; it will be found
beyond.

Apr. 18th. Spent the evening at Caberarie's, etc. Wrote to Governor Allencaster.

Sunday, Apr. 19th. In the evening at a fandango.

Apr. 20th. We this day learned that an American officer had gone on to the city of Mexico. This was an enigma to us inexplicable, as we conceived that the jealousy of the Spanish government would have prevented any foreign officer from penetrating the country; and why the United States could send an authorized agent to the viceroyalty, when the Spanish government had at the seat of our government a chargé d'affaires, served but to darken the conjectures. The person alluded to was Mr. Burling, a citizen of Mississippi Territory, whose mission is now well known to the government. We likewise received an account of a commercial treaty having been entered into between Great Britain and the United States, which by the Dons was only considered as the preliminary step to an alliance offensive and defensive between the two nations.

Apr. 21st. Presented the commanding general with a letter for General Wilkinson, which he promised to have forwarded to the governor of Texas.

Apr. 22d. Spent the day in reading and studying Spanish; the evening at Captain Villamil's.

Apr. 23d. Dined at Don Pedro Vallois'; spent the evening with Colonel Maynor; bade him adieu, as he was to march the next day. In the evening received a letter from the commandant-general, informing me my papers were to be detained, giving a certificate of their numbers, contents, etc.[13]

Apr. 24th. Spent the evening at Zuloaga's with his relations. About sundown an officer of the government called upon me, and told me that the government had been informed that, in conversations in all societies, Robinson and myself had held forth political maxims and principles which, if just, I must be conscious if generally disseminated would in a very few years be the occasion of a revolt of

---

[13] These papers, originally forming Docs. Nos. 15 and 16, were given in the App. to Pt. 3, pp. 79–82, and will be found beyond.

those kingdoms; that those impressions had taken such effect that it was no uncommon thing, in the circles in which he associated, to hear the comparative principles of a republican and a monarchical government discussed, and even the allegiance due, in case of certain events, to the court called in question; that various characters of consideration had indulged themselves in those conversations, all of whom were noted and would be taken care of; but that, as respected myself and companion, it was the desire of his Excellency that while in the dominions of Spain we would not hold forth any conversations whatsoever, either on the subject of religion or politics.

I replied that it was true I had held various and free conversations on the subjects complained of, but only with men high in office, who might be supposed to be firmly attached to the king, and partial to the government of their country; that I had never gone among the poor and illiterate, preaching up republicanism or a free government; that as to the catholic religion, I had only combated some of what I conceived to be its illiberal dogmas; that I had spoken of it in all instances as a respectable branch of the Christian religion which, as well as all others, was tolerated in the United States; and that, had I come to that kingdom in a diplomatic character, delicacy toward the government would have sealed my lips; or had I been a prisoner of war, personal safety might have had the same effect; but, being there in the capacity which I was, not voluntarily, but by coercion of the Spanish government, which at the same time had officially notified me that they did not consider me under any restraint whatever; therefore, when called on, I should always give my opinions freely, either as to politics or religion; but at the same time with urbanity, and a proper respect to the legitimate authorities of the country where I was.

He replied, " Well, you may then rest assured your conduct will be represented in no very favorable point of view to your government."

I replied, " To my government I am certainly responsible, and to no other."

He then left me. I immediately waited on some of my friends and notified them of the threat, at which they appeared much alarmed. We went immediately to consult [Malgares], who, to great attachment to his friends, joined the most incorruptible loyalty and the confidence of the government. Our consultation ended in a determination only to be silent and watch events.

We suspected [Walker] to be the informant, but whether just in our suspicion or not, I will not pretend to determine; for Robinson and myself frequently used to hold conversations in his presence, purposely to have them communicated; but he at last discovered our intentions, and told us that if we calculated on making him a carrier of news, we were mistaken; that he despised it.

Apr. 25th. At eleven o'clock I called on his Excellency, but was informed that he was engaged. About three o'clock I received a message from him by Lieutenant Walker, informing me that he was surprised I had not returned, and to call without ceremony in the evening; which I did, and presented him with a letter.[14] He then also candidly informed me my party would not join me in the territory of the king of Spain, but that they should be attended to punctually, and forwarded on immediately after me; and requested that I should give orders to my sergeant to deliver up all his ammunition, and dispose in some manner of the horses of which he had charge. I stated in reply that, with respect to the ammunition, I would give orders to my sergeant to deliver, if demanded, all they possessed, more than was necessary to fill their horns; but that as to the horses, I considered their loss was a charge which must be adjusted between the two governments, and therefore should not give any directions respecting them, except as to bringing them on as far and as long as they

[14] This letter appeared in the App. to Part. 3, where it originally formed Doc. No. 17, pp. 82, 83, dated Apr. 4th, and will be found beyond.

were able to travel. He then gave me an invitation to dine with him on the morrow.

Sunday, Apr. 26th. Dined at the general's. In the evening went to Malgares', Zuloaga's, and others'. Wrote to my sergeant and Fero; to the latter of whom I sent $10, and to the other $161.84, to purchase clothes for the party. We had been for some time suspicious that the doctor was to be detained; but this evening he likewise obtained permission to pursue his journey with me, which diffused general joy through all the party.

Apr. 27th. Spent the day in making arrangements for our departure, writing to the sergeant, etc.

I will here mention some few anecdotes relative to [Walker], with whom we boarded during our stay in Chihuahua. When we came to the city we went to his quarters, by order of the general, and considered ourselves as guests, having not the least idea that we should be charged with board, knowing with what pleasure any American officer would receive and entertain a foreign brother soldier situated as we were, and that we should conceive it a great insult to be offered pay under similar circumstances. But one day, after we had been there about a week, he presented to me an account for Robinson's and my board, receipted, and begged, if the general inquired of me, that I would say I had paid it. This naturally led me to demand how the thing originated. He with considerable embarrassment observed that he had taken the liberty to remark to the general that he thought he should be allowed an extra allowance, in order to be enabled to treat us with some little distinction. The general flew into a violent passion, and demanded if I had not paid him for our board? To which the other replied, No, he did not expect pay of us. He ordered him immediately to demand pay, to receive it, sign a receipt, and lodge it in his hands; and added that he would consult me if [to ascertain whether] the thing was done. This he never did; yet I took care, every Sunday after that, to deposit in the hands of Walker a sum which was considered the proportion for Robinson and myself. Malgares and several others of the Spanish officers having heard of the thing, waited on us much mortified, saying with what pleasure they would have entertained us had not the designation of the general pointed out his will on the subject.

[Walker] had living with him an old negro, the only one I saw on that side of St. Antonio, who was the property of some person who resided near Natchez, and who had been taken with Nolan. Having been acquainted with him in the Mississippi country, he solicited and obtained permission for old Cæsar to live with him. I found him very communicative and extremely useful. The day I arrived, when we were left alone, he came in, looked around at the walls of the room, and exclaimed, "What! all gone?" I demanded an explanation, and he informed me that the maps of the different provinces, as taken by [Walker] and other surveyors, had been hung up against the walls; but that the day we arrived they had all been taken down and deposited in a closet which he designated.

W[alker] gave various reasons for having left the United States and joined the Spanish service; one of which was, his father having been ill-treated, as he conceived, by G. at Natchez. At Chihuahua he had charge of the military school, which consisted of about 15 young men of the first families of the provinces; also of the public water-works of the city, on a plan devised by the royal engineer of Mexico; of the building of a new church; of the casting of small artillery, fabrication of arms, etc. Thus, though he had tendered his resignation, they knew his value too well to part with him, and would not accept of it, but still kept him in a subordinate station, in order that he might be the more dependent and the more useful. Although he candidly confessed his disgust at their service, manners, morals, and political establishments, yet he never made a communication to us which he was bound in honor to conceal; but on the contrary fulfilled the station of informer, which in that country is considered no disgrace, with great punctuality and fidelity. In this city the proverb was literally true, that "the walls have ears"; for scarcely anything could pass that his Excellency did not know in a few hours.

In the evening I was notified to be ready to march the next day at three o'clock.

Apr. 28th. In the morning Malgares waited on us, and informed us he was to accompany us some distance on the route. After bidding adieu to all our friends, we marched at a quarter past three o'clock, and encamped at nine o'clock at a stony spring; passed near Chihuahua a small ridge of mountains, and then encamped in a hollow.[15]

As we were riding along, Malgares rode up to me and informed me that the general had given orders that I should not be permitted to make any astronomical observations. To this I replied that he well knew I never had attempted making any since I had been conducted into the Spanish dominions.

Apr. 29th. Arrived at a settlement [Horcasitas or Bachimba?] at eight o'clock; plenty of milk, etc.

When about to make my journal, Malgares changed color, and informed me it was his orders I should not take

[15] Mapula or vicinity—perhaps on the spot noted in Wislizenus' itinerary of Doniphan's vanguard, Apr. 25th, 1847, Mem. p. 62 : "They made on that day but 14 miles, and encamped at Coursier's hacienda, near Mapula. This place is to the right of the usual road, and about five miles out of the way, but has to be resorted to for want of water, if one does not intend to go in one trip as far as Bachimba, the nearest watering place on the road, and 32 miles from Chihuahua." Mapula is marked on modern maps as on the railroad, S. E. from Chihuahua, while a Fresno appears to the right, due S. from that city. Pike is to follow the present railroad for many miles, but more or less inexactly. His "small ridge of mountains" is passed about 4 m. S. of Chihuahua; this is a range of hills which encompass the city on that side, and command a fine view. On crossing them, the main road runs S. E. in a valley 10 m. wide, bounded E. and W. by mountain ridges, with Coursier's hacienda and Mapula off to the right. About 20 m. from Chihuahua these ridges hem the valley so closely as to form a cañon 5 or 6 m. long and 1 m. or less wide ; Wislizenus notes a spring and ranche in this cañon ; qu.: now called Horcasitas? Bachimba is in the plain, about 5 m. off the cañon, on a fine running stream ; in 1847 it was a hacienda with a dozen houses.

notes ; but added, "you have a good memory, and when you get to Cogquilla [Coahuila] you can bring it all up." At first I felt considerably indignant, and was on the point of refusing to comply ; but thinking for a moment of the many politenesses I had received from his hands induced me merely to bow assent with a smile. We proceeded on our route, but had not gone far before I made a pretext to halt, established my boy as a vedet [vidette], sat down peaceably under a bush, and made my notes. This course I pursued ever after, not without some very considerable degree of trouble to separate myself from the party.

Arrived at the fort of St. Paul at eleven o'clock, situated on a small river of the same name, the course of which is N. E. by S. W. At the time we were there the river was not wider than a mill stream ; but sometimes it is 300 yards wide, and impassable. Distance 30 miles.[16]

Apr. 30th. Marched at six o'clock, and at eleven arrived at [Saucillo, on] the river Conchos—24 miles ; beautiful green trees on its banks. I was taken very sick at half past ten o'clock. Arrived at night at a small station [Las Garzas] on the river Conchos, garrisoned by a sergeant and 10 men from Fort Conchos, 15 leagues up said river. Distance 43 miles.[17]

[16] Pike marks the fort " P[residio] de S[n.] Paubla," and the river " Rio S[n] Paubla," without prejudice to the gender of the holy person concerned. Modern Ortiz is about the site of the Presidio San Pablo, on the railroad, on the N. or left bank of the river ; the latter is present Rio San Pedro, a large branch of the Conchos which falls in above Julimes. About 10 m. S. of Bachimba the road forked ; the right-hand fork went S. S. E., to Santa Cruz de Rosales, which was said to contain 5,000 inhabitants in itself and vicinity in 1847 ; it is on the Rio San Pedro, 8 m. higher up than San Pablo, to which the left-hand road leads S. E. The latter is the one Pike took ; it is shorter than the other ; both come together before Saucillo is reached. In 1847 San Pablo was reported to be " a flourishing place, with about 4,000 inhabitants": Wislizenus, Mem. p. 63. Rio San Pedro is a fine stream, over 100 m. long, heading in the mountains on the W. The plain or valley which it traverses, and in which both the roads above mentioned lie, has a varying width of 25–35 m.

[17] Pike struck Rio Conchos where the railroad does now—at Saucillo, or El Saucillo, a town on the left or W. bank of the river ; the " 24 miles " from San Pablo to this place is about right. This march was through the same valley as

May 1st.   Marched up the Conchos to its confluence with the river Florada [Rio Florido], 15 leagues from where we left the former [Conchos] river, and took up the latter [Rio Florido], which bears from the Conchos S. 80° and 50° E. On its banks are some very flourishing settlements, and they are well timbered. A poor miserable village [Santa Rosalia] is at the confluence. Came 10 miles up the Florada to dinner, and at night stopped at a private house. This property or plantation was valued formerly at $300,000, extending on the Florada, from the small place where we slept on the 30th of April, 30 leagues up said river.   Distance 45 miles.[18]

yesterday's, with a good but not such a level road, as the mountains approach each other near Saucillo, leaving S. of it a gap through which the road continues into the next valley.   The night's small station is less easily identified, but was no doubt at Las Garzas or in that immediate vicinity, where the Conchos is crossed. A Mexican league is supposed to be 5,000 varas (of about 33 inches each=about 4,583 yards, or nearly 2⅔ m.), but in itineraries is usually found to be less than this.   Las Garzas (Sp. *garzas*, "herons") is an obscure place not to be found on many modern maps ; it is beyond Concho and La Cruz (both of which are points on the railroad).   Wislizenus notes it on his journey, Mem. p. 64 : " We passed through la Cruz, a small town, and further below [further S., but higher up Rio Conchos], through las Garzas, a smaller place yet, where we crossed the Conchos."   It is the place marked " Pres[idio]" on Pike's map, which is probably in error in marking the trail as continuing up the left bank of the Conchos.

Rio Conchos is the principal river of Chihuahua, over 400 m. long, and with its many tributaries watering much of the State.   The name is said to be derived from its shells (Sp. *conchas*), and I have seen Shell r. in print.   It makes a long loop southward before turning N., and then runs about N. E. into the Rio Grande at Presidio del Norte—a place also called Presidio de las Juntas (lettered " Santas " on Pike's map) from the confluence of the two rivers.   Rios Florido and San Pedro are its principal tributaries.   Pike lays down the Conchos pretty well : notice particularly its northward course on the W. of the mountains, along what is called on his map " Puerta de la Virgin."

[18] Pike's route of May 1st probably crossed the Conchos at or near Las Garzas, and continued approximately up the right or E. bank of that river to the confluence of Rio Florido, opp. Santa Rosalia, the " poor miserable village " of the text, which stood on a hill in the point between the two rivers ; its present name is the same ; the railroad passes it now.   Writing of Apr. 30th, 1847, Wislizenus has, Mem. p. 65 : " Santa Rosalia is a town of about 5,000 inhabitants ; it lies on a hill about 100 feet higher than the river, and towards the S. spreading out on a small plateau.   Here, on the southern end of the town, the Mexicans had erected a fort against General Wool, when his division was expected to march towards Chihuahua."   The town is not marked on Pike's map,

Finding that a new species of discipline had taken place, and that the suspicions of my friend Malgares were much more acute than ever, I conceived it necessary to take some steps to secure the notes I had taken, which had been clandestinely acquired.   In the night I arose, and after making my men charge all their pieces well, I took my small books and rolled them up in small rolls, tore a fine shirt to pieces, and wrapped it round the papers, and put them down in the barrels of the guns, until we just left room for the tompoins [tampons], which were then carefully put in ; the remainder we secured about our bodies under our shirts.   This occupied about two hours, but was effected without discovery and without suspicions.

May 2d.   Marched early, and in 4¼ hours arrived at Guaxequillo,[19] situated on the river Florada, where we were to exchange our friend Malgares for Captain Barelo, who was a Mexican by birth, born near the capital and entered as a cadet at Guaxequillo near 20 years past, and who, by his extraordinary merits, being a Creolian, had been promoted to a captaincy, which was even by himself considered his ultimate promotion.   He was a gentleman in his manners, generous and frank, and I believe a good soldier.

Sunday, May 3d.   At Guaxequillo the captain gave up

which, moreover, gives his trail as crossing the Conchos there and the Florido higher up, though the usual road comes up the right bank of the Conchos and crosses the Florido at or near the mouth of the latter, to continue E. S. E. up its left side.   Rio Florido is the largest branch of the Conchos, having itself various tributaries, as R. de Barral, falling in near Bustamente, and R. Allende, with Jimenez near its mouth ; the railroad crosses both of these at the places said. Neither of these streams appears on Pike's map.   The place where he dined seems to be about that marked Santa Rita on his map.   This I do not recognize ; but it cannot have been far from Bustamente.   The evident confusion of distances in the text makes it probably imposssible to identify the "private house" at which he slept.   La Ramada was a small place on the Rio Florido, about 24 m. from Santa Rosalia.   He seems to have come beyond this point, perhaps to the vicinity of present Jimenez (on the railroad).   His legend " Camion de Monaseo " presumably stands for Camino de Monasterio (Monastery road).

    [19] Or Guajuquilla : a well-known place on the right or S. bank of the river, marked on Pike's map as a presidio or fortified town.   A citation from Wisli-

his command to Malgares. At night the officers gave a ball, at which appeared at least sixty women, ten or a dozen of whom were very handsome.

May 4th. Don Hymen Guloo arrived from Chihuahua, accompanied by a citizen and a friar, who had been arrested by order of the commandant-general, and was on his way to Mexico for trial.

May 5th. The party marched with all the spare horses and baggage.

May 6th. Marched at five o'clock; ascended the river four miles, when we left it to our right and took off S. 60° E., eight miles. Our friend Malgares accompanied us a few miles, to whom we bade an eternal adieu, if war does not bring us together in the field of battle opposed as the most deadly enemies, when our hearts acknowledge the greatest friendship. Halted at ten o'clock, and marched again at four. No water on the road; detached a Spanish soldier in search of some, who did not join us until twelve o'clock at night. Encamped in the open prairie; no wood; no water, except what the soldier brought us in gourds. The mules came up at eleven o'clock at night. Distance 30 miles.[20]

May 7th. Marched very early; wind fresh from the south. The punctuality of Captain Barelo as to hours was

zenus, Mem. p. 65, will throw some further light on the situation : " Made a strong march to-day [May 3d, 1847] of 33 miles [from La Ramada], to *Guajuquilla*. The road was constantly winding itself through endless chaparrál ; the Rio Florido on the left, and mountains and hills east and west, in the distance, from 10 to 20 miles. About half way we passed a rancho with some water ; farther on the road forks ; the right hand road leads directly to the town ; the other by a large hacienda [qu.: where Pike slept last night ?]. Before Guajuquilla we crossed the Florido, and passing through town encamped south of it. Guajuquilla looks more like a town than any other place we have seen so far, on the road from Chihuahua ; its population is from 6 to 7,000." Three miles S. of this town was the Hacienda de Dolores, " a large estate with well irrigated and cultivated fields " ; a place on the railroad is now marked " Dolores." Thence the road continued for a jornada of about 50 m. without water. Pike will proceed upon this on the 6th, the party having been sent ahead on the 5th.

[20] An unidentifiable place on the jornada, short of the first water from Guajuquilla.

remarkable. Arrived at half past nine o'clock at a spring [Ojo S. Bernarde of Pike's map?], the first water from Guaxequillo. The mules did not unload, but continued on nine miles to another spring [Ojo S Blas of Pike's map] at the foot of a mountain, with good pasturage round it; mountains on each side all day.²¹

May 8th. Marched, at five miles due west, through a gap in the mountains; then turned S. 20° E., and more south to a [Cerro Gordo or Andabazo] river about 20 feet wide, with high steep banks; now dry except in holes, but sometimes full and impassable. Halted at seven o'clock and sent on the loaded mules. Marched at five o'clock; came ten miles and encamped without water. Distance 18 miles.²²

²¹ Pike's map marks the first spring on the road as " Ojo S. Bernarde " and the next as " Ojo S Blas "—names which appear to be transposed from the order in which they come in other itineraries of this route. Thus Wislizenus, Mem. p. 66: " About eight miles from our to-night camp, we passed a spring, with a water-pool, in a ravine to the left of our road; but the water was so muddy and brackish, that the animals refused to drink, or rather to eat it. This spot is known as *San Antonio camp*. Three miles further, a few deserted houses, and a spring on the right hand of the road, (*San Blas*,) are found; but the water is equally bad, and of sulphureted taste. The first good water, and in sufficient quantity, is met about five miles beyond San Blas, in *San Bernardo*, a deserted rancho, with willows and cotton trees, built against a steep mountain wall, from whence a fine creek takes its origin. A small plain half a mile below the rancho contains also some springs and water-pools, and good grass. We pitched our camp in this plain. We have travelled to-day, according to my estimate, about 40 miles [*i. e.*, from a dry camp about 20 m. from the Hacienda de Dolores, near Guajuquilla]." It is clear that Wislizenus is on Pike's trail, and that they have reached what is practically the same camp—near the San Bernardo spring of the former's narrative, or the San Blas spring of the latter's map; and that the spring which Pike speaks of as the " first water from Guaxequillo " and maps as San Bernarde spring, was either the San Antonio camp or the San Blas spring of Wislizenus. The situation is considerably off the present railroad, and the above names are not to be found on ordinary modern maps. But my identifications are confirmed by the fact that both travelers, on decamping next day, cross a mountain gap or pass and soon come upon a river: see next note.

²² The mountain Pike passes, and the river he crosses, are easily identified; the latter is the stream known as El Andabazo (or Cerro Gordo), with a town of the latter name higher up on it. This is the first of several streams we shall cross, running to the left as we go, and sinking in the Bolson de Mapimi—for

May 9th. Marched between four and five o'clock and
arrived at Pelia [Pelayo] at eight.[23] This is only a station
for a few soldiers, but is surrounded by [copper] mines.
At this place are two large warm springs, strongly impregnated with sulphur, and this is the water obliged to be used
by the party who are stationed there. Here we remained
all day. Captain Barelo had two beeves killed for his and
my men, and charged nothing to either. Here he received
orders from the general to lead us through the wilderness
to Montelovez [Monclova], in order that we should not
approximate to the frontiers of Mexico, which we should

they are all beyond the Conchos basin, the divide of which was passed in the
course of the long dry jornada above noted. The lake that the Cerro Gordo
cr. sinks in is sometimes called Laguna de Xacco : so Hughes, Don. Exp., 1847,
p. 129. The trail Pike followed is thus described by Wislizenus, p. 66 : " We
started late, and made but 10 miles, to the *Cerro Gordo*, or *el Andabazo* creek.
Having crossed the mountain, at whose foot San Bernardo lies, we went for
a mile through a cañon, with mountains of limestone on both sides, and from
there into another valley, watered by the el Andabazo. This considerable
creek seems to run from southwest to northeast." The obscure town of Cerro
Gordo above named must not be confounded with the place in Vera Cruz which
was the scene of the famous battle of Cerro Gordo.

Pike has now passed the present interstate boundary between Chihuahua and
Durango. The line runs on a parallel of latitude from Lago de Tlahualila 60
Mex. leagues W. to a source of Rio del Fuerte near Huenote. Pike maps
Lake Tlahualila conspicuously : see the large sheet of water laid down in the
Bolson Mapimi across which is legended " Here the Indians sallied forth to
attack New Biscay and Cohuahuila," and which has a large forked stream running into it from the S. The main fork of this is the present Rio de Nasas,
which actually discharges into Laguna del Muerto ; so Pike's body of water
represents both Lake Tlahualila and the Lake of the Dead, as well as
some smaller sheets, as Laguna del Cayman, etc., all lying in the same general
depression. Pike mentions " Lac du Cayman " elsewhere and correctly says
that Rio Nassas (which he also calls Brassos) falls into it. L. de Parras, however, he lays down separately, with its own river discharging into it. The
boundaries of Chihuahua, Durango, and Coahuila all meet in Lake Tlahualila,
whence that between Durango and Coahuila runs S. for a few miles and then
S. E., while that between Chihuahua and Coahuila extends N. along the border
of the Bolson to the Rio Grande.

[23] Pelayo is the best-known place we have come to since leaving Guajuquilla,
and easily found on modern maps by this name ; it appears on Pike's map as
" P[residio]. Pelia," and has been more fully called Hacienda de San José de

have done by the usual route of Pattos [Patos], Paras
[Parras], etc.

Sunday, May 10th. Marched past one copper mine
[Oruilla], now diligently worked. At this place the proprietor had 100,000 sheep, cattle, horses, etc. Arrived at
the Cadena,[24] a house built and occupied by a priest. It is
situated on a small stream at the pass of the [Sierra de las
Mimbres] mountains, called by the Spaniards [Puerta de
Cadena, or] Door of the Prison, from its being surrounded
with mountains. The proprietor was at Sumbraretto [Som-

Pelayo. The name is thus a personal one, though some have derived it from
Sp. *pelar*, to boil, scald, with reference to the hot sulphur springs. (One
Pelayo, Latinized Pelagius, founded the monarchy of Asturias in Spain early
in the eighth century A. D. The form Palayo is also found.) The place is on
the main road, about 25 m. from the crossing of Andabazo cr. "Pelayo,"
says Wislizenus, p. 67, "is a small village, or hacienda, with several good
springs around it ; some of common, others of higher temperature. The creek
formed by them is, according to the Mexican statements, afterwards lost in
the sand. . . In Pelayo, a small but steep hill was fortified on the top, by walls
of stone. This fortification was probably intended against General Wool's
army. Two days before us [*i. e.*, May 5th, 1847] Lieutenant Colonel Mitchell
had arrived here with the vanguard [of Doniphan's troops], and seeing the
inhabitants of the place organized as a military company, he made 30 of them
prisoners, and took their arms from them ; but upon their representation that
they would by this act become a prey to the surrounding Indians, he restored
them their arms, under the condition that they be used only for defence
against Indians." That series of creeks flowing to the left, two of which have
thus far been mentioned, are all crossed by the railroad, much E. of Pike's
route ; four places at or near which such crossings occur are named Escalon,
Zavalza, Conejos, and Peronal—the two former in Chihuahua, the two latter in
Durango, and the last of these being nearest the railroad crossing of the creek
which flows through La Cadena, as about to be noted.

[24] La Cadena is present name of a place on or near the fourth one of the small
streams above noted, considerably off (?) the modern main road—say 20 m.
S. W. of Peronal, and 25 m. due W. of Mapimi. It is reached by a rough
mountain road 18 m. from Pelayo, past the copper mine of Oruilla ; the
hacienda there, of which Pike speaks as being so rich in stock, had been
deserted when Wislizenus passed in 1847. The creek comes from the Sierra
de las Mimbres, on the W. Another steep range rises about 3 m. E. of La
Cadena ; the gap between the two is the Pass of Cadena, Puerta de Cadena, or
"Door of the Prison," through which Pike goes to-day due E. in the direction
of Mapimi.

brerito], distance six days' march. This hacienda was obliged to furnish accommodations to all travelers.

Marched at five o'clock, passed the chain of mountains due east [in the direction of Mapimi] 12 miles, and encamped without water. Distance 31 miles.

May 11th. Marched and arrived at Maupemie [Mapimi [25]] at eight o'clock, a village situated at the foot of mountains of minerals, where they worked eight or nine mines. The mass of the people were naked and starved wretches. The proprietor of the mines gave us an elegant repast. Here the orders of Salcedo were explained to me by the captain. I replied that they excited my laughter, as there were disaffected persons sufficient to serve as guides should an army ever come into the country.

Came on three miles further, where were fig-trees and a fruit called by the French La Grain [*sic*], situated on

[25] Lettered " Maupeme " on the map, and so rendered in the text beyond ; same word as that in Pike's legend " Bolson de Mapini "; now usually spelled Mapimi. Hughes writes Malpimi. The meaning of the word is unknown, as it probably would not be were it of Spanish derivation ; its most frequent use is in the phrase Bolson de Mapimi, applied to very extensive tracts of low-lying ground encompassed with mountains, chiefly in the states of Chihuahua and Coahuila, but also overreaching into Durango. *Bolson* is a Spanish word which means various things, among them " purse," " pouch," or " pocket," and seems to be applied here in the same way that we use the word " hole " for several different valleys in our Rocky mts. Mapimi, as the designation of a particular place, is still the name of the town Pike comes to, now on the railroad, about 15 m. by rail from Peronal, and about 20 m. by the road he came from La Cadena Pass. It is thus the place where the highway and the railroad come together. The situation is the eastern part of an extensive valley some 20 m. wide and 35 m. long from N. to S., surrounded on all sides by mountains yielding silver mines. " Two springs, called Espiritu Santo and Agua de Leon, form here [at Mapimi] a creek, which runs through the town in an eastern direction," Wislizenus, *l. c.* This seems to be the stream that " formed a terrestrial paradise " for Pike—as well it might, with the Holy Ghost re-enforcing Ponce de Leon. Wislizenus found Mapimi " rather deserted," May 9th, 1847; but the artillery " fired a salute, in honor of the anniversary of the battle of Palo Alto " (fought May 8th, 1846). Pike's camp of the 11th of May, 3 m. E. of Mapimi, was snug under the eastern mountain chain, whence it was about 2 m. through a cañon into another valley forming a part of the series of the Bolson de Mapimi.

a little stream which flowed through the gardens, and formed a terrestrial paradise. Here we remained all day sleeping in the shade of the fig-trees, and at night continued our residence in the garden. We obliged the inhabitants with a ball, who expressed great anxiety for a relief from their present distressed state, and a change of government.

May 12th. Was awakened in the morning by the singing of the birds and the perfume of the trees around. I attempted to send two of my soldiers to town [Mapimi], but they were overtaken by a dragoon and ordered back; on their return I again ordered them to go, and told them if a soldier attempted to stop them to take him off his horse and flog him. This I did, as I conceived it was the duty of the captain to explain his orders relative to me, which he had not done; and I conceived that this would bring on an explanation. They were pursued by a dragoon through the town, who rode after them, making use of ill language. They attempted to catch him, but could not. As I had mentioned my intention of sending my men to town after some stores to Captain Barelo, and he had not made any objections, I conceived it was acting with duplicity to send men to watch the movements of my messengers. I therefore determined they should punish the dragoons unless the captain had candor sufficient to explain his reasons for not wishing my men to go to town, in which wish I should undoubtedly have acquiesced; but as he never mentioned the circumstance, I was guardedly silent, and the affair never interrupted our harmony.

We marched at five o'clock; came on 15 miles and encamped without water. One mile on this side of the little village [26] the road branches out into three. The right-hand

[26] "The little village" is not named. Pike's map makes the triple forking of the road he is about to mention in the immediate vicinity of Mapimi; but this appears to be an error, as he was already 3 m. beyond that town when he started on the 12th. His map is otherwise so far out of drawing that it does help us much more than the slender thread of text to discover exactly what way Captain Barelo took him around the Bolson to Parras. The precise stages of the journey to Parras would probably be recoverable by one thoroughly

THREE WAYS OUT OF PARADISE.

one by Pattos, Paras, Saltelo [Patos, Parras, Saltillo], etc.,
is the main road to [the city of] Mexico and San Antonio
[in Texas].   The [middle] road which we took leaves all the
villages a little to the right, passing only some plantations.
The left-hand one goes immediately through the mountains
to Montelovez, but is dangerous for small parties on account
of the savages ; this road is called the route by the Bolson
of Maupeme, and was first traveled by Monsieur de Croix,
afterward viceroy of Peru.   In passing from Chihuahua to
Texas, by this [left-hand] route, you make in seven days
what it takes you 15 or 20 by the ordinary one ; but it is
very scarce of water, and your guards must either be so
strong as to defy the Appaches, or calculate to escape them
by swiftness ; for they fill those mountains, whence they
continually carry on a predatory war against the Spanish
settlements and caravans.

We this day passed on to the territories of the Marquis
de San Miquel [Miguel], who owns from the mountains of

familiar with the ground ; but it is impossible for me to trace the route upon any
map I have been able to find.   The only road laid down on the best map before
me runs down the Rio Nasas past San Lorenzo to Mayron, at the Laguna del
Muerto, into which that river sinks, and thence to Pozo (Pozzo) and Parras.
From the railroad junction at Torreon the track runs at a distance from, but
approximately parallel with, the river and the road just indicated, through places
marked Matamoras, Colonia, and Hornos, to Mayron and thence to Pozo.
Wislizenus speaks of a place apparently about where Pike comes to on the 12th,
where the road forks, and describes a "northern" and a "southern" route.
The northern one, he says, leads by Alamito, San Lorenzo, and San Juan (all
on the Rio Nasas) to El Pozo ; it is thus identical with or very nearly the same
as the one just said to descend the Rio Nasas.   The southern one, he says,
would have taken him by San Sebastian, on the Nasas, to Gatuño, Matamoras
(or la Bega de Maraujo), Santa Mayara, by the Laguna de Parras to Alamo de
Parras, St. Domingo, and Peña, to El Pozo, and thence to Parras.   I think
that Pike's route coincides most closely with this one ; it is for the most part
S. of the railroad, passing close to the Laguna de Parras (the sink of the
Rio Guanabel); and when we find him at Parras, on the 17th, he is almost due
E. of the place where he crossed the Rio Nasas, at an air-line distance there-
from of nearly or about 40 Mexican leagues—say 100 m.

The "Monsieur de Croix" above named is Teodoro de Croix, b. at Lille,
Flanders, about 1730, d. at Madrid, Spain, Apr. 8th, 1791 ; he was viceroy of

the Rio del Norte to some distance in the kingdom of Old Mexico.

May 13th. Came on to the river Brasses [Rio Nasas,[27] on which was the] Ranche de St. Antonio, part of the marquis' .estate. My boy and self halted at the river Brasses to water our horses, having ridden on ahead, and took the bridles from their mouths in order that they might drink freely, which they could not do with the Spanish bridles. The horse I rode had been accustomed to being held by his master in a peculiar manner when bridled, and would not let me put it on again for a long time; in the meantime my boy's horse ran away, and it was out of our power to catch him again. But when we arrived at the

---

Peru from Apr., 1784, to Mar., 1790; he had previously served as commandant of the interior provinces and of Sonora, under his elder brother, Carlos Francisco de Croix, Marques de Croix, and viceroy of New Spain, 1766–1771. See the legend of his route on Pike's map.

[27] "Brasses" and "Brassos" are Pike's rendering of Brazos, name of a great river in Texas, but the stream here meant by "Brasses" is Rio Nasas (or Nazas), which flows into Laguna del Muerto, in Coahuila. This he elsewhere calls Nassas and Nassus; saying that it runs into Lake Cayman, and forms part of the boundary between Cogquilla (Coahuila) and New Biscay (his name for Chihuahua, though he means Durango). He also charts it conspicuously, but much out of drawing: see his map, first river E. of Mapimi, with "Rancho S[n] Antonio" there lettered. Some of my maps, running back 40 years, apply the name Nazas to that other stream (Rio Guanabal) which sinks in Laguna de Parras, and which Pike also charts, greatly out of position; but he is correct in his identification of the Nasas. This is a notable stream in Durango and Coahuila, which has been called "the vein and center of the Bolson" by Wislizenus, who says further, p. 69: "San Sebastian is a hacienda on the left bank of the Nasas river, and about 35 miles from Mapimi. The Nasas is here quite a deep and respectable stream, while further down it becomes flat, and disappears sometimes entirely in the sand. It comes about 150 leagues from the western part of the State of Durango, from the so-called Sianori mountains. . . The Nasas is the Nile of the Bolson de Mapimi; the wide and level country along the river is yearly inundated by its rising, and owes to that circumstance its great fertility."

On crossing Rio Nasas, or at a point on his road in that vicinity, Pike passes from the present State of Durango into that of Coahuila; but we have no mileage for the 13th. He never leaves Coahuila till he enters the Texas of his day, close to present San Antonio de Bexar, Tex. He never touches Nuevo Leon at any point.

Ranche,[28] we soon had out a number of boys, who brought in the horse and all his different equipments, which were scattered on the route. This certainly was a strong proof of their honesty, and did not go unrewarded. In the evening we gave them a ball on the green, according to custom. We here learned that one peck of corn, with three pounds of meat per week, was the allowance given a grown person.

May 14th. Did not march until half past four o'clock [p. m.]. About nine o'clock [a. m.] an officer arrived from St. Rosa [29] with 24 men, with two Appaches in irons. They were noble-looking fellows, of large stature, and appeared by no means cast down by their misfortunes, although they knew their fate was transportation beyond the sea, never more to see their friends and relations.

Knowing as I did the intention of the Spaniards toward those people, I would have liberated them if in my power. I went near them, gave them to understand we were friends, and conveyed to them some articles which would be of service if chance offered.

This day the thermometer stood at 30° Raumauer [Réaumur], 99½° Fahrenheit. The dust and drought of the road obliged us to march in the night, when we came 15 miles and encamped without water. Indeed, this road which the general obliged us to take is almost impassable at this season for want of water, whilst the other is plentifully supplied.

May 15th. Marched early and came on five miles, when we arrived at a pit dug in a hollow, which afforded a small

[28] El Rancho de San Antonio, already indicated as on the Rio Nasas, but exact location in question. I cannot find the name on any modern map. It does not seem to be the same place as the San Sebastian mentioned by Wislizenus. But the general locality is near the present interstate boundary of Coahuila and Durango, not far from the place where the two railroads cross each other, known as El Torreon (The Tower).

[29] Santa Rosa, one of the principal Coahuilan towns, about half-way between Monclova and Presidio del Rio Grande, on waters of the Upper Rio Sabinas, and on the road which General Wool took during the invasion of Mexico.

quantity of water for ourselves and beasts.[30]   Here we were obliged to remain all day in order to travel in the night, as our beasts could enjoy the benefit of water.   Left at half past five o'clock and came on 15 miles by eleven o'clock, when we encamped without water or food for our beasts. Passed a miserable burnt-up soil.   Distance 20 miles.

May 16th.   Marched two miles and arrived at a wretched habitation [El Pozo?], where we drew water from a well for all the beasts.   Marched in the evening and made 15 miles further [*sic*].   The right-hand road we left on this side of Maupeme [Mapimi], and joined it about four miles further. Distance 15 [*sic*] miles.[31]

[30] See Pike's map, place legended " Well of Putrid Water."

[31] The text is contradictory concerning mileage, and ambiguous in the matter of the road which came in.   The place whence water was drawn is that legended " Well of Mineral Water " on Pike's map.   I am not sure that this is El Pozo of various maps and itineraries before me, called " Pozzo " on the most modern ones ; but am inclined to think it is.   Pozo is a well-known place where the railroad now crosses a highway, and whence there is a regular road S. W. to Alamos de Parras, and another S. E. to Parras itself. Under date of May 13th, 1847, Wislizenus has, Mem. p. 71 : " We travelled to-day 25 miles from San Juan to *el Pozo.*   The road was more gravelly than sandy, at first quite level, afterwards slightly ascending.   A few miles to our right a steep mountain chain was running parallel with our road ; to the left rose more distant mountains. . . . About half way we passed by a deserted rancho, ' Rufugio,' with a well. Near El Pozo the valley becomes narrower."   Dr. W. describes a fight with Lipan Indians which had occurred at Pozo two days before, and continues, p. 72 : " *El Pozo* (the well) is a hacienda, belonging to Don Manuel de Ibarra, and consists of but one large building, in which many families live.   The place is distinguished for its ingenious water-works.   It consists of a deep and very spacious well, from which the water is drawn by mule power in the following way : Over a large wheel in the upper part of the well a strong and broad band of leather is stretched, moving around with the wheel ; to the band, in regular distances, many buckets of leather are attached, which, by the equal circular motion of the wheel and the band, are descending on one side of the well, and fill themselves with water, while they are drawn up on the other side, and, emptying their water into a basin, return again to the well.   To receive the drawn water, two large basins of stone, about 40 feet wide and 100 feet long, have been made, and on the outside of the basins runs a long line of troughs, all of stone, for the watering of the animals. . . . The same Indians which our men fought here, the Lipans, used to frequent this well very freely, and carried their impudence even so far that they notified the Mexicans at what time they wanted to

Sunday, May 17th.   Marched ; about seven o'clock came in sight of Paras [Parras], which we left on the right and halted at the Hacienda of St. Lorenzo, a short league to the north of said village.[32]   At the Hacienda of St. Lorenzo was

have the basins full, and the Mexicans did not dare to disobey.   Although the idea of this water-wheel is by no means a new one, it is certainly very simply and well executed, and the more gratifying to the traveller, as this is the only watering place between San Juan and Parras, a distance of about 50 miles."

[32] No mileage for the 17th ; but Paras is a notable place, easily discovered on ordinary maps.   Sp. *parras* means means grapevines, especially such as are trained on a trellis, and various vineyards have given geographical names in Mexico, as Laguna de Parras, Alamo de Parras, etc.   The latter is a phrase coming near what is meant by our traditional " vine and fig-tree " ; it now designates a place further W., not to be mistaken for Parras itself.   " Paras " and the San Lorenzo hacienda above said are both marked on Pike's map ; the latter must not be confused with present town of San Lorenzo on Rio Nasas, much further W.   The map is entirely out of drawing in these parts, but not irrecognizably, and we can make the requisite adjustments.   In particular, Laguna de Parras is put down over 100 m. from its true position, and the course of its feeder (Rio Guanabal) is still further out of the way.   His route passed near this laguna, between it and Laguna del Muerto.   We must not forget that he was traveling under compulsion, propulsion, and perpetual irritation—circumstances unfavorable to the accuracy of such notes as he could take by stealth and afterward supplement from memory, and under which he could not be expected to improve Humboldt's map !

Some extracts from Dr. Wislizenus, Mem. pp. 72, 73, will give a better idea of Parras than Pike's glimpse affords : " *May* 14 [1847].   We left [Pozo] this morning for *Parras*, in the State of Coahuila. . . .   Our road ran parallel with a near mountain chain on the right, and was mostly ascending.   In the latter part of our march we saw from a hill Parras, at the foot of the same chain, which here makes a bend towards southeast.   The first sight of the town reminded me of el Paso, on account of the great many gardens and vineyards that surround it.   Entering the town, I was struck with the luxuriant growth of pomegranates, figs, and fruits of all sorts, and with the enormous height and circumference of the common opuntias and agaves, which I had already seen in the State of Chihuahua, but much smaller.   The opuntias had trunks of one foot in diameter, and the agave americana grew to the height of from 10 to 15 feet, making excellent hedges.   The town itself was much handsomer than I had expected.   It has some fine streets, with old substantial buildings, a large ' plaza,' and a general appearance of wealth and comfort.   We encamped in the Alameda, a beautiful public walk, shaded with cotton trees and provided with seats of repose.   Early in the morning a concert of thousands of birds, many mockingbirds among them, that live here quite undisturbed, awoke us from our slumber.   These Alamedas, fashionable in all the Mexican cities, do honor to

a young priest, who was extremely anxious for a change of government, and came to our beds and conversed for hours on the subject.

May 18th.   Marched early and came through a mountainous tract of country, well watered, with houses situated here and there amongst the rocks.   Joined the main road at a Hacienda of [Cienega Grande], belonging to the Marquis de San Miquel [Miguel]; good gardens and fruit; also a fine stream.[33]   The mules did not arrive until late at night, when it had commenced raining.

May 19th.   Did not march until three o'clock, the captain

the general taste of the Mexicans for flowers, gardens, and natural embellishments.   To prevent any injury to the trees our horses were kept outside the Alameda.   Parras was probably built towards the end of the seventeenth century, and received its name from its vine, parra meaning vine-branch.   The cultivation of the vine is at present a principal object of industry in Parras.   The vineyards are mostly on the hilly slopes of the limestone mountains west of town.   They produce a white and a red wine, both of very pleasant taste, resembling somewhat the wine of el Paso, but more heating and stronger. . . . We rested in Parras two days, and left it on the morning of *May* 17, on our road to Saltillo.   From Parras we marched about five miles in an eastern direction, through a a plain, to *San Lorenzo*, or, as it is commonly called, *Hacienda de Abajo*, a large, splendid hacienda, belonging to the above mentioned Don Manuel de Ibarra.   The road from el Pozo leads directly to this place ; by going to Parras, several leagues are lost."   This " lower hacienda" is the one which Pike names above, and where he camps to-night.

[33] No distance or direction given, and no place named—but we can discover Pike by extraneous means.   Dr. Wislizenus says, p. 73 : " From here [San Lorenzo] the road was winding over a hilly and rocky country, till we arrived in *Cienega Grande*, a hacienda of Don Rey de Guerrero, (25 miles from Parras.) " This is no doubt the place Pike reaches, on his way to Patos.   The unnamed hacienda of the text is so marked on his map, on the above " fine stream." This creek requires attention.   Pike lays it down as one of the headwaters of Rio Tigre, also called Rio San Francisco del Tigre, which he mistakes it to be, and so runs it off into the Gulf of Mexico, about where Tiger r. does in fact empty.   But Pike was never on any tributary of Tiger r.—never in that watershed at all—never in Nuevo Leon.   His " fine stream " is a headwater of that river which falls into the Rio Grande by Ringgold Barracks, and whose two main forks are known as Rio San Juan and Rio Salinas.   Saltillo, once known as Leona Victoria, and present capital of Coahuila, is on a branch of the Salinas (Rio Meteros) ; and Monterey, present capital of Nuevo Leon, is on a branch of the San Juan.

not being very well.   He here determined to take the main
road, notwithstanding the orders of General Salcedo.   Came
on 10 miles [vicinity of Rancho Nuevo and Castañuela [34]].
Met a deserter from Captain [Francis] Johnston's company
[then probably of the 2d Infantry].   He returned, came to
camp, and begged me to take him back to his company ;
but I would not give any encouragement to the scoundrel—
only a little change, as he was without a farthing.

May 20th.   Came to the Hacienda of Pattos [Patos] by
nine o'clock.   This is a handsome place, where the Marquis
De San Miquel [Miguel] frequently spends his summers, the
distance enabling him to come from [the City of] Mexico in
his coach in 10 days.   Here we met the Mexican post-rider
going to Chewawa [Chihuahua].   Don Hymie [Hymen],
who had left us at Paras [Parras], joined in a coach and six,
in which we came out to a little settlement called the
Florida, one league from Pattos, due north.   Distance 18
miles.[35]

[34] Before coming to Patos and Florida, we will see what Wislizenus says, Mem.
p. 73 : " *May* 18.   Through a wide valley, with mountains to the north and
south, we went to-day (18 miles) to *Rancho Nuevo*, and encamped about one
mile southeast of it, in a valley. . . . Some miles from our camp, in a corner,
amidst mountains, lies *Castañuela*, an old but small town, from which a shorter
but very rough road leads over the mountains to Parras.   A fine creek runs by
it, descending from the southwest mountains and turning towards the northeast."
This seems to be about the place to which Pike was brought on the 19th.

[35] " Pattos " is marked " Hacienda Poloss " on Pike's map, where it is set down
about a day's journey due W. of " Saltello " ; " Florida " is also marked, nearly
as far off to the N. E.   But these are mere crudities of engraving ; any good
modern map will show Patos, about 35 m. W. by S. from Saltillo, and about 16
m. S. by W. from San Antonio de Jaral ; which latter is 12 m. S. E. of a place
on the railroad now called Pastora.   As to Patos and its vicinity we will hear
from Dr. Wislizenus, Mem. p. 74 : " *May* 19.   Marched 25 miles [from Rancho
Nuevo] to *Vequeria*, a small place on a creek of the same name.   The very
tortuous road led over a hilly and broken country.   From one of the hills we
perceived, towards the E. N. E., the distant mountains of Saltillo.   About five
miles from Vequeria we passed a creek with very clear water, the San Antonio,
which unites below, near *Patos*, with the Vequeria creek. . . . Northeast from
Vequeria is an opening in the surrounding mountains, through which the mountain chain of Saltillo appears again.   The route through this pass is the shortest
and most direct from Saltillo, but with wagons one has to take a southeastern

The Hacienda of Pattos was a square inclosure of about 300 feet, the building being one story high, but some of the apartments were elegantly furnished.   In the center of the square was a jet d'eau, which cast forth water from eight spouts, extended from a colossean female form.   From this fountain all the neighboring inhabitants got their supply of water.   The marquis had likewise a very handsome church, which, with its ornaments, cost him at least $20,000; to offi- ciate in which, he maintained a little stiff superstitious priest. In the rear of the palace, for so it might be called, was a fish-pond, in which were immense numbers of fine fish.   The population of Florida is about 2,000 souls.   This was our nearest point to the city of Mexico.

May 21st.   Marched down the [San Antonio] water-course over a rough and stony road about 10 miles, when we left it on the right [crossed it from E. to W.], and came on eight miles further to a horse-range of the marquis', where he had four of his soldiers as a guarda caballo [herders].   Halted at half past nine o'clock.[36]   At this place we had a spring of bad water.

May 22d.   Marched [north] at three o'clock; came on 16 miles to a small shed, and in the afternoon to la Rancho, eight miles to the left of the main road, near the foot of

course to avoid the mountains. About one mile from Vequeria, in the pass leading to Saltillo, lies *Patos*, a small town." The name of the place Dr. W. calls "Vequeria" is preferably spelled Vaqueria ; the word means simply stock- farm or cattle-ranch ; vaqueros are the cowboys of such places, whom I used to hear called "buckeros" when I was in New Mexico, perhaps by unconscious confusing of "vaqueros" with the bucking bronchos they rode.

Here we regret to take leave of our accomplished fellow-traveler, who has set up finger-posts on Pike's route all the way from El Paso to Patos. Dr. Wis- lizenus keeps on eastward to meet General Wool's forces at Buena Vista and Saltillo. Pike has turned northward, down the San Antonio cr., and camps at Florida, less than 3 m. N. of Patos, in the direction of San Antonio de Jaral.

[36] Route of the 21st northward, past if not through San Antonio de Jaral, down the right side of San Antonio cr., and across this from E. to W.; thence continuing northward to some point probably on the present railroad and in the vicinity of the station now known as Sauceda (Willows). Pike's map shows the crossing, at a point below certain forks he delineates, probably not far from half-way between Sauceda and Pastora.

the mountain, where was a pond of water, but no houses. Some Spanish soldiers were here. We left Pattos mountain on our left and right, but here there was a cross mountain [El Monte de los Tres Rios] over which we were to pass in the morning.[37]

The marquis maintains 1,500 troops to protect his vassals and property from the savages. They are all cavalry, as well dressed and armed as the king's, but are treated by the king's troops as if vastly inferior.

May 23d. Marched early and came to a spring in the mountain.[38]

Sunday, May 24th. Marched at an early hour and passed through [El Paso de los Tres Rios in] the mountains, where there was scarcely any road, called the Mountain of the Three Rivers. At the 13th mile joined the main road, which we had left to our right on the 22d instant, and in one hour after came to the main Mexican road from the eastern provinces; thence northwest to the Rancho, nine miles from Montelovez, whence the captain sent in an express to give notice of our approach.[39]

---

[37] Route N., thus bearing off from the river, main road, and line of present railroad, all of which run along together about N. N. E.; camp at or near no named place, but about 8 m. due W. of a place on the railroad (Treviño or Venadito) where a branch turns off to go to Monterey. "La Rancho" of the text, better written El Rancho, or simply ranch, is beyond the place marked on the map as an Indian village by the name of "Rambo"—unless this is the ranch itself, a little misplaced.

[38] Route about N., 15–20 m. to the foot of the pass in the cross mountain, at the place marked "Rivera" on Pike's map.

[39] On making Three Rivers Pass in the morning, Pike goes over the "cross mountain" which forms the divide between the waters of the San Juan and Salinas basin, and comes upon the water-shed of Rio Sabinas (which river he will cross to reach the Rio Grande). The main road which he strikes at the 13th mile is also the railroad line, and he strikes them both at or near Bajan, 5 m. above Joya, where the main road now comes in from points eastward. We have no mileage for the 24th, but it was a good day's journey to get only 9 m. short of Montelovez (Monclova).

As several of Pike's daily mileages are missing, we cannot say exactly how many miles he made it out to be from the Mapimi locality to Montelovez. If we average up the missing ones with the rest of the 14 days, it makes 15 m. a

May 25th. In the afternoon Lieutenant Adams, commandant of the company of Montelovez, arrived in a coach and six to escort us to town, where we arrived about five o'clock. In the evening visited Captain de Ferara [qu.: Don Juan Joaquin de Ferrero?], commandant of the troops of Cogquilla, and inspector of the five provinces.

Lieutenant Adams, who commanded this place, was the son of an Irish engineer in the service of Spain. He had married a rich girl of the Passo del Norte, and they lived here in elegance and style, for the country. We put up at his quarters and were very hospitably entertained.

May 26th. Made preparations for marching the next day. I arose early, before any of our people were up, and walked nearly round the town; and from the hill took a small survey, with my pencil and a pocket compass which I always carried with me. Returned and found them at breakfast, they having sent three or four of my men to search for me. The Spanish troops at this place were remarkably polite, always fronting and saluting when I passed. This I attributed to their commandant, Lieutenant Adams.

May 27th. Marched at seven o'clock, after taking an affectionate leave of Don Hymen, and at half past twelve arrived at the Hacienda of Don Melcher [Michon on the map], situated on the same stream of Montelovez.[40]

Don Melcher was a man of very large fortune, polite, generous, and friendly. He had in his service a man who had deserted from Captain Lockwood's[41] company, first regi-

day, or a total of 210 m. Those who are better informed than myself concern-
• ing the kind of country passed over can judge how near right these figures may
be. It seems to me rather scant measure for the most direct route by which
the Bolson could have been flanked by anything like the curve the railroad
now takes. Pike certainly never made such a fishhook-shaped trail as that
delineated on his map, if he only went 210 m.

[40] Route N., down E. bank of the river on which Monclova is situated, along
the main road and present railroad. No mileage; but 5½ hours on a road
should make 16–18 m., and set Pike near Hermanos, at the place Don Melcher
or Michon had his real estate.

[41] Benjamin Lockwood of Ohio had been an ensign in the levies of 1791 when

ment of infantry, by the name of Pratt.   From this man he had acquired a considerable quantity of crude indigested information relative to the United States, and when he met with us his thirst after knowledge of our laws and institutions appeared to be insatiable.   He caused a fine large sheep to be killed and presented to my men.

May 28th.   Marched early and arrived at Encina Hacienda [42] at ten o'clock.   This place was owned by Don Barego [Borages on the map].

When we arrived at the Hacienda of Encina, I found a youth of 18 sitting in the house quite genteelly dressed, whom I immediately recognized from his physiognomy to be an American, and entered into conversation with him. He expressed great satisfaction at meeting a countryman, and we had a great deal of conversation.   He sat at a table with us and partook of a cold collation of fruits and con_ fectionery ; but I was much surprised to learn, shortly after we quit the table, that he was a deserter from our army ; on which I questioned him, and he replied that his name was Griffith ; he had enlisted in Philadelphia, arrived at New Orleans, and deserted as soon as possible ; the Spaniards had treated him much better than his own countrymen, and he should never return.   I was extremely astonished at his insolence, and mortified that I should have been betrayed into any polite conduct toward the scoundrel.   I told him that it was astonishing he should have had the impertinence to address himself to me, knowing that I was an American officer.   He muttered something about being in a country where he was protected, etc.; on which I told him that if he again opened his mouth to me, I would

he was appointed a lieutenant of Infantry, Mar. 7th, 1792, and arranged to the 4th sub-Legion, Sept. 4th of that year ; he was attached to the 4th Infantry, Nov. 1st, 1796, made a captain July 10th, 1797, transferred to the 2d Infantry Apr. 1st, 1802, and to the 1st Infantry Sept. 2d of that year ; and died July 29th, 1807.

[42] The present town of Encinas (The Oaks) is on the road, 20 m. from Hermanos, and presumably at or near the site of the old Barego estate.   Pike is fairly in the valley of Rio Sabinas.

instantly chastise him, notwithstanding his supposed protection. He was silent; I called up one of my soldiers
and told him in his hearing, that if he attempted to mix
with them to turn him out of company; which they executed by leading him to the door of their room a short
time after, when he entered it. When dinner was nearly
ready, I sent a message to the proprietor, that we assumed
no right to say whom he should introduce to his table, but
that we should think it a great indignity offered to a Spanish officer to attempt to set him down at the same board
with a deserter from their army; and that if the man who
was at the table in the morning were to make his appearance again, we should decline to eat at it. He replied that
it was an accident which had produced the event of the
morning; that he was sorry our feelings had been injured,
and that he would take care he [Griffith] did not appear
again whilst we were there.

Our good friend Don Melcher here overtook us, and
passed the evening with us.

This day we passed the last mountains, and again entered
the great Mississippi valley, it being six months and 13 days
since we first came in sight of them. Distance 20 miles.

May 29th. Marched at seven o'clock and came to the
Millada river and a Rancho. [Distance 20 miles.⁴³]

May 30th. Marched at five o'clock and arrived at the
Sabine river at eight; forded it. Marched in the evening
at four o'clock, at ten encamped at the second ridge without water. Distance 27 miles.⁴⁴

⁴³ Millada r. of Pike is the main fork of Sabinas r., and the one whose upper
waters he left at Hermanos. Leaving it there, the road through Encinas to
Alamo cuts off a bend of the river which the railroad now meanders by way of
Baroteran, Aura, Obeya, and so on. The ranch was at present site of Alamo,
a well-known crossing where several roads still concenter, 10 or 12 m. above
the forks. It used to be called Alameda Arriba or, as we should say, "Upper
Cottonwoods"; whence I imagine that Pike got his name "Millada." This
river flowed to his right as he faced N.; the letter " w " of the word " which "
is engraved on the map at precisely the point he crossed this stream : see next
note.

⁴⁴ The main stream of Sabinas r. is crossed at the place now called Potrillo,

Sunday, May 31st.   Marched early and at nine o'clock arrived at a Rancho on fine running water ; course east and west.   Marched eight miles further to a point of woods, and encamped.   No water.   Distance 23 miles.[45]

and also Juarez, 10 m. from Alamo. This sets Pike at a point 17 m. further on a bee line for the Presidio Grande. His mapping of the " Millada " and Sabinas rivers is faulty to the last degree : see the map on this point. 1. The Millada (on which the letter " w " is engraved) should turn above that point and connect with the stream on which " Montelovez " is situated. 2. The main Sabinas (identifiable on the map by " △ Kan " engraved alongside Pike's trail) should have been carried clear up N. W., 100 m. or more. 3. The great river which Pike fetches into the Rio Grande at Presidio Grande, and which he runs down to this point from " Montelovez," does not exist. It is an imaginary river, compounded of about equal parts of upper portions of the two forks of the Sabinas, cut off from their proper connections lower down, and run into the Rio Grande about 100 m. too high up. The rest of the river (E. of Pike's trail) is connected with the Rio Grande about right—that is to say, below Laredo. Observe that Pike says nothing about crossing the mouth of any such river as his map shows just where his trail comes to the Rio Grande. It is a sheer blunder, which has baffled many a person who naturally supposed that Pike fetched up at the mouth of Sabinas r., some 40 m. below Laredo, but never could see how he got there, or how he got thence to San Antonio, or what in the name of geography the two rivers he crossed were anyhow. In fine, this affair of the Sabinas r. befogged the whole trail for several hundred miles, both in Mexico and in Texas. For my own part, I first tried to bring Pike to the Rio Grande at the mouth of Sabinas r., and very soon lost him in Nuevo Leon—to say nothing of the impossibility of trailing him thence to San Antonio. Then I tried the roads to Laredo, observing that this would do pretty well for the Texan side ; but again I lost him in Nuevo Leon. Though the map itself indicated that Pike never was in Nuevo Leon (where General Salcedo, in fact, had no business to send troops, as it was out of his jurisdiction), yet political boundaries nearly a century old go for little on their face, and I was almost tempted to give the puzzle up. But I thought that I would try the experiment of disregarding the map altogether, and trailing Pike solely by his itinerary in the text. It was a week's work to satisfy myself that he was never over the present boundary of Coahuila after he left Durango, and probably never 25 m. on either side of the railroad from Mapimi to Sabinas r. There he was within two days of the Rio Grande, heading straight for the Presidio Salto ; and a glance at his map showed me what the trouble was with that unlucky river.

[45] Directly on the main road to Presidio Salto—the Presidio Grande, or del Rio Grande, of Pike. The running water, on which was situated a ranch, was one of the several *small* affluents of the Rio Grande which run E. along here on the Mexican side.

CHAPTER III.

MONDAY, June 1st. Arrived at the Presidio Rio Grande[1] at eight o'clock. This place was the position to which our friend Barelo had been ordered, and which had been very highly spoken of to him; but he found himself miserably mistaken, for it was with the greatest difficulty we obtained anything to eat, which mortified him extremely.

When at Chihuahua, General Salcedo had asked me if I had not lost a man by desertion, to which I replied in the negative. He then informed me that an American had arrived at the Presidio Rio Grande in the last year; that he had at first confined him, but that he was now released and practicing physic; and that he wished me to examine him on my arrival. I therefore had him sent for; the moment he entered the room I discovered he never had received

---

[1] Pike is now seen to have been all the while on the old Spanish trail from Coahuila into Texas—for it was the "old" trail of his day, a century ago. The place is 40 m. below Eagle Pass or old Fort Duncan, and 90 m. above Laredo or old Fort McIntosh. It is thus the middle one of three places on the river within easy striking distance of San Antonio, Tex. From each of the three roads still converge to the latter point ; but this most historic place on the lower Rio Grande has in the course of time fallen between two stools, so to speak. For now one railroad runs from San Antonio nearly S. to Laredo, by the way of Pearsall, Derby, Cotulla, Encinal, Webb, and Sanchez, and another comes W. to Laredo from Corpus Christi on the Gulf ; while a third railroad connects San Antonio with Eagle Pass by way of Castroville, Salinal, and Brackettville (Fort Clark). The last named one is that which Pike kept so close to on his way out of Mexico ; the one from Laredo runs in Nuevo Leon to Monterey and so on. Eagle Pass is roundly 500 m. up the Rio Grande, by any practicable road, but less than half as far from the Gulf in a direct line. Forty years ago it had

a liberal education, or been accustomed to polished society. I told him the reason I had requested to see him, and that I had it in my power to serve him if I found him a character worthy of interference.

He then related the following story: That his name was Martin Henderson; that he was born in Rock Bridge County, State of Virginia; that he had been brought up a farmer; but that, coming early to the State of Kentucky and to Tennessee, he had acquired a taste for frontier life, and that, in the spring of 1806, himself and four companions had left the Saline in the District of Saint Genevieve, Upper

a population of 300, and Fort Duncan, which adjoined the town, was our uppermost military post on the river. On the other side the Mexicans had their similar establishment at a place called Piedras Negras or Black Rocks. A fine view of this place is given on one of the engravings of the U. S. and Mex. B. Survey, supposed to be bound opp. p. 72. The Ciudad Porfirio Diaz is there or thereabouts now, and another settlement called Fuentes is in the neighborhood; but Fort Duncan has disappeared, except from history. Fuentes is on a small river which falls in just above; higher up on the same is San Fernando de Rosas, or Zaragoza, a point whence various roads radiate. Laredo or Loredo is a very old place, whose history dates back to the early Spanish occupation of the country. Emory writes that in his time, say 1850, it was a decayed place of 600 inhabitants, having been ravaged by savage hordes, and being then supported mainly by old Fort McIntosh, which was built a mile above the town. He thinks that the countless herds of horses which had been stampeded and stolen by the Indians were the progenitors of the mustangs which roamed the plains of Texas thence N. and E. Laredo is now a focal point of roads from every direction, including two railroads; and a place called Nuevo Laredo is established across the river. At 61 or 62 m. by the road below Laredo, and thus opposite the mouth of Rio Sabinas (which takes the undesirable name of Rio Salado below its forks), a fortified trading-post was built, and called Bellville. This name appears on maps of 40 years ago, but has lapsed, like that of Redmond's Ranch by which it was once known, and there is nothing on the American side to show for what would supposably be a marked place—the confluence of so large a river with the Rio Grande. But there is a town of Carrizo a few miles below, on the Texan side. The Mexican town of Guerro or Guerrero is located on the N. bank of Rio Salado, 4 m. up; and 3 m. further are the handsome falls, a colored plate of which should be found opp. p. 65 of the Report last named. Forty miles below this confluence, Rio Alamo, also known as Rio Alcontre, falls in on the Mexican side, and 4 m. up this river is the town of Mier, on its S. bank. Mier, or a town of that name in this vicinity, must be an old place; Pike marks a Mier on the Texan side. The Mier of the Mexican War became a celebrated place, during the Texan invasion of 1840, when

Louisiana, in order to penetrate through the woods to the province of Texas; that his companions had left him on the White [Arkansaw] river, and that he had continued on ; that in swimming some western branch his horse sunk under him, and it was with difficulty he made the shore with his gun. Here he waited two or three days until his horse rose, and he then got his saddle-bags; but all his notes on the country, courses, etc., were destroyed. He then proceeded on foot for a few days, when he was met by 30 or 40 Osage warriors, who, on his telling them he was going to the Spaniards, were about to kill him ; but on his

a desperate fight occurred on its plaza. It was then a town of 2,000 or 3,000 inhabitants, and had many stone buildings among the straw-thatched huts. It made much history, and was a point of strategic importance, being the starting-place of the shortest and most direct road to Monterey. Military operations on the Rio Grande during the American occupation of Mier are said by Emory to have altered the channel of the river, with the result of throwing the island of Los Adjuntos over to the Mexican side, and thus changing what had been the United States and Mexican boundary. About 5 m. further down the Rio Grande stands Roma, a town on the American side, notable as the head of ordinary steamboat navigation. Below this, at the distance of 16 or 17 m., are the adjoining localities of Rio Grande City and Ringgold Barracks. These notable places are opposite the mouth of the San Juan r., on some of whose headwaters Pike was found in the country W. of Saltillo, and which is the first considerable stream that falls in on the Mexican side above the Gulf. The town of Camargo is built on its E. bank, about 4 m. up. The original establishment of Fort Ringgold is old (for our young history on the Rio Grande) ; it was a mean place in 1850, when Rio Grande City had a population of about 300, but came into prominence during the years of the Boundary Survey, when it was a base of various operations, and a point of observation : distance from the sea, 241 m. by the river; alt. 521 feet ; lat. 26° 22′ 27.79″ N.; long. 98° 46′ 32.85″ W. (Emory, *l. c.*). All the points here in mention, between and including Ringgold Barracks and Laredo, are in Texas or in Tamaulipas ; for Nuevo Leon is cut off from the Rio Grande by the Tamaulipan " Panhandle" which runs up to Coahuila. To return now from our trip up and down the river to the famous place where we left Pike : The name of Presidio Rio Grande which Pike uses is not yet entirely obsolete, but the place is now better known as Presidio Salto—that is, " Fort Falls," or the Mexican military post which was established near the falls of the Rio Grande. Las Isletas, or The Islets, is the name of the place in the river where the usually impassable falls or rapids occur, and just above these is the crossing. The scene is well shown on the plate opp. p. 68 of the Report cited. The latitude of Las Isletas was determined by Michler in 1853 to be 28° 16′ 11.5″ N.

saying he would go to the Americans, they held a consultation over him, and finally seized on his clothes and divided
them between them; then his pistols, compass, dirk, and
watch, which they took to pieces and hung in their noses
and ears; then they stripped him naked, and round his
body found a belt with gold pieces sewed in it; this they
also took, and finally seized on his gun and ammunition,
and were marching off to leave him in that situation; but
he followed them, thinking it better to be killed than left
in that state to die by hunger and cold. The savages after
some time halted, and one pulled off an old pair of leggings
and gave him, another mockinsons, a third a buffalo robe,
and the one who had carried his heavy rifle had by this
time become tired of his prize, they never using rifles; they
counted him out 25 charges of powder and ball, then sent
two Indians with him, who put him on a war-trace, which
they said led to American establishments; and as soon as
the Indians left him he directed his course as he supposed
for Saint Antonio. He then killed deer and made himself
some clothes. He proceeded on and expended all his ammunition three days before he struck the Grand Road,
nearly at the Rio Grande. He further added that he had
discovered two mines, one of silver and the other of gold,
the situation of which he particularly described; but that
the general had taken the samples from him. That he
would not attempt to pass himself on us for a physician,
and hoped, as he only used simples and was careful to do
no harm, we would not betray him. He further added that
since his being in the country he had made, from information, maps of all the adjacent country; but that they had
been taken from him.

   I had early concluded that he was an agent of Burr's, and
was revolving in my mind whether I should denounce him
as such to the commandant, but feeling reluctant from an
apprehension that he might be innocent, when one of my
men came in and informed me that it was Trainer, who had
killed Major Bashier [?] in the wilderness between Natchez

and Tennessee, when he was his hireling. He shot him, when taking a nap at noon, through the head with his own pistols. The governor of the State and the major's friends offered a very considerable reward for his apprehension, which obliged him to quit the State ; and with an Amazonian woman, who handled arms and hunted like a savage, he retreated to the source of the White river; but, being routed from that retreat by Captain Maney [James B. Many], of the United States army and a party of Cherokees, he and his female companion bore west ; she, proving to be pregnant, was left by him in the desert, and I was informed arrived at the settlements on Red river, but by what means is to me unknown. The articles and money taken from him by the Osages were the property of the deceased major. I then reported these circumstances to Captain Barelo, who had him immediately confined, until the will of Governor Cordero should be known, who informed me, when at Saint Antonio, that he would have him sent to some place of perpetual confinement in the interior. Thus vengeance has overtaken the ingrate and murderer when he least expected it.

In the evening we went to see some performers on the slack-rope, who were no wise extraordinary in their performances, except in language which would bring a blush on the cheek of the most abandoned of the female sex in the United States.

June 2d. In the day time were endeavoring to regulate our watches by my compass, and in an instant that my back was turned some person stole it. I could by no means recover it, and I had strong suspicions that the theft was approved, as the instrument had occasioned great dissatisfaction.

This day the captain went out to dine with some monks, who would have thought it profanation to have had us as their guests, notwithstanding the priest of the place had escorted us round the town and to all the missions ; we found him a very communicative, liberal, and intelligent man. We saw no resource for a dinner but in the inventive genius of a little Frenchman who had accompanied us from Chihuahua, where he had been officiating one year as cook to the general, of whom he gave us many interesting anecdotes, and in fact was of infinite service to us; we supported him and he served as cook, interpreter, etc. It was astonishing with what zeal he strove to acquire news and information for us; and as he had been four times through the provinces, he had acquired considerable knowledge of the country, people, etc. He went off and in a very short time returned with table-cloth, plates, a dinner of three or four courses, a bottle of wine, and a pretty girl to attend on the table. We inquired by what magic he had brought this about, and found that he had been to one of the officers and notified him that it was the wish of the commandant that he should supply the two Americans with a decent dinner, which was done; but we took care to compensate them for their trouble. This we explained to Barelo in the evening, and he laughed heartily.

We parted from the captain with regrets and assurances of remembrance. Departed at five o'clock, escorted by Ensign [Blank] and [blank] men; came on to the Rio Grande, which we passed, and encamped at a Rancho on the other side. Distance seven miles.[2]

June 3d. The mosquitoes, which had commenced the first night on this side of Montelovez, now became very troublesome. This day saw the first horse-flies; saw some wild horses; came on in the open plain, and in a dry time, when there was no water. Distance 30 miles.

June 4th. Came 16 miles to a pond and dined; great sign of wild horses; in the afternoon to the river Noissour [Nueces], swimming where [*i. e.*, too deep to ford when] we arrived, although it was not more than ten steps wide. Distance 36 miles.[3]

[2] N. E., heading straight for San Antonio de Bexar, on the old trail, to the vicinity of Carrizo springs, Maverick Co.

[3] The Nueces (R. des Noix of F. maps, as Vaugondy, 1783; Neuces on

June 5th. After losing two horses in passing the river, the water having fallen so that we forded, we crossed and continued our route. Passed two herds of wild horses, which left the road for us. Halted at a pond on the left of the road, 15 miles, where we saw the first oak since we left New Mexico, and this was scrub oak. Passed many deer yesterday and to-day. Came on to a small creek at night, where we met a party of the company of Saint Fernandez returning from the line. Distance 31 miles.[4]

June 6th. Marched early and met several parties of troops returning from Texas, where they had been sent to

Winterbotham's, 1795) is the first one of the large series of rivers which drain Texas to the S. E. and S., and fall into one another or separately into the Gulf. Among these are the San Antonio, the Guadalupe, the Colorado (Red river of Texas), the Brazos, the Trinity, the Nechez, and the Sabine—all of which Pike had to cross, in the order in which they are here named, to reach Natchitoches on the Red r. in the present State of Louisiana. During this journey to the last named he continued in what was then the Spanish province of Coahuila until he was almost to San Antonio, and thereafter traversed the then province of Texas, though he passed into what is now the U. S. State of Texas on crossing the Rio Grande.

[4] Those three streams which Pike lays down across his trail, before the San Antonio is reached, are the Nueces; the Leona, a branch of the Frio; and the Frio, main branch of the Nueces. These are successively crossed in the order here given. To-day's pond is marked on the map, between the Nueces and the Leona; a second pond is also marked, between the Leona and the Frio. Pike letters the Frio " Cold Creek," and runs the Nueces into the Rio Grande at or near Mier (see note [1]); but it empties separately into the Gulf of Mexico near Corpus Christi. Fort Ewell was built on the Nueces, on the road between San Antonio and Laredo (Fort McIntosh); near the headwaters of the Leona was situated Fort Inge, on the road from San Antonio to Eagle Pass (Fort Duncan).

My maps differ irreconcilably concerning a certain Rio Quihi, tributary to the Nueces system. The best one, of 1857–58, makes it a large branch of the Leona, reaching across the direct route from Presidio Salto to San Antonio, and therefore across Pike's trail. *This* Quihi r. is the present San Miguel r., which joins the Frio in McMullen Co. On an earlier map, 1849, there is no such river, but an insignificant Quihi cr., branch of a Rio Hondo, branch of a Rio Seco, branch of the Rio Frio. Some of these maps lay down a branch of the Frio called Artaceoasa cr. in one instance, and Atascosa cr. in another; this name is the same as that of a place Pike marks "Astecostota," and of present Atascosa Co., in which the creek runs to fall into the Frio in Live Oak Co.

re-enforce, when our troops were near the line. Immense numbers of cross-roads made by the wild horses. Killed a wild hog [peccary, *Dicotyles torquatus*], which on examination I found to be very different from the tame breed, smaller, brown, with long hair and short legs; they are to be found in all parts between Red river and the Spanish settlements.

Passed an encampment made by the Lee Panes [Lipans[5]]; met one of said nation with his wife. In the afternoon struck the woodland, which was the first we had been in from the time we left the Osage nation. Distance 39 miles.

Sunday, June 7th. Came on 15 miles to the [Medina] river Mariano—the line between Texas and Cogquilla—a pretty little stream, [on which was a] Rancho. Thence in the afternoon to Saint Antonio.[6] We halted at the mission of Saint

[5] " Lee Panes " looks at first sight as if intended for Les Panis, the Pawnees. But this is Pike's way of rendering Lipans. These were a tribe cognate with Apaches, and therefore of Athapascan stock. They were often called Lipan Apaches, and sometimes Sipans. Pike elsewhere speaks of " the language of the Appaches and Le Panis," showing what he means.

[6] The trip from the Rio Grande to the San Antonio r. made about 151 m. by Pike's estimates, serving to show the course of the old Spanish trail as the most direct route then practicable. Pike's Mariano is now called Medina r.; on this is Castroville, seat of Medina Co., and the river mostly separates this county from Bexar Co. Pike sets San Antonio on the N. bank of an affluent of a fork large enough to look as if it were Rio Cibolo ; but this last comes in much further down the San Antonio, and no doubt he intended simply to delineate the small forked San Pedro, on one of whose branches the city was situated. The San Antonio itself is represented as joining the Guadalupe high up; but these two great rivers only come together as they approach the coast, to fall into Espiritu Santo bay opposite Matagorda isl., between Indianola and Arkansas City. On some old maps, as that in Winterbotham's History, 1795, San Antonio is set on a stream called Rio Hondo, which is run separately into the Gulf of Mexico between the Nueces and the Guadalupe. The early importance of the Mariano or Medina r. as a political boundary ceased of course with the retirement of Coahuila beyond the Rio Grande, and thus the extension of Texan territory, through what had been Coahuilan territory, to New Mexico. The city was formerly more fully called San Antonio de Bexar, Bejar, Behar, Bexer, etc., to distinguish it from uncounted other places dedicated to the patron saint of highways by highwaymen and other persons, and is still the seat of Bexar Co.; pop. lately 37,673 (scarcely less than that of Dallas). The mission of " St. Joseph," commonly called San José, is figured on p. 69 of Major Emory's

Joseph [San José]; received in a friendly manner by the priest of the mission and others.

We were met out of Saint Antonio about three miles by Governors Cordero and Herrara, in a coach. We repaired to their quarters, where we were received like their children. Cordero informed me that he had discretionary orders as to the mode of my going out of the country ; that he therefore wished me to choose my time, mode, etc.; that any sum of money I might want was at my service ; that in the mean-time Robinson and myself would make his quarters our home ; and that he had caused to be vacated and prepared a house immediately opposite for the reception of my men. In the evening his levee was attended by a crowd of officers and priests, among whom were Father M'Guire and Dr. Zerbin. After supper we went to the public square, where might be seen the two governors joined in a dance with people who in the daytime would approach them with reverence and awe.

We were here introduced to the sister of Lieutenant Mal-gares' wife, who was one of the finest women we saw. She was married to a Captain Ugarte, to whom we had letters of introduction.

June 8th. Remained at San Antonio.

June 9th. A large party dined at Governor Cordero's, who gave as his toast, "The President of the United States— Vive la." I returned the compliment by toasting "His Catholic Majesty." These toasts were followed by "General Wilkinson." One of the company then gave "Those gentlemen ; their safe and happy arrival in their own country; their honorable reception, and the continuation of

reports, probably looking much as it did when Pike was received there by the priest ; and the steel engraving which forms the frontispiece of the same volume shows the plaza of the city. San Antonio is a very old place, having been occu-pied for military and ecclesiastical purposes before 1720, was long the most important one in Texas, was styled Thermopylæ of Texas after the massacre of Texans by Mexicans at Fort Alamo, Mar. 6th, 1836, and is now the second in size, though the capital of the present State is Austin, on the Rio Colorado of Texas.

the good understanding which exists between the two countries."

June 10th. A large party at the governor's to dinner. He gave as a toast, "My companion, Herrara."

June 11th. Preparing to march to-morrow. We this evening had a conversation with the two governors, wherein they exhibited an astonishing knowledge of the political character of our Executive, and the local interests of the different parts of the Union.

June 12th. One of the captains from the kingdom of [Nuevo] Leon having died, we were invited to attend the burial, and accompanied the two governors in their coach, where we had an opportunity of viewing the solemnity of the interment, agreeably to the ritual of the Spanish church, attended by the military honors which were conferred on the deceased by his late brethren in arms.

[As I ascertained to-day,] Governor Cordero gave the information of my intended expedition to the commandant-general as early as July [1806], the same month that I took my departure. His information was received via Natchez.

June 13th. This morning there were marched 200 dragoons for the sea-coast, to look out for the English, and this evening Colonel Cordero was to have marched to join them. We marched at seven o'clock, Governor Cordero taking us in his coach about two leagues, accompanied by Father M'Guire, Dr. Zerbin, etc. We took a friendly adieu of Governor Herrara and our other friends at Saint Antonio.

It may not be improper to mention here something of Father M'Guire and Dr. Zerbin, who certainly treated us with all imaginable attention while at Saint Antonio. The former was an Irish priest, who formerly resided on the coast above [New] Orleans [in present Louisiana], and was noted for his hospitable and social qualities. On the cession of Louisiana, he followed the standard of "the king, his master, who never suffers an old servant to be neglected." He received at Cuba an establishment as chaplain to the mint of Mexico, whence the instability of human affairs carried him to Saint Antonio. He was a man of chaste classical taste, observation, and research.

Dr. Zerbin formerly resided at Natchez [in present Mississippi], but in consequence of pecuniary embarrassments emigrated to the Spanish territories. Being a young man of a handsome person and an insinuating address, he had obtained the good-will of Governor Cordero, who had conferred on him an appointment in the king's hospital, and many other advantages by which he might have made a fortune; but he had recently committed some very great indiscretions, by which he had nearly lost the favor of Colonel Cordero, though whilst we were there he was treated with attention.

I will here attempt to portray a faint resemblance of the characters of the two governors whom we found at Saint Antonio; but to whose superexcellent qualities it would require the pen of a master to do justice.

Don Antonio Cordero is about 5 feet 10 inches in height, 50 years of age, with fair complexion and blue eyes; he wore his hair turned back, and in every part of his deportment was legibly written "the soldier." He yet possessed an excellent constitution, and a body which appeared to be neither impaired by the fatigues of the various campaigns he had made, nor disfigured by the numerous wounds received from the enemies of his king. He was one of the select officers who had been chosen by the court of Madrid to be sent to America about 35 years since, to discipline and organize the Spanish provincials, and had been employed in all the various kingdoms and provinces of New Spain. Through the parts which we explored he was universally beloved and respected; and when I pronounce him by far the most popular man in the internal provinces, I risk nothing by the assertion. He spoke the Latin and French languages well, was generous, gallant, brave, and sincerely attached to his king and country. Those numerous qualifications advanced him to the rank of colonel of cavalry, and governor of the provinces of Cogquilla and Texas. His usual residence was Montelovez, which he had embellished a great deal, but since our taking possession of Louisiana he had removed to San Antonio, in order to be nearer the frontier, to be able to apply the remedy to any evil which might arise from the collision of our lines.

Don Simon de Herrara is about 5 feet 11 inches high, has a sparkling black eye, dark complexion and hair. He was born in the Canary islands, served in the infantry in France, Spain, and Flanders, and speaks the French language well, with a little of the English. He is engaging in his conversation with his equals; polite and obliging to his inferiors, and in all his actions one of the most gallant and accomplished men I ever knew. He possesses a great knowledge of mankind from his experience in various countries and societies, and knows how to employ the genius of each of his subordinates to advantage. He had been in the United States during the presidency of General Washington, and had been introduced to that hero, of whom he spoke in terms of exalted veneration. He is now lieutenant-colonel of infantry, and governor of the kingdom of New Leon. His seat of government is Mont Elrey [Monterey]; and probably, if ever a chief is adored by his people, it is Herrara. When his time expired last, he immediately repaired to Mexico, attended by 300 of the most respectable people of his government, who carried with them the sighs, tears, and prayers of thousands that he might be continued in that government. The viceroy thought proper to accord to their wishes *pro tempore*, and the king has since confirmed his nomination. When I saw him he had been about one year absent, during which time the citizens of rank in Mont Elrey had not suffered a marriage or baptism to take place in any of their families, until their common father could be there, to consent and give joy to the occasion by his presence. What greater proof could be given of their esteem and love?

In drawing a parallel between these two friends, I should

say that Cordero was the man of greatest reading, and that Herrara possessed the greatest knowledge of the world. Cordero has lived all his life a bachelor. Herrara married an English lady in early youth, at Cadiz; one who by her suavity of manners makes herself as much beloved and esteemed by the ladies as her noble husband is by the men. By her he has several children, one now an officer in the service of his royal master.

The two friends agree perfectly in one point—their hatred to tyranny of every kind; and in a secret determination never to see that flourishing part of the New World subject to any other European lord except him whom they think their honor and loyalty bound to defend with their lives and fortunes. But should Bonaparte seize on European Spain, I risk nothing in asserting that those two gentlemen would be the first to throw off the yoke, draw their swords, and assert the independence of their country.

Before I close this subject, it may not be improper to state that we owe it to Governor Herrara's prudence that we are not now engaged in a war with Spain. This will be explained by the following anecdote, which he related in the presence of his friend Cordero, and which was confirmed by him. When the difficulties commenced on the Sabine,[7] the commandant-general and the viceroy consulted each other, and mutually determined to maintain inviolate what they deemed the dominions of their master. The viceroy therefore ordered Herrara to join Cordero with 1,300 men, and both the viceroy and General Salcedo ordered Cordero to cause our troops to be attacked, should they pass the Rio Oude [sic]. These orders were positively reiterated to Herrara, the actual commanding officer of the Spanish army on the frontiers, and gave rise to the many messages which

---

[7] Sabine r. still forms a portion of the boundary between Texas and Louisiana—that is, from the Gulf to 32° N., the remainder being along a meridian to 33°. In consequence of its delimiting office, it was formerly called Rio Mexicano and Mexican r. Thus "Mexicano R." appears on the map accompanying Winterbotham's History, N. Y., J. Reid, 1795.

he sent to General Wilkinson when he was advancing with our troops. Finding they were not attended to, he called a council of war on the question to attack or not, when it was given as their opinion that they should immediately commence a predatory warfare, but avoid a general engagement; yet, notwithstanding the orders of the viceroy, the commandant-general, Governor Cordero's, and the opinion of his officers, he had the firmness or temerity to enter into the agreement with General Wilkinson which at present exists relative to our boundaries on that frontier. On his return he was received with coolness by Cordero, and they both made their communications to their superiors. " Until an answer was received," said Herrara, " I experienced the most unhappy period of my life, conscious I had served my country faithfully, at the same time that I had violated every principle of military duty." At length the answer arrived, and what was it, but the thanks of the viceroy and the commandant-general for having pointedly disobeyed their orders, with assurances that they would represent his services in exalted terms to the king. What could have produced this change of sentiment is to me unknown, but the letter was published to the army, and confidence again restored between the two chiefs and the troops.

Our company consisted of Lieutenant Jn. Echararria, who commanded the escort; Captain Eugene Marchon of New Orleans, and Father José Angel Cabaso, who was bound to the camp at or near the [river] Trinity; with a suitable proportion of soldiers. We came on 16 miles to a place called the Beson, where we halted until the mules came up. Marched again at four o'clock, and arrived at the river of Guadalupe at eight o'clock. Distance 30 miles.[8]

[8] Striking the Guadalupe at about the nearest point, in the vicinity of present town of New Braunfels; to reach it, Rio Cibolo was crossed, and there was the place called El Beson. There is no such disparity of size between the Guadalupe and San Antonio rivers as Pike's map indicates. The former has two main forks, the western one retaining the name Guadalupe, for which Pike letters " Buenacus." The other is called Rio San Marco, or San Marcos; it falls in at or near Gonzales, about 40 m. (direct) below New Braunfels.

Sunday, June 14th. When we left Saint Antonio, every-thing appeared to be in a flourishing and improving state, owing to the examples and encouragement given to indus-try, politeness, and civilization by the excellent Governor Cordero and his colleague Herrara ; also to the large body of troops maintained at that place in consequence of the difference existing between the United States and Spain.

Came on to the Saint Mark [river, Rio San Marco] in the morning; in the afternoon came on 15 miles further, but was late, owing to our having taken the wrong road. Dis-tance 30 miles.[9]

June 15th. Marched 20 miles in the morning to a small pond, which is dry in a dry season, where we halted. Here commenced the oak timber, it having been musqueet [mes-quit, *Prosopis juliflora*] in general from Saint Antonio. Prairie like the Indiana territory. In the afternoon came on six miles further to a creek, where we encamped early. Distance 26 miles.[10]

June 16th. Marched early, and at eight o'clock arrived at Red river [Rio Colorado of Texas [11]]. Here was a small

[9] Camp in vicinity of the present town of Lockhart (?).

[10] Camp short of Bastrop, a comparatively old place on the Rio Colorado, located at the point where the Spanish trail crossed the river, about 35 m. below Austin, and present seat of the county of the same name. Bastrop is a mere village, pop. about 1,650, but the name was famous in the early annals of Texas, when the Baron Bastrop had his immense estate on the Washita. Dunbar and Hunter, in their well-known Observations, etc., which formed one of the tracts accompanying Jefferson's Message to Congress of Feb. 19th, 1806, inform us that the Baron's great grant of land from the Spanish government began near the Bayou Bartholomew, about 12 leagues above the post on the Washita, and consisted of a square 12 leagues on each side, or over a million French acres (London ed. 1807, p. 83). Bastrop seems to have been a prototype of the modern " cattle barons," or " cattle kings," as they are styled, who generally manage to cover more ground than Queen Dido did when she stretched a bull's-hide around her famous city.

[11] This Red r. or Rio Colorado requires attention to discriminate it from several others of the same name ; they are all great streams, not to be con-founded, in spite of their homonymity : 1. Red r. of the North, flowing into British America between North Dakota and Minnesota : see Part I., *passim*. 2. Red r., the uppermost and smallest one of three branches of the Arkan-

Spanish station and several lodges of Tancards—tall, hand-some men, but the most naked savages I ever saw, without exception. They complained much of their situation. In the afternoon passed over hilly, stony land ; occasionally we saw pine timber. Killed one deer. Encamped on a small run. Distance 26 miles.

June 17th. Came on by nine o'clock to a large encamp-ment of Tancards,[12] more than 40 lodges. Their poverty

saw which have been so called. This was oftenest called Negracka r., but is now usually known as the Salt fork of the Arkansaw : see note [10], p. 552. 3. Red r., the middle one of three branches of the Arkansaw which have been so called, now known as the Cimarron r.: see note [10], p. 553. 4. Red r., the lowest and largest of the three branches of the Arkansaw which have been so called ; it is the main fork of the Arkansaw, often known as the Red r. of Arkansas, oftenest now as the Canadian r.: see note [17], p. 558. 5. The Red r. of Louisiana, the Red r. of Natchitoches, the Red r. of the Mississippi—*the* Red r. of Pike's Expedition, which he never found. This is the first (lowest) great branch of the Mississippi from the W., and the one now most commonly known as the Red r., without any qualifying phrase, probably never called Colorado r. One of its Indian names is Kecheahquehono, to be found on some maps. 6. The Red r. of Texas, the one Pike crosses this 16th of June near Bastrop, and which flows into the Gulf of Mexico at Matagorda, between the Guadalupe and the Brazos rivers. This is also the Rio Roxo or Rojo, and the Rio Colorado, of the Spanish, sometimes qualified as Rio Colorado del Este, or Colorado r. of the East (though it is the southernmost of the lot), to distinguish it from : 7. Red r. of the West ; Rio Colorado del Occidente ; Colorado r. of the West, flowing into the Gulf of California. This has seldom been called Red r., and is always now known as the Colorado, without qualifying terms, as we very early adopted the Spanish name. We hear of cowboys who " paint the town red " in carrying their jags, but that is nothing to the way these rivers have rubricated maps. Easy alliteration of the words " red " and " river " has doubtless tended to spread the phrase, in the lack of nomenclatural resources, and in ignorance of the connections of several of these rivers.

[12] The " Tancards " of whom Pike speaks on the 16th and 17th, also called Tankahuas, Tonkawans, Tankaways, etc., were a remarkable people—a sort of Ishmaelites who roamed about, and seemed to belong nowhere in particular. Powell styles them a " colluvies gentium " or fusion of tribes ; and what little we know of their local habitation is derived mainly from Dr. Sibley's notes, supplemented by the above passages in Pike's narrative. Dr. Sibley's historical letter to General Dearborn, dated Natchitoches, Apr. 5th, 1805, and first pub-lished with other tracts in Jefferson's Message to Congress of Feb. 19th, 1806, is one of the bases of the literature on this subject. " The Tankaways (or Tanks, as the French call them)," says Sibley, p. 45 of the London ed., 1807,

was as remarkable as their independence.   Immense herds
of horses, etc.   I gave a Camanche and Tancard each a
silk handkerchief, and a recommendation to the commandant at Natchitoches.   In the afternoon came on three
hours and encamped on a hill, at a creek on the right-hand
side of the road.   Met a large herd of mules escorted by
four soldiers ; the lieutenant took from them some money
which they had in charge.   Distance 30 miles.

June 18th.   Rode on until half past ten o'clock, when we
arrived at the river Brassos.[13]   Here is a stockade guard of

" have no land, nor claim the exclusive right to any, nor have any particular
place of abode, but are always moving, alternately occupying the country
watered by the Trinity, Braces [Brazos], and Colerado, towards St. a Fé.
Resemble, in their dress, the Cances [Kanzas] and Hietans [Comanches], but
[are] all in one horde or tribe.   Their number of men is estimated at about 200;
are good hunters ; kill buffaloe and deer with the bow ; have the best breed of
horses ; are alternately friends and enemies of the Spaniards.   An old trader
lately informed me that he has received 5000 deer skins from them in one year,
exclusive of tallow, rugs and tongues.   They plant nothing, but live upon fruits
and flesh : are strong, athletic people, and excellent horsemen."   The history of
the tribe dates back of Sibley and Pike nearly a century, if the first mention of
these Bedouins of the Texan sands in 1719 be taken as its starting-point.   In
1876 Gatschet had collected a vocabulary of about 300 words, upon which linguistic material he classed the people as a separate stock called Tonkawa, from
the Caddoan or Wakoan word *tonkaweya,* implying that these Indians kept by
themselves, aloof from other tribes.   The Tonkawan family is recognized by
Powell as one of the 58 distinct linguistic stocks he adopts in his classification ;
his map locates the tribe agreeably with the above indications, and his text
adds : "About 1847 they were engaged as scouts in the United States Army, and
from 1860–62 (?) were in the Indian Territory ; after the secession war till 1884
they lived in temporary camps near Fort Griffin, Shackleford County, Texas, and
in October, 1884, they removed to the Indian Territory (now on Oakland Reserve).
In 1884 there were 78 individuals living ; associated with them were 19 Lipan
Apache " (Seventh Ann. Rep. Bur. Ethn., 1885–86, published 1891, p. 126).
Two other Tonkawan tribes, the Mayes and Yakwal, are extinct or merged in
the former ; and several minor bands have been known by name.
    [13] The full style of this river was el Rio de los Brazos de Dios, River of the
Arms of God, which seemed neither blasphemous nor sacrilegious to the admirable fanatics who so solemnly theographized geography in their excursions for
the salvation of souls, ad majorem Dei gloriam.   It is difficult for us to realize
what a queer lot they were, with their "Monastery Road" to the "Opening of
the Virgin," their Corpus Christi in one place and Sangre de Cristo elsewhere,
Holy Ghost bay, Todos Santos collectively when they ran out of individual

one corporal, six men, and a ferry-boat. Swam our horses over; one was drowned and several others were near it, owing to their striking each other with their feet. We then came on about two miles on this side of a bayou called the Little Brassos, which is only a branch of the other, and which makes an impassable swamp at certain seasons between them. Distance 31 miles.

June 19th. Came on through prairies and woods alternately 20 miles to a small creek, Corpus Christi, with well-wooded, rich land. In the afternoon came on ten miles, and passed a creek which at high water is nearly impassable four miles. Overflows swamps, ponds, etc. Encamped about one mile on this side, on high land to the right of the road. Met the mail, Indians, and others. Distance 30 miles.[14]

June 20th. Came on 16 miles in the morning; passed several herds of mustangs or wild horses; good land, ponds and small dry creeks, prairie and woods, alternately. It

saints, and Rio Trinidad for the whole Trinity after the members of the divine family had been separately complimented. It is fortunate that we cannot commit the intellectual anachronism of putting ourselves in the place of these very sincere servants of a very moderate polytheism, though the result be that the Brazos is also called Brasses and Braces r., bringing up a ludicrous association of ideas with the buttons and suspenders which uphold our trousers, ad majorem pudorem virorum. Other names of this stream are Rivière Ste. Thérèse (or Rio Santa Teresa), and R. Maligne; thus the phrase "St. Théreseor or Maline R." appears on the map in Winterbotham's History, 1795. The river is the largest one of the series Pike is crossing; it drains a great area in Texas from the Llanos Estacados or Staked Plains to the Gulf, which it reaches between Galveston and Matagorda. The point at which the old Spanish trail struck it is indicated by Pike's mention of the Little Brazos, a sort of bayou or side-sluice which runs close to the E. side of the main stream for a great distance. The crossing was near the mouth of this bayou.

[14] The streams passed to-day are tributaries of the Brazos, the larger one mentioned being that afterward known as Navasota r., which falls in a good way below, at or near a place which was once named Washington. The high land on the other side, on which was camp, represents some of the elevation which forms the water-shed between Brazos and Trinity rivers, and which is passed over next day. The clause of the text reading " impassable four miles. Overflows swamps, ponds, etc.," I suppose may be read " impassable for (some) miles (along its course, where it) overflows (in) swamps, ponds, etc."

rained considerably. We halted to dry our baggage long before night. Distance 20 miles.

Sunday, June 21st. Came on to the river Trinity [Rio Trinidad [15]] by eight o'clock. Here were stationed two captains, two lieutenants, and three ensigns, with nearly 100 men, all sick, one scarcely able to assist another. Met a number of runaway negroes, some French, and Irishmen. Received information of Lieutenant Wilkinson's safe arrival. Crossed with all our horses and baggage, with much difficulty. Distance 20 miles.

June 22d. Marched the mules and horses in the forenoon, but did not depart ourselves until three o'clock. Father José Angel Cabaso separated from us at this place for the post of [300 Spanish troops cantoned further down Trinity river], where he was destined. Passed thick woods, and a few small prairies with high rich grass. Sent a dispatch to Nacogdoches. Distance 22 miles. [16]

June 23d. Came on 20 miles in the forenoon to a small creek of standing water; good land and well timbered. Met a sergeant from Nacogdoches. In the afternoon made 20 miles and crossed the river Natches [or Neches, [17]] run-

[15] The original Rio Trinidad has become better known under its equivalent English name of the Trinity, and there is a place lower down on it which is or was called Trinidad or Trinity (now Swartwout?). It empties into Galveston bay, and so into the Gulf. The Spanish trail from the crossing led on to a place called Crockett, in Houston Co., at or near which camp of the 21st was pitched. A little above the crossing, on the E. bank of the river, we are informed by Dr. Sibley, was the residence of the Keyes or Keychias, a Caddoan tribe which in 1805 mustered 60 men. These are now called Kichais, and now or lately consisted of about 60 persons.

[16] For Nacogdoches see next note. The above lacuna in the text may be presumptively supplied from Pike's map, where the post is marked to that effect.

[17] Natches and Neches are obviously the same Indian word, the root of which appears in Natchitoches and various other names. The two have run through the usual range of variation in spelling in the course of writing and printing; but of late years the form Natchez has become fixed as the name of the well-known city on the Mississippi below Vicksburg, while the designation of the river has perhaps acquired stability in the form of Neches. The latter is the principal stream between the Trinity and the Sabine; it runs south approxi-

ning N. W. and S. E., 20 yards wide, belly-deep to horses at this time, but sometimes impassable. Two miles on this side encamped on a hill in a little prairie. The mules and loads arrived at twelve o'clock. The sandy soil and pine timber began again this afternoon, but there was good land near the river. Distance 40 miles.

June 24th. The horses came up this morning; lost six over night. We marched early and in 15 miles came to the river Angeline [Rio Angelina], about the width of the Natchez, running N. and S.; good land on its borders. Two miles further was a settlement of Barr and Davenport's, where were three of our lost horses; one mile further found two more of our horses, where we halted for dinner. Marched at four o'clock, and at half past eight arrived at Nacogdoches, where we were politely received by the adjutant and inspector [Don Francisco Viana], Captain Herrara, Mr. Davenport, etc. This part of the country is well watered, but sandy; hilly soil; pine, scrub oak, etc. Distance 37 miles.

June 25th. Spent in reading a gazette from the United States, etc. A large party at the adjutant and inspector's

mately parallel with both, and falls into the Gulf through Sabine l., as the Sabine does ; in fact, it is collateral with the Sabine, and has been considered a branch of the latter. The Spanish trail crossed it high up. Its own main branch is that eastern one known as Rio Angelina or Angeline r., which Pike crosses on the 24th ; and E. of a small branch of the latter was the site of Nacogdoches. It is now an obscure village, pop. about 1,200, seat of the county of its own name, which occupies a space between Angelina and Atoyac rivers ; but the place is an old one, which, like all the others which the Spanish trail went through, has a long ethnic, civil, and military history. Neches or Natches r. is to be particularly noted as the ancient seat of a tribe of Indians who, though a mere handful a century ago, left their name as a legacy for all time. Sibley (*l. c.*, p. 43) speaks of "a small river, a branch of the Sabine, called the Naches," on which lived the " Inies, or Tachies (called indifferently by both names)," and adds : " From the latter name the name of the province of Tachus or Taxus is derived," *i. e.*, Texas. Among the permutations of the word and its derivatives not the least singular is the English adjective and noun *Texican*—a word obviously formed upon the model of *Mexican* from *Mexico*. I suppose this is modern, and what may be termed cowboy dialect ; I used to hear it constantly when I was in those parts.

to dinner : 1st toast, " The President of the United· States ";
2d, " The King of Spain "; 3d, " Governors Herrara and
Cordero."

June 26th. Made preparations to march the next day.
Saw an old acquaintance ; also, Lorrimier's son-in-law, from
the district of Cape Jerardeau [Girardeau]. Dined with
the commandant, and spent the evening at Davenport's.

June 27th. Marched after dinner and came only 12
miles. Was escorted by Lieutenant Guodiana and a military party. Mr. Davenport's brother-in-law, who was taking
in some money, also accompanied us.

Don Francis Viana, adjutant and inspector of the Internal
provinces, who commanded at Nacogdoches, is an old and
veteran officer, and was one of those who came to America
at the same time with Colonel Cordero. Possessing a mind
of frankness, he unfortunately spoke his opinions too freely
in some instances, which, finding their way to court, prevented his promotion. But he is highly respected by his
superiors, and looked up to as a model of military conduct
by his inferiors. He unfortunately does not possess flexi-
bility sufficient to be useful [to us] in the present state of
the Spanish kingdoms. He is the officer who caused Major
Sparks and Mr. Freeman to return from their expedition on
the Red river [see p. 412].

Sunday, June 28th. Marched early and at nine o'clock
crossed the little river called [Toyac [18]], whence we pushed

[18] Three lacunæ in this sentence, two of which I fill, omitting the other, which
was a long dash in place of the Frenchman's name. We seem bound by Pike's
map to supply " Toyac " as the missing name of the river he means, though
there is certainly no such large river as he lays down between the Neches and
the Sabine. The map is evidently at fault here, for he runs the Neches into
Trinity r., and thus into Galveston bay, and his " Rio Toyac" comes nearer
exhibiting the proper relations of the Neches with the Sabine. Exactly what
his great " Rio Toyac " may pass for is thus questionable, but the " little river "
of the text, which he crosses after leaving Nacogdoches, must be the present
Atoyac r. (the branch of the Angelina which separates Nacogdoches Co. from
San Augustin Co., for the most part). The route continues to-day past San
Augustin, which was on the Spanish trail, and on or near another small branch
of the Angelina, which runs between San Augustin Co. and Sabine Co. The

on in order to arrive at the house of a Frenchman, [about nine] miles distant from the Sabine. We stopped at a house on the road, where the lieutenant informed me an American by the name of Johnson lived; but was surprised to find he had crosed the line with his family, and a French family in his place. When we began conversing with them they were much alarmed, thinking we had come to examine them, and expressed great attachment to the Spanish government. They were somewhat astonished to find I was an American officer; and on my companions stepping out, expressed themselves in strong terms of hatred to the Spanish nation. I excused them for their weakness, and gave them a caution. Fine land, well watered and timbered; hickory, oak, sugar-tree, etc. Distance 40 miles.

June 29th. Our baggage and horses came up about ten o'clock, when we dispatched them on. Marched ourselves at two o'clock, and arrived at the river Sabine by five. Here we saw the cantonment of the Spanish troops, when they were commanded by Colonel Herrara, in the late affair between the two governments. Crossed the Sabine river and came about one league on this side to a little prairie, where we encamped. Distance 15 miles.[19]

place where he stopped on the 28th, only three hours' march from the Sabine, and where he found both Frenchmen and Americans, was evidently the exact locality of which Sibley speaks concerning certain Caddoan Indians known as Aliche, Eyeish, or Eyish. They were then on the verge of extinction, having been in 1801 reduced by the smallpox till only 25 of them were left in 1805. Writing in the latter year he says (*l. c.*, p. 43) that "they were, some years ago, a considerable nation, and lived on a bayau which bears their name, which the road from Nachitoch to Nacogdoches crosses, about 12 miles west of Sabine r., on which a few French and American families are settled." These data fix Pike's camp with precision.

[19] The former office of the Sabine or Mexican r. in delimiting Spanish from American possessions continues to-day in so far as it represents the boundary between Texas and Louisiana. On crossing it, our fervid young patriot passed from the military protection of his Catholic Majesty to that of his Brother Jonathan and Uncle Sam—the former of these two, by the way, being as actual a person as King Charles IV. of Spain, and no other than Jonathan Trumbull of Connecticut. The Spanish trail entered what is now the State of Louisiana at a point between Hamilton and Sabinetown, both of which were places on the

Parted with Lieutenant Guodiana and our Spanish escort. Here I think proper to bear testimony to the politeness, civility, and attention of all the officers who at different periods and in different provinces commanded my escort, but in a particular manner to Malgares and Barelo, who appeared studious to please and accommodate, all that lay in their power ; also, the obliging, mild dispositions evinced in all instances by their rank and file.

On this side of the Sabine I went up to a house, where I found 10 or 15 Americans hovering near the line, in order to embrace an opportunity of carrying on some illicit commerce with the Spaniards, who on their side were equally eager. Here we found Tharp and Sea, who had been old sergeants in General Wayne's army.

June 30th. Marched early and came 15 miles to a house at a small creek, where lived a Dutch family named Faulk, and where we left a small roan horse which had given out. Marched 12 miles further to a large bayou, where had been an encampment of our troops, which I recognized by its form, and took pleasure in imagining the position of the general's marquee and the tents of my different friends and acquaintances. Distance 28 [27] miles.[20]

July 1st. Finding that a horse of Dr. Robinson's, which

Texan side of the river. The crossing was but little above Sabinetown, and between two small watercourses known as Bayou San Patricio and Bayou San Miguel, both running in Sabine Co., La. His camp of the 30th seems to have been between Bayou Miguel and the next below, now called Lennan ; and these two I suppose to be the ones he lays down as running into the Sabine together, as they do, pretty nearly.

[20] General Wilkinson's " marquee," the location of which Pike took pleasure in imagining, was the large tent used by field and general officers ; the name is not often heard now, though the word is hardly obsolete. Old Fort Jesup was built directly on the continuation of the Spanish trail in Louisiana, rather less than half-way from the Sabine to Red r. A short distance S. of this was a place whose name appears on various maps as Many, Manny, Maney, and by accident Mary—the latter on Emory's, 1857–58, which I think is one of the most accurate and altogether useful maps ever drawn to a scale of 1 : 6,000,000. A glance at this shows Pike's trail from the Rio Grande to the Red r. in all its main features ; and though many desirable details are necessarily lacking, not one is misleading.

had come all the way from Chihuahua, could not proceed, was obliged to leave him here. Yesterday and to-day passed many Choctaws, whose clothing, furniture, etc., evidently marked the superiority of situation of those who bordered on our frontiers, to that of the naked, half-starved wretches whom we found hanging round the Spanish settlements. Passed a string of huts, supposed to have been built by our troops, and at a small run a fortified camp but half a mile from the hill where anciently stood the village Adyes [Adayes on the map [21]]. We proceeded to a spring where

[21] This short clause brings up a number of interesting points. The hill is among the slight elevations which together form the water-shed between the Sabine and Red r. This rise of ground corresponds in a general way with the boundary between Sabine and Nachitoches cos. in Louisiana, parting the numberless and mostly unnamed small waters which make on either hand for their respective outlets in the two rivers. Pike is already on the Red River side, among the runs which discharge into the body of water known as the Spanish l., and which finds its way into Red r. by various channels. This is the place where " anciently stood," as he informs us, the village of the mysterious tribe of Indians he calls Adyes and Adayes. These have a long history ; but the literature of the subject is mainly a presentation of our ignorance. Powell says that the first mention of them occurs in the Naufragios of Cabeça de Vaca, who calls them Atayos, about 1540, and that they are also noted by various early French explorers of the Mississippi, as d'Iberville and Joutel. The fortified camp of which Pike speaks was built in 1715 and known as the Mission of Adayes. From documents preserved in San Antonio de Bexar, examined by Mr. A. S. Gatschet in 1886, it appears that 14 Adai families emigrated to a place S. of that town in 1792 ; these were afterward lost sight of. According to Baudry de Lozieres, as cited by Powell, 100 Adaizans were left at home in 1802. Turning to Sibley (l. c. p. 42), we find that in 1805 there were 20 men and more women living " about 40 miles from Natchitoches, below the Yattassees [a tribe that lived on Bayou Pierre or Stony creek], on a lake called Lac Macdon, which communicated with the division of Red river that passes by Bayau Pierre. They live at or near where their ancestors have lived from time immemorial. They being the nearest nation to the old Spanish fort, or Mission of Adaize, that place was named after them, being about 20 miles from them, to the south." Dr. Sibley collected a vocabulary of about 250 words, the sole basis we have for the modern scientific classification of the tribe, upon the only sure principle of natural generation as indicated by mother-tongues. " Their language differs from all others," says Dr. Sibley, "and is so difficult to speak or understand, that no [other] nation can speak ten words of it : but they all speak Caddo, and most of them French." He adds that they were always attached to the latter, with whom they sided against the Natchez ; and that after the

we halted for our loads. Finding the horses much fatigued, and not able to proceed, we left them and baggage and proceeded. We arrived at Natchitoches[22] about 4 p. m.

Language cannot express the gayety of my heart when I once more beheld the standard of my country waved aloft. "All hail!" cried I, "the ever sacred name of country, in which is embraced that of kindred, friends, and

Natchez massacre of 1798, while the Spanish occupied Fort Adaize, the priests took much pains in vain to make them believe what was told them about Catholic dogma. This is practically the sum of what is known of these evidently intelligent and manly people ; the rest of the literature is mainly the conclusions reached upon the subject by various authors. The consensus of opinion very properly classifies the Adaize, Adaizi, Adaise, Adaes, Adees, Adayes, Adyes, Adahi, or Adai, as a distinct linguistic stock, lately called the Adaizan family, whose affinities, more or less remote, are with the Caddoan.

[22] Natchitoches, or some other form of this word, was originally the name of a certain tribe of Indians of the Southern Caddoan family, and of the island on which they dwelt in Red r., at the site of the town which later arose there and is still so called. We hear of these people and their place very early in French colonial history. In Sept., 1688, Henri de Tonti was visited at his Fort St. Louis on the Illinois, by Couture, one of his men whom he had left at Arkansas Post in 1686, who apprized him of La Salle's tragic death. He set off (he says, in Oct., 1689—probably a wrong date from memory) in Dec., 1688, descended the Illinois and Miss. rivers to Red r., and went up this, reaching the Natchitoches Feb. 17th and the Caddodaquis Mar. 28th, 1689 : so Parkman's La Salle, etc., p. 439. He was told that some of the assassins or those in the plot to murder their leader were at a village of the Naouadiches, some 85 leagues S. W., whither he went, but found no trace of Hiens and his confederates. After much suffering, including an illness at his Arkansas Post, he regained Fort St. Louis Sept., 1689 : Wallace, Hist. Ill. and La., 1893, p. 188 seq. According to this authority the present town dates from Jan., 1717, when Antoine de la Mothe Cadillac, governor of Louisiana under Crozat, sent a sergeant and some soldiers to establish a post on the island, which was commanded ca. 1721–28 by Louis Juchereau de St. Denis (b. Quebec, Sept. 18th, 1676, d. post 1731). This notable character, uncle of D'Iberville's wife, Chevalier, etc., is the "Mons. St. Dennie" of Sibley's notice of the Natchitoches, p. 49, where it is said he was still in command after the Natchez massacre of 1728 ; "the Indians called him the Big Foot, were fond of him, for he was a brave man." According to Gayarré, Hist. La., II. p. 355, the foreign population of Natchitoches was 811 by a census made under Gov. O'Reilly, ca. 1769, or when the French had been in Louisiana 70 years. Sibley, writing at Natchitoches Apr. 5th, 1805, says that an elderly French gentleman then living had shortly before informed him that the informant remembered when the Natchitoches were 600 men strong : this should represent ca. 3,000 total souls.

every other tie which is dear to the soul of man!" Was affectionately received by Colonel Freeman, Captains Strong and Woolstoncraft, Lieutenant Smith, and all the [other] officers of the post.[23]

[23] Constant Freeman of Massachusetts had been a captain in the Revolutionary army when he was made major of the 1st Regiment of Artillerists and Engineers, Feb. 28th, 1795 ; promoted to be lieutenant-colonel of Artillerists, Apr. 1st, 1802 ; transferred to corps of Artillery, May 12th, 1814 ; and honorably discharged June 15th, 1815 ; he had been brevetted colonel July 10th, 1812, and he died Feb. 27th, 1824.

Elijah Strong of Connecticut was an ensign of the 1st sub-Legion Feb. 23d, 1793 ; lieutenant, July 1st, 1794 ; transferred to 1st Infantry, Nov. 1st, 1796 ; captain, Oct. 23d, 1799 ; major, 7th Infantry, Dec. 15th, 1808 ; and died June 9th, 1811.

Charles Wollstonecraft of England was appointed from Pennsylvania to be a lieutenant of the 2d Artillerists and Engineers, June 4th, 1798 ; he became a lieutenant of Artillerists, Apr. 1st, 1802 ; captain, Mar. 15th, 1805 ; was transferred to the corps of Artillery, May 12th, 1814 ; on the 15th of March, 1815, he was brevetted major for 10 years' faithful service in one grade, and Sept. 28th, 1817, he died.

Thomas A. Smith of Virginia was appointed from Georgia a second lieutenant of Artillerists, Dec. 15th, 1803 ; became first lieutenant, Dec. 31st, 1805, and captain of Rifles, May 3d, 1808 ; he was a brigadier general in 1814, resigned Nov. 10th, 1818, and died in a few weeks.

Meteorological Observations made by Captain Pike during a Tour through the Internal Provinces of New Spain, in the year 1807.[24]

Date.	[Réaumur's] Thermometer.			Sky.	Wind.	
	sun-rise.	3 p. m.	sun-set.		Course.	Force.
Mar. 3	4	....	....	cloudy and snow	W	fresh
4	1	....	2	snow	E	do.
5	4	....	....	clear	N W	gentle
6	....	....	2	cloudy and snow	N	do.
7	1	....	....	hail	N	....
8	....	....	3	cloudy	W	....
9	3	....	4	clear	W	....
10	0	....	6	hail and snow	S W	....
11	1	....	6	....	W	fresh
12	3	....	3	....	W	gentle
13	1	....	....	....	N	fresh
14	3	....	6	cloudy	S W	....
15	0	....	6	....	W	....
16	7	....	2	clear	S W	gentle
17	4½	....	7	....	E	....
18	6	....	6	....	E	fresh
19	2	....	7	....	....	....
20	....	....	....	....	E	....
21	9	....	....	clear and cold	....	....
22	....	....	....	snow and hail	S E	....
23	....	....	....	....	....	....
24	2	....	6	clear	E	gentle
25	....	....	....	do.	....	....
26	1	....	6	do.	E	gentle
27	1	....	....	do.	S	fresh
28	2	....	8	do.	S	gentle
29	2	....	9	....	N	fresh
30	1	14	4	....	N	....
31	5	....	11	....	W	gentle
Apr. 4	13	16	15	....	....	....
5	14	17	15	....	S	....
6	15	16	14	....	....	....
7	13	15	16	cloudy	....	....
8	14	16	17	....	....	....
9	13	17	15	....	....	....
10	14	16	14	....	....	....
11	15	18	15	....	....	....
12	13	19	17	....	....	....
13	14	17	18	light snow	....	....
14	15	19	15	....	....	....
15	14	20	18	....	....	....
16	13	18	16	....	....	....
17	16	20	15	....	....	....
18	17	19	16	....	....	....
19	18	18	15	....	....	....
20	15	18	16	....	....	....
21	14	13	15	....	....	....
22	16	18	16	....	....	....
23	15	19	19	....	....	....
24	13	19	16	....	....	....
25	15	19	16	clear	....	....
26	14	18	17	....	....	....
27	15	19	17	....	....	....
28	14	17	16	....	....	....
29	15	24	20	....	....	....
30	15	....	20	....	....	....

[24] In the orig. ed. this weather diary occupied an unpaged leaf following p. 278 of the main text of Pt. 3, being thus pp. 279, 280. I leave it in the same relative position, and pass it without further remark.

Meteorological Observations made by Captain Pike (Continued).

Date.	[Réaumur's] Thermometer.			Sky.	Wind.	
	sun-rise.	3 p. m.	sun-set.		Course.	Force.
May 1	11	....	....	....	....	....
2	12	24	17	....	....	....
3	15	23	16	some rain	....	....
4	14	24	17	clear	....	....
5	17	23	16	....	W	....
6	17	28½	16	....	S	....
7	14	29	15	....	S W	....
8	12	27	15	....	W	....
9	9	26	20	....	....	....
10	11	24	17	....	W	....
11	....	25	....	....	....	....
12	15	27	....	....	E	....
13	27	20	....	....	S W	....
14	10	30	20	....	S E	....
15	11	32½	....	clear	S	....
16	....	25	....	cloudy	....	....
17	....	23	20	some rain	....	....
18	29	24	21½	rain	....	....
19	20½	....	15	cloudy	E	gentle
20	13	24	....	some rain	....	....
21	....	22	19	cloudy	....	....
22	....	24	....	rainy morning	....	....
23	15	23	15	clear	W	....
24	14	22	21	....	....	....
25	16	24	23	....	W	....
26	15	23	22	cloudy and rain	....	....
27	14	21	18	rain	....	....
28	15	23	15	cloudy	S	....
29	19	....	....	do.	....	....
30	....	30	20	do.	....	....
31	22	27	25	do.	S	....
June 1	17	2	....	....	S E	....
2	....	25	....	cloudy	....	....
3	....	26	....	....	....	....
4	....	30	....	....	....	....

CHAPTER IV.

OBSERVATIONS ON NEW SPAIN.[1]

𝕿HE kingdom of New Spain [2] lies between 16° and 44° N. lat., and 96° and 118° W. long. It is divided into two separate and independent governments, and these again into various subdivisions.

[1] Chapter IV., which I introduce to accommodate Pike's Observations on New Spain, as the article may be briefly entitled, consists of the leading piece of the App. to Pt. 3 of the orig. ed., pp. 1–51 ; it had no number, but as it came first and was followed by a piece presented as No. 2, it is of course to be taken as No. 1, *pro forma*. The original heading was : Geographical, Statistical, and General Observations made by Capt. Z. M. Pike, on the Interior Provinces of New Spain, from Louisiana to the Vice Royalty, and between the Pacific Ocean, Gulph of California and the Atlantic Ocean or Gulph of Mexico. This was by far the most important article in the whole work, bringing news of great public interest in 1810. Much of it was original ; how much of it was borrowed without acknowledgement could only be said after careful examination of prior works on the same subject. It should be compared with Humboldt and Bonpland's Political Essay on the Kingdom of New Spain, with a Physical and Geographical Atlas, etc., 2 vols., 4to, with atlas, folio, of 20 plates. Pike's two maps of Mexico will be best understood in connection with the same source of information : see Memoir, *anteà*.

[2] Nueva España (New Spain) is a term whose geographical and political connotation has varied much. As the colonial name of what we call Mexico it was first applied to Yucatan and Tabasco by Grijalva, in 1518, and next extended to all the Cortesian conquests. The kingdom of New Spain proper was a region under the audience of Mexico, which corresponded closely to the modern states of Yucatan, Campeche, Tabasco, Vera Cruz, Hidalgo, Guanajuato, Michoacan, Colima, Mexico, Morelos, Tlascala, Puebla, Guerrero, Oajaca, and Chiapas. The viceroyalty of New Spain, dating from 1535, when the first viceroy, Mendoza, entered in possession, was much more comprehensive, as it embraced all the Spanish possessions in Central and North America, from the S. boundary of Costa Rica, as well as the West Indies and the Spanish East Indies. Its political composition was the five audiences of Mexico, Guadalajara, Guatemala, Santo Domingo, and Manila, and the captaincy-general of Florida. During the eighteenth century the East Indies and Guatemala were excluded from the viceroyalty. The viceroyalty of New

I. The viceroyalty includes :

1. The administration of Guadalaxara,² which lies between 18° 30′ and 24° 30′ N. lat., and 104° and 109° W. long., and is bounded south and west by the South Sea, north by the

Spain, as the term was most generally used, long consisted of the three " kingdoms " of New Spain, New Galicia, and New Leon. This corresponded to modern Mexico, plus then undefined territories of Texas, New Mexico, and California, now parts of the United States. On the separation in 1793 of the Provincias Internas or Internal Provinces, the viceroyalty of New Spain corresponded to the present Mexico, plus the Californias, but minus southern Coahuila, Durango, Sinaloa, Chihuahua, and Sonora. Spanish viceroyalty ceased in 1821, but " New Spain " was not finally " Mexico " till 1824 (during the Empire under Iturbide, 1822-28). The term " Provincias Internas " was vaguely used, as early as the seventeenth century, for the northern parts of New Spain or Mexico. " In 1777 (by order of Aug. 22, 1776) a new government was formed under this name, completely separated from the viceroyalty of New Spain, and comprising Nueva Vizcaya ([New Biscay] Durango and Chihuahua), Coahuila, Texas, New Mexico, Sinaloa, Sonora, and the Californias. The Capital was Arizpe in Sonora, and the audience of Guadalajara retained its judicial authority ; the governor was also military commandant. In 1786 and 1787-93 the government was again subordinate to the viceroy. When the final separation was made in 1793, California was attached to Mexico," Cent. Cyclop., 1894, *s. v.*, p. 828. This last " New Spain" is Pike's ; and the present article is mainly devoted to the Provincias Internas of this New Spain—excepting that nothing is said of the Californias.

³ El Reino de Nueva Galicia, or New Galicia, was a prime division of colonial New Spain, whose limits fluctuated, like those of most Mexican political divisions, but for most of the seventeenth and eighteenth centuries corresponded nearly to the modern states of Jalisco, Aguas Calientes, and Zacatecas, plus a small part of San Luis Potosí. The audience of Guadalajara, originating in 1548, had jurisdiction over this Nueva Galicia ; in 1786 the latter became the intendency of Guadalajara ; and after 1792 the Provincias Internas were judicially subordinate to the audience of Guadalajara. Pike's " administration of Guadalaxara " corresponds inexactly to the present State of Jalisco or Xalisco. This lies on the Pacific coast, bordered by the states of Sinaloa, Durango, Zacatecas, Aguas Calientes, Guanajuato, Michoacan, and Colima ; area, 27,261 sq. m.; pop., 1,280,500 ; capital, Guadalajara. The situation of this city is lat. 21° N., long. 103° 10′ W.; it was founded in 1542, and is now the second largest city in Mexico, pop. 95,000. That " one of the Gusman family," who Pike says built it " in 1551 " was probably Nuño or Nuñez Bertrande Guzman, b. Guadalajara (in Spain) about 1485, d. there 1544 ; he was the enemy of Cortés, and the conqueror of New Galicia. Rio Grande de Santiago is the largest river in the state, and Lago de Chapala, which lies mostly within its limits, is the largest lake in Mexico ; area, over 1,300 sq. m.

provinces of Biscay [Nueva Viscaya] and Sinaloa ; N. E. by the administration of Zacatecas; E. by the administration of Guanaxuato, and S. E. by that of Valladolid. It is 350 miles in length from northwest to southeast, and 250 in width east and west. Its population may be estimated at 100,000. It is one of the most luxuriant and rich administrations in the viceroyalty ; and is watered from east to west by the great river de Santego [Rio Grande de Santiago], which receives most of its waters from Lac [Lago] de Chapala. Guadalaxara, the capital, was built by one of the Gusman family in 1551, and in 1570 the bishopric was removed from Compostela to that place. It is the seat of the audience of Guadalaxara, which includes Guadalaxara and the administration of Zacatecas. The population of this city may be estimated at 75,000; it stands in N. lat. 20° 50′, W. long. 105°.

2. The administration of Valladolid[4] lies between 22° 10′ and 18° 12′ N. lat., and 102° and 105° W. long., and is bounded south by the South sea [Pacific ocean] and part of Mexico, east and northeast by the latter, and north by that of Guanaxuato. Its greatest length from northeast to southwest is 230 miles, and its greatest width, east and west, 190 miles. Its population may be estimated at 360,000. Its capital of the same name is situated in about 20° N. lat., 103° 25″ W. long. Population unknown.

3. The administration of Mexico[5] lies between 21° 30′

---

[4] Valladolid was the name of an old Castilian province in Spain, and of the capital of that province ; it was applied to a political division in Mexico which has entirely disappeared, though corresponding to some extent to the present State of Michoacan. The capital of this was also called Valladolid until 1828, when it was changed to present Morelia, in honor of the patriot priest José Maria Morelos y Pavon, b. there Sept. 30th, 1765 ; joined the revolt of Hidalgo, 1810 ; was captured Nov. 15th, 1815 ; executed Dec. 22d, 1815, near the City of Mexico.

[5] This administration has been so changed and subdivided that it is not easily compared in a word with existing divisions which represent its former extent. In general terms it was a south central portion of Mexico with an extensive Pacific coast line, but cut off from the Atlantic by Vera Cruz and Puebla, and bordered on the N. by San Luis Potosí, etc. The present State of Mexico is

and 16° 30' N. lat., and 99° and 105° W. long., and is bounded south by the South Sea, east by the governments of La Puebla and La Vera Cruz, north by that of St. Louis, and west by Valladolid and Guanaxuato. Its greatest length, north and south, may be 360 miles, and its greatest width, which is on the Western Ocean, is 200 miles. Its population may be estimated at 1,500,000 souls. The capital of this administration, and of the whole kingdom, is Mexico ; a particular description of which is deemed unnecessary. From every information I could obtain from persons who had resided in it for years, it does not contain more than 200,000 inhabitants. Its being the residence of the viceroy, whose court is more splendid than that at Madrid ; its central position as to the ports of Acapulco and Vera Cruz ; together with the rich and luxuriant vale which surrounds it, will, whenever the Spanish Americans burst the present bonds of slavery in which they are bound, give to Mexico all those advantages which great wealth, a large population, and a commanding situation concentrate, and assuredly make it one of the greatest cities in the world. In point of population, it is now in the second rank, and in beauty, riches, magnificence, and splendor, in the first.

4. The administration of Oxaca [Oaxaca or Oajaca[6]] lies between 18° and 16° N. lat., and 98° and 112° W. long., and is bounded south by the South Sea, west by the government of La Puebla, north by Mexico and Vera Cruz,

an area of somewhat over 9,000 sq. m., bounded by Querétaro, Hidalgo, Tlascala, Puebla, Morelos, Guerrero, and Michoacan. Its capital is Toluca ; for the City of Mexico, capital of the republic, is in a small Federal District set apart from the rest of the state (like our District of Columbia), with an area of only 463 sq. m. The pop. of the present State of Mexico is about 830,000 ; the capital city of the republic has a pop. of 330,000 ; its situation is lat. 19° 25' 45" N., long. 99° 7' 18" W., at an alt. of about 7,500 feet.

[6] The present State of Oajaca has an extensive Pacific coast-line on the S., Guerrero and a small part of Puebla on the W., Puebla and Vera Cruz on the N., Vera Cruz and Chiapas on the E.; area, about 28,800 sq. m.; pop. about 816,000. The capital city of the same name is on the Rio Verde or Atoyac, about 200 m. S. E. of the City of Mexico ; pop. 29,000.

and east by the province of Gualamalia [Guatemala]. Its greatest length, east and west, is 230 miles, and its width, north and south, 175 miles. Its population may be estimated at 520,000 souls. Its capital is Oxaca, in 17° 30′ N. lat., 99° 25′ W. long.

5. The administration of Vera Cruz[7] lies between 17° and 22° N. lat., and 98° and 101° W. long., and is bounded north and east by the gulf of Mexico, south by Oxaca, west by Puebla and Mexico. Its greatest length, N. W. and S. E., is 430 miles, and its width, E. and W., not more than 60 miles. Its population may be estimated at 220,000. Its capital is Vera Cruz, which is the sole port of entry for all the kingdom on the Atlantic ocean, as that of Acapulco is on the Western. Its population may be estimated at 30,000 souls, and is in 19° 10′ N. lat. and 98° 30′ W. long. This city was taken and sacked by the English on the 17th of May, 1683, since which the works for its defense [present Castle of San Juan de Ulúa] have been made so very strong as almost to bid defiance to an attack from the sea.

6. The administration de la Puebla[8] lies between 20° and

---

[7] Vera Cruz is the long, narrow maritime state of Mexico, with the Gulf on the E., Tamaulipas on the N., and then bordered on the W., S., and E., successively, by San Luis Potosí, Hidalgo, Puebla, Oajaca, Chiapas, and Tabasco. The land is low along the Gulf, or in the *tierra caliente*, but soon rises to the mountainous *tierra fria* of most of the state. The whole area is 27,450 sq. m.; pop. 642,000. The long-famous seaport of Vera Cruz is the principal city, pop. 24,000, in lat. 19° 12′ N., long. 96° 9′ E. This was founded near the present site by Cortés in May, 1519, by the name of Villa Rica de la Vera Cruz; site changed to the Rio de la Antigua in 1525; to present position in 1599; became City of Vera Cruz in 1615; was taken by the French in 1838, by the Americans in 1848, by the Allies in 1861. The celebrated Picacho of Orizaba, 10 m. N. of Orizaba, alt. 18,314 feet, is on the boundary between Vera Cruz and Puebla. This is the highest mountain of N. America, except Mt. St. Elias.

[8] Present State of Puebla is entirely cut off from the sea, being wedged in among Vera Cruz on the E., Oajaca on the S., Guerrero on the S. W., and Morelos, Mexico, Tlascala, and Hidalgo, on the W.; area 12,740 sq. m.; pop. lately, 845,000; capital, La Puebla de los Angeles, so called from a pious taradiddle; pop. about 110,000; it is a very old city, founded about 1530, and was taken by the French in 1863. The famous peak of Popocatepetl, or

16° N. lat., and 100° and 102° W. long., and is bounded south by the South sea, east by Oxaca and Vera Cruz, north and west by Mexico; it is near 300 miles in its greatest length from north to south, and 120 in its greatest width from east to west. Its population may be estimated at 800,000 souls. Its capital is the city of La Puebla, estimated at 80,000 souls, which is in 19° 12' N. lat., and 100° 50' W. long.

7. The administration of Guanaxuato [or Guanajuato[9]] lies between 21° 30' and 23° 30' N. lat., and 103° and 105° W. long., and is bounded south by Valladolid, east by Mexico, south by St. Louis [and] Zacataca, and west by Guadalaxara. Its greatest extent, from north to south, is 75 miles, and from east to west, 85. Its population may be estimated at 500,000 souls. Its capital city is Guanaxuato, in lat. 21° N., long. 103° W.

8. The administration of Zacataca [Zacatecas[10]] lies between 21° 20' and 24° 52' N. lat., and 103° and 105° 30' W. long., and is bounded north by the internal province of Biscay, east by St. Louis, west by Guadalaxara, and south by Guanaxuato. Its greatest length is 210 miles, north and south, and its greatest width is 145 miles, from east to west. Its population may be estimated at 250,250 souls. The capital, Zacataca, stands in 23° N. lat. and 104° W. long.

9. The administration of St. Louis [San Luis Potosí[11]]

Smoking mt., a volcano about 17,800 feet high, is on the boundary between this state and Mexico, 45 m. S. E. of the city of the latter name; and N. of that peak is another volcano, Ixtaccihuatl or the "Woman in White," over 16,000 feet high.

[9] Guanajuato is a small central state, surrounded by Zacatecas, San Luis Potosí, Querétaro, Michoacan, Jalisco, and Aguas Calientes; area, 11,370 sq. m., pop. over 1,000,000; capital of same name, about lat. 21° 1' N., long. 100° 35' W.; pop. 52,000.

[10] Zacatecas has altered less than some of the administrations, the present state being bounded N. by Coahuila, N. and N. W. by Durango, W. and S. W. and S. by Jalisco, S. by Aguas Calientes, E. by San Luis Potosí; area, 25,230 sq. m.; pop. 585,640; capital of same name, about lat. 22° 40' N., pop. about 60,000.

[11] Pike's "St. Louis" corresponds, though inexactly, to present State of San

lies between 21° 20′ and 28° 50′ N. lat., and 99° and 102°
W. long., includes Texas and St. Ander [Nuevo Santander]
in this dimension, and is bounded north by New Leon,
east by the province of St. Ander, south by Guanaxuato
and Mexico, and west by Zacataca. Its greatest length
from north to south is 200, and its width from east to west
is 170 miles. Its population may be estimated at 311,500
souls. Its capital is St. Louis de Potosi, the population of
which is 60,000; it stands in 22° N. lat., 103° W. long.,
and was founded in 1568 [1576].

II. The province of Nuevo San Ander [Santander [12]] is
bounded north by the province of Texas, west by Nuevo
Leon and Cogquillo [Coahuila], south by St. Louis, and
east by the Atlantic Ocean; from north to south it is about
500 miles in length, but from east to west not more than
150. Its population may be estimated at 38,000 souls.
The capital, New San Ander [Nuevo Santander], is on the
river of that name [also known as the Rio Jimenez, and
Rio de las Palmas], about 40 miles from the sea, in 23° 45′
N. lat. and 101° W. long.

III. The kingdom of New Leon [Nuevo Leon [13]] is

Luis Potosí, lying among Nuevo Leon, Tamaulipas, and a small extent of
Vera Cruz on the E., Zacatecas on the W., Coahuila on the N., and Guanajuato, Querétaro, and Hidalgo on the S.; area, 24,450 sq. m.; pop. about
550,500; capital of the same name, 223 m. N. N. W. of City of Mexico;
pop. 62,600.

[12] Nuevo Santander, whose history is something of a political curiosity, was
originally a division of colonial New Spain, and continued to be known as a
colony until 1786. The extent was about that of the present State of Tamaulipas, bounded substantially as Pike says, though it once overreached the Rio
Grande into what is now Texas. Tamaulipas has Texas on the N., separated
by the Rio Grande; the Gulf of Mexico on the E.; Nuevo Leon and Coahuila
on the W.; San Luis Potosí on the S. W. and S.; with a small extent of Vera
Cruz on the extreme S.; area, 29,350 sq. m.; pop. about 173,000; capital,
Cuidad Victoria. The river, on one of whose headwaters this city is situated,
falls into the Gulf near the Barra de Santander, as it is still called, about 60
Mexican leagues S. of the mouth of the Rio Grande, and rather less than 40
such leagues N. of Tampico; its length is supposed to be about 150 m.

[13] Or Nuevo Reino de Leon, as it was long styled. This was a division of
colonial New Spain, corresponding to the present State of Nuevo Leon, but,

bounded east by New San Ander, north by Cogquilla, west by Biscay, and south by St. Louis and Zacataca; its greatest length north and south is 250 miles; width, east and west, 100 miles. Its population may be estimated at 30,000 souls. Its capital, Mont El Rey [Monterey], is situated on the headwaters of Tiger river, which discharges into the gulf of Mexico. The city of Mont El Rey contains about 11,000 souls, and is the seat of the bishop, Don Dio Premiro, who visited the port of Natchitoches when it was commanded by Captain Turner, of the 2d U. S. regiment of infantry. His episcopal jurisdiction extends over Nuevo San Ander, New Leon, Cogquilla, and Texas, and his salary is equal to $100,000 per annum. Mont El Rey is situated in 26° N. lat. and 102° W. long. There are many rich mines near the city of Mont El Rey, whence, I am informed, there are taken to be coined 100 mule-loads of bullion in silver and gold monthly, which may be presumed to be not more than the three-fifths of what is taken from the mines, as there are many persons who prefer never

when a kingdom, including certain portions of what are now Tamaulipas and San Luis Potosí; it was attached to the intendency of the latter in 1786. New Leon still has Tamaulipas along the whole of its E. border, excepting that its northern panhandle is environed by Coahuila, which thence extends on its W. side to San Luis Potosí, which latter thence curves to meet Tamaulipas at the end of the southern panhandle. The shape of some of the Mexican states would show, in the absence of all history, that earthquakes and volcanoes were not the only agitations against which New Spain contended in the settling of some of her geographical problems. Area of New Leon, 24,000 sq. m.; pop. 272,000; capital, Monterey: for Pike's location of Monterey on "Tiger" r., see note [33], p. 682, May 18th, 1807. The position of this city is about lat. 25° 40′ N., long. 100° 25′ W.; pop. 46,000; it is best known to us as a prize captured by the U. S. forces under Z. Taylor, Sept. 23d, 1846. The Count of Monterey was one Caspar de Zuñiga y Azevedo, b. ca. 1540, d. Lima, Peru, Feb. 10th, 1606, viceroy of Mexico, Oct. 5th, 1595–1603, of Peru, Nov. 28th, 1604, till death; Monterey bay, Cal., named for him. The American officer whom Pike names was Edward D. Turner of Massachusetts, who entered the army as an ensign of the 2d Inf. Mar. 4th, 1791; became a lieutenant July 13th, 1792: captain of the 2d sub-Legion Nov. 11th, 1793, and of the 2d Inf. Nov. 1st, 1796; served as brigade inspector from Nov. 1st, 1799, to Apr. 1st, 1802; was retained as a captain of the 1st Inf. from the latter date, and resigned Nov. 30th, 1805.

getting their metal coined, as then it is not so easily ascertained what they are worth, which is an all-important secret in a despotic government.

The foregoing nine administrations or intendencias, the province of Nuevo San Ander, and the kingdom of [Nuevo] Leon, are included in the two audiences of Guadalaxara and Mexico, and form, as I believe, the whole political government of the viceroy of Mexico; but I am not positive whether his jurisdiction does not include the audience of Guatimalia [Guatemala], which lies to the south, and includes the province of that name, that of Chiapa [Chiapas], Yucatan, Veraqua [Veragua], Costa Rica, and Honduras. An audience is the high court of appeals in which the viceroy presides and has two votes; it is intended as a check on his power and authority.

The administrations are governed by intendants, who are offiers of high rank, and always Europeans.

The longitude given is from the meridian of Paris.

In the general view of New Spain,[14] I shall take some notice of the manners, customs, political force, etc., of the viceroyalty; but, as I do not pretend to be correctly informed as to that quarter of the kingdom, and there have been so many persons who have given statements on those heads, I shall confine my observations principally to the internal provinces through which I passed, and on which I made my observations.

[14] This comes at the end of the present dissertation, when Pike has finished with his account of the Internal Provinces, to which he now proceeds. Two of these, Sonora and Sinaloa, are "internal" to the extent of bordering on the Gulf of California and not on the high sea. These he never saw; those he traversed correspond to the present three Mexican states of Chihuahua, Durango, and Coahuila, and to our Territory of New Mexico, State of Texas, and a small part of the State of Louisiana. Most of the commentary that would otherwise be here offered has already been put upon Pike's itinerary through these regions; but some points will come up for further criticism or explanation.

INTERNAL PROVINCES.

1. NEW MEXICO. [*Geography.* The province of New Mexico] lies between lat. 30° 30' and 44° N., and long. 104° and 108° W., and is the most northern province of the kingdom of New Spain. It extends northwest into an undefined boundary, is bounded north and east by Louisiana, south by Biscay and Cogquilla, and west by Senora and California.[15]

[15] New Mexico, as long as it was a province of New Spain, could not be satisfactorily bounded, for the simple reason that its boundaries were never clearly defined. Pike's ascription of lat. 44° N. sends it up to the shadowy border of " the Oregan "—that No Man's Land till Lewis and Clark descended the Columbia to the South Sea. This is no place to open the celebrated quarrel over boundaries that hovered in the air like clouds on political paper ; suffice it, that when the Oregan became an undisputed possession of any nation, it already belonged to the United States. Away from the Pacific coast, Spanish dominion never exceeded 38° N. in fact, whatever it may have been on paper at any time. Shortly after Pike's time, *i. e.*, from Feb. 22d, 1819, an intelligible theoretical boundary was agreed upon by the United States and Spain, though it was never run upon the ground. This line, aside from any question of the still unsettled boundary of Texas, ran from the Red r. to the Arkansaw r. on the meridian of 100° W. from Greenwich, up the Arkansaw to its source, thence due N. on whatever the meridian might prove to be to lat. 42° N., thence on that parallel due W. to the Pacific. Spanish Nuevo Mejico was quietly captured without resistance by the U. S. Army of the West under Kearny in 1846 ; formally ceded in 1848 ; organized as a U. S. territory in 1850 ; its southern boundary changed by the acquisition of the Gadsden purchase and definitely established in 1853 ; Arizona detached on the W. in 1863 along the meridian of 109° W.; eastern boundary, the meridian of 103° W.; present area, 122,460 sq. m.; pop. in 1890 given as 153,593. Thus, to all intents and practical purposes, Pike's " New Mexico " is our New Mexico and Arizona, and thence indefinitely northward. Present Arizona has an area of 112,920 sq. m.; pop. 59,620 by the census of 1890. In December, 1863, Governor John N. Goodwin and Secretary Richard C. McCormick, with other new Territorial officials, entered into possession on the ground, and formally proclaimed their functions. They proceeded to establish the capital on Granite cr., a tributary of the Rio Verde, and named it Prescott, for the historian, after having deliberated whether to call it Audubon, for the ornithologist. The log house built for the gubernatorial, secretarial, and all other functions was there when I last saw it, in 1892, and still the residence of one of the original party, Judge Fleury, who in the course of time exercised his versatile talent in every capacity, from cook to acting governor. Arizona is thus politically in its 32d year now (1895). Its historic period dates from 1540 or 1536 ; the prehistoric compass of time, since it

Its length is unknown; its breadth may be 600 miles; but the inhabited part is not more than 400 miles in length and 50 in breadth, lying along the river del Norte, from lat. 37° to 31° 30' N.; but in this space there is a desert of more than 250 miles.

Air and Climate. No persons accustomed to reside in the temperate climate of lat. 36° and 37° N. in the United States can form any idea of the piercing cold which is experienced on that parallel in New Mexico; but the air is serene and unaccompanied by damps or fogs, as it rains but once a year, and some years not at all. It is a mountainous country. The grand dividing ridges which separate the waters of the rio del Norte from those of California border it on the line of its western limits, and are covered, in some places, with eternal snows, which give a keenness to the air that could not be calculated upon or expected in a temperate zone.

Timber and Plains. The cotton tree [*Populus*] is the only tree of this province, except some scrubby pines and cedars at the foot of the mountains [and many other species there and elsewhere]. The former borders the banks of the rio del Norte and its tributary streams. All the rest of the country presents to the eye a barren wild of poor land, scarcely to be improved by culture, and appears to be only capable of producing sufficient subsistence for those animals which live on succulent plants and herbage.

Mines, Minerals, and Fossils. There are no mines known in the province, except one of copper situated in a mountain on the west side of the rio del Norte, in lat. 34° N. [see note [26], p. 637]. It is worked, and produces 20,000 muleloads of copper annually. It also furnishes that article for

was first inhabited, is very likely not exceeded by the Christian era—to judge from recent exhumations in the valley of the Gila, revealing a cluster of cities 6 m. long. Those who named the present capital Phœnix builded better than they knew—the name, I mean, not the mud hovels and wicker-work jacals which adorn some portions of that new center of political intrigue to which were lately shifted the inevitable dissensions that arose between the northern mountaineers and the southern deserteers.

the manufactories of nearly all the internal provinces. It contains gold, but not quite sufficient to pay for its extraction; consequently it has not been pursued.

There is, near Santa Fe, in some of the mountains, a stratum of talc, which is so large and flexible as to render it capable of being subdivided into thin flakes, of which the greater proportion of the houses in Santa Fe, and in all the villages to the north, have their window-lights made.

Rivers. The river del Norte takes its source in the mountains which give birth to the headwaters of California, the Plata [South Platte], Pierre Jaune ["Yellowstone," *i. e.,* North Platte] of the Missouri, and Arkansaw of the Mississippi, in lat. 40° N. and long. 110° W.[16] Its distance from its source to the gulf of Mexico may be, by its meanders, estimated at 2,000 miles, passing through the provinces of New Mexico, part of Biscay, Cogquilla, and New San Ander, where it falls into the gulf at lat. 26° N. It cannot, in any part of its course, be termed a navigable stream, owing to the sand-bars. In the flat country and mountains in the upper part, with which its course is interrupted, small boats might ascend as high as the Presidio de Rio Grande in Cogquilla, and it might be navigable for canoes in various parts of its course. In the mountains above Santa Fe it afforded amply sufficient water for canoe navigation, and even more

---

[16] To correct in detail all such statements would hardly come within the scope of cursory notes, and I usually pass them over, as anyone can easily inform himself of the adjustment required for geographical precision. But in this particular instance it is well to remember that Pike had acquired an erroneous notion of the source of the Yellowstone, from considering the *South* Platte to be the whole Platte, thus throwing the *North* Platte out of court. Having no knowledge of this great river, he fancied there was some spot whence he could walk in a day to the source of any one of the four he names—a feat for which the seven-leagued boots of fable would be required: see note [5], p. 524. For some particulars concerning the Rio Grande, see note [32], p. 642. To the different names which the river had in different regions, add Rio Abajo and Rio Arriba for lower and upper sections, not well defined but conveniently recognized, of Rio del Norte above El Paso. Pike is quite right in the matter of Rio Bravo—a name never applied to the river in any portion of its course which he traversed in New Mexico.

than appeared to be flowing in its bed in the plains. This must be attributed to numerous canals and the dry sandy soil through which the river courses, where much of the water which flows from the mountains must be absorbed and lost. In the province of New Mexico it is called the Rio del Norte ; below it is termed the Rio Grande ; but in no instance did I hear it called the Rio Bravo, as many of our ancient maps designate it.

There are also, in the limits of this province, to the west, the rivers San Rafael, San Xavier, de los Dolores, also de los Anamas or Nabajoa, all of which join and form the great Rio Colorado of California.[17]   The two first take their

---

[17] Whatever the real implication of names bestowed upon actual or alleged branches of the Colorado by the early explorers from whom Pike drew his inspiration, as Escalante 1777, it is not difficult to identify those he uses, even when his text does not agree with his map, as happens in some cases. From the Rio Gila, for which see note [19], we will follow his map upward. 1. "Rio S^n. Maria" of the map, not in the text. The name Santa Maria held for many years for the branch of the Colorado now called Bill Williams' fork. This is composed of two main streams, to one of which the name Santa Maria is now usually restricted ; the other is called Big Sandy. Bill Williams' fork does not head in Bill Williams' mountain, being cut off from that by the Rio Verde, etc.; its basin lies entirely W. of Aubrey and Chino valleys, and of the Prescott plains. This river drains westward from the Santa Maria, Granite, Juniper, Weaver, and other ranges in Arizona, and falls into the Colorado from the E. at a place called Aubrey City, the site of which was pointed out to me by a native when I navigated the Colorado in 1865, though I saw nothing like a city. 2. There is no mention in the text, nor any sign on the map, of the Colorado Chiquito, otherwise Little Colorado r., though this is a large water-course which, when it runs, drains an extensive area in N. Arizona. This stream heads about the White, Mogollon, and other ranges on or near the confines of New Mexico ; receives from the Zuñian mts. its main fork, Rio Puerco of the West ; flows N. W. past (E. of) the San Francisco and Bill Williams' peaks, and falls into the Colorado from the S. E., well up in the Grand Cañon of the latter ; its own lower courses are terribly cañonous for a great distance, its bed being riven in chasms comparable even with the awful abyss of the Colorado itself. 3. Non-appearance of the Colorado Chiquito affects to some extent the identification of the river called in the text "de los Anamas or Nabajoa" and lettered on the map "Rio Jasquevilla." This is laid down as a large eastern branch of the Colorado which falls in *above* the Grand Cañon, and on which lived the "Nahjo" (Navajo) and "Cosninas" (Cojnino) Indians, and *south* of which were the "Indiens Moqui, Independent since 1680," in four villages lettered "Oraybe," "Mosanis,"

sources in the same mountains as the Rio del Norte, but on the west side.

The river Colorado, by its meanders, may be about 1,000 miles in length, from its sources to its discharge into the head of the gulf of California, in the 33d degree of N. lat. [about 32°]. It has been represented to me, by men of

" Songoapt," and " Gualpi "—for, though the Moki legend is set astride of the river itself, it belongs to these four villages S. of the river. The stream in question certainly was meant for the Colorado Chiquito ; but most of its ascribed characters are those of Rio San Juan of N. W. New Mexico, N. E. Arizona, and S. E. Utah. The leaning toward the Colorado Chiquito is shown by the location of the Cojnino Indians on this stream, and its passage next N. of the circle of ten peaks lettered " Sierra de los Cosninas "—these indicating the San Francisco, Bill Williams', and other mountains of central Arizona ; but identification with the San Juan is possible by the location of the Navajos on its headwaters and of the Mokis further S., as well as by its entrance into the Colorado *above* the Grand Cañon—for Pike charts the upper end of the cañon as the " Puerto del Bacorelli." Rio San Juan heads in N. W. New Mexico, next W. of the Rio Grande basin, having numerous collateral sources there and in contiguous parts of N. E. Arizona and S. W. Colorado ; hence it enters S. E. Utah and runs to the Colorado around the base of Mt. Navajo, thus including in its ramifications adjacent corners of two states and two territories ; two of its affluents retain to this day the names Rio de las Animas and Rio Navajo, respectively. Among its larger tributaries may be mentioned Rio Chusco, Chasco, or Chaco, and especially Rio Chelly—the lattei being that one the mystery of whose famous Cañon de Chelly was fathomed by Captain J. H. Simpson in 1859. The two strange words which Pike uses in this connection, " Bacorelli " and " Jasquevilla," both treated in the Index, are not the same as Jicarilla, present name of certain mountains in Arizona and of a certain tribe of Indians called in Arizona " Hickory " Apaches. 4. The fact that the Grand Cañon of the Colorado is indicated on Pike's map may be certified in more than one way: (*a*) He marks below it certain " Indiens Chemequaba," *i. e.*, Chemehuevi, a Shoshonean tribe then as now living in Arizona below the cañon, and thus isolated from their parent stock among Apaches of Athapascan lineage. (*b*) Pike's term " Cosninas," for certain Indians and mountains, is still an alternative name for the Cosnino, Cojnino, or Cataract Cañon, a side-spur of the Grand Cañon, and still the residence of a curious cave-dwelling tribe called Yavasupai, Havasupi, or Aguazul, who numbered 214 when I visited them in 1881. (*c*) The trans-continental route via the Arkansaw and Colorado rivers, which Pike suggests as the " best communication from ocean to ocean," need not be supposed to run through the Grand Cañon, but rather to approximate that lately achieved by the Atlantic and Pacific R. R., connecting on the E. with the A., T., and S. F. R. R., on the W. with the So. Cala. R. R. 5. West of the Grand Cañon Pike traces a problematical " Rio de los Panami des surfurcas on information and research, to be navigable for square-rigged vessels at least 300 miles from the gulf. By this river and the Arkansaw there could be the best communication established between the Pacific and the Atlantic oceans. There are represented to be various numerous and warlike nations of Indians on its banks. Through the whole of its course its banks are entirely destitute of timber, and indeed I was

ignore l Embouchure," without beginning or end. This suggests Virgin r., whose junction with the Colorado in Nevada was then unknown. 6. Above the Grand Cañon, Pike forks the Colorado distinctly into two main branches, referable of course to the Grand and the Green rivers. 7. The main course of Grand r. is lettered " Rio de los Duimas," for which read Las Animas—but not "Los Anamas or Nabajoa" of Pike's text, already accounted for. This " Duimas " may be taken as intended to represent the whole course of Grand r. and its branches, as the Gunnison, etc. 8. The main course of the " Duimas " or Grand r. is what Pike means by Rio " de los Dolores " of the text, nameless on his map. This is the Dolores r. of present geography, running chiefly in Colorado, but joining the Grand in Utah. Pike forks this ; one of these forks is the continuation of the Dolores ; the other is present San Miguel r. of Colorado. 9. Green r. is the one lettered " Rio Zanguananos," as the main continuation of the Colorado itself. This is correct, though the singular S-shaped course in which it is laid down is so far out of drawing that the two branches of it which he names are thrown in the wrong direction. These two are the San Rafael and San Xavier of both text and map. The first one of them is present San Rafael r.; and if we take Pike's San Xavier to be the next above on the same side, it corresponds to Price r. We must not seek for any streams higher up the Grand than Price r.; the early Spanish travelers did not get very far in that direction ; and Pike sets all these streams considerably S. of Great Salt l., not beyond the latitude he assigns to the head of the Rio Grande. The old Spanish trail from Colorado into Utah passed a certain Sierra La Sal, or Salt mt., which is situated near the confluence of the Green and the Grand ; continued across both these rivers a little above their junction, and so on westward between the San Rafael r. and the San Xavier or Price r., into the basin of present Sevier r. and Sevier l. Now Pike sets his " Montaigne de Sel," or Mountain of Salt, close to the main Rio Zanguananos or Green r., and directly against the mouth of his San Rafael. This particular combination could not have been accidental, and seems to show what was really mapped, though so distortedly. As intimated in beginning this note, I have attempted identifications without prejudice to any original implication of the Spanish records, but solely according to what I find in Pike. The early names themselves seem open to the interpretation here offered, and I know from several futile attempts which I made that Pike's geography of the Colorado basin would be hard to square with the facts in any other way. Should the present identifications be acceptable, some hitherto unsurmounted difficulties would prove to have been overcome.

informed that for 300 miles there was not a tree ten inches in diameter.

The river S. Buenaventura empties into the Pacific ocean to the north of California in 39° 30′ N. latitude, and takes its source in the Sierre Madre to the north of the Colorado and del Norte.[18]

[18] This paragraph is contradicted by the map, on which "Rio de Sta. Buenaventura" runs W. into a nameless lake, S. of a certain Lac de Timpanagos, and is the first river, N. and W. of Green r., that does not connect with the Colorado. The Buenaventura is a ghost-river which haunted geography for many years. Nothing like such a river as this was represented to be exists—it is as much of a myth in Utah and California as Lahontan's fabulous Long r. in Minnesota and Dakota. But it is a rule with hardly an exception that every myth has some basis of fact. In so far as Pike's Buenaventura represents anything in nature, I imagine it to be an adumbration of Sevier r., and its sink to be Lake Sevier, in the western part of Utah, S. of Great Salt l. True, the Buenaventura is laid down very much out of the actual course of the Sevier; but not more wrongly than Green r. is, and the very curious way in which the Sevier winds about to reach its sink would hardly have been discovered and correctly delineated by those early travelers in the "Great American Desert." The nameless lake itself is not very far out of the way on Pike's map. Possibly also, the mysterious river, "whose mouth is unknown," may be intended for some section of the Sevier; for, if we were to connect this trace with Pike's Buenaventura, we should have a recognizable representation of the Sevier. But Pike heads his Rio S. Buenaventura, by a principal branch called "Rio de S^n. Clemente," in that portion of the continental divide he marks "Sierra Verde," i. e., Green mts., also the source of present Green r. We should note further in this connection the appearance on Pike's map of New Mexico of a certain river running northward, lettered "Rio de Piedro Amaretto del Missouri." Here, "Amaretto" is a mistake of the engraver for *Amarillo*, the phrase being Sp. Piedra Amarilla=F. Pierre Jaune or Roche Jaune=E. Yellow Stone, a principal branch of the Missouri. As we have repeatedly seen already, Pike was determined to interlock the headwaters of the Yellowstone, Platte, Arkansaw, and Rio Grande in some one spot in the Rocky mts.—and here we have it, just over the divide that separates these Atlantic waters collectively from those of the general basin of the Colorado. Observe, also, how nearly the dotted trail of the "Country explored by a Detachment of American Troops commanded by Captain Pike" reaches to the supposed Yellowstone.

The Sevier r. possesses a melancholy interest as the scene of the wanton and brutal murder by Piute Indians of Captain John Williams Gunnison and most of his companions, near Sevier l., Oct. 27th, 1853. The particulars are given by Lieutenant E. G. Beckwith, P. R. R. Rep., II. 1855, pp. 72–74. The massacre occurred at break of day of the 27th, not on the 26th, as usually reported. There was no provocation whatever, and no thought of danger on the part of

The Rio Gila[19] heads opposite the copper-mines, and

the devoted band. Those killed, besides Captain Gunnison, were Mr. E. H. Kern, topographer and artist ; Mr. F. Creuzfeldt, botanist ; Mr. Wm. Potter, a citizen of Utah, guide ; John Bellows, an employee ; and three men of the military escort, which consisted of a corporal and six privates ; only four of the whole party escaped with their lives. Lieutenant Beckwith expressly exonerates the Mormons from complicity in the outrage ; public opinion thought otherwise ; and the official record of Captain Gunnison's death stands " Killed 26 Oct. 53 by a band of Mormons and Inds near Sevier Lake Utah." The lamented and accomplished officer met his fate while conducting explorations and surveys for a railroad route near the 38° and 39° parallels of N. lat. He had graduated from the U. S. Military Academy at West Point July 31st, 1837, when he became a second lieutenant of the 2d Artillery ; was transferred with that rank to the corps of Topographical Engineers July 7th, 1838 ; became first lieutenant May 9th, 1846 ; and obtained his captaincy Mar. 3d, 1853.

[19] Pike acquired a good idea of the Gila, for one who never saw it, and it is well laid down on his map ; though it joins the Colorado a considerable distance above the head of the Gulf of California, the confluence is below 33°, being in lat. 32° 43' 32" N., long. 114° 36' 10" W. The Gila was known to the whites before the Mississippi was discovered ; it was long better known than the Rio Grande, and down to the present century was far better known than the Rio Colorado. The valley of the Gila was the first seat of semi-civilization within the present limits of the United States ; and Tucson, on the Santa Cruz r., disputes with St. Augustine in Florida the record of being the oldest continuously inhabited white settlement in our country ; but St. A. was founded by Spaniards about the middle of the sixteenth century. An early if not the first name of the Gila was Rio de los Apostolos, more fully Rio Grande de los Apostolos, as the legend appears, for example, on Vaugondy's map, 1783, where so many apostolic and canonical towns are marked along the river as to give its valley the appearance of a well-settled region, including even that ancient and celebrated structure, the Casa Grande, still extant. Rio de los Apostolos or Apostles' r. appears on maps of the present century, as for example on the one which Captain Clark drew at the Mandans in the winter of 1804-5, and which Captain Lewis dispatched to President Jefferson April 7th, 1805, but which was never published of full size till September, 1893. Pike's first branch of the Gila is called " Rio de la Asuncion," with Rio Verde as its main fork. This is correct ; for the river of the Assumption of the B. V. M., whatever may be the myth upon which such an extraordinary assumption was based, is that now known as Rio Salinas, Rio Salado, and Salt r., into which the Verde falls near Mt. McDowell and the fort of the same name. The confluence of Salt r. with the Gila is below Phœnix, present capital of Arizona, and but little above the point where the Agua Fria also falls into the Gila. The Verde is the principal river of central Arizona, for the most part flowing southward, though it starts northward by the headwater called Granite cr. and then makes a loop ; this creek is the site of Prescott, first capital of Arizona on the establishment of the Terri-

discharges into the gulf of California, just below the Colorado, in the 33d degree of N. latitude.

tory in 1863, and of Fort Whipple, established by the troops to which I was attached in July, 1864. Pike's small branch of the Gila lettered " Rio de Ozul," for which read Rio Azul or Blue r., is the present San Carlos, of which we lately heard a good deal on account of the unruly Apaches at the agency of that name. Present Blue cr. is a small branch higher up on the same side, near Pike's Rio San Francisco, which latter he rightly charts as one of the initial forks of the Gila. His Rio San Pedro, still so called, is the principal Gileño tributary from the S. It acquired special importance in connection with the U. S. and Mexican Boundary Survey. Near this stream he marks " Pres[idio] de Tubson," at the town of " Sn. Xavier del bac," in the " Senora " (Sonora) of that day.

The Indian tribes of the Gila valley which are located on the map may be here noted, as their names do not come up elsewhere in this work, and with these may also be conveniently considered those which Pike marks on the Colorado above the Gila. Such are, on the Gila : The Yumas (Cuchans) ; the " Cojuenchis " ; the " Cucapa " (Cocopas) ; the Papagos ; the " Cocomaricopas " (Maricopas) ; and on the Colorado : the " Chemequaba " (Chemehuevis, who are of Shoshonean stock, as we have already seen) ; the " Jalchedum " ; the " Yabijoias " (Yavapais) ; the " Yamaya " (Amaquaqua, Amaqua, Majave or Mohave). All these Indians lived within the present territory of the United States, occupying the valley of the Gila on both sides from above the junction of the San Pedro down to the Colorado, and up the Colorado, on the Arizona side at least, to the Grand Cañon, to the almost entire exclusion of other tribes. They were bounded on the N. by Shoshonean tribes in California, Nevada, Utah, and a small part of Arizona ; on the E. by Athapascan tribes, especially the Apaches ; on the S., they stretched throughout Lower California, and far into Mexico. With the single exception just said, the names that I can identify all are now classed under two main family groups or linguistic stocks, Piman and Yuman ; and all belong to the latter, excepting the Papagos and the Pimas themselves. 1. The Piman family is mainly Mexican, as of its nine tribes or divisions only three are Arizonian. Of these, the Sobaipuri, who lived on the Santa Cruz and San Pedro branches of the Gila, have entirely disappeared. The Pimas proper, Upper Pimas, or Pimas Altas (so called in distinction from the Lower Pimas, Pimas Bajas, or Nevomes, of Mexico), have lived for 200 years on the Gila and Salado, in the position assigned by Pike to the Cocomaricopas. The Papagos lived further S. and extended into Mexico. According to late official returns (for 1890), there were 4,464 Pimas and 5,163 Papagos under the Pima Agency on the Gila. 2. The Yuman family is less summarily to be disposed of, as the area of its distribution in the United States is more extensive and its divisions are more numerous, and several of them are entirely extralimital in Lower California and Mexico. The name *Yuma* is given by Whipple as a Cuchan word meaning " sons of the river." In the early days of our occupation of Arizona some of the tribes

The Rio Puerto [Pecos[20]] is a branch of the Rio del Norte ; it comes from the north and joins that river about 100 miles below the Presidio del Norte.

along the Colorado were hostile ; but since the subjugation of the Yumas and Mohaves, followed by the establishment of Fort Yuma and Fort Mohave, they have given very little trouble, with the exception of the Hualapais or Walapais. These may be properly classed as Yuman by linguistic affinities, but they are rather mountain than river Indians, and have within comparatively few years been most decidedly hostile.   In January, 1865, it was my misfortune, which I shall never cease to regret, to be concerned in a cruel massacre—for I cannot call it a fight—in which about 30 Hualapais were killed, in the Juniper mts., a very few miles from the spot where Camp Hualapais was later established. My friend, the late Colonel William Redwood Price, when major of the 8th Cavalry (d. Dec. 30th, 1881), had the handling of the Hualapais after this ; in 1867 they were about 1,500 people, with probably 400 warriors ; he killed probably 175 of them, mostly men, and brought them to terms in 1869, when a batch of prisoners was sent to San Francisco.   In 1881, when we reoccupied Camp Hualapais and named it Camp Price, a threatened outbreak was averted by putting a chief in irons.   The Hualapais now number perhaps 750, in N. W. Arizona, and are almost the only members of the Yuman stock in the Territory whom we have not entirely broken down, pauperized, and debauched. The shocking syphilization of all the Yuman Indians along the Colorado has been notorious for many years.   The Yumas or Umas proper, or Cuchans, have been segregated ; there are or were lately about 1,000 at the Mission Agency in California, and 300 at the San Carlos in Arizona.   Of the Mohaves, some 650 are at the Colorado River Agency in Arizona, 800 at San Carlos, and perhaps 400 at large.   The disestablishment of Fort Mohave is quite recent ; I was post surgeon there in 1881.   There are about 300 Maricopas at the Pima Agency in Arizona.   The Cocopas are a small tribe whose census is uncertain; they live on the California side of the Colorado up to the vicinity of the Gila. The Yavasupai or Aguazul Indians, who live in Cojnino or Cataract cañon, to the number of about 200, as already said, note [17], are entirely cut off from the world in the bottom of the chasm selected for their abode.   Some of them I found occupying holes in the rock, which they walled up like old-fashioned cliff-dwellers ; while others were sheltered in wickiups scattered about the few acres of arable ground they could find to irrigate for the cultivation of their corn, beans, melons, squashes, peaches, apricots, and sunflower-seeds.

[20] This is the main fork or largest branch of the Rio Grande.   As already remarked, note [23], p. 632, Pike maps it too high up ; for it runs entirely E. of the mountains (Sacramento, Guadalupe, White, etc.), W. of which he traces it, and its mouth is 346 m. by the channel of the Rio Grande below the site of Presidio del Norte, in lat. 29° 40′ N., long. 101° 20′ W.   The length of the river is supposed to be between 700 and 800 m.   The Pecos heads in the mountains immediately W. of Santa Fé—on the E. side of the Santa Fé range and W. side of Las Vegas range, among such peaks as the Truchas, Cone,

None of the foregoing streams present any evidence of civilization on their shores excepting the Rio del Norte.

Lakes. I heard of no lakes in the province, except that

Baldy, Lake, etc., there flowing due S. before it bears off to the left. It receives numerous small tributaries, both above and below the point where it passes by the cañon, old pueblo, and modern town of Pecos. The name is derived from the old pueblo, which was situated on one of those tributaries in the mountains, some 25 m. S. E. of Santa Fé. The Pecos have for many years been currently reported to have been among the straitest sect of the Montezuman faith, and the belief is general that they were those who longest guarded the holy fire in their estufas and looked to the east for the advent of their paraclete. This is a traditional taradiddle which has no foundation in fact. Not that Montezuma Ilhuicamina and Montezuma Xocoyotzin were not real historical persons ; nor that the latter, Montezuma II., was not euhemerized and apotheosized ; simply, that the Pecos people never worshiped him. The myth recrudesced during the old Santa Fé trade, and was found in full swing on our peaceable conquest of New Mexico in 1846. *Pecos* is corrupted from the (Tañoan) Jemez word *Paquiu*, applied later than the aboriginal name *Tshiquite*, rendered *Cicuique* in old Sp. chronicles. Pecos "was in 1540 the largest Indian village or pueblo in New Mexico, containing a population of about 2,000 souls, which formed an independent tribe speaking the same language as the Indians of Jemez. In 1680 the Pecos rebelled with the others, but surrendered peaceably to Vargas in 1692, and thereafter remained loyal to Spain," Cent. Cyclop. Names, *s. v.* " What with the massacres of the second conquest, and the inroads of the Comanches, they gradually dwindled away, till they found themselves reduced to about a dozen, comprising all ages and sexes ; and it was only a few years ago that they abandoned the home of their fathers and joined the Pueblo of Jemez," Gregg, Comm. Pra., I. 1844, p. 271. The pueblo was desolate and in ruins when our Army of the West came by in 1846 : see Lieut. Emory's report, Ex. Doc. 41, 30th Congr., 1st Sess., pub. 1848, p. 30, with plate facing it ; also, a different view, on the plate facing p. 447 of Lieut. Abert's report in the same volume. The latter says, p. 446 : " In the afternoon [Sept. 26th, 1846] I went out on the hills to see the ancient cathedral of Pecos. The old building and the town around it are fast crumbling away under the hand of time. The old church is built in the same style as that of San Miguel ; the ends of the rafters are carved in imitation of a scroll ; the ground plan of the edifice is that of a cross. It is situated on a hill not far from the winding course of the river. High ridges of mountains appear to converge until they almost meet behind the town, and through a little gap one catches sight of a magnificent range of distant peaks that seem to mingle with the sky." Abert was told that the surviving remnant went to live with the Zuñis ; but Gregg's statement is no doubt correct, especially as Emory says, *l. c.*, that " they abandoned the place and joined a tribe of the original race over the mountains, about 60 miles south." The modern small village of Pecos grew up close by the original site, which was abandoned in 1840.

of Tampanagos, the existence of which I consider very doubtful. It is said to commence, according to Father Escalante, in the 40th deg. N. lat., and to have been explored to the 42d deg. in a N. W. direction, where it enlarged its dimensions, and the discoverer thought proper to return.[21]

Animals. North Mexico produces deer, elk, buffalo, cabrie, the gresley [grizzly and] black bear, and wild horses.

Population. Its population is not far short of 30,000 souls, one-twentieth of which may be Spaniards from Europe, or Chapetones [Gachupines[22]], four-twentieths Creoles, five-twentieths Metifs, and the other half civilized Indians.

The capital is Santa Fe, situated on a small stream which empties into the east side of the Rio del Norte, at the foot of the mountains which divide the waters of that river from the Arkansaw and the Red river of the Mississippi, in 36° N. lat. and 100° W. long. It is an oblong square, extending about one mile from east to west on the banks of the creek. In the centre is the public square, one side

---

[21] Here we enter the legendary land where we are liable to be soon confronted with the standard specter of the northwest passage to India, and other well-dressed phantoms. The body of water which the map shows probably represents Utah l., south of Great Salt l., and connected therewith by the short course of the Jordan. This seems to be what Pike means by the legend: "This lake is known as high as the 40° of Lat. there it opens wider to the West and receives the Waters of the Rio Yampancas"; for we can readily understand this as a way of saying that the lake is connected with a larger one to the W. Utah l. is meridionally E. of Great Salt l. by a few miles, and entirely S. of it; the Jordan is a very short stream between them. In a broad sense, then, Pike's Lac de Timpanagos or Lake of Tampanagos includes both these bodies of water; and his Rio Yampancas answers to Bear r., the large stream which falls into Great Salt l. at Bear River bay. His Sierra de Tampanagos covers the mountains on the E. and S. E. of Great Salt l. A different form of the same word appears in his " Indiens Yamparicas " of that region, and yet another in the legend : " The Lake of Tampanagos is supposed to be the same as the Lake of Thequaio in the Chart d'Alzate de Thequao placed in 40° of Lat. some Historians pretend that the Aretiqui comes from this Lake."

[22] *Chapetones* is a word which, with several variants in form, is pretty well

of which forms the flank of the soldiers' square, which is closed and in some degree defended by the round towers in the angles which flank the four curtains; another side of the square is formed by the palace of the governor, his guard-houses, etc.; the third side is occupied by the priests and their suite, and the fourth by the Chapetones who reside in the city. The houses are generally only one story high, with flat roofs, and have a very mean appearance on the outside; but some of them are richly furnished, especially with plate.

The second cities in the province are Albuquerque and Passo [El Paso] del Norte. The latter is the most southern city of the province, as Tons [Taos] is the most northern. Between the village of Sibilleta and the Passo there is a wilderness of near 200 miles [including the Jornada del Muerto].

Trade and Commerce. New Mexico carries on a trade direct with Mexico through Biscay [Nueva Viscaya], also with Senora [Sonora] and Sinaloa; it sends out about 30,000 sheep annually, tobacco, dressed deer and cabrie skins, some furs, buffalo robes, salt, and wrought copper vessels of a superior quality. It receives in return, from Biscay and Mexico, dry goods, confectionery, arms, iron, steel, ammunition, and some choice European wines and

known, and to be found in many dictionaries, though its origin may never have been satisfactorily shown, or at least agreed upon. In its application to un-American Spaniards in America the sense implied seems to have been always reproachful—perhaps something as our cowboys and other "rustlers" in the wild and woolly West would speak of a "tenderfoot" or "greeny." In Mexico the word corresponding to Chapeton or Chapetone was *Gachupin* or *Gachupine,* "applied to natives of Spain who are called Chapetones in Peru and Maturrangos in Buenos Aires," as one of the authorities before me says. I am afraid that it is significant of some unpleasant matters already noted, to find Pike here using the word said to be current in Peru, instead of that which was usual in Mexico: see Memoir, *anteà.* Geo. W. Kendall's Narrative of the Texan Expedition of 1841, 2 vols., small 8vo, London, 1845, II. p. 75, speaks of "the *Gachupines,* or natives of Old Spain"; and p. 76: "the *Gachupines* were indiscriminately slaughtered," etc. Gregg, Comm. Pra., I. 1844, p. 170, has : "*Gachupin*—a term used to designate European Spaniards in America." Wislizenus uses *Gachupins.*

liquors; from Senora and Sinaloa, gold, silver, and cheese. The following articles sell in this province, as stated, which will show the cheapness of provisions and the extreme dearness of imported goods: Flour sells, per hundred, at $2; salt, per mule-load, $5; sheep, each, $1; beeves, each, $5; wine del Passo, per barrel, $15; horses, each, $11; mules, each, $30; superfine cloths, per yard, $25; fine cloths, per yard, $20; linen, per yard, $4, and all other dry goods in proportion.

The journey with loaded mules from Santa Fe to Mexico, and returning to Santa Fe, takes five months. They manufacture rough leather, cigars, a vast variety and quantity of potters' ware, cotton, some coarse woolen cloths, and blankets of a superior quality. All those manufactures are carried on by the civilized Indians, as the Spaniards think it more honorable to be agriculturists than mechanics. The Indians likewise far exceed their conquerors in their genius for, and execution of, all mechanical operations.

About two miles above the town of Passo del Norte is a bridge over the river, where the road passes to the west side, at which place is a large canal [acequia]. This takes out an ample supply of water for the purpose of cultivation, which is here carried on in as great perfection as at any place that I visited in the provinces. There is a wall bordering the canal the whole way on both sides, to protect it from the animals; and when it arrives at the village, it is distributed in such a manner that each person has his fields watered in rotation. At this place were as finely cultivated fields of wheat and other small grain as I ever saw; and numerous vineyards, from which were produced the finest wine ever drank in the country, which was celebrated through all the provinces, and was the only wine used on the table of the commanding general.

Agriculture. They cultivate corn, wheat, rye, barley, rice, tobacco, vines, and all the common culinary plants cultivated in the same latitude in the United States. New Mexico has the exclusive right of cultivating tobacco. They

are, however, a century behind us in the art of cultivation ;
for, notwithstanding their numerous herds of cattle and
horses, I have seen them frequently breaking up whole
fields with a hoe. Their oxen draw by the horns, after
the French mode. Their carts are extremely awkward and
clumsily made. During the whole of the time we were
in New Spain I never saw a horse in a vehicle of any
description, mules being made use of in carriages, as well
as for the purposes of labor.

Antiquities. On the river St. Francis,[23] a large branch of

[23] That is, Rio San Francisco, one of the initial forks of the Gila : see the
map, and note [19]. The other is the main continuation of the Gila, sometimes
called Rio San Domingo. The confluence is in Arizona, a few miles over the
New Mexican border. There are mountains in this region called the San
Francisco divide, and others known as the San Francisco range—both by no means
to be confounded with the San Francisco mt. of the range in north-central Arizona. Whether the ruins of which Pike speaks as on this river be the work of the
aboriginal colonists of Old Mexico from the northwest is, of course, in question ;
he simply renders a prevalent opinion of his time. The oldest *authentic* ruins
known to exist in Arizona have only very recently been brought to light by the
exhumations conducted by my friend, Mr. Frank H. Cushing, of the Hemen-
way Archæological Expedition, in 1886–88, in the valley of the Salado or Salt
r., near the town of Tempe, and not far from Phœnix. An account of these
discoveries, from the pen of Dr. Washington Matthews, U. S. A., forms part
of the Seventh Memoir of Vol. VI. of Mem. Nat. Acad. Sci., 1893, pp. 142–
161, figs. 1–22. Mr. Cushing dug up mounds he supposes to be from 1,000
to 2,000 years old, full of bones and pottery, and revealing structures, some
of which recall the long famous Casa Grande itself. The buildings represented
by the cluster of mounds crowded an area some 6 m. long and ½ to 1 m.
wide. Five of the best marked mounds, standing in the places of groups of
houses, have been named Los Muertos, Los Guanacos, Los Hornos, Las Cano-
pas, and Las Acequias. Four kinds of architecture have been recognized as
priest-temples (style of Casa Grande) ; sun-temples, in some cases 200 feet long
by 150 broad ; certain great communal houses, a sort of several-storied proto-
types of our modern city flats ; and ultramural huts, jacals, or wickiups. I
should have called them respectively hierœcias, heliœcias, synœcias, and
excœcias. Those old Saladoans had an extensive system of irrigation, the lines
of acequias madres or mother-ditches alone representing over 150 m. of dug-
way ; some of these canals are now utilized by the new-comers. It took many
thousand people many years to leave monuments like these. Their actual
antiquity is unknown ; that it is very great is obvious ; it is great enough to
have resulted in the disappearance of everything but bone and clay. There is
no sign of wood-work or textile fabric. Conjecture of a thousand years or more

the river Gila, which heads near the copper mines in New
Mexico and discharges into the Red river of California,
are the remains of old walls and houses which are ascertained to have been the work of the Mexicans on their
route emigrating from the northwest to the plains of Mexico, where they finally established themselves.   Those walls
are of a black cement, the durability of which increases

may reasonably be based on comparison of the natural rate of decay of structures
known since the historic period, 1540.   Thus, the Casa Grande has not changed
perceptibly in our day, except from vandalism, and probably looks much as it
did 350 years ago.   It would appear also that the same indefatigable explorer
has settled the long-mooted question of the Seven Cities of Cibola (Cebola,
Sibola, Zibola), against any theory of their being the Moki (Tusayan) villages,
or being anywhere else than in the vicinity of Zuñi itself.   The names which
have come down to us since Coronado, 1541, are : (1) Ahacus, Avicu, Aquico,
Jahuicu, Havico ; (2) Canabe ; (3) . . .; (4) Aquinsa ; (5) Alona ; (6) Musaqui,
Maçaque, Maçaquia ; (7) Caquina.   According to a certain phonetic system
the preferable spelling is given as : (1) Hawiku ; (2) Kyanawe ; (3) Ketchup-
awe ; (4) Apina or Pinawan ; (5) Halona ; (6) Matsaki ; (7) Kyakima.   All
these were in what is now Valencia Co., N. M.; two were some miles S. W.
of Zuñi, near the village of Ojo Caliente ; two were nearer Zuñi, but E. of it ;
two were within 3 m. of Zuñi, S. of it; while one, Halona, occupied in part,
at least, the site of the present pueblo.   The ruin of Hishota–uthla, classed as
"Cibolan" though not as one of the Seven Cities, is 12 m. N. E. of Zuñi, on
the road to Fort Wingate ; excavation there has revealed "a compactly-built,
many-storied stronghold of stone containing a population of probably more than
a thousand people," supposed to have been dead and gone long before Coronado passed that way.   Zuñi, now one of the best known of all the extant
pueblos in New Mexico, is also the best living exemplar of such places.   Its
antiquity is great, though hardly estimable with precision.   Some of its inhabitants made a tour of the United States under Mr. Cushing's management in
1881 and 1882.   Immense collections of implements, utensils, and the like
were made about that time by the late Colonel James Stevenson, and deposited in our museums.   I visited the town in the summer of 1864, when it
was far from having been as well exploited as it has since become ; so my own
observations are obsolete.   The Zuñi nation, otherwise Çuni, Sune, Soone,
Suinyi, Shiwina, etc., sole member of the Zuñian linguistic stock, has but one
permanent pueblo, though it also inhabits at times three other small villages,
of the nature of " summer resorts," as we should say of our similar æstival
refuges.   These Indians numbered 1,613 by the census of 1890.   They are
well distinguished by their speech from all the various Tusayan, Tañoan, and
Keresan pueblonians of New Mexico, Arizona, and Chihuahua : for some of
which, see next note.

with its age, so that it has hitherto bid defiance to the war of time. Its composition is now entirely lost. There is also found at this place many broken pieces of earthenware, which still possess the glazing as perfectly as when first put on.

Aborigines.[24] The Kyaways [Kiowas] wander on the

---

[24] I can find no better place than this to bring up some matters which require attention concerning certain pueblos which Pike locates on his map, but which, being off his route, he does not notice in his text. The Tañoan pueblos have been pretty fully noted in the foregoing itinerary, but the Tusayan and Keresan have not been sufficiently treated. We must first come to an under- standing of the term " Pueblo Indians." This is simply a convenient phrase, or *façon de parler*, to designate various tribes which, in New and Old Mexico, and Arizona, settled in permanent habitations, became attached to the soil, practiced agriculture, kept flocks, and built the kind of towns called " pueblos." They are thus collectively distinguished from all roving and more or less warring tribes ; they are settlers, not nomads ; farmers and graziers rather than hunters, and of peaceful rather than predatory proclivities. This step in the direc- tion of civilization was not however taken without some sacrifice of the strength of the natural wild animal, and they have suffered in consequence. They are never " bad " Indians ; simply poor, tame ones, who for ages have been the prey of the priest, the trader, and the wild Indian. But the point to be insisted on is, that " Pueblo Indian " does not mean all one kind of Indians. It includes various tribes of distinct ethnic characters, the representatives of several linguis- tic lineages, who have severally yielded to their environments, and thus become collectively modified in a way that brings about that appearance of affinity which does not exist, and tends to obscure those radical distinctions of race which do exist. We say, for instance, " New Yorker," meaning anyone who lives in New York ; but it would be as far from the fact to suppose that all Pueblo Indians are of one race as that all New Yorkers are Americans. The differences in language, and therefore in lineage, of the Tusayan, Keresan, Tañoan, and Zuñian pueblonians is as great as that of the English, French, German, and Spanish peoples. We must not be misled by the convenience of a phrase : see note [3], p. 578. The Pueblonians to be here noted belong either (1) to the Tusayan federation, or (2) to the Keresan linguistic family.

1. Pike marks, W. of the Continental divide and in the region of the Colo- rado Chiquito, S. of the San Juan r., six Indian villages, which he calls Oraybe, Mosanis, Songoapt, Gualpi, Chacat, and Cumpa. For the last two, see note [21], p. 630 ; the other four are the well-known Moki Indians, living on the four Moki mesas, about 50 m. N. E. of the Colorado Chiquito, in N. E. Arizona. With a single (Tañoan) exception, those Indians are of Shoshonean stock ; and without exception, they form the Tusayan confederacy. The ethnic affinities of Mokis are with such Indians as the Snakes, Utes, Comanches, and other well-known mem- bers of the Shoshonean race which overran so vast an area in western parts of the

sources of La Platte and are supposed to be 1,000 men
strong.   They possess immense herds of horses, and are at
war with both Pawnees and Tetaus [Ietans, Comanches],
as well as the Sioux.   They are armed with bows, arrows,
and lances, and hunt the buffalo.   This nation, with the
Tetaus and Utahs, all speak the same language.   The Utahs
wander at the sources of the Rio del Norte, are supposed
to be 2,000 warriors strong, are armed in the same manner,

United States.   But these settled down in Arizona and built pueblos, isolated
from their kindred and surrounded by Athapascan (Navajo and Apache) tribes.
They are at present the only Shoshonean tribe in Arizona, excepting the handful of Chemehuevis who live among Yuman tribes on the Colorado Grande,
and unless there be also a few Kwaiantikwokets on the northern border about
Mt. Navajo.   The Mokis have resided in their present position for more than
200 years.   This habitat is the plateau of moderate extent, commonly called the
Moki mesa, some special elevations of which are well-known landmarks by the
name of the Moki buttes, in full view from the main road which passes S. of
them.   Three of the most conspicuous of these buttes are called Chimney,
Signal, and Spring.   The mesa is between long. 110° and 111° W., in lat. 36°
N. and southward, and thus to the S. W. of the Navajos ; the locality is some-
times called the " Province of Tusayan."   Here the Mokis proper, of Shosho-
nean stock, built six villages ; and a seventh village, probably also about 200
years old, called Hano (or Tewa) was built with them by Tañoan (Tewan or
Teguan) refugees from the Rio Grande.   Thus even the compact and isolated
Moki establishment is not quite homogeneous, ethnically speaking.   The
Tusayan census is about 2,000 ; the Tañoans there were lately counted as 132.
Among the names of the seven villages, the four which Pike gives can be recognized under their modern spellings, as Oraybe=Oraibi, etc.   One authority I
have consulted renders Oraibi, Shipauliwisi, Shongapavi, Mishongnivi, Shicho-
amavi, Walpi (or Hualpee), and Tewa (i. e., Hano).   Another, and probably
preferable set of orthographies, is Oraibi, Shupaulovi, Shumepovi, Mashong-
navi, Sichumovi, Walpi, and Hano.   The name Tusayan, which varies to
Tuçayan, Tuzan, etc., is derived from a Zuñian word Usaya, applied to
certain pueblos once inhabited by the confederacy.   The Tusayans' name of
themselves is a word variously rendered Hopituh, Hapitu, Hopee, Hopi, Opii,
etc.   Other words designating them, or some of them, are Cinyumuh, Shenoma
or Shinumo, and Totonteac.   The term now usually rendered Moki was
longest current as Moqui ; it is also found as Maqui, Magui, Mohace, Mohotse,
and "Monkey."

2. The Keresan family consists entirely of Pueblo tribes who live in New
Mexico along the Rio Grande and some of its tributaries, where their pueblos
are interspersed with others of Tañoan stock, in the moderate area to which
their range is thus restricted.   The family name is variously rendered by differ-

and pursue the same game, as the Kyaways. They are, however, a little more civilized, from having more connection with the Spaniards, with whom they are frequently at war, but were then at peace, and waging war with the Tetaus.[25]

A battle was fought between them and the Tetaus in September, 1806, near the village of Tons [Taos]: there

ent authors, as Keres, Keran, Kera ; Queres, Queris, Quera, Quirix ; Chuchacas or Chuchachas ; also, Keswhawhay. Some ethnists divide these people into two dialectal groups: one including the pueblos of Acoma and Laguna and their outliers ; the other, all the rest of the pueblos about to be named. Acoma is the only pueblo which exists on the site occupied at the date of the earliest Spanish annals. Laguna dates from 1699. There were five Keresan pueblos in 1582 ; there had been seven in 1542. The full list of Keresan pueblos, as given by Powell in alphabetical order, with the census for 1890, is : 1. Acoma, including the summer pueblitos of Acomita and Pueblita ; pop. 566. 2. Cochití, on the W. bank of the Rio Grande, 27 m. S. W. of Santa Fé ; pop. 268. " The inhabitants formerly successively occupied the Potrero de las Vacas, the Potrero San Miguel, the now ruined pueblo of Cuapa, and the Potrero Viejo," Cent. Cyc., s. v. 3. *Hasatch. 4. Laguna, including the eight other places whose names are here starred ; pop. 1,143. Laguna is thus really a group of small pueblos situated on and near Rio San José, W. of the Rio Grande. The original foundation was by Zuñians as well as by Keresans, and the place was called Kawaiko. 5. *Paguate. 6. *Punyeestye. 7. *Punyekia. 8. *Pusityitcho. 9. San Felipe ; pop. 554. This is called by the name of the mission which the Spanish founded there. 10. Santa Ana, pop. 253, on the Rio Jemez, W. of the Rio Grande. This Spanish name is also that of a mission, usurping the native name Tamaya. 11. Santo Domingo ; pop. 670. 12. *Seemunah. 13. Sia, on the Jemez ; pop. 106 ; also called Chea, Chia, Cia, Cilla, Silla, Tsea, Tsia, Tzia, Zia. " In 1582 Sia was said to be the largest of five villages forming a province called Punames. The recent pueblo dates from about 1692, when the village formerly occupied was abandoned. The tribe, which was once comparatively populous, now numbers but 106. The decrease is attributed largely to infectious disease and to the killing of persons accused of witchcraft," Cent. Cyc., s. v. 14. *Wapuchuseamma. 15. *Ziamma. Total pop. 3,560 for the 17 places, of which 15 (all but Acomita and Pueblita) are permanent pueblos, and 7 are officially rated as principal and distinct. Those which are given by Pike in his itinerary have been already noted, along with the Tañoan pueblos as they occur in his text.

[25] For remarks on the Indians mentioned in this paragraph which would be introduced here had I not recently given them elsewhere, the reader is referred to Lewis and Clark, ed. 1893, p. 55, note [7]; p. 58, note [11]; p. 60, note [15] ; and p. 477, note [3].

were about 400 combatants on each side, but they were separated by a Spanish alcalde riding out to the field of battle. There were 8 or 10 killed on each side. The Utahs gave all the horses taken to the Spaniards. This shows in a strong degree the influence the Spaniards have over those Indians.

The Nanahaws [Navajos [26]] are situated to the N. W. of Santa Fe. They frequently war with the Spaniards, and are supposed to be 2,000 warriors strong. They are armed in the same manner as the two preceding nations. This nation, as well as all the others to the west of them bordering on California, speak the language of the Appaches and Le Panis [Lipans [27]], who are in a line with them to the Atlantic.

[26] The Navajos, Navahos, or, as they call themselves, Tennai, are one of the three main divisions of the southern group of Athapascan Indians (the other two being the Lipans and the Apaches). They have always lived, so far as is known to history, in the country where they do now, and whence they raided in every direction before their final subjugation in our times. They focused on the upper waters of the Rio San Juan, in N. W. New Mexico, whence they habitually ranged down the river in Colorado and Utah, and S. of it in Arizona. They were thus in contact and conflict with Shoshonean tribes on the N., and warred when they pleased with the various Apache tribes of their own stock which were about them; they were of course a terror to the peaceful Pueblonians, who had to hold their own as best they could against all the battlesome savages by whom they were beset on every hand. They were powerful, and are still one of the largest tribes with which we have to do, like the Comanches and some of the divisions of the Sioux. A late census returns about 17,000, nearly all on the large Navajo reservation which occupies the contiguous N. W. corner of New Mexico and N. E. corner of Arizona.

An interesting account of the expedition of Colonel Doniphan and some of his officers to the Navajos in 1846, together with the text of the first treaty of peace concluded between them, the New Mexicans, and Americans, at Ojo Oso (Bear spring), Nov. 22d, occupies Chaps. IX–XI of Hughes' Don. Exp., 8vo, ed. of 1847, pp. 61–76.

[27] The Lipans or Sipans cut no figure now in the United States, where they are practically extinguished, though the case may be different in Mexico. They were a numerous and roving tribe of stalwart Indians who scoured the plains of Texas from Red r. to the Rio Grande. They were a sort of Apaches, having their nearest affinities with the latter, and in fact might be considered the Apaches of the plains as distinguished from those of the mountains. They have been commonly called Lipan Apaches, and such is no incorrect designa-

The Appaches[28] are a nation of Indians who extend from the Black mountains in New Mexico to the frontiers of Cogquilla, keeping the frontiers of three provinces in a continual state of alarm, and making it necessary to employ nearly 2,000 dragoons to escort the caravans, protect the villages, and revenge the various attacks they are continually making on the subjects of his Catholic Majesty. This nation formerly extended from the entrance of the Rio Grande to the Gulf of California, and have waged a continual warfare, excepting short truces, with the Spaniards,

tion, though they are rather more distinct from most bands of Apaches than these are from one another. They extend in Mexico as far S. as Durango. A Lipan collision which made some history, and enriched the cabinet of S. G. Morton, the craniologist of Philadelphia, may be read in Hughes' Don. Exped., pp. 130–132, and Wislizenus, Mem., pp. 71, 72 : see also note [5], p. 697.

[28] There is no historic period when the Apaches were not the scourge of the country they inhabited, down to the time when they were brought to terms by General Crook, in his Arizona campaigns of 1872 *seq.*, and even since then their repeated escapades are matters of recent notoriety. They always warred with other Indians, always warred with the whites, and not seldom with one another. In Arizona particularly, so far as we are concerned, they did more to retard the development of the country than all other causes combined. For some years after the Territorial government was established, it was at the risk of life that one went out of sight of Prescott or Fort Whipple alone or with a small party. The Apaches lurked behind every rock, and hid in every bush ; or, failing that, under cover of every three blades of grass—a trick they did to perfection— and reddened with blood every trail that led to the capital or the post. People were killed and stock was run off within a few hundred paces of both these places, and more than one pitched battle came off within ear-shot. A regular part of my business for two years was the extraction of Apache arrow-heads. The arrows used by the tribes nearest us were exactly such as Pike describes, though, so far as my observation went, the heads were all of stone, quite small and sharp, and very brittle, so that they usually shivered when they struck a bone and the fragments were not easily removed. They were only held in place with gum in the shallow notch at the end of the small hardwood stick that was set in the large reed, and thus were always left in the wound when the stick was pulled out. It is within my certain knowledge that they were in some cases poisoned ; the common opinion was that the septic substance was derived from a deer's liver into which a rattlesnake had been made to inject its venom, and which was then left to putrefy in the sun ; but how this case may really be, I never ascertained to my satisfaction. We continually hunted Apaches and killed a good many ; a particular friend of mine, Mr. Willard Rice, who saved my life on a very ticklish occasion, when we were on a deer-

from the time these pushed their enterprises back from Mexico into the internal provinces. It is extremely difficult to say what are their numbers at the present day, but they must be very much reduced, from their long and constant warfare, the wandering and savage life they lead in the mountains, which is so injurious to an increase of population, and in which they are frequently extremely pinched by famine.

At the commencement of their warfare the Spaniards used to take them prisoners and make slaves of them ; but finding that their unconquerable attachment to liberty

hunt together without other companions, and who is still living near Prescott, is to be credited with at least 20 "good" (dead) Apaches—none of the score women or children, either. But such desultory operations as we could conduct in those years seemed to make little difference ; it required Crook's systematic campaigns, on a large scale, to render the country inhabitable. The other side of the picture is, that the Apache has never committed an atrocity that we have not exchanged in kind, with the sole exception that we have probably never put a prisoner to death by slow torture, as was the Apache custom ; that the Apache has not broken faith with us oftener than we are proud to say we have with him, and has not robbed us of more than we would like to take from him, if he had anything left to steal and we had an opportunity. The secrets of Indian agencies, like those of the Roman confessional, only leak out under great pressure. The Apaches that troubled us most in that particular vicinity of which I speak were known or supposed to be those of the Tonto basin, commonly called Tontos (Pinal Coyoteros). In scientific classification the Apache tribes and sub-tribes are numerous. The alphabetical list now recognized by high authority is : Arivaipa, Chiricahua, Faraone, Gileño (Gilans, or Apaches of the Gila, with four sub-tribes, Coyotero, Mimbreño, Mogollon, and Pinal Coyotero or Tonto), Jicarilla, Lipan, Llanero, Mescalero, Naisha, Querecho, Tchikun, Tchishi. All the Apaches within our jurisdiction have been brought under military subjection and restraint. The largest body of Apaches is now on the San Carlos reservation ; their number is uncertain, say 2,000, representing several different tribes. Nearly as many more are in charge of the military at Camp Apache, in Arizona, say 1,900, known collectively as White Mountain Apaches. About 800 Jicarillas are on the Southern Ute Reservations in Colorado ; some 500 Mescaleros are on the reservation of that name in New Mexico ; and 300 other Apaches are on the Kiowa, Comanche, and Wichita Reservation in Indian Territory. After a recent outbreak had been quelled 356 prisoners were sent to Mount Vernon Barracks in Alabama. There are about 150 children at school in Carlisle, Pa. The total of perhaps 6,000 Apaches with which we have still to deal is not large in comparison with the numbers of some other tribes—but it is enough.

made them surmount every difficulty and danger in returning to their mountains, they adopted the mode of sending
them to Cuba. This the Appaches no sooner learned than
they refused to give or receive quarter, and in no instance
have any been taken since that period, except those surprised when asleep, or knocked down and overpowered.

Their arms are the bow and arrow, and the lance. Their
bow forms two demi-circles, with a shoulder in the middle;
the back of it is entirely covered with sinews, which are
laid on in so nice a manner, by the use of some glutinous
substance, as to be almost imperceptible; this gives great
elasticity to the weapon. Their arrow is more than the
" cloth yard " of the English, being three feet and a half
long, the upper part consisting of some light rush or cane,
into which is inserted a shaft of about one foot, made of
some hard, seasoned light wood ; the point is of iron, bone,
or stone, and, when the arrow enters the body, in attempting to extract it the shaft comes out of its socket and the
point remains in the wound. With this weapon they shoot
with such force as to go through the body of a man at a
distance of 100 yards, and an officer told me that in an
engagement with them, one of their arrows struck his shield
and dismounted him in an instant. Their other weapon of
offense is a lance of 15 feet in length, with which they
charge with both hands over their heads, managing their
horses principally with their knees. With this weapon they
are considered an overmatch for any Spanish dragoon
single-handed ; but, for want of a knowledge of tactics,
they can never stand the charge of a body which acts in
concert. They all carry shields. Some few are armed
with guns and ammunition taken from the Spaniards.
Those, as well as the archers, generally march to war on
foot ; but the lancemen are always mounted. Numerous
are the anecdotes I have heard related of their personal
bravery and the spirit of their partisan corps. Not long
before I went into that country a cornet, with 63 dragoons,
between New Mexico and Biscay, was surrounded by about

200 Apaches' infantry. Instead of charging through them, as [he should have done, since] it was on the plain, he ordered his dragoons to dismount and fight with their carabines ; in consequence of which he and his whole party fell a sacrifice.

Malgares related an instance when he was marching with 140 men and they were attacked by a party of Appaches, both horse and foot, who continued the fight for four hours. Whenever the Spanish dragoons would make a general charge, the Appaches' cavalry would retreat behind their infantry, who met the Spaniards with a shower of arrows, who immediately retreated ; and even the gallant Malgares spoke of the Spanish cavalry's breaking the Appaches infantry as a thing not to be thought of.

Malgares assured me that, if the Appaches had seconded the efforts and bravery of their chieftain, the Spaniards must have been defeated and cut to pieces; that in various instances he rallied his men and brought them up to the charge, and that when they fled, he retired indignantly to the rear. Seeing Malgares very actively engaged in forming and bringing up the Spaniards, the Appache chieftain rode out ahead of his party and challenged him to single combat with his lance. This my friend refused, as he said that the chief was one of the stoutest men he knew, carried a remarkably heavy lance, and rode a very fine charger ; but one of his corporals, enraged to see the Spaniards thus braved by this savage, begged permission to meet the " infidel." His officer refused his request and ordered him to keep his ranks ; but he reiterating the request, his superior in a passion told him to go. The Indian chief had turned his horse to join his party, but seeing an enemy advancing, he turned, gave a shout, and met him at full speed. The dragoon thought to parry the lance of his antagonist, which he in part effected ; but not throwing it quite high enough, it entered his neck before and came out at the nape, when he fell dead to the ground, and his victorious enemy gave a shout of victory, in which he was joined by all his followers.

This enraged the Spaniards to such a degree that they made a general charge, in which the Indian cavalry again retreated, notwithstanding the entreaties of their gallant leader.

In another instance a small smoke was discovered on the prairie; three poor savages were surrounded by 100 dragoons and ordered to lay down their arms; they smiled at the officer's demand, and asked him if he could suppose that men who had arms in their hands would ever consent to become slaves. The officer, being loath to kill them, held a conference for an hour; when, finding that his threats had as little effect as his entreaties, he ordered his men to attack them at a distance, keeping out of the reach of their arrows, and firing at them with their carabines, which they did, the Indians never ceasing to resist as long as life remained.

In a truce which was held a Spanish captain was ordered to treat with some of the bands. He received their deputies with hauteur, and they could not come upon terms. The truce was broken, and the Indians retreated to their fastnesses in the mountains. In a day or two this same officer pursued them. They were in a place called the Door in the Mountain, where but two or three dragoons could enter at a time, and there were rocks and caves on the flanks behind which the Indians secreted themselves until a number of the Spaniards had come in. Then the Indians sounded a trumpet; the attack began, and continued on the side of the Appaches until the Spanish captain fell, when the Indian chief caused the firing to cease, saying that the man who had so haughtily spurned the proffered peace was now dead. On this occasion they deviated from their accustomed rule of warfare, and made a prisoner of a young officer, who, during the truce, had treated them with great kindness, and sent him home safe and unhurt.

Some of the bands have made temporary truces with the Spaniards, and received from them 25 cents per diem each. Those people hang round the fortifications of the country, drink, shoot, and dissipate their time; they are haughty and independent. Great jealousy exists between them and the Spaniards. An officer was under trial, when I was in the country, for anticipating an attack on his fortress by attacking the chiefs of the supposed conspiracy, and putting them to death before they had time to mature and carry their plan into execution. The decision of his case I never learned; but those savages who have been for some time about the forts and villages become by far the most dangerous enemies the Spaniards have, when hostile, as they have acquired the Spanish language, manners, and habits, pass through the populated parts under the disguise of civilized and friendly Indians, commit murders and robberies, and are not suspected. There is in the province of Cogquilla a partisan by the name of Ralph, who, they calculate, has killed more than 300 persons. He comes into the towns under the disguise of a peasant, buys provisions, goes to the gambling-tables and to mass, and before he leaves the village is sure to kill some person or carry off a woman, which he has frequently done. Sometimes he joins people traveling on the road, insinuates himself into their confidence, and takes his opportunity to assassinate them. He has only six followers, and from their knowledge of the country, activity, and cunning, he keeps about 300 Spanish dragoons continually employed. The government has offered $1,000 for his head.

The civilized Indians of the province of New Mexico are of what were formerly 24 different bands, the different names of which I did not become acquainted with, but the Keres were one of the most powerful; they form at present the population of St. Domingo, St. Philips, Deis, and one or two other towns.[29] They are men of large stature, round full visage, fine teeth, appear to be of a gentle, tractable disposition, and resemble the Osage more than any nation

[29] See note [13], p. 615, note [14], p. 616, note [15], p. 618 ; also, note [24], p. 743, The towns here mentioned are those usually called San Domingo, San Felipe, and Sandia—the latter being the Tañoan one Pike elsewhere speaks of as St. Dies.

of whom I possess any knowledge. They are not the vassals of individuals, yet may properly be termed the slaves of the State, for they are compelled to do military duty, drive mules, carry loads, or, in fact, perform any other act of duty or bondage that the will of the commandant of the district, or of any passing military tyrant, chooses to ordain.

I was myself eye-witness of a scene which made my heart bleed for those poor wretches, at the same time that it excited my indignation and contempt, that they would suffer themselves, with arms in their hands, to be beaten and knocked about by beings no ways their superiors, unless a small tint of complexion could be supposed to give that superiority. Before we arrived at Santa Fe, one night, we were near one of the villages where resided the families of two of our Indian horsemen. They took the liberty to pay them a visit in the night. Next morning the whole of the Indian horsemen were called up, and because they refused to testify against their imprudent companions, several were knocked down from their horses by the Spanish dragoons with the butt of their lances; yet, with the blood streaming down their visages, and arms in their hands, they stood cool and tranquil—not a frown, not a word of discontent or palliation escaped their lips. Yet what must have been the boiling indignation of their souls at the indignities offered by the wretch clothed with a little brief authority! The day of retribution will come in thunder and in vengeance.

Those savages are armed with bow and arrows, and with lances, or escopates. Although they are said to be converted to Christianity, they still retain many of their ancient rituals, feasts, and ceremonies, one of which is so remarkable it must not be passed unnoticed. Once a year there is a great feast prepared for three successive days, which they spend in eating, drinking, and dancing. Near this scene of amusement is a dark cave, into which not a glimpse of light can penetrate, and in which are prepared places to repose on. To this place persons of all description, of both sexes and of all ages, after puberty, repair in the night, when there is an indiscriminate commerce of the votaries, as chance, fortune, and events direct. Those revels certainly have great affinity to some of the ancient mystic rites of Greece and Rome.

Government and Laws. The government of New Mexico may be termed military, in the pure sense of the word; for although they have their alcaldes, or inferior officers, their judgments are subject to a reversion by the military commandants of districts. The whole male population are subject to military duty, without pay or emolument, and are obliged to find their own horses, arms, and provision. The only thing furnished by the government is ammunition. It is extraordinary with what subordination they act when they are turned out to do military duty. A strong proof of this was exhibited in the expedition of Malgares to the Pawnees. His command consisted of 100 dragoons of the regular service and 500 drafts from the province. He had continued down the Red river until their provision began to be short; they then demanded of the lieutenant where he was bound and the intention of the expedition. To this he haughtily replied, "Wherever my horse leads me." A few mornings after he was presented with a petition, signed by 200 of the militia, to return home. He halted immediately, caused his dragoons to erect a gallows, and then beat to arms. The troops fell in; he separated the petitioners from the others, then took the man who had presented the petition, tied him up and gave him 50 lashes, and threatened to put to death, on the gallows erected, any man who should dare to grumble. This effectually silenced them, and quelled the rising spirit of sedition; but it was remarked that it was the first instance of a Spaniard receiving corporal punishment ever known in the province.

Morals, Manners, etc. There is nothing peculiarly characteristic in this province that will not be embraced in my general observations on New Spain, except that, being on the frontier and cut off, as it were, from the more inhabited parts of the kingdom, together with their continual wars with some of the savage nations who surround them, renders the people the bravest and most hardy subjects in New Spain ; being generally armed, they know the use of arms. Their want of gold and silver renders them laborious, in order that the productions of their labor may be the means of establishing the equilibrium between them and the other provinces where those metals abound.   Their isolated and remote situation also causes them to exhibit, in a superior degree, the heaven-like qualities of hospitality and kindness, in which they appear to endeavor to fulfill the injunction of the scripture which enjoins us to feed the hungry, clothe the naked, and give comfort to the oppressed in spirit; and I shall always take pleasure in expressing my gratitude for their noble reception of myself and the men under my command.

Military Force.   There is but one troop of dragoons in all New Mexico of the regular force, which is stationed at Santa Fe, and is 100 strong.   Of this troop the governor is always the captain, entitling himself captain of the royal troop of Santa Fe dragoons; but they are commanded by a first lieutenant, who is captain by brevet.   The men capable of bearing arms in this province may be estimated at 5,000, of which probably 1,000 are completely armed, 1,000 badly, and the rest not at all.

Religion.   The catholic religion is practiced in this province after the same manner as in the other provinces, and will hereafter be taken notice of generally.

History.   In the year 1594 two friars came out from Old Mexico to New Mexico, and were well received by the savages.   They returned, and the ensuing year Juan de Ouate,[30] a monk, went out, explored the country, and returned. After this 100 troops and 500 men, women, and children

[30] Juan de Oñate, first governor of New Mexico, b. Guadalajara, Mex., about 1555, d. after 1611. " He was a son of the founder of Guadalajara, and was married to a granddaughter of Hernando Cortés. In 1595 his proposition to settle New Mexico was accepted by the viceroy Velasco, and after much delay the grant was confirmed by the Count of Monterey. Oñate left Zacatecas in Jan., 1598, with 130 men besides Indians, a large wagon- and cattle-train, etc.;

came out and settled on the Rio del Norte, at some no very great distance from where Santa Fe now stands. They entered into an arrangement with the Indians on the subject of their establishment; but a few years after [in 1680] the Indians rose *en masse*, fell on the Spaniards by surprise, killed most of the soldiers, and obliged them to retreat to the Passo del Norte; whence it acquired its name. Here they awaited a re-enforcement from Biscay, which they received, of 70 men and two field-pieces, with which they recommenced their march and finally arrived at Santa Fe, then the capital Indian village, to which they immediately laid siege. The Indians maintained themselves 22 days, when they surrendered and entered into a second negotiation; since which time the Spaniards have been engaged in continual warfare with the various savage tribes which surround them on all sides. These have been near ruining the Spaniards several times, and obliged them to apply for re-enforcements from Biscay and Senora. A few years since the Tetaus carried on a warm and vigorous war against them, but are now at peace and considered as their firmest allies.

In the history of New Mexico it may not be improper to record the name of James Pursley, the first American who ever penetrated the immense wilds of Louisiana, and showed the Spaniards of New Mexico that neither the savages who surround the deserts which divide them from the habitable world, nor the jealous tyranny of their rulers, was sufficient to prevent the enterprising spirit of the Americans from penetrating the arcanum of their rich establishment in the new world. Pursley was from near Baird's town, Kentucky, which he left in 1799. In 1802, with two companions, he left St. Louis and traveled west, on the head of the Osage

reached the Rio Grande, probably at El Paso, April 20; took formal possession April 30; crossed the river; and in Aug. founded the first capital, San Juan (Santa Fé was founded later). After the first year he had little trouble with the Indians. Early in 1599 he explored a part of Arizona, and in 1604 followed the Gila river down to the Gulf of California. He probably ceased to rule as governor in 1608." (Cent. Cyc. Names, *s. v.*) (See Nadal and Niza, in the Index.)

river, where they made a hunt; thence they struck for the White river of the Arkansaw, and intended to descend it to Orleans; but, while making preparations, the Kans stole their horses. They secured their peltries, and pursued the Kans into the village. The horses were there, but the Indians refused to give them up. Pursley saw his horse, with an Indian on him, going to the water at the edge of the town, pursued him, and with his knife ripped open the horse's bowels. The Indian returned to the village, got his gun, and came and snapped it at Pursley, who pursued him into the village with his knife. The Indian took refuge in a lodge surrounded by women and children. This struck the chiefs with astonishment and admiration of the "mad Americans," as they termed them, and they returned the other horses to the hunters. This anecdote was related by traders who had been in the village at the time.

Pursley and his companions then returned to where they had buried their peltry, and determined to pursue the route by land to St. Louis; but some persons stole their horses a second time, when they were at no great distance from the Osage river, on which they formed a rough canoe and descended that stream. Near the entrance of the Missouri they overset their canoe and lost their whole year's hunt, but saved their arms and ammunition, which is always the primary object in a desert. On the Missouri they met Monsieur [Blank] in his barge, bound to the Mandanes. Pursley embarked with him for the voyage; his two companions preferred returning to their homes. On their arrival at the point of destination, his employer dispatched Pursley on a hunting and trading tour with some bands of the Paducahs and Kyaways, with a small quantity of merchandise. In the ensuing spring they were driven from the plains by the Sioux into the mountains which give birth to La Platte, the Arkansaw, etc., and it was their sign which we saw in such amazing abundance on the headwaters of La Platte [in South Park, Col., Dec. 16, 1806]. Their party consisted of near 2,000 souls, with 10,000 beasts. The

Indians, knowing they were approximating to New Mexico, determined to send Pursley, with his companions and two of their body, into Santa Fe, to know of the Spaniards if they would receive them friendly and enter into a trade with them. This being acceded to by Governor Allencaster, the Indian deputies returned for their bands; but Pursley thought proper to remain with a civilized people, among whom a fortuitous event had thrown him—a circumstance of which, he assured me, he had at one time entirely despaired.

He arrived at Santa Fe in June, 1805, and has been following his trade as a carpenter ever since; at this he made a great deal of money, except when working for the officers, who paid him little or nothing. He was a man of strong natural sense and dauntless intrepidity. He entertained me with numerous interesting anecdotes of his adventures with the Indians, and of the jealousy of the Spanish government. He was once near being hanged for making a few pounds of gunpowder, which he innocently did as he had been accustomed to do in Kentucky, but which is a capital crime in these provinces. He still retained the gun which he had with him his whole tour, and said confidently that if he had two hours' start not all the province could take him. He was forbidden to write, but was assured he should have a passport whenever he demanded it, and was obliged to give security that he would not leave the country without permission of the government. He assured me that he had found gold on the head of La Platte, and had carried some of the virgin mineral in his shot-pouch for months; but that, being in doubt whether he should ever again behold the civilized world, and losing in his mind all the ideal value which mankind have stamped on that metal, he threw the sample away. He had imprudently mentioned it to the Spaniards, who had frequently solicited him to go and show a detachment of cavalry the place; but, conceiving it to be in our territory, he had refused, and was fearful that the circumstance might create a great obstacle to his leaving the country.

2. BISCAY. *Geography.* [The province of Nueva Vizcaya [31]]
lies between lat. 33° and 24° N., and long. 105° and 111° W.
It is bounded on the north by New Mexico, on the west by
Senora and Sinaloa, and on the east by New Leon and
Cogquilla. It is 600 miles in length from northwest to
southeast, and 400 miles in width from east to west, taking
it at its greatest extent.

Air and Climate. The air is dry and the heat very great
at that season of the year which precedes the rainy season,
which latter commences in June and continues until September by light showers. During the other part of the
year there is not the least rain or snow to moisten the earth.
The atmosphere had therefore become so electrified that
when we halted at night, in taking off our blankets the
electric fluid would almost cover them with sparks, and in
Chihuahua we prepared a bottle with gold-leaf as a re-
ceiver, and collected sufficient electric fluid from a bear-skin
to give a considerable shock to a number of persons. This
phenomenon was more conspicuous in the vicinity of Chihuahua than in any other part that we passed over.[32]

Mines and Minerals. This province abounds in silver
and gold mines, which yield an immense quantity of those
metals, but not so great a revenue to the king as those
which are nearer the mint, and consequently present a
greater facility to coinage. I am not acquainted with the

[31] The province which Pike calls indifferently Biscay and New Biscay was
properly Nueva Vizcaya. It was named Reino de la Nueva Vizcaya by Francisco de Ibarra, who invaded it about 1560-70, and retained the name until
after the independence. As a colonial division of New Spain it had been
originally called Copala, and was much more extensive than Pike's Biscay, as it
corresponded to the present states of Sonora, Sinaloa, Chihuahua, Durango,
and a southern part of Coahuila. This region was included among the Provincias Internas in 1777, and such was its status in Pike's time ; but meanwhile
it had become contracted in extent by the exclusion of Sonora and Sinaloa, so
that in Pike's time it was little if any more than equivalent to the two present
states of Chihuahua and Durango. Present Chihuahua has Sinaloa and Durango
on the S. Present Durango is surrounded by Sinaloa, Chihuahua, Coahuila,
Zacatecas, and Jalisco.

[32] Wislizenus, Mem., p. 55, quotes this passage, and adds : " By rubbing the

proportion of the metals which the mineral yields in any instance, except in one of the silver mines at Chihuahua, which belonged to a friend of mine, who informed me that his mine yielded him $13.50 per cwt.   I one day, with Robinson, went through many of these furnaces and noticed the manner which they pursued in analyzing the mineral and extracting the metals; but, as I had previously asked several Spanish officers to accompany me, who had always declined or deferred it to a future period, I conceived it probable it was too delicate a subject to make a minute inquiry into.   I, however, so far observed the process as to learn that the mineral was brought from the mines in bags, on mules, to the furnace; it was then ground or pounded into small lumps, not more than the size of a nut, and precipitated into water, in a sieve which permitted the smaller particles to escape into a tub, through several progressive operations.   From the small particles which remained at the bottom of the tubs, after it had been purified of the earthy qualities, there was a proportion of metal extracted by a nicer process; but the larger parts were put into a furnace similar to our iron furnaces, and when the mass was in a state of fusion, it was let out into a bed of sand prepared for it, which formed it into bars about the size of our common pig iron, averaged in value at about $2,500.   The gold was cast into a mold similar to a bowl and stamped with its value, as was each bar of silver, by the king's assayer of metals.   They were worth from $8,000 to $10,000.   These masses of silver and gold are received into the king's trea-

hair of cats and dogs in the dark, I could elicit here a greater mass of electricity than I had ever seen produced in this way.   Some persons, entitled to confidence, informed me that by changing their woollen under-dress in the night, they had at first been repeatedly frightened by seeing themselves suddenly enveloped in a mass of electrical fire.   The remarkable flames that appeared after a thunder-storm in the mountains south of El Paso, already mentioned by me [Mem. p. 43], were no doubt connected with electricity.   I recollect also, from an account published in relation to the battle of Buena Vista, that during a sultry evening electrical flames were seen on the points of the bayonets among the sentinels stationed in the mountains."

sury in payment, and in fact have a currency through the kingdom; but there are vast speculations made on the coinage, as people who have not large capital prefer selling their bullion in the internal provinces, at a considerable discount, to being obliged to transport it to Mexico, in order to have it converted into specie.   The present C[ommandant?], I was informed, was engaged in this traffic, on which, from the province of Senora, he sometimes made 25 per cent. Numbers of the proprietors who have no immediate use for their bullion put it into their cellars, where it remains piled up for their posterity, of no service to themselves or the community.

There are at Chihuahua and in its vicinity 15 mines, 13 silver, one gold, and one copper, the furnaces of all of which are situated round the town and suburbs, and present, except on Sundays, volumes of smoke arising to the eye in every direction, which can be seen from a distance long before the spires of the city strike the view.   It is incredible the quantity of cinders which surround the city in piles 10 or 15 feet high; next the creek they have formed a bank of it to check the encroachments of the stream, and it presents an effectual barrier.   I am told that an European employed some hands and wrought at the cinders, which yielded $1.25 for each per day; but that this not answering his expectations, he ceased his proceedings.

At Mausseme [Mapimi] there are one gold and seven silver mines.   At Durango there are many rich mines, but the number to me is unknown.   There are also gold mines in the Sierra Madre, near Alomas [Alamos], and many others of which I have no knowledge.   There is in the province, about 100 miles south of Chihuahua, a mountain or hill of loadstone.   Walker, who had been on the ground and surveyed it, informed me it appeared to be in solid strata, as regular as those of limestone, or any other of the species. He had brought home a square piece of near a foot and a half, was preparing some to be sent to Spain, and likewise forming magnets to accompany it, in order that their comparative strength might be ascertained with magnets formed in Europe.

Rivers.[33]   Rio Conchos is the largest in the province.   It takes its source in the Sierra Madre, near Batopilis, in lat. 28° N., and discharges itself into the Rio del Norte [at the Presidio del Norte] in lat. 31°, after a course of about 300 miles.   It is the largest western branch of the Rio del Norte, and receives in its course the Rio Florido from the east and San Paubla [now San Pedro] from the west.   Where we struck the Conchos, it appeared to be nearly as large as the Rio del Norte at the Passo.

The Rio San Paubla is the largest western branch of the Conchos; it heads in lat. 28° 50′ N., and empties into the latter at Bakinoa [?].   Its whole course is about 150 miles ; in summer it is nearly dry, and in the rainy seasons impassable.

The Rio Florido takes its rise in lat. 26° 30′ N., and after a course of about 150 miles discharges into the Conchos. Guaxequillo is situated on its east bank, about its center.

The Rio Nassas [Nasas] is in part the line between Biscay and Cogquilla; it runs north and sinks in the lake du Cayman [Laguna del Muerto]; it is nearly dry in the dry seasons, but at some seasons it is impassable.

Lakes.   Lac du Cayman and lac du Parras are two small lakes situated at the foot of the mountains [in the Bolson de Mapimi], and are full of fish.

Animals, Insects, etc.   There are some few bears, deer, and wild horses, but they are not in abundance.   The scor-

---

[33] For these, see the itinerary, Apr. 30th–May 13th, pp. 668–678, and notes there. The lakes Pike proceeds to mention are in or on the border of present Coahuila. The situation of the Presidio del Norte, where the Conchos discharges, is lat. 29° 33′ 53″ N., long. 104° 36′ 27″ W., by the river 346 m. above the mouth of the Pecos, and 348 below El Paso—both of these distances much in excess of the direct line between these points. " Batopilis " is very far out for the source of the Conchos, unless Pike refers to some other place than the modern Batopilas. This is situated below lat. 27° N., and in the Pacific water-shed, being on a branch of the Rio del Fuerte, which runs from Chihuahua through Sinaloa and empties into the Gulf of California at Point Ahome.

pions of Durango are one of the most remarkable instances of the physical effects of climate or air that I ever saw recorded. They come out of the walls and crevices in May, and continue about a fortnight in such numbers that the inhabitants never walk in their houses after dark without a light, and always shift or examine the bed-clothes and beat the curtains previous to going to bed; after which the curtains are secured under the bed, similar to the precautions we take with our mosquito curtains. The bite of those scorpions has been known to prove mortal in two hours. The most extraordinary circumstance is that by taking them 10 leagues from Durango they become perfectly harmless and lose all their venomous qualities. Query: Does it arise from a change of air, sustenance, or what other cause? [34]

[34] Before undertaking to answer this query, it would be well to ascertain the fact. The scorpions which Pike describes are known by the Spanish name *alacran*, and I presume are closely related to the widely distributed *Androctonus biaculeatus*, if not the same species. Kendall's Narrative of the Texan Expedition of 1841, pub. Lond., 1845, II. p. 114, cites Pike in this connection, and also has: " I believe that the city of Durango is somewhat celebrated for the beauty and talent of its women—I know that it is noted for the numbers and venomous qualities of its *alicrans*, or scorpions. Frequently, while travelling through the State of Durango, were we regaled with Mexican stories of the swarms of poisonous *alicrans* which infest the capital. . . A bounty of some three or six cents . . . is paid by the authorities for each insect secured, and according to some of the stories told us, no inconsiderable business is carried on in catching and bottling the much dreaded scorpions." When Gregg was in Durango, March, 1835, he noted that city "as being the headquarters, as it were, of the whole scorpion family. During the spring, especially, so much are the houses infested by these poisonous insects, that many people are obliged to have resort to a kind of mosquito bar, in order to keep them out of their beds at night. As an expedient to deliver the city from this terrible pest, a society has already been formed, which pays a reward of a *cuartilla* (three cents) for every *alacran* (or scorpion) that is brought to them. Stimulated by the desire of gain, the idle boys of the city are always on the look-out; so that, in the course of a year, immense numbers of this public enemy are captured and slaughtered. The body of this insect is of the bulk and cast of a medium spider, with a jointed tail one or two inches long, at the end of which is a sting whose wounds are so poisonous as often to prove fatal to children, and are very painful to adults. The most extraordinary peculiarity of these scorpions is, that they are far less dangerous in the north than in the south, which in some manner accounts for the story told Capt. Pike, that even those of Durango lose

Population and Chief Towns. The population of Biscay may be estimated at 200,000 : of these three-twentieths may be Spaniards from Europe, five-twentieths Creoles, five-twentieths Metifs and Quatroons, and seven-twentieths Indians. Durango [or Guadiana] was founded in 1550. It is the principal city, the seat of government for the province of Biscay and of the bishopric of Durango. Its population may be estimated at 40,000 souls. It is situated in lat. 25° N. and long. 107° W.

Pallalein, situated somewhere at the foot of the Sierra Madria [Madre], is supposed to contain 25,000 souls.

Chihuahua,[35] the place of residence of the commandant-general of the internal provinces, was founded in 1691 ; it

most of their venom as soon as they are removed a few miles from the city," says Gregg, very sensibly, Comm. Pra., II. 1844, p. 89. Hughes, Doniphan Exp., p. 128 : "the soldiers would sometimes shake their blankets, toss . . . the lizards and *alacrans*, exclaiming angrily, ' d——n the scorpion family ! ' "

[35] Gregg, Comm. Pra., II. 1844, p. 114, cites Pike in his own description of Chihuahua, as it appeared to him in 1839, and the two accounts may be here brought together. Noting the regularity of the city in comparison with Santa Fé, the dressing of the best buildings with hewn stone, the paving of some of the streets, and the population of about 10,000, this author continues :

" The most splendid edifice in Chihuahua is the principal church, which is said to equal in architectural grandeur anything of the sort in the republic. The steeples, of which there is one at each front corner, rise over 100 feet above the azotea [roof]. They are composed of very fancifully-carved columns ; and in appropriate niches of the frontispiece, which is also an elaborate piece of sculpture, are to be seen a number of statues, as large as life, the whole forming a complete representation of Christ and the 12 Apostles. This church was built about a century ago, by contributions levied upon the mines (particularly those of Santa Eulalia, 15 or 20 miles from the city), which paid over a percentage on all the metal extracted therefrom ; a *medio* [6¼ cents], I believe, being levied upon each *marco* of eight ounces. In this way, about a million of dollars was raised and expended in some 30 years, the time employed in the construction of the building. It is a curious fact, however, that, notwithstanding the enormous sums of money expended in outward embellishments, there is not a church from thence southward, perhaps, where the interior arrangements bear such striking marks of poverty and neglect. If, however, we are not dazzled by the sight of these costly decorations for which the churches of Southern Mexico are so much celebrated, we have the satisfaction of knowing that the turrets are well provided with bells, a fact of which every person who visits Chihuahua very soon obtains auricular demonstration. One, in particular, is situated in lat. 29° N., long. 107° 30' W. Its population may be estimated at 7,000. It is an oblong square, on the east side of a small stream which discharges into the river Conchos. On its south extremity is a small but elegant church. In the public square stands the principal church, royal treasury, town-house, and the richest shops. At the

is so large and sonorous that it has frequently been heard, so I am informed, at the distance of 25 miles.

"A little below the *Plaza Mayor* stand the ruins (as they may be called) of San Francisco—the mere skeleton of another great church of hewn stone, which was commenced by the Jesuits previous to their expulsion in 1767, but never finished. By the outlines still traceable amid the desolation which reigns around, it would appear th⁻ᵗ the plan of this edifice was conceived in a spirit of still greater magnificence than the Parroquia which I have been describing. The abounding architectural treasures that are mouldering and ready to tumble to the ground bear sufficient evidence that the mind which had directed its progress was at once bold, vigorous, and comprehensive.

"This dilapidated building has since been converted into a sort of state prison, particularly for the incarceration of distinguished prisoners. It was here that the principals of the famous Texan Santa Fé Expedition were confined, when they passed through the place, on their way to the City of Mexico. This edifice has also acquired considerable celebrity as having received within its gloomy embraces several of the most distinguished patriots, who were taken prisoners during the first infant struggles for Mexican independence. Among these was the illustrious ecclesiastic, Don Miguel Hidalgo y Costilla, who made the first declaration at the village of Dolores, September 16, 1810. He was taken prisoner in March, 1811, some time after his total defeat at Guadalaxara ; and being brought to Chihuahua, he was shot on the 30th of July following, in a little square back of the prison, where a plain white monument of hewn stone has been erected to his memory. It consists of an octagon base of about 25 feet in diameter, upon which rises a square, unornamented pyramid to the height of about 30 feet. The monument indeed is not an unapt emblem of the purity and simplicity of the curate's character.

"Among the few remarkable objects which attract the attention of the traveller is a row of columns supporting a large number of stupendous arches which may be seen from the heights, long before approaching the city from the north. This is an aqueduct of considerable magnitude which conveys water from the little river of Chihuahua, to an eminence above the town, whence it is passed through a succession of pipes to the main public square, where it empties itself into a large stone cistern ; and by this method the city is supplied with water. This and other public works to be met with in Chihuahua, and in the southern cities, are glorious remnants of the prosperous times of the Spanish empire. No improvements on so exalted a scale have ever been made under the republican government. . . . *¡Ojalá por los dias felices del Rey!*"

western extremity is another church for the military, a
superb hospital belonging formerly to the Jesuits' possessions, the church of the monks of St. Francis, St. Domingo,
the military academy, and quartel del tropa. On the northwest were two or three missions, very handsomely situated
on a small stream which comes in from the west. About
one mile to the south of the town is a large aqueduct which
conveys the water round it, to the east, into the main stream
below the town, in the center of which is raised a reservoir
for the water, whence it is to be conducted by pipes to the
different parts of the city, and in the public square is to be
a fountain and *jet d'eau*, which will be both ornamental and
useful. The principal church at Chihuahua was the most
superb building we saw in New Spain. Its whole front was
covered with statues of the apostles and the different saints,
set in niches of the wall, and the windows, doors, etc., were
ornamented with sculpture. I never was within the doors,
but was informed by Robinson that the decorations were
immensely rich. Some men, whom we supposed entitled to
credit, informed us that the church was built by a tax of
$12\frac{1}{2}$ cents laid on each ingot of gold or silver taken out of
the mines in the vicinity in [blank] years. Its cost, with
decorations, was $1,500,000, and when it was finished there
remained $300,000 of the fund unappropriated. At the
south side of Chihuahua is the public walk, formed by three
rows of trees whose branches nearly entwine over the heads
of the passengers below. At different distances there are
seats for persons to repose on. At each end of the walks
there were circular seats, on which, in the evening, the
company collected and amused themselves with the guitar,
and songs in Spanish, Italian, and French, adapted to the
voluptuous manners of the country. In this city, as well as
all others of any consideration, there are patrols of soldiers
during the night, who stop every person at nine o'clock
and examine them. My countersign was " Americans."

Trade, Commerce, and Manufactures. Biscay trades with
North Mexico, Senora, and the viceroyalty, from the latter

of which places they bring on mules all their dry goods, European furniture, books, ammunition, etc.   They furnish a great quantity of horses, mules, sheep, beeves, and goats, to the parts of the kingdom which are more populous and have less spare ground for pasturage, etc.   Some persons make large fortunes by being carriers from Mexico to Chihuahua, the freight being $8 per cwt., and they generally putting 300 pounds on each mule.   The merchants make their remittances twice a year in bullion.   Goods sell at Chihuahua at about 200 per cent. on the prices of our Atlantic seaport towns.   Their horses average at $6, but some have sold as high as $100; their trained mules at $20, but extraordinary matches for carriages have sold at $400 per pair.   Rice sells at $4 per cwt.   They manufacture some few arms, blankets, stamped leather, embroidery, coarse cotton and woolen cloths, and a species of rough carpeting.   Their blankets average $2, but some sell as high as $25.

Agriculture.   They cultivate wheat, corn, rice, oats, cotton, flax, indigo, and vines.   What I have said relative to the cultivation of those articles in New Mexico will equally apply to this province; but it may be proper to observe here that one of Nolan's men constructed the first cotton-gin they ever had in the province, and that Walker had caused a few churns to be made for some private families, and taught them the use of them.

Timber, Plains, and Soil.   To the north of Chihuahua, about 30 miles to the right of the main road, there is some pine timber; at a spring on this side of Carracal [Carrizal] we saw one walnut tree, and on all the small streams there are shrubby cotton trees.   With these few exceptions the whole province is a naked, barren plain, which presents to the eye an arid, unproductive soil, more especially in the neighborhood of mines; even the herbage appears to be poisoned by the mineral qualities of the soil.

Antiquities.   There are none in the province which came within my notice but the Jesuits' college and church at Chihuahua, which were about a century old, and used as hospitals. In these there was nothing peculiar, except a certain solidity and strength, in which they appeared to surpass the other public buildings of the city.

Aborigines. There are no uncivilized savages in this province except the Appaches, of whom I have spoken largely. The Christian Indians are so incorporated amongst the lower grades of Metifs that it is scarcely possible to draw the line of distinction, except at the ranchos of noblemen or large landholders, where they are in a state of vassalage [peonage]. This class of people laid a conspiracy, which was so well concerted as to baffle the inquiries of the Spaniards for a length of time, and to occasion them the loss of several hundred inhabitants. The Indians used to go out from their villages in small parties; in a short time a part would return with the report that they had been attacked by the Indians; the Spaniards would immediately send out a detachment in pursuit, when they were led into an ambuscade and every soul cut off. They pursued this course so long that the whole province becamed alarmed at the rapid manner in which their enemies multiplied; but some circumstances leading to suspicion, they made use of the superstition of those people for their ruin. Some officers disguised themselves like friars and went round amongst the Indians, pretending to be possessed of the spirit of prophecy. They preached up to the Indians that the day was approaching when a general delivery from Spanish tyranny was about to take place, and invited the Indians to join in concerting with them the work of God. The poor creatures came forward, and in their confessions stated the great hand that had already been put to the work. After these pretended friars had ascertained the nature and extent of the conspiracy, and had a body of troops prepared, they commenced the execution and put to death about 400 of the unsuspecting Indians. This struck terror and dismay through the Indian villages, and they dared not rise to declare their freedom and independence.

Government and Laws. In this province there is some

shadow of civil law ; but it is merely a shadow, as the following anecdote may illustrate : An officer, on arriving at
a village, demanded quarters for himself and troops. The
supreme civil officer sent him word that he must show his
passport. The military officer immediately sent a file of
men, who brought the judge a prisoner before him, when
he severely reprimanded the judge for his insolence and
obliged him to obey his orders instantly. This was done
by a subaltern, in a city of 20,000 inhabitants. The only
laws which can be said to be in force are the military
and ecclesiastic, between which there is a perfect understanding.

The governor is a brigadier-general, resides at Durango,
and receives $5,000 in addition to his pay in the line. It is
proper to observe that there are ordinances to bear on each
subject of civil discussion ; but the administration of them
is so corrupt that the influence of family and fortune generally procures the determination that they have right on
their side.

In each town is a public magazine for provisions, to which
every farmer brings whatever grain and produce he may
have for sale, and where he is sure to find a market ; and
should there be a scarcity the ensuing year, it is retailed out
to the inhabitants at a reasonable rate. To this place all
the citizens of the town repair to purchase.

Morals, Manners, etc. There is nothing peculiar in the
manners or morals of the people of this province, but a
much greater degree of luxury among the rich, misery
among the poor, and a corruption of morals more general
than in New Mexico. As to military spirit, they have none.
At a muster of a regiment of militia at Chihuahua one of my
men attended, and informed me that there were about 25
who had fire-arms and lances, 50 with bows and arrows and
lances, and the balance with lances or bows and arrows only.

Military Force. The regular military force of Biscay consists of 1,100 dragoons, distributed as follows : On the
frontiers of the deserts of New Mexico and Senora, at the

forts of Elisiaira [Elizario], Carracal [Carrizal], San Buenaventura, Presidio del Norte, Janos, Tulenos, and San Juan
Baptist [Bautista]. Farther south are Chihuahua, Jeronime
[Jeronimo or Hieronimo], Cayone, San Paubla [Pablo],
Guaxequillo [Guajuquilla], and Conchos, with several other
places which are appendages of those positions. The com-
plement of each of those posts is 150 men, but may be averaged at 1,100 in all, say 100 at each post. The militia are
not worthy of particular notice.

Religion. Biscay is in the diocese of Durango, the bishop's
salary being estimated at $100,000 per annum. The catho-
olic religion is here in its full force, but the inferior clergy
are very much dissatisfied. The people's superstition is so
great that they run after the holy father in the streets, endeavoring to kiss the hem of his garment; and should the
bishop be passing the street, the rich and poor all kneel.

History. I shall not presume to say anything on this
subject, except that I believe this province has been populated about 270 years.

3. SENORA. *Geography.* The province of Senora lies between lat. 33° and 27° N., and long. 110° and 117° W. Its
greatest length from north to south is about 420 miles, and
its width from east to west 380 miles. It is bounded north
by New Mexico, west by California, south by Sinaloa and
the gulf, east by Biscay and New Mexico.[36]

Air and Climate. Dry, pure, and healthy generally, but
near the gulf the ground is marshy, and it is, in some of the
districts, unhealthy.

Mines, Minerals, and Fossils. On this subject I can only

[36] Sonora then was nearly the same as the present State of that name, but lost
a northern strip (the Gadsden Purchase) to our Arizona, and also lost its New
Mexican line. For the present boundary between it and the United States,
running on lat. 31° 20' N. to long. 111° W., see note [32], p. 645. In Mexico
Sonora is now bounded on the E. by Chihuahua, on the S. by Sinaloa, and on
the W. by the Gulf of California, except the short extent to which the Colorado
r. separates it from Lower California. Area, 77,550 sq. m.; pop. 140,500;
capital, Hermosillo, pop. 7,000; principal seaport, Guaymas, pop. 5,500, situated in lat. 27° 56' N., long. 110° 36' W.

speak in general.   Senora abounds in rich gold and silver mines, but more especially the former, inasmuch as gold does not preserve its usual exchange with silver in this province.   General Salcedo told me that in this province the largest piece of pure gold had been found ever yet discovered in New Spain, and that it had been sent to the king to be put in his cabinet of curiosities.

Rivers.[37]   Rio de l'Ascencion is a short river which enters the Gulf of California about 31° N. lat.   Rio Yaqui heads on the borders of Biscay and Senora, and discharges into the Gulf of California in Guyamas [Guaymas], lat. 23° N.

Timber, Plains, and Soil.   This province is, like Biscay, destitute of timber, but has some rich soil near the gulf.

Animals.   There are deer, cabrie, and bear; there are also remarkably large lizards [*Ctenosaura teres* of Harlan], which are said to weigh ten pounds; these are perfectly harmless, tamed by the inhabitants, and trained to catch mice.

Population and Chief Towns.   The population of Senora may be estimated at 200,000 souls, of which three-twentieths probably are Spaniards, four-twentieths Creoles, six-twentieths Metifs, and seven-twentieths Indians.

Arispea [Arizpe[38]], the capital of Senora, and until 20

[37] The whole Sonoran water-shed is Pacific, and the river-system runs on general S. and S. W. courses to the Gulf, in a series of somewhat parallel streams.   The northernmost one of these, of any size, which Pike calls Ascencion r., I find lettered Rio Altar ; its main branch is Rio Magdalena ; some of its ultimate sources are in Arizona, in the country about Arivaca, Tubac, and old Fort Mason ; it discharges between George's bay and Cape Tepoca.   The Sonora is much larger, with a main branch called San Miguel ; it discharges opposite Tiburon isl.   Arizpa, which Pike speaks of as near the head of the Yaqui, is high up on the right bank of the Sonora ; lower down is Hermosillo (lat. 29° 10′ N., long. 110° 45′ W.).   The Yaqui is the largest Sonoran river, falling into the Gulf below Guaymas and above Point Lobos.   It has two main forks, Rio Moctezuma and Rio Bavispe.   Rio Matape, a small river, is the one that falls in at Guaymas, and not the Yaqui.   Another small one, Rio Mayo, falls in below Vacamora and Point Rosa.   Rio Alamos, which heads in Sonora, falls over the Sinaloan boundary.

[38] Arizpe is now a small place, with a population of probably 4,000, and is of interest chiefly to the antiquarian.   The original mission of Arizpe was already

years past the seat of government of the internal provinces, is situated in lat. 31° N. and long. 111° W., near the head of the river Yaqui. It is celebrated throughout the kingdom for the urbanity and hospitality of its inhabitants, and the vast quantity of gold table utensils made use of in their houses. Its population is 3,400 souls. Sonora and Terenate are the next cities in magnitude in the province, the latter to the north and the former to the south of the capital.

Trade and Commerce. Senora trades with New Mexico and Biscay for the productions of those different provinces, and with Old Mexico both by land and sea, through the gulf of California. It is celebrated for its cheese, horses, and sheep.

Agriculture. They cultivate the same as in Biscay.

Aborigines. There are a number of savage nations bordering on Senora, which obliges the king to keep up a number of military posts on the north and west frontiers ; but the names of the tribes, or any of their distinguishing characters, I am unacquainted with. However, it may not be improper to observe that they are armed with bows, arrows, shields, and lances, like their savage neighbors. The civilized Indians are in the same situations as in the other provinces.

Government and Laws. Similar to Biscay, the governor being a brigadier-general and receives $7,000 in addition to his pay in the line.

Morals and Manners. In every respect similar to Biscay, except that they are more celebrated for hospitality.

Military Force. The regular military force of this prov-

over 150 years old in Pike's time, and the place is believed to have been an Opata village as early as 1540. The derivation of the name is given as the Opata word *arit*, meaning "ant." The name *Arizpe* suggests the obvious conjecture, that the root of the word *Arizona*, the derivation of which has been so much mooted, may be here found. How this may be, I do not know ; but *Arizona* does not appear to be Spanish, and certainly any such etymology as Lat. *arida zona*, which has been adduced among others, is fictitious.

ince is 900 dragoons and 200 infantry, stationed as follows:
Tubson, San Cruz, Tubac, and Altac on the north, with 100
dragoons each for a garrison; Fiuntenas, Bacuachi, Bavista,
and Horcasites in the center, with 300 dragoons and 200
infantry; Buenavista on the south, with 100 dragoons as a
garrison.[39] The infantry mentioned above are of a nation
of Indians called the Opejas, and are said to be the best
soldiers in New Spain. I saw a detachment of them at
Chihuahua who appeared to be fine, stout, athletic men,
and were the most subordinate and faithful troops I ever
knew, acting like a band of brothers and having the greatest attachment for their officers.

Religion. Catholic, in the diocese of the bishop of
Durango.

History. I am unacquainted with it, except that the seat
of government of the internal provinces was formerly at
Arispea, at which time the government of California was
also under the commandant-generalcy of the internal
provinces; but the removal of the seat of government to
Chihuahua and the disjunct situation of California induced
his Majesty to annex it to the government of the viceroyalty. The increasing magnitude of the relations of
New Spain with the United States also gave an importance
to the eastern interests which induced the continuance of
the seat of government at Chihuahua.

4. SINALOA. *Geography.* The province of Sinaloa lies

[39] Tubson is now Tucson, Ariz. San Cruz is Santa Cruz, also in Arizona,
on or near the branch of the Gila of that name. Tubac is likewise now Arizonian, being a place about on long. 111° W., N. W. of Nogales, and not far
from old Forts Mason and Crittenden. Altac is Altar, on the Sonoran river
of that name. "Fiuntenas" I take to be a misprint for Fronteras, a place on
one of the headwaters of the Yaqui, about lat. 31° N. Bacuachi is on one of
the branches of the Sonora r., above Arizpe. Bavista is Bavispe, a place high
up on the river of that name, close to the eastern border of the State. Horcasites, to judge from its location on Pike's map, was on or near the Sonora r.,
in the vicinity of present Ures; but I have not found the place. Near it
Pike locates a Presidio San Antonio, omitted from the text. Buenavista is a
place low down on the Yaqui r.; the present road from Punta de Agua on Rio
Matape goes through it to Batacoso, Alamos, and so on.

between lat. 23° and 28° N., and long. 108° and 111° W.
It is bounded north by Senora and Biscay, east by the
latter, south by the administration of Guadalaxara, and
west by the gulf of California; in its greatest length it is
300 miles north and south, and in width from east to west
150 miles.[40]

Air and Climate. On the sea-coast humid, but back [of
the coast] dry and pure.

Mines, Minerals, and Fossils. There are both gold and
silver mines; but with their relative value or productions I
am unacquainted.

Rivers.[41] Rio [del] Fuerte takes its source in lat. 27º N.
and long. 110° W., and disembogues into the gulf of California. It crosses the whole province, and is nearly 150
miles long. Rio Culican [Culiacan] is not more than 50
miles in length, and enters the gulf of California in lat.
25° N.

Timber, Plains, and Soil. No timber; soil similar to
that of Senora.

Animals. Domestic only.

Population and Chief Towns. Its population may be estimated at 60,000, not more than three-twentieths of whom
are Spaniards; the remainder Creoles, Metifs, and Indians.

Sinaloa is the capital, but its population, extent, etc., to
me is unknown.

Trade and Commerce. Unacquainted with.

[40] Sinaloa or Cinaloa is practically the same as it was, but would be now
said to be bounded by Sonora, Chihuahua, Durango, and Jalisco; its whole S.
W. length is sea-coast, on the Gulf of California and Pacific Ocean. Area,
36,180 sq. m.; pop. 245,700; capital, Culiacan, on the river of that name,
in lat. 24° 50′ N., long. 107º 20′ W.; pop. 8,000. The principal city and
port is Mazatlan, in lat. 23º 15′ 36″ N.; pop. 12,000.

[41] Sinaloa has a long series of comparatively short rivers, with a general
S. W. trend to the sea. Rio del Fuerte (River of the Fort) is the largest and,
excepting Rio Alamos, the northernmost. The Sinaloa is the next one of
any size; on this is Sinaloa, in Pike's time the capital, but not now a place
of special importance. Further S. come successively, Rio San Lorenzo,
Rio San Miguel, Rio Piaxtla, Rio Mazatlan, and Rio El Rosario; the latter is
charted by Pike, who empties it into the Gulf, near 23°, which is about right.

Agriculture. The same as Senora.

Aborigines. None who are not civilized.

Government and Laws. Unacquainted with.

Military Force. One hundred dragoons for expresses, and a guard for the governor.

Religion. Catholic, in the diocese of the bishop of Durango.

History. To me unknown.

5. COGQUILLA. *Geography.* The province of Cogquilla lies between lat. 31° and 33° 30' N., and long. 101° and 105° W. Its greatest length north and south may be 500 miles, and its greatest width east and west 200 miles. It is bounded north by New Mexico and Texas, east by the latter, San Ander, and New Leon, south by the administration of Zacataca, and west by Biscay.[42]

Air and Climate. Pure and healthy, except about the middle of May, when the heat is intense, and sometimes a scorching wind is felt, like the flame issuing from an oven or furnace, which frequently skins the face and affects the eyes. This phenomenon is felt more sensibly about the setting of the sun than at any other period of the 24 hours.

Mines, Minerals, and Fossils. I know of no mines in this province, except at Montelovez and San Rosa, with the value of which I am unacquainted; but those of San Rosa are reputed to be as rich as any silver mines in the kingdom. Montelovez has none very considerable.

Rivers. This province has no river of magnitude or consequence but the Rio Grande, which crosses its northern part in a S. E. direction.[43]

[42] Coahuila, or Coahuila de Zaragoza, or Cohahuilla, or Quagila, etc., has much the same limits now, excepting of course the cis-Grandean portion which is now a part of Texas. On the eastern side there is a curious peninsula or panhandle of the State, which is wedged between two similar projections of Nuevo Leon and Tamaulipas respectively. On the S. are San Luis Potosí as well as Zacatecas, and on the W. the former Biscay gives Chihuahua and Durango. Area, 60,500 sq. m.; pop. 178,000; capital, Saltillo, about lat. 25° 25' N., long. 101° 4' W., founded 1586; pop. 23,000.

[43] The Rio Grande does not now cross Coahuila, but forms its whole U. S.

Lakes. There is a small lake called the Aqua [Agua] Verde, situated on its western extremities, which gives rise to a small stream that discharges into the Rio del Norte.

Timber, Plains, and Soil. From the river Nassus [Nasas] to the east there is the palmetto, which grows to the height of 20 and 25 feet, with a trunk of 2 feet in diameter. Its leaves are in the shape of a spear, and cover all the trunk when young, but fall off as the tree grows old. Its wood is of a spongy nature, and from every information I could procure, is of the same species as that of the same name in the Southern States.[44] One hundred miles to the east of the Rio Grande oak timber commences, being the first we saw in the provinces; but it is very small and scrubby, and presents from this to the line of Texas (the river Mariana [Medina, near San Antonio, Tex.]), a very perceptible gradation of the increase of timber, both in quantity, luxuri-

border on the N. W., N., and N. E.   But there are a good many rivers in Coahuila, some of them notable.   1. Prominent among these is the whole course of the Sabinas, and of its main fork on which is Monclova, together with their respective tributaries, down to where the two are joined, to continue under the name of Rio Salado to the Rio Grande ; the Salado cuts across the tip end of New Leon, but again becomes Coahuilan to the extent of separating Coahuila from Nuevo Leon before entering Tamaulipas.   The "Aqua Verde" lake which Pike names, and which is rather centrally than westerly located, is the Laguna de Agua Verde ; which, with a neighboring one called Santa Maria, belongs to the water-system of the Sabinas.   2. The two rivers which flow into Lag. del Muerto and Lag. de Parras enter Coahuila.   3. The headwaters of the Rio San Juan, on one of which Saltillo, the capital, is situated, are in Coahuila. 4. A series of Coahuilan streams falls into the Rio Grande at successive points from below Presidio Salto to above Presidio San Vincento.

[44] The tree is not the palmetto of the Southern States, *Sabal palmetto*, but one of the large woody yuccas, of the same genus as the small shrubby ones commonly called Spanish bayonets, from the character of the leaves Pike notes. *Yucca treculeana* (or *canaliculata*) is a Mexican species sometimes 25 feet high and 2 feet thick, thus answering to the requirements of the text.   The one best known in our country is the tree yucca, *Yucca arborescens*, very similar to the last named.   This grows abundantly in some parts of Southern California in the valley of the Mohave r., sometimes so thickly as to make a sort of forest.   Multitudes may be seen along the line of the Atl. and Pac. R. R. in the desert, where there is for many miles no sign of anything else that looks like a tree.

ance, and variety.   The country here becomes very similar to the Indiana territory.

Animals.   Deer, wild horses, a few buffalo and wild hogs [peccaries].

Population and Chief Towns.   Montelovez [Monclova[45]] is the capital of Cogquilla.   It is situated on a small stream of water in lat. 26° 30′ N. and long. 103° 30′ W.   It is about one mile in length, on a course N. 70° E. by the main street. It has two public squares, seven churches, a powder magazine, mills, king's hospital, and quartel del tropa [soldiers' barracks].   This is the principal military depot for the provinces of Cogquilla and Texas.   Its population may be estimated at 3,500 souls.   This city being the stated residence of his Excellency Governor Cordero, he has ornamented it with public walks, columns, and fountains, and made it one of the handsomest cities in the internal provinces.

Santa Rosa, about 38 miles N. W. of Montelovez, is represented to be the most healthy situation in the province, and to have the best water and fruit.   It is on the headwaters of the river Millada [read here Sabinas].   Its population is represented at 4,000 souls.   Paras [Parras] is situated on a small stream ; with its suburbs it is supposed to contain 7,000 souls, and San Lorenzo, three miles to the north, 500 souls.   This place may be termed the vineyard of Cogquilla, the whole population pursuing no other occupation than the cultivation of the grape.   Its name denotes the Branches of the Vine.   At the Hacienda of San Lorenzo, where we halted, there were 15 larger stills, larger cellars, and a greater number of casks than I ever saw in any brewery of the United States.   Its gardens were delightfully interspersed with figs, vines, apricots, and a variety of fruits which are produced in the torrid zone ; fine summer-houses, where were wine, refreshments, and couches to repose on, and where the singing of the birds was delightful.   There were, likewise, mills and a fine water-fall.

[45] For various places mentioned in this and the following paragraphs, see the itinerary of May 16th to June 1st, pp. 680–689, and notes along there.

The Presidio [Salto] of Rio Grande is situated on that river, and is remarkable for nothing but three or four handsome missions with which it is surrounded, a powder magazine, quarters for the troops, and a few iron field-pieces on miserable truck carriages.   Population 2,500 souls.

The population of this province may be estimated at 70,000 souls, not more than 10,000 of whom are Spaniards.

Trade, Commerce, and Manufactures. This province receives all its merchandise from Mexico by land, and in return gives horses, mules, wines, gold, and silver.   There is an annual fair held at Saltelo [Saltillo], in New Leon [Coahuila], where an immense quantity of merchandise is disposed of, and where merchants of very large capitals reside.

Agriculture. They cultivate the vine principally, with grain and corn sufficient for their own consumption, and to supply the greatest part of Texas.

Aborigines. The Appaches cover the northwest frontier.   The Lee Pawnees [Lipans : see note [27], p. 746] are a nation who rove from the Rio Grande to some distance into the province of Texas.   Their former residence was on the Rio Grande, near the sea-shore.   They are at present divided into three bands, of 300, 350, and 100 men each. They are at war with the Tetaus and Appaches, and at peace with the Spaniards.   They have fair hair, and are generally handsome, armed with bows, arrows, and lances. They pursue the wild horses, of which they take numbers, and sell them to the Spaniards.

Government and Laws. Military and ecclesiastical power is all that is known or acknowledged in this province ; but its administration was mild under their excellent Governor Cordero.   The governor's civil salary is $4,000 per annum.

Morals and Manners. It was evident to the least discerning eye that, as we diverged from these parts which produced such vast quantities of the precious metals, the inhabitants became more industrious, and there were fewer beggars.   Thus the morals of the people of Cogquilla

were less corrupt than those of Biscay or New Leon, their
neighbors.

Military Force. There are 400 dragoons maintained in
this province, and stationed at Montelovez, San Rosa, Pres.
Rio del Norte, and San Fernandez.

Religion. Catholic, but mild. It is in the diocese of
Durango.

History. Cogquilla had not pushed its population as far
as the Rio Grande in the year 1687, as at that time La Salle [46]
established himself at the entrance of that river, it being a
wilderness; but Montelovez was established some time
before this era. Of its particular history I have no
knowledge.

6. TEXAS. *Geography.* The province of Texas lies between lat. 27° 30' and 35° N., and long. 98° and 104° W.,
bordered north by Louisiana, east by the territory of
Orleans, west by Cogquilla and New Mexico, and south by
New San Ander. Its greatest length from north to south
may be 500 miles, and breadth from east to west 350.

Air and Climate. One of the most delightful tempera-
tures in the world; but, being a country covered with

[46] Robert Cavelier, Le Sieur de la Salle, b. Rouen, Normandie, France,
Nov. 22d, 1643, murdered by Duhaut in conspiracy with other assassins, in
Texas, on a branch of the Trinity, or of the Brazos, Mar. 19th or 20th, 1687,
was never at the mouth of the Rio Grande. La Salle sailed from France with
four vessels and about 280 persons, July 24th, 1684; three of the vessels sighted
Florida Jan. 15th, 1685; landed at St. Louis, later St. Bernard, now Matagorda, bay, in Feb., 1685; one vessel sailed away in Mar., 1685, leaving La
Salle with about 180 adventurers or colonists. He founded Fort St. Louis at
or near present La Vaca, in Apr., 1685, giving a color of French claim that did
not entirely fade away till 1803, though the settlement speedily aborted. The
remainder of 1685 and the year 1686 were mainly passed in fruitless wanderings
and warrings in different directions, with misery and disaster at every turn. La
Salle's people dwindled down to about 20 who were left at the fort, and 17 who
started with their leader, Jan. 7th, 1687, overland to Canada. This *verloren
hoop* included : La Salle; Father Jean Cavelier, his brother ; their two nephews,
Moranget and Cavelier ; Sieur de Marla, Friar Anastase Douay, who afterward
wrote of the journey, a witness of La Salle's death ; Joutel, a trusty soldier,
whose account (pub. 1713) is to be preferred to Douay's when the two differ ;
Teissier, a pilot, one of the conspirators ; Liotot, the surgeon, ditto; Hiens,

timber, the new emigrants are generally sickly, which may justly be attributed to putrescent vegetation, which brings on intermittent and bilious attacks, and, in some instances, malignant fevers. The justice of these remarks is proved by the observations of all the first settlers of our western frontiers, that places which in the course of 10 or 15 years become perfectly healthy, were the first two or three years quite the reverse, and generally cost them the loss of two or three members of their families.

Mines, Minerals, and Fossils. The only one known and worked is a mine of lead.

Rivers.[47] The river St. Antonio takes its source about one league to the northeast of the capital of the province, St. Antonio, and is navigable for canoes to its source, affording excellent fish, fine mill seats, and water to every part of the town. It is joined from the west by the river Mariana, which forms part of the line between Cogquilla and Texas, and then discharges into the Rio Guadelupe about 50 miles from the sea. At the town of St. Antonio it is about 20 yards wide, and in some places 12 feet in depth. The river Guadelupe takes its source about 150

a German ex-buccanier, ditto ; Duhaut, the actual assassin ; Jean Archevêque, his servant and accomplice ; Saget, La Salle's servant ; Nika, a Shawanoe hunter ; another Indian, and some other persons. This party had crossed the Colorado and Brazos Mar. 15th, 1687. After a quarrel which arose over some buffalo meat, in a detached party who were 6 m. away from La Salle, Duhaut, Liotot, Hiens, and others conspired to kill Moranget ; Liotot brained him ; Saget and Nika were also then and there killed. La Salle left Joutel and others in their own camp and proceeded to the scene of this tragedy, accompanied only by Father Douay, and an Indian, Mar. 19th or 20th. On his approach, Duhaut shot him in the head from ambush ; Liotot and others mocked and buffeted his corpse. Some time in May Duhaut was murdered by Hiens ; at the same time Liotot was murdered by one Ruter. Some survivors of this bloody expedition reached Poste aux Arkansas in July. The colony left at Fort St. Louis had been utterly extirpated by Indian massacre and dispersion of the few survivors, before Apr. 22d, 1689, when the spot, void of all but the dead there buried, was visited by a Spanish party under Don Alonzo de Leon. See note [21], p. 560.

[47] For the several rivers about to be treated here, see the itinerary, June 7th–29th, and notes there.

miles to the northwest of St. Antonio ; where we crossed it, it was a beautiful stream, at least 60 yards in width. Its waters are transparent and navigable for canoes. After receiving the waters of the St. Antonio and St. Marco it discharges into the southwest end of the bay of St. Bernardo [Matagorda]. At the crossing of this river there is a range for the horses of St. Antonio and a guarde de caballo, with an elegant site for a town.

The river St. Marco takes its source about 100 miles north, 20 west of St. Antonio, and at the crossing of the road is 30 yards in width, a clear and navigable stream for canoes. By the road this river is only 14 miles from the Guadelupe, into which it discharges.

The Red [or Colorado] river [of Texas] takes its source in the province of Cogquilla in lat. 33° N. and long. 104° 30′ W., but, bending to the east, enters the province of Texas, and after a winding course of about 600 miles disembogues into the bay of St. Bernard [Matagorda], in lat. 29° N. Where the road traverses it, it is at least 150 yards wide, and has a guard of dragoons stationed on its banks. Its waters are of a reddish cast, whence it probably derived its name. This stream is navigable for boats of three or four tons burden.

The river Brassos [Brazos] takes its source in the province of Cogquilla in lat. 34° N. and long. 105° W., enters the province of Texas, and discharges into the gulf of Mexico in lat. 28° 40′, after a course of 750 miles. It is the largest river in the province, and, where the road crosses, is 300 yards wide and navigable for large keels. From the appearances on its banks it must rise and fall 100 feet. Its waters were red and turbid ; its banks well timbered, with a rich, prolific soil. Here was kept the only boat I recollect to have seen in the provinces.

The river Trinity takes its source in lat. 34° N. and long. 99° W., and discharges into Galueston's [Galveston] bay in lat. 29° 30′ N. By its meanders it is about 300 miles in length. Where the road crosses it is about 60 yards in width, with high, steep banks covered with timber, and a rich, luxuriant soil.

The Nachez [Neches] and Angelina are small rivers, of about 20 yards in width, which, after forming a junction, discharge into the Trinity. The river Toyac is a small stream, which discharges into the gulf of Mexico, at the same bay with the Sabine, in about lat. 29° 50′ N. and long. 97° W.[48]

The Sabine river, the present limits between the Spanish dominions and the territories of the United States in that quarter, takes its source in about lat. 33° N., and enters the gulf of Mexico in 29° 50′. It may be 300 miles in length by its meanders, and at the road about 50 yards in width. Here the Spaniards keep a guard and a ferry-boat.

Lakes. Some small ones near the head of the Guadelupe and some branches of Red river.

Timber, Plains, and Soil. This province is well timbered for 100 miles from the coast, but has some small prairies interspersed through its timbered land; take it generally, it is one of the richest, most prolific, and best watered countries in North America.

Animals. Buffalo, deer, elk, wild hogs [peccaries], and wild horses, the latter of which are in such numbers as to afford supplies for all the savages who border on the province, the Spaniards, and vast droves for the other provinces. They are also sent into the United States, notwithstanding the trade is contraband. They go in such large gangs that it is requisite to keep an advanced guard of horsemen in order to frighten them away; for should they be suffered to come near the horses and mules which you drive with you, by their snorting, neighing, etc., they

---

[48] This description of the Nachez, Angelina, and Toyac (Atoyac) rivers agrees with the map, and with the misapprehension under which Pike labored. As already indicated, note [18], p. 710, the three are branches of one, which falls into the Gulf in the same bay with the Sabine; but Pike cuts off the Nachez and Angelina from the Toyac and turns them into the Trinity as branches of the latter, thus leaving the Toyac alone to pursue the course all three should have taken together.

would alarm them, and frequently the domestic animals
would join them and go off, notwithstanding all the exertions of the dragoons to prevent them.   A gentleman
told me he saw 700 beasts carried off [stampeded] at one
time, not one of which was ever recovered.   They also in
the night frequently carry off the droves of travelers' horses,
and even come within a few miles of St. Antonio, and take
off the horses in that vicinity.

The method pursued by the Spanish in taking them is as
follows: They take a few fleet horses and proceed into
the country where the wild horses are numerous.   They
then build a large strong inclosure, with a door which
enters a smaller inclosure; from the entrance of the large
pen they project wings out into the prairie a great distance, and then set up bushes, etc., to induce the horses,
when pursued, to enter into these wings.   After these
preparations are made they keep a lookout for a small
drove, for, if they unfortunately should start too large a
one, they either burst open the pen or fill it up with dead
bodies, and the others run over them and escape ; in which
case the party are obliged to leave the place, as the stench
arising from the putrid carcasses would be insupportable ;
and, in addition to this, the pen would not receive others.
Should they, however, succeed in driving in a few, say two
or three hundred, they select the handsomest and youngest,
noose them, take them into the small inclosure, and then
turn out the remainder ; after which, by starving, prevent-
ing them taking any repose, and continually keeping them
in motion, they make them gentle by degrees, and finally
break them to submit to the saddle and bridle.   For this
business I presume there is no nation in the world superior
to the Spaniards of Texas.

Population and Chief Towns.   St. Antonio, the capital of
the province, lies in lat. 29° 50' N. and long. 101° W., and
is situated on the headwaters of the river of that name; it
contains perhaps 2,000 souls, most of whom reside in
miserable mud-wall houses, covered with thatched grass

roofs. The town is laid out on a very grand plan. To the east of it, on the other side of the river, is the station of the troops.

About two, three, and four miles from St. Antonio are three missions, formerly flourishing and prosperous. Those buildings, for solidity, accommodation, and even majesty, were surpassed by few that I saw in New Spain. The resident priest treated us with the greatest hospitality, and was respected and beloved by all who knew him. He made a singular observation relative to the aborigines who had formerly formed the population of those establishments under charge of the monks. I asked him what had become of the natives. He replied that it appeared to him that they could not exist under the shadow of the whites, as the nations who formed those missions had been nurtured, taken all the care of that it was possible, and put on the same footing as the Spaniards; yet, notwithstanding, they had dwindled away until the other two missions had become entirely depopulated, and the one where he resided had not then more than sufficient to perform his household labor; from this he had formed an idea that God never intended them to form one people, but that they should always remain distinct and separate.

Nacogdoches is merely a station for troops, and contains nearly 500 souls. It is situated on a small stream of the river Toyac.

The population of Texas may be estimated at 7,000. These are principally Spanish, Creoles, some French, some Americans, and a few civilized Indians and half-breeds.

Trade and Commerce. This province trades with Mexico by Mont El Rey and Montelovez for merchandise, and with New Orleans by Nachitoches; but the latter trade, being contraband, is liable to great danger and risks. They give in return specie, horses, and mules.

Agriculture. The American emigrants are introducing some little spirit of agriculture near Nacogdoches and the Trinity; but the oppressions and suspicions they labor under prevent their proceeding with that spirit which is necessary to give success to the establishment of a new country.

Aborigines. The Tancards [note ¹², p. 705] are a nation of Indians who rove on the banks of Red river, and are 600 men strong. They follow the buffalo and wild horses, and carry on a trade with the Spaniards. They are armed with the bow, arrow, and lance. They are erratic and confined to no particular district ; are a tall, handsome people ; in conversation they have a peculiar cluckling, express more by signs than any savages I ever visited, and in fact language appears to have made less progress. They complained much of their situation and the treatment of the Spaniards ; are extremely poor, and, except the Appaches, were the most independent Indians we encountered in the Spanish territories. They possess large droves of horses.

There are a number of other nations now nearly extinct, some of which are mentioned by Dr. Sibley in a report he made to the government of the United States on these subjects. A few, and very few indeed, of those nations have been converted by the missions, and these are not in that state of vassalage in which the Indians further to the south are held. [Notes ¹⁷, ²¹, ²², pp. 709, 713, 714.]

Government and Laws. Perfectly military, except as to the ecclesiastical jurisdiction.

Morals and Manners. They being on the frontier, where buffalo and wild horses abound, and not engaged in any war with savages who are powerful, have adopted a mode of living by following those animals, which has been productive of a more wandering disposition round the capital (St. Antonio) than in any other of the provinces. Cordero, restricting by edicts the buffalo hunts to certain seasons, and obliging every man of family to cultivate so many acres of land, has in some degree checked the spirit of hunting or wandering life which had been hitherto so very prevalent, and has endeavored to introduce, by his example and precepts, a general urbanity and suavity of manners which rendered St. Antonio one of the most agreeable places that we met with in the provinces.

Military Force. There were in Texas at the time I came through 988 [888?] men, from the actual returns of the troops which I have seen, 500 of whom were from St. Ander and New Leon, under command of governor Herrara. The disposition of those troops is as follows: 388 at St. Antonio, 400 [300?] at the cantonment of [Blank, 300 marked on map low down] on the Trinity, 100 at the [crossing of the] Trinity, and 100 at Nacogdoches. The militia, a rabble made somewhat respectable by a few American riflemen who are incorporated amongst them, are about 300 men, including bow and arrow men.

Religion. Catholic, but much relaxed.

History. To me unknown, except what can be extracted from various authors on that subject.

GENERAL REMARKS ON NEW SPAIN.

To become acquainted with all the civil and political institutes of a country requires a perfect knowledge of the language, a free ingress to the archives, and a residence of some years; even then we can scarcely distinguish between the statute laws and common law, derived from custom, morals, and habits. Under those circumstances, it cannot be expected that I shall be able to say much on the subject, as I possessed none of the above advantages. I will, however, offer a few observations. To a stranger it is impossible to define the limits of the military and ecclesiastical jurisdictions; in every affair which relates to the citizens, and in fact with the soldiery, the force of superstition is such that I am doubtful whether they would generally obey one of their officers in a direct violation of the injunction of their religious professions. The audiences of Mexico and Guadalaxara were formed, no doubt, as a check on the immense power of the viceroy. The number of members composing each is to me unknown, but they are formed of the viceroy as president, with two votes, generals, and bishops. To their jurisdictions the appeals from the judgment of the intendants and all subordinate officers may be made in civil cases; but the military and ecclesiastical decisions are distinct. Notwithstanding all this semblance of justice, should an individual dare to make the appeal and not succeed in establishing the justice of his claim to redress, he is certainly ruined. Where justice is so little attended to, when opposed to power and wealth, as in the Spanish provinces, the appeal is a desperate remedy. This tribunal or legislative body enacts all the laws for the general regulations of their divisions of the kingdom.

The captain-generalcy of the internal provinces appeared to me to be much more despotic, for the laws or regulations were issued in the form of an order merely, without any kind of a preamble whatsoever, except sometimes he would say, " By order of the king "; and such was the style of governors of provinces.

Morals, Manners, etc. For hospitality, generosity, and sobriety the people of New Spain exceed any nation perhaps on the globe; but in national energy, patriotism, enterprise of character, or independence of soul, they are perhaps the most deficient. Yet there are men who have displayed bravery to a surprising degree, and the Europeans who are there cherish with delight the idea of their gallant ancestry.

Their women have black eyes and hair, fine teeth, and are generally brunettes. I met but one exception to this rule, at Chihuahua—a fair lady, who, by way of distinction, was called " the girl with light hair." They are all inclining a little to enbonpoint; but none or few are elegant figures. Their dress generally is short jackets and petticoats and high-heeled shoes, without any head-dress. Over the whole dress they have a silk wrapper,[49] which they always wear

---

[49] The reboso, with which the women muffle their faces, in a characteristic manner perhaps traceable back to the Moors, or to the wives of the prophet himself, is as indispensable an article of attire as a fan. The Spaniards have a

and, when in the presence of men, affect to bring over their
faces, but from under which you frequently see peeping a
large sparkling black eye.   As we approached the Atlantic
and our frontiers, we saw several ladies who wore the gowns
of our countrywomen, which they conceived to be much
more elegant than their ancient costume.   The lower class
of the men are generally dressed in broad-brimmed hats,
short coats, large waistcoats, and small clothes always open
at the knees (owing, as I suppose, to the greater freedom it
gives to the limbs on horseback), a kind of leather boot or
wrapper bound round the leg somewhat in the manner of
our frontier-men's leggings, and gartered on.   The boot is
of a soft, pliable leather, but not colored.   In the eastern
provinces the dragoons wear, over this wrapper or boot, a
sort of jack-boot made of sole-leather, to which are fastened,
by a rivet, the spurs, the gaffs of which are sometimes near
an inch in length ; but the spurs of the gentlemen and officers, although clumsy to our ideas, are frequently ornamented with raised silver-work on the shoulders, and the
straps embroidered with silver and gold thread.   They are
always ready to mount their horses, on which the inhabitants of the internal provinces spend nearly half the day.
This description will apply generally to the dress of all the
men of the provinces for the lower class ; but in their cities,
among the more fashionable, they dress after the European
or United States modes, with not more variation than we
see in our cities from one six months to another.

phrase *de reboso*, equivalent to the Italian *in petto*, Latin *sub rosa*, to indicate
secrecy, intrigue, and the like.   The reboso varies much in size, shape, color,
texture, price, and other qualities ; and, according to one distinguished author,
it has various uses : "The church was crowded with women of all conditions,
and the horrid *reboso*, which the poor use for shawl, bonnet, handkerchief, and
spit-box, sent out an odor which the incense from the altar failed to stifle,"
says Emory, Ex. Doc. 41, 30th Cong., 1st Sess., 1848, p. 41.   Some say that
the large mobile lips of Mexican señoras acquire their osculatory capacity by the
habitual use of those features in gesticulation as well as articulation ; their hands
and arms being kept bundled up with their heads in that comprehensive article
of attire, they are obliged to use their lips for pointers.

Both men and women have remarkably fine hair, and pride themselves in the display of it. Their amusements are music, singing, dancing, and gambling. The latter is strictly prohibited, but the prohibition is not much attended to. The dance of —— is danced by one man and two women, who beat time to the music, which is soft and voluptuous, but sometimes changing to a lively, gay air. The dancers exhibit the motions of the soul by gestures of the body, snapping the fingers, and sometimes meeting in a stretched embrace. The fandango is danced to various figures and numbers. The minuet is still danced by the superior class only. The music made use of is the guitar, violin, and singers, who, in the first-described dance, accompany the music with their hands and voices, having always some words adapted to the music.

Their games are cards, billiards, horse-racing, and cock-fighting, the first and last of which are carried to the most extravagant lengths, losing and winning immense sums. The present commandant-general is very severe with his officers in these respects, frequently sending them to some frontier post in confinement for months, for no other fault than having lost large sums at play. At every town of consequence is a public walk, where the ladies and gentlemen meet and sing songs, which are always on the subject of love or the social board. The females have fine voices, and sing in French, Italian, and Spanish, the whole company joining in the chorus.

In their houses the ladies play the guitar, and generally accompany it with their voices. They either sit down on the carpet cross-legged, or loll on a sofa. To sit upright in a chair appeared to put them to great inconvenience; although the better class would sometimes do it on our first introduction, they soon took the liberty of following their old habits. In their eating and drinking they are remarkably temperate. Early in the morning you receive a dish of chocolate and a cake; at twelve you dine on several dishes of meat, fowls, and fish, after which you have a variety of confections, and indeed an elegant dessert; then drink a few glasses of wine, sing a few songs, and retire to take the siesta, or afternoon's nap, which is taken by rich and poor. About two o'clock the windows and doors are all closed, the streets deserted, and the stillness of midnight reigns throughout. About four o'clock they rise, wash and dress, and prepare for the dissipation of the night. About eleven o'clock some refreshments are offered, but few take any, except a little wine and water and candied sugar.

The government has multiplied the difficulties of Europeans intermarrying with the Creoles or Metifs to such a degree that it is difficult for such a marriage to take place. An officer wishing to marry a lady not from Europe is obliged to acquire certificates of the purity of her descent 200 years back, and transmit it to the court, when the license will be returned; but should she be the daughter of a man of the rank of captain or upward this nicety vanishes, as rank purifies the blood of the descendants.

The general subjects of conversations among the men are women, money, and horses, which appear to be the only objects, in their estimation, worthy of consideration. Uniting the female sex with their money and their beasts, and having treated them too much after the manner of the latter, they have eradicated from their breasts every sentiment of virtue or ambition, either to pursue the acquirements which would make them amiable companions, instructive mothers, or respectable members of society; their whole souls, with a few exceptions, being, like those of Turkish ladies, taken up in music, dress, and the little blandishments of voluptuous dissipation. Finding that the men only regard them as objects of gratification to the sensual passions, they have lost every idea of that feast of reason and flow of soul which arise from the intercourse of two refined and virtuous minds.

The beggars of the City of Mexico are estimated at 60,000 souls; what must be the number through the whole kingdom, and to what reason can it be owing that, in a country superior to any in the world for riches in gold and silver, producing all the necessaries of life and most of its luxuries, there should be such a vast proportion of the inhabitants in want of bread or clothing? It can only be accounted for by the tyranny of the government and the luxuries of the rich. The government strives, by all the restrictions possible to be invented without absolutely driving the people to desperation, to keep Spanish America dependent on Europe.

Trade, Commerce, Manufactures, and Revenue. The trade and commerce of New Spain are carried on with Europe and the United States by the port of Vera Cruz solely, and with the East Indies and South America generally by Acapulco ; and, even at these ports, under such restriction as to productions, manufactures, and time, as to render it of little consequence to the general prosperity of the country. Were all the numerous bays and harbors of the gulfs of Mexico and California opened to the trade of the world, and a general license given to the cultivation of all the productions of which the country is capable, with freedom of exportation and importation, with proper duties on foreign goods, the country would immediately become rich and powerful, and a proper stimulus would be held out to the poor to labor, when certain of finding a quick and ready sale for the productions of their plantations or manufactories. The country abounds in iron ore, yet all the iron and steel, and articles of manufactures, are obliged to be brought from Europe, the manufacturing or working of iron being strictly prohibited. This occasions the necessary articles of husbandry, arms, and tools to be enormously high, and is a great check to agriculture, improvements in manufactures, and military skill. The works of the Mexicans, in gold, silver, and painting, show them naturally to have a genius which, with cultivation and improvement, might rival the greatest masters of either ancient or modern times. Their dispositions and habits are peculiarly calculated for sedentary employments, and I have no doubt, if proper establishments were made, they would soon rival, if not surpass, the most extensive woolen, cotton, or silk manufactures of Europe; their climate being proper to raise the finest cotton in the world, and their sheep possessing all the fineness of wool for which they are so celebrated in Spain. Under these circumstances, together with the immense quantities of the raw materials which they have on hand, wool sells for a mere trifle; and, in fact, they scarcely take half from the fleece of the sheep, for the coarse manufactures of the country and to make beds.

I cannot presume to state the revenues of the country from official documents, but the following statements I have had from so respectable a source, and they are so confirmed by my own observations, that I think much reliance may be placed on their correctness. The mint coins, per annum, at least, $50,000,000 in silver and $14,000,000 in gold, the one-fifth of which (the duty) is equal to $12,800,000.[50] The duties on foreign goods and the amount paid by the purchasers of monopolies may be estimated at $4,000,000; which, with the duty on gold and silver, makes the annual revenue $16,800,000. The civil list of the kingdom is $580,000, the military $7,189,200; these together amount to $7,760,200, which, deducted from the gross revenue of $16,700,000, leaves a clear revenue for the king from his Mexican dominions of $9,030,800. The money paid for the support of the clergy is not included in this estimate, as they receive their revenue through its own proper channel. The best paid officers under the govern-

[50] Humboldt, in his Personal Narrative, etc., p. xxii of the Philada. ed. of 1815, takes express exception to these statistics, in the following terms : " The numerous statistical data, which Mr. Pike has collected in a country of the language of which he was ignorant, are for the greater part very inaccurate. According to this author the mint of Mexico coins every year 50 millions of piastres in silver, and 14 millions in gold; while it is proved by the tables annually printed by order of the Court, and published in the Political Essay [of Humboldt and Bonpland], that, the year in which the produce of the mines was the most abundant, the coinage amounted only to 25,806,074 piastres in silver, and to 1,359,814 piastres in gold."

ment cost the king nothing in a direct line, yet the oppressive manner in which they pay themselves and impoverish the people would render it better policy to abolish their impositions and pay them out of the public treasury by a direct salary.

Return of Military Force in New Spain.

Provinces and Places.	Disciplined and Regular European Troops.			Regular Troops of the Country.			Militia with Regular Field Officers and under Pay.			Probable Armed Citizens.	
	Cavalry.	Artillery.	Infantry.	Cavalry.	Artillery.	Infantry.	Cavalry.	Artillery.	Infantry.	Fire-arms.	Bows, arrows, and lances.
Xalapa Ina. Vera Cruz...............	....	200	2000	2000	....	....	3000	....	1000	....	....
Vera Cruz and sea-ports..............	....	800	2000	....	....	....	600	....	2000	....	....
Mexico.............................	1000	....	....	....	....	1000	3400	1000	....	....	....
Provinces and viceroyalty............	....	....	....	....	....	....	....	....	....	15000	80000
New Mexico.........................	....	....	....	100	....	....	....	....	....	1000	4000
Biscay..............................	....	....	....	1100	....	....	....	....	....	5000	8000
Senora..............................	....	....	....	900	....	200	....	....	....	5000	3000
Sinaloa.............................	....	....	....	100	....	....	....	....	....	3000	6000
Cogquilla...........................	....	....	....	400	....	....	....	....	....	1000	2000
Texas...............................	....	....	....	488	....	....	....	....	....	500	1000
Total.......................	1000	1000	4000	5088	....	1200	7000	1000	3000	30500	109000

	Cavalry.	Artillery.	Infantry.
Regular troops, European.	1000	1000	4000
Regular troops, Mexican..	5088	....	1200
Trained militia..........	7000	1000	3000
Total.................	13088	2000	8200

Cavalry.... 13088
Artillery ... 2000
Infantry.... 8200

Total..... 23288 disciplined and effective force.
30500 undisciplined militia.
109000 bow, arrow, and lance men.
162788 total force.

The European troops are some of the choicest regiments from Spain; consequently, we may put them on the supposition that they are well disciplined, and officered by men of honor and science.

The regular troops of the kingdom who are in the viceroyalty, acting from the stimulant of ambition and envy, are supposed to be equal to their brethren from Europe. The militia, with the regular officers, are likewise good troops, but are not held in so high estimation as the other corps.

Those three corps, forming a body of 23,288 men, may be called the regular force of the kingdom, as the militia of 139,500 would, in my estimation, be of no more consequence against the regular troops of any civilized power than the ancient aborigines of the country were against the army of Cortes.

The particular observations which follow must be considered as applying to the troops of the internal provinces, unless it is stated to the contrary.

The appearance of the Spanish troops is certainly, at a distance, à la militaire ; their lances are fixed to the side of the saddle under the left thigh and slant about five feet above the horse. On the right the carabine is slung in a case to the front of the saddle, or pommel, crosswise, the breech to the right hand ; and on each side of the saddle, behind the rider, is a pistol ; below the breech of the carabine is slung the shield, which is made of sole leather three doubled, sewed together with thongs, with a band on the inside to slip the left arm through ; those of the privates are round, and are about two feet in diameter. The officers and non-commissioned officers have their shields oval, bending on both sides, in order to permit the arrow to glance, and they have in general the arms of Spain with Don Carlos IV. gilt on the outside, with various other devices, which add much to the elegance of their appearance on horseback, but are only calculated to be of service against savages who have no fire-arms. The dragoons of the viceroyalty do not make use of the lance or shield, but are armed, equipped, and clothed after the modern manner, as are also the dragoons of the eastern provinces. When they recently expected to be opposed to the American troops they were deprived of the lance and shield, and received the straight cutlass in their stead.

Their dress is a short blue coat, with red cape and cuffs, without facings, leather or blue cotton velvet small-clothes and waistcoat, the small-clothes always open at the knees, the wrapping-boot with the jack-boot and permanent spur

over it, a broad-brimmed, high-crowned wool hat, with a rib-
bon round it of various colors, generally received as a present
from some female, which they wear as a badge of the favor
of the fair sex and a mark of their gallantry.

Their horses are small and slender-limbed, but very active
and capable of enduring great fatigue. The equipments of
the horses are, to our idea, awkward ; but I believe them
superior to the English, and they have the advantage over
us in the skill of the rider, as well as in the quality of the
beast. Their bridles have a strong curb, which gives so
great a mechanical force to the bridle that I believe it almost
practicable with it to break the jaw of the beast. The saddle is made after the Persian mode, with a high projecting
pommel or, as anciently termed, bow, and is likewise raised
behind. This is merely the tree ; it is then covered by two
or three covers of carved leather and embroidered workman-
ship, some with gold and silver in a very superb manner.
The stirrups are of wood closed in front, carved generally
into the figure of a lion's head, or that of some other beast ;
they are very heavy, and to us present a very clumsy appearance. The horseman, seated on his horse, has a small
bag tied behind him, his blankets either under him, or lying
with his cloak between his body and the bow, which makes
him at his ease. Thus mounted, it is impossible for the
most vicious horse ever to dismount them. They will catch
another horse with a noose and hair rope, when both are
running nearly at full speed, with which they soon choke
down the beast of which they are in pursuit ; in short, they
are probably the most expert horsemen in the world.

At each post is a store, called the king's, where it was the
original intention of the government that the soldiers should
be supplied with provisions, clothing, arms, etc., at a cheap
rate ; but it being a post generally given to some young
officer to make his fortune, they are subject to great impositions. When a dragoon joins the service he receives from
the king five horses and two mules, and this number he is
always obliged to keep good from his own pocket ; but

when he is discharged, the horses and mules receive the discharge mark and become his private property. They engage for five or ten years, at the option of the soldier, but in the bounty there is a very material difference. It is extremely easy to keep up their corps, as a private dragoon considers himself upon an equality with most of the citizens and infinitely superior to the lower class, and not unfrequently you see men of considerable fortune marrying the daughters of sergeants and corporals.

The pay of the troops of New Spain varies with the locality, but may be averaged, in the internal provinces, as follows :

Colonel, $4,500 ; lieutenant-colonel, $4,000 ; major, $3,000 ; captain, $2,400 ; first lieutenant, $1,500 ; second lieutenant, $1,000 ; ensign, $800 ; sergeant, $350 ; corporal, $300 ; private, $288. With this pay they find their own clothes, provisions, arms, accouterments, etc., after the first equipments.

Corporal punishment is contrary to the Spanish ordinances. They punish by imprisonment, putting in the stocks, and death. As a remarkable instance of the discipline and regularity of conduct of those provincial troops, although marching with them and doing duty as it were for nearly four months, I never saw a man receive a blow or put under confinement for one hour. How impossible would it be to regulate the turbulent dispositions of the Americans with such treatment ! In making the foregoing remark I do not include officers, for I saw more rigorous treatment exercised toward some of them than was ever practiced in our army.

The discipline of their troops is very different from ours. As to tactics or military maneuvers, they are not held in much estimation ; for, during the whole of the time I was in the country, I never saw a corps of troops exercising as dragoons, but frequently marching by platoons, sections, etc., in garrison, where they serve as infantry with their carabines. In these maneuvers they are very deficient. On a march a detachment of cavalry generally encamp in a circle. They relieve their guards at night; as soon as they halt the new guard is formed on foot with their carabines, and then marched before the commandant's tent, where the commanding officer of the guard invokes the holy virgin three times; the commanding officer replies, "It is well." They then retire and mount their horses, and are told off, some to act as guard of the horses, as cavalry, others as guard of the camp, as infantry. The old guards are then paraded and relieved, and the new sentinels take post. Their sentinels are singing half the time, and it is no uncommon thing for them to quit their post to come to the fire, go for water, etc.—in fact, after the officer is in bed, frequently the whole guard comes in; yet I never knew any man punished for those breaches of military duty. Their mode of attack is by squadrons, on the different flanks of their enemies, but without regularity or concert, shouting, hallooing, and firing their carabines; after which, if they think themselves equal to the enemy, they charge with a pistol and then a lance. From my observation on their discipline I have no hesitation in declaring that I would not be afraid to march over a plain with 500 infantry and a proportionate allowance of horse artillery of the United States army, in the presence of 5,000 of these dragoons. Yet I do not presume to say that an army with that inferiority of numbers would do to oppose them, for they would cut off your supplies, and harass your march and camp, night and day, to such a degree as to oblige you in the end to surrender to them without ever having come to action. If, however, the event depended on one single engagement, it would eventuate with glory to the American arms. The conclusion must not be drawn that I consider they are more deficient in physical firmness than other nations, for we see the savages, 500 of whom on a plain fly before 50 bayonets, on other occasions brave danger and death in its most horrid shapes, with an undaunted fortitude never surpassed by the most disciplined and hardy veterans. It arises solely from the want of discipline and confidence in each other, as is always the case with undisciplined corps, unless stimulated by the godlike sentiment of love of country, of which these poor fellows know little. The traveling food of the dragoons in New Mexico consists of a very excellent species of wheat biscuit, and shaved meat well dried [charqui], with a vast quantity of red pepper [chile colorado], of which they make bouilli and then pour it on their broken biscuit, when the latter becomes soft and excellent eating.

Farther south they use large quantities of parched corn-meal and sugar [pinole], as practiced by our hunters, each dragoon having a small bag. In short, they live, when on command, on an allowance which our troops would conceive little better than starving, never, except at night, attempting to eat anything like a meal, but biting a piece of biscuit, or drinking some parched meal with sugar and water, during the day.

From the physical as well as moral properties of the inhabitants of New Spain, I do believe they are capable of being made the best troops in the world, possessing sobriety, enterprise, great physical force, docility, and a conception equally quick and penetrating.

The mode of promotion in the internal provinces is singular, but probably productive of good effects. Should a vacancy of first lieutenant offer in a company, the captain commanding nominates, with the senior second lieutenant, who by seniority would fill the vacancy, two other lieutenants to the general, giving his comments on all three. The general selects two for a nomination to the court, from whom is selected the fortunate candidate, whose commission is made out and forwarded. As the letters of nomination are always kept a secret, it is impossible for the young officers to say who is to blame if they are disappointed, and the fortunate one is in a direct way to thank the king only for the ultimate decision. And thus with superior grades to the colonel.

The king of Spain's ordinances for the government of his army are generally founded on justice and a high sense of honor. I could not get a set from any of the officers to take to my quarters, consequently my observations on them were extremely cursory. They provide that no old soldier shall ever be discharged the service, unless for infamous crimes. When a man has served with reputation for 15 years and continues, his pay is augmented; 20 years, he receives another augmentation; 27 years, he receives the brevet rank and pay of an ensign; and 32, a lieutenant, etc. Those circumstances are a great stimulant, although not one in a thousand arrives at the third period, when they are permitted to retire from the service with full pay and emoluments. All sons of captains, or of grades superior, are entitled to enter the king's schools as cadets, at the age of 12 years.

The property of any officer or soldier who is killed on the field of battle, or dies of his wounds, is not liable to be taken for debt, and is secured, as well as the king's pension, to the relatives of the deceased.

Courts-martial for the trial of commissioned officers must be formed of general officers; but this clause subjects the officers of the provinces to a great species of tyranny, for the commanding general has taken it upon himself to punish for all offenses not capital, and consequently according to his own judgment and prejudices, from which there is only an appeal to the king, and difficult it is indeed for the complaints of a subaltern to reach his majesty through the numerous crowd of sycophants who surround him, one-half of whom are probably in league with his oppressor. It likewise deprives an officer of the most sacred of all rights, that of being tried by his peers; for, should he be sent to Mexico or Europe for trial, it is possible he cannot take half the testimony which is necessary to complete his justification.

There is another principle defined by the ordinances, which has often been the cause of disputes in the service of the United States. The commandant of a post in the Spanish service, if barely a captain, receives no orders from a general, should one arrive at his post, unless that general should be superior in authority to the person who posted him ; for, says the ordinance, he is responsible to the king alone for his post.   That principle, according to my ideas, is very injurious to the country which adopts it.   For example, we will say that a post of great importance, containing immense military stores, is likely to fall into the hands of the enemy; an officer superior to the commandant receives the information, repairs to the post, and orders him immediately to evacuate it.   The commandant, feeling himself only responsible to the authority who placed him in that position, refuses to obey, and the magazines and place are lost.   The principle is also subversive of the very root of military subordination and discipline, where an inferior should in all cases obey a superior, who alone should be responsible for the effect arising from the execution of his orders.   It will readily be believed that, in my thus advocating implicit obedience to the orders of a superior, that I do not suppose the highest improbabilities or impossibilities, such as an order to turn your arms against the constituted authority of your country, or to be the ensign of his tyranny or the pander of his vices.   Those are cases where a man's reason must alone direct him, and are not —indeed, cannot be—subject to any human rule whatever.

Religion.   It forms a subject with which I am very imperfectly acquainted ; but, having made some inquiries and observations on the religion of the country, I will freely communicate them, fearful at the same time that I lay myself open to the severe criticism of persons who have in any degree applied themselves to the study of theology or the ritual of the catholic church.

The kingdom of New Spain is divided into four archbishoprics, viz.: Mexico, Guadalaxara, Durango, and St. Louis Potosi.   Under these again are the sub-bishoprics—deacons, curates, etc., all of whom are subject and accountable to their immediate chief for the districts committed to their charge, and the whole are again subject to the ordinances of the high court of inquisition held at the capital of Mexico, whence are fulminated the edicts of their censure against the heresies and impious doctrines of modern philosophy, both as to politics and religion. I am credibly informed that the influence of that tribunal is greater in his Catholic majesty's Mexican dominions than in any Catholic country in Europe or perhaps in the world. A few years since they condemned a man to the flames, for asserting and maintaining some doctrine which they deemed heretical; and a Jew who was imprudent enough to take the image of Christ on a cross, and put it under the sill of his door, saying privately he would make the dogs walk over their God. They likewise examine and condemn to the flames all books of a modern sentiment, either as to religion or politics, and excommunicate anyone in whose hands they may be found. I recollect to have seen a decree of theirs published in the Mexican gazettes, condemning a number of books, " as heretical and contrary to the sacred principles of the holy Catholic church, and the peace and durability of the government of his Catholic majesty." Amongst these were mentioned Helvetius on Man, J. J. Rousseau's works, Voltaire's, Mirabeau's, and a number of others of that description; even at so great a distance as Chihuahua a officer dared not take Pope's Essay on Man to his quarters, but used to come to mine to read it.

The salaries of the archbishops are superior to those of any officers in the kingdom; the bishop of Mexico's being estimated at $150,000 per annum, when the viceroy's is $80,000, with $50,000 allowed for his table, falling short of the bishop's $20,000.

Those incomes are raised entirely from the people, who pay no tax to the king, but give one-tenth of their yearly income to the clergy, besides the fees of confessions, bulls, burials, baptisms, marriages, and a thousand impositions which the corruption of priestcraft has introduced, and which have been kept up by their superstition and ignorance. Notwithstanding all this, the inferior clergy, who do all the slavery of the office, are liberal and well-informed men ; I scarcely saw one who was not in favor of a change of government. They are generally Creoles by birth, and always kept in subordinate grades, without the least shadow of a probability of rising to the superior dignities of the church. This has soured their minds to such a degree that I am confident in asserting that they will lead the van whenever the standard of independence is raised in that country.

Politics. It has often been a subject of discussion with politicians, in what manner a mother country should treat her distant and powerful colonies, in order to retain them longest in their subjection ; for the history of all nations and all ages has proved that no community of people separated from another by an immense ocean, feeling their power, strength, and independence, will remain long subject to the mother country, purely from the ties of consanguinity and similarity of habits, manners, and religion. Society itself having arisen from the mutual wants, fears, and imbecility of the infancy of human institutions, a large body of that society will remain no longer subject to another branch, at the immense distance of 1,000 leagues, than until they feel their maturity, and capability of providing for their own wants and their own defense. Therefore we may draw a conclusion that no political course of conduct whatever will eventually prevent the separation ; but there is a line of conduct which certainly must retard it in a great measure ; and prudence would dictate to the mother country the policy of giving way without a struggle to an event beyond her power to prevent.

The two great examples of English and Spanish America are before our eyes. England gave us liberty to pursue the dictates of our own judgment with respect to trade, education, and manners, by which means we increased in power, learning, and wealth, with a rapidity unknown in the annals of the world, and at the first attempt to infringe the rights which we had hitherto enjoyed, asserted that claim which nature and the locality of our situation gave us a right to demand and a power to defend.   Had Great Britain yielded to the storm with grace and dignity, she would have secured our gratitude, ancient prejudices, and affections in her favor; on the contrary, by a long and arduous conflict, the murder of thousands of our citizens, the destruction of our country, the profanation of our altars, and the violation of every right, divine and human, she implanted in the breast of the Americans an antipathy approaching nearly to horror, a desire of revenge almost hereditary; and destroyed the bonds of brotherhood which might have subsisted between the two countries.   It will take ages of just conduct from her to the United States to eradicate this.   Spain pursued a different line of conduct toward her Mexican dominions, which were settled by Europeans 60 years previous to any part of the United States, and might be termed a conquered kingdom, rather than the settlement of a savage country.   This country she has therefore bound up in all the ligatures of restrictions, monopolies, prohibitions, seclusions, and superstitions; and has so carefully secluded all light from bursting in on their ignorance, that they have vegetated like the acorns in the forest, until the towering branches have broken through the darkness of the wild which surrounded them and let in the light of heaven.   The approximation of the United States, with the gigantic strides of French ambition, have begun to arouse their dormant qualities, and to call into action the powers of their minds on the subject of their political situation.

An instance of their disposition for independence has been exhibited in their feeble attempts at a revolution on the 15th of January, 1624, under the viceroyalty of Don Diego Carrello Galves; the insurrection on the 8th of June, 1692; and more recently, in 1797, under the Count de Galves,[51] when they proclaimed him king of Mexico in the

---

[51] Bernardo Galvez y Gallardo, viceroy of Mexico from June 16th, 1785, until his death at Tacubaya, Nov. 30th, 1786. He was b. at Marcharavieja July 23d,

streets of the capital, and 130,000 souls were heard pro-
claiming, "Long live Galvez, king of Mexico!" It was
then only for him to have willed it, and the kingdom of
Mexico was lost to Charles IV. forever. But preferring his
loyalty to his ambition, he rode out attended by his guards
to the mob, with sword in hand, crying out, " Long live his
Catholic majesty, Charles IV.," and threatening to put to
instant death with his own hand any persons who refused
immediately to retire to their houses. This dispersed the
people. In another quarter of the kingdom an immense
number had also collected and proclaimed him king. He
sent 10,000 men against them, dispersed them, and had four
beheaded. Those firm measures saved the country at that
period, and for them he received the greatest honors from
the court of Spain ; but was poisoned a short time after, ful-
filling the maxim that " it is dangerous to serve a jealous
tyrant." For such always conceive that the same power
which stilled the ocean's rage can by its will raise the storm
into all the majesty of overwhelming fury. Thus, by taking his life, it relieved them from the dread of his influence
with the Mexicans.

England would naturally have been the power they would
have looked up to, in order to form an alliance to secure
their independence ; but the insatiable avarice and hauteur
exhibited by the English in their late descents at La Plate
[La Plata, in South America], with the disgrace of their
arms, has turned their views from that nation.

They therefore have turned their eyes toward the United
States, as to a sister of the same soil, in their vicinity—one
who has within her power ample resources of arms, ammunition, and even men, to assist in securing their independence, and who in that event would secure to herself the
almost exclusive trade of the richest country in the world for
centuries, and [the opportunity] to be her carriers as long
as the two nations exist. For Mexico, like China, will never

1746, was son of Mathias de Galvez, and had a very eminent career as
soldier and statesman.

become a nation of mariners, but will receive the ships of all the world into her ports, and give her bullion in exchange for the productions of their different countries. Then, what would not be the advantages the United States would reap from the event! Our numerous vessels would fill every port, and our vicinity would enable us to carry off at least nine-tenths of her commerce; even on the coast of the Pacific no European nation could vie with us. There would also be a brisk inland trade carried on with the Spanish provinces via Red river; and having a free entrance into all their ports, we should become their factors, agents, guardians—in short, their tutelar genius; as they fear but hate France and all French men and measures. It therefore remains for the government of the United States to decide whether, if Bonaparte should seize the crown of Spain, the States would hold out a helping hand to emancipate another portion of the western hemisphere from the bonds of European tyranny and oppression: or, by a different policy, suffer 6,000,000 people to become, in the hands of French intrigue, enterprise, and tactics, a scourge on our southwestern boundaries, which would oblige us to keep up a large and respectable military force, and continually lay us liable to a war on the weakest and most vulnerable part of our frontiers.

Twenty thousand auxiliaries from the United States under good officers, joined to the independents of the country, are at any time sufficient to create and effect the revolution. These troops can be raised and officered in the United States, but paid and supplied at the expense of Mexico. It would be requisite that not only the general commanding, but that every officer, down to the youngest ensign, should be impressed with the necessity of supporting a strict discipline, to prevent marauding, which should in some instances be punished with death, in order to convince the citizens that we come as their friends and protectors, not as their plunderers and tyrants. Also, the most sacred regard should be paid not to injure the institutions of their religion ; thereby showing them we have a proper respect for all things in any way connected with the worship of the Deity, at the same time that we permit every man to adore him agreeably to the dictates of his own judgment.

The details requisite for the equipment, organization, etc., of the corps, so as to adapt it to the locality of the country and the nature of the service, could be easily formed, but would be impertinent here.

Should an army of Americans ever march into the country, and be guided and governed by these maxims, they will only have to march from province to province in triumph, and be hailed by the united voices of grateful millions as their deliverers and saviors, whilst our national character resounds to the most distant nations of the earth.

WASHINGTON, April 12th, 1808.

CHAPTER V.

CORRESPONDENCE.[1]

Art. 1.   Letter, Pike to Allencaster.   (Orig. No. 8, pp. 69, 70.)

[TRANSLATION.]

SANTA FE, March 3d, 1807.

SIR :

On the arrival of your troops at my encampment, last month, under the command of Lieutenant Don Ignacio Saltelo and Mr. Bartholomew, they informed me that your Excellency had directed them to assure me that I should be escorted through your dominions to the source of Red river, as our being on the frontiers of your province gave cause to suspicion.   I conceived it more proper to comply with the request and repair to Santa Fe, in order to explain to your Excellency any circumstance which might appear extraordinary; but on my arrival here I am informed by

---

[1] The Appendix to Pt. 3 of the orig. ed. was the most extraordinary hotch-potch I ever saw in type—a lot of letters and other papers bundled together in no intelligible or imaginable order.   There being no evidence of design or purpose, the first step toward bringing an appearance of order out of this confusion must be taken by disregarding the original helter-skelter entirely, and by rearranging the various pieces of which this Appendix consisted as freely as if they were loose manuscripts accidentally disordered.   The documents with which we have to do were disarranged as follows :

No. 1. Pike's Observations on New Spain, the leading article, not numbered, making pp. 1–51, or more than half of the whole Appendix.   (This I have disposed of in the foregoing Chap. IV.)

No. 2, pp. 52, 53.   A fragmentary vocabulary of Mississippi place-names, having no connection with Pt. 3 of the book.   (This I have made Chap. IX., pp. 355, 356, of Pt. 1, where it belongs.)

No. 3, pp. 53–55.   A letter from Pike to Wilkinson.

No. 4, pp. 55–57.   A letter from Wilkinson to Pike.

No. 5, pp. 57–63.   A letter from Pike to Wilkinson.

No. 6, pp. 64–68.   A Congressional report, with accompanying documents, including matter relating to all three of Pike's expeditions, yet lacking one of

your Excellency that it is necessary for myself and troops to pass by Chihuahua in the province of Biscay, more than 200 leagues out of my route. I have demanded of your Excellency to know if we are to be considered as prisoners of war. You inform me that you do not consider us in that light. Not to embarrass your Excellency with many demands, I only request to receive it from under your hand, in what manner I am to consider myself, and the orders for my passing into the country; also, whether the expense of the voyage is to be considered as defrayed by the government of Spain or of the United States. Excuse my language, as I am not much accustomed to writing in French, but your Excellency's having no person who understands English obliges me to attempt that language.

I am, Sir, etc.,

[Signed] Z. M. PIKE.

the most important of the papers belonging to it (see No. 13, below). (All these I shall relegate to the following Chap. VI.)

No. 7, p. 69. A mere paragraph about a priest. (This I have simply interpolated in the text of the itinerary, Chap. II., pp. 603, 604—the place where it belongs.)

No. 8, pp. 69, 70. A letter from Pike to Allencaster.

No. 9, p. 70. A certificate from Allencaster to Pike.

No. 10, p. 71. A letter from Pike to Allencaster.

No. 11, p. 72. A letter from Pike to Salcedo.

No. 12, p. 72. A letter from Salcedo to Pike.

No. 13, pp. 73-77. The missing document which belongs to No. 6 (see above), being a brief sketch of Pike's Arkansaw Expedition and of his Mexican Tour, no date, no place, no addressee. (This, of course, goes with No. 6, in the following Chap. VI.)

No. 14, pp. 78, 79. A letter from Pike to Salcedo.

No. 15, pp. 79, 80. A letter from Salcedo to Pike.

No. 16, pp. 80-82. Inventory of papers seized by the Spanish authorities, with accompanying certificate.

No. 17, pp. 82, 83. A letter from Pike to Salcedo.

No. 18, pp. 83-85. A letter from Pike to Salcedo.

No. 19, pp. 86, 87. A letter from Salcedo to Wilkinson.

By eliminating from the above No. 1, No. 2, No. 6, No. 7, and No. 13, as above indicated, the residuum consists entirely of correspondence relating to the Mexican Tour, which is easily rearranged in the chronological order of the several letters, and thus forms the present Chapter V.

Art. 2.   Certificate, Allencaster to Pike.   (Orig. No. 9, p. 70.)

[TRANSLATION.]

SANTA FE, March 3d, 1807.

The first lieutenant of the Anglo-American troops, of the name of Z. Montgomery Pike, with the party of soldiers under his command, having been met with by the troops under my orders, at four days' journey from the seat of government, in this province, which is under my charge, he was required personally to appear, which he voluntarily did; and, complying with the orders of the commanding-general of these internal provinces, I bade the said lieutenant proceed on his march, with his party, equipped with horses, provisions, and equipage, under the charge of an officer and 60 men of our troops, with orders to introduce him to the said commanding-general in the town of Chihuahua.

I permitted said party to carry their arms and ammunition, being actuated by proper consideration, and in order to grant said Anglo-American's petition.

I certify the foregoing contents to be accurate.

[Signed]   JOACHIN RL. ALLENCASTER.

Art. 3.   Letter, Pike to Allencaster.   (Orig. No. 10, p. 71.)

ST. FERNANDEZ, March 7th, 1807.

SIR :

On my arrival at this village, and meeting with Dr. Robinson, he informed me he had acknowledged to Lieutenant Malgares to belong to my party.   As this acknowledgment, in fact, only interested himself, I am constrained to explain to your Excellency my reasons for having denied his connection with me.   He marched from St. Louis with my detachment as a volunteer, after having with much pain and solicitation obtained permission from the general for that purpose.   On our arrival on the Rio del Norte, then supposed to be Red river, he left the party in order to come to Santa Fe, with a view of obtaining information as to trade, and collecting some debts due to persons in the Illinois. On my being informed of his embarrassments, I conceived it would be adding to them to acknowledge his having accompanied a military party to the frontiers of the province, and conceived myself bound in honor and friendship to conceal it; but his scorning any longer the disguise he assumed has left me at liberty to make this acknowledgment to your Excellency, which I hope will sufficiently exculpate me in the opinion of every man of honor, and of the world, for having denied a fact when I conceived the safety of a friend, in a foreign country, was concerned in the event.

The above statement will be corroborated by General Wilkinson, and he will be reclaimed by the United States as a citizen, agreeably to our treaties with Spain regulating the intercourse, commerce, etc., between the two nations.

I felt disposed to enter into an expostulation with your Excellency, as to the deception practiced on me by the officers who came out with your invitation to enter the province; but will omit it, and only request that my sergeant and party may be ordered to follow with all possible dispatch, as he has all my astronomical instruments, and clothing, except what I now wear.

I have found Lieutenant Malgares to be what you stated, a gentleman and a soldier, and I sincerely wish the fortune of war may one day enable me to show the gentlemen of the Spanish army with whom I have had the honor of forming an acquaintance, with what gratitude I appreciate their friendship and politeness, and none more highly than your Excellency's.   With sincere, etc.,

[Signed]   Z. M. PIKE.

Art. 4. Letter, Pike to Salcedo. (Orig. No. 17, pp. 82, 83.)

CHIHUAHUA, April 4th, 1807.

SIR:

I hope your Excellency may not attribute it to presumption or a disposition to intrude, when I address you on a

subject foreign to my official duties, and on which I can only
speak as an individual ; for I should feel myself wanting in
humanity, and that attention which every man owes to his
fellow-creatures in distress, should I remain silent, more
especially when those who are compatriots, and some of
them former companions, are now in a strange country, lan-
guishing out their days far from their friends and relations,
with scarcely a dawn of hope remaining of ever again being
blessed with a view of their native homes.   It is scarcely necessary to add that I allude to the unfortunate companions
of [Captain Philip] Nolan, who, having entered the territories of his Catholic Majesty in a clandestine manner,
equally in violation of the treaties between the two governments, the laws of the United States, and those of Spain,
could not be reclaimed or noticed by their own country.
Yet, from every information I have received on the subject,
the men of the party were innocent, believing that Nolan
had passports from the Spanish governor to carry on the
traffic of horses.   I pretend not to justify the many irregularities of their conduct since [they have been] in the Spanish dominions ; but hope that these may be viewed with an
eye of clemency, as the men are most of them very illiterate,
possessing scarcely any part of an education.

David Fero was formerly a subaltern in a company of
infantry of the United States commanded by my father at
the time I served as a volunteer, but left the service, as I
have been informed, owing to some irregularities of conduct.
His having been once my companion entitles him at present
to my particular attention ; yet I will here mention to your
Excellency a circumstance which may appear, if known, in
an unfavorable light, viz.: About 15 days past I was informed Fero was in town, and that he desired to see me.   I
was extremely mortified at receiving the information, as I
conceived he must have left his post in a clandestine
manner ; yet I could not find it in my heart to refuse
the interview, which I gave, but determined at the same
time to inform you of the circumstance, conceiving that

you could not look on it as a matter of much criminality. [Note ¹¹, p. 660.]

But to conclude, I have to beg of your Excellency, if it be in your power and consistent with the line of conduct you conceive proper to pursue, to inform me if anything can be done toward restoring these poor fellows to their liberty, friends, and country ; and in a particular manner I intercede for Fero. If it is out of the power of the general to grant them leave to return to the United States, I beg to know if there be any objection to my taking letters to their fathers, wives, etc. I should not have addressed this letter to the general, had I not conceived the fate of those men to be at his disposal, as he had suffered one of them to join the service of his Catholic Majesty; neither do I request the honor of any other than a verbal reply, as I write in the character of an individual, not as an officer of the United States.

                    I am, Sir,
                         With high consideration,
                              Your humble, obedient servant,
                                   [Signed]   Z. M. PIKE.
          His Excellency,
     GENERAL NIMESIO SALCEDO.

----

*Art. 5.*²   *Letter, Pike to Salcedo.*   (*Orig. No. 11, p. 72.*)

                         CHIHUAHUA, April 6th, 1806 [*i. e.*, 1807].
SIR :

Having been for near the space of a year absent from my country, the probability of its yet being two or three months before I arrive in the territory of the United States, and the

---

² On this subject I can throw a little further light, as reflected from some documents which I find on file in the Archives of the War Department. The following letter is in a clerk's hand, with Pike's signature :

                         WASHINGTON CITY Feby. 10th. 1808.
SIR,

Being informed that the Chevalier Don Fownda, Charge des affaires from his Catholic Majesty to the United States, has forwarded to your office an account

necessity of passing through some hundred leagues of foreign territory, with the distressed situation of my troops, have induced me to apply to your Excellency for a necessary supply of money. Any arrangement which may be conceived proper for the remuneration I will cheerfully adopt, to pay it either to the Spanish consul at New Orleans, or the ambassador of his Catholic Majesty at Washington.

The sum which I conceive will answer the present purposes of myself and troops is $1,000, for which I will give such vouchers·as your Excellency may conceive proper.

I have the honor to assure your Excellency
of my high respect, and
to be your obedient servant,
[Signed]   Z. M. PIKE.

His Excellency,
GENERAL SALCEDO.

of expenses said to have occurred in consequence of my being *obliged* to pass thro' the internal provinces of New Spain, amounting to a sum, exceeding 21,000 Dollars.—I have thought it proper to state to you the following circumstances. On my being informed by the Govr. at Santa fé that I should be obliged to go to Chihuahua, I addressed a letter to him in which amongst other topics—I demanded to be advised if myself and troops were to be supported at the expense of the U States or his Catholic majesty—On this subject he was silent in his reply—but the day I marched from that city sent me a small sum of money, which I was informed was the subsistence money of my party to Chihuahua— at which place I refunded said sum to an officer of the Gov^{rs}. acquaintance & took his receipt for the same—at the seat of goverment I received $1000 and gave triplicate receipts making my goverment responsible for the same—and on the close of my correspondence with Gen^l. Salcedo was informed that I should be conveyed to our territories in the same manner I had been from New Mexico to Chihuahua—That was to find our own subsistence—but all other expences to be paid by the Spanish officers.—I left a requisition that my party in the rear might be allowed 2\frac{61}{100}$ per diem for their subsistence, and as this was for the support of our troops, when in their country, it remains to be decided by our Gov^t. whether they will refund the money—At the first place where I changed my escort on this side of Chihuahua, pay was demanded for the services of the mules, and horses, which I positively refused—but finding the officer was embarassed, I gave him a receipt agreable to the enclosed copy and date.—at^r S^t. Antonio I received $200 of Gov$_r$. Cordero—whereof the account stands enclosed—but I presume in justice no part should be allowed except the cash advanced, and the mens subsistence—as agreable to the Chevaliers own maxim

Art. 6.   Letter, Salcedo to Pike.   (Orig. No. 12, p. 72.)

[TRANSLATION.]

CHIHUAHUA, April 7th, 1807.

Acceding to the solicitation you have made in your letter of yesterday, that from the royal treasury of this place there should be delivered you one thousand dollars, which you say are necessary for the accommodation of the troops of the United States of America which you have under your charge, or whatsoever other sum you choose to demand, and that the government of the said United States shall

—" *the Goverment which unnecessarily produced the expenditures ought in justice to defray them* "—.

I have the honor to be,

Sir,

With high consideration

Your most obt. Servt.

[Signed]   Z. M. PIKE Captain

The Honable.   1st UStates Regt. Infy

JAMES MADISON,

Secy. Dept. State

The foregoing letter has two inclosures.   One is the following form of account :

" U. States to

the Spanish Govt.—   Dr.

7th. April 1807.   To cash furnished on receipt to Cap: Pike at Chihuahua, $1000

11th. June, 07.   To cash furnished Cap: Pike at St. Antonio, on receipt,   200

To a requisition for subsistence of my party in the rear at

2\frac{81}{100}$ from . . . . . . to . . . . ———

* To amount of five recepts worded in substance as

below—not exceeding   250

*————07. $

———————

I acknowledged to have been furnished by . . . . with . . . mules

. . . horses for the transport of my party and baggage from . . . . . . to

. . . . . .   The hire of said beasts to be hereafter adjusted between the Govt. of the U. States and that of his Cath. Majesty—

" (Signed) Z. PIKE.

" N. B.   The whole of those charges (the latter of which I by no means conceive the U States under any just obligation to discharge) cannot if my men have refund the said sum to the Señor Marquis de Cassa Yrujo, I have directed the formula of four corresponding and quadruplicate receipts for you to sign.

God preserve you many years.

[Signed] NIMESIO SALCEDO.

For the 1st Lieutenant,
    MONTGOMERY PIKE.

Art. 7. Letter, Salcedo to Wilkinson. (Orig. No. 19, pp. 86, 87.)

[TRANSLATION.]

CHIHUAHUA, April 8th, 1807.

EXCELLENT SIR :

On the 16th of February last, John Robinson appeared before the governor of New Mexico, saying that he was a Frenchman, an inhabitant of St. Louis, which place he left on the 15th of June last year, with the view of going to the country of the Pananas [Pawnees], to make recoveries [of certain debts]; that, having received information that his debtors had directed their steps to said province [of New Mexico], he had concluded to follow them, in company with 15 other persons, who went for the purpose of hunting on the rivers of Arcs,[3] Arkansaw, and Colorado (Red river); that in the neighboring mountains of the two last [named rivers] his company had left him, for which reason he saw himself under the necessity of proceeding to

recently left the country, amount to more than $2000.   1200 of which I only pledged the faith of the Gov^t. for— Pike "

The other one of the two inclosures is the following memorandum or indorsement of the State Department :

" The account against Pike inadmissible save the $1200 advanced him in Cash —and what may have been advanced to his men left in Mexico at the rate of 2\frac{81}{100}$ p. day—the Sum he asked for their subsistence— It appears to have been understood by Capt Pike that he was to find subsistence for himself & Party and that the Spanish Govert would meet the other expences of his Journey."

[3] Rivière au Bois d'Arc of the French, as we should say Bodark, Bowdark, or Bowwood r., meaning the Osage.   The reference is to the bois d'arc

the Yutas Indians [Utes], to whom he exposed his situation, and who accordingly agreed to conduct him [to Santa Fé].

On the 25th of the same month of February, at the distance of four days' march from the town of Santa Fe, and nine leagues west of its settlement, at the place called the Ojocaliente (Hot Spring), near the confluence of Rio Grande del Norte (Great North river), and that known under the name River [Rio] de los Conejos ([River] of Rabbits), a detachment of the garrison of said province of New Mexico met Montgomery Pike, first lieutenant of the infantry of the United States, with eight men of the said infantry; who, on being given to understand that he must be conducted to said town, consented to accompany them. It was then settled that two of his [Pike's] men should remain on the spot with half of his Catholic Majesty's detachment, to wait for six others [of Pike's men] who had not yet arrived; while he proceeded to the governor's, to whom he declared that his being in that neighborhood was owing solely to his having been lost, and having mistaken the Rio del Norte for the Colorado. But this [Spanish] officer, in compliance with the orders of his superior officer, forwarded the said first lieutenant [Pike], with the six men of the American army and the above mentioned John Robinson, to this capital.

They arrived here on the 2d instant, and said officer [Pike], on being presented to me, laid before me, in the same manner as he had done to the governor of Santa Fe, the papers relative to his mission, the correspondence he had carried on with your Excellency since it commenced, his journals, and note books.

Your Excellency is not ignorant of the repeated representations made by the king's minister in the United States, and by the Marquis of Cassa Calva while he was in

---

or bowwood, the Osage orange, *Maclura aurantiaca*, a well-known tree of the lower Mississippi valley, whose wood was formerly in great request for the purpose indicated in the vernacular name. It is very thorny, bears pruning well, and has come to be much cultivated for hedges. Its botanical affinities are with the mulberry.

Louisiana, summoning[4] the American government to carry
into effect any projects of extending its expeditions into
territories unquestionably belonging to his Majesty. You
must therefore, without any further observations or remarks
on my part, be satisfied that the documents contain evident,
unequivocal proofs that an offense of magnitude has been
committed against his Majesty, and that every individual of
this party ought to have been considered as prisoners on
the very spot. Notwithstanding such substantial and well-
grounded motives as would have warranted such a measure,
also wishing to give the widest latitude to the subsisting
system of harmony and good understanding, and, above all,
being finally persuaded that your Excellency would take such
steps as your judgment might suggest as best calculated
to prevent any bad consequences on the occasion, I have
concluded to keep in this general government all the papers
presented by Lieutenant Pike, and to give him and his
men full liberty to return to your Excellency, after having
treated them with attention, and offered them every assistance they stood in need of.

I am, without reserve, and beyond expression, your most
obedient, humble, respectful, and faithful servant, who
prayeth God may preserve your Excellency many years.

[Signed] SALCEDO.

GENERAL JAMES WILKINSON.

---

*Art. 8. Inventory and Certificate, Valasco and Walker to
Pike. (Orig. No. 16, pp. 80–82.)*

[TRANSLATION.]

Inventory of papers which [from] the lieutenant of infantry of the United States of America, Montgomery Pike, in
the superior government, and [by the] commandant general

---

[4] The meaning of the clause is clear, though it may not be obvious on its face,
owing to the use of " summoning " in a particular sense : compare Pike's use of
" summons " in Art. 11, p. 825. Agreeably with etymology, " summoning "
might be written *submonition*, on the model of *admonition;* the radical meaning of these two words is much the same, both conveying the idea of warning,

of the internal provinces of New Spain, [were taken] as belonging to a voyage which he executed from St. Louis up [of] the Illinois to the population [settlements] of New Mexico, to visit the Indian nations, and reconnoiter the country and intermediate rivers, as it appears his expedition was undertaken by provision of the government of the said United States and the orders of General Wilkinson :

1. Letter from General Wilkinson to Pike, dated 24th June, 1806.

2. Another from the same to Pike, 18th July, 1806.

3. Another from the same to the same officer, 19th July, 1806.

4. Another from the same to Pike, dated 6th August, 1806.

5. Letter from Lieutenant Wilkinson to his father, 27th October, 1806.

6. Another from the same to the same, 28th October, 1806.

7. Letter from Pike to General Wilkinson, 22d July, 1806.

8. Letter from Lieutenant Wilkinson to Lieutenant Pike, 26th October, 1806.

9. Proclamation of General Wilkinson, prohibiting any citizen of the United States from trading with the Indian nations without his permission or that of the government, dated 10th July, 1805.

10. A letter from Charles Junot, Agent for the Indians, to General Wilkinson, dated 10th July, 1806.

11. Notes of Lieutenant Pike on the voyage from New Mexico to Chihuahua, of four pages.

12. A rough manuscript [draught] of the Missouri and Osage rivers.

13. Letter from Sergeant Ballenger to General Wilkinson, without date.

---

with the implied force of enjoining, restraining, etc. Salcedo simply reminds Wilkinson that the Spanish government had warned the United States off those premises, and consequently that the latter should not have carried into effect any projects of, etc.

14. Letter from Lieutenant Wilkinson to Pike, without date.

15. A certificate, in the French language, of a certain Baptist Lamie [note⁴⁴, p. 388] found among those nations, specifying his motive for being there.

16. A bundle of papers, in the French language, which contain notes on the harangues and manifestoes which Lieutenant Pike delivered to the Indian nations.

17. A passport of Lieutenant Pike to the Indian Winapi-cane, a captain of the little Osage.

18. A small draught or map of the country which is situated between the Mississippi and Santa Fe, with a description of that town, and of having met with 3,000 Camanches.

19. A book, 8vo, manuscript, which contains the diary of Lieutenant Pike, from January, 1807, to the 2d March of the same year, when he arrived at Santa Fe, in 75 pages.

20. A book, 4to, manuscript, in pasteboard, with copies of letters to the secretary of war and General Wilkinson, and various observations relative to the commission of the lieutenant, in 67 pages.

21. A manuscript book, in folio, containing different plans of countries, etc., with a diary with rhumbs, distances, and worked observations and meteorological tables, which arose from a revisal of the voyage, by the said Lieutenant Pike, in 40 pages.

Don Francisco Valasco, first officer of the secretaries of the commandant-generalship of the internal provinces of New Spain, and Juan Pedro Walker Alferez,⁵ of the company of horse of the royal presidio of Janos:

We certify that the lieutenant of American infantry, Montgomery Pike, when presented to the commandant general of the before mentioned provinces, Don Nimesio Salcedo, likewise produced a small trunk which he brought with him ; * and that, in the presence of the undersigned,

---

⁵ *Sic*—but "Alferez" is not a part of Walker's name, being his rank in the Mexican cavalry : read "Walker, ensign of," etc.

* The want of candor exhibited in the certificate is manifest. It was an

[he] opened [it] himself, and took out different books and papers; when, having separated with his own hands, under our cognizance, all that appeared to be, or that he said was, private, or had no connection with the voyage, [he] delivered the remainder to the demand of the commandant general, which [papers delivered] were solely those comprehended in the foregoing inventory which we have formed, and for the verification of which we have signed these presents at Chihuahua, the 8th of April, 1807.

[Signed]   FRANCISCO VALASCO.
JUAN PEDRO WALKER.

Art. 9.   Letter, Pike to Salcedo.   (Orig. No. 14, pp. 78, 79.)

CHIHUAHUA, April 14th, 1807.
SIR :

On my marching from Santa Fe, Governor Allencaster informed me that my papers would be considered as a sacred deposit until my arrival at this place, when your Excellency would examine and take them into consideration.

When they were examined and taken possession of, I explained without disguise the nature and contents of each, conceiving that those only which had any relation to the object of my expedition could be interesting, and that merely a copy of the chart and a translation of the official papers would be taken. You must be conscious, Sir, that it was in my power to have secreted or destroyed every trace of my voyage and plans previous to my arrival at Chihuahua; but, resting satisfied that no rupture had taken place between his Catholic Majesty and the States I have the honor to serve, which would have been a justification for the seizure of my papers, I preferred leaving them *in statu quo*, to using that duplicity which in some degree always implicates the character of a military man.

Admitting the country which I explored to be contested

imbecile attempt to show that all my actions were voluntary, and that in the delivery of my papers there was no degree of constraint. [Orig. note.]

between the two governments, each would naturally wish to gain some information as to its geographical situation, in order that they might each form correct ideas as to what would be their mutual interests, founded on justice and the honor and dignity of the nation, in forming the line of demarcation. This was the view of the United States government in the expedition which I had the honor to command; the loss of the geographical sketches taken might be the occasion of a suspension of the final line of limits, and consequently the delay of an amicable adjustment of the differences now existing between the two governments.

Your Excellency may not have an intention of detaining my papers, which I had begun to suppose from your returning only part of them by Lieutenant Walker; in which case you will please to excuse this intrusion. But I will add that, if you have it in view to detain the papers, I request you will be pleased to examine them with particular care. You will find that there are letters from General Wilkinson, as well as his son, to me; also, from the latter to his father and mother; and others which, being by no means of a political nature, or at least not relative to the relations existing between the government of Spain and the United States, therefore can by no means be interesting to your Excellency. The book which contains my charts also contains part of the blotters of a voyage to the source of the Mississippi, which I presume cannot be interesting to the Spanish government.

But, to conclude, I have only to request of your Excellency to know if it is your intention to detain my papers now in your possession; and if so, that you may cause me to be furnished, or suffer me to take, a copy of them, and that I may receive a certificate from under your hand of the number, nature, etc., of the said papers, and the reasons for their seizure and detention, in order that my government may be enabled to make the proper application to the Spanish court for an explanation. My reason for applying to your Excellency so early on this subject is that, on the

arrival of my men who are still in the rear, I may be prepared to march in a short period of time; for, under the
present aspect of affairs, I feel conscious that I am as anxious to arrive on the territories of the United States as your
Excellency must be for me to quit the dominions of his
Catholic Majesty.

In all events, I hope you will believe me to be, with the
highest sentiments of personal respect,

Your most obedient servant,

[Signed] Z. M. PIKE.

His Excellency, Brigadier-general Don Nimesio Salcedo, Commanding-general of the Interior Provinces of the kingdom
of New Spain.

---

*Art. 10.   Letter, Pike to Wilkinson.   (Orig. No. 3,
pp. 53–55.)*

CHIHUAHUA, April 20th, 1807.

MY DEAR GENERAL :

Never did I sit down to address you with a heart so
oppressed with anxiety and mortification ; but knowing the
uncertainty which must exist as to the fate of myself and
party, I conceive it proper to attempt a communication,
although I think it extremely uncertain, owing to the
difficulty of the route, whether it may ever come to hand,
or at least, previous to my arrival at the territories of the
United States, owing to the various circumstances which
are not to be communicated in a letter.   I was detained in
the mountains of Mexico [*i. e.*, present State of Colorado]
until the month of January, and in February found myself
with eight of my party only, on the head branches of the
Rio [Grande] del Norte, which I then conceived to be the
sources of the Red river, our information making the latter
extend the whole distance between the former and the
Arkansaw, although its sources are some hundred miles
below either of the others.

Here I was encountered by two officers and 100 men,

who bore orders from the governor of New Mexico to cause me and my party to march to the capital of said province. His request was in the most polite style, and in fact the commanding officer assured me there was not the least constraint, but that his Excellency desired a confer- ence, and that I should be conducted by the most direct route to the navigable part of the Red river, whence I could immediately descend to Nachitoches. Although dubious of the faith of the invitation, and in a situation where I could have defended myself as long as my provision lasted, or until I might probably have escaped in the night; yet, knowing the pacific intentions of our government, and the particular instructions of my general as to my conduct in case of a rencounter with a body of Spanish troops, I conceived it most proper to comply with the demand and repair to Santa Fe; and, as the balance of my party who remained in the mountains were, many of them, invalids and not in a situation to be able to return, I conceived it most proper to leave orders for them to follow, accompa- nied by an escort of Spanish troops left for that purpose.

On my arrival in Santa Fe, his Excellency Governor Allencaster informed me it was necessary that I should immediately march to Chihuahua, Province of Biscay, in order to present myself to his Excellency, Commandant-gen- eral N. Salcedo, for further orders. This being so different from what I had been taught to expect, I demanded of Governor Allencaster, in a written communication, to know if I were to consider myself and party as prisoners of war. He replied in the negative. We marched on the following day, and arrived on the 2d instant at this place, whence, I am informed by the general, I shall march, on the arrival of the remainder of my party, for Nachitoches.

I must here acknowledge myself and party under infinite obligations to the friendship and politeness of all the Spanish officers, and in a particular manner to the commandant- general of those provinces.

Should the politics of our country make it necessary to

augment the army previous to my arrival, I hope the general will approve of my aspiring to a considerable promotion in the new corps. Should the line of demarcation be amicably adjusted between the United States and Spain, I hope to obtain the appointment of one of the commissioners, as I make bold to assert that, with respect to the arrangements necessary, and knowledge of the country through which the line must pass, I am better instructed than any other officer of my age in our service; and, if joined to a colleague of profound astronomical knowledge, we could surmount every difficulty. I likewise beg leave to suggest to your Excellency that I conceive the information I hold to be of considerable consequence in the determination of the line of limits, and that if it be not already determined I can throw considerable light on the subject.

I hope your Excellency will be pleased to forward orders for me to Nachitoches, informing me if I am to descend to [New] Orleans or proceed to the Federal City; and if the latter, permitting me to pass by Louisiana, in order to visit and arrange the affairs of my family, to whom I beg the favor of my general to communicate the certainty of the existence of myself and Dr. Robinson, who begs to be sincerely remembered to you.

Please to present my respectful compliments to your lady; and the doctor's and mine to James [Lieutenant Wilkinson], who, I hope, has long ere this arrived in safety.

The general will pardon the requests I have made of him, knowing the confidence of my heart in the paternal and soldierly esteem which he has manifested for him who has the honor to be,

With every sentiment of esteem,
Respect, and high consideration,
Dear General,
Your obedient humble servant,
[Signed]   Z. M. PIKE.

His Excellency,
GENERAL WILKINSON.

Art. 11. Letter, Salcedo to Pike.   (Orig. No. 15, pp. 79, 80.)
[TRANSLATION.]

CHIHUAHUA, April 23d, 1807.

Of the papers connected with the expedition which by orders of the United States government you have made from the St. Louis of the Illinois unto the settlements of New Mexico, and which you yourself* separated from those [others] which you brought here and put into my hands the day you arrived in this town, there have been formed an inventory, and a certificate respecting each of them accompanying it, to you, and in the office, the 17th current, for the purpose therein expressed, the judgment on which remains for the decision of the king, my lord, and shall be reported in the secret archives of this captain-generalcy. Meditating that you have indicated, in your official summons to this government, the greatest desire to arrive at the territories of the United States, [I] have resolved that you prepare to continue your voyage in two or three days, in consequence of which the arrangements necessary shall be made, such as you, with the people of your expedition, have experienced until your arrival at this place.

God preserve you many years.
[Signed]   NIMESIO SALCEDO.

MONTGOMERY PIKE, 1st Lieutenant of Infantry.

Art. 12. Letter, Wilkinson to Pike. (Orig. No. 4, pp. 55–57.)

NEW ORLEANS, May 20th, 1807.

DEAR SIR :

After having counted you among the dead, I was most agreeably surprised to find, by a letter from General Salcedo, received a few days since, that you were in his possession, and that he proposed sending you, with your party, to our frontier post.   I lament that you should lose

* See my account of the seizure of my papers, April 1st, 1807.   [Orig. note. Read Apr. 2d, and see p. 658.]

your papers, but shall rely much on your memory. Although it was unfortunate that you should have headed Red river, and missed the object of your enterprise, yet I promise myself that the route over which you have passed will afford some interesting scenes, as well to the statesman as the philosopher.

You will hear of the scenes in which I have been engaged, and may be informed that the traitors whose infamous designs against the constitution and government of our country I have detected, exposed, and destroyed, are vainly attempting to explain their own conduct by inculpating me. Among other devices, they have asserted that your and Lieutenant Wilkinson's enterprise was a premeditated co-operation with [Aaron] Burr. Being on the wing for Richmond, in Virginia, to confront the arch-traitor and his host of advocates, I have not leisure to commune with you as amply as I could desire. Let it then suffice for me to say to you, that of the information you have acquired, and the observations you have made, you must be cautious, extremely cautious, how you breathe a word; because publicity may excite a spirit of adventure adverse to the interests of our government, or injurious to the maturation of those plans which may hereafter be found 'necessary and justifiable by the government.

I leave Colonel Cushing[6] in command of the district, with plenary powers, and have informed him that you have leave to repair to St. Louis by the most direct route, the moment you have communicated to me in duplicate the

[6] Thomas Humphrey Cushing of Massachusetts, a captain in the Continental Army, became a captain of the 2d Infantry, Mar. 4th, 1791; he was arranged to the second sub-Legion Sept. 4th, 1792 ; promoted to be a major in the first sub-Legion Mar. 3d, 1793, and assigned to the 1st Infantry Nov. 1st, 1796 ; he acted as inspector of the army from Feb. 27th, 1797, to May 22d, 1798, and became lieutenant-colonel of the 2d Infantry April 1st, 1802 ; he acted as adjutant and inspector-general from Mar. 26th, 1802, to May 9th, 1807, was promoted to the colonelcy of the 2d Infantry Sept. 7th, 1805, to a brigadier-generalship July 2d, 1812, and honorably discharged June 15th, 1815 ; he died Oct. 19th, 1822.

result of your travels, voluntary and involuntary, in relation to clime, country, population, arts, agriculture, routes, distances, and military defense. The president will be impatient to have whatever you have acquired ; to the detailed account a sketch must be added, and the original and duplicate addressed to me at the city of Washington, with the least possible delay. You may make up your report at Natchitoches, and proceed thence to the Wascheta [Washita] and thence to the Arkansaw, or you may descend to Fort Adams, and proceed thence to St. Louis by the most convenient route. Colonel Cushing, whom I leave in command of the district, has my orders in your favor, and will give you every indulgence ; but as an expedition is now in motion up the Arkansaw, to explore it to its source and further northwest, it is highly important that you should, either in person or by two or three confidential men, send forward to the Arkansaw every information which you may deem essential to the success of the enterprise. A Mr. Freemen [Thomas Freeman], under the chief direction of Mr. [William] Dunbar of Natchez, has control of this operation. The escort, which consists of 35 select non-commissioned officers and privates, is commanded by Lieutenant Wilkinson, seconded by Lieutenant T[homas]. A. Smith. This detachment, with two boats suitably equipped, will reach Natchez in eight or ten days from the present, and will proceed with all possible dispatch. You will address your communications to Lieutenant Wilkinson, who, after many hardships and difficulties, reached this place about the 1st of March. He has finished a pretty good traverse of the river, and his journal is interesting. I think the present party will winter near the Arkansaw Osages, about 600 miles by the river from the Mississippi.

The president mentioned you and your explorations to the source of the great river, in his address to Congress, in handsome terms. I am convinced he has a proper sense of your merits, and will do you ample justice. I offer you leave to go immediately to your family, because I apprehend it will be most desirable; yet, if you possess in your information aught which you may desire to communicate in person, you are at liberty to proceed, by the shortest route, to the seat of government, near which you will find me, if alive, three or four months hence.

I pray you to attend particularly to the injunctions of this hasty letter, and to believe me, whilst I am your general,

Your friend,
[Signed]   JAMES WILKINSON.

CAPTAIN PIKE, U. S. Army.

Art. 13.   Letter, Pike to Wilkinson. (Orig. No. 5, pp. 57–63.)

NACHITOCHES, July 5th, 1807.

DEAR GENERAL :

Once more I address you from the land of freedom and under the banners of our country.   Your esteemed favor of the 20th of May now lies before me, in which I recognize the sentiments of my general and friend, and will endeavor, as far as my limited abilities permit, to do justice to the spirit of your instructions.

I must premise to your Excellency that my letter of the 20th of April, dated at Chihuahua, went through a perusal by General Salcedo, previous to his forwarding it.

That letter stated the mode of my being brought into Santa Fe, and I will now state to your Excellency the proceedings on the subject of my papers.   I will omit the hauteur of the reception given me by Governor Allencaster, for a more particular communication; it changed afterward to extreme politeness.   Being under no restrictions previous to arriving at Santa Fe, I had secreted all my papers which I conceived it necessary to preserve, leaving my book of charts, my orders, and such others as should induce the governor to know me in my proper character, and prevent his suspicions being excited to a stricter inquiry.

On examining my commission, orders, etc., he told me to

remove my trunk to my own quarters, and that on the morrow he would converse with me on the subject. I had
caused my men to secrete my papers about their bodies, conceiving this safer than [leaving them] in the baggage ; but
in the evening, finding the ladies of Santa Fe were treating
them to wine, etc., I was apprehensive their intemperance
might discover the secret, and took them from all but one,
who had my journal in full, but who could not be found,
and put them in my trunk, conceiving that the inspection
was over. But next morning an officer, with two men,
waited on me and informed me that he had come for me to
visit the governor, and brought these two men to take up
my trunk. I immediately perceived I was outgeneraled.
On my arrival at the governor's house, his Excellency demanded if I had the key. My reply was in the affirmative ;
when he observed, " It is well " ; my trunk should be a
sacred deposit in the charge of the officer who would escort
me to Chihuahua, for which place I marched after dinner,
under the escort of Lieutenant Don Facundo Malgares and
65 men. His character I beg leave to introduce to the
attention of your Excellency as that of a European possessing all the high sense of honor which formerly so evidently
distinguished his nation, the commandant of the 600 troops
who made the expedition to the Pawnees, an officer of distinguished merit, who in his mode of living fully justified
the pomp and style of his actions, who outshines many of
the governors of provinces, and whom in my future reports
I shall have frequent occasion to quote. He observed to
me : " The governor informs me, Sir, your trunk is under
restrictions ; but your word of honor as a soldier that no
papers shall be taken out, and you have free ingress, as
usual." I gave it, and I presume it is scarcely necessary to
add it was religiously adhered to.

On our arrival at Chihuahua the general demanded my
trunk, and on its being opened and the papers laid on the
table, he took them in hand one by one and demanded what
was the purport of each, which truth obliged me to declare ;

had I been disposed to equivocate, Ensign Walker, of his Catholic Majesty's service, who stood present and assisted in the examination, could have immediately detected the fraud; also, his Excellency understands sufficient of the English language to discover the general purport of any paper.

After going through them in this manner and separating them into two piles, he observed to me: "You will leave those papers for my inspection, and in the meanwhile, in concert with Ensign Walker, who will give the Spanish translation, you will give me a detailed account of your route, views, destination, etc., during which time I will examine the papers now before me." With this I complied, flattering myself that it was his intention to return me my papers, by his demanding a sketch; also, so great was my confidence in the all-protecting name of my country, I conceived it was a greater step than the general would venture to take, to seize on the papers. But when I had finished the proposed sketch and presented it, and found a still further delay, I addressed the general on the subject. After a few days, some were returned, but I was officially informed that the remaining papers had been seized, but would be kept in the secret cabinet of that captain-generalship until the pleasure of his Catholic Majesty should be known. At the same time I was presented with a certificate specifying the number and contents of those detained, and adding that they were assorted by my own hand, and voluntarily. This assertion was so contrary to truth, honor, or the line of conduct a general should have pursued with a young gentleman, that I took the liberty of telling one of the officers who signed said certificate that it was incorrect. But as Sergeant Meek was still in the rear with nearly all my baggage, I took care to give him orders that none of said baggage should be opened, except by force; which will evince that, although I preferred acting like a gentleman to obliging General Salcedo to resort to rough treatment, yet that it was not a volunteer surrender of my papers.

But the general will please to recollect that my journals were saved at Santa Fe, were continued, and are entire to this post ; for the fortunate circumstance of the doctor's having copied my courses and distances through all the route, except an excursion we made to the source of the river La Platte, unto the Spanish territories, preserved them. These will enable me to exhibit a correct chart of the route, although not so minute as the one seized on, which was plotted daily by the eye and angular observations.   Thus the only essential papers lost were my astronomical observations and meteorological tables, and a book containing remarks on minerals, plants, etc., with the manners, population, customs, etc., of the savages.   But the results of the former were in part communicated, and probably my journal may supply part of the balance, while our memories will make the loss of the latter of but little consequence. While in the Spanish territories I was forbidden the use of pen and paper, notwithstanding which I kept a journal, made meteorological observations, and took courses and distances from the time I entered their country until my arrival at this place; all of which I brought safe off in the men's guns, where I finally secreted my papers without detection.

From our unremitting attention day and night, the immense territory they led us through, and the long time we were in their country, I make bold to assert I have been able to collect a correct account of their military force, regular and irregular; also, important and interesting information on geographical situations, political sentiments and dispositions of the people of every class, manners, arts, resources, riches, revenues, situation, value, and productions of their mines, etc.; also, the annual revenues paid to Bonaparte.   Had we possessed as great a knowledge of the Spanish language when we entered the territories as when we left them, our information would have been nearly as complete as I could wish it, if sent expressly for the purpose of acquiring it, by the open authority of his Majesty.   But the French language, in which my communications were sometimes made, was greatly beneficial.

By the sergeant, who is still in the rear and was never suffered to join me, as General Salcedo conceived he would probably procure some information from him, which he could not if [the sergeant were] immediately under my orders, I expect many other communications of importance from many individuals who promised to forward them by him. But I presume the general has found himself in error; as I perceive by a letter from him to Governor Cordero, the sergeant killed one of his [7] men, in consequence of some improper conduct, and the general accuses him of great intractability, as he is pleased to term it.

From the foregoing statement your Excellency will observe that I yet possess immense matter, the results of one year's travel in countries, desert and populated, which have both been long the subject of curiosity to the philosopher, the anxious desires of the miser, and the waking thoughts and sleeping dreams of the man of ambitious and aspiring soul—results which, in our present critical situation, I do conceive to be immensely important, and which open a scene for the generosity and aggrandizement of our country, with a wide and splendid field for harvests of honor for individuals. But my papers are in a mutilated state, from the absolute necessity I was under to write on small pieces in the Spanish country; also, from being injured in the gunbarrels, some of which I filed off three times to take out the papers. These circumstances make it necessary, in the first

[7] It will be observed that Pike's syntax leaves the personal pronoun equivocal. We naturally read that Sergeant Meek killed one of his own men, *i. e.*, a man of Pike's party; and I have been more than once summonsed, during my editorial function, to say who this man was. But there is no record that I can discover, and no other intimation than the above ambiguous clause, that any man of Pike's or Meek's party was killed by Meek. On the contrary, Pike's final word about his men accounts for every one of them: see p. 855, and note there. In the absence of any further evidence, we must understand that Sergeant Meek killed one of General Salcedo's men; and if so, might easily be accused of "great intractability."

place, to take a rough copy as they stand; then it will be necessary to assort the matter, as military, political, moral, mercantile, meteorological, agricultural, etc., all now forming an undigested mass. Then, Sir, the combining each, the plotting, etc., would take up a time of considerable extent for one man; and to make duplicates after they are in order could not be done in three months. The general may recollect it was nearly that period before my reports were completed last year, although I was assisted by Mr. [Antoine] Nau and the sergeant-major, and sometimes by Lieutenants [James B.] Wilkinson and [Henry Richard] Graham.[8] Also, with respect to the Spanish country, I must know the extent of the objects in view, in order to embrace those points in my reports; and further, my dear sir, my health is by no means the most perfect, my eyes being so extremely weak that it is almost impossible for me to continue for one hour with the pen in my hand, and by that time I have a considerable pain in my breast.

From those circumstances my general will perceive the almost impracticability of my complying with the contents of his letter as to duplicate reports from this place; but I shall immediately commence the business of arranging and digesting my papers, and will proceed with the labor with every perseverance my situation will permit until the arrival of my sergeant and the balance of the party, should they not be retarded more than 20 days, when I shall proceed immediately to St. Louis, and thence through Kentucky, Virginia, etc., to the Federal City, making no unnecessary delay, and during the whole of the route prosecuting my business at every leisure moment. When at Washington, I flatter myself with your assistance and advice. As I propose taking courses, distances, etc., hence to St. Louis, it will

[8] Of Virginia, appointed from Kentucky a second lieutenant of the 3d Infantry Feb. 16th, 1801, and transferred to the 2d Infantry Apr. 1st, 1802: became a first lieutenant of the same Dec. 20th, 1803, and resigned Jan. 31st, 1808; was made a captain of the first Rifles Mar. 8th, 1809, and appointed major Aug. 12th, 1814, but the appointment was negatived by the Senate Dec. 10th, 1814; he was honorably discharged June 15th, 1815, and died in 1819.

be making the tour of the greatest part of Louisiana, crossing the main rivers at different points. I am certain that from the survey of the Missouri by Captains Lewis and Clark, my own of the Mississippi, Lieutenant Wilkinson's of the lower Arkansaw, which river I surveyed to its sources, and Mr. Dunbar's of Red river, can be formed the completest survey of Louisiana ever yet taken.

As to the instruments I had with me I wish the general to inform me in what light they stood, as most of them were ruined in the mountains by the falling of the horses from precipices, etc., and I left an order at Chihuahua for the sergeant to sell them at a certain price, as the addition of a land carriage of 500 leagues would not add to their benefit.[9] Baroney, if alive, is with my sergeant; he has proved a noble fellow in his line, and I beg liberty to recommend him to some appointment near the Kans, should any offer. I must further add the following anecdote of my men, in whose breasts lay the whole secret of my papers, and whom I frequently, when in the Spanish territories, was obliged to punish severely for outrages committed in a state of intoxication, yet who never once offered, or showed a disposition to discover it. It is certain they knew instant death would follow; still, their fidelity to their trust is remarkable. I have charged them as to communications, and shall dispose of them in such a manner as not to put it in their power to give things much publicity.

Dr. Robinson has accompanied me the whole route, is still with me, and I take pleasure in acknowledging I have received important services from him, as my companion in dangers and hardships, counselor in difficulties, and one to whose chemical, botanical, and mineralogical knowledge the expedition is greatly indebted—in short, Sir, he is a young gentleman of talents, honor, and perseverance, possessing, in my humble opinion, a military turn of mind, and

---

[9] That is, Captain Pike wishes to know how he is to account for instruments which were damaged, or which he had ordered to be sold, to prevent further injury on a long march.

would enter, I believe, in case of an augmentation of the army, if he could obtain a rank above a subaltern.

I hope the general will be pleased to have my copies forwarded by Lieutenant Wilkinson, so that I can command the use of them at Washington; also all my letters written him during the expedition, as they contain information I wish to refer to, and the copies were seized. Dr. [John] Sibley has informed me that the expedition up the Arkansaw is suspended, which supersedes the necessity of my sending the express ordered.

I congratulate the general on the safe arrival of Lieutenant Wilkinson, and am sorry to hear of the difficulties he encountered. I have been obliged to draw money of the Spanish government, which I have to pay to their ambassador at Washington. I supported those of my men who were with me all the time in the Spanish country. Being separated from my baggage and never permitted to have it join me, and having been presented to the commandant-general in a blanket cappot,[10] I was under the necessity of going to very considerable expense to support what I considered not only my own honor, but the dignity of our army. This, when a captain's pay is $2,400 per annum, was a ruinous thing to my finances; but I hope it may be taken into due consideration.

After making myself pretty perfect in the French language, I have obtained such a knowledge of the Spanish as to make me confident in asserting, in three or four years I will with ease make myself sufficiently master of the latter, Italian, and Portuguese, to read them all, and speak and write Spanish. The doctor has even exceeded me in that point. I mention this to the general, as I know the interest he takes in the improvement of his military protégé.

[10] That is, F. *capote*, some sort of surtout, overcoat, or cloak, constantly confounded with F. *capot*, meaning hood. Among the Canadian voyageurs and other French in America, *capote* was the most general name of any such outer garment. It constantly occurs, for example, in annals of the fur-trade of the Northwest, capotes being made of several regulation sizes and styles, for barter with the Indians, as well as for wear of the men of the N. W. Company.

We heard in the Spanish dominions of the convulsions of the western country, originating in Mr. Burr's plans, and that you were implicated; sometimes that you were arrested, sometimes superseded, etc. Those reports, although I never credited them, gave me great unhappiness, as I conceived that the shafts of calumny were aimed at your fame and honor, in a foreign country where these had hitherto stood high and been revered and respected by every class. At St. Antonio Colonel Cordero informed me of the truth of the statement [*i. e.*, falsity of those reports], which took a load from my breast and made me comparatively happy ; I hope ere long the villainy will be unmasked, and malignity and slander hide their heads. The before mentioned gentleman sent you by me a box of Spanish chocolate, which I shall forward to Colonel Cushing. Governor Herrara said the maliciousness of the world was such as to forbid his writing, but begged to be sincerely remembered to you. A letter addressed to me at Cincinnatti, Ohio, may possibly reach me on my route, when I hope to receive your approbation of my conduct. Many letters written to me, addressed to this place, have been secreted or destroyed ; possibly the general can give me a hint on the subject.

Those ideas have made a deep impression on my mind, and did not an all-ruling passion sway me irresistibly to the profession of arms and the paths of military glory, I would long since have resigned my sword for the rural cot, where peace, health, and content would at least be our inmates, should not our brows be crowned with laurel.

I must now conclude, as this letter has far exceeded the bounds proposed when commenced ; but the effusions of my heart on its contents are such that I could not limit them to a more contracted space. Excuse my scrawl, as I am entirely out of practice, but believe me to be,

Dear General,

With high respect and esteem,

Your obedient servant,

GENERAL WILKINSON.   [Signed]   Z. M. PIKE, Captain.

Art. 14.   Letter, Pike to Salcedo.   (Orig. No. 18, pp. 83-85.)

NATCHITOCHES, August 20th, 1807.

SIR :

Previous to my departure from Chihuahua, we had entered so fully into the subject of the seizure of my papers, that I should never have made another appeal until I made one through our government to the ambassador of his Catholic Majesty, had I not received orders to that effect ; it not being known, at the time those instructions were given, that the propriety of the seizure had been contested between your Excellency and myself.   But as you have now had time fully to reconsider the business, it may not appear in the same light that it did when I had the honor to address you before.   Your Excellency may be induced to conceive that the measure of seizing my notes, plans, meteorological and astronomical observations, etc., for parts of the Mississippi, Missouri, Osage, Kans, and Arkansaw rivers—waters acknowledged by the Spanish government to be within the known territories of the United States—may not be justifiable.   Whatever may be your opinion on those subjects, I am at an entire loss to conceive how, and upon what principle, you could involve in that seizure letters from individuals to individuals, the contents of which could in no wise be interesting to the Spanish government.

I have therefore once more to appeal to your Excellency, with the hope that the time you have had for deliberation may induce you to conceive it proper, and but an act of justice, to deliver up the papers seized at Chihuahua ; and hope your Excellency will have the goodness to address them to me in a packet, to the care of the commanding officer of this place.

If the continuation of an amicable understanding between the two nations be an object of estimation in the mind of your Excellency, the final demarcation of limits must be considered as the first great step to be taken toward its accomplishment.   To enable my government to form a cor-

rect idea on that subject, it was requisite they should be
well acquainted with the geographical situation of the heads
of the Arkansaw and Red rivers.   The former part of this
[requirement] I had accomplished, and could with all ease
have carried the remaining part of that object into execution, after discovering my mistake of the Rio del Norte for
the Red river, had I been permitted by the governor of
New Mexico.   Instead of which, I was hurried through the
country to Chihuahua, without having time given for the
absent part of my party and baggage to join me; by which
means I was obliged to appear in a garb and manner
entirely incompatible with the rank I have the honor to
hold, and in some degree an indignity [was thus offered] to
the country whose commission I bear.   To add to my
mortification, I was then deprived of the information I had
obtained at the risk of our lives, and the suffering of unknown miseries.   The information contained in my notes
was not only of a geographical nature, but also such as
would enable the executive of the United States to take
some steps to ameliorate the barbarous state of various
savage tribes whom I visited; and, I may be permitted to
add, would have added in some small degree to the acquire-
ment of science, which is for the general benefit of makind.

When I left Chihuahua, I was informed that my sergeant
and party were detained near the place, in order that they
should not be permitted to join me, [and to the end] that
by a separate examination they might be intimidated to
make a declaration to justify the conduct observed toward
us.   This I am conscious must have failed; but I am at an
entire loss to conceive why they should have been detained
until this time, when your Excellency assured me they
should follow immediately.   Their detention has been of
considerable private injury to myself, and an insult to my
government.

When I marched from Chihuahua, your Excellency
officially informed me that everything had been prepared for
my transport to our lines.   I was much surprised to have to

pay for the hire of horses, etc., demanded of me at the first place where we changed our escorts, as I neither conceived it just that I should pay for an involuntary tour I had taken through your territories, nor was I prepared to do it; but as your officers were responsible, and gave their receipts for the transport, and from the orders received by Captain Viana at Nacogdoches, I was obliged to hire beasts to take me to Natchitoches, although an escort of your troops were furnished. [See note ², p. 814].

I here with the greatest pleasure embrace the opportunity of acknowledging the polite treatment I received from your officers in general on my route, but in particular from Colonels Cordero and Herrara, Captains Barelo and Viana, and Lieutenant Malgares ; to all of whom it would be my greatest pleasure to have it in my power to return the compliment.

Will your Excellency do me the honor to present my high respects to your lady, and my compliments to Mr. Truxillo and Father Rocus.

I am, Sir,

      With the most profound consideration,

              Your obedient servant,

          [Signed]   Z. M. PIKE, Captain.

His Excellency,
GOVERNOR SALCEDO.

CHAPTER VI.

CONGRESSIONAL REPORT AND ACCOMPANYING DOCUMENTS.[1]

(*Orig. No. 6, pp. 64–68, and No. 13, pp. 73–77.*)

The committee of the House of Representatives of the Congress of the United States, to whom was referred the resolution to inquire whether any, and if any, what compensation ought to be made to Captain Zebulon M. Pike, and his companions, for their services in exploring the Mississippi river, in their late expedition to the sources of the Osage, Arkansaw and La Platte rivers, and in their tour through New Spain, report :

That it appears by the documents accompanying this report, that the objects of each of the exploring expeditions, together with the instructions for executing them, were communicated to and approved by the president of the United States; that the conduct of Captain Pike, in each of the expeditions, also met with the approbation of the president, and that the information obtained and communicated to the executive on the subjects of his instructions, and particularly in relation to the source of the

[1] This chapter, which appears to be a number of disjointed pieces, whose connection is not obvious, is really all of a part, being a certain Congressional matter. It is easily traced to its source in American State Papers, as the set of documents which Pike brought to bear on Congress for legislative action in his case, when he was trying to secure some appropriation to recompense himself and his companions for what they had undergone and accomplished during his two expeditions. Barring the way in which it was botched in this book, Nos. 6 and 13 are substantially the same as Doc. No. 259 of the 2d Session of the 10th Congress, being the report of a committee laid before the Ho. Reps. Dec. 16th, 1808, with accompanying papers, and as such will be found printed in American State Papers, folio, Washington, Gales and Seaton, 1834, pp. 942–944. The

Mississippi and the natives in that quarter, and the country generally, as well on the Upper Mississippi as that between the Arkansaw and the Missouri, and on the borders of the latter extensive river to its source, and the country adjacent, is highly interesting in a political, geographical, and historical view; and that although no special encouragement was given to the individuals who performed these laborious and dangerous expeditions, yet it was but reasonable for them, should they fortunately succeed in the objects, to expect some reward from government; that the zeal, perseverance, and intelligence of Captain Pike, as commander, have been meritorious, and the conduct of the individuals generally who composed the parties respectively, has been faithful, and the exertions arduous. The committee therefore are of opinion that compensation ought to be made by law to Captain Pike and his companions.

same volume contains, on p. 719, Doc. No. 248 of the 1st Session of the 10th Congress, being a previous report of a committee, communicated by John Montgomery, chairman, to the Ho. Reps., Mar. 10th, 1808. The same volume also contains, on p. 463, Doc. No. 212 of the 2d Session of the 9th Congress, a Report on Exploration of Western Waters, communicated by Mr. Alston to the Ho. Reps., Dec. 22d, 1806, mentioning Lewis and Clark, Pike, and Freeman, and recommending an annual appropriation for the purpose of such explorations. But none of these bills passed or became a law, though in Pike's own case they were, as we see, entirely favorable to his claim for extra remuneration. The case was reopened by Pike's widow, many years after his death; but nothing ever came of it. This seems hard, especially as Lewis and Clark and their men were well rewarded by Congressional legislation; but acts of Congress are as inscrutable as the ways of Providence, in any question of right or wrong. As to the composition of this chapter, see note [1], p. 807, and observe that we have: (1) The Report of the Congressional Committee of which Mr. Montgomery was chairman, recommending an appropriation. (2) A letter from the Secretary of War to this chairman, inclosing copies of instructions Pike received from Wilkinson for each of his expeditions. (3) A copy of *one* of these instructions, namely, for the Mississippi voyage, but no copy of the other which ought to appear here—for the reason, no doubt, that Pike had put it already in his book, as a sort of preface to Pt. 2: see note [1], p. 562. Both or neither of these instructions should have come here. (4) Dearborn's complimentary letter to Pike. (5) Pike's return of men, etc., or roster of his two parties, furnished for the information of Congress upon the question of who were the persons for whom reward was claimed.

[ACCOMPANYING DOCUMENTS.]

WAR DEPARTMENT, Dec. 7th, 1808.

SIR :

I herewith inclose copies of the instructions to Lieutenant Pike, for the government of his conduct on the two exploring expeditions alluded to in your letter; and likewise lists of the names of the men composing those parties. You will perceive that the instructions were given by General Wilkinson; the objects, however, of each party, together with the instructions, were communicated to and approved by the president of the United States.

Although no special encouragement was given to the individuals who performed these laborious and dangerous expeditions, yet it was but reasonable for them, should they fortunately succeed in their objects, to expect a liberal reward from the government; and as there can be no reasonable doubt of the zeal, perseverance, and intelligence of the commander, or of the faithful conduct and arduous exertions of the individuals generally, composing the respective parties, it may, I trust, be presumed that no objection will be opposed to a reasonable compensation for such meritorious services.

I am very respectfully, Sir,

Your obedient servant,

H. DEARBORN.

[Secretary at War.]

HON. J. MONTGOMERY, Chairman, etc.

HEADQUARTERS, ST. LOUIS, July 30th, 1805.

SIR :

Having completed your equipments, you are to proceed up the Mississippi with all possible diligence, taking the following instructions for your general government, which are to yield to your discretion in all cases of exigency.

You will please to take the course of the river, and calculate distances by time, noting rivers, creeks, highlands, prairies, islands, rapids, shoals, mines, quarries, timber, water, soil, Indian villages and settlements, in a diary, to comprehend reflections on the winds and weather.

It is interesting to government to be informed of the population and residence of the several Indian nations, of the quantity and species of skins and furs they barter per annum, and their relative price to goods; of the tracts of country on which they generally make their hunts, and the people with whom they trade.

You will be pleased to examine strictly for an intermediate point, between this place and the Prairie des Chiens, suitable for a military post, and also on the Ouiscousing, near its mouth, for a similar establishment; and will obtain the consent of the Indians for their erection, informing them that they are intended to increase their trade and ameliorate their condition.

You will proceed to ascend the main branch of the river until you reach the source of it, or the season may forbid your further progress without endangering your return before the waters are frozen up.

You will endeavor to ascertain the latitude of the most remarkable places in your route, with the extent of the navigation and the direction of the different rivers which fall into the Mississippi, and you will not fail to procure specimens of whatever you may find curious, in the mineral, vegetable, or animal kingdoms, to be rendered at this place.

In your course you are to spare no pains to conciliate the Indians and to attach them to the United States, and you may invite the great chiefs of such distant nations as have not been at this place, to pay me a visit.

Your own good sense will regulate the consumption of your provisions, and direct the distribution of the trifling presents which you may carry with you, particularly your flags.

I wish you a speedy, pleasant, and safe tour, and am, Sir, with sentiments of respect and esteem,

Your obedient servant,

[Signed] JAMES WILKINSON.

P. S. In addition to the preceding orders, you will be pleased to obtain permission from the Indians who claim the ground, for the erection of military posts and trading-houses at the mouth of the river St. Pierre, the falls of St. Anthony, and every other critical point which may fall under your observation; these permissions to be granted in formal conferences, regularly recorded, and the ground marked off.

[Signed] J. W.

LIEUTENANT Z. M. PIKE,
  1st Regt. Infantry.

WAR DEPARTMENT, Feb. 24th, 1808.

SIR :

In answer to your letter of the 22d instant, I can with pleasure observe, that although the two exploring expeditions you have performed were not previously ordered by the president of the United States, there were frequent communications on the subject of each between General Wilkinson and this department, of which the president of the United States was from time to time acquainted; and it will be no more than what justice requires to say that your conduct, in each of those expeditions, met the approbation of the president; and that the information you obtained and communicated to the executive, in relation to the source of the Mississippi and the natives in that quarter, and the country generally, as well on the Upper Mississippi as that between the Arkansaw and the Missouri, and on the borders of the latter extensive river to its source and the country adjacent, has been considered highly interesting in a political, geographical, and historical view. And you may rest assured that your services are held in high estimation by the president of the United States; and if any opinion of my

own can afford you any satisfaction, I very frankly declare
that I consider the public much indebted to you for the enterprising, persevering, and judicious manner in which you
have performed them.

I am, very respectfully, Sir,

Your obedient servant,

[Signed]   H. DEARBORN.

[Secretary at War.]

CAPTAIN ZEBULON M. PIKE.

----

*Sketch of an Expedition made from St. Louis, to explore the
internal parts of Louisiana, by order of his Excellency,
General James Wilkinson.* (*Orig. No. 13, pp. 73–77.*)

I embarked at Belle Fontaine, on the Missouri, near its
confluence with the Mississippi, with a command of one
lieutenant, one doctor (a volunteer), two sergeants, one corporal, 17 [16] privates, and one interpreter;[2] having under
my charge eight or ten Osage chiefs who had recently
returned from a visit to the city of Washington, together
with about 40 men, women, and children of the same nation,
redeemed from captivity from another Indian nation ; and
two Pawnees who had likewise been to the city of Washington [making a total of 51 Indians].

We ascended the Missouri river to the river of the Osage,
up which we ascended to the Osage towns, and arrived on
or about the 18th of August [p. 385], and delivered to their
nation in safety their chiefs, women, and children, with
speeches to the nation.

[2] This roster is at variance with that given in the itinerary, p. 358, where it
stands one lieutenant (Wilkinson), one doctor (Robinson, who was the volunteer), two sergeants (Ballenger and Meek), one corporal (Jackson), 16 privates
(Boley, Bradley, Brown, Carter, Dougherty, Gorden, Huddleston, Kennerman,
Menaugh, Miller, Mountjoy, Roy, Smith, Sparks, Stoute, Wilson), and one
interpreter (Vasquez). Compare note [2], pp. 358–360, and note [50], p. 510.
Numerous other slips in this sketch, notably of dates, indicate that it was
written from memory.

Here I remained making astronomical observations, and preparing for my march by land, until the 1st of September, when we took our departure for the Pawnee Republic, accompanied by some Osage chiefs, who were deputed by their nation to form a treaty of peace and amity with the nation of the Kans with whom they were then at war, under the auspices of the United States. I arrived at the Pawnee Republic about the 25th of said month [p. 409], where I caused to be held a conference between the Osage and Kans chiefs, and mediated a peace for the two nations. Having held councils with the Pawnees, made astronomical observations, etc., I marched from the said village on the 7th of October, and arrived at the Arkansaw on the 11th [read 15th] of said month, where we remained until the 28th, preparing canoes, etc., for Lieutenant Wilkinson, who descended the said river, with one sergeant, six men, and two Osage Indians.[3] During my stay at said river, I likewise made astronomical observations.

On the said day I marched with the remainder of the party up the Arkansaw. Nothing occurred worthy of note until about the middle [on the 22d] of November, when we met a party of Pawnees, of 60 warriors, who were returning from an expedition against the Kayaways. At first our conference was of the most friendly nature, and I made them some small presents ; but as they commenced to steal and plunder whatever they could with impunity, we were finally obliged to take to our arms, and were on the point of coming to hostilities, when the Pawnees retired, and we pursued our march.

We arrived where the Arkansaw enters the mountains, on the 4th or 5th [5th] of December, where we remained until the 9th [10th], searching for the route across the mountains, when we marched by a trace which we discovered, leaving the main Arkansaw to our left. Much to our astonishment

---

[3] It appears from Lieutenant Wilkinson's own report that he had but five men with him, the sergeant and four privates. Pike's enumeration of "six men" besides the sergeant includes the two Osages, whom he thus counts twice, to an aggregate of nine persons.

we arrived about the middle of said month [Dec. 13th] on a water of the Missouri, which I ascertained to be the [South fork of the] river Platte, on which we discovered signs of immense numbers of Indians. Here we remained a few days searching for those Indians, in hopes to obtain from them information as to a route to cross the mountains to the west; but not discovering any, we crossed a large chain [Park range] by a practicable route [Trout Creek pass] and fell on a large branch of water which I then conceived to be the head of the Red river [but which was the Arkansaw]. Here we remained a few days [till Dec. 21st] to recruit our horses and ourselves, when I ordered the party to proceed down said river, and I with two men ascended it [nearly] to its source, where I made some observations. I then returned and overtook the party, when we continued to descend said stream, until the perpendicularity of the rocks [of the Grand Cañon of the Arkansaw] and other difficulties rendered it impossible to proceed any further with horses, several of which had already been killed by falling from the rocks, etc.

I then caused sleds to be constructed, and soldiers to draw the baggage on the ice, and ordered a few men to endeavor to conduct the horses by a more eligible route out of the mountains; at the extremity of which we all arrived by the 9th of January, and found that we had descended the main branch of the Arkansaw, conceiving it to be the Red river, and were again at the same point [Cañon City] we had left on the 9th [10th] ult.

My remaining horses not being in a situation to allow me to hope for any further assistance from them, unless permitted further to recover, and as this would have engrossed a long time, I determined to leave some men with the horses and part of the baggage, and proceed with the remainder and the articles absolutely necessary, on foot. On the 14th of January, having constructed a small place for my men and baggage who remained, we marched, proceeding up a western branch [Grape creek] of the Arkansaw, which appeared to lead in a direct route through the mountains. On the 20th of said month, being obliged to cross a prairie [Wet Mountain valley] of some leagues in breadth, late in the evening, and many of the soldiers having their feet wet, we had it not in our power to make fire until eight or nine o'clock at night. We were so unfortunate as to ascertain that nine of the party were frozen. The ensuing day, discovering that they were not all able to march, we remained a few days to lay in provisions. Here I left two soldiers and four loads of our baggage, and proceeded on our march; but on the third day, finding another of my men not able to march, I was obliged to leave him encamped, having previously furnished him with sufficient provision. We then crossed another chain [Sangre de Cristo] of mountains, and on the 1st of February [31st of January] arrived on the waters of the Rio del Norte, which I then conceived to be the Red river, as some maps which I held portrayed the source of the Red river to lie between those of the Arkansaw and Rio del Norte. I then proceeded to choose a station [on the Rio Conejos] where there was sufficient wood to form canoes or rafts, in order to descend the supposed [Red] river to Natchitoches.

Having in many instances experienced the insolence and presuming dispositions of the Indians, when in superior numbers, I conceived it proper to throw up a small work for the protection of ourselves and baggage, until we should be prepared to descend the river.

Four or five days [seven] after I dispatched five men to return to those I had left in the mountains, and bring them on, if capable of marching; if not, to supply them with provision and bring on the baggage. Dr. Robinson, who had hitherto accompanied me as a volunteer, having some pecuniary demands in the province of New Mexico, conceived that this would be the nearest point from which he could go in and probably return, previous to my being prepared to descend the river. He left me on the 7th of February with that view.

A few days after [on Feb. 16th], hunting with one of my men, I discovered two men on horseback. I would have avoided them, agreeably to my orders; but, finding they continued to pursue us, I conceived it most proper to bring them to a conference. This, with great difficulty, I effected, as they appeared to be apprehensive that my intentions were hostile toward them. I conducted them to my camp, informed them of my intention to descend the river, and made them some small presents. Had they then informed me of my being on the Rio del Norte, I should have immediately retired; but, having executed their commission, they returned the following day on the immediate route to the [Spanish] settlements. The following day [Feb. 17th] the party I had detached for the men whom I had been compelled to leave in the mountains, returned with one only, and all the baggage, the other two not being able to come on. I then immediately [Feb. 19th] dispatched my sergeant and one man, to order and conduct on the men, horses, and baggage left on the Arkansaw, by a route which I conceived practicable.

On the 24th or 25th [26th] of February, in the morning, two Frenchmen arrived at my camp, and informed me that an officer and 50 men of his Catholic Majesty's troops had marched from Santa Fe, in order to protect me from the Utahs, who had exhibited a disposition to attack me, and would probably be at my camp in two or three days. In the course of two or three hours, I was informed by a sentinel, whom I always kept on a hill, of the approach of a party of strangers; and in a short period there arrived two officers and 100 men, at a small distance from the camp. The lieutenant commandant, having entered my works by my invitation, informed me that the governor of New Mexico had been informed of my situation; and, understanding I was bound for Red river, offered me any assistance which lay in his power to accommodate me. I replied that I stood in no need of assistance; that I could descend the river with craft which I proposed constructing. He then informed me I was on the Rio del Norte, which astonished me extremely, and that the source of the Red river was eight days' march below Santa Fe ; and that the governor, being informed that I had missed my route, offered mules, horses, etc., to conduct me to the Red river, and wished to see me at his seat of government. I told him that if the whole of my party were here, I would not hesitate to pay my respects to his Excellency, with one or two men. He then assured me that there was not the least constraint; that I could go in before or after the arrival of my party, as my inclination dictated ; that if I went in now he would leave an Utah interpreter and one man, with the men of my party I chose to leave, in order to conduct the sergeant and party when they arrived. I finally concluded it would be more con- sistent with the good understanding which existed between the government of the United States and his Catholic Majesty, to proceed to Santa Fe, and give to Governor Allencaster an explanation of my being on his frontiers. We then marched for his [the Spanish lieutenant's] camp, about 12 miles distant, leaving the [Utah] interpreter, one Spanish soldier, a corporal [Jackson] and one private [Carter] of my detachment, with orders for the conduct of my sergeant [Meek] when he should arrive.

The next day I was much surprised to find that the lieutenant and all the regular troops, except 10, were to remain, and that the militia officer was to conduct me to Santa Fe ; the lieutenant giving as a reason the particular orders to see all my party in safety at the capital. We arrived at the town in four or five days [Mar. 3d], where I was received at first in a manner very different from what I had been taught to expect from the proffers of the lieu- tenant in the name of the governor. The arms of my men being taken possession of by the guard the first night of my arrival, without my knowledge, and my being likewise in- formed that Dr. Robinson was a prisoner at some leagues' distance, they induced me to believe that a rupture had taken place between Spain and the United States, and to address a letter to the governor, demanding if I was to consider myself and party as prisoners of war, and if the expense arising from the detention of myself and party was to be defrayed by the United States or his Catholic Majesty. To this his Excellency gave me a very polite verbal answer, assuring me that I was by no means to consider myself as a prisoner; that the arms of my men were taken unknown to him, and should be immediately restored; but that it was necessary I should march immediately to join Lieutenant Malgares and party, who were waiting for me at the village of St. Fernandez, in order to conduct me to Chihuahua, to be presented to the commandant-general with my papers for an explanation.   On my arriving at said village, I addressed a letter to the governor, informing him that Dr. Robinson had accompanied my party as a volunteer.   This I had not acknowledged at Santa Fe, as I was apprehensive that his coming on to the frontiers of the province with a military party, in case of a rupture between the two governments, might place him in a critical position.[4]

[4] As a pendent to the foregoing sketch, which was prepared for the information of Congress, may be presented a hitherto unpublished letter which Pike wrote to the Secretary of War soon after his arrival in Washington, when he transmitted reports of his Western Expedition. It is printed literally and punctually true to the manuscript now on file in the archives of the War Department.

WASHINGTON CITY .08
Jany. 26 . . .

SIR !

I am at length enabled to present you with the reports of my late expidition from the period of our sailing from Belle Fontain on the 15th. of July 1806 ; to my leaveing my Stockade on the Rio del Norte under escort of the Spanish Cavalry ; on the 27. Feby. 07.

They should have been presented some time since, had I not have been imployed by the Commander in Chief, for a very consedrable proportion of my time since my arrival at the seate of Goverment :—It must be recollected that the Spanish General seized on all my Documents in his power ; Amongst which [were] the book of Charts protracted, daily, from my notes and the eye ; and although I retained a Copy of Courses, Distances, &c—by which I have been enabled to retrace my plans, and routes, yet they necessarily are not so perfect as the Original and daily protractions would have made them :   They likewise

The lieutenant [Pike] only further observes that he has not entered into the particulars of the hardships undergone, such as enduring thirst or famine for three or four days, at different periods; marching over rugged mountains, through snows three or four feet deep, exposed to every inclemency of the weather for want of clothes, carrying at the same

obtained, and retained a note book engrossed with Observations on the manners, morals, and habits of the Aborigines of the countries through which we passed ; the loss of which naturally abridged my desertation on those heads ; also all my Meteorological tables to the entrance of their country where [were] amongst the papers sized [seized] :   But what I regret the most was my Astronomical Observations having taken at Several of the most important points, the necessary Data, from which on my arrival at the United States, and having it in my power to refer to the appropriate tables and Calculations, I could have fixed the Latt. and Longitude and thereby secured the Great Geographical Object of giving a Determinate position to Various and important points of our Country, from having it in my power to correct the Chart which I now present you agreeably to the true principals of spherical projections.   The few notes you see of the Latt. are ascertained from letters I wrote Gen[l]. Wilkinson at different periods and the Longitude would have been preserved in the same manner had I have had tables with me which would have enabled me to calculate the immersions & emersions ;—as well as angular distances at the time the observations were taken.—In the Chart herewith I have included all the Country between the La Platte of the Missouri and the Red river of the Mississsippi ; and although it is, and from the nature of our information, of that immense district *must be*, very imperfect ; yet I do not hesitate to assert it is the best extant :   I have carefully remarkd on said Chart all the parts by actual survey and the Gentleman by whom surveyed, in order that each, may lay claim to his proper proportion of fame.—You have also herewith L[t]. Wilkinsons report of his expedition after I detached him down the Arkensaw, (and his seperate Chart on a large scale), in which he encountered immense dificulties in the accomplishment of the desired end.

I have not the talents nor passions requisite for the Botanist or Mineralogist, but had I have possessed them ; the various duties I was oblidged to perform of commanding Officer, Surveyor ; Astronomer ; hunter ; and advanced guard, together with the dreary season in which we travelled part of the route ; with our minds much more actively employed in forming resources for our preservation from famine ; and defence against any savage enemy who might assail us, then [than] examining the productions of Nature which was under our feet and Instead of our eyes being directed to the Ground ; they were endeavouring to peace [pierce] the Wild before us—or giveing distinction and form to moveing Bodies on the distant Prairies—or enjoying the rapturous sublimity of the unbounded prospects which were frequently presented to our View's.   Yet Doc[r]. Robinson who possessed both talents, and taste for those pursuits ; has promised

time packs of 60 or 70 pounds' burden—in short, every
hardship to which a savage life in its greatest state of barbarity is exposed.   These are circumstances only calculated
to excite humanity, and not to give explanation as to the
general chain of events connected with the voyage.   He
therefore refers his Excellency [President Jefferson] to the

to enclose me some remarks which no doubt will be interesting ; and if received
shall be presented to the War Department.

   After I entered the Spanish Dominions I was as careful to conceal any notes
or observations, I made on their country as I had been indifferent to all that
related to what was in the conceived Territories of the United States ; Trusting
to the dignified title of an American Officer ; the Caution with which I conceived the Spanish Goverment would act and an Idea I had eroneously formed
of their want of Energy ; yet owing to some Indications I was induced to conceal my journal and other papers, leaving the Book of Charts &c for to lull any
suspicions which might arise from their being no papers in the trunks.   I now
wish General Dearborne to signify to me the extent he wishes me to enter in
the of my involuntary Tour through the Internal Provences of New Spain if it
is thought proper :   I can give (from the Notes and Documents in my possession) in addition to *my Diary and Corrispondences with the Spanish Governors
relative to my Detention, seizure of my papers, the subsistence of my party &c* ;
A General Idea of the Commerce, morals, manners, Arts, and Sciences :   A
correct account of their Military posts, with a well founded estimate of the
whole Militia of the Provences ; their population, and relative connexion with
each other.   Also, an Idea of their Annual revenue, the monies coined at the
mint &c.   Some suggestions on the sate [state] and influence of the Catholc
Religion, The Dispositions of the Inferior Clergy—to close whole with a view
of the general tendency of the Country to a revolution, the interests of the
United States in case of that event ; or the best mode of Treating with New
Spain in case of a rupture with the Mother Country ; with a General Chart of
those parts of the provinces through which we passed.   This may be takeing to
wide a field for the time, the Goverment may wish to allow me in making the
report ; or they may possess, information on those subjects from pens far abler
than mine, who may have anticepated those suggestions in their full extent.

   I beg leave at this moment to call the attention of the Secy of War to the situation of the remaining part of my Detachment in New Spain which consists of
one Interpreter, a Young man of Good family in upper Louisiania whose salary
is 500 Dollars pr—Annum, one Sergeant, one Corporal and five privates ; several of those poor fellows have become cripples from their limbs being frozen,
and are in a strange country amongst people whose language they cannot understand, from their long detention without any information from their native
Land, dispair will seize their minds, and will picture to their immaginations
Years of Confinement in a foreign Country—I who was late their Companion
in dificulties and Dangers cannot so soon forget our forlorne situation, and the

commander-in-chief of the United States army, for an explanation of the general intent and nature of the expedition, and to his notes, astronomical observations, and charts, for the courses, situations, etc., of the different points and rivers alluded to in the foregoing sketch.

———————

Return of persons employed on a tour of disovery and exploration to the source of the Mississippi, in the years 1805 and 1806 [and to the source of the Arkansaw in the years 1806 and 1807].

Lieutenant Z. M. Pike; Interpreter Pierre Rosseau; Sergeant Henry Kennerman; Corporal William E. Meek; Corporal Samuel Bradley.

Privates John Boley; Peter Branden; John Brown; Jacob Carter; Thomas Dougherty; William Gorden; Solomon Huddleston; Jeremiah [R.] Jackson; Hugh Menaugh; Theodore Miller; John Mountjoy; David Owings; Alexander Roy; Patrick Smith; John Sparks; Freegift Stoute; David Whelply.

This party left St. Louis the 9th of August, 1805, but had been detached for that duty from the 1st of July. They returned the 30th of April, 1806.

From this time until the 15th of July, I was preparing for the second expedition, to the westward, which consisted of the following persons, to wit:

obligations I am under to them for the promtitude with which they encountered danger, and fortitude they exhibited, and the fidility and attachment they evinced to their Military Commander, and leader, through those scenes; as not to exert myself to call forth the attention of the Government in their favour: I therefore hope that General Dearborne will take such measures as may be deemed expediant in order to restore those poor Lads to the service of their Country.

I am Sir With High Respect and
Consideration
Your Obt. Sert.

The Honl.   [Signed]   Z. M. PIKE Captain
HENRY DEARBORNE.   1st UStates Regt. Infy
Sec. of War.

Captain Z. M. Pike; Lieutenant James B. Wilkinson*; Dr. John H. Robinson; Interpreter Baroney Vasquez†; Sergeant Joseph Ballenger*; Sergeant William E. Meek†; Corporal Jeremiah [R.] Jackson †.

Privates John Boley*; Samuel Bradley*; John Brown; Jacob Carter†; Thomas Dougherty†; William Gorden; Solomon Huddleston;* Henry Kennerman [deserted]; Hugh Menaugh; Theodore Miller†; John Mountjoy†; Alexander Roy; Patrick Smith†; John Sparks†; Freegift Stoute; John Wilson*.

* Those thus marked descended the Arkansaw river, and arrived at New Orleans some time about the   of February, 1807.

† Those thus marked are still detained in New Spain.[5]

The balance [except Kennerman] arrived at the Nachitoches on or about the 1st of July, 1807.   But it may probably be better to leave the whole time undefined, to be regulated by the honorable secretary of war.

[5] The dagger set at Mountjoy's name is probably an error : see note [2], pp. 358–360, and note [50], p. 510.   Mountjoy was certainly one of those who accompanied Pike from the Rio Conejos into Mexico, and there is no evidence that he was dropped anywhere in that country.   Also, Pike says that only " five " privates were detained in Mexico when he made a report to the Secretary of War, dated at Washington, Jan. 26th, 1808 : see p. 853.   Furthermore, witness the following hitherto unpublished document, which I find in the archives of the War Department, and in which Mountjoy's name does not appear :

" Return of a Detachment of Infantry of the Army of the U: States, detained at Chihuahua, the Seat of Government for the Internal Provinces of New Spain, by Order of the Commandant General of those Provinces, in the year 1807.—

———

" Baroney Vasquez—Interpreter
    William E. Meek—Sergeant
    Jeremiah Jackson—Corporal
    Thomas Dougherty—Private
    Jacob Carter—   Ditto
    John Sparks—   do.
    Theodore Miller—   do.
    Patrick Smith—   do.

                  " [Signed] Z. M. PIKE Captain
                        " 1st UStates Regt Infy "

Above in clerk's hand, Pike's signature.   Rec'd at War Dept. May 3d, 1808.

INDEX.

N. B.—This index covers all the matter of the two preceding volumes, both of main text and notes thereto. It is mainly an index of names, proper and common, without analysis of what comes under them. All proper names are intended to be indexed in every place where they occur, except a few of incessant recurrence, in the cases of which some selection is made. Of common names the list is quite full, though it is exclusive, as a rule, of mere mention or allusion. Proper are distinguished from common nouns by capitalization, the same as they would be if occurring in ordinary sentences. The arrangement of the entries is intended to be strictly alphabetical, without regard to the logical order in which phrase-names and phrases would follow one another; thus, Mountjoy's name comes between Mt. Hosmer and Mt. Keyes; various Sandy things interrupt the canon of Spanish saints whose names begin with San; and so on. Contractions and abbreviations are alphabetized as if they were spelled out. Place-names which are phrases are entered as usually spoken or written, but a great many of them are also re-entered in another form or in other forms; as, Rio Conejos and Conejos r. Alternative and variant names of the same thing are all entered, but cross-references are made only in special cases. Roman numerals all refer to pages of the introductory matter in Vol. I.; the unbroken pagination of the rest of the work obviates reference by vol. for the Arabic figures. Besides serving the usual purpose, this index has been made the depository of various belated items, which do not appear elsewhere in the work, and really contains no little additional information, with here and there a correction.

Usual abbreviations or contractions for names of States and Territories, civic and military titles, etc.; also, the following:

Ark. r., Arkansaw river; br., branch (of a stream); chf., (Indian) chief; co., county; cr., creek; fk., fork (of a stream); Ind., Inds., Indian, Indians; isl., island; l., lake; ldg., landing; Miss. r., Mississippi river; Mo. r., Missouri river; Mt., mt., Mount, mountain; pk., peak; pra., prairie; pt., point; r., river; rap., rapid or rapids; res., (Indian) reservation; R. R., Ry., railroad, railway; sl., slough; spr., spring, springs; st., street; St., Saint; sta., (railroad) station; tp., township.

A

Aaiaoua, 22
Abadie, d', 213, 214
Abajo, Hacienda de, 682
Abboinug, 31
Abert, J. J., 334
Abert, J. W., 429, 446, 607, 615, 617, 630, 633, 645, 737
Abicu, N. M., 604
Abies balsamea, 132, 318, 320
Abilene, Kas., 403, 404
Abricu, N. M., 605

Abrupt Discharges, see Kapuka
Abstract of Indians, etc., 590, 591
Abstract of Nations, etc., 346, 347
Acanza, 559
Acapulco, Mex., 721, 722, 791
Accault, M., 3, 5, 13, 35, 64, 65, 68, 70, 71, 91, 95
accountants, 286
acequias, 621, 652, 740, 741
Acer saccharinum, 157
Achipoe is a form of the word Ojib way or Chippewa

Aco, Acoma, N. M., 630, 745
Acomita, N. M., 745
Act of Congress, see Congress
Acts of Minnesota Legislature, 74, 164
Adaes, Adahi, Adai, Adaise, Adaizan, Adaize, Adaizi, 713, 714
Ada, Kas., 405
Adams co., Ill., 6, 9, 11
Adams, Gov. A., xlix, lv, 457, 471, 490
Adams isl., 26
Adams, Lieut., 686
Adams, Mrs. Ann, 84
Adams, Prest. J., lxx
Adana sta., Col., 442
Adayes, Adees, 713, 714
Adobe, Col., 462
Adobe cr., 446
Adyes, 713, 714
Africa, 525
Agate cr., 468
agave, 681
agricultural establishment, 15, 16, 211
agriculture of Osages, 532
Agua Caliente, N. M., 597, see Ojo Caliente
Agua de Leon, 675
Agua Fria, N. M., 614
Agua Fria r., Ariz., 734
Agua Nueva, Mex., 653
Aguas Calientes, State of, 719, 723
Agua Verde l., 776
Aguazul Inds., 731, 736, see Havasupai
Ahacus, 742
Ahmokave, Hamookhabi, are same word as Mojave, and said by some to mean "three mountains"
Aiatans, 412
Aiavvi, 22
Aile pra., 206
Aile Rouge, 69, 202, 205, 257, 347
Aiowais, 346, 347
Aird, George, 24
Aird, James, 24, 32, 225, 293
Aishkabugakosh, Aishkebugekoshe, Aishkibugikozsh, 169
Aitkin, Alfred, see Aitkin, Wm.
Aitkin co., Minn., 134, 135, 137, 143, 175, 314
Aitkin l., 137
Aitkin, Minn., 134, 135, 136, 137, 157
Aitkin, Robert, see Aitkin, Wm.
Aitkin's ferry, 122
Aitkin's post is that referred to, 138
Aitkinsville, see Aitkin, Wm.

Aitkin, Wm., or Wm. A., or Wm. R., or Robert, 330, believed to be the same "Mr." Aitkin. Among licensed traders in Minnesota in 1833 were W. A. Aitkin, at Fond du Lac, and Alfred Aitkin, at Sandy l. Wm. Aitkin, of Little Rock, signed a memorial in 1848. In Minn. Hist. Coll., I. 86, J. F. Williams speaks of W. A. Aitkin as at Sandy l. in 1832; see op. cit., V. 483; on p. 382 it says W. A. Aitken was given the trade of the Amer. Fur Co. in Fond du Lac dept., 1826; died 1851, "and lies buried at Aitkinsville (Swan river)." The Hist. Up. Miss. Vall., 1881, says Wm. Aitkin located at Swan r., 1848. His half-breed son Alfred, doubtless the one above mentioned, was murdered at Leech Lake post, 1836. Name varies also to Aitken, Aikin, Aiken
Ajuntos isl., 692
Akansa, 559
Akaque, 347
Ako l., 166, named for M. Accault by Hon. I. V. D. Heard
Alabama, cx, cxi, 748
alacrans, 763
Alameda Arriba, Mex., 688
Alameda, N. M., 619
alamedas, 681, 682
Alamito, Mex., 677
Alamo de los Pinos, N. M., 621
Alamo de Parras, Mex., 677, 681
Alamo de Peña, 652
Alamo, Mex., 688, 689
Alamo r., br. of Rio Grande, 691
Alamos, 761
Alamosa, Col., 494
Alamosa cr., 494, 497
Alamosa de Parras, 680
Alamosa r., in N. M., 637
Alamos r., 774
Alamos, Sonora, 773
Alarcon, Alarchon, Hernando de, discovered Colorado r. of the West, Aug. 26th, 1540; said he navigated it 85 leagues; returned same year without joining Coronado
Albach's Annals, 438
Albany Argus, xxiii
Albany, Ill., 26
Albany, N. Y., liii, lxx, lxxiii
Albion, Minn., 128

Alboquerque, A. d', 619
Albuquerque, Alburquerque, N. M., 619, 621, 625, 626, 739, old town founded about 1701. See H. H. Bancroft's Arizona and New Mexico, notes to pp. 168, 228, 231 seq.
Albykirk, Albykirky, 619
Alchedoma, see Jalchedum
Alcontre r., 691
Alder r., 137
Aldrich, Hon. Chas., preface and xlix
Alencaster, Alencastre, see Allencaster
Aleutian isls., 53
Alexander, Gen., 82
Alexandria, Mo., 14
Algodones, N. M., 616, 617, 619
Algona l., 310
Algonquian, Algonquin Inds., 289, 337, 341, 346, 351, 353
Alice l., 162
Aliche, 711
alicrans, 763
Alim8pigoiak, Alinoupigouak, see Assiniboine
Allamakee co., Ia., 38, 41, 42, 305
Allan, see Allen
Alleghany, Allegheny mts., 444, 454, 523
Allen, Allan, Maj. W., ciii
Allen, Andrew H., preface
Allencaster, Don Joachin or Joaquin del Real, xlvii, 504, 508, 509, 608, 609, 610, 611, 612, 613, 622, 758, 807, 808, 809, 823, 828, 850, was governor 1805–08
Allencaster's brother, 648
Allen co., Kas., 395, 397
Allende r., 670
Allen, J. A., see Coues and Allen
Allen, Judge C. H., 390
Allen l., 128, 332, named by Brower for Lieut. James Allen
Allen, Lieut. Jas., 97, 101, 102, 103, 104, 122, 124, 127, 143, 147, 156, 161, 163, 167, 309, 328, 329, 330, 331, 332, 335
Allenoga r., 162, name compounded by Schoolcraft of Allen + oga
Allen's bay, 157, 158, 160, 332
Allouez, 288
Alma bluffs, 58
Almagra, Almagre r., 452
Almansa, see D'Almansa
Alma, Wis., 55, 56, 57, 59, 60, 62
Almighty, the, 352, 353
Alomas, 761, see Alamos

Alona, 742
Alnwick, Col., 465
Alston, Mr., 841
Altac, Altar, in Sonora, 773
Altar r., 771
Alton, Ill., 2, 5
Alvarado, Hernando de, August, 1540, was sent by Coronado from Cibola (Zuñi) to Cicuye (Pecos) via Acuco (Acoma) and Tiguex (near Bernalillo, N. M.), and returned to Tiguex
Amaqua, Amaquaqua, 735, also Amacava, Amajava
Amaranth isl., 6
Amazon bend, 2
Amazonian woman, 694
Amelia l., 90
American Antiquarian Society, xxxiv
American Fur Company, 156, 204, 298
American Philosophical Society, 77
American State Papers, 10, 840
Americus sta., Col., 470
amusements, Spanish, 789
Anakigi, 66
Analectic Magazine, lxxix
Anamas r., 445, 730, see Animas r.
Andabazo cr. or r., 672, 673
Andaig r., in Schoolcraft, 1855, for Karishon or Crow r.
Andalusia, Ill., 23, 24
Anderson, Col. A. L., 634
Anderson, Geo., 154, 155, 172, 180, 202, 272, 280, 283
Anderson, Geo., his brother, 202
Anderson, Mrs. M. B., preface
Andes, 461
Andreas' Historical Atlas, 17
André, Maj., lxvi
Androctonus biaculeatus, 763
Andromeda, 67
Andrus cr., 163, named by Brower for the treasurer of the Minnesota Game and Fish Commission
Andrusia l., 160, named by Schoolcraft for Andrew Jackson, president 1829–37
Andrusian lakes of Eastman, 1855, are Elliott Coues and Pamitascodiac or Tascodiac
Angelina, Angeline r., 709, 710, 782
Angle isl., 7
Anglo-American, xlvi, xlvii, 809
Anglojibway, 31
Animas r., br. of Rio Grande, 637
Anitons, 313
Annals of Iowa, xlix

Barre, Gov. de la, 72
Barrionuevo, Francisco de, on Coro-
nado's expedition, discovered
Taos in 1541
Bar r. of Pike, 6, 7, 290, is identified
with South Two Rivers by Beck,
Gaz., 1823, p. 316
Barrois, Céleste, 388
Barroney, see Vasquez
Bartholomew, Mr., 609, 613, 614,
615, 807
Bartlett, J. R., 645
Barton, Capt. J. L., cviii
Barton co., Kas., 423, 424, 425, 433,
522
Barton co., Mo., 385
Baie Verte, see Baye, La. In 1785,
it had about 55 pop. in 7 families,
in 1812 about 250 pop.
Bashier, Major, 692
Bas Lac aux Cèdres Rouges or du
Cèdre Rouge, 135, 356
Bass brook, 147
Bassett's cr., 94
Bass l., near Minneapolis, Minn., 90
basswood, 315
Bastonnais, Bastonnaise, 188
Bastrop, Baron, 704
Bastrop, Tex., 704, 705
Batacoso, 773
Bates co., Mo., 370, 385, 390
Bates, Frederick, 10, 388
Bates' isl., 366
Bates, Moses D., 9
bathytaphy, 73
Baton Rouge, La., liv, 564
Batopilas, Batopilis, 762
battle, see names of battles
Battle cr. and isl., 45
Battleground, in Kas., 439
Battle rap., 98
Batton Rouge, 564
baugahudoway, 150
Bavbien, C., 607
Bavispe, Bavista, 771, 773
Bayard sta., Kas., 397
Bay City, Wis., 63
Bay cr., Ill., 6
Baye des Puans or Puants, 298
Baye, La, 298, 299
Baye Verde, 356
Bay of Puante, 68
Bay of the Holy Spirit, 444
Bayogoula, Bayoucogoula, i. e., peo-
ple of the bayou, bayouc, or
bayouque ; see N. Y. Nation,
Nov. 15th, 1894
Bayou au Roi, 5

Bayou Bartholomew, 704
Bayou chute, 11
Bayou Lennan, 712
Bayou Pierre, 713
Bayou Roi, 5
Bayou St. Charles, 8, 10
Bayou San Miguel, 712
Bayou San Patricio, 712
Bay r. of Pike, 364, 365
Bay St. Charles, 9, 10
Bay Settlement, 129
Baxter sta., 129
Bazar, Kas., 401
Bean cr. is given in Beck's Gaz., 1823,
p. 89, as a name of Rivière au
Fèvre, i. e., Galena r.
Bean, Ellis, liii
Beans cr., N. M., 604
Bear r., br. of Fountain r., in Col.,
452
Bear cr., br. of May cr., in Col., 492
Bear cr., br. of Miss. r., in Minn.,
163
Bear cr., br. of Miss. r., in Mo., 8
Bear cr., br. of Osage r., in Mo., 373,
382, 383
Bear Creek cañon, 456
Bear Creek isl., 370
Bear cr. is Loose cr., 370
Bear cr. is Noir cr., 7, 290
Bear cr. is translation of Makoqueta
cr., which see
Beard, Jack, 384
Beard, Mr., 437
Bear isl., 153, in Leech l.
Bear isl., 99, in Miss. r., Sect. 2, tp.
33, range 29, 4th M.
Bear pt., at Lake Itasca, 167, was
named by Peter Turnbull in 1883
Bear r. is Loose cr., 370
Bear r., Utah, 738
Bear spr., N. M., 746
Beau or Beaux, a chf., 172, 173, 175,
189
Beautiful Bird, a chf., 384, 552, 591
Beaver, Col., 462
Beaver cr., br. of Ark. r., in Col.,
462
Beaver cr., br. of Ark. r., Kaw Agency,
550
Beaver cr., br. of Osage r., 377, 378
Beaver depot, Col., 462
Beaver isl., Ia., 26
Beaver isl. is the largest (middle) one
of the Coon isls., near Coon cr.,
Anoka co., Minn.
Beaver isls. of Pike, 99, 192, 193
Beaver or Chabadeba r., 51

Bowwood r., 815
Boy l., 155
Boynton's isl., 99
Boy or Boy's r., 153, 155, 156, 320, 334
Braba was a name of Taos in 1541
Braces r., 706, 707
Brackenridge's Travels, 361
Brackettville, Tex., 690
Braddock's defeat, 438, 531
Bradford, Col., 490, 491, 492
Bradley, Corp. or Sergt. Samuel, 1, 20, 54, 56, 108, 114, 115, 117, 124, 127, 128, 131, 136, 137, 138, 139, 172, 173, 177, 193, 359, 360, 372, 373, 401, 428, 432, 547, 845, 854, 855
Braggers, 345, 349
Brainerd, Minn., 129, 130, 131, 135, 177, 179, 318
Branches of the Vine, 777
Branden, Pvt. Peter, 1, 854
Brandy r., 96
Brannan, lxxix, lxxxiii, ci
Bras Cassé, Bras Casse, Brasse Casse, a chf., 88, 338, 347
Brasses, Brassos r., Mex., 673, 678
Brasses, Brassos, Brassus r., Tex., lii, 678, 706, 707
Bravo r., 641, 642, 643, 644, see Rio Grande and Rio del Norte
Brazeau, Marie, 388
Brazito, battle and tract, 640
Brazos, Col., 596
Brazos pk., 597
Brazos r., Brazos de Dios r., lii, 560, 705, 706, 707, 779, 780, 781
Breche, Brèche-dent, a chf., 176, 189, 190
Breck l., 166
brelau, brelaw, 96, 432
Brent's, N. M., 637
Brevoort, Capt. H. B., xxvi, xxviii, see also Michigan Pioneer Collections, I. p. 373, VIII. p. 449
Bridge cr., 518
Bridgeport, Kas., 403, 404
Bridgeport, Mo., 366
Bridgeport, Wis., 38
Brigade order, Pike's, lxxx
Brisbois, Mr., 36
Briscoe, Pvt., 332
British generalities not indexed
British medals, 551
British sergeant killed, xc
Britt's ldg., 49
Brock, Gen., c
Brockman, Mo., 373

Brock's, Ill., 4
Brockway, Minn., 102
Broken Arm, a chf., 88, 338, 347
Broken Arrow sl., 50
Broken Gun channel, 52
Broken Teeth or Tooth, a chf., 134, 176, 347
Brook Luta, 402, 403
Brooks, officer of artillery, lxxx
Broolay, Stephen, 30
Brother Jonathan, 711
Brotherton, Mo., 361
Brouisseau, J. Le F. d'I. de, 214
Broulé r., in Schoolcraft, 1855, see Bois Brûlé r.
Brower, Hon. J. V., preface, 101, 105, 158, 159, 160, 163, 164, 165, 166, 167, 288, 326, 328, 331, 332, 336
Brower isl., in Hernando de Soto l., named by a committee consisting of Capt. R. Blakely, Mr. Chas. D. Elfelt, and Hon. I. V. D. Heard, for Hon. J. V. Brower
Brower ridge, 165, 166
Brower r. is the name I have given to that stream which flows into Lake Winnibigoshish and is commonly reckoned as III. or Third r., which see: see also Annals of Iowa for Apr., 1895, p. 22
Brown cañon, 472
Brown Cañon sta., Col., 472
Brown, Clara or Clarissa, xxx, xxxiii
Brown co., Ind., cxi
Brown co., Wis., 298, 299
Brown, Browne, Dr. Jos., 388, 579
Brown, Gen. John, xxx, xxxiii, lix
Browning, Hon. D. M., preface
Brown, John, 394
Brown, Pvt. John, 1, 115, 359, 360, 373, 432, 454, 457, 476, 482, 488, 489, 490, 510, 845, 854, 855
Brown's cr., br. of Ark. r., 472
Brown's cr., br. of Miss. r., 90
Brown's fall, 90, 92
Brown's isl., 98
Brownsville, Minn., 49, 206
Brownsville, N. Y., lxxxii
Brûlé l., 153, 155
Brunet, F., 334, 335
Bruno cr., 401
Brusha for Brèche-dent, 176
Brush cr., 519
Brush Hollow cr., 462
Brushy cr., 559
Brushy Mound, see Timbered Hill
Bruske, Bruské, Brusky, Chas., 139
Bruslé, Étienne, 30

cisely on the site of the older one of two Indian villages which were replaced by Santa Fé, N. M.
Fort Marsiac, Massac, xxv, 656, 657
Fort Mason, 771, 773
Fort Mellon, lxxxvii
Fort Mohave, Mojave, 736
Fort Niagara, lxxvi, cvi
Fort Osage (or Clark), 520
Fort Oswego, ciii
Fort Perrot (various or alleged), 54, 59
Fort Pike, La., cx
Fort Pike, N. Y., civ, cx
Fort Point (Clark or Osage), 520
Fort Prince Charles, 358
Fort Recovery, 43⁹
Fortress Monroe, 45
Fort Reynolds, 451
Fort Riley, 404, 405, 408, 425
Fort Ringgold, 692
Fort Ripley (old), 127, site selected by Gen. Geo. Mercer Brooke, surveyed Sept. 24th, 1848, by Lieuts. Geo. Hasket Derby and Robert Stockton Williamson, both then of U. S. Top. Engrs., former of Phœnixiana and Squibob fame, latter noted in connection with Pac. R. R. expls. and surveys; see Harper's Mag., XIX, 1859, p. 54
Fort Ripley (town), Minn., 127, 179
Fort Rouillé, lxxv, lxxvi, lxxxiii, xcii, cii
Fort St. Anthony (Snelling), 30, 58, 82, 83, 328, 329
Fort St. Antoine, Beef r., 58
Fort St. Antoine, Lake Pepin, 65
Fort St. Croix, 309
Fort St. Louis, Ill., 560, 714
Fort St. Louis, Ia., 13
Fort St. Louis, Mo., 269
Fort St. Louis, Tex., 560, 779, 780
Fort St. Pierre, 80
Fort Sarah, 425
Fort Scott, 394, 395
Fort Selden, 636, 638, 639, 640
Fort Smith, 559
Fort Snelling, 30, 58, 75, 82, 83, 84, 85, 90, 91, 236, 243, 310, 328, 334, 358, 405 : see also Ex. Doc. No. 9, Ho. Reps., 40th Congr., 3d Sess.
Fort Stanton, 447
Fort Thorn, 638
Fort Tompkins, ciii
Fort Toronto or Rouillé, lxxv, cii
Fort Toronto or York, lxxvii

Fort Towson, 519
Fort Whipple, 735, 747
Fort William (British), 169
Fort William, Col., 446
Fort Wingate, 607, 619, 629, 742
Forty-niners, cxi
Fort York, lxix, lxxiii, lxxiv, lxxvi, lxxvii, lxxviii, lxxix, lxxx, lxxxiii, lxxxiv, lxxxv, lxxxvii, xcii, xciii, xciv, xcv, xcvii, c, ci ; and see York
Fort Yuma, 646, 736
Fort Zara, Zarah, 425 ; gone before 1866
Foster, Dr. Thos., 85, 86, 87, 88
Fountain cave, 75, 199, 200, 201
Fountain City bay, 57
Fountain City, Wis., 55, 56
Fountain cr., 452
Fountain r., 445, 451, 452, 453, 454, 459, 463
Four Brothers isls., 4
Fourche de la Côte du Kansas, 423
Four Mile cr., 399
Fourth rap., 104
Fowlshiels, xlv
Fownda, Chevalier Don, 812, 813
Fox Inds., 26, 31, 35, 36, 301, 330, 338, 339, 346, 347
Fox isl., 12, 13
Fox pra., 12
Fox r., Ia., 12, 13
Fox r., Wis., 291, 294, 295, 298, 299, 301, 302, 338, 340, 341, 347
Fox sl., 13
Fox-Wisconsin portage, route, traverse, 24, 35, 68, 294, 302
Fra Cristobal, 634, 635, 639
Fra Cristobal mt. or pk., 633, 637
Frame cr., 366
France, 213, 701, 805
Francisco, Don, 618
Francis r., 377, 378
François r., 95, 313
Franconia, 309
Frank, a Pawnee, 402, 408, 416, 569
Franklin co., Kas., 520
Franklin co., Mo., 363, 364, 365, 366
Franklin mts., 631, 640
Franklin, Tex., 643
Franquelin, J. B., 3, 13, 24, 35, 48, 49, 51, 71, 72, 73, 81, 91, 95, 309, 313
Fraser, Lieut., lxxxiv, lxxxvii, xc, xcix
Fray Cristobal, 635, 636
Frazer City, Minn., 318
Frazer, Jas., 37, 40, 42, 44, 48, 49,

Gunnison, Capt. J. W., 408, 425, 433, 437, 439, 491, 733, 734
Gunnison, Col., 469
Gunnison r., 466, 467, 468, 471, 596, 732
Guodiana, Lieut., 710, 712
Gusman family, 719, 729
gutta serena, 81
Guttenberg channel, 34
Guttenberg, Ia., 34
Guyagas spr., 652
Guyamas, 771
Guy Fawkes, cvi
Guzman l., 650
Guzman, N. B., 719
Guzzler's gulch, 429
Gwin's cr., 6
Gypsum City, Kas., 403, 404
Gypsum cr., 403, 404

H

Hacienda de Abajo, 682
Hacienda de Cienega Grande, 682
Hacienda de Dolores, 671, 672
Hacienda del Petrero, 653
Hacienda de Patos, 683, 684
Hacienda de San José de Pelayo, 673
Hacienda de San Lorenzo, 681, 777
Hacienda Encina, 687
Hacienda Poloss, 683
hackmetack, 319
Hackley's chute and isl., 13
Hacuqua is Zuñian name of Aco or Acoma, according to Cushing
Haddock sl., 57
Hadley cr., 6
Haha Inds., 348
Halcheduma, see Jalchedum
Haldemand cr., 400
Haldimand, U. C., xci
Hale l., 143
Half Dozen, a chf., 88
Half Moon battery, lxxvii, lxxxviii
Half Moon cr., 471
Half Moon l., 131, 177
Halfway house, 456
Half-way r., 559
Hall, Edwin S., 167, 336, opened first road in Itasca l. basin for G. L. O. survey in 1875
Halley, Col. A., 384, settled about 1839 at Halley's Bluff
Halley's Bluff, 384, on S. side of Osage r., in N. E. ¼ of Sect. 34, T. 38, R. 30, 2 m. S. of West Bellevoir
Hallico r., 380

Hall l., near Itasca l., named for E. S. Hall by Brower
Hallock, Chas., 326
Hallock, Minn., 326
Hall's ferry, 361
Halona, 742
Ham, a mythical person, 56
Hamburg bay, 6
Hamburg, Ill., 5, 6
Hamburg, Mo., 362, 363
Hamilton, a ship, lxxxiii
Hamilton co., Kas., 441
Hamilton, Gov. H., xcviii
Hamilton, Ill., 14, 15
Hamilton, Lt.-Col. Wm. S., 36
Hamilton, Tex., 711
Hamish is Jemez
Hammond, Kas., 394
Hammond's chute, 52
Hamookhabi is same word as Mohave
Hampton, Gen., lxv
Hampton, Ill., 25
Hamtramck, Col. J. F., xxvi
Hamtramck, J. F., xxvi
Hamtramck, Mich., xxvi
Hancock co., Ill., 13, 15, 17, 18
Hancock isl., above Dayton, Minn.
Hancock's bottom, 363, 364
Hanging Kettle l., 135
Hannibal and St. Jo. R. R., 8
Hannibal, Mo., 8, 9, 10, 211
Hano, 744
Hanover, N. H., lxxxi
Hapita, 744
Harding, Kas., 396
Hardscrabble, Col., 453
Hardscrabble cr., 462, 488
Harkness cr., 6
Harland, Kas., 440
Harlan, Dr. Richard, 771
Harmon's Journal, 278
Harmony Mission, Mo., 385
Harpe, B. de la, 77, 78, 79
Harper and Brothers, 553, 554
Harper cr., Kas., 399
Harper, F. P., preface
Harper's Ferry, Va., 41
Harper's Gazetteer, 554
Harper sl., 41, 42
Harper's Magazine, 326
Harriet l., 90
Harrison, ex-Prest. B., preface, xxxii
Harrison, Gen. Wm. H., xxx, 11, 222
Harrison, J. C. S. or Symmes, xxx, xxxii
Harrison's ldg., 369
Harrison, W. H., xxxii, xxxiii
Harris sl., 28

Medora, Mo., 370
Meeker co., Minn., 97
Meek, Sgt. W. E., xlvi, I, 114, 115, 118, 178, 359, 360, 432, 482, 490, 506, 509, 510, 595, 830, 832, 845, 850, 853, 854, 855
Mekabea Sepe, 29
Melcher or Michon, more probably Melchior, Don, 686, 688
Meles taxus, 96
Meline, Col. J. F., xlvi, xlvii, lv, cxii
Melish, John, 553
Menard, 51, 71, 295, 296
Menasha, 300
Menaugh, Pvt. H., I, 359, 360, 432, 482, 490, 506, 510, 845, 854, 855
Menchokatonx, 313
Mendesuacantons, 313
Mende Wahkantoan, 345, 348
Mendota, Minn., 76, 81, 83
Mendoza, a viceroy, 718
Meno Cockien, 356
Men of Achievement Series, xlviii
Menomene Inds., see Menomonee Inds.
Menomene r., 340
Menomeny-sibi, 138
Menomine, Menominie Inds., see Menomonee Inds.
Menomonee cr., Ill., 32
Menomonee Inds., 38, 39, 183, 299, 330, 340, 341, 346, 347
Menomonee settlement, 300
Mer a Doge, 26
Mercer co., Ill., 21
Mercer co., O., 438
Mercer cr., 400
Merchant, a chf., 268
Mercier, Mr., 243
Mer Douce, 30
Merior, Maj., 411
Merriam, Kas., 519
Merrimac isl., 74, was the nidus of a spiritualists' camp, 1892–93
Merrimac, Minn., 74
Mesa Prieta, 634
Mescalero Apaches, 631, 632, 748
Mescalero res., 748
Meschaouay r., 50
Meschasipi r., 288
Meschetz Odeba r., 35
mesquite, 704
Mesquite, N. M., 640
Messchsipi r., 288
Messila, N. M., 640
Messipi, Messisipi r., 288
Meteorological Observations, 216, 217, 218, 219, 220, 716, 717

Meteros r., 682
Metifs, 510, 738, 764, 768, 771, 774, 790
Metoswa raps., 160, were so named by Schoolcraft, 1855, because he supposed they were 10 in number
Meunier, Pierre, see Archevêque
Mexican boundary, 641, 642, 644, 645, 646, 647, 691, 692, 735
Mexican claims, 647
Mexican mts., in Col., 444, 445, 822
Mexicano or Mexican r., 702, 711
Mexican tour, Pike's, begins 595, runs to end of Vol. II.
Mexican waters, 164
Mexico, in various applications, *passim* throughout Pt. 3, and 270, 340, 677, 683, 684, 718, 720, 721, 722, 723, 724, 726, 735, 739, 740, 742, 743, 746, 765, 786, 790, 800
Meyer, Wm., 238
Miakechesa, Mia Kechakesa, 345, 349
Miami co., Kas., 519
Miami rap., xxvi
Miawakong r., 316
Michals, Mr. Myers, 20
Micheli–, see Michil–
Michigan, State or Territory, xxx, 45
Michilimackinac, 20, 68, 70, 181, 183, 229, 247, 250, 261, 276, 280, 281, 294, 295, 298, 303, 304, 306, 327, 345, 346, 352
Michi Sepe, 288
Michler, Lt. Nathaniel, 645, 647, 692
Michoacan, 718, 719, 720, 721, 723
Michon, see Melcher
Micissypy r., 288
Mico, 288
Middle cr., br. of Cottonwood r., 401
Middle cr., br. of Mo. r., 369
Middle Nicollet l., 165
Middle or Half-way r., 559
Middle park, Col., xlviii, 479
Middle r., br. of Mo. r., 369
Midway, Col., 469
Midway Reservoir, at Clarke l. and vicinity, named by Brower
Mier, Mex., 691, 692, 696
Migadiwin cr., 98
Migiskun Aiaub l., 317
migrations of Pawnees, 535
Mikenna l., in Itasca basin, named by A. J. Hill
Milakokia r., 295
Milan, Ill., 4, 24, 293
Military Academy, see West Point
military discipline, Spanish, 797

Mississipy r., 288
Missourians of Doniphan's Exp., 654
Missouri Geological Report, 372
Missouri Inds., 338, 346, 525, 526, 536, 591
Missouri, Kansas, and Texas R. R., 8, 385, 397
Missouri Pacific R. R., 365, 370, 379, 385, 390, 403, 404, 448
Missouri r., not indexed—Pt. 2 to 369 and elsewhere passim
Missouri River Commission, 363, 364, 365, 366, 369
Missouri, State of, cx, cxi, and in Pt. 1 to 14, in Pt. 2 to 395, also 518, 519
Missouriton, Mo., 363
Mitchell co., Kas., 421
Mitchell, Lt.-Col., 674
Mitchell, Lt.-Col. G. E., ci, ciii
Mitchell, S. A., 553, 554
Mitschaoywa r., 50
Mobile isl., 2
Moctezuma r., 771
Modenas pass, 491
Moeng8oana r., 13
Mogollon Apaches, 748
Mogollon, Mogoyon mts., 730
Mohace, 744
Mohave Inds., 736
Mohave r., 776
Mohotse, 744
Moingana, Moingoana r., 13
Mojave, 735
Mojou, Joseph, 87
Moki, 630, 731, 742, 743, 744
Moki buttes or mesas, 743, 744
mole., 97
Moline chain, 25
Moline, Ill., 25
Moloch, priests of, 41
Mommytaw r., 386
Monastery Road, 670, 706
Monclova, 776, 777
Monegaw Springs, Mo., 384
Monistique r., 296
Monkey, see Moki
Monk r., 14
Monmouth, lxvi
Monongahela r., 438
Montagne de Salines, 631, 632
Montagne qui Trempe à l'Eau, 52, 54, 206, 356
Montaigne de la Prairie, 348
Montaigne de Sel, 732
Montana, xlix, cxi
Montbrun's tavern, 368, 369
Montebello, 14

Monte de los Tres Rios, 685
Monte Largo, 619
Montello, 301
Montelovez, 673, 677, 685, 686, 689, 695, 701, 775, 777, 779, 784
Mont Elrey, El Rey, 701, 725, 784
Monterey bay, 725
Monterey, Count of, 725, 755
Monterey, Mex., 685, 690, 692, 701, 725, 784
Monte Rito Alto, 483
Montezuma I., II., 737
Montezuma, Kas., 437
Montgomery co., Kas., 400, 555
Montgomery co., Mo., 4, 366, 367, 368
Montgomery, Hon. John, lxiii, 841, 842
Monticello, Minn., 97, 98, 99
Mont La Garde is Schoolcraft's name for La Grange, at Red Wing, Minn.
Montoso mt., 598
Montoyo, Tex., 640, 643
Montpelier, Ia., 23, 24
Montreal, Can., lxxvii, 77, 167, 312
Montreal, Ill., 18
Montreal r., Wis., 306
Montrose, Ia., 16, 291
Montrose isl., 16
Montville, Col., 493
Monument cr., 452
Moon cr., 400
Moore, Dr. John, 616
Moore, Geo. H., 326
Moorhead, Minn., 318
Moors, 787
Moose rap., 137
Moqui, 730, 731, 744
Moquino pueblo, 630
morals, 754, 755, 769, 787
Moranget, 779, 780
Morantown, Kas., 397
Morelos, Mex., 718, 721, 722
Morelos y Pavon, J. M., 720
Morgan co., Mo., 371, 374, 377
Mormon battalion, 333, 639
Mormon cr., Wis., 50
Mormons, 15, 734
Moro r., 559
Morris co., Kas., 521
Morrison, Allan, 326, 327, guided Chas. Lanman to Lake Itasca in 1846
Morrison co., Minn., cx, 102, 103, 107, 122, 123, 125, 127, 128, 179
Morrison hill, 165, named by Brower for Wm. Morrison

Rum r., 94, 95, 96, 101, 194, 196, 311, 313, 314, 343, 350, 351, 356
Running sl., 6
Running Turkey cr., 522
Ruque, see Rocque and Rocque's
Rural Cemetery, 357
Rush co., Kas., 425
Rush cr., br. of Ark. r., 460
Rush cr., Ill., 27
Rush cr., Minn., 63
Rush cr. of Lewis and Clark, 369
Rush cr., Wis., 42
Rush isl., 19
Rush l., bay of Leech l., 153
Rush l., Little Winnibigoshish l., 325
Rush l., Otter Tail series, 318
Rush l., Wis., 301
Rush pt., 325
Russell co., Kas., 404, 423
Russia, 571
Ruter, 780
Ruxton cr., 452, 456
Ruxton, G. F., 457, 598

S

Sabal palmetto, 776
Sabinal, Sabinal sta., N. M., 629
Sabinas r., 679, 685, 687, 688, 689, 691, 777
Sabine bay or l., 709, 782
Sabine co., La., 712, 713
Sabine co., Tex., 710
Sabine l., 709, 782
Sabine r., bet. La. and Tex., 1, 407, 696, 702, 708, 709, 710, 711, 712, 713, 782
Sabine r., in Mex., see Sabinas r.
Sabinetown, Tex., 711, 712
Sabinez, N. M., 628, 629
Sabin's Bibl. Amer., xxxiv
Sable l., 120, 241, and see Sandy l.
Sabula, Ia., 27
Sac and Fox boundary, war, and treaty, 9, 11, 45, 367
Sac Inds., 5, 15, 16, 19, 20, 24, 31, 101, 210, 211, 293, 330, 337, 338, 339, 361, 384, 526, 551, 570, 591, and see Fox Inds.
Sackett's Harbor, lxxiii, lxxx, lxxxii, lxxxiii, xcii, xciv, xcvii, ciii, civ, cx
Sack r., 101, see Sauk r.
Sacque, see Sac Inds.
Sacramento mts., 631, 736
Sacramento r., 654, 655
Sac r., br. of Miss. r., 315, see Sauk r.
Sac r., br. of Osage r., 381, 383, 384, 385, 514

Sacs and Foxes, see Sac Inds. and Fox Inds., also Sac and Fox
Sac village, see Sac Inds.
Saddle mt., 464, 465
Sagatagon r., 103
Saget, 780
Saguache co., Col., 491, 492
Saguache mts., 596
Saint, Sainte, as follows, abbrev. St., Ste., see also San, Santa, and Santo
St. a fé, St. Affe, St. Affee, lii, liii, 706, see Santa Fé
St. Albans, Mo., 362, 363
St. Ander, 724, see Santander and New San Ander
St. Anthony, 289
St. Anthony's falls, 70, 75, 82, 83, 90, 91, 92, 93, 94, 195, 196
St. Antoine, fort on L. Pepin, 71
St. Antonio r., 780
St. Antonio, Tex., liii, 666, 692, 697, 783, 784, 785, 786, 813, 814, 836, see San Antonio de Bexar
St. Aubert, Mo., 369
St. Aubert's isl., 370
St. Aubert sta., Mo., 370
St. Augusta, Minn., 99, 100, 194
St. Augustine, Fla., 734
St. Bernard bay, 779, 781
St. Charles bayou, 8, 11
St. Charles co., Mo., 3, 4, 360, 363, 364
St. Charles district, lvi, 10, 360
St. Charles, Mo., 214, 229, 360, 361, 511, 512, 567, 568, 569
St. Charles r., 451, 454, 463, 488, 490
St. Clair co., Mo., 371, 381, 383, 384, 385
St. Clair, Gen. A., 438
St. Cloud, Minn., 99, 100, 101, 120, 193, 315
St. Croix falls, 309, 310
St. Croix, fort, 71
St. Croix l., 72, 308
St. Croix, Ste. Croix, a trader, 71, 72
St. Croix, Ste. Croix r., 48, 52, 58, 60, 62, 65, 70, 71, 72, 73, 77, 80, 95, 205, 227, 231, 243, 279, 306, 308, 309, 338, 342, 347, 348, 350
St. Denis, St. Dennie, L. J. de, 714
St. Dies mts., 616, see Sandia mts.
St. Dies pueblo, 619, see Sandia
St. Domingo, Mex., 677, 766
St. Domingo, N. M., 615, 752
St. Elias mt., 722
St. Elizabeth, Mo., 372
Ste. Thérèse r., 707

Shokauk cr. or r., 18
Shokokon sl., 18, 19
Shongapavi, 744
Shooter, a chf., is Wacouta
Shooters at Leaves, 349
Shoshonean, 731, 735, 743, 744, 746
Shoshones, 341
Shouchoir pt., 296
Shumepovi, Shumopavi, 744, is Pike's Songoapt
Shupaulovi, 744
Shute de la Roche Peinture, 123, 316
Shute de St. Antoine, 356
Sia, 604, 745
Sibilant l., named by Brower from its shape of the sibilant letter S
Sibilleta, N. M., 628, 632, 739, see Sevilleta
Sibley, Dr., 77, 559, 705, 706, 708, 709, 711, 713, 714, 785, 835
Sibley, Gen. H. H., 40, 76, 86, 204, 239, 333
Sibley l., 129
Sibley, Mo., 520
Sibley, Mr., U. S. Commissioner, 518
Sibola, 742
Sichumovi, 744
Siegfried cr., 166, named by Brower for A. H. Siegfried
Sienega, Sieneguilla, see under C
Sierra Blanca, Col., 448, 483, 493
Sierra Blanca, N. M., 631
Sierra Christopher, 632, 633, 639
Sierra co., Cal., cx
Sierra co., N. M., 637, 638
Sierra de el Sacramento, 631
Sierra de Guadalupe, 631
Sierra de la Cola, 640
Sierra de las Mimbres, 674
Sierra de los Caballos, 635, 637, 638
Sierra de los Cosninas, 731
Sierra de los Organos, 631
Sierra de Tampanagos, 738
Sierra la Sal, 732
Sierra Madre, 733, 761, 762, 764
Sierra Magdalena, 632
Sierra Magillez, 632
Sierra Obscura, Oscura, 631, 632
Sierra Verde, 733
siesta, 660
Sieur Dacan, d'Acau, d'Accault, d'Ako, 64
Signal butte, 744
Silla, 745
Silver Cliff, Col., 482, 483, 484
Silver cr., Col., 483
Silver cr., Kas., 401
Silver cr., Minn., 98, 99

Silver Creek Siding, Minn., 99
silver mines, 759, 760, 761
Simcoe, Gov. J. G., lxxvi, lxxvii
Simcoe l., lxxv
Simpson, Kas., 408
Simpson, Lieut. J. H., 598, 615, 619, 630, 645
Sinaloa, city, 774
Sinaloa r., 774
Sinaloa, State, 719, 726, 739, 740, 759, 770, 773, 774, 775
Sinecu pueblo, 643
Singonki-sibi, 143
Singuoako r., 132
Sinipee, Sinipi, Sinope, Ia., 32
Sinsinawa, Sinsinaway, Sinsinniwa, Sissinaway cr. or r., 28, 32
Siouan, 345, 412, 559
Sioux, passim throughout Pt. 1, esp. 30, 31, 43, 44, 45, 46, 47, 50, 82, 91, 341, 342, 343, 344, 345, 346, 347, 348, 349, 352, 353, 354, passim in Pt. 2, 744, 746, see also following
Sioux-Chippewa boundary, 72, 101
Sioux councils, 83, 84, 207
Sioux l., 313
Sioux of the Prairie, 81
Sioux outbreak of 1862, 85
Sioux, Pike's speech to, 46
Sioux r., 95, 313
Sioux r. of Beltrami, 97
Sioux sl., 41
Sioux treaty, Pike's, 227, 231, 233, 234, 235, 236, 237, 238, 239
Sioux village, old, 348
Sipans, 746, see Lipans
Sirens, The, 126
Sisibakwet l., 147
Sisitoans, Sisitonwans, Sissetons, Sissitons, 120, 208, 313, 343, 345, 346, 347, 348, 349
Sister bluffs, 297
Sitgreaves, Capt. L., 645
Sivola is Cibola
Six, a chf., 88, 348
Six Mile cr., Col., 462
Six Mile cr., Ill., 6
Six Mile cr., Kas., 401
Sixth rap. of Nicollet, 126
Sketch of Arkansas journey, 845 to 854
Skidis, 412
Skin cr., 559
Skunk r., 18
slack-rope, 694
Slate cr., br. of Ark. r., 549
Slate or Martin's cr., 465

Tancards, 705, 706, 785
Tandy, D. C., 358
Tandy, R. E., 358
Tankahuas, Tanks, 705
Tanner, H. S., 553, 554
Tañoan pueblos, 598, 601, 604, 605, 615, 619, 643, 737, 742, 743, 744, 752
Tanos, 653
Taoapa, 88, 348
Taos co., N. M., 598
Taos cr., 598
Taoses mt., 598
Taos, N. M., xlvii, 438, 446, 453, 598, 606, 607, 618, 739, 745, 758, discovered 1541 by Barrionuevo of Coronado's army
Taos r., 598
Taos valley, 492
Taoyatidoota, 85
Tapage, 412
Tapatui, 288
Tapoueri Inds., 48
Taracone Apaches, see Faraone
Tarehem, 591
Target l., 50
tariff of prices in exchange, 283
Tascodiac l., 160
Tassé, 194
Tatamane, Tatamene, 203, 347
Tatanga, *i. e.*, Buffalo Sioux, named first in Radisson's Journal, pub. by Prince Society of Boston
Tatangamani, 69, 342
Tatangashatah, 347
Tatankanaje, 349
Tatanka Yuteshane, 349
Tate cr., 400
tattoo, 72
Tatunkamene, 69
Taucos is found for Tewa
Tau-formed peninsula, 153
Taui is Taos
Tavern cr., 363, 369
Tavern, The, 363
Tawangaha, 591
Tawanima, 559
Taxidea americana, 96, 432
Taxus, 709
Taylor co., Wis., 52
Taylor isl., 8
Taylor, Z., 17, 45, 725
Tcawi, 412
Tchahtanwahkoowahmane, Tchaypehamonee, 85
Tchikun, 748
Tchishi, 748
Teabo creeks, see Big and Little

Teakiki r., 3
Tears, Lake of, 65
Tebo creeks, see Big and Little
Tebo r., br. of Mo. r., 379
Tecumseh st., Toronto, lxxviii
Teepeeota pt., 59, 60
Tegatha was a name of Taos
Teguan, 744
Teissier, 779
Tell, Wm., 289
Tempe, Ariz., 741
Teneriffe, Peak of, 461
Ten Mile cr., br. of Blue r., 471
Ten Mile cr., br. of Bull cr., 519
Ten Mile cr., br. of Oil cr., 465
Tennai, 746
Tennessee, liii, liv, cxi, 691, 694
Tennessee fk. of Ark. r., 471
Tennessee r., 656
Tepeedotah, Tepeeota pt., 59, 60
tequesquite, 654
Terenate, 772
Terre Beau, 379
Tesugue, Tesuque, 605, 606, 625
Tetankatane, 348
Tetans or Tetaus, 407, 412, 413, 441, 449, 459, 526, 535, 536, 537, 563, 566, 570, 571, 574, 587, 588, 590, 591, 592, 600, 620, 744, 745, 756, 778
Tête du Mort, des Morts cr., 28
Tetilla pk., 614
Tetoans, 349
Tetobasi, 528, 591
Tetons, 343, 346, 347
Tewa, Tewan, 744
Texan expedition of 1841, 739, 765
Texas, xxxii, lii, liii, 436, 559, 560, 640, 641, 642, 643, 644, 645, 661, 678, continuously from 690 to 711, 719, 724, 725, 726, 727, 746, 775, 777, 778, 779, and to 786
Texas cr., in Col., 475, 483
Texas Creek sta., Col., 475
Texican, 709
Texus, lii
Teyde, Pico de, 461
Tharp, Sgt., 712
Theakiki r., 3
Thequaio l., 738
Thequao, A. de, 738
Thermopylæ, 571
Thermopylæ of Texas, 698
Thieves' isl., 21
Thinthonhas, 313
Third fk. of Ark. r., 451, 463
Third rap. of Nicollet, 101
Third r., 324

Ute cr., 494
Ute cr. = Brush Hollow cr., 462
Ute Inds., xlvi, 448, 453, 492, 596, 743, 816
Ute pass, 456, 464
Utica, N. Y., xlvi

V

Vacamora, 771
Vache Blanche, 347
Valasco, F., 817, 819, 820
Valencia co., N. M., 628, 629, 742
Valencia, N. M., 618, 628
Valladolid, Mex., 720, 721, 723
Valladolid, Spain, 720
Vallance, J., 553
Valley City, Ia., 25
Vallois, Don P., 661, 662
Vallois, Señora M., 659
Valverde ford is near the ruins of Valverde, and about 5 m. N. of Fort Craig, N. M.
Valverde, N. M., 633, 634
Van Bibber, Mr., 367
Van Buren, Ark., 559
Van Buren, M., 358
Vandals, 632
Van Dalsem, Capt. H. H., cviii
Vandermaelen l., 160
Vaqueria, 684
vaquero, 684
vara, 669
Varennes, P. G. de, 254
Vargas, 737
Vasquez, A. F. B., or " Baroney," lxiv, 359, 360, 361, 362, 364, 365, 368, 371, 386, 387, 390, 393, 401, 403, 414, 416, 420, 421, 422, 429, 432, 435, 449, 459, 470, 472, 474, 477, 478, 480, 481, 482, 490, 506, 509, 510, 545, 579, 580, 612, 834, 845, 853, 855
Vaugondy, 559, 695, 734
Veau, Mr. Jacques, 194, 195
Vegas, Col., 459
Velasco, see Valasco, F.
Velasco, viceroy, 755
Vellita, N. M., 629
Venadito, 685
Venus' spr., 651
Vequeria cr., 683
Vequeria, Mex., 683, 684
Vera Cruz, administration or State of, 673, 718, 720, 721, 722, 723, 724
Vera Cruz, city of, 721, 722, 791
Veragua, Veraqua, 726
Verdegris r., 400

Verde r., Ariz., 727, 730, 734
Verde r., Mex., 721
Verdigris, Kas., 400
Verdigris, Verdigrise r., 399, 400, 515, 532, 555, 556, 557, 560, 584
Verendrye, Le Sieur de, 254, 255, 256
Veritas, Caput, 331
Vermijo r., 558
Vermilion cr., br. of Osage r., 377, 378
Vermilion r., br. of Ark. r., 395, 400, 514, 515, 555, 557
Vermilion r., br. of Miss. r., Cass co., Minn., 147
Vermilion r., br. of Miss. r., Dakota co., Minn., 72, 73
Vermilion r. of Beltrami = Deer r., Minn., 147
Vermilion sea, old name of the Gulf of California, for Red sea
Vermilion sl., 73
Vermillion isl., 298, 356
Vermillion r. of Pike, br. of Osage r., 379
Vermont, 570
Vermonter, 242
Vernon co., Mo., 370, 385
Vernon co., Wis., 49
Verte, Isle, 297
Verte r., 77, 78
Verum Caput, 165, 331
Verumontanum, 165
Verwyst, 101
Veta pass, 492, 494
Viana, Capt. or Don F., 412, 709, 710, 839
Viceroyalty of New Spain, 719
Vicksburg, Miss., 708
Victoria City, Mex., 724
Victoria, Wis., 49
Victor, Kas., 422
Victory, Wis., 45
Vide-poche, 215
Vieau, Jacques, 194
Vieux Desert l., 128
Vigil, D., 607
Village Creek, Ia., 43
Village de Charette, 568, 572
Villamil, Don B., 659, 661, 662
Villa Rica de la Vera Cruz, 722
Villiers, N. de, 214
Villineuve, a person, 413
Vimont's Relations, 31
Vine cr., 559
vineyards, 681
Vingt-une isl., 361
Viola, Wis., 41
Virginia, a boat, 84

Virginia, a State, xxvii, xxviii, liii, lxxxviii, 656, 691, 715, 826, 833
Virgin r., 732
Visscher, Capt. N. J., xxvi, xxvii
Vitior, 613, 614. This baffling name is clearly a misprint, Mr. F. W. Hodge believes, for Sienega (Cienega), place on a cr. of same name, br. of Santa Fé r., 2 m. S. E. of Cieneguilla, which appears on most maps of to-day. Cienega and Cieneguilla were both towns of Santa Fé co. in 1844, but La Bajada may be later. Cienega had pop. 500, and Cieneguilla, pop. 300, in 1853–54, according to Whipple, P. R. R. Rep. III., Pt. 3, p. 12
Vocabulary, etc., 355
volcano, 723
Volcano sta., N. M., 597
Volney, Count, 154
Voltaire, 154, 801
Vulgate, 182

W

Wabasha, 43, 171, 206, 260, 342, 347, 348
Wabasha I., II., III., 44
Wabasha co., Minn., 56, 57, 64
Wabasha, Minn., 57, 59. 60, 61
Wabasha st., St. Paul, 74
Wabashaw, 44, 88
Wabash r., 68, 438
Wabash Ry., 8, 15
Wabash, St. Louis, and Pacific R. R., 360
Wabesapinica, Wabezipinikan, Wabisapencun, Wabisapincun, Wabisipinekan r., 26
Wabezi r., 122
Wabiscihouwa, 44
Wabisipinekan r., 293
Wabizio-sibi, 122
Wablo cr., 383
Waboji, 338
Wacanto, Wacantoe, 343, 347
Wachpecoutes, 263
Waconda, Mo., 12
Waconda, Wacondaw pra., 12
Wacouta, Wacouta, 69
Wacouta, Goodhue co., Minn., 63
Waddapawmenesotor, 81
Wadena co., Minn., 128
Wade, Pvt., 332
Wadub r., 101
Wagoner's cr., 15

Wahkantahpay, 88
Wahkanto, 349
Wahkootay is Wacouta, 88
Wahkpakotoan, 344, 345, 349
Wahkpatoan, 345, 349
Wahpatoota, 349
Wahpaykootans, 88
Wahpeton Sioux, 85
Wahpetonwans, 118
Wajhustachay, 61
Wakan-tibi, 200
Wakarusa pt., 520
Wakarusa r., 408, 520
Wakoan, 706
Wakomiti is the Ojibway name of the stream misnamed Hennepin r., and should stand : see Annals of Iowa, Apr., 1895, p. 26
Wakon-teebe, 198
Wakouta, 62, 69
Wakouta, Goodhue co., Minn., 63
Wakpatanka is Sioux name of the Miss. r., meaning Great river
Wakpatons, 313
Wakuta, Wakute, see Wacoota, 69
Walapais, 736
Walbach, Gen. J. De B., xxvii, xxviii
Walker, Capt. Joel P., of Cal., 446
Walker, Lt. J. P., 656, 658, 660, 664, 665, 666, 761, 767, 817, 819, 820, 821, 830
Walking Buffalo, a chf., 69, 88
Wallace co., Kas., 404
Wallace, Joseph, 531, 532, 560, 714
Wallace, N. M., see Santo Domingo, N. M.
Wall, a Mr., xxi
Walnut cr., br. of Ark. r., 424, 425, 426, 429, 517, 518, 522, 545, 546, 547
Walnut cr., or White Water r., 549
Walnut Hills, lii, 657
Walpi, 744, is Pike's Gualpi
Walworth, Capt. John, lxxxvii, lxxxviii
Wamaneopenutah, 347
Wamdetanka, 85
Wamendetanka, 348
Wamendi-hi, 118
Waminisabah, 347
Wanomon r., 147
Wanotan, 349
Wanyecha cr., 94
Wapahasha, Wapasha, Wapashaw, 43, 44, 61, 86, 348
Wapello, Louisa co., Ia., named for a chf. who had his village on Iowa r. near present city
Wapsipinecon, Wapsipinicon r., 26

Winnebago pra., Stearns co., Minn., between Watab raps. and Brockway
Winnebago rap., 300
Winnebago village, 300
Winnebeegogish l. of Schlc., 1855
Winnepegoosis l., 322
Winnepeg or Winnibigoshish l., 322
Winneshiek sl., 42
Winnibigoshish l., 138, 149, 152, 153, 158, 159, 168, 317, 322, 323, 324, 325
Winnipec or Winnibigoshish l., 322, 327
Winnipeg l., 351, 353
Winnipegoos is Winnibigoshish l., D. Thompson, 1798
Winnipek is Winnibigoshish l., Schlc., 1855
Winona, a maiden of myth, 66
Winona co., Minn., 52, 53, 57
Winona, Minn., 54, 55, 56, 88, 206
Winship, W. W., preface
Winsor, J., 296
Winterbotham's map, xli, 696, 697, 702, 707
wintering grounds, 99
Winter's ldg., 53
Wisconsan r., 35
Wisconsin Central R. R., 302
Wisconsin r., 3, 34, 35, 71, 78, 224, 295, 302, 303, 304, 338
Wiscoup, 156, 259, 347, 351
Wise Family, a chf., 591
Wise, Kas., 397
wishtonwish, 429, 430, 431
Wislizenus, Dr., 339, 437, 446, 518, 521, 631, 635, 649, 650, 652, 653, 654, 667, 668, 669, 670, 671, 672, 674, 675, 680, 681, 682, 683, 684, 739, 747, 759
Wissakude r., 309
Withlachoochee r., lxxxvii
Without Ears, a chf., 591
Without Nerve, a chf., 591
Wiyakonda, Mo., 12
Woco-sibi, Wokeosiby, 127
Wolf cr., br. of Ark. r. in Col., 442
Wolf cr. of Pike, 103, 184
Wolfe, Gen., lxxxiii, c
Wolf Inds., 35, 338
Wolf r., 300, 301, 356
Wollstoncraft, Maj. C., 715
Wolverine cr., 396
Woman in White mt., 723
women and children, 286
Woodbridge, N. J., lix
Woodcock, 88

Wood cr., br. of Miss. r., 2
Wood cr., br. of Mo. r., 363, 364
Wood, Mr., 201, 202, 205, 206, 207
Woodruff, J. C., 554
Woods, Lake of the, 279, 281, 351
Woods, Mr., 37, 42
Woodson co., Kas., 395, 398, 399
Wool, Gen. J. E., 669, 674, 679, 684
Woolstoncraft, Capt., 715
Wooster, Maj. Gen. D., cvi
Worcester, Mass., xxxiv
Word of God, 182
wounded, see killed and
Wright co., Minn., 96, 97, 98
Wright's cr., 381
Wright's isl., 379
Wrightstown, 299
Wuckan l., 340
Wuckiew Nutch, 208, 343, 347
Wukunsna, 347
Wyaconda, Mo., 12
Wyaconda r., 9, 291
Wyaganage, 86, 342, 347
Wyalusing, Wis., 34
Wyoming co., N. Y., cx
Wyoming, Ia., 23
Wyoming sl., 23

X

Xacco l., 673
Xalisco, 719
Xaxales, 628, 629, has been thought to have been so called as once a temporary Apache rancheria of huts, jacales, or xacales ; but see Jarales. The form Xarales is also found
Xenia, Kas., 396, 397
Xicarilla for Jicarilla, in Don José Cortez, 1799
Xila is Gila
Xisuthros, 182
Xocoyotzin, 737
Xougapavi is Shongapavi
X. Y. Company, 139, 277
X. Y. Z., one, 336

Y

Yaatze, see San Marcos
Yabijoias, 735, of Pike, simply error in copying Indiens Yabipias à longues barbes from Humboldt's map
Yahowa r., 22, see Iowa r.
Yahowa r., 44, see Upper Iowa r.
Yakwal, 706

THE END.